ECONOMICS

THE BASICS

The McGraw-Hill Series Economics

ESSENTIALS OF ECONOMICS

Brue, McConnell, and Flynn
Essentials of Economics
Fifth Edition

Mandel
M: Economics: The Basics
2024 Release

Schiller
Essentials of Economics
Twelfth Edition

PRINCIPLES OF ECONOMICS

Asarta and Butters
Connect Master: Economics
Third Edition

Colander
Economics, Microeconomics, and Macroeconomics
Twelfth Edition

Frank, Bernanke, Antonovics, and Heffetz
Principles of Economics, Principles of Microeconomics, Principles of Macroeconomics
2024 Release

Frank, Bernanke, Antonovics, and Heffetz
Streamlined Editions: Principles of Economics, Principles of Microeconomics, Principles of Macroeconomics
Fourth Edition

Karlan and Morduch
Economics, Microeconomics, and Macroeconomics
2024 Release

McConnell, Brue, and Flynn
Economics, Microeconomics, Macroeconomics
Twenty-Third Edition

McConnell, Brue, and Flynn
Brief Editions: Microeconomics and Macroeconomics
Third Edition

Samuelson and Nordhaus
Economics, Microeconomics, and Macroeconomics
Nineteenth Edition

Schiller
The Economy Today, The Micro Economy Today, and The Macro Economy Today
Seventeenth Edition

Slavin
Economics, Microeconomics, and Macroeconomics
Twelfth Edition

ECONOMICS OF SOCIAL ISSUES

Guell
Issues in Economics Today
Tenth Edition

Register and Grimes
Economics of Social Issues
Twenty-First Edition

DATA ANALYTICS

Prince
Predictive Analytics for Business Strategy
First Edition

MANAGERIAL ECONOMICS

Baye and Prince
Managerial Economics and Business Strategy
Tenth Edition

Brickley, Smith, and Zimmerman
Managerial Economics and Organizational Architecture
Seventh Edition

Thomas and Maurice
Managerial Economics
Fourteenth Edition

INTERMEDIATE ECONOMICS

Bernheim and Whinston
Microeconomics
Second Edition

Dornbusch, Fischer, and Startz
Macroeconomics
Thirteenth Edition

Frank
Microeconomics and Behavior
2024 Release

ADVANCED ECONOMICS

Romer
Advanced Macroeconomics
Fifth Edition

MONEY AND BANKING

Cecchetti and Schoenholtz
Money, Banking, and Financial Markets
2024 Release

URBAN ECONOMICS

O'Sullivan
Urban Economics
Ninth Edition

LABOR ECONOMICS

Borjas
Labor Economics
Ninth Edition

McConnell, Brue, and Macpherson
Contemporary Labor Economics
Twelfth Edition

PUBLIC FINANCE

Rosen and Gayer
Public Finance
Tenth Edition

ENVIRONMENTAL ECONOMICS

Field and Field
Environmental Economics: An Introduction
2024 Release

INTERNATIONAL ECONOMICS

Appleyard and Field
International Economics
Ninth Edition

Pugel
International Economics
Eighteenth Edition

ECONOMICS

THE BASICS

2024 Release

Michael Mandel

Chief Economist, Progressive Policy Institute

Senior Fellow, Mack Institute for Innovation Management at The Wharton School of the University of Pennsylvania

Former Chief Economist, *BusinessWeek*

Mc Graw Hill

ECONOMICS

Some ancillaries, including electronic and print components, may not be available to customers outside the United States.

This book is printed on acid-free paper.

1 2 3 4 5 6 7 8 9 LKV 29 28 27 26 25 24

ISBN 978-1-266-94051-4
MHID 1-266-94051-0

Cover Image: *Rawpixel.com/Shutterstock*

mheducation.com/highered

DEDICATION

To Eleanor

ABOUT THE AUTHOR

Courtesy of Michael Mandel

Michael Mandel

Michael Mandel delights in translating complex economic concepts into understandable, relevant, and exciting examples for a broad audience. He received his PhD in economics from Harvard University, where he studied the intricacies of game theory. He is currently Senior Fellow at the Mack Institute for Innovation Management at The Wharton School of the University of Pennsylvania, as well as Chief Economist and Vice President at the Progressive Policy Institute in Washington, DC. He writes about the policy implications of innovation, regulation, and growth, both domestically and internationally.

Previously, Mandel was Chief Economist of *BusinessWeek* (now *Bloomberg Businessweek*), where he regularly tackled such hot topics as the economics of immigration, the power of technological innovation to drive growth, the importance of foreign trade, and consequences of tax policy.

Mandel's columns and cover stories won numerous awards, including the Excellence in Economic Journalism Award from the Institute on Political Journalism, given to the writer "who has done the most to shape public opinion by giving the public a better understanding of economic theory and reality"; the Gerald Loeb Award, the most prestigious prize for economic and financial journalism; and the Economic Journalist of the Year Award from the World Leadership Forum. He was also named one of the top 100 business journalists of the 20th century.

Mandel is the author of several books, including *Rational Exuberance: Silencing the Enemies of Growth and Why the Future Is Better Than You Think* and *The High-Risk Society.* He also helped revise the 1995 edition of Paul Samuelson's classic economics textbook.

Mandel lives in Washington, DC, not far from the White House and the Capitol, with his wife Laura Gramling.

PREFACE

We live in an ever-changing world where economic issues and debates are more important than ever before. I have three goals in writing the 2024 release of this textbook. First, I want to clearly explain basic economic principles, using the tools that I learned during my years as an economist and an economic journalist. Second, I aim to provide an introduction to the forces of globalization, technology, and financial markets that are driving the vibrant, but increasingly perplexing economy that we all live in. Third, I want to help you understand the economic issues affecting your life.

What you see here is the result of my continuing effort to achieve these three goals. The first half of the textbook, which includes the introduction and 11 core chapters, presents the essential economic concepts. I **designed this section to be accessible to students with a wide range of economic and mathematical backgrounds.** The second half of the textbook covers topics such as financial markets, globalization, technological change, labor markets, health care, and environmental economics.

I am also dedicated to keeping the textbook up-to-date with the latest events and forces in the global economy. To this end, throughout the text I've woven in examples from the COVID-19 pandemic, the Russian invasion of Ukraine, the unprecedented pandemic relief legislation, supply chain disruptions, the Fed's efforts to fight inflation, and the rise of artificial intelligence.

Fundamental Goals

To summarize, I want to accomplish three goals with this textbook:

- To help you acquire the basic tools of economics, enabling you to understand today's world in a new way.
- To give you better insights into the forces of globalization, technology, and financial markets that are so important for today and our future.
- To help you understand the economic issues affecting your life.

Distinguishing Features and Organization

This textbook emphasizes the main forces shaping today's economy: technological change, globalization, and the evolution of financial markets. The basic tools of economics are presented in the first 12 chapters to lay a foundation for understanding how the economy evolves and changes.

Current and Real Examples

Economic concepts and ideas are illustrated in recent newsworthy events to help you see that economics is in action everywhere around you.

Relevant to You

Every chapter now has at least one section on *Your Economic Life*. These sections relate the chapter material directly to student lives.

Clear and Simple Graphs

This book's simple, easy-to-follow graphs translate complex economic concepts into effective visual tools for the beginning student.

Historical Context

Economic Milestone boxes sprinkled throughout each chapter provide interesting historical facts and references that relate to the material at hand.

Assurance of Learning Ready

Many educational institutions today are focused on the notion of assurance of learning, an important element of many accreditation standards. *Economics: The Basics, 5e* is designed specifically to support your assurance of learning initiatives with a simple yet powerful solution.

Each chapter in the book begins with a list of numbered learning objectives, which appear throughout the chapter as well as in the end-of-chapter assignments. Every Test Bank question for *Economics: The Basics, 5e* maps to a specific chapter learning objective in the textbook as well as topic area, Bloom's Taxonomy level, and AACSB skill area. You can use our Test Bank software, *EZ Test,* or *Connect Economics* to easily search for learning objectives that directly relate to the learning objectives for your course. You can then use the reporting features of *EZ Test* to aggregate student results in similar fashion, making the collection and presentation of assurance of learning data simple and easy.

AACSB Statement

McGraw-Hill is a proud corporate member of AACSB International. Understanding the importance and value of AACSB accreditation, *Economics: The Basics, 5e* recognizes the curricula guidelines detailed in the AACSB standards for business accreditation by connecting selected questions in the Test Bank and end-of-chapter material to the general knowledge and skill guidelines in the AACSB standards.

The statements contained in *Economics: The Basics, 5e* are provided only as a guide for the users of this textbook. The AACSB leaves content coverage and assessment within the purview of individual schools, the mission of the school, and the faculty. While *Economics: The Basics, 5e* and the teaching package make no claim of any specific AACSB qualification or evaluation, we have, within *Economics: The Basics, 5e,* labeled selected questions according to the six general knowledge and skills areas.

Tegrity: Lectures 24/7

Tegrity in Connect is a tool that makes class time available 24/7 by automatically capturing every lecture. With a simple one-click start-and-stop process, you capture all computer screens and corresponding audio in a format that is easy to search, frame by frame. Students can replay any part of any class with easy-to-use, browser-based viewing on a PC, Mac, iPod, or other mobile device.

Educators know that the more students can see, hear, and experience class resources, the better they learn. In fact, studies prove it. Tegrity's unique search feature helps students efficiently find what they need, when they need it, across an entire semester of class recordings. Help turn your students' study time into learning moments immediately supported by your lecture. With Tegrity, you also increase intent listening and class participation by easing students' concerns about note-taking. Using Tegrity in Connect will make it more likely you will see students' faces, not the tops of their heads.

Changes in the 2024 Release

M Series

Mandel's 2024 Release is part of the M Series at McGraw-Hill. M Series products are unified through a magazine-like layout, succinct coverage, student-friendly examples, and innovative digital support. *M: Economics: The Basics* is written specifically for the one semester survey course, designed to convey core concepts and principles at a level that is approachable for the widest possible audience.

The narrative in all chapters has been completely evaluated to reflect recent economic events. Every chapter includes at least one section on *Your Economic Life,* speaking directly to the role of the chapter material in the daily life of students. Content and data updates to the figures, tables, problems, and chapter narrative have been made throughout the book to reflect news events. Select *Spotlight* and *How It Works* boxes have been updated or replaced to provide scenarios from today's economic landscape. Additionally, all of the end-of-chapter problems are assignable through McGraw-Hill *Connect,* and select problems are available as algorithmic variations (for more information on *Connect* please refer to pp. xiv and xv). Chapter-by-chapter changes are as follows:

Chapter 1 Introduction was substantially revised to reflect recent economic events and debates. In particular, the chapter now highlights new disagreements in economics such as the appropriate level of spending on pandemic relief. Figure 1.1 was updated, as were all of the figures and tables in the appendix ("The Basics of Graphs") to reflect current, real-world data.

Chapter 2 Demand and Supply: The Basics of the Market Economy has been updated with current examples, including an explanation of how telemedicine can turn local markets into national markets. Numbers were updated in many examples to reflect the higher levels of prices in the economy.

Chapter 3 Market Equilibrium and Shifts now incorporates pandemic-related market supply and demand shifts. The impact of the Russian invasion of Ukraine on supply and demand curves for oil is highlighted in Figure 3.9. Figure 3.2 and Figure 3.12 were updated to reflect new data. Problems are updated to reflect current data.

Chapter 4 How Businesses Work updates chapter examples to keep them fresh and current, including a pandemic-related example on personal protective equipment (PPE).

Chapter 5 Competition and Market Power has updated examples, including introducing Zoom as an example of a product that differentiated itself from rivals. It is noted that the rise in the price of new vehicles in 2021 and 2022 was not the result of market power.

Chapter 6 Government and the Economy is systematically updated in light of the unprecedented scale of pandemic-related government actions, and the continuing debate about whether the government intervened too much or too little during the pandemic. A new section is added to the pandemic response. A new Table 6.2 is added to the main pieces of pandemic-related legislation. The chapter now incorporates new examples, including the FTC taking action against Microsoft's proposed purchase of Activision Blizzard, and the argument for federal subsidies for COVID vaccinations.Figures 6.1 and 6.2 are updated, and a figure on comparing government spending as a percentage of GDP globally is removed. The appendix is updated with current data.

Chapter 7 The First Step into Macroeconomics is updated to reflect post-pandemic context for macroeconomic discussions. Figures and tables now take into account the most recent data, including Table 7.1 and Figures 7.1, 7.2, 7.3, and 7.4.

Chapter 8 Inflation now highlights the inflationary surge that started during the pandemic. A new box on why inflation surged in 2021 and 2022 was added. The *Your Economic Life* section on the relative price of housing for different regions was updated, as were the figures on changes in the real wages over the course of the pandemic. Table 8.1, Figure 8.1, Figure 8.2, Table 8.2, and Table 8.3 were updated, as was the economic data used in the problems.

Chapter 9 Growth now reflects the latest economic events The global travel example was rewritten to account for pandemic restrictions. The *Spotlight* on Chinese growth was revised to account for recent developments in that country. Figure 9.1, Table 9.1, Table 9.2, Figure 9.5, Figure 9.6, Figure 9.8, and Figure 9.9 were all updated, as were the economic data in the problems.

Chapter 10 Business Cycles, Unemployment, and Inflation now incorporates the pandemic recession into the discussion of business cycles. The *Economic Milestone* on job cutbacks was updated to account for the pandemic. Figure 10.5 and Figure 10.6 now track real GDP and private sector jobs, respectively, through the Great Recession of 2008–2009 and the pandemic recession. The *Spotlight* on recession-resistant industries to include the experiences of the pandemic, which is very different than most recessions.

Chapter 11 Fiscal Policy has been substantially restructured to cover the impact of the unprecedented pandemic relief legislation. Tables and figures were revised to account for current data, including Figure 11.6 tracking budget deficits.

Chapter 12 Monetary Policy is significantly revised to include the Fed's response to the pandemic and to the post-pandemic inflationary surge. Figure 12.5 has been updated to reflect the Fed's direct lending in the early days of the pandemic. The appendix to Chapter 12 adds a new section on using aggregate supply and demand to analyze the pandemic.

Chapter 13 The Financial Markets added a new *How It Works* section on cryptocurrencies and fintech. All data were updated in the chapter, including Figure 13.6 on the stock market and Table 13.3, on how credit scores affect the interest rates borrowers pay. The *Economic Milestone* on mortgage rates was update to reflect a new low for the 30-year mortgage rate.

Chapter 14 International Trade has been substantially revised to take into account the current policy debates over trade, including the worries about supply chain disruptions that arose during the pandemic, and new concerns about China. The discussion of the global nature of the game industry has been updated. The discussion of offshoring was expanded to include two important new concepts, reshoring and nearshoring. A figure on labor costs in manufacturing unfortunately had to be removed for lack of data. The argument for protecting crucial industries was expanded to account for pandemics. Updates include Figure 14.1, Figure 14.2, Figure 14.4 Table 14.1, Figure 14.6, and Figure 14.7.

Chapter 15 Technological Change now incorporates the story of the successful rapid development of the COVID-19 vaccines, including a new *Spotlight* on Operation Warp Speed. The discussion of space tourism is expanded to include recent milestones. The discussion of innovation clusters was expanded to include artificial intelligence. Figures and tables were updated, including Figure 15.1 and Figure 15.2.

Chapter 16 Economics of the Labor Market now incorporates the impact of the pandemic, artificial intelligence, and remote work on the labor market. Wages and prices in the examples are updated to be more consistent with inflation. Figure 16.5, Figure 16.6, Figure 16.9, and Table 6.2 are updated with the most recent data.

Chapter 17 The Distribution of Income has updated figures and tables with current data, including Figure 17.1, Table 17.1, Figure 17.2, Figure 17.3, Figure 17.4, Figure 17.5, Figure 17.6, Figure 17.7, Figure 17.8, and Figure 17.9

Chapter 18 Economics of Health Care and Retirement was significantly revised to address pandemic-related issues in health care. Updates were made to Figure 18.1, Figure 18.2, Table 18.1 ,Table 18.3, Figure 18.3, Table 18.5, Figure 18.6, and Figure 18.7. The discussion of retirement now incorporates the impact of new retirement laws (specifically SECURE 2.0).

Chapter 19 Economics of Energy, the Environment, and Global Climate Change was revised to incorporate the rise in energy prices driven by Russia's invasion of Ukraine and the increased certainty of global climate change. Figures and tables were updated throughout the chapter, including Figure 19.1, Figure 19.2, and Table 19.1.

SUPPLEMENTS

Economics: The Basics, 2024 Release comes with a complete array of instructor and student tools that make both teaching and learning easier.

Test Bank

Available in Connect, as Microsoft Word files, and via Test Builder, the test bank includes a full complement of multiple-choice and short answer/essay questions to choose from.

Test Builder in Connect

Available within Connect, Test Builder is a cloud-based tool that enables instructors to format tests that can be printed or administered within an LMS. Test Builder offers a modern, streamlined interface for easy content configuration that matches course needs, without requiring a download.

Test Builder allows you to:

- access all test bank content from a particular title.
- easily pinpoint the most relevant content through robust filtering options.
- manipulate the order of questions or scramble questions and/or answers.
- pin questions to a specific location within a test.
- determine your preferred treatment of algorithmic questions.
- choose the layout and spacing.
- add instructions and configure default settings.

Test Builder provides a secure interface for better protection of content and allows for just-in-time updates to flow directly into assessments.

PowerPoint Presentations

Learn as graphs come alive! The PowerPoint presentations that accompany Mandel's text incorporate both the fundamental concepts of each chapter and the graphs essential to each topic. Where appropriate, the graphs themselves are animated to demonstrate movement within a coordinate axis—something printed figures simply cannot do. The PowerPoint presentations successfully enhance the lessons in the text *without* providing a substitute for chapter reading or class attendance.

Instructor's Manual

The Instructor's Manual includes pop quiz resources, common student stumbling blocks, and lecture notes. The manual is an invaluable resource for professors new to the course, as well as for TAs or other graduate instructors.

Solutions Manual

Suggested answers to the end-of-chapter questions are provided in this manual.

Proctorio

Mc Graw Hill connect + proctorio

Remote Proctoring and Browser-Locking Capabilities.

Remote proctoring and browser-locking capabilities, hosted by Proctorio within Connect, provide control of the assessment environment by enabling security options and verifying the identity of the student.

Evergreen

Content and technology are ever-changing, and it is important that you can keep your course up to date with the latest information and assessments. That's why we want to deliver the most current and relevant content for your course, hassle-free.

Environmental Economics uses an Evergreen delivery model, which means it has content, tools, and technology that are regularly updated and relevant, with updates delivered directly to your existing McGraw Hill Connect® course. Engage students and freshen up assignments with up-to-date coverage of select topics and assessments, all without having to switch editions or build a new course.

McGraw Hill Customer Care Contact Information

We understand that getting the most from new technology can be challenging. That's why our services don't stop after you purchase our products. You can reach our Product Specialists 24 hours a day to get product training online. Or you can search our knowledge bank of Frequently Asked Questions on our support website. For Customer Support, call 800-331-5094, or visit www.mheducation.com/highered/contact.html. One of our Technical Support Analysts will be able to assist you in a timely fashion.

ACKNOWLEDGMENTS

I want to thank Gwendolyn Ball for her research assistance on the 2024 release of the text. A special thanks to Aparna Lhila and Tianxu Chen for their contributions to the Connect offer that accompanies this edition.

I also want to thank the following people who were good enough to read and comment on chapters from the previous editions of this text, including Geordan Hull, Jelena Nikolic, Mahjuja M. Taznin, and John Ifediora.

Michael Mandel

SUPPORT AT every step

Education for all

McGraw Hill works directly with Accessibility Services departments and faculty to meet the learning needs of all students. Please contact your Accessibility Services Office, and ask them to email **accessibility@mheducation.com**, or visit **mheducation.com/about/accessibility** for more information.

Affordable solutions, added value

Make technology work for you with LMS integration for single sign-on access, mobile access to the digital textbook, and reports to quickly show you how each of your students is doing. And with our Inclusive Access program, you can provide all these tools at the lowest available market price to your students. Ask your McGraw Hill representative for more information.

Solutions for your challenges

A product isn't a solution. Real solutions are affordable, reliable, and come with training and ongoing support when you need it and how you want it. Visit **supportateverystep.com** for videos and resources both you and your students can use throughout the term.

Updated and relevant content

Our new Evergreen delivery model provides the most current and relevant content for your course, hassle-free. Content, tools, and technology updates are delivered directly to your existing McGraw Hill Connect® course. Engage students and freshen up assignments with up-to-date coverage of select topics and assessments, all without having to switch editions or build a new course.

BRIEF CONTENTS

CONTENTS

CH 01

INTRODUCTION

stdmrz/123RF

LEARNING OBJECTIVES

After reading this chapter, you should be able to:

LO1-1 Understand the importance of markets in today's economy.
LO1-2 Identify three of the main forces shaping today's economy.
LO1-3 Explain the debate over the role of government in the economy.
LO1-4 Define economics and discuss how prosperity is measured.
LO1-5 Name some key disagreements in economics.

On March 11, 2020, the fast-moving COVID-19 viral outbreak was officially declared a global **pandemic**. Over the next several months, the United States and most other countries saw a sharp drop in economic activity as many businesses and schools closed to reduce the spread of the virus. People shifted to remote work and education, but not everyone had the capability to do that. The number of unemployed Americans rose from 6 million before the pandemic to 23 million a month later. At the same time, the unemployment rate—the share of the labor force without a job—rose to almost 15 percent.

Pandemic
An infectious epidemic that crosses international borders

Nevertheless, the U.S. economy rebounded from the initial shock of the pandemic, aided by the rapid development of COVID-19 vaccines. Fiscal stimulus policies, started under President Donald Trump and continued under President Joseph

Biden, helped cushion the economic impact of the pandemic. As of the end of 2022, the unemployment rate was down below 4 percent.

Yet as of early 2023, many Americans still felt like the economic recovery was uneven and incomplete. Rising prices for essentials like gasoline, food, and housing were putting the squeeze on household budgets. Many businesses that had made it through the worst of the pandemic were still struggling to make a profit. The Federal Reserve was boosting interest rates to fight inflation, raising the possibility of an economic recession.

The economic picture was equally mixed in much of the rest of the world. Russia's February 2022 invasion of Ukraine, in addition to causing great human suffering, had helped push up energy prices in European countries such as Germany. China's "zero-COVID" policy, while greatly holding down COVID-related deaths in that country, also slowed growth and led to popular discontent.

The question now is what the future will bring. Despite the recovery, in early 2023 many Americans were still ambivalent about the future of the economy. They worried that they would have a lower standard of living than their parents and that their kids would have an even tougher time. These concerns played an important role in the presidential campaign of 2020, which put Joseph Biden in the White House, and in the midterm elections of 2022, which gave the Republican Party control of the House of Representatives.

But here, history offers a reason for optimism. Back in 1929, the United States was hit by the Great Depression, an economic crisis that was far deeper and lasted longer than either the Great Recession of 2008–2009 or the pandemic-induced economic problems of 2020–21. At the low point of the Great Depression in the 1930s, roughly one-quarter of the American workforce was unemployed. Construction came to a halt, farmers were desperate, and banks were closing. That terrible period—which seemed like it would never end—lasted a full decade.

But surprise! The Great Depression was followed by 75 years of strong economic growth and rising living standards. Someone who graduated from high school during the Great Depression may have had a miserable time finding a first job but probably ended up enjoying a lifetime of rising wages, improved health, bigger homes, better education, and far more options for travel and entertainment. One example: In 1929, air travel was a rarity, available only to a few people. Today, traveling by air across the United States or to other countries is common. Or consider health: Despite the pandemic, people are far more likely to live 65 years or more today than they were in 1929, when illnesses such as diphtheria and tuberculosis were major causes of death.

Looking forward from today, what will the next 75 years bring? Change happens so quickly now that even 5 or 10 years can dramatically alter our lives. By some forecasts, China could pass the United States as the world's largest economy within the near future. The Internet brings us more entertainment and information every day, as well as increasing amounts of misinformation and opportunities for fraud. Advances in health technology may significantly reduce the death toll from cancer and other medical conditions, increasing the societal complications brought about by a growing elderly population. The threat of global climate change has increased pressure to move away from fossil fuels such as coal and oil to other energy sources such as solar, wind, and nuclear power.

One key question: What actions, if any, should government take to affect these trends? Or to put it another way, how much should governments intervene in the economy?

> **Artificial intellligence**
> Computer systems that perform tasks that normally require human intelligence, including sophisticated decision making.

There are no easy answers. Should the federal government increase its regulation of large tech companies, such as Alphabet and Meta, or would too many rules slow down innovation and economic growth? Is **artificial intelligence** (AI) a boon to economic growth, or should it be regulated more intensely?

Consider also the hot-button issues of immigration and trade. How many immigrants should the federal government let into the United States, and what qualifications should they have? Should the United States raise tariffs on imported goods or should we keep tariffs low?

Finally, the pandemic showed the importance of government decisions about the health care system and public health. Medicare, Medicaid, and other government programs already pay for roughly half of health care spending. The Food and Drug Administration, a federal agency, also decides whether new pharmaceuticals and medical devices are safe and can be sold.

Yet there is still intense disagreement about whether the government needs to get even more involved in the health care system. Some people argue for less government intervention in health care decisions and spending, while others want to see the government taking an even bigger role.

THE BIG PICTURE (LO1-1)

LO1-1 Understand the importance of markets in today's economy.

This textbook will accomplish three goals for you. *First,* you'll get the basic tools of economics, starting in **Chapter 2** with supply and demand. When you're finished, you won't be an economist, but you will have learned a new way of thinking about today's world.

Second, using these tools of economics, you can begin to understand **markets** and the 21st-century **global market economy**. In a market, buyers and sellers come together–not necessarily in the same place–to voluntarily exchange goods and services for money. It may be the smallest of transactions, such as an individual downloading an iPhone app for 99 cents, or an airline paying $200 million or more for a new passenger jet. The market economy consists of all the different markets going on simultaneously.

markets
A way for buyers and sellers to voluntarily exchange goods and services for money.

global market economy
A collection of all the different participating markets in the world interacting simultaneously.

market transactions
The activity of exchanging goods and services that other people are willing to pay for.

Today, the vast majority of economic activity worldwide is organized by **market transactions**: activities that produce and exchange goods and services that other people are willing to pay for. From poor rice farmers in Cambodia to multimillionaire investment bankers on Wall Street, markets are essential, and this book will show you how they work.

Third, you'll see the ways in which the possibilities and choices of today's economy are expanding. At any moment, households must make purchasing choices based on their income and according to the range of products and services available (you can't yet buy your own spaceship). Businesses must make production choices based on the technology available to them and by their past investments in factories, processes, and materials. Governments must make spending choices based on the taxes they collect and the money they can borrow.

But these constraints change every day. Some things that were impossible or very expensive a few years ago have now become commonplace. Ecommerce has become so common that people can buy almost anything online and have it delivered the next day. Countries that were once poor, such as China, have become productive dynamos that are challenging the United States in many markets. The stock market and other financial markets are now far more accessible to ordinary people and small businesses.

For all these reasons, we'll pay special attention to the main forces driving change in today's economy.

ECONOMIC MILESTONE

1983 THE FIRST COMMERCIAL MOBILE PHONE

The first commercial mobile phone was sold in 1983 by Motorola. It cost $4,000 and weighed almost 2 pounds. This phone was fondly called "the brick phone" because of its size and weight. Nevertheless, it marked a major turning point in technological history. For the first time, ordinary people could buy a portable communication device.

KEY FORCES SHAPING TODAY'S ECONOMY (LO1-2)

LO1-2 Identify three of the main forces shaping today's economy.

Let's look individually at three of the main forces shaping today's economy: technological change, globalization, and the evolution of financial markets.

Technological Change

The forward progress of technology and science is the primary force for economic growth–not just in the United States, but everywhere. From the development of the steam engine, the automobile, and electricity through the creation of computers and the Internet, technological change has been the critical factor in raising living standards.

technological change
An improvement in knowledge that increases the quantity and range of goods and services an economy can deliver.

Technological change, broadly speaking, is any improvement in knowledge that increases the quantity and range of goods and services the economy can deliver. One example of technological change is the introduction of a new electronic product, such as the first microprocessor or the first mobile telephone, that lets people do things they couldn't do before (see the "**Economic Milestone**" box). Other examples of technological change include the expansion of online shopping, the development of vaccines for diseases such as COVID-19, and the testing of self-driving cars and trucks, otherwise known as autonomous vehicles.

The term "technological change," as economists use it, also applies to new ways of organizing work. For example, in the 1950s, McDonald's became immensely profitable by adapting assembly-line methods to the restaurant industry. The result was "fast food" mass-produced at low prices. Technological change includes creativity in entertainment as well. Walt Disney, who died in 1966, created the animated feature film. Originally hand-drawn by teams of animators, those early films evolved into the computer animation we know today. The evolution of the early video games into today's sophisticated multiplayer games also represents a form of technological change. Electric scooters, now found in many cities, are an interesting example of technological change transforming mobility.

Ray Kroc, founder of McDonald's
Bettmann/Getty Images

Successful technological change or innovation is much more difficult than it looks. Plenty of ideas look promising at first, but they take years or decades to get turned into successful products or businesses. For example, the first video telephone, which allowed you to see the person on the other end of the call, was demonstrated at the 1964 World's Fair in New York City. This was the AT&T Picturephone, and it was a commercial failure. It wasn't until many years later that videoconferencing became available–first, for businesses, and then for individuals through programs such as Skype and FaceTime.

Most products take multiple attempts to become practical. For example, the Apple iPhone was introduced in 2007. Before that, mobile phones could be used to talk with other people, but they had far less usefulness in terms of downloading information, entertainment, or games.

Technological change is uneven, moving much faster in some industries than others. Although information technology has evolved rapidly in recent decades, the pace of change in energy technologies has been much slower. Despite the rise of electric cars, the great majority of vehicles sold in the United States are still powered by internal combustion engines–a technology first invented in Germany in the 1880s. Nuclear power has turned out to be far more expensive and troublesome than expected, and the 2011 disaster at Japan's Fukushima nuclear power plant has raised more questions about safety. Meanwhile, renewable energy sources, such as solar, wind, and hydropower, provided only 13 percent of U.S. energy needs as of 2022.

However, with global climate change on everybody's minds these days, and the price of oil so high, companies and governments have more incentive to invest in developing new energy technologies that either are cheaper or emit fewer greenhouse gases. As a result, the pace of energy-related technological change may accelerate.

ECONOMIC MILESTONE

1997: THE FIRST TOYOTA PRIUS

In 1997, Japan-based carmaker Toyota introduced its innovative Prius model in Japan, which came to the United States in 2000. The Prius was the first mass-produced hybrid vehicle, combining both gasoline and electric propulsion systems to achieve higher gas mileage with less pollution. The Prius, still being sold as of 2023, set the stage for fully electric vehicles, such as the ones made by Tesla.

Globalization

globalization

The increasing exchange of goods, services, ideas, and people among countries.

Globalization is the increasing exchange of goods, services, ideas, and people among countries. The United States imports cheese from New Zealand, television sets from Taiwan, fish from Ecuador, tires from Romania, clothing from Turkey . . . the list is almost endless.

But trade in manufactured goods and foodstuffs is only one aspect of globalization. More and more international trade–both exports and imports–consists of intangible services. For example, when you call customer support for your new computer, you may get routed to a call center in India. The services of those Indian customer representatives are being imported into the United States or wherever you might be located.

Global flows of information–ideas, research, entertainment, and other forms of communication–have vastly increased as well. Before the pandemic, many more people were also crossing international borders for business, for tourism, or to immigrate permanently. For example, tourist arrivals increased over 63 percent between 2009 and 2019, only to fall sharply in 2020 as world travel shut down during the COVID-19 pandemic.

Why are countries so much more interconnected these days? Technological change is one reason. It is now possible to communicate from virtually any spot on the globe to virtually any other spot at almost no cost. If a retailer like Walmart in the United States is running low on, say, size 12 jeans, it can immediately flash a new order to a clothing factory in India, Vietnam, or wherever the production is done.

Technology by itself, however, is not enough to explain the pull of globalization. Most people accept that being open to the global economy brings enormous advantages. Incomes in countries such as Korea, China, and India started rising at a rapid rate only when they focused on becoming exporters–that is, when they produced what the rest of the world wanted.

For a rich country like the United States, a big benefit of foreign trade is access to cheaper goods and services. The price of most clothing to American consumers is lower today than in the 1990s, mainly because of soaring imports from low-cost producers overseas. In addition, a global economy greatly expands the size of the potential market for exporters. Companies such as Boeing and Intel, the giant U.S. semiconductor manufacturer, get much of their revenue from outside the United States.

Globalization also acts as a reality check. In an economy walled off from the global economy, it's easy for companies and workers to grow complacent and sluggish. Foreign competition shakes things up, forcing everyone to try harder and to look for better ways of doing things.

Of course, the impact of the global economy is not all positive. Foreign competition can wipe out jobs at home, force down wages and profits, and cause deep-seated insecurity. The flood of cheap imports in recent decades, while clearly benefiting American consumers, has ravaged manufacturing industries in the United States, eliminating millions of domestic jobs.

tariffs

Extra charges or taxes levied on imports by a country.

In response to such effects, it's tempting to pull up the drawbridge, close the gates, and pretend the outside world doesn't exist. In 2018, President Trump raised **tariffs** on a wide variety of imported goods, including steel, aluminum, washing machines, and solar panels. He further raised them in 2019.

Now, the United States is a big country; in theory, U.S. factories could produce almost everything we import today, from toys to clothing to computers. Moreover, the stunning rise in domestic oil and gas production over the past two decades has greatly lessened the U.S. dependence on oil imports.

Yet today, every successful national economy is tied into the broader global economy. Closed economies–that is, ones that are cut off from the rest of the world–may do better in the short run, but history shows they quickly lose their vitality and fall behind. Over time, it has become clear that countries that are open to international trade do better than those that are isolated (see **"Spotlight: The Chinese Economy"**).

SPOTLIGHT: THE CHINESE ECONOMY

If you check the label on your clothing, there's a good chance it will say "Made in China." The same is true for many smartphones, laptop computers, toys, motorcycles, appliances, and all sorts of other goods.

Forty-five years ago, it would have been almost impossible for you to find anything in the United States that was made in China. In 1978, China was the most populous country in the world, with a billion people. But it was also one of the poorest countries, barely able to feed itself and certainly possessing no ability to compete economically with the United States.

Since then, China has undergone one of the great economic transformations in history. Starting in the late 1970s, the government relaxed some aspects of its control over the economy, encouraged markets, and took steps to foster trade with the rest of the world.

The result: China is now the largest global exporter of goods, and has become a key leader in new technologies such as artificial intelligence. Perhaps more important, many Chinese are far better off than their parents were 30 years ago.

To be clear, there are significant issues with the Chinese model of growth. The country's economic policies have led to ongoing trade and political disputes with the United States. China still has political unrest and poor regions, and rapid growth has caused problems like severe air pollution in Beijing and Shanghai. But overall, China is a global economic success story.

The Evolution of Financial Markets

financial markets

The parts of the economy connected with borrowing, investing, or transferring money. It is also called the *financial system*.

financial system

See *financial markets*.

cryptocurrency

A digital currency, such as Bitcoin, which uses encryption to track transactions.

The third force driving today's economy forward is the evolution of the financial markets. The **financial markets** (sometimes also called the **financial system**) encompass all parts of the economy that have to do with borrowing, investing, or transferring money. That includes the stock market, where investors can buy and sell shares of companies; the residential mortgage market, where people can borrow money to buy homes; and the venture capital market, where start-up companies can raise funds to finance their early years. The financial markets also include banks, brokerage firms, mutual funds, credit card providers, and **cryptocurrency** traders. Government regulators, which in the United States include such agencies as the Securities and Exchange Commission and the Federal Reserve Board, are part of the financial markets as well.

Over the long run, the spread of financial markets has helped fuel economic growth. Companies, individuals, and governments can use financial markets to raise money for useful activities. As just one example, Tesla, the electric vehicle company, was able to expand faster, hire more workers, and make more cars because it could borrow billions of dollars.

Most people justifiably have mixed feelings about financial markets, which can experience violent swings. Over the long run—say, 20 years—the stock market has historically almost always gone up. But in the short run, it is subject to wide swings that can create large fortunes or steal hard-earned investments. Pick the right stock, and you can turn a small stack of money into a much larger pile. But make a bad investment or get caught in a stock market crash, and you can see your life savings disappear. For Americans who have invested their retirement savings in the stock market, these downturns can seem devastating, even if the long-term trend is upward.

Great Recession of 2008–2009

The deep economic downturn that started in December 2007 and lasted through June 2009.

COVID-19 pandemic

The global pandemic that was officially declared in March 2020.

financial crisis

An economic disruption that starts in the financial sector.

The last two decades illustrate very well the ups and downs of the financial markets, including both the **Great Recession of 2008–2009** and the **COVID-19 pandemic**, which officially started in March 2020. We will read much more about these crises later in the textbook, but here we will give a quick summary. The Great Recession of 2008–2009 was triggered by a **financial crisis,** which sent the economy, the stock market, and housing prices all plunging together. The problems hit many financial institutions as well, which had lent large sums of money under the assumption that home prices would keep going up. The result: billions of dollars of losses at big financial institutions. Moreover, there was a danger of a chain reaction, where the losses at one big bank or other financial institution would cause it to fail, and pull down other companies with it. As a result, the governments of the United States and other countries had to intervene very actively in the financial markets in 2008 and 2009 to keep them from collapsing.

By contrast, the beginning of the COVID-19 pandemic saw a sharp drop in stock prices followed by a rapid rebound. Overall, an investor who put all of his or her money in the stock market in 2002 and kept it there over the next 20 years could have done very well, despite the financial crisis and the pandemic. Still, many people were fearful of another stock market plunge and held on to their money as cash or placed it in other safe investments.

THE ROLE OF GOVERNMENT (LO1-3)

LO1-3 Explain the debate over the role of government in the economy.

In response to the COVID-19 pandemic, the U.S. government took aggressive steps to protect Americans from the new and deadly virus, while cushioning the economic impact of the pandemic on individuals and businesses. Nevertheless, Washington policymakers were intensely criticized both for not doing enough and for interfering too much in the economy.

This debate is an example of a more general concern: Should the economy be guided by politicians and government regulators, or should individuals and private businesses be allowed to make business decisions as they please? This question comes up in all sorts of situations. At one extreme is a **centrally planned economy**, in which most economic activities are controlled by the government. In the past, the Soviet Union—which collapsed in 1991—approached this mode. The government owned all the factories and decided what they would produce, how much, and at what selling price. At the other extreme would be an imaginary economy with few or no government regulations or laws at all—what economists call a **laissez-faire economy**.

centrally planned economy
An economy in which most economic activities are controlled by the government.

laissez-faire economy
An economy with few government regulations or laws.

Obviously, neither of these two extremes is workable. But virtually every debate over economic policy boils down to finding the right balance between government intervention and free competition. Let's get a better idea of what these terms mean.

Economic Competition

The common definition of competition is "a rivalry between contestants to achieve a goal or reward." Workers compete for jobs and promotions. Universities compete to attract good students. Companies compete for customers or for market dominance. States compete to attract new businesses.

Economic competition is the effort by people and businesses to achieve a desirable outcome, given what everyone else is doing. The most important economic competition happens within the context of a market. Buyers compete to get the best deals at the lowest prices; sellers compete to sell the most products for the highest prices. McDonald's competes with Wendy's to sell hamburgers, while Boeing competes with the European company Airbus to sell passenger airplanes.

economic competition
The effort by people and businesses to achieve a desirable outcome, given what everyone else is doing.

History suggests that economic competition—conducted within a fair set of rules—is the most consistent force for growth and progress. A company has a much stronger incentive to innovate and to produce a better and cheaper product if it knows that its rival down the block or across the ocean is trying to take its customers. The influx of inexpensive, reliable cars from Japan in the 1980s forced General Motors, Ford, and Chrysler to improve the reliability of their own cars and to come up with a whole new type of vehicle—the minivan. More recently the success of the hybrid gas-electric cars from Toyota and Honda compelled U.S. auto manufacturers to move more quickly to introduce their own hybrid and electric models.

The most competitive large economy in the world, by most reckonings, is the United States. Developing countries such as China and India have prospered by introducing more elements of a U.S.-style economy, including more competition, start-ups of new companies, and much less top-down management by the government.

What is the attraction of the U.S. economic model? The simplest answer is that it has a long track record of success. Despite recent problems, the United States has enjoyed consistently strong economic growth over time. Most people living in the United States enjoy a high living standard, meaning they have ample access to necessities such as food, clothing, and shelter and luxuries such as entertainment and travel. U.S. companies and workers have also shown a remarkable ability to adapt to new technologies and a changing global economy, in part because they have always been used to competing.

Still, the idea of unbridled economic competition with no government intervention troubles many people because it seems to lead to insecurity, waste, and unnecessary hostility. After all, if there is a winner, there must be losers. If companies are competing for the same customers, the one who comes in second may be forced to lay off workers. And economic competition seems to leave behind large pockets of poverty—people who are jobless and homeless.

Government Intervention

Government intervention represents the actions taken by government to affect the economy. Indeed, it would be impossible to do business without basic laws governing fraud and contracts. The government issues money, insures bank deposits so people can trust banks, and regulates the banks and the financial system. Regulations govern the details of daily life. They dictate how our homes are wired and whether our cars have seat belts or airbags, and they ensure that you can use your computer in the same room as your television without the signals creating interference on the screen. The Food and Drug Administration must approve new drugs for safety and usefulness before they can be sold in the United States, and the Federal Aviation Administration certifies new aircraft before they can be flown.

government intervention
Actions taken by the government to affect the economy.

Moreover, the government generally takes responsibility for making sure the economy doesn't fall into deep slumps in which millions of people lose their jobs. This role has been highlighted during the Great Recession of 2008-2009 and the pandemic. In 2008, the Federal

Reserve—the central bank of the United States—lent financial institutions billions of dollars to ensure that they would not fail and drag down the economy when the overheated housing market crashed. Also in 2008, President George W. Bush signed into law the Troubled Asset Relief Program (TARP), which made $700 billion available to help prop up the troubled financial sector. After President Obama took office in 2009, he signed the American Recovery and Reinvestment Act (ARRA), which spent almost $800 billion in an effort to create jobs across the whole economy. After the Great Recession ended, the Federal Reserve kept interest rates low for many years to ensure that the economy did not slip back into a downturn again.

Similarly, in the early days of the pandemic, President Donald J. Trump signed into law the mammoth Coronavirus Aid, Relief, and Economic Security (CARES) Act, the largest economic stimulus package in U.S. history. That was followed by several significant pieces of legislation, including the $1.9 trillion American Rescue Plan of 2021, enacted under President Joseph R. Biden. We'll discuss the pandemic relief legislation in more detail in **Chapters 6** and **11**.

Even during normal times, every country draws a different line between the appropriate role of the government and the appropriate role of private businesses and individuals. In Canada and the United Kingdom, health care is provided by the government. And the Chinese government regularly exercises control over where its citizens live and how many children they can have. For years, families in China were limited to only one child. That "one-child" policy was changed to a "two-child" policy in 2016, but the government control still exists. Indeed, China exercised strict control over its citizens' movements during the pandemic.

In practice, centrally planned economies seem to do poorly over the long run. Top-down management reduces insecurity, but at the cost of reducing incentives to innovate and make improvements. In a competitive economy, businesses react quickly to changing conditions; they don't have any choice if they want to stay in business. And unlike businesses in planned economies, they can use new technology without waiting for permission from a central authority.

deregulation
The process of reducing government control over markets.

Over the past 30 years, most countries have moved in the direction of less intervention by government, a process known as **deregulation**. For example, in the United States, President Jimmy Carter started reducing government control over the airline and trucking industries in the late 1970s. That process was greatly accelerated by President Ronald Reagan when he took office in January 1981.

About the same time on the other side of the globe, Chinese leader Deng Xiaoping began the process of shifting China away from a centrally planned economy. Today, China still has many people working in state-owned factories, but it also has a vibrant private business sector that has made China the largest exporter in the world.

YOUR ECONOMIC LIFE: Finding the Right Role for Government

In practice, you will find that government and competition are both present in every part of your economic life. For example, one big issue is how far the government should go in protecting your online privacy. On the one hand, you probably like the free and innovative services provided by tech companies, including e-mail, messaging, photo sharing, search, and navigation. Companies like Alphabet (which provides Google Search and Gmail) and Meta (which provides Facebook and Instagram) support these services by helping companies target their advertisements to the right people. For example, if you just shopped online for a pair of shoes, you are more likely to see shoe ads.

On the other hand, you may worry sometimes that the large tech companies know too much about you. Data can sometimes be sold and used in ways that might make you feel uncomfortable. Policymakers in the United States and around the world are currently debating what rules will protect your privacy without choking off innovation and raising prices.

Government also has a key role to play in determining what kind of housing is available to you, and how much it will cost. Most homes are built by private developers, not by the government. But developers and builders must work within a framework of zoning rules and construction codes set by the government. That's good, because you don't want to live in a building that will collapse. However, too many regulations will raise the cost of constructing housing, and push up housing costs and rents.

THE DEFINITION OF ECONOMICS (LO1-4)

LO1-4 Define economics and discuss how prosperity is measured.

Economics is a very broad subject that covers everything from the impact of gasoline prices on household budgets to the supply of new apartments in cities to the use of satellites to deliver Internet service to rural areas. That's why we need a broad definition. From a wide perspective, economics is about how we make decisions, given that we can't have everything. To put it more precisely, **economics** is the study of how individuals, businesses, and governments make decisions and trade-offs in the face of scarce resources.

economics

The study of how individuals, businesses, and governments make decisions and trade-offs in the face of scarce resources.

You could be a home owner trying to decide whether to allocate your money to buying a new car or to repairing your roof. Or you could be a business manager trying to decide whether to open a new store or put money into fixing up an existing one. Or you could be a government official choosing whether to create more educational scholarships or fund COVID-19 vaccines for the elderly. In each of these cases, it's necessary to make a trade-off because only a limited amount of money is available.

This way of thinking about economics will be very important in this textbook, especially when we consider the behavior of consumers, workers, and businesses in the following chapters. It reflects the reality of the world.

Indicators of Prosperity

Economics is always concerned with what can be done to improve people's lives, keeping in mind the need to make trade-offs. Ultimately, we judge the success or failure of an economy by the prosperity of its inhabitants. Of course, this leaves open the question of how to precisely measure prosperity. As you will see in this textbook, economists like to quantify (or put numbers on) the things they study, and there are lots of different ways to measure how well an economy and its members are doing.

For example, we can look at the total output of an economy, also called its **gross domestic product** (GDP) (see "**How It Works**"). In an important sense, the more goods and services an economy can produce, the better it is doing. That's why economists want to make sure the total output of the economy keeps growing.

gross domestic product (GDP)

The dollar value of the total output of an economy. Based on final goods and services produced in a year.

But economists look at other measures as well to gauge economic success. For example, government statisticians produce reams of data on wages and benefits. That's certainly one indicator of how well people are doing. Another important statistic is annual household income, which includes pay for workers plus other sources of money such as Social Security and income from investments. Economists also keep an eye on household consumption, which is the amount of goods and services a typical household consumes in a year.

Individuals may look better or worse off depending on which indicator we observe. For example, a student in college may have no income but may still have a good standard of living, including travel and a steady flow of online entertainment. A rich person who is not working won't receive any wage payments but may still have plenty of money from investments.

Then there are non-monetary measures of prosperity. We can survey people and ask them how happy or satisfied they are. Or we can look at whether life expectancy–the number of years that people are expected to live–is rising or falling. Indeed, the life expectancy at birth of Americans was basically flat from 2010 to 2019, as improvements in medical care were balanced out by other factors such as drug overdoses and a rise in diabetes. Not surprisingly, life expectancy fell sharply in 2020 and 2021 because of the pandemic.

Environmental indicators are important measures of prosperity as well. An economy that is growing while harming the environment is not helping future generations. We'll look more closely at the economics of energy, the environment, and global climate change in **Chapter 19**.

The Safety Net

Any successful modern economy must allow all its members to share in its prosperity. It's not politically or morally acceptable for most of the population to live good lifestyles while a smaller number are much worse off.

safety net

Government programs that provide a measure of economic security for the poor, the sick, and the vulnerable.

That's why the United States and other industrialized countries have a **safety net**, the government programs that provide a measure of security for the poor, the sick, and the vulnerable. In the United States, the safety net consists of a wide array of programs with familiar names: Social Security, Medicare, Medicaid, unemployment insurance, food stamps, housing subsidies, and tax credits for low-income wage earners.

HOW IT WORKS: GROSS DOMESTIC PRODUCT

Suppose you had to fill out a government form that asked, "How big are you?" You could give your height, your weight, your waist size, your shoe size, your hat size, or any other possible physical measurement.

Similarly, there are plenty of ways to measure an economy. But one key indicator is known as **gross domestic product (GDP)**, which is the dollar value of the total output of a national economy over a year.[1] GDP includes the value of all the food produced in the country, the value of its cars and trucks, and the amount of money spent on health care plus more. GDP also includes the value of tickets for sporting events, the money paid by consumers for phone service, and the cost of all the goods and services provided by federal, state, and local governments, such as defense, education, and road repair.

In the United States, the value of GDP is calculated by the Bureau of Economic Analysis, one of the major statistical agencies of the federal government. For 2022, the GDP of the United States was approximately $25.5 trillion, an almost unimaginably large number. This comes to roughly $75,000 for every woman, man, and child in the country. (We'll look at GDP in more detail in **Chapter 7**.)

Other countries calculate GDP as well, using roughly the same set of rules as the United States. **Figure 1.1** shows the 10 largest economies in the world in 2022, measured by GDP.

Figure 1.1

The 10 Largest Economies in the World in 2022. This chart shows the gross domestic product (GDP), measured in dollars, of the 10 largest economies in the world. The United States leads with a GDP of $25.5 trillion. China is number 2 with a GDP of $18.3 trillion.

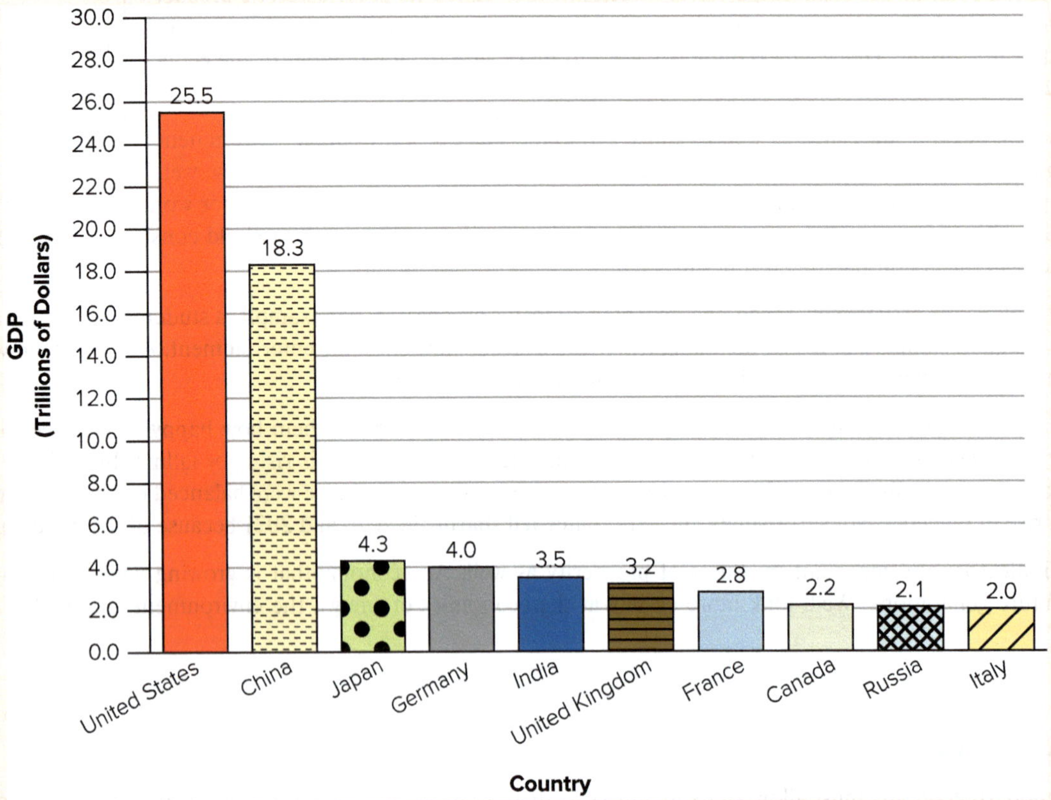

Source: International Monetary Fund estimates as of October 2022. The estimate for the United States is from early 2023.

[1] Taking care not to double count.

The safety net makes an enormous difference in the well-being of low-income households. The food stamp program, for example, provided low-cost food to roughly 42 million Americans in 2021, with the average person getting $2,600 in benefits. About 82 million low-income Americans were enrolled in the Medicaid program in June 2022, receiving help with medical costs.

Still, there is widespread disagreement about whether the U.S. government is doing enough to help the poor. The income and wealth gap between rich and poor has increased over the past decade, so that the top 20 percent of U.S. households get about half the country's income. In 2021, the Census Bureau reported that there were 39 million Americans who were officially designated as living below the poverty line.

By comparison, European countries such as France and Germany pride themselves on the strength of their social safety nets, which offer comprehensive medical care, better retirement benefits, and more job security than in the United States. Yet, until very recently, many of these countries also consistently suffered from a worse unemployment problem than the United States. Although the United States clearly has problems today, despite all its shortcomings, no one has yet come up with an economic model clearly superior to that of the United States.

DISAGREEMENTS IN ECONOMICS (LO1-5)

LO1-5 Name some key disagreements in economics.

In some areas of economics, there is little disagreement. However, economists are divided when it comes to several key areas of government policy.

Consider, for example, the government's role in cushioning the economic impact of the COVID-19 pandemic. Starting in March 2020, under President Donald J. Trump, and going through 2021 and 2022, under President Joseph R. Biden, Congress passed several large pieces of COVID-related legislation. These bills had many different valuable purposes, including funding vaccination research and development; providing cash directly to individuals and small businesses; expanding unemployment insurance; supporting state and local governments; and providing money to expand broadband service in rural areas.

Yet the appropriate level of pandemic relief is an issue of continuing controversy. Some economists believed that the U.S. government could have done more to control the pandemic, while others were concerned that the federal government spent too much and took on too much debt, leading to higher inflation.

Another area of dispute is the right level of federal taxes. In 2017, Congress passed the Tax Cuts and Jobs Act, which was signed into law by President Donald Trump on December 22, 2017. The legislation reduced tax rates for corporations and many Americans. The Congressional Budget Office projected this would lower future tax revenues and increase the amount of money the government would have to borrow. Some economists argued that this legislation would increase economic growth, while others worried that the new law would increase inequality and impose a bigger debt burden on future generations.

This level of disagreement is not unusual for changes in the tax law. President Bill Clinton raised federal income taxes in 1993 to reduce the federal budget deficit, and his actions were applauded by many well-known economists. But when President George W. Bush sharply cut taxes in 2001 and 2003, he received applause from equally well-known economists.

Politicians continue to argue about whether taxes should be raised on high-income households. There is simply no consensus in the economics profession about this question (and don't let anyone tell you there is).

Equally contentious is the debate over the government's role in the health care system. As we will see in **Chapter 18**, the Affordable Care Act (ACA) of 2010—also called Obamacare—greatly altered the country's health care system. Some critics of the ACA argue that it called for too much government interference in the private sector, and have repeatedly tried to repeal it. Meanwhile, other economists believe that health care should be completely funded by the government through higher taxes.

Likewise, although everyone agrees that education is crucial, there is no consensus among economists—or anyone else, for that matter—about how best to improve elementary and high-school education. Many economists argue that "money talks," so spending more resources on education, especially for the younger grades, is the right thing to do. But an influential group of economists believes, based on empirical studies, that spending money to reduce class size has little impact on educational achievement.

And then there are colleges and other forms of higher education. Some economists want the federal government to provide more scholarship funds, enabling more poor children to go to college. Others argue that if the government provides more scholarship funds, colleges will simply cut their financial aid packages or raise tuition by the same amount, leaving poor students in the same quandary.

Economists also have differing views about the government's best approach to stimulating technological innovation. Should tech giants such as Alphabet, Meta, Apple, and Amazon be more tightly regulated, or will government interference hold back new products and services and thus hurt consumers? Should government agencies pass new rules for self-driving cars—also known as autonomous vehicles—or should companies be allowed to experiment? And on the subject of cars, should the government force auto manufacturers to sell more fuel-efficient vehicles, or would that deprive us of our right to drive gas-guzzling sport utility vehicles?

Why do economists disagree about so many vital policy questions? In many cases, we don't have enough data to be sure of the right answer. Other times, the controversy is aggravated by the political agendas of those who stand to gain or lose from policy changes. In this textbook, we will present both sides of controversial issues and help you understand the reasoning behind each.

Economics is a dynamic subject, always evolving to keep up with changes in the economy. With any luck, this textbook will help you better understand both the subject of economics and the economy we live in.

01 SUMMARY

1. The basic tools of economics developed in this textbook, such as supply and demand, are essential for understanding markets and today's global market economy. ***(LO1-1)***
2. Three key forces shaping today's economy are *technological change*, *globalization*, and the evolution of *financial markets*. Technological change is an improvement in knowledge that increases the range of products and services the economy can deliver. Globalization is the increasing exchange of goods, services, ideas, and people among countries. And financial markets affect any person or business who borrows, invests, or spends money. ***(LO1-2)***
3. An important economic policy debate is the appropriate role of government in the economy—that is, the degree to which individuals and private businesses can make decisions as they please without interference from politicians and government regulators. Most economists believe that economic competition—conducted within a fair set of rules—is the most consistent force for growth and progress. ***(LO1-3)***
4. Economics is defined as the study of making decisions in the face of scarce resources. The goal of economic policy, broadly defined, is to raise the prosperity of the inhabitants of a country. ***(LO1-4)***
5. Economists often disagree about the right way to raise prosperity. Important economic policy debates include the nature of the government's role in such areas as health care, education, and regulating innovative industries, as well as setting the level of taxes. ***(LO1-5)***

KEY TERMS AND CONCEPTS

pandemic
artificial intelligence
markets
global market economy
market transactions
technological change
globalization
tariffs
financial markets (financial system)
cryptocurrency
Great Recession of 2008–2009
COVID-19 pandemic
financial crisis
centrally planned economy
laissez-faire economy
economic competition
government intervention
deregulation
economics
gross domestic product (GDP)
safety net

connect PROBLEMS

1. Economic activity around the world is mainly organized by ______ ***(LO1-1)***

   a) Internet connections.
   b) family connections.
   c) informal arrangements.
   d) market transactions.

2. The COVID-19 viral outbreak was declared a pandemic in March 2020. The immediate response of the labor market was _____ *(LO1-1)*

   a) a decline in unemployment.
   b) a rise in the number of jobs.
   c) a sharp rise in the number of unemployed workers.

3. Technological change ______ *(LO1-2)*

   a) moves faster in some industries than others.
   b) is found equally in all parts of the economy.
   c) moves fastest in the energy sector.
   d) never benefits the economy.

4. One benefit of globalization is ______ *(LO1-2)*

   a) higher prices for most consumers.
   b) lower prices for most consumers.
   c) less international communication between businesses.
   d) a lower standard of living for most people.

5. Many people have mixed feelings about financial markets because financial markets ______ *(LO1-2)*

   a) can experience violent swings.
   b) can work only in a centrally planned economy.
   c) only hurt the economy.
   d) always go down.

6. For each of the following, indicate whether it is more likely to be the result of economic competition or government intervention. *(LO1-3)*

   a) Protection against unsafe drugs.
   b) Rapid innovation.
   c) Help for poor families.
   d) Strong economic growth.

7. At its extreme, a laissez-faire approach to the economy means no government regulation at all. Let's suppose we got rid of the rule that you need a medical degree to practice medicine. One disadvantage of such a change would be ______ *(LO1-3)*

   a) more time spent in waiting rooms.
   b) fewer doctors.
   c) a higher price for most medical care.
   d) a lower quality for most medical care.

8. One indicator of prosperity is gross domestic product. Gross domestic product measures the economy by ______ *(LO1-4)*

   a) adding up annual household income.
   b) looking only at household consumption.
   c) counting the dollar value of the total output of a national economy over a year.
   d) measuring annual wages and benefits.

9. If the government safety net were to disappear, which of the following outcomes would be likely to occur? *(LO1-4)*

   a) Elderly Americans would live longer.
   b) Poor families would be able to buy more food.
   c) The income and wealth gap between rich and poor would narrow.
   d) The U.S. government would spend less on health care.

10. Disagreements among economists are ______ *(LO1-5)*

    a) unusual.
    b) limited to health care and education.
    c) frequent when considering the appropriate degree of government intervention.
    d) rare when considering new technologies.

11. Is the following statement true or false? Reputable economists agree that the government response to the pandemic was the appropriate level of intervention. ***(LO1-5)***

APPENDIX

THE BASICS OF GRAPHS

LEARNING OBJECTIVES

After you read this appendix, you should be able to:

LO1A-1 Read data from a line graph or a bar graph.
LO1A-2 Plot points on a graph using data from a table.

In this textbook, we use several different kinds of graphs. But don't be scared: The purpose of graphs is to help you by giving a visual representation of economic concepts or numerical relationships. For example, we can compare the sizes of two economies with numbers, or we can use the visual representation of a bar graph, as in **Figure 1.1.** We also use graphs to plot the behavior of individuals or firms in markets, or to help understand the behavior of the whole economy.

READING DATA FROM GRAPHS (LO1A-1)

LO1A-1 Read data from a line graph or a bar graph.

bar graph
A graph where the height of vertical bars represents quantities.

horizontal axis
A horizontal reference line on a graph, usually labeled to show values.

Graphs can be used to convey economic information visually. **Figure 1.1**, reproduced here as **Figure 1A.1**, is a **bar graph** that compares the size of different economies, measured in dollars. A bar graph conveys information using vertical bars. This graph has a **horizontal axis** (sometimes called the *x*-axis) and a **vertical axis** (sometimes called the *y*-axis). In this graph, the horizontal axis contains a list of countries, and the vertical axis reports the size of each country's economy. The height of the bars represents the size of each economy. So the United States has a bigger economy than France, measured in dollars.

Figure 1A.1 An Example of a Bar Graph
The 10 Largest Economies in the World in 2022

Source: International Monetary Fund estimates as of October 2022. The estimate for the United States is from early 2023.

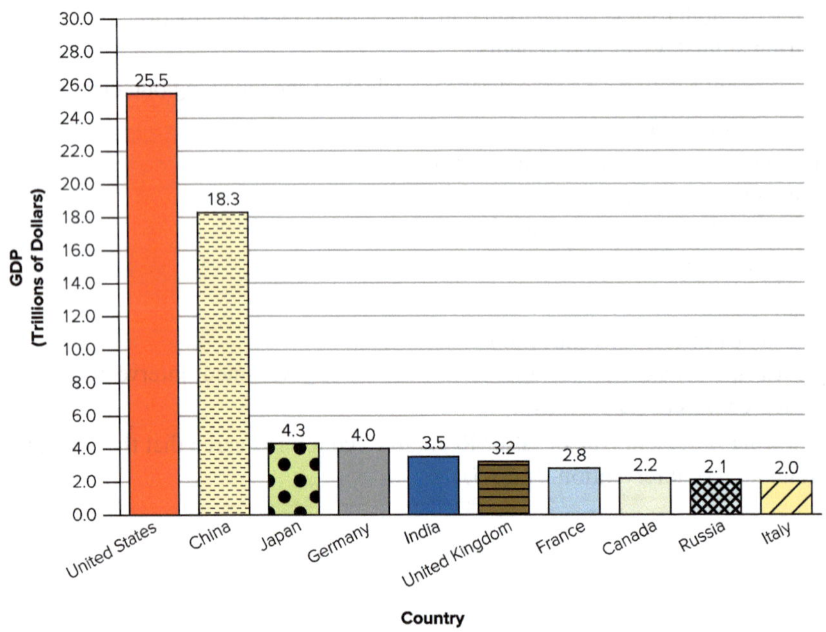

We can read the size of each economy from the graph. For example, the bar labeled "Germany" goes up to the line labeled 4.0. That means Germany's gross domestic product (GDP) in 2022 was $4.0 trillion.

vertical axis

A vertical reference line on a graph, usually labeled to show values.

Another type of data graph is a **line graph**. A line graph, as the name shows, conveys information using a line. For example, **Figure 1A.2** shows the population of the United States from 1995 to 2021. To determine, for example, the population of the United States in 1999, we start from 1999 on the horizontal axis and trace straight up until we reach the line. Then we look to the vertical axis and see that there were just under 280 million Americans in 1999.

line graph

A type of graph that uses a line to convey information.

Figure 1A.2 An Example of a Line Graph: The U.S. Population

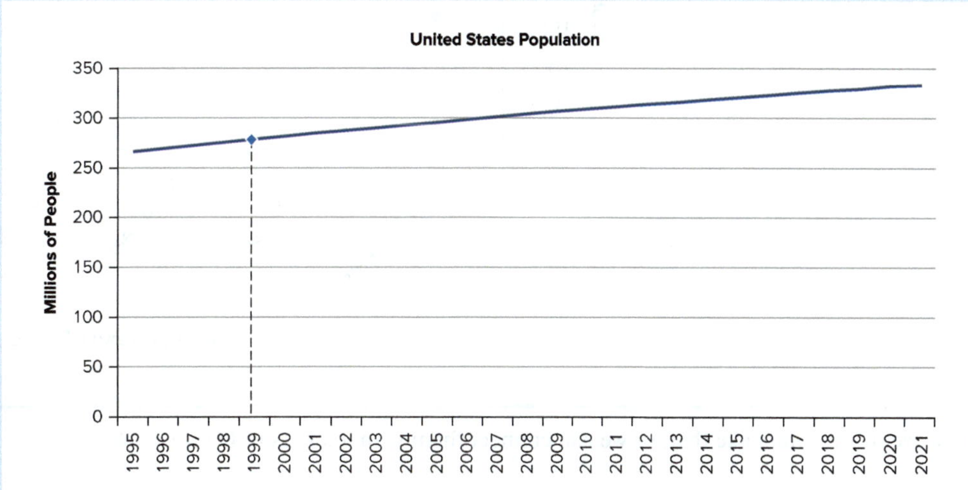

Source: Census Bureau.

PLOTTING GRAPHS FROM DATA (LO1A-2)

LO1A-2 Plot points on a graph using data from a table.

With the data graphs just described, you can read the data from the graph. But often in economics, you will be asked to go the other direction: Given a table of numbers, you have to be able to graph it. That is, you plot the data points on the graph, one by one. Then if necessary you connect the points.

Consider **Table 1A.1**, which reports on entertainment spending in 2021 for households headed by people of different ages. For example, a household headed by a person 45-54 years old will spend $4,700 per year, on average, on entertainment. Entertainment spending includes tickets for sporting events, movies, and concerts; purchases of consumer electronics, sports equipment, and toys; and spending on pets.

Table 1A.1 Age and Entertainment Spending

Household Headed by Person	Amount Spent on Entertainment for Household*
Under 25 years old	$1,700
25–34 years old	3,200
35–44 years old	4,300
45–54 years old	4,700
55–64 years old	3,700
65 and older	2,900

*Rounded to nearest $100.
Source: Bureau of Labor Statistics. Consumer Expenditure Survey, 2021.

How do we turn this into a graph? The first column of categories–in this case, the different age groups–goes along the horizontal axis. Then for each number, we go to the corresponding level of the vertical axis. Therefore, for a household headed by a 45-54-year-old, we run our finger up until we get to the $4,700 level, and that's where we put our point. We do that for each category on the horizontal axis, as shown in **Figure 1A.3**.

Figure 1A.3 Age and Entertainment Spending

Source: Bureau of Labor Statistics, *Consumer Expenditure Survey*, 2021.

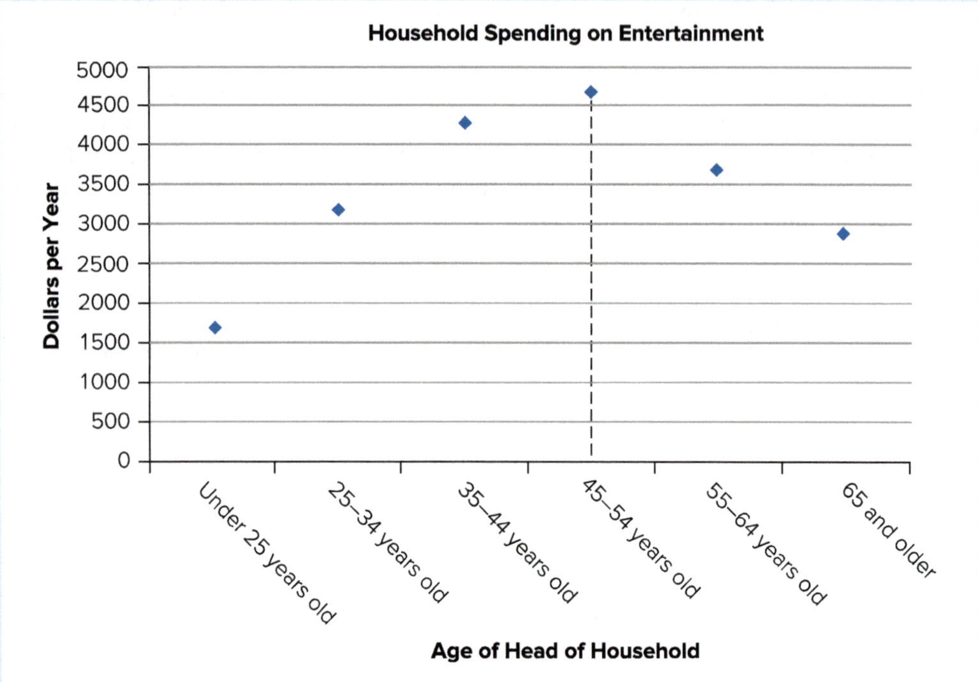

We can leave those points like that, or we can connect them with lines, as in **Figure 1A.4**.

Figure 1A.4 Age and Entertainment Spending (with Connected Lines)

Source: Bureau of Labor Statistics, *Consumer Expenditure Survey*, 2021.

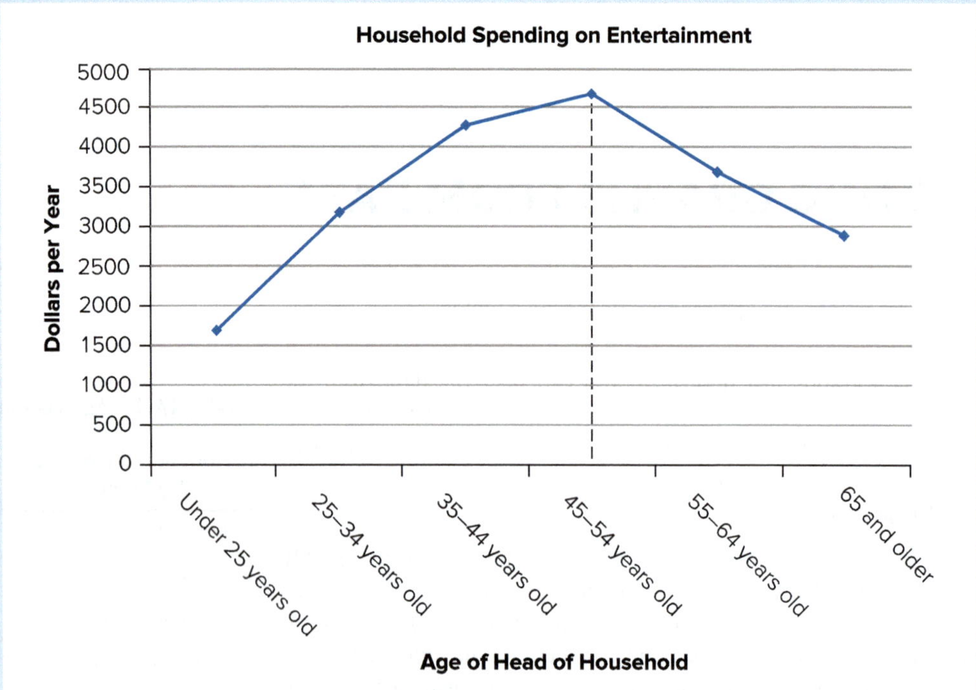

One thing to notice about **Figure 1A.4** is that the line is **upward-sloping** from the category "under 25 years" to the category "35–44 years." That means the line goes from the bottom left to the top right, so that higher values on the horizontal axis are generally associated with higher values of spending on the vertical axis. An upward-sloping line means, in this case, that entertainment spending per household increases as the age of the head of the household increases from under 25 years old to 35–44 years old.

Let's look at another graph. Since 1950, the population of the city of Cleveland, Ohio, has been steadily falling, as shown in **Table 1A.2**.

We will graph these data in **Figure 1A.5**. The first column, which is the years, goes on the horizontal axis. The vertical axis is the population. As before, we begin by plotting each data point, starting from the horizontal axis and moving up. For example, the population of Cleveland in 1990 was roughly 500,000 people, so we go up from 1990 to the line labeled 500 and put a point there. Then we connect the points in sequence.

Table 1A.2 Population of Cleveland, Ohio

	(Thousands)
1950	915
1960	876
1970	751
1980	574
1990	506
2000	477
2010	396
2020	372

Source: Census Bureau.

upward-sloping
A graph where higher values on the horizontal axis are generally associated with higher values on the vertical axis.

Figure 1A.5 Population of Cleveland

Source: Census Bureau.

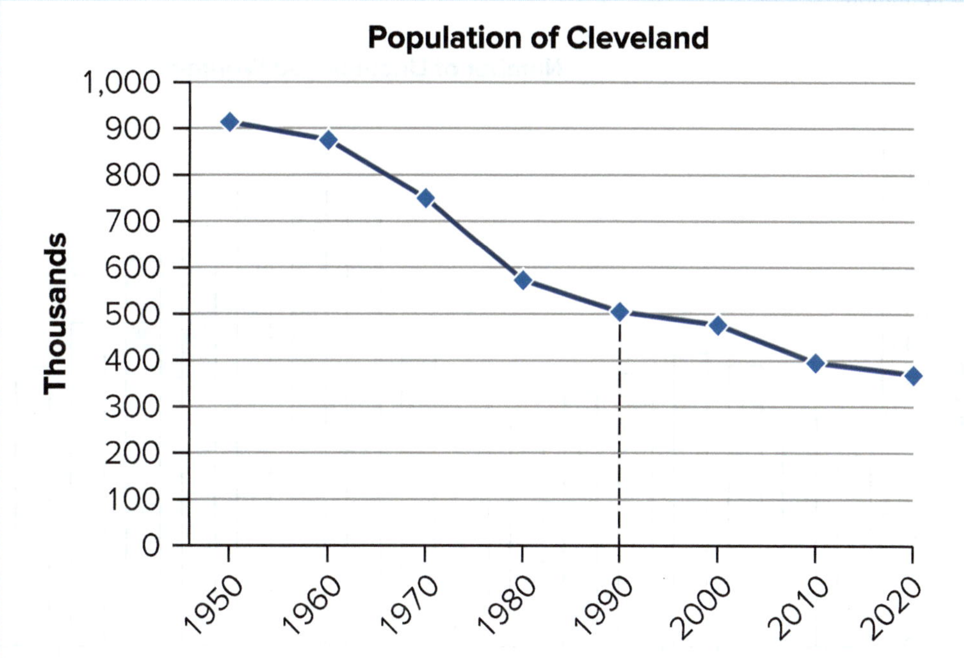

This graph is **downward-sloping**, which means that higher values on the horizontal axis are generally associated with lower values on the vertical axis. In this case, the population of Cleveland decreases as we move to the right along the graph to later years.

downward-sloping
A graph where higher values on the horizontal axis are generally associated with lower values on the vertical axis.

CONCLUSION

This appendix has described the basics of graphs. As we move on in the textbook, we will see more ways that graphs can be used to understand the markets that make up the economy.

KEY TERMS AND CONCEPTS

bar graph
horizontal axis
vertical axis
line graph
upward-sloping
downward-sloping

connect PROBLEMS

1. The following graph plots the number of unemployed workers in the United States from 2000 to 2022. What is the number of unemployed workers in 2007? ***(LO1A-1)***

   a) 4 million
   b) 7 million
   c) 9 million
   d) 14 million

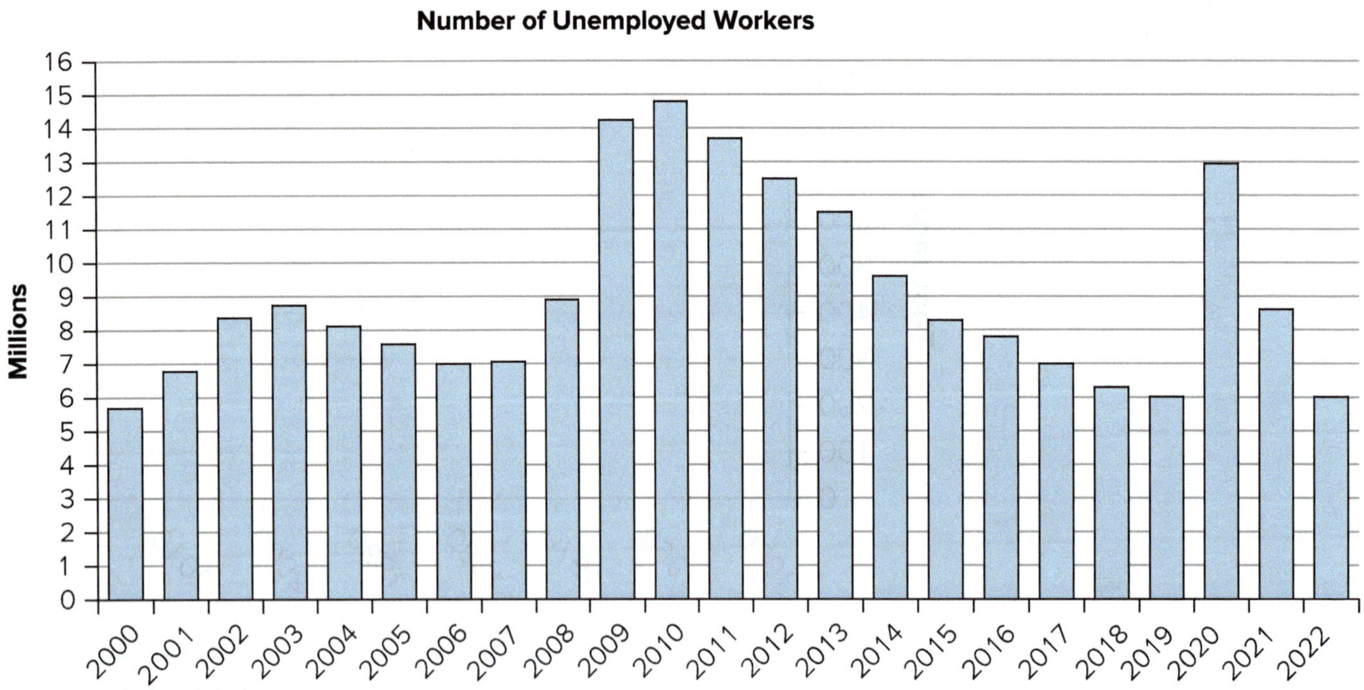

Source: Bureau of Labor Statistics.

2. Which year in the graph shows the largest number of unemployed workers? Which year shows the lowest number of unemployed workers? ***(LO1A-1)***
3. The following table reports on the average price of a gallon of unleaded gasoline in the United States, rounded to the nearest 10 cents. ***(LO1A-2)***

Average Price of a Gallon of Unleaded Gasoline*

2007	2.80
2008	3.30
2009	2.40
2010	2.80
2011	3.50
2012	3.60
2013	3.50
2014	3.40
2015	2.40
2016	2.10
2017	2.40
2018	2.70
2019	2.60
2020	2.20
2021	3.10
2022	4.10

*To the nearest 10 cents.
Source: Bureau of Labor Statistics.

a) Plot the points to make a line graph.
b) From 2014 to 2016, is the line upward-sloping or downward-sloping?
c) From 2020 to 2022, is the line upward-sloping or downward-sloping?
d) In what year is the price of gasoline the highest?

4. At a (hypothetical) minor league baseball stadium, the team owner has tried four different prices for tickets and has found that attendance per game varies, according to the table shown at right. Graph this data, with attendance on the horizontal axis and ticket price on the vertical axis. Is this graph upward- or downward-sloping? ***(LO1A-2)***

Attendance per Game (in Thousands)	Ticket Price
5	$15
10	10
15	5
20	3

CH 02

DEMAND AND SUPPLY: THE BASICS OF THE MARKET ECONOMY

astudio/Shutterstock

LEARNING OBJECTIVES

After reading this chapter, you should be able to:

LO2-1 Describe the key elements of a market.
LO2-2 Explain how the price in a market affects the quantity demanded.
LO2-3 Explain how the price in a market affects the quantity supplied.
LO2-4 Discuss why the number of markets can increase.

market economy
A collection of all the different markets in a given area.

Remember Legos, those little plastic building blocks? A **market economy**, such as that of the United States, is a bit like a Lego tower. It's an economic system made up of smaller "building blocks" of individual markets for trading all the different goods and services used in a country. The variety of different markets is almost too big to grasp. It ranges from the market for tickets to live Taylor Swift performances, to the online market for video games, to the market for airline tickets between London and Shanghai (an 11-hour flight!), to the market for pizza in downtown Missoula, Montana (which, in late 2022, included 23 pizza stores).

This chapter introduces the basics of the market economy. First, we'll explore the differences among local, national, and global markets. Next, we'll look separately at demand and supply in markets—that is, the behavior of buyers and sellers. Then, we'll briefly discuss the creation of new markets.

PRICES, BUYERS, AND SELLERS (LO2-1)

LO2-1 Describe the key elements of a market.

Any market has one or more **buyers** and one or more **sellers**. In the market, the buyer pays money in exchange for a **product**–a good or service. The sellers receive money in exchange for supplying the product. The rate at which the buyer and seller exchange money for the good or service is known as the **price**.

A simple example is the market for apples, say, in your town. There may be several sellers–the local supermarkets, the organic food store, and the corner deli. There are generally many buyers, such as people who enjoy eating apples and restaurants that make apple pie. The price is the amount a buyer pays per pound of apples.

It's usually easy to figure out who are the buyers and sellers in a market. The individuals or businesses with the cash or credit cards in their hands, or writing the checks, or using their smartphone payment systems, are the buyers. The people or businesses collecting the money are the sellers.

But keep in mind that each individual or business is typically a buyer in some markets and a seller in others. For example, the typical worker is a seller in the **labor market**. That is, workers sell their time on the job for money. Meanwhile, they are buyers in most other areas of their lives, purchasing food, coffee, video games, and other necessities and luxuries. A business such as Starbucks is a seller in the market for premium cups of coffee–but it's also a buyer of coffee beans, coffee cups, espresso machines, office computers, and the labor of its workers.

buyers

In a market, the consumers or businesses that exchange their money for goods and services from others.

sellers

Businesses or individuals who receive money in exchange for supplying goods and services.

product

A good or service.

price

The rate at which buyers and sellers exchange money for a good or service.

labor market

The market where workers sell time on the job in exchange for money.

Local, National, and Global Markets

Buyers and sellers who are geographically close to each other are part of a **local market**. For example, certain perishable food products like milk are generally sold in local markets (see "**Spotlight: The Milk Market**"). Dental services are typically local because you are unlikely to travel to a different part of the country to have your teeth cleaned. Similarly, many personal services such as haircuts, dry cleaning, and shoe repairs are handled in local markets. Even in today's global economy, no one is going to ship their dresses or shirts to India to be dry-cleaned, even if it's cheaper there!

local market

A market where buyers and sellers are geographically close to each other.

SPOTLIGHT: THE MILK MARKET

When you drink a glass of milk, there is a good chance it hasn't traveled more than a few hundred miles from the cow. Virtually every state has its own dairy industry, with distinctively named brands of milk from Shamrock Farms in Phoenix, Arizona, to Sassy Cow Creamery in Columbus, Wisconsin. As a result, the market for fluid milk is mainly local.

In theory, refrigerated milk could be safely shipped much farther than current distribution patterns. But a complicated set of government regulations—in place since the 1930s—discourages but does not prohibit long-distance shipments of fluid milk.

However, the market for dairy products such as cheese and butter is clearly global. The butter you put on a piece of bread may have come from as far away as New Zealand, and the cheese you eat may have come from France or even Lithuania.

279photo Studio/Shutterstock

national market
A market where buyers and sellers can be in different parts of a country.

In contrast, a **national market** lets buyers and sellers conduct transactions across the country. Thanks to the Internet and fast transportation, an increasing number of goods and services are traded in national markets. Do you want to open a stock account? No matter where in the United States you live, you can buy those stock-trading services from a broker anywhere else in the country. You can go house-hunting on the Internet and buy books, clothes, electronics, and music online. You can hire professionals in other parts of the country to improve your résumé or do your taxes.

global market
A market where buyers and sellers can be located anywhere in the world.

multinational
A business that operates in multiple countries.

Similarly, **global markets** allow buyers and sellers to be anywhere in the world. Crude oil has been sold on global markets for decades, as have steel, fish, natural gas, and memory chips. Global markets are often the province of globe-spanning companies called **multinationals**, which have operations in multiple countries. The online retailer Amazon, for example, operates ecommerce fulfillment centers in at least 20 countries, and ships products almost everywhere around the globe.

Indeed, one of the most remarkable changes in recent years is the seemingly overnight transformation of some local markets into vibrant national or global markets. The biggest change is the rise of ecommerce, which enables consumers to order clothes or electronics or almost any other goods from sellers around the country or the world.

telemedicine
The delivery of medical services at a distance using information technology.

Another example is the growth of **telemedicine**. During the pandemic, it became much more common to do remote appointments with health care providers such as physicians and therapists using mobile apps. Government regulations are gradually changing to make it easier to do online visits with healthcare providers in other states, potentially turning a local market for medical and psychological services into a national market.

The Market Price

In economics, we balance the wonderful complexity of the real world with the useful simplicity and clarity of economic models. In the previous section, for example, we talked about the *price* of a good or service as if there were only one price. In the real world, however, even identical cars may sell at different prices depending on which dealerships they are bought from and how well the buyers negotiate.

market price
The typical price at which a good or service sells in a market. Also, the current price at which a share of stock can be bought or sold.

That's why we define the **market price** as the *typical* price at which a good or service sells in a market. In many cases, the price for a good or service may be obvious and easy to identify. For example, the covers of most newspapers and magazines list their newsstand prices.

But sometimes, identifying the price of a good or service is not as easy as reading it off a printed list. Sellers are always adjusting their prices to pull in more customers. A **sale price**, for example, is intentionally set below the market price to stimulate purchases.

sale price
A price intentionally set below the market price to stimulate purchases.

negotiated price
A price that is determined on a case-by-case basis as a result of negotiation between individual buyers and sellers.

Then there are **negotiated prices**, which are determined by individual buyers and sellers on a case-by-case basis. Go to an auto dealer's showroom, and you will see the sticker price of a car or SUV listed on its window. But that sticker price is just the starting point for negotiation, after which different buyers may pay hundreds of dollars more or less for the same model car. Negotiated prices are more common in markets for big-ticket items like cars or homes.

volume discount
A price set below the market price to reward buyers who purchase a large quantity of items.

In many markets, buyers may be offered a **volume discount**, or a lower price for making a large purchase. For example, a hospital may charge an individual patient one price for an operation such as an appendectomy. But insurance companies may be able to negotiate a much lower price for the identical procedure, based on the large volume of operations they pay for on behalf of their customers–firms and individuals who buy medical insurance.

advance purchase discount
A reduced price given for buying in advance, so that prices differ according to when purchases are made.

In other markets, an **advance purchase discount** means that prices are lower if the good or service is purchased further in the future. For example, as of December 2022, it would cost you about $200 to fly from Baltimore (MD) to Rochester (NY) if you wanted to buy a ticket for the next day. However, if you were willing to buy the ticket a month in advance, it might cost a bit over $100.

A similar advance purchase discount holds for many events as well. It is typical for marathons and other races to offer a lower registration price to people who sign up by a particular date. In that case, two people of the same race may have paid different registration fees depending on when they signed up.

HOW PRICE AFFECTS THE QUANTITY DEMANDED (LO2-2)

LO2-2 Explain how the price in a market affects the quantity demanded.

Some words in economics have meanings different from ordinary usage. Usually, a *demand* refers to a forceful request, with the threat of consequences if the request is not met. Bank robbers demand money; babies demand their bottles.

Demand in a market, though, is a gentler concept. The **quantity demanded** by a particular buyer is the amount that a buyer is willing to purchase at a given price. For example, the weekly quantity demanded for gasoline at $3.00 per gallon is the amount a consumer is willing to buy at that price over a week.

quantity demanded
The amount of a good or service that a buyer is willing to purchase at a given price.

To really understand a market, though, it's not enough to know what consumers are buying today. We also need to know what would happen to quantity demanded if the price of a good or service went up or down. In the market for gasoline, for example, it's extremely important for government agencies and oil companies to know how much the quantity of gasoline demanded will increase if the price drops from $3.00 a gallon to $2.00 a gallon or even lower, all other things being equal.

The link between a buyer's quantity demanded and the price is called the **demand schedule**. To illustrate the demand schedule for an individual, we will focus on the decision of a person–let's call her Sally–to purchase a ticket to see a movie in a theater. Despite the ease of viewing movies online and continued worries about the pandemic, in 2021, there were almost 500 million tickets sold at movie theaters in the United States and Canada.

demand schedule
The link between a buyer's quantity demanded and the price.

But, of course, the number of times Sally goes to a movie theater in a year depends on the price of the tickets. If the price is $9.00 per ticket, Sally might see four movies each year. If the price is $2.00 per ticket, Sally might decide to see 10 movies–not just the blockbusters, but some lesser known films at well. At $40.00 a ticket, Sally might decide not to buy any movie tickets at all, and just wait for the film to be available online.

Table 2.1 shows what Sally's demand schedule might look like. The first column is the price per movie, and the second column is the number of tickets Sally would be willing to buy at that price.

In theory, we can build a demand schedule for every possible good or service that someone could buy. For example, your demand schedule for basketball tickets would reveal how many basketball games you might attend over the next year, depending on the price. Even if you are a vegetarian, we could construct your demand schedule for hamburgers. It would show zero quantity demanded at every price because no matter how low the price of hamburgers is, you wouldn't buy any.

Table 2.1 Sally's Demand Schedule for Movie Tickets

The demand schedule tells us how many movies Sally will want to see in a movie theater, given the price per ticket.

Price per Ticket (Dollars)	Quantity Demanded (Number of Movie Tickets to Be Bought in a Year)
$ 2.00	10
$ 5.00	6
$ 9.00	4
$15.00	1
$40.00	0

The **market demand schedule** sums the demand schedules for all the individual buyers in a market. So the market demand schedule in a town for hamburgers, for example, tells us how many hamburgers will be bought by the people in that town at any given price. That includes vegetarians who never buy hamburgers and people who eat a cheeseburger every day for lunch.

One final note: When we think about a demand schedule for a market, we are implicitly assuming that everything else about the buying situation stays the same when the price changes. For example, the market demand schedule for basketball tickets assumes that key factors like the quality of the team, the cost of the concessions, and the ease of traveling to the arena don't change when the price goes up or down. This assumption is called ***ceteris paribus***–Latin for "all other things equal." Economists often use this simplifying strategy to determine the effect of a single change on a complex system.

market demand schedule
A sum of the demand schedules for all the individual buyers in a market.

ceteris paribus
A Latin phrase meaning "all other things equal."

The Law of Demand

When a local supermarket wants to bring in more shoppers, it advertises a sale–lower prices for detergent, say, or for lamb chops. And when an automobile maker wants to attract more buyers for its cars or SUVs, it lowers its prices or offers rebates. The sellers expect that a lower price will increase the quantity demanded.

Alternatively, as the price of a good or service goes up, some people will simply stop buying the item, especially if it is a luxury and not a necessity. For example, if the price of a basketball ticket goes up enough, some people will simply cut basketball games out of their budgets and stop going.

law of demand
The tendency of quantity demanded to rise if the price falls, all other things being equal.

Generally speaking, the lower the price, the greater the quantity demanded. This relationship between price and quantity demanded is known as the **law of demand**. Here's a good way to think about it: If the price of a good goes up, you look at your spending and ask yourself, "Is this the best use of my money?" If it's not, you spend a little bit less on the item that has gone up in price, and a little bit more on something else.

Suppose you drink three cups of coffee a day at $3 a cup. The local coffee vendor raises the price of a cup of coffee to $4.50 a cup. Now you have to ask yourself whether that third cup of coffee is still worth it, or whether you want to spend that $4.50 on a chocolate bar or a piece of fruit. The principle works on a bigger scale as well. If tuition per class goes up, you may cut back on the number of college courses you take at a time.

Keep in mind that the law of demand is a general tendency, not an ironclad rule. In some cases, rising prices will *increase* demand. For example, when the prices of homes in a city are rising rapidly, buyers sometimes feel that they have to jump in quickly before the prices go even higher. Conversely, when the prices of homes start to fall in a market, buyers sometimes hold back from purchases hoping that home prices will decline further. However, despite such exceptions, you can usually expect that demand will fall as prices rise, and vice versa.

YOUR ECONOMIC LIFE: The Special Case of Zero Price

zero price
Occurs when an additional unit of a good or service is offered at no cost to buyers.

Economists will be the first people to tell you that there's no such thing as a free lunch. And, in fact, almost everything in your life–like your college tuition–seems to come with a price tag attached. But there actually *are* a few products that come with a **zero price** so that you can get an additional unit of a good or service at no extra charge.

HOW IT WORKS: THE iPHONE AND THE LAW OF DEMAND

Not even Apple, the creator of the iPhone, can break the law of demand. When Apple released the first iPhone in June 2007, the new phone was universally acknowledged as a great breakthrough. Still, it sold for a stunning $599—beyond the budget of most people at the time. Two months later, Apple reduced the price to $399. The result? Demand jumped. At the higher price, Apple sold just under a million iPhones, or about 14,000 per day. But after the price cut, average sales over the next four months were 20,000–25,000 per day. The price cut may not have been the only reason for the increase in sales, but it certainly helped.

leonardo255/123RF

When Apple announced the price cut, many people who had rushed to buy iPhones at the earlier higher price felt cheated. As a result, Steve Jobs, then CEO of Apple, was forced to write a letter on Apple's website apologizing and offering a $100 credit to those who had bought the phone at the higher price.

Source: Hafner, Katie. "For iPhone Owners, an Apology and a Credit," *The New York Times*, September 6, 2007, http://www.nytimes.com/2007/09/06/technology/06cnd-apple.html?_r=1.

There is no trick. In today's technology-based economy, you can consume plenty of goods and services in unlimited quantities after paying an initial fee. For example, your cell phone plan may offer unlimited calling and texting to other cell phones in the same country once you have paid your monthly rate. Similarly, at least for now, most broadband internet plans to your home allow you to connect for as long as you want for a fixed monthly charge (though virtually all mobile data plans do charge more if you go above a certain amount of data used during the month).

You may find zero prices sometimes occur outside the technology sector as well. Some restaurants offer unlimited refills on coffee, and you can still find "all-you-can-eat" buffets, even though they are less common than they used to be. So if the price for additional units is zero, why don't you consume an infinite amount?

First, you generally reach **satiation** at some point, meaning that eventually the value to you of consuming any more of the good disappears. You can drink only so much free coffee at one sitting before you get full or you start to shake from too much caffeine.

satiation
The point at which the value of additional consumption of a good or service goes to zero.

There's another consideration as well. Many products and services require some of your time to consume. For example, if you are sitting in front of the television, you are not doing something else like taking a walk, going to the mall, or spending time with friends. And no matter how adept you are at multitasking, you cannot talk on the cell phone while you are sleeping.

In other words, even at a zero price, you face an **opportunity cost** to consuming more of a good or service if it requires some of your time. In doing one thing, you are giving up the opportunity to do something else. In a world in which there are only 24 hours to the day, that's a real cost. So the opportunity cost of watching television is not zero; it's the value to you of the other activities you could be doing instead. Your long-distance calls on your cell phone may be free, but if you spend all your time on the phone, you are not studying for exams, earning money at work, or taking a walk in the park. Such trade-offs will limit how much you consume, even at a zero price.

opportunity cost
The value or benefit of the next-best alternative use of money or time.

Opportunity cost is an important concept in economics. In general, the opportunity cost of a choice or action is defined as the value or benefit of the next best alternative. This embodies the basic principle that you have to choose between different uses of their time and money. We'll meet this idea again.

Lester Balajadia/Shutterstock

Graphing the Demand Curve

Now let's look at the demand schedule for coffee consumption in a week for an individual–let's call him Tom. For many people, drinking a cup of coffee is an essential part of their day. However, one principle of economics is that even the demand for necessities responds to price.

In **Table 2.2**, the first column is the price per cup, and the second column is the number of cups demanded during the week. For example, if the price is $1.00 per cup, Tom may consume 18 cups per week. But if he must pay $5 a cup, he will restrict himself to only six cups a week.

Table 2.2 Tom's Demand Schedule for Coffee

This demand schedule represents how many cups of coffee Tom will want to buy in a week, depending on the price.

Price per Cup (Dollars)	Quantity Demanded (Cups per Week)
$1.00	18
$2.00	15
$3.00	12
$4.00	9
$5.00	6
$6.00	3

This demand schedule for coffee can be represented visually on a graph (shown as **Figure 2.1**). Going up the vertical axis of the graph are the different prices Tom could pay. Going across the horizontal axis of the graph are the different quantities he could demand. To plot the demand schedule on the graph, we start from a price on the vertical axis and move right until we get to the corresponding quantity.

We do this for every price, and then we connect the points in a line, called a **demand curve**. The demand curve shows the link between price and quantity demanded. It is the graphical counterpart to the demand schedule.

demand curve
A line on a graph showing the link between price and quantity demanded.

Figure 2.1 Tom's Demand Curve for Coffee
Each point on the demand curve says how many cups of coffee Tom will demand, given the price. Point *A* says that at $2 per cup, Tom will demand 15 cups of coffee in a week. Point *B* corresponds to a price of $3 and a quantity demanded of 12 cups.

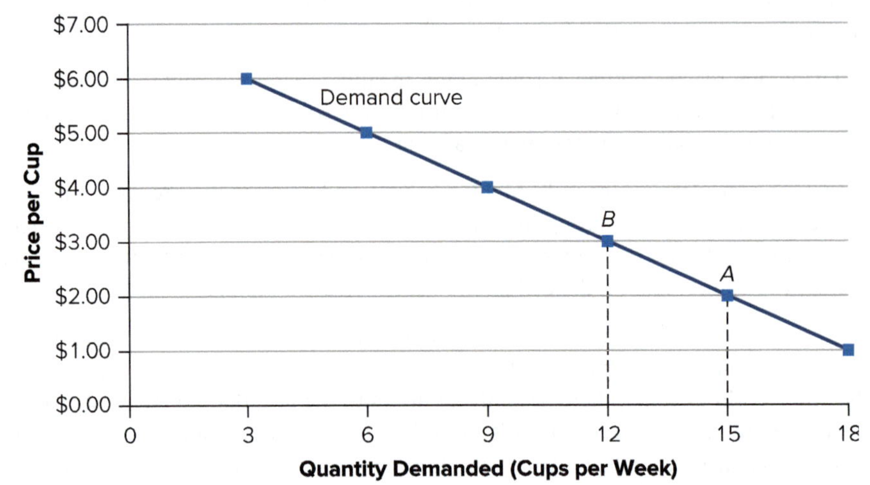

HOW IT WORKS: UNCOVERING THE DEMAND SCHEDULE

Suppose you start making necklaces in your spare time. Your friends tell you how good the necklaces look, so you decide to start selling them online. The tough question is: How much should you charge for each necklace? $0.99? $5.99? $20.99?

Obviously, the answer to this question depends on how many necklaces will be purchased at each price—the market demand schedule. For example, if the quantity demanded drops by very little when the price goes from $0.99 to $5.99, then it makes sense to charge the higher price.

But knowing the demand schedule for a market is often not easy, especially with a new product. One way to uncover a demand schedule is to survey consumers and ask them how much they would pay for a new product. Companies regularly show new products to groups of selected people and ask their opinions. The problem, though, is that consumers may say they highly value a product and then spend their money on something else.

For established products, one way to see a demand schedule is to actually look at how much consumers buy at various prices. This is most useful for widely used products, like gasoline, where economists can review how buyers have reacted to past price increases in order to predict the response to future price increases or decreases.

downward-sloping demand curve

A demand curve that is consistent with the law of demand, so that an increase in price leads to a decline in quantity demanded. As a result, the line slopes down when read from left to right.

For example, when the price is $2 per cup, the quantity demanded is 15 cups. So we find that price on the vertical axis, and go from left to right until we reach 15 cups per week (point *A* on graph). That becomes a point on the demand curve. Next, when the price is $3 per cup, the quantity demanded is 12 cups. We find the price $3 on the vertical axis and move right until we reach 12 cups (point *B*).

The result is known as a **downward-sloping demand curve** because the curve we plotted from our data starts at the top left side of the graph and slopes downward to the right. The law of demand suggests that most demand curves will slope downward because price increases reduce the quantities demanded, all other things being equal.

HOW PRICE AFFECTS THE QUANTITY SUPPLIED (LO2-3)

LO2-3 Explain how the price in a market affects the quantity supplied.

quantity supplied

The amount of a good or service that a seller is willing to supply at a given price.

Now we turn our attention to the supply side of markets. In any market, the **quantity supplied** by a particular seller is the amount of goods and services that the seller is willing to provide at a given price. As the price changes, the quantity supplied changes as well. The **supply schedule** for a good or service reports the quantity supplied at different selling prices.

For example, the supply schedule for new homes in a region reports how many homes will be built at each price. You can imagine an experienced homebuilder adding up the cost of the material, labor, and land involved in building a new home, and comparing that amount to the market price for new homes. The bigger the difference between the cost of construction and the final sale price, the more likely he will decide to build the home. If it costs $200,000 to build a home that can be sold for $500,000, you will see a lot of new houses springing up quickly. On the other hand, if the price of new homes falls to only $150,000, then new construction will probably come to a halt.

supply schedule
The link between a seller's quantity supplied and the market price.

Now let's turn to the supply schedule for women's haircuts. A hair salon hires hairstylists, who are available to shape, trim, and dry the hair of anyone who walks through the door. For simplicity, assume it takes an hour to give a good haircut. So the quantity supplied of haircuts at any price in this market is determined by the number of hairstylists employed.

Note that the quantity supplied of haircuts can exceed the quantity demanded. What does this mean? The stylists may spend part of the day not giving haircuts but reading the newspaper next to an empty chair or sweeping the floor while waiting for customers. But as long as they are available if and when someone comes in wanting a haircut, their time at work is part of the supply of haircuts.

Table 2.3 The Supply Schedule for Helen's Haircutting Salon

For any price of a haircut, this table reports how many haircuts are supplied.

Price per Haircut (Dollars)	Quantity Supplied (Haircuts Available in a Week)
$10 .00	40
$20.00	60
$30.00	80
$40.00	100
$50.00	120
$60.00	140
$70.00	160

Let's take a look at a hypothetical supply schedule for Helen's Haircutting Salon, as shown in **Table 2.3**. At a price of $10, there are only 40 haircuts available per week, with perhaps one hairstylist working full-time. As the price per haircut rises, however, running a hair salon becomes much more lucrative. At $20 per haircut, the number of haircuts available is 60 (perhaps because the existing stylist works extra hours during the week). As the price rises further, more people are put to work. At $70 per haircut, 160 haircuts are available, which reflects employment of perhaps four stylists, each working a 40-hour week and taking 1 hour for each haircut.

The **market supply schedule** adds up the quantity supplied by all the sellers in a market. For example, suppose there are 10 haircutting salons in a town, all with the same supply schedule as **Table 2.3**. Then, if the price per haircut is $40, there will be a total of 1,000 haircuts supplied (100 haircuts × 10 stores).

market supply schedule
The sum of the supply schedules for all the individual suppliers in a market.

The Law of Supply

The **law of supply** says that higher prices tend to increase the quantity supplied of a good or service, assuming nothing else changes. If the price a business can get for its goods and services rises, it has an incentive to increase production. There are plenty of ways to do that. It can hire more workers; it can have existing workers put in longer hours; it can open up a new store or a new factory; it can buy new computers or new machinery to beef up its productive capabilities.

law of supply
The tendency of quantity supplied to rise if the price rises, all other things being equal.

Suppose the market price of a haircut goes up. That will make it more attractive for a hair salon to hire more stylists. It will also increase the willingness of would-be entrepreneurs to open up their own businesses. But if the price goes down, haircutting will be less profitable; some hairstylists will be let go or be given reduced hours; and some existing salons may close. The quantity supplied will drop along with the price. This is part of the natural ebb and flow of markets.

The law of supply operates in global markets as well. Suppose a department store chain is selling blue shirts imported from China. If the price of that kind of shirt goes up—perhaps because men are dressing better—the department store chain will order more shirts from its supplier in China. The Chinese factory will need a little time to respond because it must first hire more workers and train them. But higher prices will generally lead to an increase in the quantity supplied, even though it may take a while.

A key market where the law of supply generally holds is the labor market. The price of labor is the wage rate—that is, the price per hour a worker gets paid. Generally speaking, a higher wage rate will not have much effect on the labor supplied by people who are already working full-time. However, economic research generally shows that higher wages do increase the labor supply of people who are less committed to working, such as teenagers.

SPOTLIGHT: THE GREAT ETHANOL BOOM

Most people don't think about the market for corn—but it is a great example of the law of supply in action.

In 2005, the federal government mandated that most gasoline sold in the United States had to contain some ethanol alcohol, a fuel that is usually made from corn. In 2007, that requirement was increased, with the goal of decreasing the country's dependence on foreign oil.

As a result, the demand for corn ethanol soared, and so did the demand for the corn used to make the ethanol. The price of corn skyrocketed as well, from roughly $2 per bushel in 2005 to almost $5 per bushel in 2008.

Here's where the law of supply came into effect. Farmers, the main suppliers of corn, responded to the rising price by increasing the quantity supplied. They planted more corn—a lot more corn. The result was the largest corn crop in history at the time.

Consumers were not happy about the higher price of corn, however. Not only was corn in the store more expensive, so was pork and beef, because pigs and cattle are often fed corn. The situation got even worse in 2012, when a drought hit the Midwest, cutting corn production and raising corn prices even higher.

smereka/Shutterstock

As of 2022, there was continuing debate about the level at which the government should set the ethanol mandate. A lower mandate would illustrate the law of supply in action again. Less demand for ethanol would mean lower prices for corn, which would mean that farmers would switch to other crops, lessening the quantity supplied of corn.

Source: U.S. Department of Agriculture.

Like the law of demand, the law of supply does not hold true in every circumstance. In some cases, an increased price can lower supply. For example, suppose your goal is to work enough hours during a semester to pay your expenses–let's say $2,000. If you earn $10 an hour, you will have to work 200 hours to achieve your goal. But if you earn $20 an hour, it will take only 100 hours to earn enough to pay your expenses–so a higher price for your labor will decrease, not increase, the amount of labor you supply. However, in most situations, the law of supply does hold.

Graphing the Supply Schedule

Just as we plotted the demand schedule from **Table 2.2** in **Figure 2.1**, we can plot the supply schedule for a market on a graph. Let's think about a suburban town where home owners hire other people to mow their lawns. They might be paying neighborhood teenagers or a landscape service.

Table 2.4 The Market Supply Schedule for Lawn Mowing

As the price to mow a lawn rises, so does the quantity supplied. For example, if the going market price for mowing a lawn in a town is $30, then suppliers make themselves available to mow 25 lawns.

Market Price per Lawn Mowed (Dollars)	Quantity Supplied (Lawns Mowed per Week)
$10 .00	5
$20.00	15
$30.00	25
$40.00	35

The market price per lawn determines the quantity of lawn-mowing services supplied. If the price is high enough, then teenagers tear themselves away from their video games and offer to mow their neighbors' lawns, and landscape services hire more workers.

Table 2.4 shows a hypothetical market supply schedule for the lawn-mowing market in a town. As the market price per lawn increases, so does the quantity supplied.

Now let's plot this supply schedule on a graph (**Figure 2.2**). Going up the vertical axis are the various prices that could be charged per lawn. Going across the horizontal axis is the quantity supplied–the number of lawns mowed. To plot the supply schedule, we start with a price on the vertical axis and move right horizontally until we come to the number of lawns mowed.

Figure 2.2 The Market Supply Curve for Lawn Mowing
Each point on the market supply curve says how many lawns suppliers are willing to mow, given the price. Point *A* says that at $20 per lawn, the quantity supplied is 15 mowed lawns. Point *B* corresponds to a price of $30 and a quantity supplied of 25 lawns.

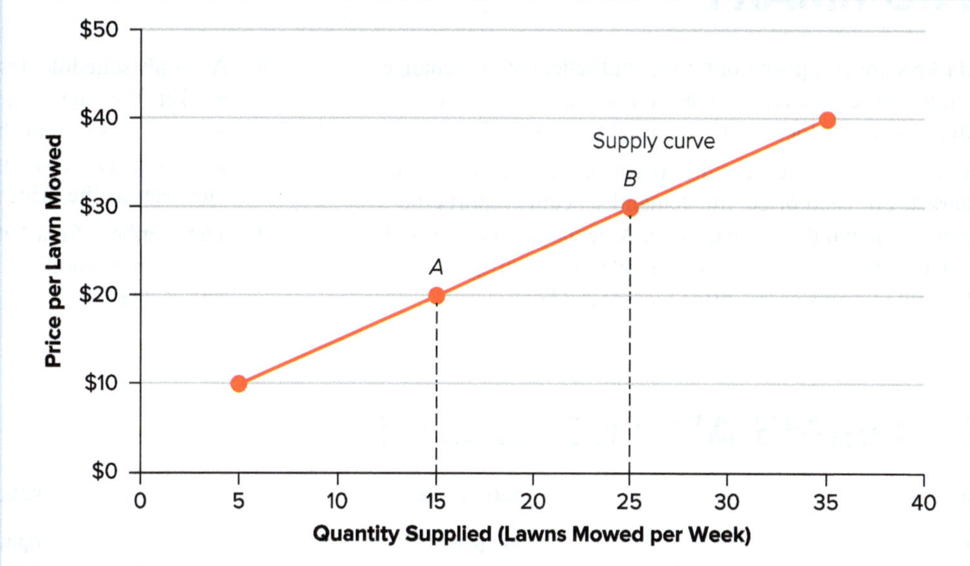

For example, if the market price is $20 per lawn, the supply schedule tells us that the quantity supplied is 15 mowed lawns. That quantity supplied corresponds to point *A* in **Figure 2.2**. Plotting all the combinations of price and quantity supplied and connecting the points gives us the **supply curve** The supply curve shows the link between the price and the quantity supplied.

supply curve
A line on a graph showing the link between price and quantity supplied.

The result is an **upward-sloping supply curve** that starts at the lower left corner and goes to the upper right corner of the graph. We have drawn it as a straight line, but real-world supply curves are generally not straight.

upward-sloping supply curve
A supply curve that is consistent with the law of supply, so that an increase in price leads to an increase in quantity supplied. As a result, the line slopes up when read from left to right.

NEW MARKETS (LO2-4)

LO2-4 Discuss why the number of markets can increase.

Here's one final note for this chapter. Demand and supply schedules describe how buyers and suppliers behave in existing markets, but the number of markets is not fixed. **New markets** are created every day to meet the changing needs of consumers and to take advantage of the changing capabilities of producers. New markets can provide new products or services, or bring in new buyers and sellers.

new markets
Markets with new products and services, or markets that include mostly new buyers and sellers.

Some goods and services we buy today were not available 10, 20, or 30 years ago, or were not available in the same form. Online video meetings have become the norm. You can go to the grocery store and buy plant-based "meat" products. Ridesharing services like Uber and Lyft, which were only founded in 2009 and 2012, respectively, are now essential to transportation in many areas. We're surrounded by new technologies and new products.

New markets also arise as incomes rise in developing countries like China and India. For example, as recently as the early 1990s, few families owned cars in China. But as the country grew richer and incomes soared, the market for automobiles in China went from minuscule to enormous almost overnight.

We will return to the notion of new markets in **Chapters 13**, **14**, and **15** when we look at financial markets, globalization, and technological change in more detail. For now, keep in mind that one of the biggest positives of a market economy is its ability to adapt quickly to changing circumstances.

02 SUMMARY

1. Markets are composed of buyers and sellers who exchange goods and services for money at a rate called the price. Markets can be local, national, or global. *(LO2-1)*
2. A demand schedule describes the behavior of buyers in a market. For each price, the demand schedule reports the quantity demanded at that price. A demand curve is usually downward-sloping, which means that the quantity demanded drops as the price increases. *(LO2-2)*
3. A supply schedule describes the behavior of sellers in a market. For each price, the supply schedule reports the quantity supplied at that price. A supply curve is usually upward-sloping, which means that the quantity supplied increases as the price increases. *(LO2-3)*
4. The number of markets is not fixed. New markets can provide new goods or services or bring in new buyers and sellers. *(LO2-4)*

KEY TERMS AND CONCEPTS

market economy
buyers
sellers
product
price
labor market
local market
national market
global market
multinational
telemedicine
market price
sale price
negotiated price
volume discount
advance purchase discount
quantity demanded
demand schedule
market demand schedule
ceteris paribus
law of demand
zero price
satiation
opportunity cost
demand curve
downward-sloping demand curve
quantity supplied
supply schedule
market supply schedule
law of supply
supply curve
upward-sloping supply curve
new markets

connect PROBLEMS

1. Which of the following is an example of a seller in a market? *(LO2-1)*
   a) An online clothing store selling a blue dress.
   b) A student paying tuition.
   c) A department store hiring a cashier.
   d) An airplane passenger buying a ticket.
2. Which of the following is an example of a buyer in a market? *(LO2-1)*
   a) An airline offering low fares for seats on a flight.
   b) A student paying for a haircut.
   c) A restaurant selling a meal.
   d) An amusement park selling admissions to a ride.
3. Which of the following is an example of a global market? *(LO2-1)*
   a) The market for haircuts in New York City.
   b) The market for dry cleaning in St. Louis.
   c) The market for homes in Dallas.
   d) The market for crude oil.
4. The typical price at which a good or service sells in a market is the _______ *(LO2-1)*
   a) sale price.
   b) market price.
   c) negotiated price.
   d) volume discount.

5. When a person becomes unwilling to consume more of a good even at a zero price, he or she has reached _______ *(LO2-2)*
   a) the market price.
   b) *ceteris paribus*.
   c) satiation.
   d) the sale price.
6. The demand curve is the graphical representation of the _______ *(LO2-2)*
   a) opportunity cost.
   b) sale price.
   c) supply schedule.
   d) demand schedule.
7. Sam lives in a small town with only one restaurant. The restaurant, run by an eccentric old gentleman, offers a dinner menu on which every dish is the same price. Each month, he posts the price of the meal in the window. The following table lists the number of times Sam goes out to dinner at the restaurant during the month, according to the posted price of the dinner. *(LO2-2)*

Price per Meal (Dollars)	Quantity Demanded (Number of Times Sam Eats at the Restaurant in the Month)
$ 6.00	24
$12.00	12
$18.00	8
$24.00	6
$30.00	4
$36.00	2

   a) Plot the demand curve for meals.
   b) How many times per month does Sam eat at the restaurant if the price per meal is $18?
8. All other things being equal, when the price of a good increases, the quantity supplied typically _______ *(LO2-3)*
   a) stays the same.
   b) decreases.
   c) increases.
9. In a small town, there's only one construction company that builds new homes. The following table lists the number of new homes built in a year at different selling prices. *(LO2-3)*

Sale Price of a New Home (Dollars)	Quantity Supplied (Number of New Homes Built in a Year)
$150,000	2
$200,000	10
$250,000	16
$300,000	20
$350,000	23

   a) Plot the supply curve for new homes.
   b) How many homes are built if the price is $250,000 per home?
10. The first true smartphone, the iPhone, was introduced in 2007. Since then, billions of smartphones have been sold globally. Which of the following statements is true? Explain your answer. *(LO2-4)*
   a) The rise of the smartphone did not lead to any new markets.
   b) The rise of the smartphone created many new markets, including the market for smartphone applications (apps).
   c) The only new market created is the market for smartphones.
   d) The price of smartphones is lower than the price of the phones they replace.

CH 03

MARKET EQUILIBRIUM AND SHIFTS

Halfpoint/Shutterstock

LEARNING OBJECTIVES

After reading this chapter, you should be able to:

LO3-1 Define excess supply and excess demand.
LO3-2 Explain market equilibrium, and identify the equilibrium point on a supply–demand diagram.
LO3-3 Describe the impact of supply and demand shifts.
LO3-4 Discuss some causes of market shifts.
LO3-5 Illustrate how changes in income affect the demand curve.
LO3-6 Review the basics of elasticity.

The economy is always changing in ways large and small. Consider the difference between the economy today compared to before the pandemic. Working from home has become more common. Online shopping has greatly increased. And the demand for surgical and other face masks is much higher now than before the pandemic started.

Each of these events affected at least one market. With more people working from home, demand for downtown office space declined in most cities. Retailers such as Amazon and Walmart hired hundreds of thousands of workers to assemble and deliver online orders. And companies that make face masks invested in new machines to increase their production capacity.

In this chapter, we will look at how markets react to change. First, we'll examine what might happen when buyers want more than sellers are prepared to produce or when sellers produce more than buyers are prepared to consume. Then, we'll outline the key concept of *market equilibrium*—that special point where both buyers and sellers are satisfied and supply equals demand. We'll see how buyers and sellers react to events, or *shifts,* that can push markets away from equilibrium. Finally, we'll discuss the basics of elasticity of demand and supply, which tell us how much buyers and sellers react to changes in their economic environment.

MATCHING SUPPLY AND DEMAND (LO3-1)

LO3-1 Define excess supply and excess demand.

Recall from the previous chapter that markets have two sides: buyers and sellers. Each side makes decisions independently, so in theory, the amount buyers wish to purchase may be very different from the amount sellers wish to provide. But as we will see in this section, one of the great strengths of a market economy is that quantity demanded tends to roughly equal quantity supplied most of the time.

The Case of Excess Demand

A market has **excess demand** if buyers desire to purchase a greater quantity than sellers are prepared to supply at the current market price. In other words, quantity demanded exceeds quantity supplied at the current market price.

excess demand
A situation in which quantity demanded exceeds quantity supplied at the current market price.

For example, during the pandemic, global **supply chains** got snarled, making it hard to move goods from factories around the world to consumers in the United States. The result was empty shelves at stores, and the inability of Americans to get the clothing, appliances, and furniture they wanted.

supply chains
The network of suppliers needed to make a particular product.

Another example of (temporary) excess demand: When you travel by air, you will sometimes see that the flight is completely full. In such cases, there may be a "standby" list of passengers who would like to get on that plane if they could.

The employment market for nursing home staff showed signs of excess demand in some regions during and after the pandemic. An aging population requires more care—but nursing home operators were often unwilling to raise wages high enough to attract the needed staff, leading to persistent job vacancies.

The Case of Excess Supply

Other markets may suffer from **excess supply** when suppliers are willing to sell more at the market price than buyers are prepared to pay for. In that situation, the quantity supplied then exceeds the quantity demanded at the current market price. For example, sometimes a clothing company will make too many shirts in a particular style that consumers don't want to buy. The company is then stuck with a mound of unsold inventory. Or sometimes a poorly performing baseball team may find itself with many empty seats in its stadium.

excess supply
A situation in which quantity supplied exceeds quantity demanded at the current market price.

Another example of excess supply is downtown office in many cities: As the pandemic led more people to work from home, businesses have needed to rent less office space. As a result, in many areas, there is an excess of office space. Similarly, changes in vacation or travel patterns can leave a formerly popular hotel with perpetually empty rooms (as we see in "**Spotlight: Excess Supply on the Boardwalk**").

The Invisible Hand

Situations of excess demand and excess supply disappoint buyers and frustrate sellers. Every day around the country, customers are walking into stores and walking out unhappy because the dress or automobile they wanted was out of stock. On the other hand, sometimes businesses spend millions advertising products—a new type of fitness gadget, perhaps—that no one wants to buy.

market mechanism
The process by which a market reaches equilibrium without a central planner. See *invisible hand.*

How do markets react to a gap between quantity supplied and quantity demanded? The difference between the two is usually closed by what economists call the **market mechanism**—or, more poetically, the **invisible hand**.

invisible hand
A term to describe a situation in which individual actions of buyers and sellers tend to result in a positive social outcome.

The reason the mechanism is "invisible" is that no central planning agency has to issue explicit orders to close the supply-demand gap; buyers and sellers act on their own. Excess supply usually puts downward pressure on prices. For example, when retailers have too many shirts or big-screen televisions in their stores, or too many new cars in the lot, they run a sale. Motels with spare rooms offer them at cut-rate prices to tour operators or online resellers. Hair salons may trim their prices by offering newspaper coupons or specials on coloring.

SPOTLIGHT: EXCESS SUPPLY ON THE BOARDWALK

A closed casino in Atlantic City.

Shutterstock / Andy Borysowski

The first legal casino outside of Las Vegas opened in Atlantic City, New Jersey, in 1978. Gamblers from both New York City and Philadelphia immediately flocked to the new casino in the seaside resort town, with its famous boardwalk. Very quickly, developers such as Donald Trump built more and more casino hotels to take advantage of the untapped demand for legal gambling. To attract visitors to Atlantic City, the casinos staged high-profile boxing matches, featuring fighters like Mike Tyson. The town glittered.

But then Atlantic City began to face competition—first from casinos on Indian reservations in Connecticut and then from legalized gambling in nearby states such as Pennsylvania, Delaware, Maryland, and upstate New York. The number of visitors to Atlantic City peaked in 2005 and 2006. When the national recession hit in 2007, many hotel rooms in Atlantic City were left empty, and the amount gambled plunged. In the end, this situation of excess supply was partly resolved by the closure of five casinos in 2014 and 2016. Not surprisingly, Atlantic City struggled during the pandemic, but as of late 2022, the city was showing signs of an economic rebound.

Source: "Atlantic City Casino Win Dropped 6.5 Percent in 2015," *Press of Atlantic City*, January 14, 2016, http://www.pressofatlanticcity.com/business/atlantic-city-casino-win-dropped-percent-in/article_b3737d92-ba2c-11e5-a83b-73a9c987a576.html.

A lower price simultaneously increases the quantity demanded and reduces the quantity supplied. A reduced price for hotel rooms, say, increases the quantity demanded by encouraging tourists to stay longer and enticing local parents to take a quick weekend break from their kids rather than just going out to eat. The lower price also eventually decreases the quantity supplied of hotel rooms. Fewer new hotels get built, and some existing ones may go out of business or get turned into apartments.

Similarly, excess demand usually puts upward pressure on prices. Just like a price decline, a price increase affects both buyers and sellers. It decreases the quantity demanded by buyers, who buy less or substitute cheaper goods. At the same time, a higher price is a lure for sellers to increase production and add capacity by building a new store or a new factory. When there is excess demand in the real estate market, several people bid for the same apartment or house, the price rises, and builders start constructing new single-family homes or new apartment houses.

MARKET EQUILIBRIUM (LO3-2)

LO3-2 Explain market equilibrium, and identify the equilibrium point on a supply–demand diagram.

Sometimes, home builders overestimate the demand for new homes, leaving some new homes empty.

Spencer Platt/Getty Images

Left to themselves, most markets will eventually reach a **market equilibrium**, where the quantity supplied and the quantity demanded are equal. Prices move up or down, buyers change the quantity they demand, and sellers adjust the quantity they supply. True, the process of adjustment may be stop-and-go (prices may go up and down and then up again), and it may take a long time, perhaps years. Consumers and businesses get accustomed to their routines and the way they've done things in the past, and change is difficult. Yet one of the truly distinguishing features of a market economy is that eventually the forces of supply and demand are enough to overcome such inertia and restore the balance.

The price at which the quantity supplied equals the quantity demanded is the **equilibrium price**. At the equilibrium price, there's a match between how much buyers want and how much sellers are willing to supply: the **equilibrium quantity**, which is the quantity supplied and demanded at the market price. For example, the market for hotel rooms would be at equilibrium if all hotel rooms were filled, but there were no potential guests standing outside in the cold with no place to sleep.

In the real world, few markets are exactly at the equilibrium price. There might be some excess demand or some excess supply. However, most markets, left to their own devices, will tend toward the equilibrium price that balances supply and demand. As a result, most markets either are near equilibrium or are trying to get there.

market equilibrium
A situation in which the quantity supplied and the quantity demanded in a specified market are equal. See *equilibrium price* and *equilibrium quantity*.

The Basic Supply–Demand Diagram

equilibrium price
The price at which the quantity supplied in a market equals the quantity demanded.

We can depict the market equilibrium by drawing the market supply and demand curves on the same graph. The price at which the two lines intersect is the equilibrium price. At that price, quantity supplied is equal to quantity demanded: the equilibrium quantity.

equilibrium quantity
The quantity corresponding to the equilibrium price. At that price, there's a match between what buyers want and what sellers are willing to supply.

Figure 3.1 is perhaps the most famous–and useful–diagram in economics. In this figure, the equilibrium price is *P*, and the equilibrium quantity is *Q*. Think about it this way: Buyers and sellers make decisions independently from each other. However, at the equilibrium price, it happens that the quantity picked by suppliers is equal to the quantity chosen by sellers.

Figure 3.1 A Market Equilibrium
We find the equilibrium price *P* and the equilibrium quantity *Q* at the point *A*, where the supply and demand curves intersect. At that price, the quantity supplied is equal to the quantity demanded.

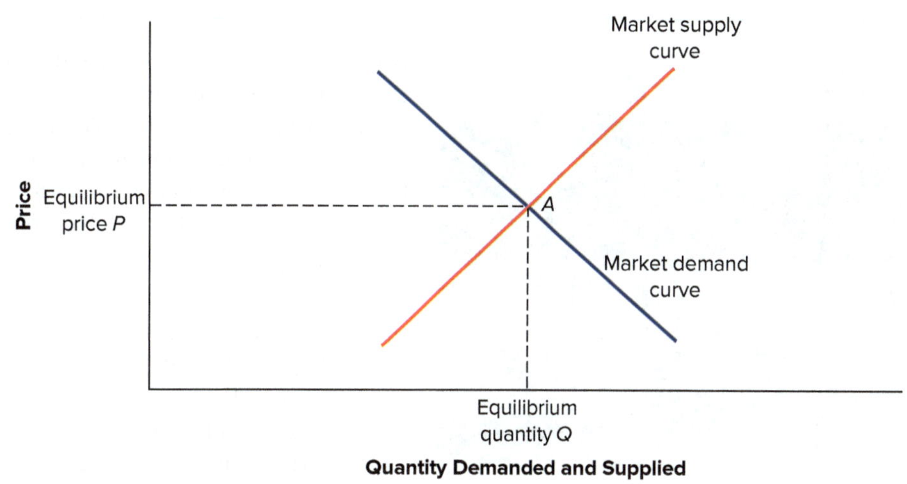

To make the idea of market equilibrium a bit more concrete, let's look at the market for new motor vehicles. We know that the demand curve for motor vehicles is downward-sloping because consumers will buy more cars, sport utility vehicles (SUVs), and other vehicles if they are less expensive. And the supply curve for vehicles is upward-sloping: If dealers can get more money for each car or SUV, manufacturers hire more workers, run the assembly lines longer, or bring in more vehicles from overseas.

Figure 3.2 illustrates the 2019 market equilibrium in the new car and light truck market, before the pandemic hit. At an average price of $36,800, vehicle manufacturers were willing to supply 17.1 million vehicles to the market. At the same price level, buyers were willing to shell out enough money to take home 17.1 million vehicles. Quantity supplied and quantity demanded are equal, making this an equilibrium.

YOUR ECONOMIC LIFE: Finding the Market Equilibrium

You've likely seen electric scooters in many towns and cities these days—you may even use them yourself to get around. A mobile app is required to unlock a scooter with an initial low price, with a per-minute charge after that. Companies like Bird and Lime pay workers to charge the scooters each night, and they replace damaged scooters.

Figure 3.2 The Market for New Vehicles in the United States
In 2019, before the pandemic hit, the quantity of new cars and light trucks supplied—by production in the United States and imports from abroad—was roughly equal to the quantity demanded. That year, new vehicle dealers in the United States sold 17.1 million cars and light trucks at an average price of $36,800 each. (The supply and demand curves are drawn as straight lines for clarity.)

Source: National Automobile Dealers Association.

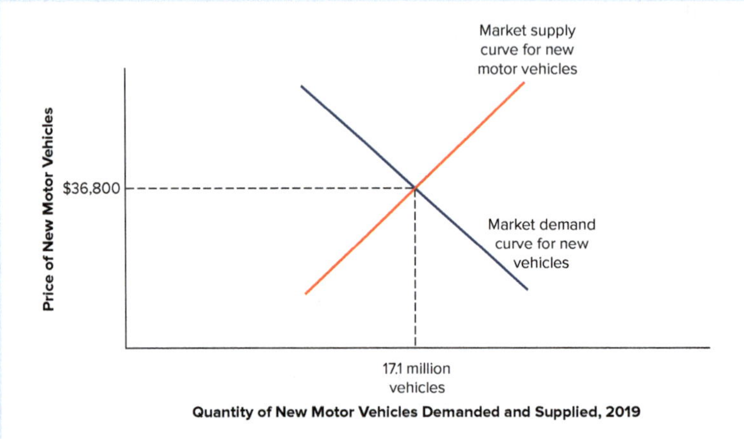

An electric scooter in action.

Simone Hogan/Shutterstock

How does this market work? On the demand side, you have alternatives to traveling by scooter: If the unlock price or the charge per minute is too high for you, you can instead walk, ride a bicycle, call a taxi, or travel by car. On the supply side, electric scooter companies are more likely to buy new scooters and fix broken ones if the rental price is higher. Both the quantity supplied and the quantity demanded of electric scooters are sensitive to price.

Table 3.1 shows hypothetical market supply and demand schedules for the electric scooter market; the left column of the table lists the price per minute (assuming that the initial unlock fee has already been paid). For any price, if you read across the table, the second column reports the quantity demanded at that price, and the third column reports the quantity supplied. For example, if the price per minute is $0.10, the market quantity demanded is 1,200 scooters and the market quantity supplied is 400. In other words, we have a situation of excess demand: More people want to ride electric scooters than are available at the going price. But if the rental price is $0.60 per minute, the quantity demanded is 200 scooters and the amount supplied is 1,400 scooters, we have a situation of excess supply. The scooter companies are willing to make more scooters available at this price than potential riders are willing to pay for.

Table 3.1 Supply and Demand in the Electric Scooter Rental Market

This table lays out hypothetical supply and demand schedules for electric scooter rentals in a city. For example, if the price were $0.50 per minute, the quantity demanded would be 400 scooters, and the quantity supplied would be 1,200 scooters.

Price per minute (Dollars)	Quantity Demanded	Quantity Supplied
$ 0.10	1,200	400
$0.20	1,000	600
$0.30	800	800
$0.40	600	1,000
$0.50	400	1,200
$0.60	200	1,400

The equilibrium for this market, as for every market, occurs at the price where quantity demanded equals quantity supplied. For this example, the equilibrium price is $0.30 per minute, where both quantity supplied and quantity demanded equal 800 electric scooters.

We can also draw the corresponding supply and demand curves on a graph, just as we did in **Chapter 2**. Look at **Figure 3.3**. The upward-sloping line is the market supply curve, and the downward-sloping line is the market demand curve. For example, start at a price of $0.60 per minute and move right. The first line we run into is the demand curve, which shows a demand of 200 scooters at this price. If we keep going right, we run into the supply curve at 1,400 scooters.

Figure 3.3 Equilibrium in the Electric Scooter Rental Market
The hypothetical supply and demand curves for electric scooters cross at the point labeled *A*. That's where the price is $0.30 per minute, and 800 electric scooters are demanded and supplied.

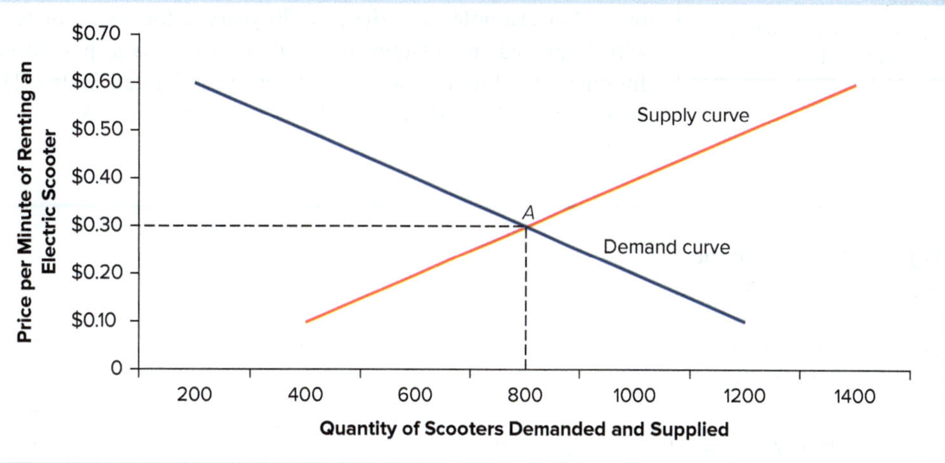

On the diagram, we can immediately identify the point *A* where the two lines intersect. Point *A* is the market equilibrium because at that price, quantity supplied equals quantity demanded.

MARKET SHIFTS (LO3-3)

LO3-3 Describe the impact of supply and demand shifts.

Markets are continually being bombarded by outside forces, large and small, that affect buyers or sellers, or both. Consider, for example, the market for music. People once mostly bought their music on compact disks (CDs). Indeed, the top year for CD sales was $13 billion in 2000. But that market was dramatically affected by the expansion of the Internet. When songs first became widely available online, potential music purchasers could download desired tracks for a low price. Now, individuals sign up for a music-streaming service such as Spotify or Apple Music, which gives them access to millions of songs at a fixed monthly fee. By 2019, before the pandemic, CD sales were down to only $630 million, even though the average price of CDs had actually fallen.

market shift
A shift of the demand or supply curve to the left or right, often as the result of events external to the particular market; a change in the quantity demanded or quantity supplied at a given price.

Economists call the changes caused by such forces **market shifts**. A **demand shift** is a market shift that affects buyers, changing the amount buyers want to purchase at any given price. For example, when music became widely available online, the demand curve for music CDs shifted to the left, as **Figure 3.4** shows.

demand shift
A change in the amount buyers want to purchase at a given price.

Figure 3.4 A Shift in the Demand for Music CDs
The ease of obtaining music from the Internet means the demand curve for music compact disks has shifted to the left. At the price *P*, the quantity demanded drops from *Q* to *Q′*.

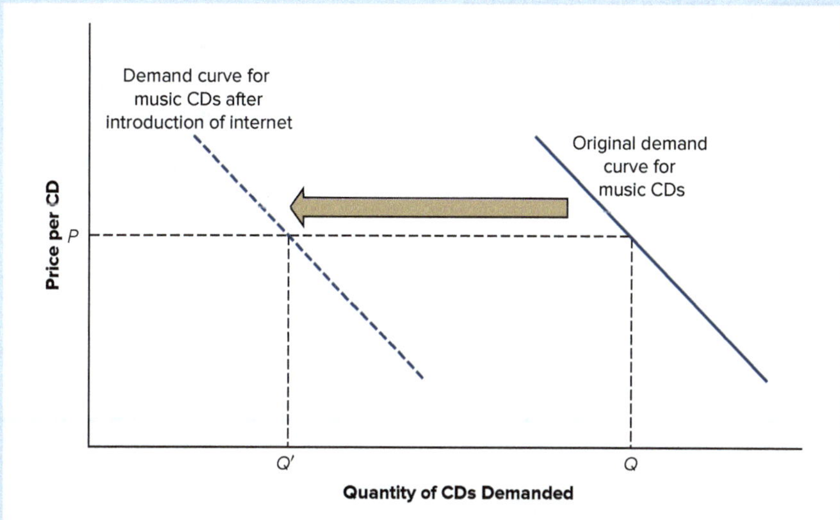

supply shift
A change in the amount sellers produce at a given price.

Similarly, a **supply shift** affects sellers, either raising or lowering the amount they supply at any given price. For example, over the past 30 years, a loosening of restrictions on clothing imports, combined with improved manufacturing capabilities overseas, has allowed countries like China, Vietnam, and Indonesia to ship a lot more clothing to the United States. The increase in imports means the supply curve for clothing shifted to the right, as **Figure 3.5** shows. For any given price, more clothing is supplied.

Figure 3.5 A Shift in the Supply of Clothing
Looser restrictions on clothing imports and increased manufacturing capabilities abroad mean that the supply curve for clothing in the United States has shifted to the right. At the price *P*, the quantity supplied rises from *Q* to *Q′*.

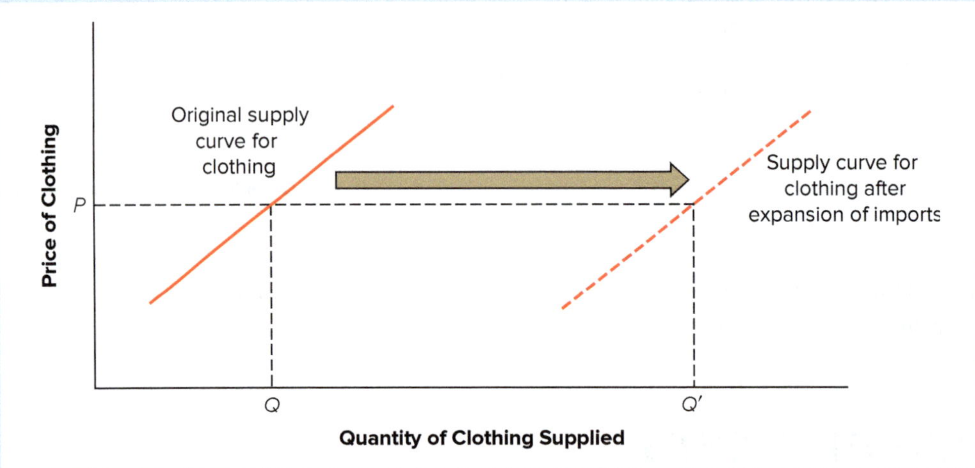

Demand Shifts and Market Equilibrium

A market shift will change the market equilibrium. After a market experiences a demand or supply shift, it eventually finds a new equilibrium. For example, if the demand curve shifts to the left–as in the case of the market for music CDs–that will temporarily create a situation of excess supply, which tends to drive down the price until a new equilibrium is reached.

Looking at **Figure 3.6**, we see that the original equilibrium in the music CD market was at point *A*, where the pre-Internet demand curve and the supply curve cross. When music downloads reduced demand for CDs, the demand curve shifted to the left and the equilibrium shifted to point *B*, with a lower price and a lower quantity supplied and demanded.

Figure 3.6 Changing Equilibrium in the Music CD Market
The decrease in demand for compact disks means that the market equilibrium shifts from *A* to *B*. The result is a lower price and a lower quantity supplied and demanded.

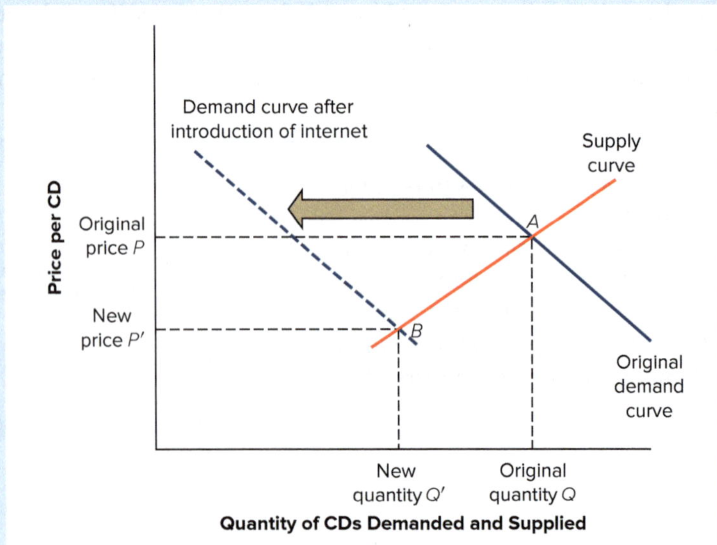

Supply Shifts and Market Equilibrium

Let's look now at the impact of a supply shift on market equilibrium. Suppose the supply curve shifts to the right, as in the case of the clothing market. That will temporarily create a situation of excess supply, which tends to drive down the price until a new equilibrium is reached.

Looking at **Figure 3.7**, we see that the original equilibrium in the clothing market was at point *A*, where the original supply and demand curves cross. The combination of fewer restrictions on clothing imports and improved manufacturing capabilities overseas caused the supply curve to shift to the right. The new equilibrium is at point *B*, with a lower price of clothing and a higher quantity supplied and demanded.

Figure 3.7 Changing Equilibrium in the Clothing Market
The increase in supply of clothing means that the market equilibrium shifts from *A* to *B*. The result is a lower price and a higher quantity supplied and demanded.

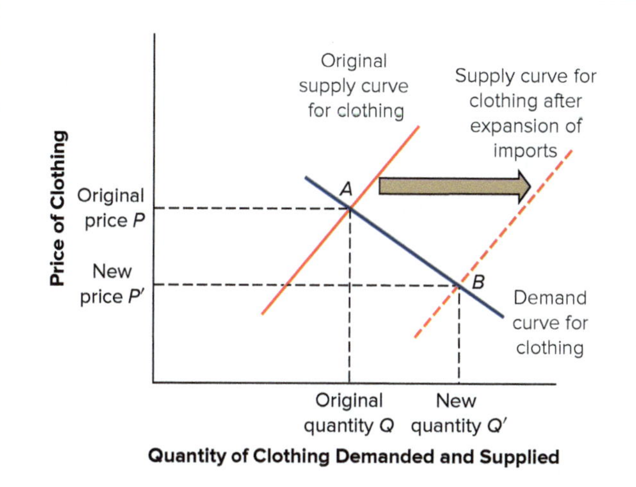

Even though these supply and demand curves are hypothetical, they generally convey what happened. Between 2000 and 2022, the average price of clothing and footwear bought by American consumers fell by 2 percent, while prices of most other goods and services soared. Government data show that purchases of clothing and footwear increased dramatically over this stretch–and that's why you have so much clothing in your closet!

YOUR ECONOMIC LIFE: Increased Demand for IT Workers

Whether you are preparing for the job market or already working, you are probably keeping a close eye on which occupations are "hot." One of the biggest shifts in recent years was the increase in demand for people with data science skills. During this time, more and more companies realized that their businesses were generating vast amounts of data that they were not taking advantage of. For example, trucking companies needed to analyze data about their customer shipping patterns, and that requires people with data science skills. Sports teams needed to analyze data about the performance of their players.

Of course, as data became more valuable, it became more tempting to hackers to steal it. That, in turn, has increased the demand for information security professionals. In fact, since 2007, the demand for virtually every IT-related skill has risen.

Figure 3.8 shows the demand-and-supply curves for IT-related occupations such as data science and information security professionals. The horizontal axis is the employment in IT-related occupations, and the vertical axis is their hourly pay. (It's not shown in the figure, but hourly pay for "software developers" in 2021 averaged almost $60 per hour, not including bonuses, incentive pay, and the like.)

The supply curve is upward-sloping because students like you are more likely to get IT-related degrees when the pay is higher. Similarly, if you already have a job in another field, you are more likely to shift to IT when pay rises.

On the other hand, the demand curve is downward-sloping because companies are going to hire fewer American IT workers as the pay goes up. Companies will either create fewer IT projects or outsource part of the work to other countries.

As **Figure 3.8** shows, when the demand for IT workers such as data scientists and information security professionals increased, the market equilibrium shifted from *A* to *B*. The result was that the wage for IT workers surged higher, and the quantity of IT workers supplied and demanded rose as well.

Figure 3.8 Demand Shifts in the Market for IT Workers
When the demand for IT workers increased, the market equilibrium shifted from *A* to *B*. The result was that the wage surged higher and the quantity of IT workers supplied and demanded rose as well.

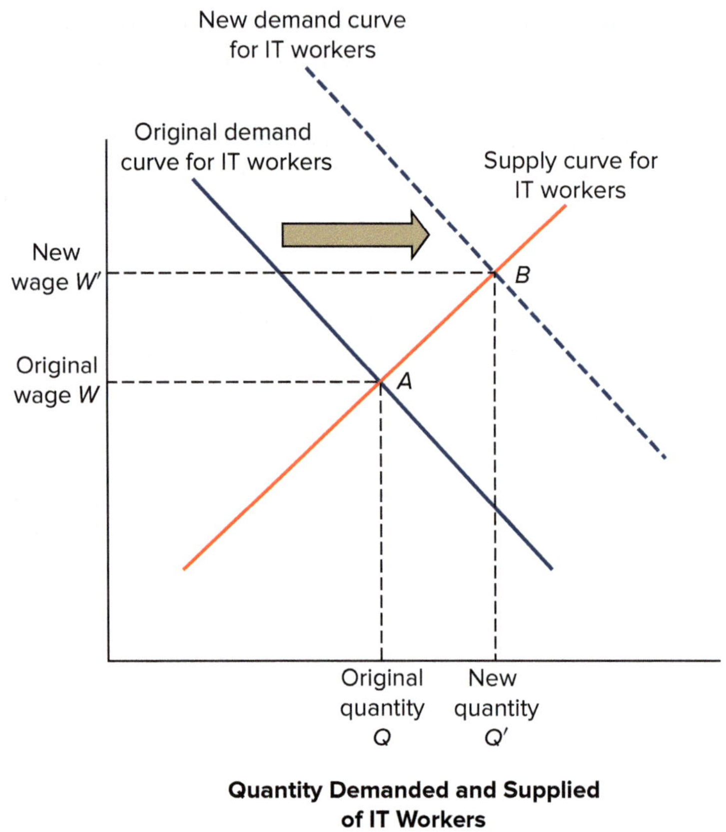

Some Examples of a Decrease in Supply

Natural disasters like hurricanes and earthquakes can hit a region very hard. When they do, they affect the supply curve for the goods and services produced in that region. For example, when Hurricane Katrina struck New Orleans in 2005, it also closed down a large number of refineries and oil rigs, both onshore and in the Gulf of Mexico. As a result, the price of gasoline jumped almost instantaneously around the country. Newspapers wrote about service stations boosting prices by $1 or more per gallon within a short period. In New Jersey, the state attorney general charged 20 gas stations with violating a 1938 law prohibiting them from raising prices more than once in a 24-hour period.

More recently, the Russian invasion of Ukraine in February 2022 led to most countries, including the United States, refusing to buy crude oil from Russia, a major oil exporter. That caused the global supply curve for oil to shift to the left.

Figure 3.9 shows the impact of the Russian invasion on the global crude oil market. Before the invasion, the market was at the equilibrium labeled *A*. The average price of crude oil was roughly $80 per barrel. After the invasion and the sanctions, the supply curve for crude oil shifted to the left. That is, at the same price, the quantity of oil supplied fell. As a result, the new equilibrium price was much higher, going as high as $120 per barrel. And because gasoline is refined from crude oil, the price of gasoline soared as well.

Shifts versus Movements

movement along a demand curve
The effect of a price change on the quantity demanded.

So far in this section, we've considered several different examples of changing markets. In two of these examples–the market for clothing and the market for IT workers–the equilibrium quantity increased. In the other two of these examples–the market for gasoline and the market for music CDs–the equilibrium quantity decreased. Yet the reason was different in each case.

Figure 3.9 The Impact of the Russia Invasion of Ukraine on the Crude Oil Market
When Russia invaded Ukraine in February 2022, most countries stopped buying oil from Russia, a major oil exporter. The effect was to shift the supply curve for crude oil to the left. The market equilibrium shifted from *A* to *B*, prices rose, and the quantity of oil supplied and bought fell.

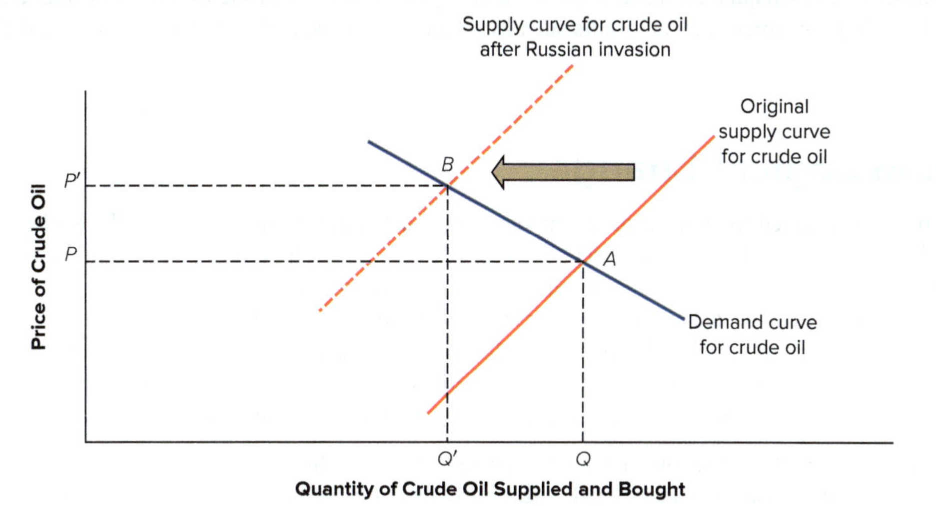

In the clothing example, the equilibrium quantity increased because the supply curve shifted and the demand curve stayed the same. This is an example of a **movement along a demand curve**. You can see in **Figure 3.7** that the equilibrium just slides along the demand curve from *A* to *B* as the supply shifts.

movement along a supply curve
The effect of a price change on the quantity supplied.

On the other hand, in the IT worker example, the equilibrium quantity increased because the demand curve shifted and the supply curve stayed the same. This is an example of a **movement along a supply curve**. You can see in **Figure 3.8** that the equilibrium just slides along the supply curve *A* to *B* as the demand shifts.

The music CD market is also an example of a movement along a supply curve, as the demand curve shifts to the left (**Figure 3.6**). And the crude oil market after the Russian invasion of Ukraine is an example of a movement along a demand curve, as the supply curve shifts to the left (**Figure 3.9**).

Michael Vi/Shutterstock

SOME CAUSES OF MARKET SHIFTS (LO3-4)

LO3-4 Discuss some causes of market shifts.

We've now seen several examples of how supply and demand shifts can affect market equilibrium. **Table 3.2** summarizes the impacts, which depend on whether the demand or supply curve is shifting, and in which direction it shifts.

Table 3.2 Summarizing the Effect of Supply and Demand Shifts

All other things being equal, an increase in demand boosts both equilibrium price and quantity. An increase in supply reduces equilibrium price and increases equilibrium quantity.

Shift and Direction	How We Say It	Effect on Equilibrium Price	Effect on Equilibrium Quantity
Demand curve shifts left.	"Demand decreases."	–	–
Demand curve shifts right.	"Demand increases."	+	+
Supply curve shifts left.	"Supply decreases."	+	–
Supply curve shifts right.	"Supply increases."	–	+

In fact, many economic changes can be described in terms of shifts in supply and demand, including the key forces driving today's economy (described in **Chapter 1**): technological change, globalization, and the evolution of financial markets. Other major causes of market shifts include government action; events such as pandemics, wars, and weather disasters; and changes in consumer tastes. Let's look at these.

Technological Change

We already mentioned the impact of technology on the demand for music CDs and IT workers. Historically, some of the biggest market shifts have been created by technological breakthroughs. Looking back a century, Henry Ford introduced the first mass-produced automobile, the Model T, in 1913. That caused the supply curve for automobiles to shift dramatically to the right, driving down prices and boosting quantities sold. Because his factories were so productive, Ford could sell cars for under $300 each–far less than the $1,000 his competitors were charging. (In **Chapter 8**, we will learn how to adjust historical prices for inflation. A car sold for $300 in 1913 would cost the equivalent of about $5,000 today–still not expensive.) The dramatically lower prices for cars enabled many more families to afford them, so the shift in the supply curve led to a movement along the demand curve.

Of course, we don't have to look back a hundred years to see technology-driven shifts. When the Internet first started becoming popular in the early 1990s, customers had to pay high hourly rates for a very slow dial-up connection. Since then, the supply of telecommunications services has been rapidly shifting to the right, in part because of advances in communications technology and in part because of hundreds of billions of dollars of investment by telecom companies. As a result, the price of an online connection, measured as the cost per unit of data transferred, has dropped sharply.

Globalization

By introducing new buyers and sellers into a market, globalization can create shifts on either the demand or supply side of a market, or both. We already mentioned the impact of China and other countries on the supply of clothing. Now let's consider the impact of globalization on the supply of furniture. Beginning around 2000, U.S.-based furniture companies started making more furniture in Chinese factories because it was considerably less expensive to produce there. As a result, the supply curve for furniture in the United States shifted to the right. The price of dining room and living room furniture dropped, and the amount of furniture purchased by American households increased, as we will see in **Chapter 5**.

Changes in Financial Markets

interest rate
The amount a borrower has to pay a lender each year in exchange for the use of the lender's money; given as a percentage of the loan.

One important cause of market shifts is a change in the cost of borrowing money. Most of us don't have enough cash on hand to pay for the car or home we want or to pay for our education. So we take out loans–auto loans, home mortgages, education loans. The price of a loan is its **interest rate**, which says how much we have to pay the lender in exchange for the use of the money. For example, a 5 percent annual interest rate means we owe the lender an extra 5 percent of the original loan value (the amount we borrowed) in return for using the money for a year. (Interest rates and loans are discussed further in **Chapter 13**.)

If interest rates rise, then cars, homes, and education become harder to pay for. So higher interest rates mean we perhaps stick with our old houses or cars for a while, or we go to school only part-time. In other words, a rise in interest rates causes demand to decline: The demand curve for autos, homes, or education shifts to the left.

Figure 3.10 shows the result of an increase in interest rates on auto loans. At any price for cars, the quantity demanded falls because potential customers are paying more for their loans. The result is that the equilibrium quantity falls, and so does the price. We'd see the same basic pattern in other markets in which many consumers use loans to buy a product or service (like education and housing).

Financial market shifts can also be caused by changes in loan standards. During the housing boom of the early 2000s, lenders offered "easy credit" for mortgages, car loans, and credit cards, making it easier for many Americans to borrow even if they didn't have much income. These easy loan standards helped shift the demand curve for houses, motor vehicles, and many other purchases to the right. The result was higher quantities purchased. Then, during the Great Recession of 2008-2009 and afterward, financial institutions tightened up on their standards for lending, making it harder for a few years to get mortgages and other loans, so demand curves shifted to the left.

Figure 3.10 The Impact of Rising Interest Rates on the Car Market
Higher interest rates cause the demand curve for cars to shift to the left. All other things being equal, that means the equilibrium shifts from *A* to *B*, leading to a lower equilibrium price and equilibrium quantity.

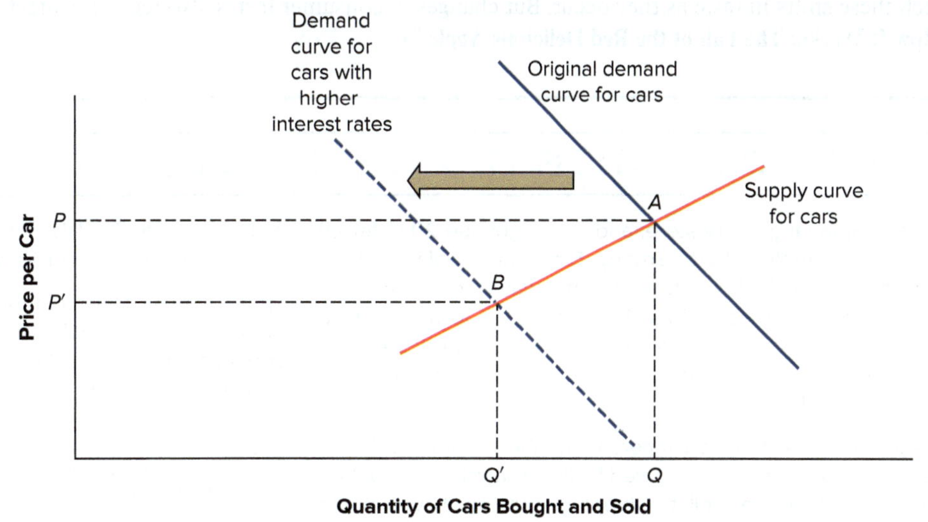

Government Action

Any type of government action–such as the creation of new rules that businesses or consumers have to follow–can cause a significant market shift, changing supply and demand in a market almost overnight. For example, if a state legislature passes a law requiring that drivers use child safety seats or booster seats for passengers through age 7, the demand curve for child car seats and booster seats immediately shifts to the right. Similarly, if a state requires that hands-free headsets be used for cell phones while people drive, that shifts the demand curve for headsets to the right.

Government action can also affect the supply side of markets. Suppose a town decides to change its land use regulations–say, by requiring builders to leave 100 feet between new homes rather than only 10 feet. That causes the supply curve for new homes in that town to shift left because now fewer homes than before can be built on the same amount of land.

Pandemics, Wars, and Weather Disasters

Finally, market demand and supply curves can be shifted by unexpected events such as pandemics, wars, and weather disasters. As we have already noted earlier in this chapter, the COVID-19 pandemic had sweeping effects on demand and supply curves across the economy. The Russian invasion of Ukraine in February 2022 caused the global supply curve for oil to shift to the left, and raising the price for crude oil and products refined from crude oil such as gasoline.

Weather events can be a major cause of supply and demand shifts across a wide range of markets. As we saw earlier, hurricanes can cause supply disruptions for goods such as gasoline, as well as cause demand shifts for goods such as plywood to cover windows. Frost can wipe out an orange crop, shifting the supply curve to the left and driving orange prices up.

One important future cause of supply shifts may be global climate change, which will affect temperature and rainfall patterns in different parts of the world. By some estimates, global warming may reduce food production in countries near the tropics, which are already hot. Areas that start off cooler–such as the northern United States, Canada, and Russia–may see a shift to the right in the supply of grain and other agricultural products. (The economic implications of environmental change and global warming are explored more deeply in **Chapter 19**.)

Shifts in Tastes

Often markets are rocked by nothing more or less than a **shift in tastes**–that is, an unexplained shift in the consumer demand curves for various products and services. One day reality shows are all the rage; the next day television viewers don't care for them. If every family needs a minivan today, next year minivans may be completely out of fashion. One month kids may want a certain brand of clothing; the next month they're onto something else.

shift in tastes

A shift in the demand curve for a good or service based on a change in consumer preferences.

Businesses learn to live with these essentially unpredictable changes. In some industries, like fashion and entertainment, the whole game is to catch these shifts in taste as they occur. But changes in consumer tastes also regularly affect more mundane industries such as food. (See **"How It Works: The Fall of the Red Delicious Apple."**)

HOW IT WORKS: THE FALL OF THE RED DELICIOUS APPLE

Go to your local grocery store, and you might see 20 different varieties of apples, from Granny Smith and Gala to Jazz, Cameo, and Pacific Rose. It wasn't that way a few years ago. Red Delicious apples—bright, firm, and easy to store—used to be the clear favorites. As recently as 1998, Red Delicious apples accounted for 40 percent of all the apples produced in the United States.

The problem was that consumers found them tasteless. Growers had spent years breeding Red Delicious apples that looked good and stood up well to shipping—but lost flavor in the process. "They eventually went too far and ended up with apples the public didn't want to eat," Lee Calhoun, an apple historian, told *The Washington Post* in 2005. The Red Delicious "is an apple that has done its duty and is on its way out."

With consumers tiring of the Red Delicious, the demand curve for that variety of apples shifted left. As a response, production and sales have been dropping, even though the apple's price remained more or less flat.

Sources: Higgins, Adrian, "Why the Red Delicious No Longer Is," *The Washington Post*, August 5, 2005; Yager, Sarah, "The Awful Reign of the Red Delicious," *The Atlantic*, September 10, 2014, http://www.theatlantic.com/health/archive/2014/09/the-evil-reign-of-the-red-delicious/379892/.

THE EFFECT OF INCOME ON DEMAND (LO3-5)

LO3-5 Illustrate how changes in income affect the demand curve.

One important influence on demand deserves special attention: income. A family earning $50,000 a year will have a very different demand curve than one earning $500,000 a year. For most goods and services, an increase in income will shift a family's demand curve to the right. For example, at price *P* a low-income household might consume *Q* of a good. But the demand curve for a high-income household is shifted to the right, so their quantity demanded is higher at *Q′*, as **Figure 3.11** shows.

Figure 3.11 Higher Income Usually Means Higher Demand
All other things being equal, consumers with higher incomes usually spend more on food, clothing, housing, and other broad categories of consumption. So for a given price *P*, the quantity demanded will rise from *Q* to *Q′*.

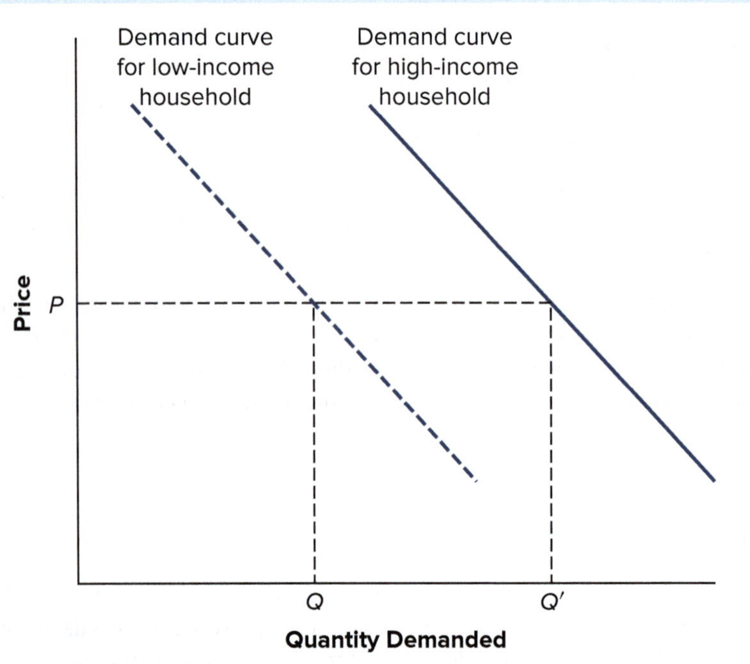

The Bureau of Labor Statistics tracks consumer spending by households with different income levels. For every major category of consumption–food, clothing, housing, transportation, health care, and entertainment–higher-income households spend more.

But if we look more closely within the spending categories, it's not simply that high-income families buy more; their whole pattern of consumption is different. For example, a family earning $50,000 a year might own a modest used car and order 1 pizza per week from the local take-out place. But a family earning 10 times as much is unlikely to own 10 modest used cars and order 10 pizzas a week.

As their incomes rise, then, people don't just consume more of the same goods. They shift their consumption patterns to other goods. Instead of a small used car, they buy a luxury automobile. They live in a bigger home, with more bedrooms and more land, and eat at expensive restaurants. They take long vacations overseas and send their kids to expensive colleges.

This shift in spending patterns holds true for countries as well. Take China, for example. As the incomes of its citizens have risen, they have bought a lot more cars and taken a lot more vacations to places like Australia and the United States. Energy use has shifted from wood stoves to electricity, and food consumption has shifted from staples such as rice to more expensive items such as meat and even imported apples.

It's helpful to classify goods and services into three different groups according to how their consumption changes with income. A **normal good** is one whose demand rises more or less in step with income, which includes a wide variety of goods and services such as housing, medical care, and motor vehicles. As you earn more, you buy more of these goods, though perhaps of different types. (By *goods,* of course, we mean goods *and* services.)

normal good

A good whose demand rises more or less in step with income.

A **luxury good** is one whose demand rises very sharply as income increases. Some examples of luxury goods include restaurant meals, travel abroad, and air travel in general, to which higher-income households devote a much larger percentage of their income. Another luxury good, of a sort, is education. High-income families are more likely to send their kids to expensive private schools and colleges rather than free public elementary and secondary schools and low-cost public universities and community colleges. As a result, high-income families put a much bigger share of their budgets toward education.

luxury good

A good whose demand rises sharply as income increases.

How much? Take a look at **Figure 3.12**, which reports education spending as a share of overall budgets. As of 2021, a household in the $30,000–$50,000 income range spent 1.0 percent of its budget on education. In contrast, a household with an income of more than $100,000 devoted 2.5 percent of its budget to education–quite a difference! (We see a similar pattern even if we look at households that are roughly the same age.)

Figure 3.12 Education Spending as a Share of Income
High-income families spend a much larger share of their budgets on education.

Source: Bureau of Labor Statistics, 2021 data.

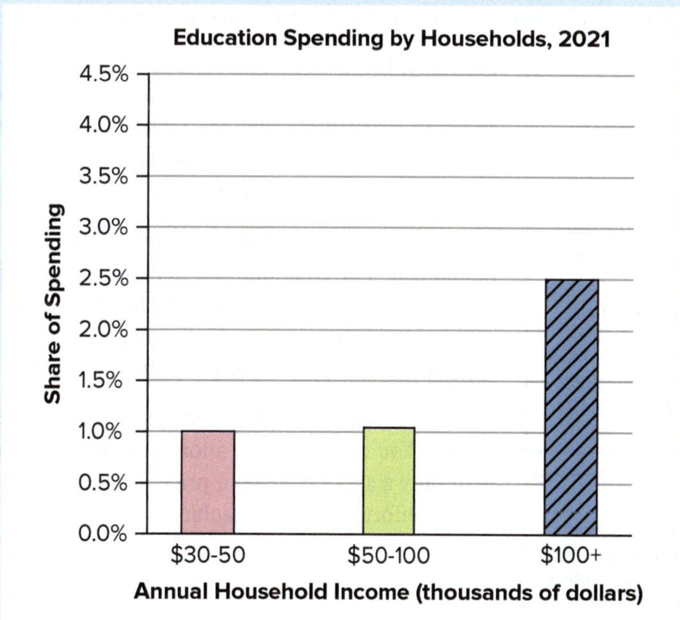

inferior good
A good for which the quantity demanded falls as income increases.

There's one more category of goods whose demand changes with income, called **inferior goods**. Inferior goods are those whose demand might actually *fall* as incomes increase. In most cities, for example, public buses are used mainly by people with low-income jobs or by students. Once people have higher incomes, they tend to buy a car rather than ride the bus, because cars offer more flexibility and generally faster trips.

Other inferior goods include cheap beer and shoddily made clothing. Rental housing is an inferior good, because households in any area are more likely to own homes as their income rises. Corporations often target different products toward low-income and high-income consumer sectors. The automakers, for example, have a range of models that run from relatively inexpensive to very pricey as a way to appeal to the widest possible array of purchasers.

A BRIEF LOOK AT ELASTICITY (LO3-6)

LO3-6 Review the basics of elasticity.

inelastic supply
A situation where the quantity supplied of a good does not change much even if the price changes significantly. More precisely, a situation where the price elasticity of supply is less than 1.

inelastic demand
A situation where the quantity demanded does not change much even if the price changes significantly. More precisely, a situation where the price elasticity of demand is less than 1.

We've seen that equilibrium price and quantity change in response to supply and demand shifts. Let's finish up by asking which will change *more*—price or quantity? If frost suddenly destroys a big portion of the orange crop—a supply shift—does that create a small increase in orange juice prices or an enormous one? A small change in the quantity of orange juice demanded or a big one? If a large number of consumers from Asian countries suddenly desire a vacation in Hawaii—a demand shift—do hotel prices there rise a lot or a little? Does the quantity supplied of hotel rooms change a little or a lot?

The answers depend on the supply and demand curves. In some markets, shifts show up mainly in price rather than quantity. For example, in the case of the consumers from Asian countries vacationing in Hawaii, the number of hotel rooms in Hawaii won't change much in the short run, so a sudden rise in tourists will cause hotel prices to fall.

In the language of economics, hotel rooms in Hawaii have an **inelastic supply**—that is, the quantity supplied doesn't change much even if the price changes a lot. Other examples of inelastic supply include the number of golf courses in California and the amount of land in New York City. Of course, eventually, new golf courses can be built and new land might be added by landfill—but it's a long process.

elastic demand
Intuitively, a situation in which a small change in price has a big impact on quantity demanded. More precisely, a situation in which the price elasticity of demand is greater than 1.

elastic supply
Intuitively, a situation in which a small change in price has a big impact on quantity supplied. More precisely, a situation in which the price elasticity of supply is greater than 1.

elasticity
The responsiveness of quantity supplied or quantity demanded to changes in price, income, or other economic variables.

Similarly, **inelastic demand** means that the quantity demanded doesn't change much even if the price changes a lot. For example, let's suppose a lot of visitors have reserved hotel rooms in a city for a big sporting event. Now suppose a hotel burns down (of course no one is hurt), which is equivalent to a decrease in supply. The price of hotel rooms is likely to skyrocket, but the quantity of rooms demanded is not likely to change much.

On the other hand, **elastic demand** means that a small change in price has a big impact on quantity demanded. For example, the demand for orange juice is elastic because many people are willing to switch to other kinds of juice or to other beverages when orange juice is too expensive. Looking at the other side of the market, **elastic supply** implies that a small price change has a big impact on quantity supplied. (**The appendix to Chapter 6** defines the concept of **elasticity** more precisely.)

The use of the word *elastic* for this economic idea makes sense when you think of a rubber band that's elastic: You can stretch it a long way without much effort—like demand or supply that changes readily with only a small change in price. A steel bar, by contrast, is inelastic and can't be bent without a great deal of effort or special machinery.

CONCLUSION

We've covered a lot of ground in this chapter. We started with the basics of market equilibrium, examined the different kinds of supply and demand shifts, and finished up with a short discussion of elasticity. Along the way, we gained better insight into how we can think about the impact of some of the most important changes in the economy, including the expansion of the Internet, the rise of China, and the large fluctuations in raw material prices.

In the next chapter, we will look more closely at the supply side of markets. In particular, we will consider how businesses make their production decisions. How do they decide how much to produce, how many people to hire, how many machines to buy, or how many stores to open? These are the key questions we will address next.

03 SUMMARY

1. Excess supply in a market means that quantity supplied is greater than quantity demanded. Excess demand means that quantity demanded is greater than quantity supplied. The gap between quantity supplied and quantity demanded is usually closed over time by the market mechanism, also known as the invisible hand. ***(LO3-1)***
2. Left to themselves, most markets eventually reach an equilibrium, which means that the quantity supplied and quantity demanded are reasonably in balance. At the equilibrium price, quantity supplied equals quantity demanded. On a graph, the market equilibrium is the point where the supply and demand curves cross. ***(LO3-2)***
3. The market equilibrium changes when either the supply or the demand curve shifts. If supply increases, equilibrium price falls and equilibrium quantity rises. If supply decreases, equilibrium price rises and equilibrium quantity falls. If demand increases, equilibrium price and quantity both rise. If demand decreases, equilibrium price and quantity both fall. ***(LO3-3)***
4. Important causes of market shifts include technological change, globalization, changes in financial markets, government action, events such as pandemics, wars, and weather disasters, and changes in consumer tastes. ***(LO3-4)***
5. Increases or decreases in income can exert a major influence on demand. Consumption patterns differ for low-income and high-income households. ***(LO3-5)***
6. If supply is inelastic, then the quantity supplied doesn't change much even if the price changes a lot. If demand is inelastic, then the quantity demanded doesn't change much even if the price changes a lot. ***(LO3-6)***

KEY TERMS AND CONCEPTS

excess demand
excess supply
market mechanism
invisible hand
market equilibrium
equilibrium price
equilibrium quantity
market shift
demand shift
supply shift
movement along a demand curve
movement along a supply curve
interest rate
shifts in tastes
normal good
luxury good
inferior good
inelastic supply
inelastic demand
elastic demand
elastic supply
elasticity

connect PROBLEMS

1. The market for new automobiles has excess demand if _______ ***(LO3-1)***
   a) potential buyers don't have to wait for the car they want.
   b) car dealers have more autos than they can sell at the market price.
   c) car dealers temporarily run out of autos to sell at the market price.

2. The following table reports the (hypothetical) market supply and demand schedules for smartphones. *(LO3-2)*

Price per Phone (Dollars)	Quantity Demanded (Millions)	Quantity Supplied (Millions)
$ 100	7	0
$250	5	1
$400	4	2
$550	3	3
$700	2	4
$850	1	5

a) Plot the supply and demand curves.
b) When the price per phone is $400, what is the quantity demanded? What is the quantity supplied? Is the market in excess supply, excess demand, or equilibrium?
c) When the price per phone is $700, what is the quantity demanded? What is the quantity supplied? Is the market in excess supply, excess demand, or equilibrium?
d) Label the equilibrium point. What is the equilibrium price for the phone market? What is the equilibrium quantity?

3. In December 2013, the new versions of Microsoft Xbox and Sony PlayStation 4 game consoles were in short supply. Many retailers ran out of stock, and especially around the holiday season, parents ran from store to store hoping to find a new game console to give their kids as a present. *(LO3-1, LO3-2)*

a) At the time, was the game console market facing a situation of excess demand, excess supply, or equilibrium?
b) The list price for the PlayStation 4 unit was $400. Was the equilibrium price higher than, lower than, or equal to $400?
c) Sony sold 4.2 million PlayStation 4 units in the United States in 2013. Was the equilibrium quantity higher than, lower than, or equal to 4.2 million?

4. The following graph represents the market for yachts. *(LO3-2, LO3-3)*

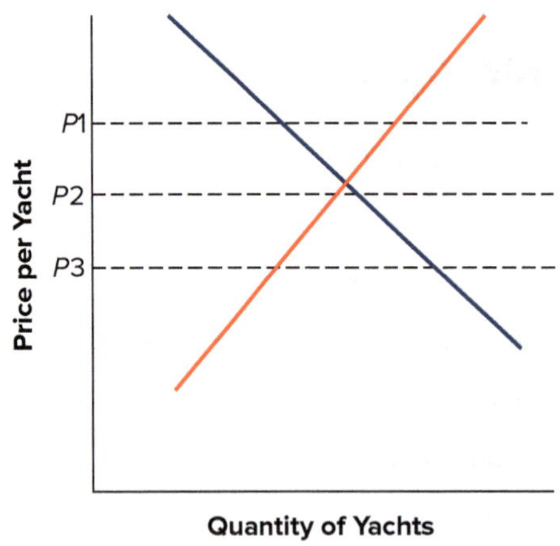

a) Label the supply and demand curves.
b) Label the market equilibrium.
c) Suppose there is a sudden increase in the demand for yachts because there are more billionaires in emerging markets. Show how the demand curve shifts, and label the new market equilibrium.

5. A sudden discovery of an enormous gold mine in Florida would mean a _______ *(LO3-3)*

a) rightward shift in the supply curve for gold.
b) rightward shift in the demand curve for gold.
c) leftward shift in the supply curve for gold.
d) leftward shift in the demand curve for gold.

6. In a shorefront tourist town, a hurricane washes away the beach. All of the town's hotels, however, are still intact, but the beach that was an added value to vacationers is no longer available. *(LO3-4)*

   a) Does the supply curve for hotel rooms shift to the left, shift to the right, or stay in the same place? Explain your answer.
   b) Does the demand curve for hotel rooms shift to the left, shift to the right, or stay in the same place? Explain your answer.
   c) After the hurricane, what happens to the equilibrium price and quantity of hotel rooms?
   d) Suppose the neighboring town still has its beach. After the hurricane, what happens to the market for hotel rooms in that town?

7. Here are some examples of new technologies and the markets they affect. Identify whether each of these is a supply or demand shift, and describe its impact on equilibrium price and quantity. *(LO3-4)*

Technological Change	Affected Market	Supply or Demand Shift?	Impact on Equilibrium Price and Quantity
A new way to cheaply generate electricity from sunlight	Market for electricity	?	?
A new car engine that gets much better gas mileage	Market for gasoline	?	?
A new additive for milk that improves its taste	Market for milk	?	?

8. The following table reports spending on food in 2021 by households with incomes of less than $70,000 and by households with incomes greater than $150,000. "Food eaten at home" refers mainly to food that is purchased at supermarkets and brought home. "Food eaten away from home" refers mainly to food eaten at restaurants, though it also includes college dining rooms and similar situations. *(LO3-5)*

	Households with Incomes Less than $70,000	Households with Incomes Greater than $150,000
Average Spending on Food Eaten at Home	$4,300	$8,600
Average Spending on Food Eaten Away from Home	$2,100	$6,200

Source: Bureau of Labor Statistics (rounded to the nearest $100).

   a) How much do households with incomes of less than $70,000 spend on food eaten at home? Do they spend more on food at home or food away from home?
   b) How much do households with incomes greater than $150,000 spend on food eaten away from home? Do they spend more on food at home or food away from home?
   c) From this table, would you conclude that food eaten away from home is a normal good, a luxury good, or an inferior good? Is food eaten at home a normal good, a luxury good, or an inferior good? Explain your answers.

9. In the early days of the Internet, relatively few Americans had online access. But as of 2021, 93% of adult Americans used the Internet. That suggests Internet access turned from ______ *(LO3-5)*

   a) a normal good into a luxury good.
   b) a luxury good into an inferior good.
   c) a luxury good into a normal good.

10. The store down the street increases the price of bananas by $2 per pound. As a result, most customers switch to buying candy instead. This is an example of what? *(LO3-6)*

   a) Inelastic supply.
   b) Inelastic demand.
   c) Elastic demand.
   d) Elastic supply.

11. If the quantity supplied doesn't change very much, even if the price doubles, then ______ *(LO3-6)*

   a) supply is inelastic.
   b) supply is elastic.
   c) demand is inelastic.
   d) demand is elastic.

CH 04

HOW BUSINESSES WORK

THIPPTY/Shutterstock

LEARNING OBJECTIVES

After reading this chapter, you should be able to:

LO4-1 Explain and apply the economic perspective on business operations.
LO4-2 Define and apply the production function, average product, and marginal product.
LO4-3 Discuss the implications of the cost function, average cost, and marginal cost. Explain the difference between variable costs and fixed costs.
LO4-4 Define and apply the revenue function and marginal revenue.
LO4-5 Determine the profit-maximizing level of output.

Many Americans work in large corporations, such as the giant retailer Walmart, which employed 1.7 million workers (called "associates") in the United States as of early 2022. Others work in small businesses, such as local bike shops, doctors' offices, or bakeries. In fact, today it's not unusual for people to start their own businesses as web designers or as creators of handcrafted items to sell online. Such small businesses are the heart and soul of any modern economy.

But no matter what its size, every business operates using the same economic principle: to produce goods and services that customers want, and thus generate enough revenue to exceed the cost of running the business. Moreover, most businesses strive to make as much money as possible, within the respective laws of their locale.

In this chapter, we study the basics of business, including production, cost, revenue, and profit maximization. These concepts are key to understanding how today's economy works.

THE NATURE OF BUSINESS (LO4-1)

LO4-1 Explain and apply the economic perspective on business operations.

Let's start with the big picture of how businesses operate, from an economic perspective. The **outputs** of a business are the goods and services it sells to customers. The **inputs** are the goods and services the business uses to produce the outputs. **Production** is the process of turning inputs into outputs.

outputs
The goods and services a business sells to customers.

inputs
The goods and services a business or an economy uses to produce outputs.

production
The process of turning inputs into outputs.

For example, think about your favorite restaurant. The outputs of the restaurant are the meals it feeds its customers. So if the restaurant serves salads and steaks, its output would be the number of salads and steaks it serves during the week.

One key input to the restaurant is human labor: the number of hours worked by the chefs in the kitchen and the staff that bring you the food and clean the restaurant. Other inputs include the food ingredients and the physical objects that make up the restaurant: the oven and refrigerators in the kitchen, the chairs and tables, and the roof over the whole thing. A final but important input is the book of recipes for the dishes on the menu; the recipes are essential because without them the dishes would come out different each time.

Let's consider a much bigger business: Procter & Gamble, which makes a wide variety of consumer products, such as those under the Crest and Gillette brands. The company's output includes toothpaste, razors, shampoos, laundry soap, and diapers, which are sold in virtually every country. The company is based in Cincinnati, Ohio, but its products are made in manufacturing facilities across the globe. As a result of this, in 2022, Procter & Gamble employed a total of 106,000 workers.

The Flow of Money

In a market economy, a business does not simply produce outputs using inputs–it also collects and spends money. **Revenue** is the money a business receives from the sales of its outputs to customers. **Cost** is what the business pays for its inputs.

revenue
The amount of money companies get from selling their products or services.

costs
The money a business pays for its inputs.

profit
The difference between revenues and costs.

For example, in the year ending June 30, 2022, Procter & Gamble received roughly $80 billion in revenues for all the toothpaste and other products it sold. The company's expenses during that period were roughly $62 billion, which were used to pay its workers, build and maintain its factories, and purchase raw materials, such as steel for its razors and plastic for its shampoo bottles.

Profit is the difference between revenues and costs. Procter & Gamble reported a profit, before taxes, of about $18 billion, which was the difference between its revenues ($80 billion) and its costs ($62 billion).

On a smaller scale, your favorite restaurant collects revenues from customers paying for meals, and it uses that money to pay its workers and suppliers. With any luck, revenues will exceed costs, so the restaurant will make a profit and be able to stay in business. **Figure 4.1** shows the basics of how a business operates.

Figure 4.1 How a Business Operates
A business uses inputs from its suppliers to produce outputs to sell to its buyers. In return, it receives revenue from the buyers, and it pays its suppliers. Any money that remains is profit.

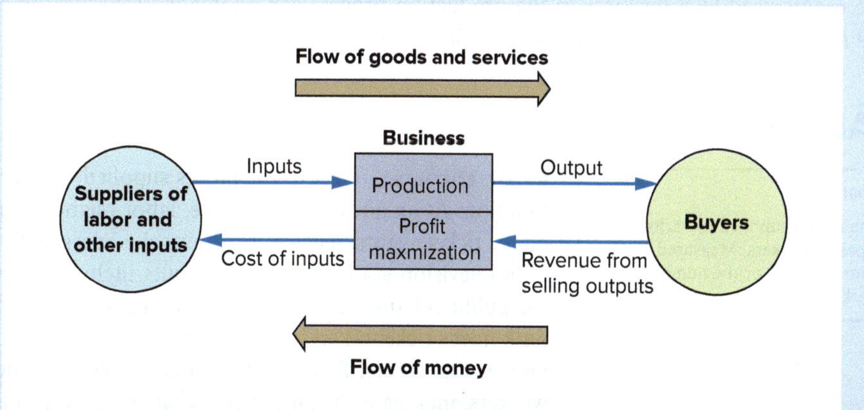

Profit Maximization

profit maximization

The main objective of a business in a market economy: finding a way to achieve the largest difference between revenue and costs.

The main objective of any business in a market economy is **profit maximization**. That is, the people running a business want to operate it in a way that yields the largest difference between revenues and costs. True, a business might have all sorts of goals, including providing jobs for the local population, giving the lazy son of the founder something to do, or being a socially responsible corporate citizen. But any business must try to make a good profit–defined as the difference between the revenue of the business and its total cost of production–or it will have trouble surviving in a competitive world.

Profit maximization is shorthand for "trying to produce something with the biggest difference between the costs and what someone is willing to pay." In the real world, maximizing the profit of a business is difficult. Running even a small business requires a multitude of large and small decisions. Managers have to deal with a constantly changing world, including tough competitors, tougher employees, machines that break down, products consumers don't want to buy, corporate scandals, pandemics, and other natural disasters.

During the early days of the pandemic in 2020, some businesses were forced to close down or drastically scale back. That meant low revenues and low or negative profits for businesses like restaurants and hotels. Meanwhile, online companies like Zoom Video Communications were reporting skyrocketing revenues and profits, as people moved to virtual meetings and online shopping.

But even during more normal times, businesses in the United States make a very wide range of profits. For example, Apple reported $119 billion in profits in 2022. That same year, other businesses large and small reported losses–that is, their costs exceeded their revenues. For example, Peloton, the maker of high-end fitness equipment, reported a $2.8 billion loss in 2022, driven by lower product sales.

The difficulty of consistently producing a good profit is the reason successful chief executives of large corporations get paid so handsomely–and it is also why the typical CEO lasts only 5 years in their job.

nonprofit organizations

Enterprises that focus on providing useful services to society rather than maximizing profits.

Of course, profit-maximizing businesses are not the only source of production because there are productive enterprises with other goals. Private universities and hospitals, for example, are sometimes set up as **nonprofit organizations**, which means they focus on providing useful services to society rather than maximizing profit. Similarly, governments are not profit-maximizing, but they provide services, such as sanitation, national security, and education. And most child care activities are still done by parents or other household members; most families are not run as profit-making enterprises.

PRODUCTION (LO4-2)

LO4-2 Define and apply the production function, average product, and marginal product.

At the core of any business is production–turning inputs into outputs that customers will buy. In this section, we take a deeper look at these inputs and production.

Types of Inputs

The inputs used by a business in the production process can be divided into five big categories–*labor, capital, land, intermediate inputs,* and *business know-how.* Let's take a closer look at each one.

LABOR

labor

The inputs supplied by various types of workers. Measured by the hours of work or the number of workers.

Labor, of course, refers to the inputs supplied by the various types of workers that enable a business to function. At an airline, for example, labor might include the hours of work put in by pilots, flight attendants, ticket agents, mechanics, crew schedulers, gate agents, menu planners, accountants, and so forth. At a television station, the labor inputs include the work time of the camera crews, the makeup staff, the public relations people, the newswriters, and of course the high-priced on-air talent. An amusement park needs ticket-takers, as well as people to maintain the rides, sell food, and perhaps dress up as well-known characters. Before the pandemic, Walt Disney World in Orlando, Florida, employed 70,000 workers, making it the largest single-site employer in the country.

We can measure labor inputs either by the number of workers a business employs or by the total number of hours worked. Measuring labor input by number of workers is especially common when the labor comes from executives and professionals because most businesses do not track the hours of their more educated workers.

CAPITAL

Capital, the second input, is another name for all the long-lived physical equipment, software, and structures a business uses in its production process. For example, an airline needs at least one airplane (usually many more) to accomplish its most important function, which is to fly passengers from one point to another. But most airlines generally also need hangars to keep the planes in, tools for the mechanics who service the planes, computers and phones for the reservation agents, and office buildings for the airline managers. A television station may have its own studios, complete with cameras, props, and equipment for transmitting its signal. And, of course, an amusement park needs its roller coasters and haunted houses. All these physical goods are part of the capital used in production.

capital
The long-lived physical equipment, software, and structures a business uses in its production process.

When businesses don't have the right capital, production becomes more difficult or impossible. During the early days of the pandemic, the United States suffered from a grave shortage of "personal protective equipment" (PPE), like the special masks worn by health care workers while treating COVID-19 patients. It turned out that the production of these masks required specific machinery that was not easily available. So before production of masks could be significantly increased, it was necessary to build new machines.

A business need not own all the capital it uses, however. For example, a law firm can either own its office building or rent it. Similarly, an airline can either own the commercial aircraft it operates, like a Boeing 747, or lease it from some other company that actually owns the plane. For example, AerCap–a company you have likely never heard of–owned about 1,800 commercial aircraft as of 2022, leasing them out to carriers around the world.

LAND

Another input to most productive activities is **land**, the actual ground used by a business. Factories need land, as do office buildings. Shopping malls, of course, require large amounts of land. Even Internet retailers such as Amazon.com require land for their fulfillment centers, offices, and data centers.

land
The actual ground used by a business. Distinct from the buildings on the land.

Agriculture and mining are especially land-intensive. It's not possible to grow wheat or extract oil from the ground without plenty of land. In fact, in these industries, land can be the major input.

INTERMEDIATE INPUTS

Intermediate inputs is really a catch-all category that refers to any goods and services purchased from other businesses and used up in production. For example, almost every business needs to buy electricity and telephone services; these are intermediate inputs. A pizzeria must buy flour, cheese, tomato sauce, pepperoni, anchovies, and all the other ingredients for its pizzas. A steel mill buys either iron ore or scrap metal as an input to its production process. A construction company buys cement, steel beams, rivets, and hard hats for its workers.

intermediate inputs
Any goods or services purchased from other businesses and used up in production.

In fact, much economic activity in the United States consists of business-to-business (B-to-B) transactions like these, in which businesses buy and sell intermediate inputs. When you, as a consumer, go into a store to buy an article of clothing, that simple sale is just the visible strand of a broad web of B-to-B transactions. The store has to pay the local electric utility for power, an accounting firm for managing its books, and a wholesaler for the clothing it sells. It pays a trucking company to bring the clothing to the store. The trucking company, in turn, pays for gasoline, truck repairs, the drivers' salaries, accident insurance, and so forth.

ECONOMIC MILESTONE

1962: The First Walmart Opens

Sam Walton opened the first Walmart in 1962 in Rogers, Arkansas, a town that, at the time, had a population of only 6,000. From these humble beginnings, Walmart has grown into the world's largest retailer. How did that happen? Walmart's executives have consistently made better use of business know-how than have their competitors. For one thing, Walmart was a pioneer in harnessing computers to track and order goods. The company was also one of the earliest retailers to extensively import cheap goods from China.

BUSINESS KNOW-HOW

business know-how

The knowledge and technology necessary for the production process.

One underappreciated input is **business know-how**, which includes all the knowledge and technology necessary for the production process. An automaker, for example, must know how to design, build, and market cars. That includes knowledge of everything from how internal combustion engines work to the wind resistance that a car encounters on the highway.

In many cases, the necessary knowledge or technology is built into or embodied in the equipment a company buys. For example, a company that buys a computer can use its capabilities without knowing the details of how the hard disk works. Similarly, the computer may come with accounting and word processing programs already installed.

Sometimes, necessary know-how is less tangible and much more specific to a particular business. A restaurant, for example, has recipes for each dish on its menu. It likely also has rules, either explicit or implicit, for how and when to clean the tables, how to manage the cash register, and what to do with unruly customers. These contribute to the business's success by ensuring that customers are satisfied enough to come back or recommend the restaurant to their friends.

Business know-how can be why a company succeeds or fails. For example, the success of Google rests on two crucial pieces of business know-how. The first is its search algorithm, invented by founders Sergey Brin and Larry Page, which typically gives users better results than any of its competitors. The second piece of business know-how is a proprietary method for pricing and selling search-based advertisements (those little ads that pop up next to Google searches). That's how the company makes most of its money. Other companies have tried to duplicate the success of Google's search ads, but this hasn't been easy.

The pharmaceutical company Pfizer was able to successfully develop and test its Covid vaccine quickly because the company's scientists had extensive experience with vaccines against other diseases. That included business know-how about how to run clinical trials and manufacture vaccines safely.

The Production Function

Economists sometimes like to think of a business as a sort of machine–a giant black box. At one end of the machine, we put in the inputs–the labor, the capital, the intermediate inputs, the land, and the business know-how. From the other end come the outputs–the goods and services the business produces, whatever they may be.

production function

The link between the inputs of a business and its outputs.

Economists give this machine a catchy name: the **production function**. A production function tells you, given the inputs, what the output is going to be. In practice, a major corporation may have hundreds of thousands or even millions of different inputs and outputs, making it nearly impossible to write down its production function. For example, Procter & Gamble, mentioned earlier, makes a very wide range of consumer products.

Table 4.1 A Simple Production Function

This table gives the production function for a small lawn-mowing business. The first column is the number of hours worked; the second column is the number of lawns mowed. For example, 2 hours of work will result in four lawns mowed.

Hours of Labor	Number of Lawns Mowed Using a Hand Mower
0	0
1	2
2	4
3	5
4	6

It's much easier to think about the production function for a small business that has only one or two inputs and one output. Consider a lawn-mowing business, which for a small fee will take care of that green expanse in front of your house (as mentioned in **Chapter 2**). The simplest such business is one consisting of your next-door neighbor's son or daughter, who for a fee will cut your lawn. This business has two inputs: cheap labor and the old push mower from the garage. The output is the number of lawns cut in a day. If you know how many hours the teenager works, you can calculate the output of the business.

Table 4.1 shows a simple production function that relates the amount of labor to the amount of output. For a given number of hours worked, it tells you how many lawns will be mowed. **Figure 4.2** graphs the same production function. For example, if the workers put in 2 hours of labor, move along the horizontal axis until you get to 12. Then move vertically until you get to the output–four lawns mowed, in this case. As the number of hours worked rises, so does the output.

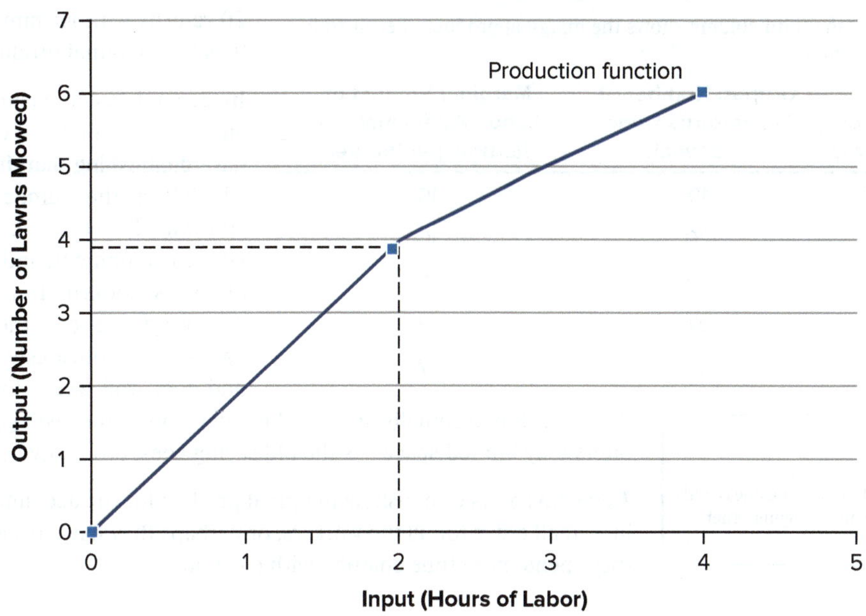

Figure 4.2 Graphing a Simple Production Function This graph corresponds to the production function in **Table 4.1**. The horizontal axis measures the input (the number of hours of labor), and the vertical axis measures the output (the number of lawns mowed). For example, 2 hours of work will result in four lawns mowed.

The Marginal Product of Labor

The production function gives an important piece of information: how much output the business can produce given its inputs. But the production function also answers another question: If the business expands by adding more workers or by having them work more hours, how much does its output increase? The **marginal product of labor** (or simply *marginal product* for short) is the extra amount of output the firm can generate by adding one more hour of labor or one more worker.

marginal product of labor
The extra amount of output a firm can generate by adding one more worker or one more hour of labor.

This is the first time in this textbook that we have encountered the idea of a *marginal* change, but it won't be the last. Economists often think about decision making in terms of small incremental steps.

We can apply this idea to the small lawn-mowing business of the previous section. The first hour of labor yields two lawns mowed. That means the marginal product of the first hour is 2, as shown in the third column of **Table 4.2**. The second hour of work yields another two lawns mowed, so the marginal product is still 2.

But what happens when the teenager works a third hour? By that time, he or she is tiring, so the marginal product of the third hour is only 1. To put it a different way, going from 2 hours worked to 3 hours worked yields only one additional lawn mowed, so the marginal product is 1.

Table 4.2 The Marginal Product of Yard Workers

In this table, the first two columns are the same as in **Table 4.1**, reporting the hours of labor and the number of lawns mowed. The third column reports the marginal product of each additional hour of work.

Hours of Labor	Number of Lawns Mowed	Marginal Product of Labor: Additional Lawns per Hour
0	0	
1	2	2
2	4	2
3	5	1
4	6	1

Let's consider a business trying to hire a worker. When a potential employee is interviewed for a job, the manager may ask, "Why should I hire you? What will you add to my company?" In effect, what the worker will add to the company is his or her marginal product–the additional output from one more worker.

Think about an accounting firm that does tax returns. The marginal product of an additional accountant is the number of tax returns he or she can complete. **Table 4.3** shows the production function for this accounting firm. The first column is the number of accountants, the second column is the output of those accountants, and the third column is the marginal product.

Table 4.3 The Marginal Product of Accountants

In this table, the third column shows the marginal product of each additional accountant.

Input: Number of Accountants	Output: Number of Tax Returns Done in a Week	Marginal Product of Labor: Additional Tax Returns per Worker
1	10	10
2	20	10
3	29	9
4	37	8
5	44	7

For example, the marginal product of the third accountant is nine tax returns. That's because the first two accountants can produce 20 returns without him and 29 returns with him. The difference, 9, is the marginal product of the third accountant.

In general, as a business adds workers without changing the amount of capital or other inputs, each additional worker will have **diminishing marginal product**. That is, the marginal product will fall as the number of workers rises, holding other inputs constant. To see this, consider a restaurant. The inputs are cooks, kitchen equipment, and ingredients, and the output is the number of meals cooked. If there's only one cook, he or she has to do everything–cut the onions, fry the potatoes, watch the pasta–which obviously limits the output of meals. Adding a second cook will likely double the output of meals just by dividing the labor. But eventually, if we add enough cooks, they will get in each other's way because the kitchen offers only limited space. As the old saying goes, too many cooks spoil the broth.

diminishing marginal product

A situation where marginal product declines as a business adds workers without changing other inputs.

Table 4.3 shows diminishing marginal product for the accounting firm. Perhaps there isn't enough room in a small office for all the workers, or perhaps they have to wait for the single copy machine, or perhaps they spend more time chatting with each other.

The Production Function with Capital

Table 4.4 The Production Function with Capital

This table gives the production function for a lawn-mowing business. The first column is the number of hours worked. The second column is the number of lawns mowed with a push mower, and the third column is the number of lawns mowed if the business uses a gasoline-powered mower.

Hours of Labor	Number of Lawns Mowed with a Push Mower	Number of Lawns Mowed with a Power Mower
0	0	0
1	2	3
2	4	6
3	5	9
4	6	11

Now let's look at what happens when we add another input: capital. In this case, capital comes in the form of a gasoline-powered mower, which cuts grass a lot faster. **Table 4.4** shows the production function of the lawn-mowing business both with and without the gasoline-powered mower. With more capital, the same number of labor hours will result in more lawns mowed. **Figure 4.3** graphs the production function with and without the power mower.

What is the marginal product of an additional hour of work, assuming that the power mower is being used? Suppose the teenager goes from working for 1 hour to working for 2 hours. Then his or her output goes from three lawns to six lawns, so the marginal product is 3.

Similarly, **Table 4.4** shows that the marginal product is 3 for 3 hours of work as well. Eventually, though, the teenager starts to get bored and a bit tired, even using the power mower. That's why the marginal product of the fourth hour of work is only 2.

Average Product

average product

The total output of a business divided by the number of labor hours or by the number of workers. Also *output per hour* or *output per worker.*

The production function also gives us a third piece of information: **average product**, which is the output divided by the number of labor hours or by the number of workers–in other words, output per hour or output per worker. For a lawn-mowing service, this would be lawns mowed per worker. For an automaker, the average product is vehicles manufactured per worker, perhaps with some adjustment so that big sport utility vehicles count more than compact cars. For an electric utility, the average product is megawatts of energy delivered per worker.

A business can raise its average product by investing in new equipment, or by reorganizing work to become more efficient. If one automaker could produce more vehicles than another automaker using the same number of workers, the first company would have an advantage.

Figure 4.3 Graphing the Production Function with Capital
This graph shows that using a power mower produces more output than using a hand mower. For example, 2 hours of labor with a power mower will yield four lawns mowed rather than two. This figure corresponds to **Table 4.4.**

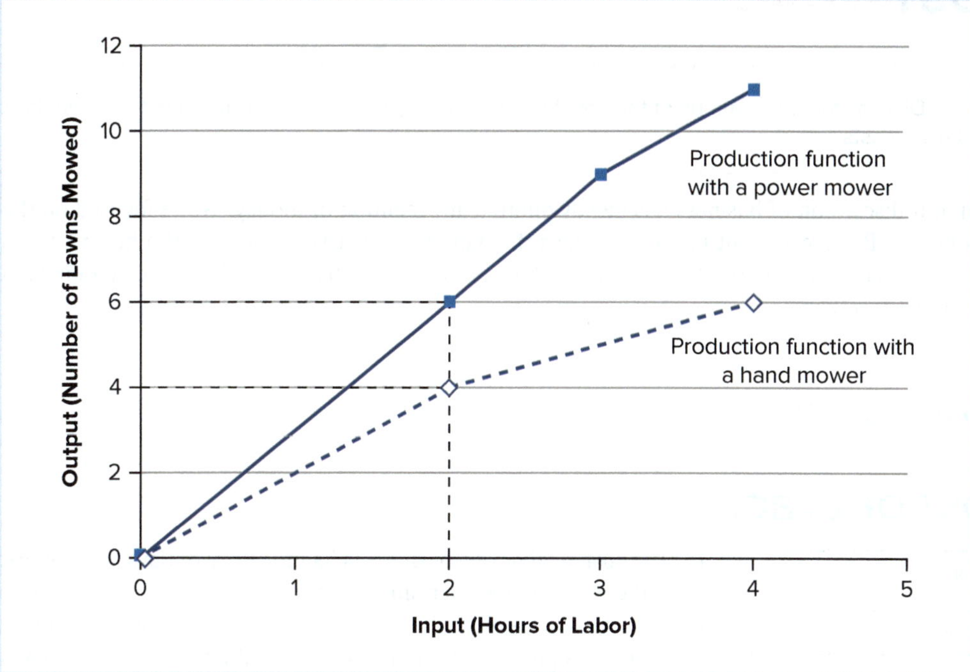

Businesses can also raise their average product by **outsourcing** part of their operations, either within the United States or overseas. That is, they hire other companies to handle tasks their own employees once did. In the 1970s and 1980s, for instance, many businesses decided they didn't want to run their own cafeterias or vacuum the office floors in the evening. Instead, they contracted out housekeeping and food services to specialized firms.

outsourcing
Shift of labor to third parties to handle tasks once done by a firm's own employees.

More recently, businesses have systematically sent their manufacturing and customer service processes overseas. Call centers and customer support operations have moved to India, the Philippines, and other low-wage, English-speaking countries. Computer companies have outsourced production of many laptop and desktop computers to Asian manufacturers. That means businesses have been able to lower their employee counts without cutting their output. This boosts the average product.

SPOTLIGHT: "CUT YOUR TREE, MISTER?"

Utility companies are supposed to be good at running power-generating plants cheaply and safely and delivering an uninterrupted supply of electricity. An important part of that task is trimming the trees and vegetation that grow alongside overhead power lines, so that they don't fall in a storm.

However, tree-trimming is a very specialized skill, so utility companies often outsource their tree work to experts. One of the biggest companies, Asplundh Tree Expert Company, reported in 2022 that it employs roughly 35,000 workers around the world.

Source: Asplundh Tree Expert Company, www.asplundh.com.

Ethan Miller/Getty Images

COST (LO4-3)

LO4-3 Discuss the implications of the cost function, average cost, and marginal cost. Explain the difference between variable costs and fixed costs.

So far, our discussion of business has mostly omitted any mention of money. We've focused on the process of production, turning inputs into outputs. But every input has a *cost*–that's the nature of a market economy. If a business wants to make the best profit-maximizing decisions, it has to know how its costs vary with its production decisions. We'll start by looking at the cost of each input and then at how they are put together.

Types of Cost

COST OF LABOR

cost of labor
Monetary outlays for labor, including benefits.

The **cost of labor** of a business is its monetary outlays for workers. In the simplest case, the cost of labor is the price of labor per unit of labor, multiplied by the amount of labor used. The price of labor is the workers' wages–either hourly wages or monthly salaries, depending on the jobs. On top of that, many businesses provide additional benefits at their own cost, such as vacation days, retirement benefits, and medical and dental insurance. Top managers at large companies often get a wide variety of other types of compensation, including use of corporate jets, health club memberships paid for by the company, and sometimes even paid housing.

COST OF CAPITAL AND LAND

cost of capital and land
Outlays for buying or renting equipment, structures, and land.

The **cost of capital and land** is the outlay for buying or renting equipment, structures, and land. Businesses can generally either buy or rent physical capital–like a building, a truck, or a computer. The same is true for land: A copper mining company will either buy land with copper ore or rent the right to mine from the owner of the land.

If a business rents a truck, the truck's cost per period is (not surprisingly) the price of the rental for that period. Similarly, if your business occupies space in somebody else's building, you generally pay rent monthly. But what happens if you buy a truck or a building yourself? There will be a big up-front cost–thousands for the truck, hundreds of thousands or even millions for the building–but you expect to use that truck or building over several years. As the business owner, you want to figure out the annual cost of your purchase and spread the initial cost over the projected life of the physical capital. If you buy a $40,000 truck and you expect it to last 10 years, you can look at your $40,000 cost as being spread over 10 years, or $4,000 a year. If you take out a loan to make your purchase, you'll also have to figure out the interest on the loan as part of your costs. We'll go into this in more detail in **Chapter 13**.

COST OF INTERMEDIATE INPUTS

cost of intermediate inputs
Outlays for goods and services purchased from other companies.

The **cost of intermediate inputs** is the money a business pays for goods and services purchased from other companies. For example, a restaurant buys ingredients for making meals–vegetables, meats, spices, and the like–from its suppliers. For many businesses, the cost of intermediate inputs can be quite large.

COST OF ACCUMULATING BUSINESS KNOW-HOW

cost of accumulating business know-how
Outlays that increase a company's knowledge and capabilities.

Finally, let's look at the **cost of accumulating business know-how**. Any outlays that increase a company's knowledge and capabilities are part of the cost of accumulating business know-how. This includes the cost of setting up scientific laboratories to research new technologies, hiring engineers and designers to develop new products, conducting marketing studies to see what customers want, bringing in management consulting firms to tell you how to run your business better, sending your workers to conferences to learn the latest techniques, paying other companies for the right to use their technologies, and so on.

Most companies do not officially report all their business know-how costs. However, they usually report their spending on research and development (R&D) on their annual financial statements. In 2021, for example, chip giant Intel spent more than $15 billion on research and development, with the goal of producing faster, cheaper, and more energy-efficient semiconductor chips.

In some cases, the cost of getting smarter is simply making mistakes and figuring out how to do things better. This is known politely as learning by doing. For now, however, we will focus on the monetary costs of accumulating business know-how.

Total Cost of Production

The **total cost** of production is the sum of costs for each of the inputs:

total cost
The sum of costs for each of the inputs used in production.

Total cost = (Cost of labor) + (Cost of capital and land) + (Cost of intermediate inputs) + (Cost of accumulating business know-how)

Here's one way to think about total cost. If you own and operate a McDonald's restaurant, your labor cost is wages and benefit payments to your hamburger flippers and cashiers. Your cost of capital and land is the rent on your store plus the cost of the food preparation equipment. The cost of intermediate inputs includes the money you pay for the beef patties, the buns, and the employees' uniforms. And the cost of accumulating business know-how is the time and money you need to go through McDonald's extensive training program for prospective owner-operators, including a stint at "Hamburger University." All of these added together make up your total cost.

The Cost Function

Imagine for a moment that you work for a company that makes candy. The members of the National Confectioners Association include candy manufacturers such as the American Licorice Company and Tootsie Roll Industries. The top company managers are going to decide how many thousands of pieces of candy to make in their factory, and they want to know how much each production level will cost.

cost function
Reports the total cost of producing each level of output.

So, you spend a week doing the calculations for each potential level of output: how many workers and candy machines are needed, the cost of the sugar and the wrapping paper, whether the company will need extra security guards if the factory has to run an extra shift at night. When you're done, you know the total cost of producing 1,000 pieces of candy, 2,000 pieces, and so on. (The appendix following **Chapter 6** goes deeper into the economics of the cost function and profit maximization.)

Your bosses don't need to know all the details of the calculation, though. All they need is the summary. The **cost function** summarizes the results of your calculations. That is, the cost function is like a calculator that tells you the total cost of producing each level of output, using the cheapest and best methods known to the company at the time.

Table 4.5 The Candy Cost Function

The left column reports the output of the factory, and the right column reports the total cost for that level of output.

Candy Produced (Pieces)	Total Cost (Dollars)
0	$ 500
1,000	$ 1,500
2,000	$ 2,500
3,000	$ 3,600
4,000	$ 4,850
5,000	$ 6,350
6,000	$ 8,100
7,000	$10,100

The cost function for your candy company might look something like **Table 4.5**. The left column of this table gives the possible levels of output for the company, while the right column reports the total cost for that level of output. The right column says, for example, that producing 3,000 pieces of candy will cost $3,600, producing 7,000 pieces of candy will cost $10,100, and producing no candy will cost $500 (the wages for the security guard, perhaps, to watch the empty factory).

We can also graph the cost function, as shown in **Figure 4.4**. If you want to know the cost of producing 5,000 pieces of candy, move across the horizontal axis until you come to 5,000. Then, the graph tells you the total cost is $6,350. The cost function is upward-sloping because it costs more to produce more candy.

Marginal Cost

Knowing the cost function for different levels of output is useful. But for profit maximization, what's more important is **marginal cost**. The marginal cost, or MC, is the added expense of producing one more unit of output. To put it a slightly different way, if a company decides to expand output by one unit, the marginal cost is the additional total cost. More precisely,

marginal cost
The added expense of producing one more unit of output.

Figure 4.4 Graphing the Candy Cost Function
The horizontal axis reports the number of candy pieces produced by the factory, and the vertical axis gives the total cost. This graph corresponds to the numbers in **Table 4.5**.

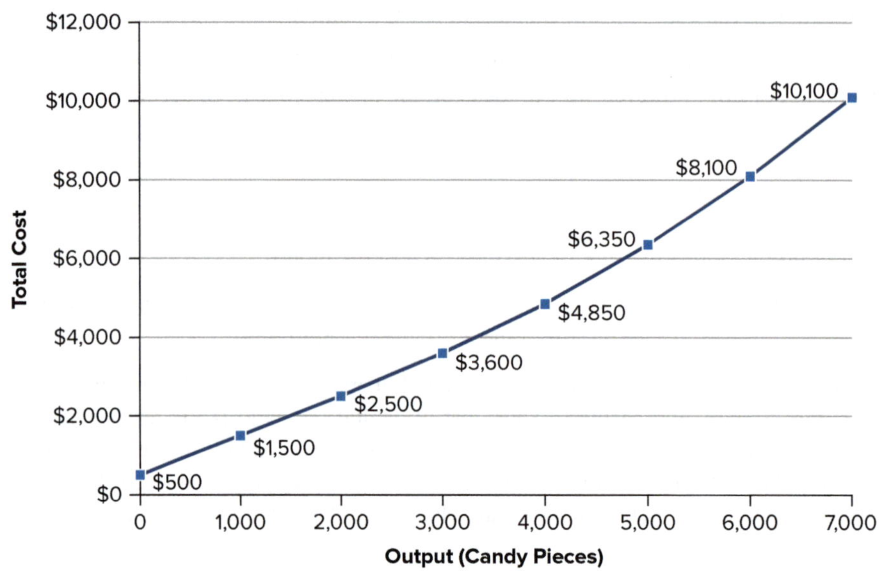

Table 4.6 Calculating Marginal Cost

For example, as the business increases production from 1,000 to 2,000 pieces of candy, the total cost rises from $1,500 to $2,500. The marginal cost is $1 per piece (the additional total cost divided by the additional number of pieces of candy).

Candy Produced (Pieces)	Total Cost (Dollars)	Marginal Cost (Dollars)
0	$ 500	
1,000	$ 1,500	$1.00
2,000	$ 2,500	$1.00
3,000	$ 3,600	$1.10
4,000	$ 4,850	$1.25
5,000	$ 6,350	$1.50
6,000	$ 8,100	$1.75
7,000	$10,100	$2.00

Marginal cost = (Added total cost of producing additional units of output) ÷ (Number of additional units of output)

Table 4.6 shows how we can calculate the marginal cost for the candy factory. Note that the first two columns repeat **Table 4.5**. For example, the cost of producing 1,000 pieces of candy is $1,500, and the cost of producing 2,000 pieces of candy is $2,500. The added cost to produce an extra 1,000 pieces (2,000 − 1,000) is $1,000 ($2,500 − $1,500), so the marginal cost in the third column is $1.00 per piece ($1,000 ÷ 1,000).

Figure 4.5 graphs the marginal cost curve. We can see from both the figure and the table that the marginal cost rises as the plant's production increases. Why should each additional piece become more expensive? Workers have to be paid overtime, machines break down more often if they run all the time, and the factory has to hire inexperienced workers who make more mistakes and require training. Generally speaking, economists tend to assume that marginal cost rises with quantity produced.

Variable versus Fixed Costs

variable costs
Costs that managers can quickly raise or lower by decisions they make today.

fixed costs
Costs that are difficult to change in the short run.

So far, we've discussed the cost function as if we could change every input equally easily. In reality, however, managers typically find some inputs easier to change than others. For example, if business at a restaurant suddenly increases, it's easier to add more waiters and cooks to prepare and serve the meals than it is to add another dining room to the restaurant.

We can think of businesses as having two types of costs: **variable costs** and **fixed costs**. Variable costs, also known as **short-term costs**, are those that managers can quickly raise or lower by decisions they make today. For example, it's easy for a retailer to adjust the number of hours its salespeople work. Similarly, advertising is a variable cost for a retailer, who can decide week to week how much advertising to buy in the local newspaper or on the Internet.

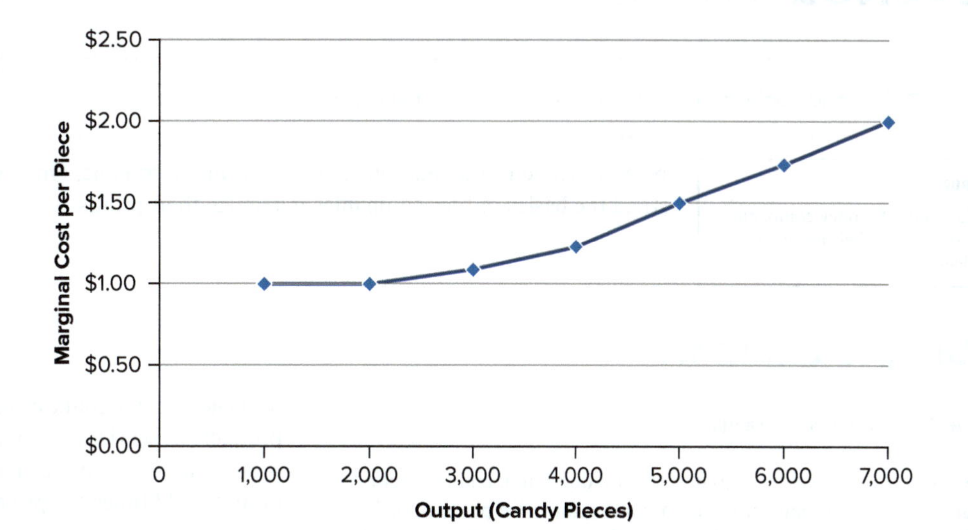

Figure 4.5 Graphing Marginal Cost
The horizontal axis measures output, and the vertical axis measures marginal cost. This graph corresponds to the third column of **Table 4.6**. In general, marginal cost rises as the output increases.

By contrast, fixed costs, also known as **long-term costs**, are harder to change; more precisely, a decision by a business to change its fixed costs will take longer to have an effect. For example, the rent a retailer pays for its building is a fixed cost. The business can certainly change that cost–but it takes a lot longer to open a new location somewhere else than it does to hire a new worker.

short-term costs
See *variable costs.*

long-term costs
See *fixed costs.*

There's one quirk you should remember about this terminology of *fixed* and *variable*. Fixed costs, of course, are not really fixed forever. The retailer could close down the store, for example. But, in the short run, it's much easier to change variable costs than fixed costs.

For that reason, variable costs are more relevant for short-term, everyday decision making, whereas fixed costs are properly the domain of long-term strategic planning. An example of variable costs can be found in your local hospital. Each day, hospital administrators have to decide how many nurses should be on duty, how many hospital gowns are needed, and how much food to order for the inpatients. These are variable costs. By contrast, spending devoted to expensive medical equipment is a fixed cost in the short term, because an MRI machine, for example, tends to last several years. Construction outlay for hospital buildings is considered a fixed cost, too.

Or consider retailers such as Starbucks, Walmart, and Home Depot. Each day or week, their managers decide how to staff their stores–how many workers to have on each shift. That's a short-term decision, which changes dramatically during the pandemic.

A key long-term decision for these companies is how many new stores to open and where. In 2022, for example, Starbucks opened 437 new company-operated stores in the United States, while closing 116 other locations. Such long-term decisions alter the fixed costs of doing business.

In some parts of the economy, hiring decisions may actually be tougher to reverse than brick-and-mortar investments. In the government sector, many workers are protected by unions and civil service rules, which make it tough to fire them except in cases of severe misconduct. On many college campuses, it is easier and faster to put up a new building than it is to fire a tenured professor.

On the other hand, outsourcing turns some decisions that used to be about fixed costs into decisions about variable costs. Suppose a U.S. company designs a new virtual reality headset and hires a Taiwanese company to make it. The cost of building and operating the factory–which is owned by the Taiwanese company–is now a variable cost for the U.S. company instead of a fixed cost.

We can distinguish between the *short-term cost function* and the *long-term cost function*. The **short-term cost function** assumes fixed costs can't be changed. If you own a building or a factory or have a long-term contract with your workers, you can't easily alter these inputs in the short term.

short-term cost function
The link between the output of a business and the cost of producing that output, assuming that fixed costs cannot be changed.

The **long-term cost function**, in contrast, puts everything up for grabs, including all the fixed costs (which are not so fixed in the long run). For example, the short-term cost function for Starbucks assumes all its retail locations are fixed. The long-term cost function, though, assumes the coffee chain can open new stores and close those that are not making a profit.

long-term cost function
The link between the output of a business and the cost of producing that output, allowing for all inputs to be changed.

REVENUE (LO4-4)

LO4-4 Define and apply the revenue function and marginal revenue.

revenue
The amount of money companies get from selling their products or services.

Now we come to the final piece of the business: revenue. Once we understand revenue, we can understand the basics of how companies maximize their profits.

A Simple Example

Table 4.7 A Revenue Example

The first column gives the output of the hot dog stand, and the second column gives the revenue amounts, assuming the price per hot dog is $1.50. Assuming all hot dogs that are made can be sold, the revenue is simply the number of hot dogs times $1.50.

Output: Number of Hot Dogs Cooked and Sold in a Day	Revenue (Assuming All Hot Dogs Can Be Sold at $1.50 Each)
10	$15
20	$30
30	$45
40	$60
50	$75

Revenue is the amount of money companies get from selling their products or services. In the simplest case, a business sells only one product at a fixed price. Then the revenue is equal to the number of units sold times the price per unit.

For example, a hot dog stand cooks hot dogs and then sells them. If the price is $1.50 each, the revenue equals the number of hot dogs sold times $1.50. **Table 4.7** shows the revenue, given the number of hot dogs sold (assuming that all the hot dogs can be sold). If the price per hot dog were higher, the revenue would be higher too.

More generally, a business may have several different ways to bring in money, beyond just selling a single product. Banks, for example, take in money by charging interest on the loans they make. But they also may charge people fees for withdrawing money from their automated teller machines. (For other examples, see "**How It Works: Finding More Revenue**" below.)

HOW IT WORKS: FINDING MORE REVENUE

One of the most important tasks of a business is finding new ways to make money from the same products. That requires figuring out what people are willing to pay for.

For example, electronics retailers get revenue from selling customers a big-screen television or computer. In addition, they get quite a bit of money from selling buyers an extended warranty—that is, a promise to fix the TV or computer if something breaks over the next few years.

Airlines generate revenue from ticket sales, but they've increasingly moved toward charging for food on board, more spacious seats, and extra baggage. Movie theaters sell access to films, of course, but they also generate revenue by selling giant candy bars, huge bags of popcorn, and cups of soda so large they could swallow a small dog.

Sports teams have had great success broadening their sources of revenue beyond game tickets. They sell parking, food, and drink. Television rights are a big money maker for most teams. And looking for more revenue, sports teams turned to selling the naming rights for their stadiums and arenas to companies that want the publicity. There's a downside, though: In some cases, the company with the naming rights gets into legal trouble or goes bankrupt, embarrassing the sports team.

Marginal Revenue

Charlie Borland/Alamy Stock Photo

Revenue typically goes up when a business expands production and sales. The question is: By how much?

The **marginal revenue** is the additional money a business gets from producing and selling one more unit of output (we're assuming at this point that the business sells everything it makes). In the simplest case, the business can sell as much as it wants at the going market price. This usually reflects the business being small relative to the total market. (We will see in **Chapter 5** that this kind of market is known as *perfect competition.*)

In this case, the marginal revenue from selling one more unit–that is, the extra revenue from the additional unit–is equal to the price. The more the business produces, the more it can sell at the same price. For our hot dog vendor, the marginal revenue is $1.50 per additional hot dog cooked and sold.

marginal revenue
The additional money a business gets from producing and selling one more unit of output; the additional money that a business gets from adding one more worker or one more hour of labor.

PROFIT MAXIMIZATION (LO4-5)

LO4-5 Determine the profit-maximizing level of output.

Now we get to the bottom line of this chapter: If profit depends on the difference between revenue and cost, both of which are affected by production, how does a business owner or manager decide *how much* to produce? The answer is that once we have both the cost and revenue functions, we can slowly increase the output of the business until we find the level that maximizes profit.

The **profit-maximizing rule** is a simple one:

A profit-maximizing business will increase production as long as marginal revenue exceeds marginal cost.

profit-maximizing rule
A profit-maximizing business will increase production as long as marginal revenue exceeds marginal cost.

That is, as long as the added revenue from an additional unit of output is greater than the additional cost of producing that unit, expansion will earn more profit for the business. For example, suppose the cost of hiring an additional landscape worker is $300 for a 40-hour week. Now suppose the extra worker can mow enough lawns to produce an additional $500 of revenue. Adding this extra worker makes sense because she can produce an additional $200 in profits over the $300 cost of hiring her.

For most businesses, marginal cost increases as output rises. Such a business will keep expanding up to the point that marginal cost is equal to marginal revenue (think about walking up to a line but no further). So the profit-maximizing rule is sometimes written this way: At the profit-maximizing output, marginal cost is equal to marginal revenue.

An Example

Let's look at an example in detail. Let's revisit the candy factory discussed earlier in this chapter.

Table 4.8 is probably the most complicated table you'll see in this textbook, so let's take it step by step. We've seen the first three columns before in **Tables 4.5** and **4.6**–the output of the factory, the cost of production, and the marginal cost. The fourth column is total revenue, assuming each piece of candy sells for $1.50 (perhaps a chocolate bar or a whole pack of gum). For example, 4,000 pieces of candy bring in $6,000 in revenue. The fifth column, marginal revenue, is the extra money the company earns by selling one more piece of candy. The final column, profit, is revenue minus costs.

Following our profit-maximizing rule, we expand production as long as marginal revenue exceeds marginal costs. For example, at the 2,000-piece level of production, marginal revenue is $1.50 and marginal cost is $1.00, so it makes sense to produce and sell more because the extra revenue exceeds the extra cost.

The expansion continues up to the 5,000-piece level of production (bolded in the table). This is the profit-maximizing level of production because, up to that point, we can still earn extra revenue. At higher levels of output, marginal cost rises to $1.75, which is more than marginal revenue. Thus, profit falls if output goes above 5,000 pieces.

One final note: It is sometimes true that there is more than one level of output that maximizes profit. In this example, an output of 4,000 pieces gives the same profit as 5,000 pieces. In such a situation, choose the output where marginal revenue equals marginal cost.

Table 4.8 The Profit-Maximizing Candy Company

The candy company will increase output as long as marginal revenue exceeds marginal cost. At an output of 4,000 pieces, the marginal revenue of $1.50 per piece is greater than the marginal cost of $1.25 per piece. At an output of 6,000 pieces, the marginal revenue of $1.50 per piece is less than the marginal cost of $1.75 per piece. The profit-maximizing level of output is 5,000 pieces, where marginal revenue equals marginal cost.

Candy (Pieces)	Total Cost (Dollars)	Marginal Cost (Dollars)	Revenue, Assuming Each Piece of Candy Sells for $1.50 (Dollars)	Marginal Revenue (Dollars)	Profit (Dollars)
0	$ 500	—	0	—	-$ 500
1,000	$ 1,500	$1.00	$ 1,500	$1.50	$ 0
2,000	$2,500	$1.00	$ 3,000	$1.50	$ 500
3,000	$3,600	$1.10	$ 4,500	$1.50	$ 900
4,000	$4,850	$1.25	$ 6,000	$1.50	$ 1,150
5,000	**$6,350**	**$1.50**	**$ 7,500**	**$1.50**	**$ 1,150**
6,000	$ 8,100	$1.75	$ 9,000	$1.50	$ 900
7,000	$10,100	$2.00	$10,500	$1.50	$ 400

HOW IT WORKS: WHO GETS THE PROFIT?

Suppose a business makes a million dollars in profit. Who gets it? The short answer is that the profit belongs to the owners of the business, but they may not always be able to take it home with them.

A small business may be owned by one person or a small number of partners. They can choose to take the profit out of the business and use it to send their kids to college. Alternatively, they can pay higher wages to their employees. Finally, they can reinvest the earnings to expand the business. Their hope in doing so is that their investment will make the business worth even more in the future.

The situation is similar for a large company. As we will see in **Chapter 13**, a large public company may have millions of shareholders who are all part owners of the company. The company will typically distribute some profit to them in the form of dividends, which are quarterly payments of cash per share of stock. The managers of the company can then use the rest of the profits to raise wages for the company's workers or reinvest it in expanding the business.

YOUR ECONOMIC LIFE: Why Are Some Stores and Restaurants Open All Night?

If you have hunger pangs at 3 a.m., where can you purchase something to snack on? In all likelihood, some restaurants and food stores near you are open all night. For example, in the Columbus, Ohio, area, Tee Jaye's Country Place Restaurants, a local chain, are open 24 hours most days. Near Atlanta, you can eat 24-hour Korean barbeque at Seo Ra Beol. Quite a few Walmart Supercenters, such as the one in Skokie, Illinois, are open around the clock.

Let's explore the decision-making process of businesses in regard to staying open all night. On the one hand, the marginal cost of the food sold is the same at night as during the day–a bag of chips is a bag of chips. The big extra costs are labor (to serve the customer and to provide security) and energy (to keep the lights on, and to heat or cool the building).

The marginal revenue from staying open at night depends on the number of potential customers who keep late hours. These often include college students and employees at nearby businesses, such as factories and hospitals, that have overnight shifts.

minimum wage

A wage floor set by the government that lifts the wages of the lowest-paid workers above their market wage.

The businesses decide whether the marginal revenue of staying open 24 hours exceeds the marginal cost. A rise in energy costs will increase the marginal cost of keeping a store or restaurant open all night. So if the price of electricity goes up, you would expect to see fewer 24-hour restaurants and stores. A rise in labor costs–say, because of a new law requiring businesses to pay a higher **minimum wage** to workers–would also likely reduce the number of all-night businesses.

So, the next time you embark on a late-night food run, think about the calculations that the managers of the business had to make in order to stay open for you.

The Law of Supply Revisited

Suppose that in **Table 4.8**, the price was $2.00 per piece rather than $1.50. What would happen to production? According to the profit-maximizing rule, the company will increase production as long as marginal revenue exceeds marginal cost. If the price is $2.00 per piece, the company will want to increase production up to 7,000 pieces of candy. In other words, a higher price leads to increased production because the company wants to maximize profit.

Now we can better understand the law of supply described in **Chapter 2**, which said that the quantity supplied in a market generally rises as the price increases. Because businesses are profit-maximizing, they can generally make more money by expanding production when the market price increases, assuming they are able to sell all they make.

Short-Term Profit Maximization and Long-Term Decisions

We can distinguish between short-term and long-term profit maximization. In **short-term profit maximization**, we focus on achieving the highest profit, assuming that fixed costs cannot be changed. The managers of the candy company make their production decisions taking the current size of the factory as a given.

short-term profit maximization

The process of running a business to achieve the greatest excess of revenues over costs, assuming that fixed costs cannot be changed.

In contrast, when we consider **long-term profit maximization**, we assume a business can vary all its inputs, even going as far as shutting down. The candy company can expand its factory; close part of it down; or move its operations to Canada, Mexico, or China.

long-term profit maximization

Profit maximization by businesses, assuming that all inputs can be changed and that there is the option to shut down.

Long-term profit maximization also includes the results of a company's big strategic decisions, like coming up with new products or entering new markets. Some companies, like Apple, maximize their profits by innovating. Others do it by offering low prices and trying to get maximum efficiency from their workforce.

For an automaker like Ford or Toyota, long-term decisions are connected with the design and development of new models–what they will look like, what performance characteristics they will have, and what market segments they will address. Take Toyota's development of the Prius, the first widely selling hybrid car, able to run on both gasoline and electricity. A team of Japanese engineers started designing the hybrid car in 1993. The biggest decision–what kind of engine to use–wasn't made until 1995. The Prius was first offered for sale in December 1997.

For executives at big drug companies, two key decisions are how much to invest in developing new drugs and where the most profitable opportunities might be. Under ordinary circumstances, it can take up to 10 years to develop a new drug in the laboratory, test it on animals, make sure it is safe for humans, run some large-scale studies to see whether it actually is beneficial, and then wait for the U.S. Food and Drug Administration (FDA) to approve the drug for sale. At each step along the way, the drug company has to decide, based on its analysis of costs and revenues, whether it makes sense to keep funding the new drug. (The development of COVID-19 vaccines was much quicker than usual, of course, though no steps were missed.)

Long-term decisions are inherently uncertain ones. Especially when companies are committing themselves to new technologies and new markets, it's tough to know what is going to happen. (For an example of long-term decision making in the airplane industry, see **"Spotlight: Boeing's Long-Term Decision."**)

SPOTLIGHT: BOEING'S LONG-TERM DECISION

The long-running competition between Boeing and Airbus, two giant commercial airplane manufacturers, offers a classic example of long-term decision making. Designing and testing a new commercial airplane is an expensive proposition requiring billions of dollars. Airplane manufacturers make investments like this in the expectation that the payoff will come over decades. For example, Boeing started developing the 747 in 1963; its first flight was in 1969; and the company was still taking orders for the cargo version of the 747 as of 2018.

In the mid-1990s, both plane makers had to place bets for the future. The executives leading Airbus chose to build the giant A380, capable of carrying up to 800 people (and requiring landing strips to be strengthened at airports around the world). Most airlines were reluctant to buy such an enormous plane. In 2019, Airbus announced it was not taking new orders for the A380.

On the other hand, Boeing designed a smaller, more fuel-efficient plane called the Dreamliner, or the 787. Boeing had a ton of orders for its new plane as of mid-2008, with the expectation that the first 787s would soon be carrying passengers. However, a series of production problems meant that the new planes did not debut until late 2011. A 3-year delay in introducing a new product would probably be disastrous for many companies. However, because the 787 will likely be sold for many years into the future, Boeing still expects to make good profits on the new model. Indeed, in 2022, Boeing received orders for 139 new 787 jets.

Thor Jorgen Udvang/Shutterstock

CONCLUSION

We started this chapter with Walmart and ended it with Boeing. In between, we looked at candy makers, lawn-mowing enterprises, giant oil producers, and fast-growing Internet search firms–all examples of profit-maximizing businesses with production, revenues, and costs. The basic logic of profit maximization that we saw here is essential for understanding how today's economy works.

In **Chapter 5**, we will show how competition–or the lack of competition–affects the production and pricing behavior of businesses, and what that means for the broader economy.

04 SUMMARY

1. A business buys inputs from its suppliers. It uses those inputs to produce output–the goods and services it sells to its customers. The money the business pays for the inputs is its cost, and the money it receives from its customers is its revenue. Profit is the difference between revenue and cost. ***(LO4-1)***
2. The inputs to production include labor, capital, land, intermediate inputs, and business know-how. The production function summarizes the output of a business, given the levels of its inputs. The marginal product of labor is the extra amount of output a business can generate by adding one more hour of labor or one more worker. ***(LO4-2)***
3. The total cost of production is the sum of the costs for all of the inputs. The cost function for a business reports how much it will cost to produce a given level of output. Marginal cost is the added cost to produce one more unit of output. Variable costs can be quickly changed by the decisions of managers. Fixed costs take longer to change. ***(LO4-3)***
4. Revenue is the amount of money companies get from selling their products or services. Marginal revenue is the added revenue from producing and selling one more unit of output. In perfect competition, the marginal revenue will be equal to the price. ***(LO4-4)***
5. A profit-maximizing business will increase production as long as marginal revenue exceeds marginal cost. Short-term profit maximization holds fixed costs constant. Long-term profit maximization allows all inputs to vary. ***(LO4-5)***

KEY TERMS AND CONCEPTS

outputs
inputs
production
revenue
cost
profit
profit maximization
nonprofit organizations
labor
capital
land
intermediate inputs
business know-how
production function
marginal product of labor
diminishing marginal product
average product
outsourcing
cost of labor
cost of capital and land
cost of intermediate inputs
cost of accumulating business know-how
total cost
cost function
marginal cost
variable costs
fixed costs
short-term costs
long-term costs
short-term cost function
long-term cost function
revenue
marginal revenue
profit-maximizing rule
minimum wage
short-term profit maximization
long-term profit maximization

connect PROBLEMS

1. A business has revenues of $40 million per month and costs of $28 million per month. Its monthly profits are _______ *(LO4-1)*
   a) $12 million.
   b) $36 million.
   c) $68 million.
   d) $144 million.
2. Some hospitals and private universities are nonprofit organizations. This means _______ *(LO4-1)*
   a) their costs exceed their revenues.
   b) they do not seek to maximize their profits.
   c) they try to maximize revenues.
   d) they do not try to minimize costs.
3. In 2020, NextEra Energy Resources, a major generator of energy from wind and solar, produced roughly 80,000 gigawatt-hours of electricity (a gigawatt-hour is a unit of electric consumption able to power about 100 homes for a year). The company had about 5,000 U.S. employees. What is the average product of NextEra Energy Resources? *(LO4-2)*
4. A medical office does MRI (magnetic resonance imaging) scans on patients. It has two MRI machines. Each scan requires a technician to run the MRI machine. The following is the production function for the office, which shows how many patients the technicians can scan. *(LO4-2)*

Number of Technicians	Number of Scans Completed per Day	Marginal Product	Average Product
1	5	?	?
2	10	?	5
3	14	?	?
4	17	3	?
5	20	?	?

   a) Fill in the table with the appropriate marginal product and average product for each level of hiring.
   b) Graph the production function.
   c) Suppose the office buys a new type of MRI machine that can do one extra scan per day. Show graphically what will happen to the production function.

5. In the previous problem, suppose that the price of the labor input (the MRI technician) is $200 per day in wages and benefits. Suppose also that the capital input (the MRI machines) has a price of $150 per day for each machine, on a long-term lease. *(LO4-3)*

   a) To do 10 scans in a day, how many technicians are needed?
   b) What is the labor cost of doing 10 scans in a day?
   c) What is the total cost of doing 10 scans per day (assuming there are two MRI machines in the office)?
   d) What is the variable cost of doing 17 scans in a day?
   e) What is the fixed cost of doing 17 scans in a day?

6. Think about a Starbucks coffee shop. Identify whether each of the following inputs is a fixed cost or a variable cost. *(LO4-3)*

   a) An espresso machine.
   b) Electricity to run the machine.
   c) The lease on the store.
   d) Workers.

7. A local handyman offers to install new windows in your home. The following is his cost function. *(LO4-3)*

Number of Windows	Total Cost (Dollars)	Marginal Cost (Dollars)
0	200	—
1	300	?
2	400	?
3	500	?
4	650	?
5	850	?
6	1,100	?

   a) Fill in the marginal cost column in the table.
   b) Graph the cost curve.
   c) What is the fixed cost of window installation?

8. All other things being equal, a business making shirts would choose not to expand when _______ *(LO4-4)*

   a) marginal revenue per shirt equals $7, and marginal cost per shirt equals $10.
   b) marginal revenue per shirt equals $20, and marginal cost per shirt equals $10.
   c) marginal revenue per shirt equals $11, and marginal cost per shirt equals $10.

9. Below is the cost function for a bicycle repair shop, including the labor cost for the repair technicians. *(LO4-4)*

Bicycles Repaired per Day (Number)	Cost (Dollars)	Marginal Cost (Dollars)	Revenue (Dollars)	Marginal Revenue (Dollars)
0	30	—	?	—
1	70	?	?	?
2	120	?	?	?
3	180	?	?	?
4	250	?	?	?
5	330	?	?	?
6	420	?	?	?
7	520	?	?	?
8	630	?	?	?

   a) Fill in the blanks for marginal cost. Is the marginal cost increasing or decreasing?
   b) Suppose the market price for repairing a bicycle is $80. Fill in the blanks for the revenue and marginal revenue.

10. Using the table in **problem 9**, answer the following questions. *(LO4-5)*

    a) How many bicycles must the store repair per day to maximize profits? (Remember the profit-maximizing rule.)
    b) Now suppose the market price for repairing a bicycle goes up to $100. How many bicycles will the shop repair?

CH 05

COMPETITION AND MARKET POWER

andresr/Getty Images

LEARNING OBJECTIVES

After reading this chapter, you should be able to:

LO5-1 Define *perfect competition* and identify its key characteristics.
LO5-2 Describe how businesses maximize profits in perfectly competitive markets.
LO5-3 Discuss the long-term outcome of perfect competition.
LO5-4 Compare and contrast the four types of market structure.
LO5-5 Explain how market power affects price and quantity supplied.

We've all been brought up on the idea of competition in sports and in life. I win, you lose; you win, I lose.

Yet, competition plays a very different role in a market economy. What economic theory says—and experience confirms—is that under the right circumstances, competition is a win–win proposition. Companies compete against each other to deliver to consumers what they want at the lowest cost. In the short run and the long run, competition in the market leads to more production, more innovation, and higher standards of living.

These benefits of competition are the key reasons the market economy remains the best way to organize an economy. If competition did not deliver a higher standard of living, there would be much more political opposition to all the insecurity and turmoil that inevitably come along with a market economy.

In this chapter, we begin by examining how perfect competition works in a single market. Then, we'll examine alternatives to perfect competition and where they fall short. Finally, we'll explain the benefits of perfect competition, which are a key justification for the market economy.

PERFECT COMPETITION (LO5-1)

LO5-1 Define *perfect competition* and identify its key characteristics.

perfect competition
A situation in which all buyers and sellers in a market are price takers.

competitive market
A market that is characterized by *perfect competition*.

price takers
Buyers and sellers who take the market price as given and make their buying and production decisions accordingly.

Let's start by looking at **perfect competition**, which is sometimes also called a **competitive market**. Perfect competition is, in some sense, an extreme type of market that is rarely found in the real world. Nevertheless, it is a useful benchmark for understanding how real market economies behave.

What makes perfect competition special is that all buyers and sellers are **price takers**. Being a price taker means just what it sounds like–buyers and sellers take the market price as given and make their buying and production decisions accordingly. Imagine that as the manager of a grocery store you are trying to decide what price to put on your all-beef frankfurters. Your competitors are selling frankfurters for $5.00 per pound (which was roughly the national price in January 2023). If you are a price taker, you charge the going rate in the market–$5.00 per pound, the same as your competitors. If you are a price taker, you'd be foolish to charge more than $5.00 because all your customers would buy their frankfurters elsewhere. And you'd be foolish to charge less because you can sell all your frankfurters at the (higher) going rate.

If you are a buyer of the frankfurters, being a price taker means that you accept the posted price as given without trying to bargain it down. In perfect competition, buyers and sellers bow to the will of the market. No seller can boost its price above the market without losing its customers to competitors. No buyer can push the price below the market because there are plenty of other buyers willing to pay the going rate.

standardized products
Outputs that differ from each other in only a small number of easily identifiable features.

Under what circumstances will we expect to see price-taking behavior? First, products have to be standardized so buyers can readily compare them. **Standardized products** differ in a small number of easily identifiable features. In the United States, corn comes in five grades, depending on factors such as the percentage of broken kernels. So, commercial purchasers of corn know that, say, one bushel of "U.S. No. 2 corn" will be roughly the same quality as any other bushel of No. 2 corn.

Likewise, it's now easier to compare the price of different desktop computers because computer capabilities are becoming increasingly standardized. Two computers with the same microprocessors, random access memory, and hard disk space are pretty much equivalent, so a purchaser can choose the cheaper one. (Laptop computers, by contrast, are not so easily standardized.) Similarly, memory chips are standardized according to size and response time.

ECONOMIC MILESTONE

1980: First Standardized Energy Use Labels

In 1980, the Federal Trade Commission started requiring makers of major appliances to label their products with estimated energy consumption or energy efficiency. Such standardized information brings the market closer to perfect competition by making it easier for consumers to compare products. Since then, energy labeling requirements have been refined and expanded several times, and now cover items such as electric vehicle chargers.

A market with perfect competition will typically have many sellers and many buyers.

Second, for price-taking behavior to occur, sellers and buyers must be well informed about what all the sellers are charging. That means if any seller lowers its prices, buyers immediately know and flock there. Similarly, if a seller raises its price, buyers immediately know they have better alternatives, and they quickly leave.

Third, and perhaps most important, a market with perfect competition will typically have many sellers and many buyers. They don't all have to be in the same place, however. In national or global markets (defined in **Chapter 2**), buyers and sellers may be in different parts of the country or different parts of the world.

Examples of Perfect Competition

Most markets do not meet all three conditions of perfect competition. Products may not be standardized; one dress, for example, is not exactly like another. It may not be easy to compare prices charged by different suppliers. And there may be relatively few buyers or sellers; in any area, there are usually few providers of cell phone service, for example.

> In perfect competition, a profit-maximizing business will expand until its marginal cost equals the market price.

However, in some ways, today's economy is moving closer to perfect competition with the rise of the Internet and globalization. As markets become global, individual businesses, no matter how large, are less able to affect prices. Buyers have access to many more potential suppliers–not just in their town or their state, but around the world. And many businesses in the United States have to worry about matching prices charged by Asian or European competitors.

Some markets that are close to perfect competition include basic foods such as wheat and corn. There are many suppliers and buyers in the United States and around the world, the products are standardized, and the current market price can be seen by anyone with access to a computer. For example, on January 25, 2023, the market price for corn was $6.75 per bushel.

Some manufactured products also trade in markets that are close to perfect competition, with many suppliers and many buyers, and standardized products. For example, memory chips for personal computers are made by many companies, the chips are standardized, and it's possible to find the current market price for memory chips of different sizes.

PROFIT MAXIMIZATION IN PERFECT COMPETITION (LO5-2)

> **LO5-2** Describe how businesses maximize profits in perfectly competitive markets.

Remember from **Chapter 4** that a profit-maximizing business increases production as long as its marginal revenue (MR) is greater than its marginal cost (MC). In perfect competition, the business can sell as much as it wants at the market price (P), so the marginal revenue from selling an extra unit of output is just equal to P.

In general, marginal cost rises as production increases. Thus, in perfect competition, a profit-maximizing business will expand until its marginal cost equals the price (P = MC). Once we know the market price, we also know the level of production for the firm in perfect competition.

For example, a company producing low-end desktop computers today is in a market that's close to perfect competition because the machines' capabilities are so similar. Suppose the company can sell its computers for $500 each. Then it will produce up to the point where its marginal cost of producing the next computer is equal to $500 (see **Table 5.1**).

Table 5.1 **Marginal Cost and Marginal Revenue Schedule for a Computer Maker**

This table gives the marginal cost schedule for a computer maker. For example, the marginal cost of the 4,000th computer is $500.

Output (Number of Computers)	Marginal Cost (Dollars)	Marginal Revenue (Assuming the Market Price is $500 per Computer) (Dollars)
1,000	$200	$500
2,000	$300	$500
3,000	$400	$500
4,000	$500	$500
5,000	$600	$500

For an individual business in a competitive market, the supply curve is the same as the marginal cost curve. Look at **Figure 5.1**. To see how much the business will produce at a market price of $500, we find point *A* where marginal cost is equal to $500. That gives us the profit-maximizing output of 4,000 units.

Figure 5.1 Profit Maximization by a Single Business in a Competitive Market
If the market price is $500 per computer, the profit-maximizing business expands to the point where marginal cost is equal to $500 (labeled *A*). This figure corresponds to the numbers in **Table 5.1**.

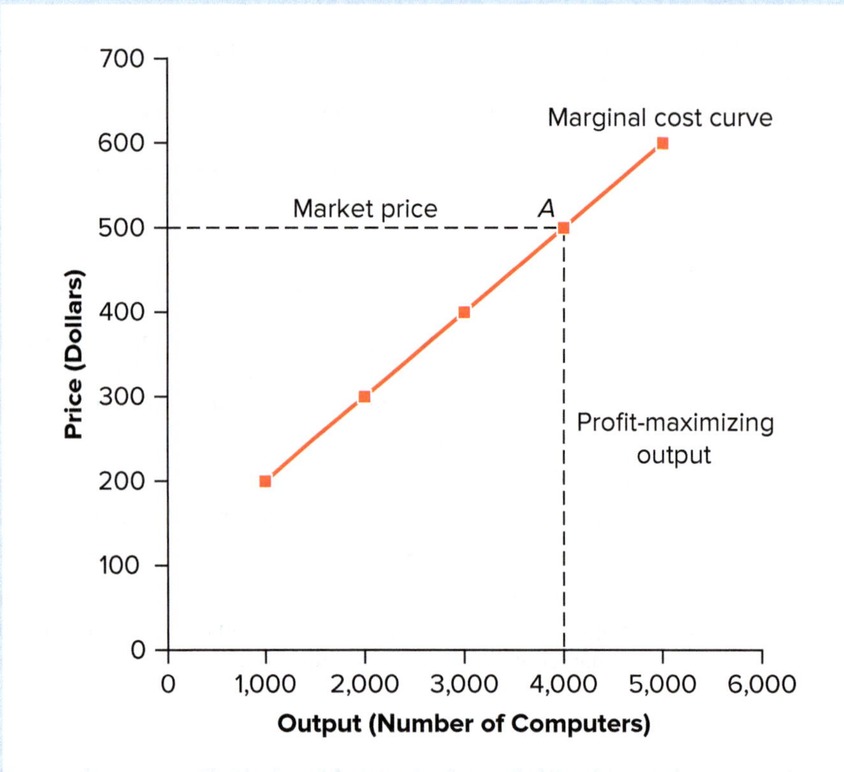

As we saw in **Chapter 2**, the market supply curve is the sum of the individual supply curves. For example, if there are 10 identical businesses with the same marginal cost schedule shown in **Table 5.1**, then at each price the quantity supplied to the market will be 10 times the individual quantity supplied. **Figure 5.2** shows the market supply curve. Note that at a market price of $500, the quantity supplied is 40,000 computers ($10 \times 4{,}000$).

Figure 5.2 Market Supply with 10 Identical Businesses
In perfect competition, all businesses in the market produce at the point where the market price equals marginal cost. In this case, with 10 computer makers, each produces 4,000 computers.

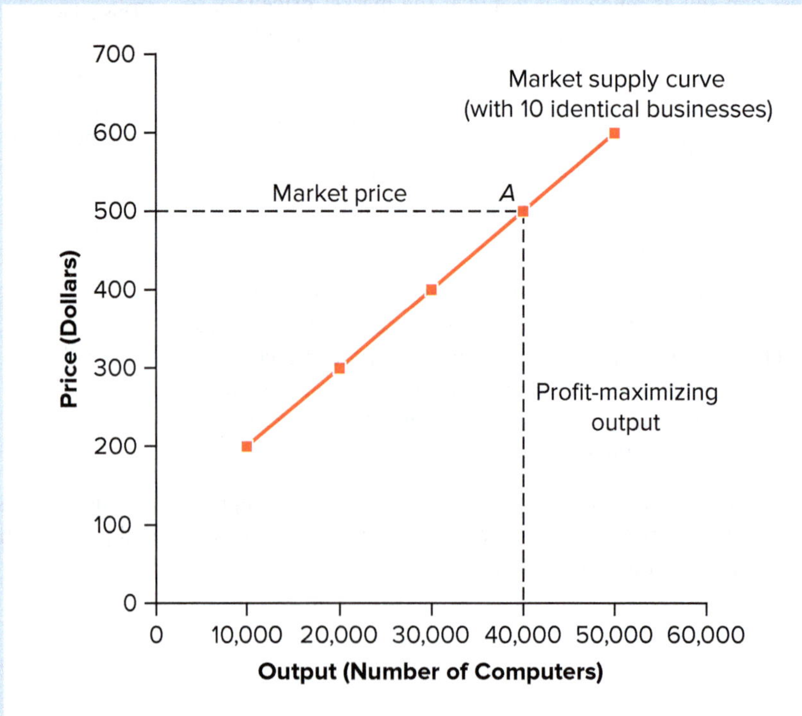

Market Equilibrium in Perfect Competition

As in any other market, equilibrium for a perfectly competitive market occurs where market quantity supplied equals market quantity demanded. At the market equilibrium, price equals the marginal cost of production for each business. If price were greater than the marginal cost, the business would have an incentive to expand production. If price were less than the marginal cost, the business would reduce production. As a result, all businesses end up producing at the same marginal cost, which is equal to the market price.

Let's stick with the example of the market for computers. Take a look at **Figure 5.3**, which shows the market supply curve that we have already seen in **Figure 5.2**. In addition, **Figure 5.3** includes a possible market demand curve. The market equilibrium is point *A* where quantity supplied equals quantity demanded–that is, the point where the two curves cross.

Figure 5.3 Graphing Market Equilibrium
This graph corresponds to the supply and demand schedules for computers shown in **Table 5.2**. Point *A* identifies the market equilibrium.

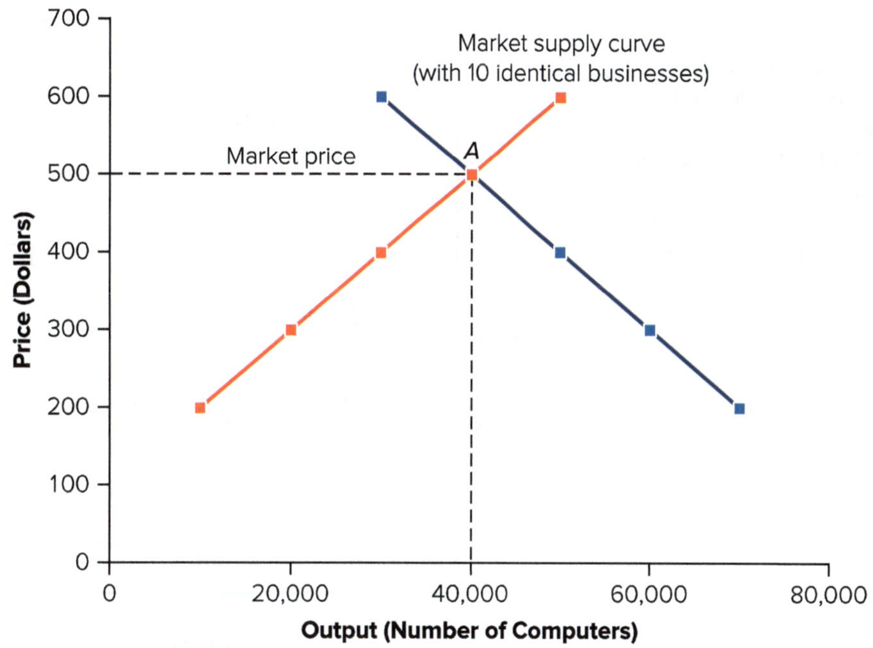

Table 5.2 shows the numbers corresponding to the supply and demand curves. At a market price of $500, the quantity demanded is 40,000 computers and so is the quantity supplied. But we know even more than that. Each of the 10 computer manufacturers produces 4,000 computers–and at that level of production, their marginal cost is $500, according to **Table 5.1**. In perfect competition, marginal cost is equal to the market price.

Table 5.2 An Example of a Market with Perfect Competition

In this market, there are 10 computer suppliers, all of them price takers, with the marginal cost curve shown in **Figure 5.1**. The equilibrium for this market comes where the price is $500 per computer, and the quantities supplied and demanded are both 40,000.

Price (Dollars)	Quantity Demanded by All Buyers (Number of Computers)	Quantity Supplied by All Sellers (Number of Computers)
$200	70,000	10,000
$300	60,000	20,000
$400	50,000	30,000
$500	40,000	40,000
$600	30,000	50,000

PERFECT COMPETITION IN THE LONG RUN (LO5-3)

LO5-3 Discuss the long-term outcome of perfect competition.

new entrants
New businesses competing in an existing market, or existing businesses that are expanding into a new market.

What happens in a competitive market in the long run? If businesses in a market are making a profit, those profits attract new entrants to the market, just as sugar attracts ants. **New entrants** are just what they sound like—new businesses competing in the same market or existing businesses in other markets that are expanding into a new market. In fact, if there is nothing to stop them—such as government regulations or high start-up costs—a market will have new entrants as long as it looks profitable. **Figure 5.4** shows how the market equilibrium changes with new entrants.

Figure 5.4 New Entrants Drive Down the Market Price
As new businesses enter a competitive market, the market supply curve shifts to the right, and the market price falls.

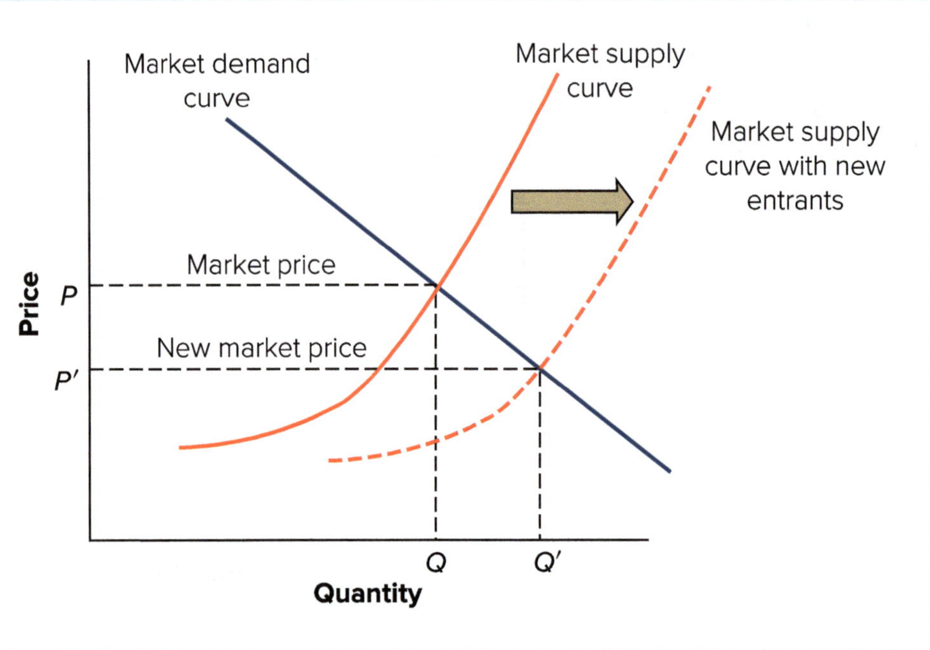

Most RadioShack stores have closed.
Michael D Edwards/Shutterstock

What happens when a new dentist opens an office in a small town? Let's assume all the dentists offer the same services: cleaning, filling cavities, and so forth. Each new dentist office increases the supply of dental services and causes the supply schedule to shift to the right. That drives down the price for everyone. Eventually, profits fall low enough that no one else is willing to take the plunge and enter the dental market in that town.

Let's call this the Big Squeeze. As more and more competitors move into a market, any business with a higher-than-average cost function finds it harder to survive. For example, in the laptop computer industry, many computer manufacturers that couldn't match low-cost producers such as Dell, Asus, and Acer have been squeezed out. In retailing, Amazon's ability to consistently offer low prices and rapid delivery has given consumers an alternative to higher-priced competitors. Eventually, those that cannot attract enough consumers to make a profit have to go out of business.

If there are no barriers to entry, only the lowest-cost businesses survive over the long run in a market with perfect competition.

In a market with perfect competition, as long as there is enough time and there are no barriers to entry, profits will tend toward zero. A **barrier to entry** is anything that might make it difficult for a competitor to enter a market. For example, if a new hospital wanted to open up in a town, it might need approval from the town government, especially if it needed a change in zoning laws. In this case, government regulation is a barrier to entry. Another barrier to entry is the lack of a key resource. Perhaps not enough land is available in town to put up another hospital, or it might take a long time for a large enough parcel of land to become available.

barrier to entry
Anything that makes it difficult for a new competitor to enter a market.

Long-Term Survival

The Big Squeeze leads us to another implication of perfect competition. If there are no barriers to entry, only the lowest-cost producers survive over the long run. Let's suppose you'd like to buy a tuna sandwich from a local restaurant or some other store that sells food. Thus, you are a buyer in the market for tuna sandwiches. Now suppose there are two types of restaurants. One type–the high-cost producers–can make a tuna sandwich at a marginal cost of $3 per sandwich (ingredients and labor). The second type of restaurant–the low-cost producers–can make the sandwich at a marginal cost of $2 (using the same ingredients but a much faster, more efficient sandwich-making technique).

Over the long run, the low-cost providers will consistently be able to drive down the price below $3, and at that price, the high-cost providers won't be able to make a profit. After they lose enough money, they will have to close or adopt the same sandwich-making techniques as their rivals. Indeed, in the long run, a market with perfect competition is driven by survival of the fittest.

This process by which the low-cost producers drive out the high-cost producers over the long run occurs in any industry in which there are no barriers to entry. Consider department stores. Remember Marshall Field's? How about Stern's? Or Bradlees? Probably not–but all these were department store chains that either closed or were sold over the past two decades. We've seen massive consolidation in the department store industry–the result of intense competition from online retailers such as Amazon and mammoth chains such as Walmart and Target. Many existing retailers simply could not cut costs low enough to compete.

From 2000 to 2022, department stores lost some 600,000 jobs. But over the same period, warehouse clubs and supercenters, like Target and Walmart, added more than 800,000 jobs. E-commerce sellers such as Amazon also added hundreds of thousands of jobs in their fulfillment centers. The result was a net plus for employment.

The long-run shift to low-cost producers is a central trend in manufacturing as well, especially for such products as basic clothing. As mentioned in **Chapter 3**, most apparel manufacturing has moved to low-cost countries like China and Vietnam because U.S.-based factories simply can't match the prices of the imports. More recently, furniture manufacturing has been moving to lower-cost producers overseas (see "**Spotlight: The Furniture Industry**").

SPOTLIGHT: THE FURNITURE INDUSTRY

Few parts of the U.S. economy have been affected so quickly or so completely by Chinese competition as the furniture industry. In 1998, the United States imported only $2 billion worth of furniture from China. By 2000, furniture imports from China had risen to $5 billion; by 2018, the pre-pandemic peak, furniture imports from China totaled more than $25 billion.

U.S. furniture makers located in states such as North Carolina found themselves suddenly competing with literally thousands of Chinese furniture factories, all vying to offer anything consumers wanted at the lowest possible cost.

In effect, the market moved much closer to perfect competition. That benefited consumers because the price of furniture in the United States fell by 17 percent from 2000 to 2018, before rising again during the pandemic years. In other words, consumers could buy a lot more furniture for the same money.

The downside? The furniture manufacturing industry in the United States lost about 42 percent of its jobs from 2000 to 2018, and the decline continued during the pandemic. Competition, foreign or domestic, is a tough taskmaster.

Source: Census Bureau, Bureau of Labor Statistics.

YOUR ECONOMIC LIFE: Why Your Favorite Business Closed

All of us know the feeling. You have a favorite coffee shop, restaurant, or bookstore, and one day it's gone. Closed. Or perhaps the business "temporarily" closed its doors during the pandemic, and just never re-opened again. Or there's a website you like to browse, and unexpectedly you get the dreaded message "This site cannot be reached."

shutdown decision

A business decision to keep operating or not, based on the level of profits.

Businesses close all the time. It's a natural part of the market economy. So, let's take a closer look at the **shutdown decision**–the decision of whether to keep operating a business.

So, why did your favorite business close down? Simply put, probably because its costs, including labor and rent, exceeded its revenues. That could be true even if the place seemed very popular. Perhaps the coffee shop had too many people buying one cup of coffee and lingering for hours staring into their laptop. Perhaps the website you liked had too many free users and not enough paid ads.

Sometimes the problem is that the restaurant is in an area that suddenly has fewer customers. Perhaps people are working from home rather than coming into the office, so that fewer workers are stopping by for lunch or dinner. Can the restaurant change its menu to appeal to local residents rather than office workers? If not, it will eventually close.

However, businesses don't make shutdown decisions simply because they lose money for one or two years. New businesses almost invariably lose money at first, and even many established companies record losses during economic downturns. Businesses shut down because it becomes clear that they are going to keep losing money–or they simply run out of cash to pay their bills.

Escaping Perfect Competition

Perfect competition is good for consumers because it drives down prices. But before finishing this section, let's note there's a force pushing against perfect competition over the long run. When businesses find themselves stuck in anything that looks like a perfectly competitive market, they try to escape it. They want to show potential customers that they are different and better than the competition in order to charge higher prices.

How can a business escape perfect competition? The best way is to build a better product–or at least do something that differentiates your product from those of your rivals. Consider, for example, the mobile phone. When Apple introduced the first iPhone in 2007, there were already plenty of mobile phones on the market. But Apple was able to differentiate itself through much better design, more powerful chips, better access to the Internet, and ease of writing third-party applications ("apps"). As a result, the iPhone quickly became the market leader and the standard to beat.

Apple was able to differentiate its iPhone from other mobile phones on the market.

Peer Grimm/EPA/Shutterstock

Another example of a product that differentiated itself was Zoom, the videoconferencing application. Its advantage over video conferencing rivals was ease of use, combined with clear video and audio. These factors vaulted it to the top when the pandemic hit.

Another way to differentiate a product is through **advertising**. Advertising, of course, is paid communication with potential customers through a public medium, such as television, the Internet, a magazine, or a billboard. One role of advertising is to provide information about what a product does and how much it costs, but good advertising also has an emotional impact. It gives potential buyers a sense of comfort or excitement, along with a reason to buy. Advertising is especially valuable for brand names such as Crest, Tide, and Coke, to which consumers can become intensely loyal (see "**How It Works: Well-Known Brand Names**").

For example, go into a drugstore and take a look at the haircare products. In many stores, you will find perhaps 40 different kinds of shampoo for men and women. They all accomplish the same thing–cleaning hair. However, they have different ingredients and perhaps different levels of effectiveness. They all have different brand names and brand images, aided by copious amounts of advertising. And unlike goods in a perfectly competitive market, they can sell for very different amounts, ranging from $2 to $20 for 16 ounces.

advertising

Paid communication with potential customers through a public medium such as television, print, or a website.

Some economists argue that consumer devotion to a well-advertised brand name is justified because all that advertising creates a reputation effect. This means a company that spends millions of dollars advertising a product–especially one that is used repeatedly like shampoo or razors–will want to make sure its financial investment in the ad campaign will pay off and not be eroded by consumer complaints or well-publicized problems with the product. So economists argue that heavy advertising often means a product does indeed deliver what its producer promises. (By contrast, heavy advertising of a single-use product like a new movie may just be a way of getting people into the theater before they hear how bad the film is.)

HOW IT WORKS: WELL-KNOWN BRAND NAMES

A well-known and respected brand name helps differentiate a product and allows a company to charge higher prices and earn higher profits compared to perfect competition. In 2022, Interbrand published a list of the "most valuable" brands—that is, products whose brand names helped boost sales and profits. The list was led by Apple, Microsoft, Amazon, Google, and Samsung, followed by Toyota, Coca-Cola, Mercedes-Benz, Disney, and Nike. In all these cases, the companies' names convey positive messages about their products and services.

Source: Interbrand, https://interbrand.com/best-global-brands/.

MARKET STRUCTURE (LO5-4)

LO5-4 Compare and contrast the four types of market structure.

If a market does not operate under perfect competition, how do we describe it? Economists have classified markets into several different types, or **market structures**, according to the number of buyers and sellers and the intensity of competition. Other than perfect competition, the main types of market structure are *monopolistic competition, oligopoly,* and *monopoly*.

market structure
Market classification according to the number of buyers and sellers and the intensity of competition.

Monopolistic Competition

Perhaps the most common market structure in today's economy is **monopolistic competition**. This type of market is characterized by a large number of sellers with similar, but not standardized, products.

monopolistic competition
A situation where a market has many sellers with similar but not standardized products.

A good example of monopolistic competition consists of restaurants in a neighborhood. There may be 5 or 10 restaurants within a short distance of each other, all offering the basics–a meal and a clean place to sit. But some may be quiet, others noisy. Some may offer pizza, others Thai food. And some may be expensive, while others serve meals for a few dollars.

These restaurants are competitors in the sense that they are all trying to attract the same pool of potential diners. However, it is not perfect competition–no market price applies to all the restaurants. Each offers a different meal or dining experience from the others, so each can charge a different price.

What's more, the restaurants are not price takers. If a restaurant lowers its prices, it knows it will take business away from the other restaurants and boost its number of diners. If it raises its prices, its quantity demanded will fall, but it will still keep the customers who really like its food. In other words, monopolistic competitors each face a downward-sloping demand curve.

PROFIT MAXIMIZATION WITH MONOPOLISTIC COMPETITION

The rule for profit maximization from **Chapter 4** was that a business boosts output as long as marginal revenue exceeds marginal cost. For perfect competition, marginal revenue is equal to price because a business can sell as much as it wants at the market price.

But for a monopolistic competitor, marginal revenue is typically less than the price. The reason is that if the business wants to sell another unit of output, it will have to cut the price it is charging everyone. That means it will lose some revenue from the goods and services it was originally selling, even as it gets additional revenue from the added sales.

Think about a restaurant serving 100 meals a night at $20 each. To attract new customers and increase sales to 110 meals a night, it might have to lower the menu price of the meals to $19. You might think that its revenue then goes up by $190: 10 additional meals at $19 each. But that's not correct.

The original nightly revenue was $2,000 (100 × $20). The new nightly revenue, with the lower price, is $2,090 (110 × $19). So, revenue only goes up by $90. The restaurant gets additional revenue from the extra meals, but it loses some money due to the lower price of the first hundred meals it was already selling.

HOW IT WORKS: PERFORMERS AS MONOPOLISTIC COMPETITORS

Musicians and actors—or indeed any kind of performers—are great examples of monopolistic competition. Performers who play the same type of music—whether classic rock, hip-hop, or country—obviously compete for the same audience. Listeners have only a limited amount of money and time, and the more they spend on concerts and music downloads for one performer, the less money and time they have for others. If too many performers are giving concerts in the same city at the same time, it becomes harder for any of them to sell out their shows.

If the market for music were perfectly competitive, all performers would have to charge the same price for their concerts. (Or perhaps they would charge by the hour so that longer concerts would cost more!) And it wouldn't matter to you which performer you went to see.

In reality, performers do not produce a standardized product. No one would ever mistake Taylor Swift for Bad Bunny, two of the highest grossing musicians in 2022 (or substitute any two performers of your choice). So some performers can charge much higher prices than others without losing all their ticket sales.

Auto dealers face the same problem. Typically, auto dealers are monopolistic competitors. They compete with other dealers in the same area selling other models of cars. The Ford dealer competes with the GM dealer, the Toyota dealer, and the Tesla dealer, who may be on the same block or even across the street.

Table 5.3 Marginal Revenue and Marginal Cost at a Car Dealer

A car dealer who is a monopolistic competitor knows that selling more cars requires lowering the price. The profit-maximizing output comes where marginal revenue equals marginal cost–in this example, at three cars sold per day.

Cars Sold per Day	Price per Car (Dollars)	Total Revenue (Dollars)	Marginal Revenue (Dollars)	Marginal Cost (Dollars)
1	$30,000	$ 30,000	$30,000	$24,000
2	$29,000	$ 58,000	$28,000	$25,000
3	$28,000	$ 84,000	$26,000	$26,000
4	$27,000	$108,000	$24,000	$27,000
5	$26,000	$130,000	$22,000	$28,000

To make things simple, imagine that the dealers post prices for the cars on their lots, and they have to offer these prices to everyone (there's no individual negotiation). The price each dealer picks depends on how many cars he or she wants to sell–that is, on the output of the dealership. To attract more customers, the dealer has to set a lower price, which lures customers away from the dealers across the street.

However, two things happen when a dealer sells one more car. The dealer gets the revenue from the additional car, but the lower price means he or she also has to give up a bit of revenue from the other cars that were already selling. As a result, the marginal revenue will be less than the price.

Table 5.3 gives an example of a revenue function, a marginal revenue function, and a marginal cost function for a car dealer. If the dealer sets the price at $30,000 per car, he or she can sell one car per day. But to sell two cars, the dealer must lower the price to $29,000 for both cars. How much extra revenue comes in? The original revenue from selling one car was $30,000. The revenue for the two cars is $29,000 per car, or $58,000 in total. Hence, the marginal revenue is $28,000 ($58,000 minus $30,000).

So the marginal revenue from selling the second car ($28,000) is lower than the price ($29,000). You can see from the table that it's true at every level of sales–the marginal revenue is less than the price.

How many cars will the dealer sell? The dealer will expand output until marginal revenue equals marginal cost. In this example, the profit-maximizing output is three cars sold per day.

MONOPOLISTIC COMPETITION IN THE LONG RUN

Generally, monopolistic competitors compete not only on price but also on other attributes of their products. For example, restaurants may try to distinguish themselves by quality of food or by friendliness of service. The more successful they are in differentiating themselves positively from their rivals, the more they can escape perfect competition, and the more they can raise their prices without fear of losing customers.

But here's a big problem for a business in monopolistic competition: If you successfully differentiate yourself from your competitor, what's to stop your competitor, or a new entrant, from imitating you? Suppose you run a restaurant, and you have been successful with your "Hawaiian Pizza." For a while that draws big crowds, but soon the other restaurants in town are offering their own versions, and your competitive edge disappears.

In the long run, monopolistic competition starts looking more and more like perfect competition as more businesses enter the market. The big challenge for successful businesses is to continually come up with new ways of defending their competitive advantage or creating new points of difference.

In fact, this is one of the great advantages of a market economy. The pressure to escape perfect competition forces successful companies to devote considerable resources to creating new products and services or to refining and upgrading their existing ones. In a market economy, standing still is a sure way to lose ground.

Oligopoly

Oligopoly occurs when a small number of sellers in a market produce similar products. (*Small* is usually defined in this context as four or fewer.) For example, except for the most heavily traveled routes, most cities are served by only a few air carriers. These suppliers are oligopolists.

oligopoly
A situation where a market has only a small number of sellers producing similar products.

In some situations, oligopolists can compete intensely. They can wage price wars to lure each other's customers away. Such intense rivalry can make an oligopoly look much like perfect competition, at least for a time.

collusion
An illegal practice in which two or more oligopolists work together to keep the prices of their products artificially high.

Alternatively, two or more oligopolists can engage in illegal **collusion**, working together to keep the prices of their products artificially high and to split the market. For instance, two local drugstores could agree that they'll both sell shampoos or tissues at a higher price and neither will try to undercut the other.

implicit collusion
Occurs when oligopolists let one company–the market leader–set prices in the market without direct communication.

Sometimes, oligopolists engage in **implicit collusion**. That means they do not communicate directly about price; however, they let one company–the market leader–set prices in the market. Whatever price the leader sets, the others follow. For example, two or three airlines may fly between the same two cities. When one airline raises ticket prices by $10, the other two follow immediately. This is not officially collusion, but it has the same effect of keeping prices higher than they would otherwise be.

In practice, however, it's difficult for oligopolists to collude effectively without talking to each other. There will always be temptation for one party to cheat, which means undercutting the oligopoly price by a bit to sell a lot more. Cheating in an oligopoly that actually benefits consumers by lowering prices.

Monopoly

At the opposite extreme from perfect competition is a **monopoly**. A monopoly is a market in which there is only one seller, and buyers have no good alternatives. As you might expect, a profit-maximizing monopolist will push up its price to take advantage of its control over the market. If you own the only gas station for miles around, you can charge more than if you face a lot of competition.

monopoly
A situation where a market has only one seller, and buyers have no good alternatives.

But to charge a higher price, a monopolist has to restrict its output. That's because buyers generally obey the law of demand–higher prices mean lower quantity demanded. Because quantity supplied equals quantity demanded in equilibrium, higher prices mean supply has to be reduced.

How high can a monopolist raise prices? It depends in part on the elasticity of market demand, as defined in **Chapter 3**. If demand is inelastic–that is, if buyers don't react much to price changes–then the monopolist can raise the price high above the competitive level. Suppose on an island, only one store sells food. This store can push prices up a lot because there are no alternatives for food buyers.

ECONOMIC MILESTONE

1960: Biggest Oligopoly Founded

For many years, the title of the biggest oligopoly went to OPEC, the Organization of Petroleum Exporting Countries. OPEC started with 5 members and now has 13, led by Saudi Arabia, which has one-fourth of the world's proven oil reserves. Historically, OPEC members met regularly to set the price of oil and to allocate quotas for how much each country will produce. However, several large oil-producing countries, including the United States, Russia, Norway, and Mexico, are not part of OPEC. Moreover, the United States has been able to use new technologies to boost oil production in recent years. As a result, OPEC lost much of its power to control the international price of oil until the Russian invasion of Ukraine in 2022, which cut down the global supply of oil and made OPEC relevant again.

But in a monopolistic market in which demand is elastic, consumers will significantly reduce their purchases when prices go up even a little. Then the monopolist won't be able to boost prices much above the competitive level. For example, suppose you have exclusive rights to sell something few people want, such as land in the middle of the desert. Your monopoly on the land won't do you much good; if you try to raise prices much above the competitive level, your potential buyers will look elsewhere.

True monopolies are even harder to find than markets with perfect competition. For example, the National Basketball Association is the only professional men's basketball league in the United States, so it has a monopoly on providing professional men's basketball games. But there are plenty of close substitutes for your sports entertainment dollar, including women's professional basketball, other major league men's sports, and college games. For that reason, there's a limit to how far NBA teams can raise their ticket prices despite their monopoly power in men's basketball (though to be honest, the price of courtside seats for popular teams such as the Golden State Warriors keeps going up and up).

Most monopolies have been undermined, to a large extent, by globalization and technology. The local department store in a small town, which once was the main source of clothing and hardware, now faces competition from online sellers such as Amazon.com that ship anywhere in the world. People have access to nearly infinite sources of news, classified ads, and other information, rather than just the local newspaper. And even when only one company manufactures a product in a country (Boeing is the only manufacturer of commercial airliners in the United States), it is not a monopoly because it must contend with competition from overseas companies, like Airbus.

natural monopoly

An industry in which it may make economic sense to have only one supplier.

Even so-called natural monopolies have been eaten away by technological change. A **natural monopoly** is an industry in which it may make economic sense to have only one supplier. The classic example is the old AT&T (known originally as American Telephone & Telegraph), which for most of the 20th century, was the sole provider of telephone service to most of the United States. At that time, all telephones had to be physically connected to each other by wires that ran from people's homes to central switching offices. That was an expensive investment; once the wires were installed, it didn't cost the phone company much to provide the service. Moreover, everyone had to be tied into the same network. As a result, it didn't make economic sense to have more than one provider of telephone service.

Today, of course, there are multiple sources of telephone service in your home. You can use a cell phone, get your phone service from your cable company, or make calls over the Internet. As a result, the conditions for a natural monopoly no longer exist.

Other natural monopolies used to include the local electric power company, cable company, and water company. These all shared two characteristics with the old telephone company. First, they had large *fixed costs* for infrastructure (wires, pipes, power stations, water filtration equipment) and low *variable costs* for providing service. Second, customers had to be tied into physical networks, so they could not easily switch.

Technological advances have made it possible to choose which company generates the electricity you use, even though there is still generally only one supply conduit to your home. And you can get your television shows from the local cable company, the local phone company, or a satellite TV company.

Speaking of technology, there's an ongoing debate about whether large tech companies such as Google and Facebook are monopolies. Google, for example, is the biggest Internet search engine in many countries, including the United States. Competing search engines exist, but have a comparatively small market share.

Google offers its search engine for free, so users don't have to pay. To compensate, Google makes most of its revenues by selling advertising. In this advertising market, Google is competing with other online companies that sell ads, as well as television networks and other media trying to reach consumers. So, Google is not a monopoly in the advertising market. We will visit this debate later in the textbook.

Probably the simplest way to keep a monopoly or oligopoly these days is to have the government protect it for you. Occupations such as manicurists and beauticians are licensed by the government in many parts of the country, which means they are protected against competition from people who don't have the right licenses.

PERFECT COMPETITION VERSUS MARKET POWER (LO5-5)

LO5-5 Explain how market power affects price and quantity supplied.

Why have we made such a big deal about the difference between perfect competition and other types of market structure? Why does it matter how many competitors are in a market and whether they are price takers?

The Benefits of Perfect Competition

The essence of a market economy is that all economic activities in a market are voluntary. Businesses choose to produce and sell because they benefit by earning the highest profit possible. Buyers make purchases because the value of the goods or services to them is greater than the prices they pay. In a market, all trades of money for goods and services are mutually beneficial–both buyers and sellers win.

But perfect competition goes further. In a market with perfect competition, businesses are price takers. As long as the market price exceeds the marginal cost, businesses automatically choose to increase output. To put this another way, as long as buyers are willing to pay enough to cover the extra costs of production, suppliers will oblige them.

To better understand the benefits of perfect competition, think again about that tuna sandwich you might buy at a local restaurant. Suppose you are willing to pay $3 or less for it. Now suppose its marginal cost–the cost of the ingredients and of the cook's time to make it–is only $2.50. As long as the price of the sandwich is between $2.50 and $3.00, the restaurant can profitably sell the sandwich, and you will be willing to buy it.

In perfect competition, that tuna sandwich will always be made and eaten. If a restaurant is not willing to make it for you, the one next door will. In essence, that's what perfect competition means–there are plenty of potential suppliers.

This idea holds not just for sandwiches but for any other type of good or service sold in perfect competition. Perhaps you want to buy an office chair. As long as the marginal cost of producing that chair is less than the price you are willing to pay, in perfect competition you will be able to find a business willing to make and sell the chair to you.

The Downsides of Market Power

A profit-maximizing monopolist will always charge a higher price than a perfect competitor would. More generally, monopoly, monopolistic competition, and oligopoly all feature sellers with some degree of **market power**. Market power is the ability to raise prices above the level that perfect competition would produce–by restricting the quantity supplied.

market power
The ability to raise prices above the level that perfect competition would produce by restricting the quantity supplied.

Higher prices and lower quantities supplied lead to higher profits for a business with market power. These higher prices hurt customers, of course. What's more, businesses with market power have to artificially hold down production and sales to keep up their prices.

Let's examine the general problem of market power using **Figure 5.5**. In perfect competition, suppliers and buyers reach the market equilibrium *A* where price equals marginal cost. Now let's suppose suppliers have some degree of market power. They band together and raise the price a bit to boost their profits. Buyers cut back on purchases because of the higher price (the result of a downward-sloping demand curve). The new market equilibrium is point *B* on the graph, and the new quantity supplied is less than the original quantity supplied.

Figure 5.5 Comparing Market Power and Perfect Competition
In perfect competition, market equilibrium occurs at point *A*. When businesses have market power, they can charge a price higher than the price with perfect competition, pushing the market to point *B* and reducing the amount produced and sold.

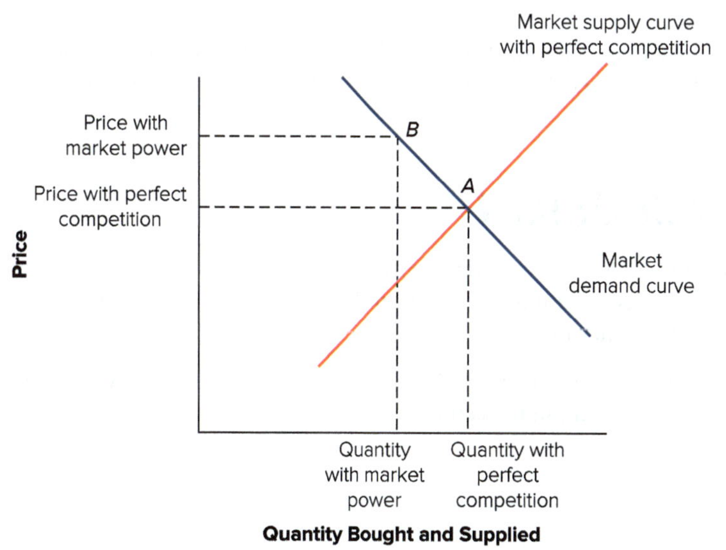

Suppose a town has lots of restaurants engaged in cutthroat competition. As a result, the restaurants charge $10 per person for their meals, just enough to cover the cost of the ingredients in the meals plus the labor required to prepare and serve them. Everyone in this town, even relatively poor people, can afford to eat out once a week. The restaurants are not making much money–just enough to stay in business. This is point *A* in the diagram.

Now imagine that the restaurant owners get together and agree to raise the prices they charge for their meals. So instead of charging $10 per person for dinner, they charge $15. What happens? In the diagram, the new market equilibrium corresponds to point *B*. The poorer people in this town stop eating out. The middle class eats out less often. The number of meals served drops significantly.

The restaurant owners are making more money–or they wouldn't have raised their prices. The people of the town are worse off–paying more and eating out less. But perhaps most important, dinners that could have been served aren't. This decrease in production and consumption represents a real loss to society.

SPOTLIGHT: THE AUTO INDUSTRY

For many years after World War II, the Big Three automakers—GM, Ford, and Chrysler—controlled the U.S. auto market. They were able to keep prices high enough to earn good profits and often made local car dealers wealthy. Autoworkers did well too. They were among the best-paid factory workers, with generous benefit packages that included free health care even after retirement.

The market power of U.S. automakers began disappearing in the 1970s, when competition arrived in the form of Toyota and other foreign automakers selling small, fuel-efficient cars that the Big Three didn't have. Detroit's market power gradually ebbed, and the Big Three could no longer boost prices as fast as overall inflation. In fact, from 1997 to 2020, the average price of new vehicles sold in the United States, adjusted for quality, barely rose, which benefited car buyers. The price of new vehicles did rise in 2021 and 2022, but that was due to shortages of key parts that shifted the supply curve for new vehicles to the left. Automakers still did not have any sustainable increase in market power.

Source: Bureau of Labor Statistics.

Market power has other consequences, in addition to higher prices for buyers. Managers at a business with market power have little incentive to cut costs. As a result, they can choose to raise wages for themselves or for their employees above what similar workers are getting paid. This helps workers at those businesses at the expense of consumers. Market power can make work easier for managers and workers–but it may not be the best thing for society.

Alternately, businesses with market power have sometimes used their high profits to research new products and technologies with long-term payoffs. The classic example is the old AT&T, which had a near-monopoly on telephone service in the United States until 1982. It used its powerful position to do some of the most important research in the country such as the invention of the transistor and the laser. Businesses with market power have also been big contributors to charity and cultural institutions–once again drawing on their higher profits.

Nevertheless, most economists believe that an economy with more competition performs better in the sense that it has higher production levels and lower costs. As we proceed through this textbook, we will return to this theme.

CONCLUSION

This chapter could be summarized with the phrase "why competition among sellers is (usually) a good thing for buyers." Competition yields lower prices and more production. Lack of competition leads to higher prices and, sometimes, a lack of incentives for businesses to try as hard as they might.

Yet there are economic situations for which competition and markets are not the right solution. That's why the next chapter is devoted to the role of government in the economy.

05 SUMMARY

1. In perfect competition, buyers and sellers are price takers. Perfect competition is more likely if products are standardized, if buyers and sellers are well informed about what other sellers charge, and if there are many buyers and sellers. *(LO5-1)*
2. In perfect competition, a profit-maximizing business will set its output level so that price (P) is equal to marginal cost (MC). *(LO5-2)*
3. In a market with perfect competition and no barriers to entry, profits will tend toward zero in the long run. New entrants will come in and drive down prices. Only the lowest-cost businesses will survive over the long run. Businesses with higher costs will shut down if they keep losing money. Businesses try to escape perfect competition by differentiating their products from those of their rivals. *(LO5-3)*
4. Perfect competition is just one type of market structure. The other types are monopolistic competition, oligopoly, and monopoly. Monopolistic competition is characterized by many sellers with similar but not standardized products. Oligopoly features a few sellers with similar products. Monopoly has one seller with no good alternatives for buyers. *(LO5-4)*
5. In monopolistic competition, profit-maximizing businesses choose an output level so that marginal revenue (MR) equals marginal cost (MC). Prices in markets with monopolistic competition are often driven down in the long run by the entry of other competitors. *(LO5-4)*
6. A business with a monopoly will also choose an output level so that marginal revenue equals marginal cost. That means a higher price and a lower quantity supplied and demanded than in a comparable market with perfect competition. This is true whenever businesses have market power. *(LO5-4)*
7. In general, markets that are closer to perfect competition perform better than markets where suppliers have more market power. As markets have more competition, production rises and costs fall over the long run. *(LO5-5)*

KEY TERMS AND CONCEPTS

perfect competition

competitive market

price takers

standardized products

new entrants

barrier to entry

shutdown decision

advertising

market structure

monopolistic competition

oligopoly

collusion

implicit collusion

monopoly

natural monopoly

market power

connect PROBLEMS

1. Answer the following questions. *(LO5-1)*
   a) Are standardized products easy to compare, hard to compare, or high priced?
   b) Are markets with one or two sellers more likely to be perfectly competitive, less likely to be perfectly competitive, or more likely to be innovative?
   c) In a perfectly competitive market, do buyers and sellers need information about prices so they can identify cheaters, gain market power, or find the current market price?
2. Consider the following products. For each one, identify whether the market has one, few, or many sellers. *(LO5-1)*
   a) Lettuce in the grocery store.
   b) Plane tickets from New York to Seattle.
   c) Tickets to a professional football game in your town.
   d) Passenger train service.
   e) Smartphones.

3. The following table shows the cost function for a business producing beach chairs. *(LO5-2)*

Quantity of Beach Chairs Produced (Number)	Total Cost (Dollars)	Marginal Cost (Dollars)
0	$ 3	—
1	$ 13	?
2	$ 24	?
3	$ 36	?
4	$ 49	?
5	$ 63	?

a) Fill in the column for marginal cost.
b) Assume the business is operating under conditions of perfect competition. If the market price is $14 per chair, how many chairs does the business produce? What is the total profit of the business?
c) If the market price is $13 per chair, how many chairs does the business produce? What is the total profit of the business?

4. The following table shows the maximum amount five potential buyers are willing to pay for a car. *(LO5-2)*

	Maximum Amount He or She Would Pay for the Car
Buyer 1	$40,000
Buyer 2	$35,000
Buyer 3	$30,000
Buyer 4	$25,000
Buyer 5	$20,000

a) What is the quantity demanded if cars sell for $30,000 each?
b) Under conditions of perfect competition, how many cars are bought if the marginal cost of producing a car is $25,000?
c) How many cars are bought if the marginal cost of producing a car falls to $20,000?

5. There are 15 hair salons in town, and the local haircut market is operating under conditions of perfect competition. *(LO5-3)*
a) What happens to the market supply curve in the short run if one of the hair salons goes out of business? Show your answer on a graph.
b) What happens to the price of haircuts sold? Show your answer on a graph.
c) What happens to the number of haircuts sold? Show your answer on a graph.

6. Someone wants to open a new restaurant in town. Identify which of the following would be a barrier to entry. Explain. *(LO5-3)*
a) None of the available property in town is zoned for business use.
b) The price of tablecloths has risen.
c) Consumers buy only from businesses they know.
d) The town requires all businesses to pay a hefty annual permit fee.
e) The town requires new businesses to pay a hefty permit fee.

7. You are running a restaurant under conditions of monopolistic competition. For each of the following situations, explain whether the demand curve you face shifts right, shifts left, or stays the same. *(LO5-4)*
a) Another restaurant opens across the street.
b) You advertise in the local newspaper.
c) You develop a tasty new dish that appeals to the local population.

8. A small business makes 1970s-style lava lamps (do an online search if you don't know what these are). There aren't many competitors. The business can sell the first few lamps for $30 each, but the business owners have found that they need to reduce the price if they want to sell more. *(LO5-4)*

Number of Lava Lamps Sold	Price	Revenue	Marginal Revenue
10	$30	?	
20	$25	?	?
30	$23	?	?
40	$21	?	?
50	$19	?	?

a) Fill in the table with the revenue and marginal revenue for each level of output. (Marginal revenue is calculated here as the change in revenue divided by the change in quantity sold.)
b) Suppose the marginal cost of making each lamp is $14. How many lamps should the business make to get the highest profit?

9. The following table shows the maximum amount five potential car buyers are willing to pay for each level of sales. Suppose that the cars are being sold by a car dealer operating as a monopoly (perhaps because there are no other car dealers in the market). *(LO5-4)*

	Maximum Amount He or She Would Pay for the Car
Buyer 1	$40,000
Buyer 2	$35,000
Buyer 3	$30,000
Buyer 4	$25,000
Buyer 5	$20,000

a) What is the revenue if the price of the car is $30,000?
b) If the marginal cost of each car is $20,000, how many cars will the monopolistic car dealer want to sell? What will the price be?
c) How many cars will be sold in perfect competition?

10. In December 2022, Google performed 88 percent of all online searches in the United States. *(LO5-5)*

a) Clearly, Google is the choice of many people for searching. If Google started charging consumers for each search, would demand for its services go down a lot or a little?
b) Does Google have market power in the market for searches, as defined in this chapter?
c) Google does charge advertisers for placing their ads next to related searches. For example, if you search for "Toyota," you will see car-related ads. Do you think Google has market power in the market for online search advertising? Explain.

11. In general, as markets have _______ *(LO5-5)*

a) more competition, production rises, and costs fall over the long run.
b) less competition, production falls, and costs fall over the long run.
c) more competition, production falls, and costs fall over the long run.
d) less competition, production rises, and costs rise over the long run.

CH 06

GOVERNMENT AND THE ECONOMY

Stockbyte/Getty Images

LEARNING OBJECTIVES

After reading this chapter, you should be able to:

LO6-1 Discuss the changes in the economic role of the government over time, including the New Deal, deregulation, and the responses to the pandemic.
LO6-2 Explain the benefits of government action.
LO6-3 Describe the limits and downsides of government action.
LO6-4 List and illustrate circumstances in which government intervention in the economy may be useful.

In recent years, one of the most controversial issues in the United States has been the government's response to the COVID-19 pandemic. Under President Donald Trump, the federal government took an active role in developing a COVID-19 vaccine and coordinating public health interventions, while providing trillions of dollars in financial assistance to individuals, businesses, and state and local governments. Under President Joseph Biden, the federal government passed additional legislation giving Americans more aid to cushion the impact of the pandemic, and undertook key tasks such as extending the nation's broadband network to include as many Americans as possible.

Yet there was serious debate about whether the government had done too little or too much to fight COVID-19. Mask and vaccine mandates were a particularly controversial topic. Some people argued that the government could have done more to avoid the large number of pandemic-related deaths, while others felt that mask and vaccine mandates were violations of civil liberties. We'll discuss this topic further in **Chapter 18**.

Another hotly debated issue is immigration: How many immigrants, and from which countries, should the federal government allow into the United States? And what should the government do about undocumented immigrants already in the country? Under President Donald Trump, the federal government became more active in deporting undocumented immigrants. The controversy over immigration continued under President Joseph Biden. We'll examine the long-term implications of immigration policy in **Chapter 16**.

The fight over pandemic responses and immigration reform are just one example of a long-running debate: How big a role should the government play in the economy?

Generally, economists start from the belief that markets are innocent until proven guilty. That is, providing goods and services through the **private sector**—which includes privately owned businesses—is preferable to taking government action unless there's a good reason to think otherwise. Hamburgers should be sold by privately owned restaurants and fast-food chains, not by the U.S. government. Similarly, it would be absurd to expect that consumer electronics—smartphones, big-screen TVs, and the like—should be sold or subsidized by the government.

private sector
The economy outside of government, including privately owned businesses.

But it's also true that markets alone are not enough: Every successful country has a large **public sector**. In the United States, the public sector includes the federal, state, and local levels of government, which collect taxes, employ workers, allocate money, regulate industries, and participate actively in the economy. The public sector provides goods and services such as public health, police, border control, and national defense. After all, no one would seriously contemplate the idea of a nuclear weapon being privately owned.

public sector
The portion of the economy that includes the federal, state, and local levels of government.

However, the right place to draw the line between the public and private sectors is often the subject of vehement debate. Should passenger trains be partly funded by the government, as they are in the United States and in most European countries, or should train transportation be left to the private sector? Should foreign students who get degrees from American universities be allowed to remain in the country? Should state governments run liquor stores, as they do in Pennsylvania and Utah? And should the federal government be able to regulate the gas mileage of sport utility vehicles?

In this chapter, we'll explore the history of government intervention in the economy, including the latest experience with the pandemic. We'll consider the advantages and disadvantages of the public sector. Then we'll explore the different justifications for a public sector role in the economy, including public goods, externalities, regulation, and redistribution.

HISTORICAL BACKGROUND (LO6-1)

LO6-1 Discuss the changes in the economic role of the government over time, including the New Deal, deregulation, and the responses to the pandemic.

When you go to bed tonight, take a close look at your mattress. Your bedding is regulated by the federal government under the Flammable Fabrics Act, originally enacted in 1953. The U.S. Consumer Product Safety Commission (CPSC) administers this standard, giving detailed directions for manufacturers to test each mattress for resistance to burning when exposed to cigarettes. For example, the standard specifies how many cigarettes will be used to test for flammability, exactly how they should be placed, and how badly a mattress can be charred and still pass the test. The standard even explains what testers should do if a test mattress ignites (see "**Spotlight: The Cigarette Test for Mattresses**"). An additional regulation, approved by the CPSC commissioners in 2006, ensures that new mattresses will be less likely to burst into flames when exposed to candles or matches.

Or consider your car, which has to meet a long list of federal and state regulations. The gas mileage it gets, the pollution that comes out of its tailpipe, the composition of the gasoline in its tank, the seatbelt that fits securely around you—all are influenced or controlled by government action. In 2014, for example, the National Highway Traffic Safety Administration issued a rule requiring all cars and other light vehicles built after May 2018 to come equipped with "rear visibility technology" to enable drivers to see children and adults behind the vehicle. And let's not forget that the highways and streets you ride on are almost all built and maintained by local or state governments, using tax dollars or the proceeds from tolls.

You can't avoid government regulation when you go to the bank or use your credit card. Your deposits are insured by the Federal Deposit Insurance Corporation up to $250,000, so your money is safe even if your bank goes under. The Federal Reserve regulates how the bank processes your canceled checks, including whether it is obliged to provide you with paper copies. The Consumer Financial Protection Bureau and the Federal Trade Commission help protect you against abusive practices by lenders. And, of course, the $10 and $20 bills you use are printed by the Bureau of Engraving and Printing, which is part of the Treasury Department.

Higher education is a mixture of private and public, with the public predominating. About 75 percent of college students attend public institutions: four-year or two-year colleges that are funded and run primarily by state and local governments. Even at many private institutions, a significant chunk of funding comes from public sources.

SPOTLIGHT: THE CIGARETTE TEST FOR MATTRESSES

The Consumer Product Safety Commission, which is part of the federal government, gives detailed instructions for testing the potential flammability of mattresses. These instructions specify, in detail, how many cigarettes to use and how long they should be allowed to burn. Here's one example:

> Place at least 18 ignited cigarettes on each mattress surface. At least nine cigarettes are placed on the "Bare" mattress test surface, and at least nine cigarettes are placed on the "Sheet" test surface. Position the cigarettes at least 6 inches (15.2 cm) apart on the mattress surface. Do not allow more than 4 mm (0.16 inch) of the length of the cigarettes to burn before placing them on the mattress surface.

And of course, the government is concerned about the safety of testers:

> It is imperative that a test be discontinued as soon as ignition has definitely occurred. Immediately wet the exposed area with a water spray (from water bottle), cut around the burning material with a knife or scissors, and pull the material out of the mattress with tongs. Make sure that all charred or burned material is removed. Ventilate the room.

Source: Consumer Product Safety Commission, Laboratory Test Manual for 16 CFR Part 1632: Standard for the Flammability of Mattresses and Mattress Pads, 2014.

https://www.cpsc.gov/s3fs-public/pdfs/blk_media_testmatt.pdf, downloaded 1/25/2023.

Before 1929, the government played a much smaller role in the economy.

And, of course, the government has been heavily involved in the health care system, even before the pandemic. A large portion of health care funding flows through public programs such as Medicare, which provides medical care for senior citizens, and Medicaid, which does the same for poor Americans. Government agencies such as the Food and Drug Administration regulate pharmaceuticals and medical devices such as pacemakers. We'll discuss more about the government's role in the health care system at various points of the textbook, including **Chapter 18**.

The Great Depression and the New Deal

Today, the hand of the government is apparent in every corner of the economy. But if we look back about 80 years or so, we see a much different world in which the government played a considerably smaller role. The dividing line was 1929–the year the Great Depression began. We'll discuss this period in more detail in **Chapter 10**, which covers the ups and downs of the business cycle. However, the key point is that economic conditions were so bad during the Depression that almost everyone was hoping the government could help. At the low point, one of every four workers was out of a job. There were widespread bank failures, the collapse of crop prices sent many farmers into bankruptcy, and it looked like the entire economy was about to come to a shuddering halt.

New Deal
A collection of public programs that President Franklin Roosevelt instituted to alleviate economic suffering during the Great Depression.

As a result, after President Franklin Roosevelt was elected in 1932, businesses and voters demanded that the federal government do something–anything–to get the economy moving again. In an amazingly short span of time, the Roosevelt administration passed a flurry of legislation to help U.S. families and businesses. This collection of public programs to alleviate economic suffering was called the **New Deal**.

The New Deal included almost any program the Roosevelt administration thought might work. For example, the Works Progress Administration (WPA), approved in 1935, was designed to put the unemployed to work building bridges, highways, and airport landing fields, as well as painting murals on public buildings. At its peak, the WPA employed 3.4 million people, or more than 5 percent of the total labor force.

The WPA and similar New Deal work programs faded away as the economy gradually recovered at the end of the 1930s. However, many New Deal programs became a permanent part of the economic landscape and are still with us today. Social Security, for example, was a New Deal program. So were unemployment insurance, the federal minimum wage, and the Federal Deposit Insurance Corporation (see **Table 6.1**).

The Era of Government Growth

The Depression and its subsequent economic recovery were followed by World War II, which pushed government spending and employment even higher as the United States geared up for war against Japan and Germany. After the war ended in 1945, government spending and employment dropped, but they did not return to their low pre-1929 levels (see **Figure 6.1**). In fact, after a short pause in the late 1940s, the government's role in the economy gradually expanded through the 1950s, 1960s, and 1970s.

It is interesting that during these three decades, the expansion of government's economic roles took place during the terms of both Republican and Democratic presidents. For example, the interstate highway program was started by President Dwight Eisenhower, a Republican who took office in 1953. Under this program, the federal government poured huge sums of money into one of the largest public works projects in history, eventually leading to the construction of almost 50,000 miles of high-speed, limited-access highways.

Table 6.1 Legacies of the New Deal

Many government programs begun under the New Deal are still with us today, including Social Security.

Program Created during the New Deal	What the Program Does Today
Social security	Financial support for the elderly
Unemployment insurance	Financial support for the unemployed
Securities and Exchange Commission	Protection for stock market investors
Federal Deposit Insurance Corporation	Protection for bank depositors from bank failures
Federal minimum wage	Minimum wage for workers
Ban on child labor	Tight restrictions on children being forced to work
Welfare for dependent mothers and children	Financial support for poor families

Figure 6.1 Government's Share of Employment The federal, state, and local governments employed about 10 percent of all workers in 1929. The government share of employment skyrocketed during World War II, going as high as 31 percent in 1944 and 1945, including military. In 2021, the government employed roughly 16 percent of all workers.

Source: Bureau of Economic Analysis.

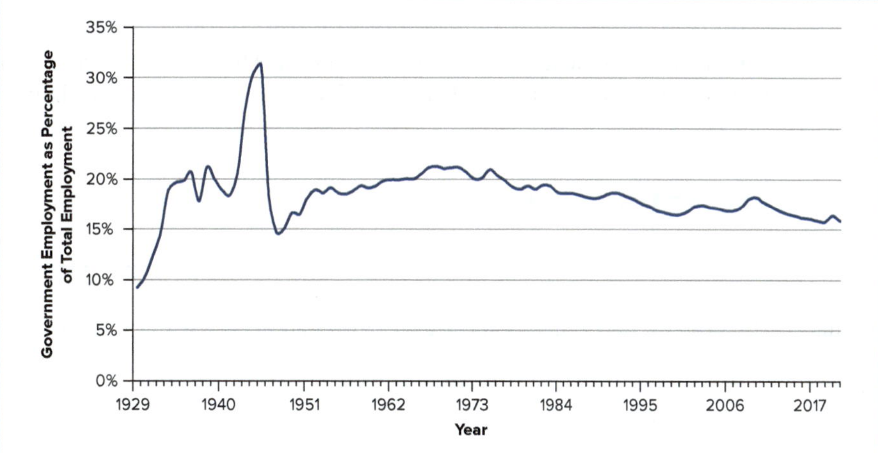

Eisenhower's successor, President John F. Kennedy, a Democrat who took office in 1961, did not stint on spending either. This is what Kennedy said in a May 1961 speech:

> I believe that this nation should commit itself to achieving the goal, before this decade is out, of landing a man on the moon and returning him safely to the earth. . . . This decision demands a major national commitment of scientific and technical manpower, materiel and facilities, and the possibility of their diversion from other important activities where they are already thinly spread.*
>
> John F. Kennedy

The manned space program Kennedy started *was* expensive and required an enormous commitment of people and resources. In fact, between 1961 and 1972, the federal government spent as much on space exploration as it did on building highways.

President Lyndon B. Johnson, a Democrat who became president when Kennedy was assassinated in 1963, made his mark with the Great Society programs, which were designed to help poor Americans. These included Head Start, which funds early childhood education for low-income children, Medicare, and Medicaid, already mentioned earlier in this chapter.

* John F. Kennedy

Landing a person on the moon required large government expenditures.

NASA.

Under Johnson, the federal government also increased its involvement in other ways. This period saw the creation of the National Endowment for the Arts and the National Endowment for the Humanities, two government agencies that fund artistic and cultural projects. Johnson also signed legislation authorizing the nonprofit, government-funded television and radio networks, Public Broadcasting Service (PBS) and National Public Radio (NPR). (Today, PBS still receives a substantial portion of its revenue from the government, whereas NPR receives little government funding.) When Richard Nixon, a Republican, took over as president in 1969, government involvement in the economy continued to grow. Nixon signed legislation approving the creation of the Environmental Protection Agency, which focuses on preserving the environment; the Occupational Safety and Health Administration, which monitors and improves worker safety; and the Equal Employment Opportunity Commission, which tries to reduce labor market discrimination. (Labor market discrimination will be discussed in **Chapter 17**. The economics of the environment will be discussed in **Chapter 19**.)

Perhaps most notably, Nixon aggressively used the power of government to control rapid price and wage increases. In an August 1971 speech, he said the following:

> I am today ordering a freeze on all prices and wages throughout the United States for a period of 90 days. In addition, I call upon corporations to extend the wage-price freeze to all dividends.
>
> I have today appointed a Cost of Living Council within the government. I have directed this council to work with leaders of labor and business to set up the proper mechanism for achieving continued price and wage stability after the 90-day freeze is over.*
>
> Richard M. Nixon

This was an amazing exercise of government control over the economy. The federal government actually told businesses what prices they could charge, and it told unions what wages they could ask for. These directives would be almost inconceivable today.

The Era of Deregulation

> The mid-1970s saw the beginning of the era of deregulation, when the role of government in the economy was reduced.

oil price shock

The events occurring in 1973 when the Organization of Petroleum Exporting Countries (OPEC) put an embargo on oil shipments to the United States and several European countries. Skyrocketing oil prices followed, which helped trigger an era of high inflation.

Starting in the mid-1970s, the public began to feel that government interference in the economy had gone far enough. The defining moment was the **oil price shock** of 1973. In October of that year, the Organization of Petroleum Exporting Countries (OPEC) put an embargo on oil shipments to the United States and several European countries that supported Israel. The result of the cutback in oil supplies was, not surprisingly, a sharp run-up in the price of gasoline and other petroleum products, which is exactly what you'd expect from a competitive market.

Americans, long used to low gasoline prices, had a strong negative reaction. President Nixon and Congress, then run by the Democratic party, responded quickly, but everything the government tried to do seemed to make things worse. For example, the government implemented odd-even gasoline rationing. If your license plate ended in an odd digit, you could buy gasoline only on odd-numbered days.

This rationing plan seemed to make sense, but in practice it worked badly. Because drivers wanted to make sure they didn't run out of gas, they started trying to keep more gasoline in their tanks than usual. Thus, the demand for gasoline actually grew. And because people were scared of running out of gas on the "wrong" days, motorists made sure to stop at a service station on their "right" days. As a result, gasoline stations were likely to have long lines of customers and sometimes to run out of fuel.

deregulation

The process of reducing government control over markets.

At the same time, the economy turned sluggish, and consumer prices rose a lot. Americans began to feel the United States had taken the wrong path–not just in response to the oil embargo, but more generally. President Jimmy Carter, a Democrat, made the first attempts at **deregulation**–the reduction of government control over markets. In particular, he rolled back government oversight of the airline and

* Richard M. Nixon

trucking industries. The Airline Deregulation Act of 1978 allowed existing airlines to change fares, abandon old routes, and start new ones without asking for government permission. New airlines could enter the industry as well, subject only to safety regulations.

However, the antigovernment movement did not get into full swing until the 1980 election of Republican President Ronald Reagan. In his first term, Reagan dramatically cut personal taxes, reduced government spending on job training programs, and generally tried to restrict the government's role in the economy. Philosophically, the idea at the time was that less government was better.

Here's one example of deregulation. From 1933 to 1980, a government rule–called "Regulation Q"–had put a ceiling on the interest rates banks could pay on savings and checking accounts. That artificially limited the interest rates small depositors could get: If a bank wanted to offer a high interest rate on its savings accounts, it wasn't allowed to do so.

Cars lined up waiting to purchase gas in 1973.

Library of Congress

In 1980, Congress–then controlled by Democrats–passed legislation that called for the elimination of interest rate ceilings, but it did not give a timetable for doing so. The Reagan administration aggressively took up this mandate, and by 1986 virtually all interest rate ceilings were a thing of the past.

Still, for all the deregulation, the antigovernment movement was a slow and moderate one rather than a revolution. Take another look at **Figure 6.1**. In the mid-1970s, the government employed about 19 percent of the total workforce, the high-water mark for public-sector hiring in the past half century. In 2021, government employed 16 percent of the U.S. workforce; this is a drop from the peak, but is still way above the pre-Depression level.

The Pandemic Response

Viewed in historical terms, the government response to the pandemic was very large and very fast. The Coronavirus Aid, Relief, and Economic Security (CARES) Act, the largest stimulus act in history, was passed by Congress and signed by President Donald Trump in March 2020, just as Americans were grappling with the reality of the pandemic. The Cares Act was followed by several other huge pieces of legislation, providing relief to every sector of society (see **Table 6.2**). As we will see later in the textbook, this mammoth response was effective in cushioning the impact of pandemic on household incomes, keeping the economy afloat while COVID-19 vaccines were developed. However, as we will discuss in **Chapter 8**, there were negative impacts as well, including higher inflation.

Table 6.2 Main Pieces of Pandemic-Related Legislation

Name of Legislation	Date	What it did
Coronavirus Aid, Relief, and Economic Security (CARES) Act	March 2020	The $2.2 trillion in the largest stimulus bill in history included stimulus checks to individuals; a moratorium on foreclosure and evictions; increased unemployment assistance; forgivable loans for small businesses; loans for large corporations; assistance to health care providers and suppliers; spending on tests, vaccine development, and medical devices; relief to state and local governments; and a variety of other provisions.
Consolidated Appropriations Act	December 2020	This bill included $900 billion in pandemic relief, with the biggest share going to additional support for small businesses, followed by checks to individuals; increased unemployment assistance; aid for schools and universities; funding for vaccines, testing and health care providers; and a variety of other provisions.
American Rescue Plan Act	March 2021	At $1.9 trillion in stimulus spending, this bill provided funding for unemployment benefits; an expanded child tax credit; aid to state and local governments; aid for schools and universities; vaccine distribution and testing; and a variety of other provisions.
Infrastructure Investment and Jobs Act	November 2021	This legislation provided $550 billion in new federal funding for rebuilding roads, bridges, and rail; extending broadband to unserved communities; boosting spending on water systems and the electric grid; and a variety of other provisions.
Inflation Reduction Act	August 2022	This bill, arguably not directly connected to the pandemic, boosted funding for clean energy and increased resources for modernizing the Internal Revenue Services, while raising money through reforming prescription drug pricing.

In addition to large spending programs, in the early days of the pandemic, many states issued "stay-at-home" orders, and required closures of schools, restaurants, and non-essential retail establishments. In response, many offices closed and people shifted to working from home if they could.

As this textbook is being revised, it is hard to know whether the aggressive role of the government during the pandemic is a one-time event, or a sign of the future. Some policymakers see a growing need for the public sector to manage large-scale climate crises, financial crises, and health crises. Others would prefer to shrink the government's role further. That will be a major debate of the coming years.

THE BENEFITS OF GOVERNMENT ACTION (LO6-2)

LO6-2 Explain the benefits of government action.

What's the biggest strength of the public sector? The government can identify a social or economic goal and, in theory, take action to achieve it directly. If it is important to improve education, then the government allocates more funds for teachers, schools, and college scholarships. If a country needs a stronger defense against external threats? Spend more on spy satellites, jet fighters, and tanks. If legislators decide that people should drive slower and waste less gasoline? Pass a law that sets the national speed limit at 55 miles per hour, as Congress did in March 1974 after OPEC cut off oil supplies in December 1973. That law, of course, is no longer in effect. Instead, the federal government sets fuel economy standards for cars and other vehicles.

Another example: When the government wanted to quickly develop a vaccine against COVID-19 in 2020, it was willing to fund development efforts at several different pharmaceutical companies simultaneously, in hopes that one would be successful (we'll discuss this further in **Chapter 15**). But the list of public-sector initiatives is nearly endless: It include bans on smoking in restaurants, bars, and office buildings; aid to the poor in the form of welfare payments, food stamps, and housing vouchers; and subsidies for wind and solar power. The government can encourage immigration of educated workers by making it easier for foreign students to remain in the country after their degrees are done, or discourage immigration by setting quotas on the number of people who can move to the United States.

ECONOMIC MILESTONE

1981: First Discount Airline

Sometimes, the best government action is to do less. Until 1978, the federal government controlled what routes airlines could fly and how much they could charge. But the deregulation of the airline industry after 1978 allowed the entry of new carriers that could offer cheap tickets.

The first of these discount airlines was People Express, which started flying in 1981. Operating from a dingy terminal at Newark Airport just outside New York City, People Express offered air fares as low as $19 off-peak to Washington, DC, and $29 to Boston. Unfortunately, this "bus in the sky" lasted only six years because the prices were too low to make a profit.

command-and-control approach
An approach to regulation that directly specifies certain market outcomes and activities to achieve desirable goals.

When the government directly specifies certain market outcomes and activities to achieve desirable goals, this is called a **command-and-control approach** to the economy. This directness can seem appealing. For example, most people agree that it's desirable for everyone to be able to receive at least a high school education. In the United States, this goal was mostly achieved by the middle of the 20th century because local governments built and staffed elementary and high schools using public money.

In other words, the goal of giving everyone at least a high school education was achieved by government action rather than by relying on markets. These public schools were open to everyone, without regard to income, family background, or gender. Such mass education caused the percentage of high school graduates to rise dramatically, with beneficial effects for the economy. This shift could not have happened so quickly or so completely if schooling had been left primarily in the hands of the private sector. What's more, every state passed a compulsory attendance law requiring children to attend school up to some level. Such laws were especially important in agricultural regions, where families could be tempted to rely on older children to work on farms instead of sending them to school.

Figure 6.2 shows the spending that resulted from these government education policies. First, government spending on public elementary and secondary schools soared, going from 1.2 percent of GDP in 1920 to around 4 percent in 1970, staying roughly at that level through today.

Government also plays an essential role in managing globalization, encouraging technological change, and shaping financial markets–the forces that guide today's economy. For example, the U.S. Trade Representative negotiates the treaties that control trade with other countries, which then have to be approved by the Senate. As we will see in **Chapter 14**, these agreements set trading rules that the private sector has to follow.

Similarly, government funds the basic research that underlies many technological advances. For example, the Defense Department sponsored much of the original research that led to the development of the Internet. And long experience has shown that financial markets work best when they are tightly supervised and regulated.

Figure 6.2 Spending on Public Education Spending on public elementary and secondary schools as a percentage of GDP has jumped over the past century, going from roughly 1.2 percent of GDP in 1920 to 3.8 percent in 2020.

Source: National Center for Education Statistics.

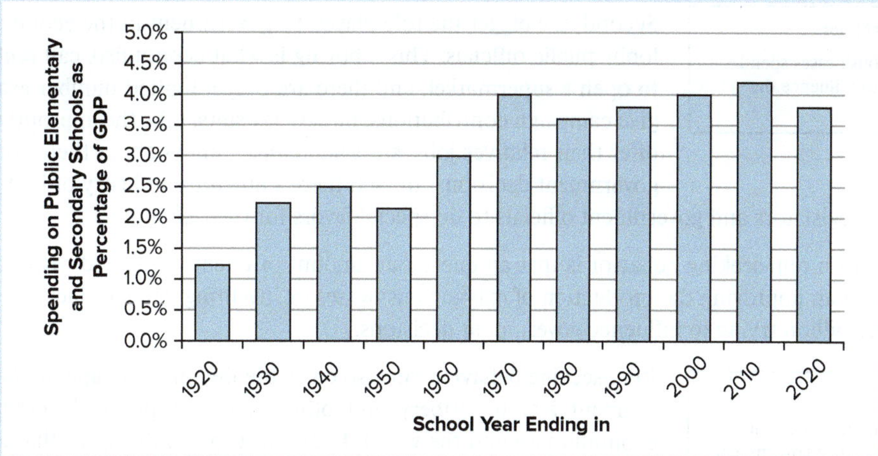

Finally, government action is also a remedy for deficiencies in private markets. The Environmental Protection Agency (EPA) sets pollution exhaust standards for passenger vehicles. Without government regulation, it's unlikely that new car buyers would spend several hundred dollars for pollution control equipment despite its benefits for overall air quality. We'll discuss the different types of government action later in this chapter.

YOUR ECONOMIC LIFE: The Hidden Benefits of Government

Sometimes the biggest benefits you get from government action are things that *don't* happen. You have a one out of six chance of getting food poisoning over the next year. That's scary, but your odds of getting seriously sick or even dying from tainted food would be a lot worse without the inspectors from the Food and Drug Administration (FDA), who monitor the safety of the nation's food supply. When a big food poisoning incident does occur, government researchers try and trace it back to its source.

Similarly, the government closely monitors the safety of motor vehicles. Sometimes, the National Highway Traffic Safety Administration (NHSTA) requires an auto manufacturer to do a "mandatory recall" of vehicles with a significant safety problem.

A final hidden benefit of government action is in your pocket. For example, if your credit card is lost or stolen, your potential liability for misuse is only $50, according to the Fair Credit Billing Act. (If your ATM card is lost or stolen, however, your potential liability depends on how quickly you report it.)

As you can see, when viewed through the lens of your own life, a market economy cannot function without government establishing the rules of the game. Finding the right balance between the private and public sectors is essential.

THE DOWNSIDES OF GOVERNMENT ACTION (LO6-3)

LO6-3 Describe the limits and downsides of government action.

So why don't we just let the government control everything? One reason is that for every clear example of the need for the public sector, there's an equally convincing case of government waste and foolishness. Most of us have had the experience of dealing with an unresponsive or obstructive government bureaucracy (such as the Department of Motor Vehicles in many states).

> **incentive problem**
> The potential lack of pressure on public-sector managers because governments don't need to make a profit.

There are several disadvantages to government intervention in the economy. First, public sector managers face an **incentive problem**. Because governments don't need to make a profit, and because they can always raise more money through taxes, there's little pressure on them to be efficient. That means a government agency can overspend unless closely watched. In contrast, private-sector managers are judged on the profits they produce, which means they have an incentive to hold down costs.

> **rent-seeking behavior**
> Occurs when businesses spend money trying to influence the government.

Second, the bigger the role played by government in the economy, the more businesses and individuals lobby public officials. This lobbying is what economists call **rent-seeking behavior**. If you need a license to open a supermarket, and there are only a limited number available, you will probably hire lobbyists, give campaign contributions, initiate lawsuits, take the appropriate politicians and bureaucrats to lunch, offer their relatives jobs, start malicious rumors about their opponents, and otherwise try to influence government decisions. In fact, there's an entire industry of lobbying firms in Washington, DC, devoted to persuading legislators and government officials to do special favors for their clients.

The problem with rent-seeking behavior is that an enormous amount of talent, time, and resources goes into beating or influencing the system rather than improving the production of existing businesses or inventing new products or services. In 2021, lobbyists in Washington spent $3.7 billion trying to influence government decisions.

> **corruption**
> Bribery or other illegal activities intended to influence government actions.

Rent-seeking behavior can also cross the line into **corruption**: illegal activities intended to influence government action. Bribery and other forms of political corruption are pervasive features of many economies around the world. Economists generally agree that government corruption slows economic growth because special favors go to businesses that are willing to cheat rather than to those offering the best products and services. (See "**Spotlight: Corruption.**")

> **lack of flexibility and innovation**
> The lack of incentive in the public sector to put technological breakthroughs into widespread commercial use.

Third, government often suffers from a **lack of flexibility and innovation**. The government can make investments in far-sighted research and development, including such breakthroughs as the internet. The problem, though, is that the public sector has little incentive to put breakthroughs into widespread use because the government can't make a profit. As a result, the private sector is far better at commercializing new technologies.

But a big argument against government intervention has to do with taxation. Let's look at that next.

The Inefficiency of Taxation

> **inefficiency of taxation**
> The reduction of production and sales that typically results from imposing a tax on a good or service.

Any government, whether it's your local town or Washington, needs money to function, and that money usually comes from taxes: payments from individuals or businesses to the government. When the government imposes a tax on a market, the seller receives less than the buyer pays, so the tax pushes the market away from the competitive equilibrium. That is, it causes less to be produced and sold than would be the case otherwise. This is known as the **inefficiency of taxation**.

Let's see how this works. If there is a tax on hotel rooms, a tourist might pay $230 a night, but the hotel keeps only $200 and must give the other $30 to the local government. (As of 2023, for example, San Francisco had a 14 percent hotel tax, which comes to $28 per night on a $200 per night room.) If there is a tax on income, the seller of labor (the worker) takes home less than the buyer of labor (the employer) pays. So if a person's yearly salary is $50,000, and she pays an income tax of $10,000, her take-home pay is $40,000.

SPOTLIGHT: CORRUPTION

Every year, Transparency International, a Berlin-based organization, calculates the Corruption Perceptions Index for most of the world's nations, based on surveys and expert assessments. According to the organization, in 2021, the least corrupt countries were Denmark, New Zealand, and Finland, all tied for the top. The most corrupt was South Sudan. The United States was the 27th least corrupt country on the list of 180—tied with Chile, and just behind Bhutan and Taiwan.

Source: Transparency International, www.transparency.org.

Imposing a tax on a market typically hurts both buyers and sellers. Adding in the tax, buyers pay more than they would in competitive equilibrium. That causes them to reduce their quantity demanded (remember the law of demand from **Chapter 2**). After taxes, sellers receive less than they would in competitive equilibrium, so they reduce their quantity supplied (according to the law of supply in **Chapter 2**).

Let's look at the effect of a simple tax on the market for chairs in **Figure 6.3**. The market equilibrium without a tax occurs where the original supply and demand lines intersect (labeled *A*). Let's suppose the government imposes a tax–say, $20–on the sale of every chair. After the tax is imposed, there is a gap between what sellers receive and what buyers pay. Whatever the buyers pay, the sellers will receive $20 less, with the difference going to the government.

Figure 6.3 How Taxes Affect a Market
This figure shows supply and demand in the market for chairs. With no tax, the market equilibrium is at point *A*. With a tax of $20 per chair, buyers pay more per chair (point *B*), and sellers receive less per chair (point *C*). The tax reduces the equilibrium quantity in the market.

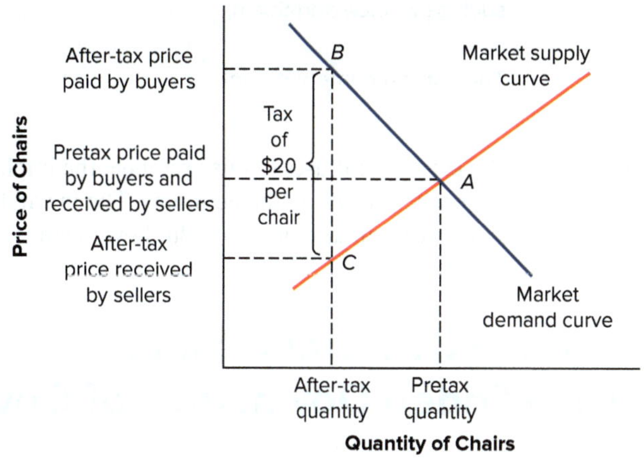

Where is the new equilibrium for this market after the tax is imposed? It still has to be true that quantity supplied and the quantity demanded are equal. But the new equilibrium quantity after the tax is imposed will be less than the old quantity. Buyers pay more (see the point labeled *B*), and sellers receive less (see the point labeled *C*) after transferring the tax money to the government.

It makes sense that a tax on something will reduce the quantity supplied and demanded. A tax on chairs makes them more expensive to buyers, which reduces the demand. The same tax, by reducing the price received by furniture manufacturers, causes them to cut back the production of new chairs.

The bigger the tax, the bigger the reduction in supply and demand in that market. At the extreme, the power to tax can be the power to destroy. Suppose every time you went to a movie theater you had to pay a $100 movie tax to the government. You would quickly stop going to the movies, and would instead stay home and watch television. If the government raises the tax on a good or service high enough, it can drive the quantity demanded down to zero.

Governments can impose taxes in many different ways (see **Table 6.3**). Each type of tax affects a different aspect of the economy. An excise tax, for example, is imposed on a specific good such as cigarettes or alcohol, and it reduces the consumption of that good. An income tax, as the name implies, lets the government take a percentage of pay. Because wages are the price of labor, an income tax reduces the amount of labor supplied and demanded, though the precise size of this effect is subject to controversy among economists. And a carbon tax, as we will discuss in **Chapter 19**, gives utilities, businesses, and individuals an incentive to use fuels that put fewer greenhouse gases into the atmosphere.

Table 6.3 Some Common Taxes

This table shows some common taxes, the markets that are taxed, and the potential impact of each tax. The biggest tax in the United States today is the income tax.

Name of Tax	What's Taxed	Potential Impact
Income tax	Most sources of money coming into a household, including wages, interest, and business profits.	People put forth less effort to earn money.
Sales tax	The purchase price of most items; some states exempt certain purchases.	Consumers spend less, save more.
Excise tax	The sale of specific items such as cigarettes, liquor, or gasoline.	People consume fewer taxed items.
Payroll tax	Wages only; the main examples are Social Security and Medicare taxes.	Employers hire fewer workers.
Corporate profits tax	Profits made by a business.	Investors are less willing to put money into businesses.
Estate tax	Value of an inheritance; also known as the "death tax," the federal estate tax in 2022 exempted the first $12 million of assets.	Controversial; if people care about how much they will leave to their heirs, the estate tax can lessen their desire to work.

Name of Tax	What's Taxed	Potential Impact
Property tax	Value of real estate.	People are less interested in buying real estate, reducing its value relative to other assets.
Capital gains tax	The increase in the value of an asset when sold.	Investors put less money into the stock market and other productive assets.
Wealth tax	Net worth of household (found in European countries such as France and Spain).	Controversial; possibly reduces the willingness of people to start new businesses because they are less likely to become wealthy.
Carbon tax	The carbon content of fuel.	People and businesses reduce their use of high-carbon fuels such as coalin order to slow climate change.

But no matter which tax the government uses to raise revenue, the implication is the same: the larger the government, the more revenue it needs to raise, and the greater the impact on the economy. The inevitable result of "too much" government intervention in the economy is a slowing of growth and a lower standard of living. But how much is "too much"? That's the question economists disagree on.

YOUR ECONOMIC LIFE: The Hidden Downsides of Government

Some of the negative consequences of government may not be immediately visible to you. For example, suppose that all local businesses have to pay high permit fees to the town government. Those fees may then be passed on to you, the consumer, in the form of higher prices, even though you have never seen a permit yourself.

More and more occupations, such as manicurists, require a license and extensive training. These rules not only protect you from incompetent workers but also raise the price of manicures because there is less competition.

Finally, it is often hard to tell how well the government is spending your tax money. Federal state and local governments all have a published budget, but it typically lacks the detail needed for ordinary people to monitor spending. In theory, the data processing systems exist to allow us to peek inside government decisions, but they are rarely used that way. In general, while government has an important role to play, it is better to not assume that the government inevitably makes better decisions than the private sector.

THE RIGHT ROLE FOR GOVERNMENT ECONOMIC POLICY (LO6-4)

LO6-4 List and illustrate circumstances in which government intervention in the economy may be useful.

In the previous section, we saw that there are arguments for and against government intervention in the economy. So now we come to the critical question of economic policy: What is the right balance between the public and private sectors? We want to identify situations where markets fail to work as well as they might and where the pluses of government action outweigh the minuses.

Obviously, this is a question about which reasonable people might disagree. However, from an economic perspective, there are four main circumstances in which government economic intervention might be appropriate: *public good provision, market regulation, externalities,* and *income redistribution.*

Public Good Provision

In the United States and most other developed countries, a long list of goods and services are provided to citizens, primarily by the government. These include national defense, police and fire protection, the road system, primary and secondary education, and public health efforts such as clean water. Individuals and businesses can add extra goods and services to these if they want–say, by hiring private security or by paying to go to private schools–but the major responsibility for national security, minimum education, and the other items on this list falls to the government.

SPOTLIGHT: DID THE GOVERNMENT CREATE THE INTERNET?

It's hard to remember a time when the Internet didn't exist. We take it for granted that we can turn on our computers and connect with other computers anywhere else in the world. Yet the communication protocols and standards enabling that miracle were encouraged and funded, in good part, by the federal government.

The key agency was the Advanced Research Projects Agency of the Defense Department, which first went by the acronym ARPA and then DARPA. Starting in the 1960s and continuing through the 1970s, DARPA funded the development of packet switching and the TCP/IP standards, which is the main way information is transmitted across the internet. Then in the 1980s, the National Science Foundation helped fund the first large-scale network, called NSFNET, and ensured that all computers followed the same communication protocol.

Today, of course, the physical elements of the Internet—the fiber-optic cables, the network routes, and the computers—are mostly privately owned and operated. Yet the standards that let all computers on the Internet communicate with each other are a public good that would have had a much tougher time coming into existence without government leadership.

Source: "A Brief History of the Internet," *Internet Society*, http://www.internetsociety.org/internet/what-internet/history-internet/brief-history-internet.

These expenditures provide what economists call **public goods**. Public goods are goods and services that benefit many people in a city, region, or country–perhaps not equally, but to some degree. In contrast, the usual sorts of private purchases, such as a car or a house, benefit only the buyer and their family.

> **public goods**
> Goods and services that benefit many people in a city, region, or country.

The classic public good is national defense because armed forces protect a whole country rather than any particular person. Fire departments generally protect all the buildings in an area, because if one goes up in flames, the others are in danger, too. And most roads are available for anyone to drive on for free (only about 5,000 miles of U.S. highways have tolls on them, out of 4 million total miles of road across the country). After all, it wouldn't do you any good to be able to drive on the road in front of your house if you couldn't drive by your neighbor's as well.

Why does it make sense for the government to provide public goods? Think about the police patrolling your neighborhood and keeping your street safe. It would almost never be worthwhile for you to pay $60,000 a year to hire that officer. However, you might be willing to band together with 100 neighbors and pay $600 each. A public good needs to be paid for collectively because it benefits everyone.

But suppose you form a voluntary association to hire a police officer and one of your neighbors refuses to pay his share. After all, the cop on the corner will deter criminals whether or not your neighbor contributes anything. This is the **free-rider problem**. You can't stop people from benefiting from a public good even if they don't pay and thus get a free ride from everyone else's contributions. After a snowstorm, plowing the road benefits everyone who uses that road. National defense benefits everyone who lives in a country; it's not possible to selectively defend one person and not another.

> **free-rider problem**
> Occurs when individuals benefit from a public good that they have not helped to pay for.

The solution to the free-rider problem is government, which has the power to compel people to pay via taxes. Thus, instead of private associations paying private security guards, the local government generally supplies police, supported by taxes. Fire departments, highway departments, and many other collective activities are also supported by taxes.

Another government activity that falls into the class of a public good is the collection of weather data and basic weather forecasting. Because it benefits everyone to know when a hurricane or blizzard is coming, it makes sense for the government to handle this activity. (See "**Economic Milestone: The First Weather Satellite.**")

Similarly, collecting basic economic data, such as the unemployment rate, benefits everyone. A private company would never be able to make enough profit to cover the costs of surveying 60,000 households every month to get this information. However, the benefits to society as a whole are high enough to make it worthwhile for us to allow the government to use tax revenues to provide this service.

One of the most important public goods the government provides is basic research. As we will see in **Chapter 15**, basic research–money spent on investigating fundamental questions such as those in physics, chemistry, biology, or mathematics–is essential for the progress of science. However, such basic research usually has no direct application in commercial products, so it's hard for private companies to invest in it. As a result, most spending on basic research comes from the government.

Once we get beyond a list of basic public goods, it becomes harder to find a political consensus about what the government should pay for. Here's one controversial example: education. Most people believe it's appropriate for the government to provide at least a high school education for everyone. However, there is intense dispute about whether the government needs to actually run the schools or whether it should just provide funding that families could use to pay for either a public or a private education for their children.

Or consider the public provision of wireless broadband service. Many cities and towns have considered setting up their own free or low-cost mobile broadband networks for residents. However, it's not clear whether it makes sense for a city to spend taxpayer money to compete with the private-sector telecom companies.

Finally, the COVID-19 pandemic raised huge questions about the public health role of the government. Few argued with the need for the federal government to fund the accelerated development and manufacture of the initial COVID-19 vaccines. And given the unprecedented nature of the pandemic, most people accepted the initial restrictions on travel and economic activities in March and April 2020.

Yet later in 2020, as it became clear that the pandemic was not coming to a quick end, many people began questioning the need for such intense government interventions into the private sector. The debate over the public health role of the government only intensified when it came time to consider imposing mandates to wear masks or to get vaccinated. We will examine this question in **Chapter 18**.

Market Regulation

Markets don't govern themselves. They run by rules that determine which actions are legal and fair–and which count as unfair or against the public interest. For example, it's illegal for a supermarket to use scales that give the wrong weights. It's also illegal for pharmaceutical companies to sell drugs that have not passed government safety standards. And "lemon laws" let buyers return cars that have to be repeatedly repaired for the same problems.

In theory, markets can enforce their own rules, up to a point. Trade associations can set rules that member companies have to follow. Consumers can choose not to patronize supermarkets that use unfair scales. Companies that make unsafe products acquire a bad reputation that consumers can research at the Better Business Bureau or on the Internet.

ECONOMIC MILESTONE

1960: The First Weather Satellite

One example of a public good is the collection of basic data about weather. The two cameras in the first weather satellite, TIROS-1, launched by the government on April 1, 1960, supplied the first continuous observations of global weather. Alas, TIROS-1 was not to have a long life, failing after only 77 days. Today, the U.S. government has several civilian weather satellites in orbit, and their pictures and data are freely available to anyone. The latest satellite, called GOES-18, was launched in 2022.

SPOTLIGHT: PRIVATE TOLL ROADS

We're used to thinking of highways as public goods, built and operated by state and local governments. Yet more and more states and municipalities, strapped for cash, are thinking about selling their toll roads to private companies that will collect the fees and handle maintenance. For example, New Jersey at one point considered selling either the New Jersey Turnpike or the Garden State Parkway—two of the most heavily traveled roads in the country. In October 2012, a Spanish company opened up a private toll road near Austin, Texas, with an 85-mile-per-hour speed limit.

The allure of private ownership is not only financial but also political. These roads need intensive maintenance, which must be paid for with tolls. But a politician who tried to raise tolls would become the immediate target of irate voters, most of whom drive. A private owner, the theory goes, would find it easier to take the unpopular step of raising tolls.

Unfortunately, the high tolls on private roads have discouraged drivers and truck traffic, at least for now. The private toll road near Austin filed for bankruptcy in 2016 (although it stayed open and emerged from bankruptcy a year later). No one yet knows whether private toll roads will turn out to be politically acceptable in the long run.

Source: Frosch, Dan, "Frugal Motorists Test Private Toll Roads," *The Wall Street Journal*, March 16, 2016, http://www.wsj.com/articles/frugal-motorists-test-private-toll-roads-1458379807.

market regulation
The role of government in setting basic rules for market competition that businesses have to follow.

But in practice it's more workable for the government to provide and enforce **market regulation**: the basic rules companies and industries have to follow. For example, consider things as simple as commercial transactions between companies and sales to consumers. Almost every state government has adopted some variant of the Uniform Commercial Code (UCC), which lays out the basic rules for such transactions; these rules are enforced by the courts. The UCC includes important provisions such as the requirement that any goods sold be "fit for the ordinary purposes for which goods of that description are used." In other words, if someone sells you something, it has to do what was promised.

The government regulates, loosely or tightly, virtually every aspect of the economy. As we will see in **Chapter 13**, government regulators keep a close watch on the financial system, including banks, insurance companies, and investment banks. State and federal regulators try to monitor the safety of products ranging from toys to cars (at the federal level, that's the job of the National Highway Traffic Safety Administration). The marketing and development of new drugs and medical devices, the allocation of frequencies for different wireless devices, and the negotiation of trade treaties with other countries all fall under the jurisdiction of one or more regulators, as **Table 6.4** shows.

Table 6.4 Examples of Regulating Markets

The government regulates almost every market to a greater or lesser extent. The first column gives the type of regulation, the second column describes the goal of regulation, and the third column lists some government agencies involved in that type of regulation.

Type of Regulation	Goal of Regulation	Examples of Government Agencies
Supervising the financial and monetary system	Investors need to be treated fairly. Bank depositors need to be assured of the safety of their money.	Federal Reserve Board, Department of the Treasury, Securities and Exchange Commission, Comptroller of the Currency, Federal Deposit Insurance Corporation, Consumer Financial Protection Bureau
Antitrust policy	Businesses have to compete fairly.	Federal Trade Commission, Department of Justice
Consumer protection	Consumers need to be able to trust the goods and services they buy.	Federal Trade Commission, Consumer Products Safety Commission, state agencies
Supervising commercial contracts	Businesses have to be able to make binding agreements.	Department of Justice, state agencies
Regulating key industries	Selected industries such as telecommunications, airplanes, and utilities need close supervision to balance industry and social needs.	Federal Communications Commission, Federal Aviation Administration, Federal Energy Regulatory Commission, state agencies
Regulating health care	Patients need to be able to depend on the drugs, vaccines, and medical devices they use.	Food and Drug Administration, Centers for Medicare and Medicaid Services, Centers for Disease Control and Prevention
Negotiating trade policy	Rules for international trade have to be negotiated with other countries.	Office of the Trade Representative, Department of Commerce, Department of State

Let's focus on two particular instances of regulation. The Federal Trade Commission (FTC) and the Department of Justice enforce **antitrust law**. Antitrust law is designed to ensure that companies don't unfairly try to get market power or reduce the amount of competition in a market or industry. These agencies have to approve large mergers and acquisitions that companies want to make so the government can ensure that the number of competitors in a market doesn't get too small. They watch for signs of collusion, a scheme in which competitors get together and try to push up prices. In other words, these government agencies are the defenders of competition.

antitrust law

Government regulation intended to maintain competitive markets and discourage unfair accumulation of market power.

For example, at the end of 2022, the Federal Trade Commission (FTC) filed to block Microsoft's proposed purchase of Activision Blizzard, a leading developer of video games such as *Call of Duty.* The FTC was worried that Microsoft would withhold best-selling games from rivals to its Xbox gaming consoles.

While the government monitors the fairness of domestic markets, it is also responsible for keeping an eye on international markets. The central government of each country has the primary responsibility for negotiating its own rules for trade–which types of beef can be imported, which airlines can fly from London to New York, and whether foreign banks can buy up domestic banks.

The regulatory role of government is always changing with the economy. The development of new technologies requires new types of regulation as well. (See "**How It Works: Regulating New Technology.**") Today, one of the biggest issues is consumer privacy and the use of online data. Large tech companies such as Google and Facebook offer free services such as search, e-mail, and photo storage. In return, they use information about consumers to sell targeted advertising. The question is whether consumer privacy is being unreasonably invaded.

The European Union passed a strict set of privacy rules, called the General Data Protection Regulation, which took effect in May 2018. The rules also affect U.S. companies that do business in Europe, which is basically every large company. In 2022, an additional set of European rules went into effect, called the Digital Markets Act, governing the actions of large tech platforms such as Facebook.

There is substantial support for passing similar rules in the United States. The problem, though, is that privacy and platform rules that are too strict may make it difficult for tech companies to develop innovative products. As usual, it is necessary to balance the benefits of regulations with the harm they might cause.

Externalities

The basic logic behind the success of a market economy is that when consumers and businesses strive to do the best for themselves, they benefit the entire economy. Thus, a profit-maximizing company competes by cutting costs, introducing better products, and otherwise behaving in a way that improves the output of the economy.

That reasoning breaks down, however, if individual actions have side effects on others. For example, if you put a 20-foot-high flamingo statue in your front yard, it may please your artistic sensibilities. But it will negatively affect the views of your neighbors and perhaps reduce the values of their homes.

HOW IT WORKS: REGULATING NEW TECHNOLOGY

Is it legal to own a nuclear power plant in your basement? What rules govern private space travel? If you copy music onto your phone, are you breaking the law? What are the rules for drones? Should humans be allowed to clone themselves?

One of the toughest tasks for government is regulating new technology. Economic progress is driven by technological change. But the dangers of new technology are usually unknown and potentially serious.

Everyone agrees that the government has the right to regulate technologies that could harm others—that nuclear power plant in your basement, for example, which could affect your neighbors. People also accept that the government needs to be able to control which new pharmaceuticals can be sold to patients. The Food and Drug Administration (FDA) requires all drugs to pass safety tests and to be shown to actually work on people as promised. (This included the new vaccines developed to deal with COVID-19.)

Or take drones—small "unmanned aircraft systems," as they are called by the Federal Aviation Administration (FAA). As drones have become more popular, the FAA has been issuing safety and operating regulations. One goal is to keep drones away from areas where they could pose a danger to aircraft.

externality

The impact that the actions of an individual or business can have on others.

negative externalities

An undesirable impact that an economic activity can have on others.

Economists call such secondary consequences of actions **externalities**. More precisely, an externality is the impact that the actions of an individual or business can have on others. Externalities can be either bad (negative) or good (positive). The classic example of a **negative externality** is pollution. A factory that emits noxious fumes is imposing a negative externality on nearby neighborhoods. In the 2011 Fukushima disaster in Japan, a tsunami from a strong earthquake caused several nuclear reactors to melt down. This imposed a negative externality on people living in a wide area around the affected areas, who were forced to evacuate permanently. On a more mundane level, if you insist on playing loud music late at night, you are imposing a negative externality on your neighbors. An airport imposes a negative externality on nearby residents in the form of noise from airplanes taking off and landing.

Pollution is a negative externality.

Fransen/Shutterstock

One of the most annoying externalities is an out-of-control car alarm. People buy alarms to deter thieves, which is an individual benefit. However, when a car alarm goes off in the middle of the night, it imposes negative externalities on everyone around–especially if it continues for a long time.

Positive externalities come about when your actions benefit other people. Suppose you have a sidewalk in front of your house that your neighbors also use. If you shovel your walk when it snows, that helps not just you but your neighbors, too. Similarly, if you paint your house, its added attractiveness helps increase the property values of your neighbors.

Here's another example of a positive externality. In the early days of the Internet, only a few people had e-mail accounts, and they could send e-mail only to each other. Now, suppose you've just signed up with an Internet service provider for the first time. Suddenly, your friends and business associates who already have accounts can e-mail you, so their connections have become more valuable to them. In effect, your decision to pay for an Internet account has a positive impact on the people already on the Internet. This is what is known as a **network externality**: Your decision to use a network affects the value of that network to other people. Social media such as Facebook show the same positive network externalities.

positive externality

A desirable impact that an economic activity can have on others.

There can be negative network externalities as well. If you decide to drive on a crowded highway during rush hour, the additional congestion you create may slow down other cars on the highway. This can be a big deal. If a road is close to capacity, then just a few additional cars can sharply slow down traffic and turn an orderly flow of cars into a traffic jam.

network externality

How the decision of a person to use a network affects the value of that network to other people.

One important purpose of government is to convince people and businesses to do fewer of the things that create negative externalities and more of the things that create positive externalities. For example, environmental regulations limit the amount of pollution a factory or a car can produce. (We'll talk more about the environment in **Chapter 19**.) Zoning regulations prevent ugly industrial buildings from being constructed in residential neighborhoods. Building codes that reduce the risk your house will catch fire increase your safety, as well as the safety of your neighbors. Some highways impose higher tolls during rush hour as a way of persuading drivers to use the road at a less congested time. In effect, the higher tolls represent the extra costs each driver imposes on other vehicles.

Here's another example: School systems have a long history of requiring students to get vaccinated for contagious diseases like measles, in part because of positive externalities. A student vaccinated against measles is highly unlikely to get infected, thus protecting fellow students from getting the measles, a classic positive externality.

The current generation of COVID-19 vaccines doesn't protect individuals from getting infected and spreading the virus to others. However, COVID-19 vaccines appear to have a different kind of positive externalities. Because they are much less likely to be hospitalized, vaccinated individuals put less pressure on emergency rooms and hospitals, and free up health care resources for people who have other kinds of health problems. However, this argument for requiring COVID-19 vaccinations remains controversial.

Income Redistribution

A final important economic function of government is **income redistribution**–shifting money from rich to poor to close big income differences. Redistribution can take place through the tax system, through the distribution of benefits such as Medicare and food stamps, or through direct transfer of money such as unemployment insurance payments or income support for poor children. During the pandemic, the federal subsidy for COVID-19 vaccinations made it possible for low-income Americans to get vaccinated without worrying about cost.

income redistribution

A policy of transferring income from high-income households to low-income households.

This is one of the most controversial economic policy topics. Should the government help the poor? Some say, of course. Others say government's main responsibility is to provide opportunities for people who are willing to work hard, not to provide handouts. There are good arguments on both sides. In **Chapter 17**, we will look at income inequality and redistribution in much more detail.

CONCLUSION

As we've gone through this chapter, we've given the arguments, pro and con, for government intervention in individual markets. It's not a debate that can end in a clean knockout for either side. Each individual case, whether it's tighter regulation of the mortgage market or requiring more tests for new drugs, has advantages and disadvantages.

However, taking a broader perspective, there's one area where everyone can agree government has a key role: providing the economic statistics that enable policymakers, politicians, and businesses to know how the economy is doing. The next chapter begins our study of macroeconomics by looking at how we measure the size of the economy.

06 SUMMARY

1. Today, the hand of the government is apparent in every corner of the economy. But before the Great Depression started in 1929, government had a much smaller role. During the Great Depression, President Franklin Roosevelt put into place a wide variety of new programs under the collective name of the New Deal. ***(LO6-1)***
2. After the Depression and World War II ended, government spending and employment dropped but did not return to their pre-1929 share of the economy. In fact, government's role in the economy gradually expanded through the 1950s, 1960s, and 1970s. Starting in the mid-1970s, the public began to feel that government intervention in the economy had gone far enough. This was the beginning of the era of deregulation. ***(LO6-1)***
3. The government response to the pandemic, starting in March 2020, was an unprecedented intervention in the economy. But it is still not clear whether this represents a one-off event or the early days of a new era of increased government intervention. ***(LO6-1)***

4. The advantage of government intervention in the economy is that it directs economic activities to achieve desirable goals. This is often called the command-and-control approach to social and economic goals. ***(LO6-2)***
5. The disadvantages include the incentive problem, rent-seeking behavior, and corruption. In addition, using taxes to raise revenues causes fewer goods and services to be produced and sold than would otherwise be the case. This is known as the inefficiency of taxation. ***(LO6-3)***
6. The critical question of economic policy is finding the right balance between the public and private sectors. There are four circumstances when government intervention in the economy might be appropriate: public good provision, market regulation, externalities, and income redistribution. ***(LO6-4)***

KEY TERMS AND CONCEPTS

private sector

public sector

New Deal

oil price shock

deregulation

mixed economy

command-and-control approach

incentive problem

rent-seeking behavior

corruption

lack of flexibility and innovation

inefficiency of taxation

public goods

free-rider problem

market regulation

antitrust law

externality

negative externality

positive externality

network externality

income redistribution

connect PROBLEMS

1. Which of the following measure the relative importance of government in the economy? ***(LO6-1)***
   a) The number of cars per person.
   b) Government employment as a share of total employment.
   c) Energy use per person.
   d) Government spending as a share of GDP.
   e) Total taxes collected.
2. Which of the following programs were part of the New Deal? ***(LO6-1)***
   a) National Public Radio.
   b) Medicare.
   c) Social Security.
   d) Federal minimum wage.
   e) Environmental Protection Agency.
3. Which of the following actions are examples of deregulation? Which are examples of increased regulation? ***(LO6-1)***
   a) In 1996, Congress passed legislation, the Health Insurance Portability and Accountability Act (HIPAA), requiring health care providers to protect the privacy of patient information.
   b) In 2010, Congress passed legislation, the Dodd-Frank Wall Street Reform and Consumer Protection Act, imposing more rules on financial corporations.
   c) In 1999, Congress passed legislation, the Financial Services Modernization Act, allowing banks, among other things, to sell insurance.
4. Which of the following is an example of a command-and-control approach? ***(LO6-2)***
   a) Requiring trucking companies to only buy new trucks that are low-pollution.
   b) Charging a fee for use of a park.
   c) Raising taxes to pay for a new bridge.
   d) Offering low-interest loans to students.
   e) Mandating COVID-19 vaccinations for health care workers.

5. The local government needs to replace all its traffic signals. Two companies are competing for this business. Company A spends $100,000 on buying a new, more efficient machine to make traffic signals. Company B spends $100,000 on campaign contributions for the city council. ***(LO6-3)***

   a) If Company B wins the contract, is this an example of perfect competition, market power, rent-seeking behavior, or monopoly?
   b) Is Company B likely to charge a higher or a lower price for the traffic signals than Company A?
   c) Would the taxpayers of the town prefer that Company A or Company B win the contract? Would the city council prefer that Company A or Company B win the contract?

6. Suppose the government taxes food according to its fat content. That is, the more fat a food contains, the higher the tax on it. ***(LO6-3)***

   a) Would this taxation raise or lower the prices consumers pay for fatty foods (including the tax)? Draw a graph to illustrate your answer.
   b) Would this tax raise or lower the amounts of fatty foods consumers buy?
   c) What effect would this tax have on the prices of nonfatty foods? (*Hint:* What happens to the demand schedule for nonfatty foods?)

7. Suppose the government decided to tax e-mail messages, text messages, and instant messages–say, at 5 cents per message. The money would be used to cut the income tax and sales tax on other goods and services. ***(LO6-3)***

   a) Suppose a student sends 10 e-mail messages, 15 text messages, and 25 instant messages each day. How much tax would be paid?
   b) Would a tax of 5 cents per message reduce your use of messaging?
   c) What effect do you think a tax on messages would have on the amount of spam sent on the Internet? Is this a desirable outcome?

8. Which of these government actions is justified by public goods, externalities, regulation, or redistribution? (More than one reason might apply in each case.) Explain your answers. ***(LO6-4)***

   a) New York City bans smoking in restaurants.
   b) Congress renews the food stamp program, which gives poor people access to groceries at a discount.
   c) Local governments open libraries that are available to anyone.
   d) School systems require measles vaccinations for students.
   e) The federal government subsidizes the cost of COVID-19 vaccinations, so that anyone can get one for free.

9. Communities sometimes take on large amounts of debt to build a new baseball or football stadium. The expectation is that a professional sports team can help create new jobs, give an area more visibility, and attract new businesses. ***(LO6-4)***

   a) Is this example of government action–taking on debt to pay for a sports stadium–an example of a public good, an externality, regulation, or redistribution?
   b) Using the concepts in this chapter, explain why government funding of a new sports stadium might not produce the desired results.

10. In 2019, the New York state government approved a congestion pricing plan for Manhattan, the central business area of New York City. The congestion pricing plan would require meaning that cars and trucks entering a specific highly congested area of Manhattan would have to pay an extra charge–perhaps more than $10 for each car. The charge could take effect as early as 2023, if it gets through certain legal and regulatory hurdles. ***(LO6-4)***

    a) Does this proposal rely on the idea of public goods, externalities, regulation, or redistribution?
    b) Show the effect of the congestion tax on a supply-demand diagram.
    c) Whom would it hurt, and whom would it help?
    d) Under what conditions is a congestion tax a good idea?

APPENDIX

DELVING DEEPER INTO MICROECONOMICS

LEARNING OBJECTIVES

After you read this appendix you should be able to:

LO6A-1 Explain the role of utility maximization in consumer choice, and use the concept of price elasticity of demand.
LO6A-2 Explain the role of cost minimization in producer decisions, and use the concept of price elasticity of supply.
LO6A-3 Explain the incidence of a tax.

Earlier in this textbook, we laid out the basics of microeconomics: supply and demand, market equilibrium, profit maximization, and competition and market power. In this appendix, we will explore several key topics in consumer choice and business decision making in more depth. These will help us understand some important issues and problems in today's economy.

First, we will lay out the logic of utility maximization, which helps explain where the demand curve comes from and how consumers react to price changes. That will give us some insight into how consumers change their behavior in response to big changes in prices for items such as food and energy.

We'll also take a deeper look at demand elasticity.

In the second half of this appendix, we'll examine the process of profit maximization, including how managers choose the best production techniques and where the cost function comes from. This will give us some insight into how companies make crucial production decisions, such as whether to move their operations to other countries.

We will finish the appendix by using the concepts of demand and supply elasticities to better understand who bears the burden of different taxes. In other words, when a tax is raised or lowered, who benefits and who loses? This is an important question as politicians debate future changes in the tax code.

CONSUMER CHOICE (LO6A-1)

LO6A-1 Explain the role of utility maximization in consumer choice, and use the concept of price elasticity of demand.

We will start by developing a framework for understanding consumer choice. Recall that in **Chapter 2**, we described the demand schedule for buyers in a market. But now we are asking an additional question: Where does a demand schedule come from? Getting the answer to this question is important for any company that makes or sells a consumer product such as shampoo, sports equipment, or motor vehicles. More importantly, it also helps us better understand the economy we live in.

The Utility Function

utility function
The link between the goods and services a person consumes and their utility.

To understand consumer decision making, economists generally start with the idea that each person has a **utility function**. You can think of a utility function as a little internal computer that accurately reflects a person's likes and dislikes. Given the actual goods and services the person is consuming, the utility function spits out a number that reflects the physical and emotional benefits the person gets–in other words, the **utility** of the person's consumption. A higher number is preferable, of course.

Each person's utility function is likely to be different. So, for example, if you like football games but don't care for opera, your utility function will give a strong positive weight to attendance at this weekend's football game and a negative weight to attendance at the opera.

utility

A measure of the physical and emotional benefits a person gets from consumption.

The utility function also tells us how much benefit a person gets from purchasing and consuming more of the same thing–say, one car versus two cars or one television versus two televisions. For example, we can write a utility function for a typical coffee drinker in **Table 6A.1**. The first column of the table shows the number of cups of coffee the person drinks in a day. The second column shows the utility she derives from those cups of coffee.

One cup of coffee might give the person four units of utility (which economists sometimes call *utils*). Two cups a day give her seven total units of utility, and three cups give her nine units of utility.

We define **marginal utility** as the added amount of utility an individual gets from one more unit of consumption, holding everything else constant. For example, in **Table 6A.1,** thc marginal utility from the third cup of coffee is two, which is the difference between the utility for the third cup (nine) and the second cup (seven). Similarly, the marginal utility from the fourth cup of coffee is one.

Table 6A.1 The Utility Function of a Coffee Drinker

As someone drinks more cups during a day, the added utility of each additional cup falls.

Cups of Coffee in a Day	Utility (Measured in Utils)	Marginal (Measured in Utils)
0	0	
1	4	4
2	7	3
3	9	2
4	10	1

Table 6A.1 also illustrates the concept of **diminishing marginal utility**–the tendency for marginal utility to decline as consumption increases. That's typical for most goods and services: the more of a good you consume, the less added benefit from increasing your consumption.

marginal utility

The added amount of utility an individual gets from one more unit of consumption of a good or service, holding everything else constant.

The Budget Constraint

Your utility function is important to your spending decisions, but it's certainly not the only factor that determines what and how much you buy. Your **budget constraint** tells you what combinations of goods and services you are able to buy, given the prices and the amount of money you have available to spend. The **rational individual** maximizes her utility, subject to her budget constraint.

diminishing marginal utility

The tendency for marginal utility to decline as the consumption of a good or service increases.

For example, suppose your entertainment budget for the month is $60. You are going to spend that on some combination of going to the movies and eating out. The local movie theater charges $10 per ticket, whereas the local restaurant charges $20 for a dinner. Given the amount of money you have available, you want to make choices that give you the highest utility. For example, if you love movies, you might decide to go to one movie every week of the month ($10 × 4 = $40) and go out to eat once ($20), thus using your budget of $60. Someone else with the same budget constraint might decide to go to the movies twice ($10 × 2 = $20) and go out to eat twice ($20 × 2 = $40).

budget constraint

The combinations of goods and services an individual is able to buy, given prices and the amount of money available to spend.

rational individual

A person who maximizes their utility, subject to a budget constraint.

The budget constraint changes when the prices do. If the restaurant in **Table 6A.2** were to cut its price to $15 per meal, your set of affordable combinations would expand. If you didn't go to any movies, you could go out to eat four times a month rather than three. Or if you had been eating out twice and seeing two movies, now you could eat out twice and see three movies and still stay within your budget.

Table 6A.2 An Example of a Budget Constraint

A person will choose how many movies and restaurant dinners to consume in a month subject to his budget constraint. In this case, the total cost, which is the sum of the cost of the movies and the cost of the meals, cannot exceed $60.

Number of Meals Eaten Out in Month	Number of Movies Seen in Month	Price per Meal (Dollars)	Price per Movie (Dollars)	Cost of Meals (Price of Meal × Number of Meals)	Cost of Movies (Price of Movie × Number of Movies)	Total Spending (Cost of Meals + Cost of Movies)
3	0	$20	$10	$60	$ 0	$60
2	2	$20	$10	$40	$20	$60
1	4	$20	$10	$20	$40	$60
0	6	$20	$10	$ 0	$60	$60

The budget constraint also changes when the amount of money you can spend goes up or down. If you had $80 available for movies and eating out, that would give you a different set of choices.

YOUR ECONOMIC LIFE: Budgeting and Savings

Having a budget doesn't mean you spend all of your income today. In addition to this month's rent, and paying for your electricity, food, and mobile service, you also need a category for savings. Savings is the category for accumulating funds for future spending on big-ticket items, such as vacations and cars, and for paying back student loans.

For example, if you are planning to take a $500 vacation on spring break, it makes sense to sock away the money before you need it. That means putting away $100 a month for the previous five months.

Savings is also about putting money away for buying a house or retirement. That may seem like a long way off in the future, but one rule of thumb is that the earlier you start saving, the better off you will be.

Utility Maximization

A rational individual will choose goods and services to maximize utility, subject to their budget constraint. Because of diminishing marginal utility, you are likely to choose a combination of goods and services rather than blowing all your money on one item. To put it a different way: Even if you enjoy riding roller coasters, and even if you say that riding roller coasters is your favorite thing to do, you are unlikely to want to ride roller coasters 12 hours a day, seven days a week. Diminishing marginal utility sets in quickly.

So the utility-maximizing decision is really about trade-offs, taking your budget constraint into account. Do you want to spend $5 on riding the roller coaster one more time, or would you rather use that money for two ice cream cones? Would you rather buy a used car or have enough money to take a trip? Would you rather spend money on a textbook or spend the same money on an extra cup of Starbucks coffee each week?

In each such case, you are weighing the marginal utility of spending your last dollar on one good or service versus another. If you can raise your utility by switching to another combination of goods and services while sticking to your budget constraint, you will.

The utility-maximizing decision depends on the prices of the goods and services you are considering. If a price of a good or service changes, so will the budget constraint and the trade-offs that you have to make.

Price Elasticity of Demand

One of the key elements of economics is being able to quantify behavior. Among other things, we can measure the size and growth of the economy, the rate of change of prices, and the ups and downs of the stock market.

We can also quantify the reaction of consumers to big changes in prices. That's critical these days, when we have seen big swings in the price of essentials like food and gasoline. How much will the quantity demanded change when prices go up or down?

price elasticity of demand
The percentage change in quantity demanded that results from a 1 percent change in price.

inelastic demand
A situation where the quantity demanded does not change much even if the price changes significantly. More precisely, a situation where the price elasticity of demand is less than 1.

In **Chapter 3**, we examined the link between a price change and the reactions of buyers and sellers. We said that demand is *elastic* if a small price change produces a big change in quantity demanded. One example is restaurant meals, for which demand drops sharply as price increases. Demand is *inelastic* if a big price change produces only a small change in quantity demanded, as is true of gasoline. (We'll consider elasticity of supply later in this appendix.)

Now we need to make these concepts more precise by assigning a number to elasticity. The **price elasticity of demand** is the percentage change in quantity demanded that results from a 1 percent change in price. This will almost always be a negative number, because an increase in price reduces the quantity demanded. But, by convention, economists usually just drop the negative sign and talk about price elasticity as a number.

For example, a price elasticity of 1 means that a 10 percent price increase leads to a 10 percent decrease in quantity demanded. An elasticity of 2 means that a 10 percent price increase leads to a 20 percent decrease in quantity demanded. An elasticity of 0.5 means that a 10 percent price increase leads to a 5 percent decrease in quantity demanded. In general, a good or service has **inelastic demand** if its price elasticity is less than 1, and has **elastic demand** if its price elasticity is greater than 1. (If it's exactly 1, we say that it has *unit elasticity*.)

elastic demand

Intuitively, a situation in which a small change in price has a big impact on quantity demanded. More precisely, a situation in which the price elasticity of demand is greater than 1.

Economists have estimated price elasticities for various goods and services. According to the Department of Agriculture, the price elasticity of food in the United States is close to 0.1, which makes it highly inelastic. That means if the price of food goes up by 10 percent, the quantity of food demanded decreases by less than 1 percent. As a result, changes in the price of food do not have very much impact on the overall consumption of food.

Most studies find that the price elasticity of gasoline is around 0.25. That is, if the price of gasoline goes up by 10 percent, the quantity demanded drops by about 2.5 percent. That's over about a year or so. There's a bigger impact if gasoline prices stay high for a longer period, because then people switch to cars with lower fuel consumption. When gasoline prices spiked over $5.00 in 2022, surveys showed that Americans cut back on driving, but they did not immediately rush out to buy fuel-efficient or electric vehicles.

Table 6A.3 The Price Elasticity of Gasoline in Action

Economic studies suggest that the price elasticity of gasoline in the short run is 0.25. That means a 10 percent increase in price will lead to a 2.5 percent decrease in the quantity demanded. In this example, the price increases by 10 percent from $3.00 to $3.30. The quantity demanded decreases by 2.5 percent from 800 gallons per year to 780 gallons.

Price (Dollars per Gallon)	Annual Quantity of Gasoline Demanded (Gallons per Year)
Before: $3.00	800
After: $3.30	780
Percentage change in price (3.30 − 3.00) / 3.00 = 10%	Percentage change (780 − 800) / 800 = −2.5%

The price elasticity of demand can be applied to either an individual demand curve or a market demand curve. **Table 6A.3** illustrates how a single individual's consumption of gasoline changes with price.

Starting from a particular combination of price and quantity, inelastic demand results in a more vertical demand curve than elastic demand. To see this, let's start with **Figure 6A.1**, which shows the demand curve that corresponds to **Table 6A.3**. Starting from the price of $3.00 per gallon and 800 gallons consumed, a 10 percent increase in the price results in a 2.5 percent decrease in the quantity demanded. This represents a price elasticity of 0.25, which indicates inelastic demand.

Figure 6A.1 Inelastic Demand for Gasoline
This figure shows the demand curve corresponding to **Table 6A.3**. With a price elasticity of demand of 0.25, a big percentage change in price produces a small change in quantity.

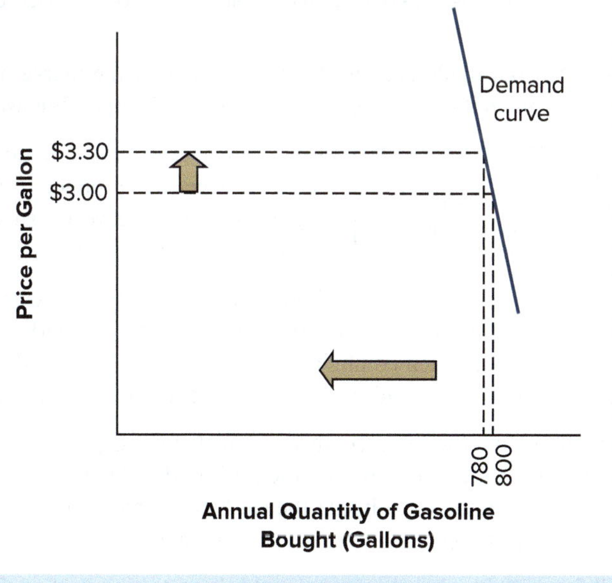

Now let's assume that the price elasticity of gasoline suddenly jumps from 0.25 to 2–that is, from inelastic to elastic. Starting from the same combination of $3.00 per gallon and 800 gallons consumed, a 10 percent increase in price now results in a 20 percent decrease in the quantity demanded. Consumption of gasoline now drops from 800 gallons per year to 640 gallons per year, as shown in **Figure 6A.2**, and the demand curve is less vertical.

Figure 6A.2 A Hypothetical Elastic Demand for Gasoline
Suppose that the price elasticity of gasoline suddenly jumps to 2. Then starting from the same combination of price and quantity, the demand curve is less vertical than it was in **Figure 6A.1**.

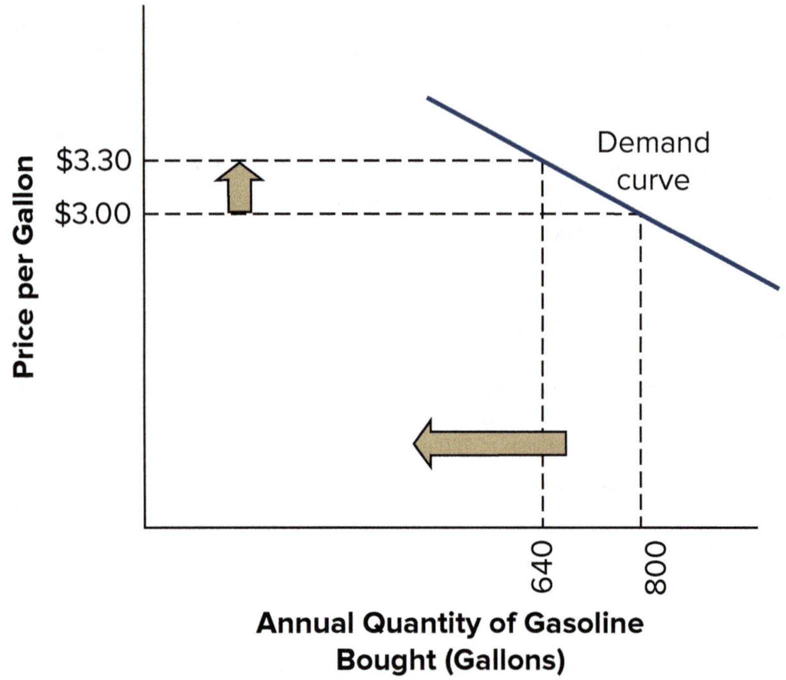

PRODUCER DECISIONS (LO6A-2)

LO6A-2 Explain the role of cost minimization in producer decisions, and use the concept of price elasticity of supply.

Now we shift our analysis from the demand side of the market to the supply side. In **Chapter 4,** we described the *cost function,* which reports how much it costs to produce each level of output. We used that information to analyze the process of profit maximization.

cost minimization
The process of choosing the lowest-cost way of producing a given level of output.

But where does the cost function come from? For any given level of output, managers have to figure out the least expensive production method. That process is known as **cost minimization**. In fact, often the biggest difference between a successful business and an unsuccessful business is which one does a better job of cost minimization.

Remember that a business usually has more than one way to produce the same output. For example, if you have a lawn-mowing business, you can use an army of workers equipped with hand mowers or one worker with a tractor. So your first step is to figure out which combination of inputs produces the desired output at the lowest cost. This cost-minimizing choice depends on the wages of the workers and the cost of the tractor and the gasoline needed to run it.

Or imagine you are the top executive of a small company creating and selling funny greeting cards. You have to ask the cost minimization questions first: Is it cheaper to print the cards in the United States or overseas? Is it cheaper to have a staff of trained greeting card writers, or should you buy the copy inside the cards from freelancers? Obviously the answers to these questions depend on the prices of inputs such as labor, printing, and international shipping.

We will first consider how businesses achieve cost minimization. Then, in the next section, we will look at pricing and output decisions.

Choosing the Right Inputs

To see a simple example of cost minimization, let's think about a lawn-mowing service (also discussed back in **Chapter 4**). Suppose the business owner has agreed to cut 20 lawns a day in the neighborhood. Now he has a choice: He can hire five workers at the going rate of $10 per hour ($80 per day for each, assuming an 8-hour day) with push mowers to do the task. Or he can hire one worker and rent a riding mower to cut the same 20 lawns. Which method should he choose?

The answer depends on the price of renting the riding mower. The option of hiring the five workers will cost \$400 per day (\$80 × 5). The option of renting the riding mower will be the daily rental cost of the mower plus the labor cost of one worker, which is \$80. So renting the mower will be the preferred option as long as its rental cost is less than \$320 per day (\$400 − \$80). But if the mower costs more than \$320 per day, it's not worth it.

In general, a producer's choice of inputs depends on its relative prices. As an input becomes more expensive, all other things being equal, a business will want to use less of it. If you are running a factory and the cost of providing health care for your U.S. workers goes up, you're likely to reduce the number of U.S. workers by automating the assembly line or by moving the operation to China or Vietnam. If the cost of renting office space rises compared to other inputs, you'll put your workers in cubicles rather than offices, or you'll buy your workers laptops and have them work from home.

Substitutes and Complements in Production

We say that one input is a **substitute** for another if, when the price of one goes up, a cost-minimizing business uses more of the other (holding output constant). For example, factory workers in China are generally thought of as substitutes for factory workers in the United States. An automated voice mail system is a substitute for human receptionists. Video conferencing is a substitute for in-person meetings.

substitute

Two inputs are substitutes if a business will use more of one when the price of the other rises.

Sometimes, though, two inputs work together, so if you use less of one, you will use less of the other as well. We say that one input is a **complement** for another if, when the price of one goes up, a cost-minimizing business will use less of the other (holding output constant). For example, freight transportation is a complement for foreign workers, because if the price of shipping freight across the ocean goes up, there is less incentive to move production overseas. Cement is a complement for construction workers, because as the price of cement goes up, less building occurs and therefore fewer workers are needed.

complements

Two inputs that are used together, such that when the price of one goes up, a cost-minimizing business uses less of the other.

Sometimes, technological changes may transform two inputs from complements to substitutes. For example, historically, trucks were complements to truck drivers. If the price of trucks fell, freight companies would buy more trucks, which would increase the demand for truck drivers. But going forward, it's only a matter of time before we see "autonomous" trucks, which are able to navigate roads without direct attention from a driver. Once autonomous trucks are introduced and their price declines, the demand for truck drivers will fall as well.

A Cost Minimization Example

Let's work through a simple example of cost minimization: If you are running a business, should you buy your own copy machine or send your documents out to a local copy shop? That's a decision many small businesses must make. If you buy a copy machine, you have to lay out anywhere from \$200 to \$1,200, depending on the speed and capacity of the machine you choose. And then there's the cost of the toner and paper, which could be 2–4 cents per copy. The alternative, of course, is to send the copying out, which could cost 10 cents or more per copy, depending on the quantity.

To make this decision, of course, we need to know the actual cost of the machine and the price per copy. **Table 6A.4** works through the cost minimization decision, assuming the cost of a copy machine is \$300, the per-page cost if you own the machine is 2 cents per copy, and the per-page cost if you go to an outside shop is 10 cents per copy.

The calculations in the table show that for low volumes of copies, it's cheaper to use an outside copy shop. But once the volume gets high enough, buying a copy machine makes sense. The result is a *cost function*: For any level of output, we can tell what the cost will be. Producing 3,000 copies, for example, will cost \$300. Producing 4,000 copies will cost \$380.

In general, the best choice of inputs depends on the price of inputs and on a producer's expected scale of output. In the example just given, the decision of whether to buy a copy machine

Table 6A.4 The Copier Decision

Few small businesses can avoid the important copier decision: Should they buy their own copy machines, with big up-front outlays and low per-page costs? Or should they use a local copy shop, with no start-up cost but a high per-page cost? The answer depends on the relative costs of the two options and the number of copies needed. The shaded regions represent the low-cost choices for selected copy volumes. For low volumes, the outside copy shop is preferable. For high volumes, buying a copier is better.

	Use Copy Shop	Buy Own Machine
Up-front cost	0	\$ 300
Per-page cost	\$ 0.10	\$ 0.02
Number of copies	Total cost	
0	\$ -	\$ 300
1,000	\$ 100	\$ 320
2,000	\$ 200	\$ 340
3,000	\$ 300	\$ 360
4,000	\$ 400	\$ 380
5,000	\$ 500	\$ 400
6,000	\$ 600	\$ 420
7,000	\$ 700	\$ 440

depends on how many copies you plan to make, holding input prices fixed. Similarly, in the case of the lawn-mowing company, the decision of whether to buy a tractor depends on how many lawns you need to mow, as well as on the relative prices of buying a tractor and renting it.

price elasticity of supply
The percentage change in quantity supplied, given a 1 percent change in price.

It's not unusual for the right mix of inputs for a small business to change as the business expands. A very small business may operate out of a spare bedroom, but a business with 10 employees needs its own office. A small business hires a part-time accountant; a bigger business has an in-house finance and legal department. These sorts of transitions make operating a business challenging.

Price Elasticity of Supply

elastic supply
Intuitively, a situation in which a small change in price has a big impact on quantity supplied. More precisely, a situation in which the price elasticity of supply is greater than 1.

inelastic supply
A situation where the quantity supplied of a good does not change much even if the price changes significantly. More precisely, a situation where the price elasticity of supply is less than 1.

perfectly inelastic supply
The quantity supplied does not change at all when the price changes.

In **Chapter 3**, we said that supply is *elastic* if a small price change leads to a large change in the quantity supplied. Similarly, supply is *inelastic* if a big price change leads to only a small change in the quantity supplied.

However, just as in the case of demand elasticity, we can be more precise. The **price elasticity of supply** is the percentage increase in the quantity supplied, given a 1 percent increase in the price. The price elasticity of supply is generally a positive number because the supply curve is usually upward-sloping. For example, if the price elasticity of supply is 3, a 10 percent price increase will lead to a 30 percent increase in the quantity supplied. **Elastic supply** means that the price elasticity of supply is greater than 1, and **inelastic supply** means that the price elasticity of supply is less than 1. **Perfectly inelastic supply** refers to when the price elasticity of supply is zero—that is, the quantity supplied doesn't change, no matter how the price changes.

Figures 6A.3, **6A.4**, and **6A.5** show, respectively, elastic supply, inelastic supply, and perfectly inelastic supply. Each figure starts from the same combination of price *P* and quantity *Q*, and shows the reaction to the same price change *P* to *P′*. The change in quantity is biggest in **Figure 6A.3**, smaller in **Figure 6A.4**, and nonexistent in **Figure 6A.5**. Starting from the same *P* and *Q*, the supply curve is more vertical when elasticity is smaller. In the case of perfectly inelastic supply, the supply curve is vertical.

Figure 6A.3 Elastic Supply
When supply is elastic, a relatively small percentage change in prices produces a relatively large percentage change in supply.

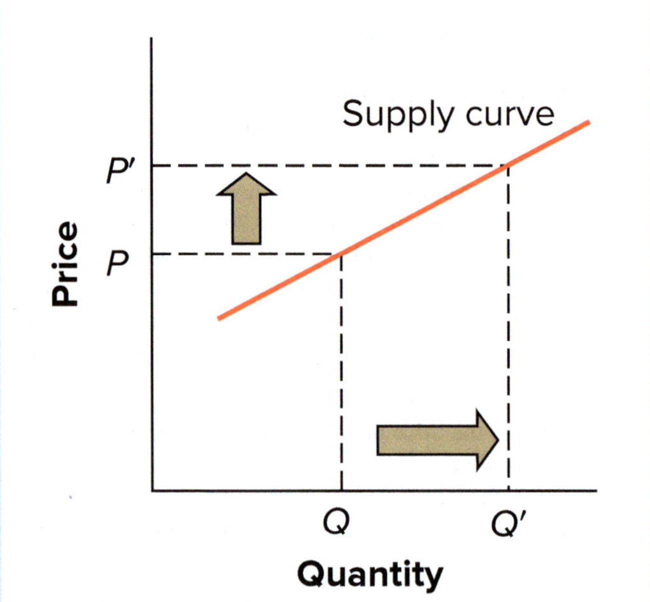

Figure 6A.4 Inelastic Supply
Starting from the same price *P* and quantity *Q*, the supply curve is more vertical when supply is inelastic than when it is elastic.

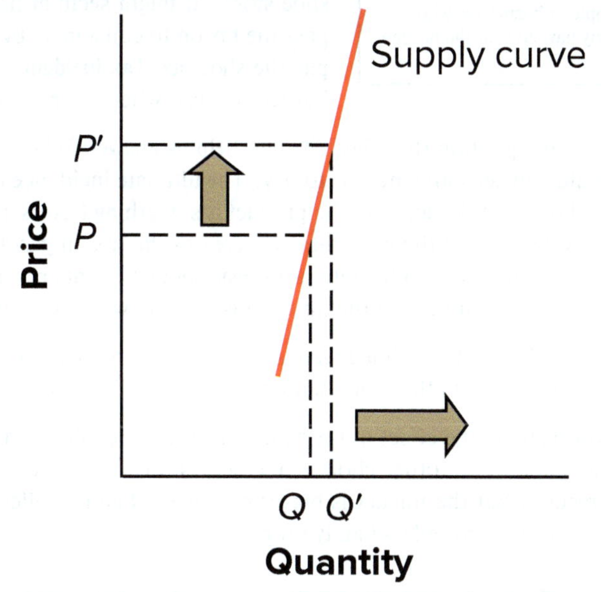

Figure 6A.5 Perfectly Inelastic Supply
Perfectly inelastic supply corresponds to a vertical supply curve. No matter what the price is, the quantity supplied remains the same.

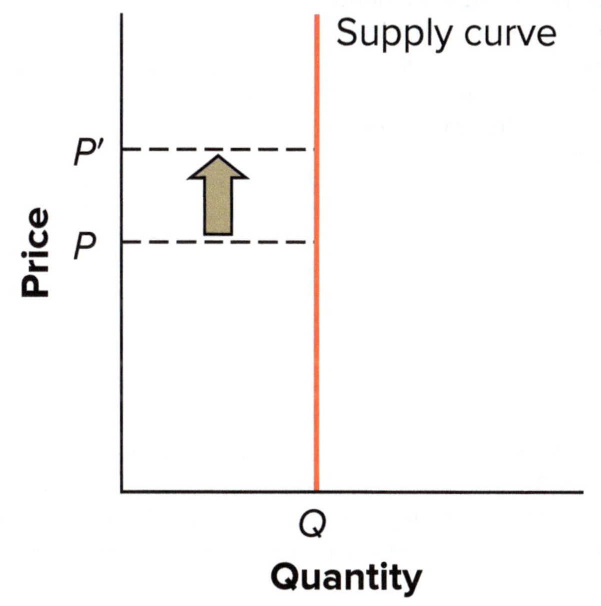

TAX INCIDENCE AND ELASTICITY (LO6A-3)

LO6A-3 Explain the incidence of a tax.

Politicians are always talking about raising or cutting taxes. In fact, Congress seems to pass some kind of tax change every year, which affects the amount that businesses and households have to pay the government.

But one of the big surprises of economics is that the ultimate *incidence* or burden of the tax may not fall on the person or company writing the check. Instead, it depends on the elasticity of supply and the elasticity of demand.

tax incidence
The people or businesses who ultimately have to bear the burden of a tax.

For example, suppose a local government levies a $5 tax per pair of shoes sold, to be collected from shoe stores. It might seem at first that shoe stores are being hurt by the tax. But the stores may try to pass the tax on to consumers by raising the prices of shoes by $5. If they are successful, consumers will pay the shoe tax. **Tax incidence** identifies the individuals or businesses that ultimately have to bear the burden of a tax, whether or not they are the ones that actually write the checks to the government.

But here's the question that elasticity can help us answer: When can we pass a tax on to someone else? If you were the one being taxed, when could you get someone else to pay? The ultimate incidence of a tax depends on which side of the market–buyers or sellers–is more inelastic. For example, suppose the product is something buyers absolutely need, at least in the short run–say, gasoline to drive their cars to work. Now suppose the government increases the tax on gasoline (as of early 2019, the average tax on gasoline in the United States, a combination of federal and state taxes, was about 52 cents per gallon). Then, in the short run, gas stations will be able to simply boost their prices by the amount of the tax because drivers won't have any choice but to pay the higher prices.

To put this a different way, if *demand* is inelastic, buyers have few alternatives, and they won't be able to object if sellers try to boost prices to pass along a tax. On the other hand, if *supply* is inelastic, sellers will be forced to absorb a tax themselves.

Figure 6A.6 shows the effect of taxing a market in which demand is inelastic and supply is elastic, as is true for gasoline. In other words, purchasers don't have other choices, but sellers do. The tax shows up as the difference between what buyers pay and what sellers ultimately receive. But the impact is bigger on buyers than on sellers. In **Figure 6A.6**, the after-tax price to buyers rises a lot, whereas the after-tax price paid to sellers barely drops.

Figure 6A.6 Taxation with Inelastic Demand
Imposing a tax on a market with inelastic demand means that the after-tax price for buyers will increase by almost as much as the amount of the tax.

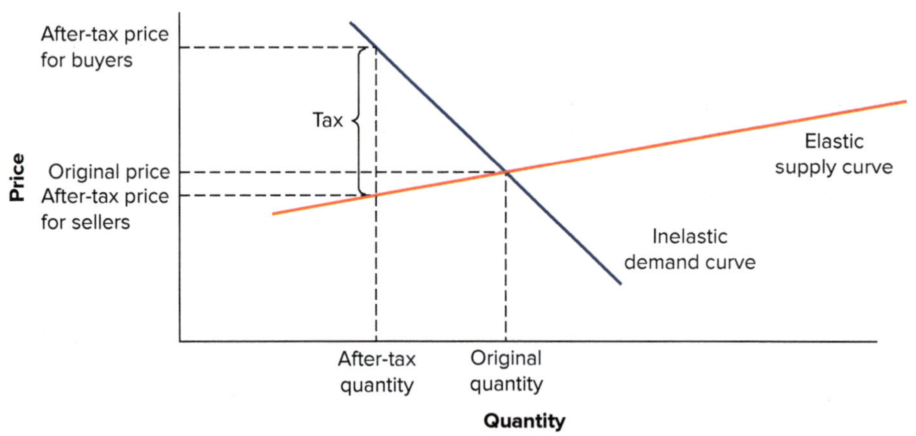

However, this may not be the final word on the incidence of the tax. There can be a difference between short-run and long-run elasticity in a market. Even if buyers don't have many options in the short run, in the long run, they may be able to make big changes. Faced with higher gas taxes, for example, drivers will eventually buy more fuel-efficient cars, take public transportation, switch jobs to avoid long commutes, or move closer to their jobs. So, in the short run, a gasoline tax falls on drivers, but in the long run, it may fall on the sellers of gasoline.

YOUR ECONOMIC LIFE: What Can You Change Easily?

Suppose the government put a tax on something important in your daily life, like your smartphone. Could you easily give it up? Probably not! The demand for smartphones is inelastic, so the burden of a tax on the phone is likely to fall on you, not the seller of the phones.

Go through some of the things you buy and use daily. If these were taxed, how easy would it be to give them up or reduce consumption? A tax on your gym membership might lead you to work out at home. The incidence of that tax is therefore likely to fall on the gym.

Or what about a tax on dog food? If you already own a dog, you are not likely to cut back on the dog's food just to save a few pennies. Therefore, the incidence of a dog food tax is likely to fall on pet owners, rather than the pet food sellers. However, over the long run, a tax on dog food is likely to lead to fewer people deciding to own a dog.

The implication: Understanding the impact of a new tax on your life requires some thought to understand what your reaction will be. You may or may not be bearing the burden of the tax.

CONCLUSION

The fundamental lesson of this appendix is that as prices change, so does the behavior of consumers and businesses. The better we can understand these reactions, the better we can understand the economy around us. That's the virtue and importance of a deeper look at microeconomics.

06 SUMMARY

1. A utility function reports a number that reflects the physical and emotional benefits a person gets from consuming different combinations of goods and services. Every person's utility function is different. Typically, people get diminishing marginal utility from increasing consumption of the same good or service. ***(LO6A-1)***
2. A budget constraint tells you what combinations of goods and services you can buy, given their prices and the amount of money you have available to spend. A rational person maximizes their utility subject to the budget constraint, which requires making trade-offs between different goods and services. ***(LO6A-1)***
3. The price elasticity of demand measures the response of quantity demanded to price changes of a good or service. It is the percentage change in quantity demanded that results from a 1 percent change in price. Demand is inelastic if the price elasticity is less than 1, and it's elastic if the price elasticity is greater than 1. ***(LO6A-1)***
4. For any given level of output, the managers of a business have to figure out the least expensive production method. The cost-minimizing combination of inputs depends on the prices of the inputs. Two inputs are substitutes if raising the price of one increases the use of the other, holding output constant. Two inputs are complements if raising the price of one decreases the use of the other, holding output constant. ***(LO6A-2)***
5. The price elasticity of supply is the percentage increase in the quantity supplied, given a 1 percent increase in the price. Supply is elastic if the elasticity is greater than 1, and it's inelastic if the elasticity is less than 1. Supply is perfectly inelastic if the elasticity is zero—that is, if a change in price does not change the quantity supplied. ***(LO6A-2)***
6. The incidence of a tax reflects who ultimately absorbs the burden of the tax. In general, the incidence of a tax depends on which side of the market—buyers or sellers—is more inelastic. ***(LO6A-3)***

KEY TERMS AND CONCEPTS

utility function

utility

marginal utility

diminishing marginal utility

budget constraint

rational individual

price elasticity of demand

inelastic demand

elastic demand

cost minimization

substitute

complements

price elasticity of supply

elastic supply

inelastic supply

perfectly inelastic supply

tax incidence

connect PROBLEMS

1. Diminishing marginal utility means that _______ ***(LO6A-1)***

   a) marginal utility falls as consumption increases.
   b) marginal utility gets smaller over time.
   c) utility falls as consumption increases.
   d) utility gets smaller over time.

2. In the following table, the first column is the number of baseball games you attend in a month. The *second column is the utility you get from attending these games.* ***(LO6A-1)***

Number of Baseball Games Attended in the Month	Total Utility	Marginal Utility
0	0	
1	10	?
2	40	?
3	60	?
4	70	?

   a) Fill in the third column with the marginal utility of each additional game.
   b) Is this a situation of diminishing marginal utility? Explain.
   c) Would you expect everyone to have the same utility function for baseball games? Why or why not?

3. You have $10 to spend on desserts for a week. You need to split it between cookies, which are $1 each, and ice cream cones, which are $2 each. ***(LO6A-1)***
   a) What is the maximum number of ice cream cones you can buy in a week?
   b) If you buy four cookies, how many ice cream cones can you buy?
   c) Suppose the price of ice cream cones drops to $1. Write down all the combinations of cookies and cones that now meet your budget constraint.

4. Suppose the price elasticity of demand for sports cars is 2. When the price is $40,000 per car, a local dealer sells 50 cars over a year. ***(LO6A-1)***
   a) If the price per car rises to $44,000, what is the percentage change in the price?
   b) What is the percentage change in sports car sales, given the elasticity?
   c) What is the new sales level for sports cars?
   d) What was the original revenue of the auto dealership from sports car sales? What is the new revenue? Did the price increase reduce or increase revenue?

5. The price of homes affects the number of new homes built–the higher the price rises, the more new homes are built. Economic literature suggests that a reasonable value for the price elasticity of supply for home construction is 3, so a 1 percent price increase generates a 3 percent increase in new home construction. ***(LO6A-2)***
   a) Suppose the average price of homes in a town is $300,000, and 200 new homes are constructed in the town each year. Now suppose the average price of homes goes up to $330,000. What is the new rate of home construction per year?
   b) Instead of rising, suppose the average price of homes in the town falls from $300,000 to $270,000. What is the new rate of home construction per year?

6. A town decides to impose a new tax of 30 percent on food sold in its area. ***(LO6A-3)***
   a) Suppose the town is in the middle of the desert, so there are no other places nearby for people to buy food. Is the burden of the tax more likely to fall on food stores or food purchasers? Is this the result of inelastic demand, elastic supply, elastic demand, or inelastic supply? Explain your answer.
   b) Now suppose the town is in the middle of a densely populated region of the country, so it's easy for food shoppers to go to stores in other towns. Is the burden of the tax more likely to fall on food stores or food purchasers? Is this the result of elastic demand, elastic supply, inelastic demand, or inelastic supply? Explain your answer.

7. Economists disagree about the magnitude of elasticity of labor supply. The labor market is a key part of the economy. Workers choose how many hours they will work, or even if they are going to take a job at all, depending on the wage they can get. The elasticity of labor supply tells us how much labor supply responds to changes in the wage. Some argue that it is quite low; others say that the elasticity of labor supply is much greater than 1.

   This debate has important policy consequences. Let's consider what happens when the government imposes a tax on wages, so there is a gap between the wage paid by employers and the wage received by workers. ***(LO6A-3)***
   a) Suppose the elasticity of labor supply is very low at the current level of employment. Does this tax have more effect on the wage received by workers, or on the quantity of labor supplied?
   b) Now suppose the elasticity of labor supply is high at the current level of employment. Does this tax have more of an effect on the wage received by workers, or on the quantity of labor supplied?
   c) Suppose you are a politician deciding whether to raise revenues by increasing taxes on high-income workers. Would you prefer that their supply of labor is elastic or inelastic? Explain.

CH 07

THE FIRST STEP INTO MACROECONOMICS

Valeria Cantone/Shutterstock

LEARNING OBJECTIVES

After reading this chapter, you should be able to:

LO7-1 Define *gross domestic product (GDP),* and distinguish between final goods and services and intermediate inputs.
LO7-2 List and discuss the components of GDP.
LO7-3 Explain what GDP does not include.
LO7-4 Compare GDP and GDP per capita across countries.

Up to this point, we have focused our attention on the behavior of individual markets. We considered supply and demand in a single market, looked at profit-maximizing businesses, and discussed how government can affect a market.

Now we are going to take our first steps into **macroeconomics**—the study of the whole economy. This is the big picture that we read about online or see on television. What's happening to unemployment? Is inflation accelerating or slowing down? Are we slumping into a recession or going into a boom? And what should Congress, the president, or the chair of the Federal Reserve do about it?

> **macroeconomics**
> The study of the overall economy.

Macroeconomics addresses these questions and more. Over the next six chapters, we will look at the core concepts of output, inflation, growth, and unemployment. We will discuss the unusual economic roller coaster of the pandemic and the inflationary surge that followed. Then, we will examine how government spending and taxation can influence the economy and the impact the Federal Reserve, the country's central bank, can have on interest rates and economic activity.

Keep in mind, however, that there are quite a few macroeconomic topics about which economists don't agree. That's to be expected because macroeconomics explores the complicated interactions of many different parts of the economy. A decision by the federal government to spend billions on new fighter planes can affect employment in the states where the planes are built. That increase in employment may affect the demand for new homes, which in turn may boost the demand for mortgage borrowing. Every part of the economy is interconnected.

The other reason for disagreement is the intensely political nature of many macro policy decisions. Republicans and Democrats in Washington differ on how much to spend, what kind of taxes to increase or cut, and how actively the government should intervene in the economy. As a result, disputes about macroeconomic policy quickly turn into political conflicts. President George W. Bush, a Republican who took office in 2001, was repeatedly attacked by congressional Democrats for running big budget deficits. Then, after President Barack Obama took office in 2009, Republicans attacked the Obama administration for running a big budget deficit. Democrats attacked President Donald Trump for increasing the federal budget deficit by cutting taxes, followed by Republicans attacking President Joseph Biden for spending too much.

This chapter, however, will examine a relatively noncontroversial topic: the basic measure of the size of the economy, which is the gross domestic product, or GDP for short. We mentioned GDP in **Chapter 1**, but we will look at it more closely now. GDP is the starting point for all macroeconomics—and for any discussion of the overall economy. We will discuss the different components of GDP and will finish by comparing the size of the U.S. economy with the economies of other countries.

MEASURING THE ECONOMY (LO7-1)

LO7-1 Define *gross domestic product (GDP),* and distinguish between final goods and services and intermediate inputs.

An ammunition plant during WWII. The government needed a measure of the economy to know how many wartime goods it could produce.

Everett Historical/Shutterstock

When you visit a hospital or a doctor's office, a nurse generally takes your blood pressure, pulse, and temperature; weighs you; and perhaps draws blood samples. These measurements have three purposes. First, if anything has changed since your last visit, that could indicate a problem. Second, if you have a complaint, the measurements help pinpoint the cause. Finally, the information helps guide your treatment.

Measuring the economy has the same purposes: to identify economic problems, diagnose their causes, and figure out the right policy fixes. But taking the temperature of an economy as big as that of the United States is not an easy job. In fact, before the mid-1930s, economists had no systematic way of measuring or tracking the economy as a whole. Government statisticians and industry trade associations could provide some information, such as the amount of freight being hauled by railroads or the amount of canned corn coming out of the nation's factories (a whopping 100 million cans in 1893, for those of you taking notes). But there was nothing anyone could point to and say, "*This* is how big the economy is."

When the Great Depression arrived in 1929, it suddenly became more important for us to know how the economy was doing. As we saw in the previous chapter, the economy was very sick during that time. There were loud calls for the government to do something about it, and economists were forced to come up with new tools and new ways of thinking. For the first time, we needed an overall measure of the economy to see how bad economic conditions were and whether they were getting better. In the 1930s, economist Simon Kuznets, who later won the Nobel Prize in Economics, worked with a small staff to construct the first overall measure of the U.S. economy.

Kuznets's work represented a major breakthrough in economics. However, it was just the start. Over the next 10 years, the nation's economic statistics steadily improved. One major motivation for improving economic analysis was the international conflict between Germany and Japan in the early 1940s. Government military planners needed to know how big the economy was so they could figure out how many tanks, ships, and planes it could produce.

By the time World War II ended in 1945, the foundations for the current system of gathering economic statistics were in place. Today, the Bureau of Economic Analysis (BEA), the Bureau of Labor Statistics (BLS), the Census Bureau, and the Federal Reserve are the main statistical agencies in Washington. They conduct surveys, collect information, and regularly publish reports on key economic statistics, such as unemployment, inflation, productivity, and foreign trade.

The Basics of Gross Domestic Product

The BEA is charged with estimating output of the U.S. economy. The **gross domestic product** *or* **GDP** is the dollar value of the total output of the economy in a year. Collectively, all the statistics that feed into this process of estimating GDP are known as the **system of national accounts** (The BEA also estimates quarterly GDP, which is economic output in each quarter of the year.)

gross domestic product (GDP)
The dollar value of the total output of an economy. Based on final goods and services produced in a year.

system of national accounts
All the statistics that feed into the process for estimating the quarterly and annual output of the U.S. economy.

personal consumption
The goods and services bought by households.

nonresidential investment
The buildings, equipment, and software that businesses purchase to use in production.

residential investment
The construction of new homes and the renovation of existing homes.

change in private inventories
Increase or decrease of inventories at manufacturers, wholesalers, and retailers.

government consumption and investment
The goods and services purchased by the government.

net exports
The difference between exports and imports.

Measuring the output of the largest economy in the world is a complicated task. GDP includes a wide range of goods and services–we'll explain next which ones belong and which ones don't. For now, think of that range as a long list going from automobiles and light trucks (13.8 million sold in 2022) to baseball games (64 million fans attending in 2022), to college classes (almost 19 million students enrolled in higher education in 2020), to military strategy (615 generals and admirals in the U.S. armed forces as of 2023), to haircuts (123,000 barbers and 720,000 hairdressers, hairstylists, and cosmetologists hard at work making customers look good in 2022), to paintball (an estimated 2.6 million people participated in 2021). No one really knows just how many different items this list contains, but it's certainly well into the millions for the United States, depending on how finely we cut it.

Such a list, even if we could compile it, would be interesting but not terribly useful. The different types of goods and services are all measured in different units. What have automobiles to do with admirals besides beginning with the same letter? Not much. And there's no easy way to add them all up.

But here's the key: If we can express each item on the output list as a dollar amount, the statisticians at the BEA can sum them into a figure for the total production of the economy. For example, in 2022, U.S. households spent $154 billion on pets, pet products, and related services such as veterinary care. We can add that to the billions spent for haircuts, the total amount spent on knee replacements, and the revenues collected by zoos and aquariums. After we have added our entire list of products and services, we have the output of the economy!

The Components of GDP

What goes into GDP? Here are its components:

- **Personal consumption**: goods and services for household use.
- **Nonresidential investment**: the long-lived buildings, equipment, and software that businesses purchase to use in production.
- **Residential investment**: the construction of new homes and the renovation of existing homes.
- **Change in private inventories**: goods produced by businesses that are not immediately purchased.
- **Government consumption and investment**: goods and services purchased by the government.
- **Net exports**: the difference between exports and imports.

Each of these amounts is measured in dollars, and GDP consists of the sum of all of these:

GDP (in dollars) = Personal consumption + Nonresidential investment + Residential investment + Change in private inventories + Government consumption and investment + Net exports

Table 7.1 shows how the different components of GDP added up in 2022. For example, residential investment totaled $1127 billion. Note that net exports were negative because the United States imported more than it exported (we'll discuss imports and exports later in the chapter).

Table 7.1 The Components of Gross Domestic Product, 2022

Below are the main components of GDP, along with their descriptions.

Category	Billions of Dollars in 2022	Explanation
Personal consumption	17,361	Vehicles, food, housing, medical care, education, consumer electronics, and everything else that households can consume.
Nonresidential investment	3,345	Computers, factory machinery, software, office buildings, airplanes, and all the other long-lived capital investments that businesses use for production.
Residential investment	1,127	Construction of new homes and renovation of existing homes.
Change in private inventories	159	Increase or decrease of inventories at manufacturers, wholesalers, and retailers.
Government consumption and investment	4,447	Salaries and benefits of government employees; purchases of supplies and equipment; and construction of buildings, highways, and other infrastructure.
Net exports of goods and services	−974	Exports of goods and services to other countries, minus imports of goods and services from other countries.
Gross domestic product	25,464	

Source: Bureau of Economic Analysis, www.bea.gov (as of February 2023).

No Double-Counting

We've listed the main components of GDP, but we seem to have left out some economic activity. For example, no category of GDP corresponds to, say, the spending by a business on janitorial services or electricity. In fact, all the intermediate inputs of businesses (described in **Chapter 4**) appear to be left out.

final goods and services
The goods and services that are bought by ultimate users.

intermediate inputs
Any goods or services purchased from other businesses and used up in production.

There's a reason for that. To eliminate double-counting, BEA statisticians count only the purchases of **final goods and services**–that is, goods and services that are bought by their ultimate users. Purchases of intermediate inputs are left out of GDP. **Intermediate inputs** include any goods and services bought by a business that are completely used up in production in less than a year.

Why do statisticians leave out intermediate inputs? Think about a restaurant that buys apples to make apple pie, which it then serves to customers. The apples are an intermediate input, and the apple pie is part of personal consumption expenditures. We don't want GDP to include both the apples and the apple pie because that would count the apples twice. Similarly, a printing company uses paper and ink to produce a book for sale to readers–say, a textbook. To avoid double-counting, only the purchase price of the book is counted as part of GDP.

However, a business can make some purchases that are included as part of GDP, like nonresidential investments in buildings, equipment, and software. What makes these different is that they are long-lived–that is, they don't get used up within a year. When the printing company buys a printing press–which may have a useful lifetime of 10 years–that's counted as a nonresidential investment. Similarly, the purchase of a commercial oven by the restaurant to bake the apple pies is a nonresidential investment and is included in GDP.

HOW IT WORKS: A TRILLION HERE, A TRILLION THERE...

The total GDP of the United States in 2022 was roughly $25.5 trillion. None of us sees a trillion of anything in our daily lives, so it's hard to get our heads around a number that big. With that in mind, let's figure out how big it really is.

The thickness of a $1 bill is roughly .0043 inches. If we stacked up 25.5 trillion-dollar bills, they would make a pile more than a million miles high. That's more than four times the distance to the moon.

By contrast, if you make $50,000 per year, those dollar bills piled up would be 18 feet high—not nearly as impressive.

UNDERSTANDING GDP (LO7-2)

LO7-2 List and discuss the components of GDP.

Let's take a closer look at each component of GDP in more detail.

Personal Consumption

The biggest category of GDP is personal consumption, which accounted for more than $17 trillion in 2022. This enormous sum includes all sorts of goods that households spend money on, such as food, telephone services, personal computers, automobiles, and gasoline.

SPOTLIGHT: CONSPICUOUS SPENDING

When the BEA totals up spending on personal consumption or residential investment, it makes no judgment about an item's usefulness or social value. For example, from 2013 to 2022 the residential investment component of GDP included construction costs of $190 million for an enormous mansion being built in the ritzy Bel Air section of Los Angeles. The house, including a 30-car garage and five swimming pools, was originally expected to be listed for sale for $500 million. The actual selling price: $126 million, far less than the cost.

Meanwhile, the personal consumption component of GDP includes spending on flashy jewelry, plastic surgery, expensive parties, and all the champagne that professional athletes pour on each other when they win the championship. If you can spend it, the BEA can count it.

Sources: "California Dreaming: Record $500 Million Tag on L.A. Home," *Bloomberg*, May 26, 2015.

"Once Listed For $500 Million, Bel Air Mansion "The One" Just Sold At Auction For A Big Loss," *Celebrity Net Worth*, March 7, 2022.

Residential investment: Bel Air mansion.

Bloomberg/Contributor/Getty Images

The category of personal consumption also includes the money consumers spent on pet food and on greeting cards. So, when you buy holiday cards, you are contributing toward personal consumption and GDP. Religious intangibles–contributions to your local church, synagogue, or mosque–are counted as part of personal consumption. So are spending on education and contributions or bequests to universities. Gambling losses count as personal consumption, too, as does the latest mobile game app.

One oddity of GDP statistics is that medical spending counts as part of personal consumption even if a health insurer or the federal Medicare system pays the bill. The reason is that the individual is the ultimate consumer of medical spending. If Medicare pays for your grandfather's heart surgery, that counts as personal consumption for him even though the money never touched his hands.

ECONOMIC MILESTONE

1950: Auto's Share of Spending Hits Peak

Following World War II, factories switched from making tanks and planes to producing cars—lots of them. In 1950, spending on motor vehicles and parts exceeded 7 percent of personal consumption, an all-time record, as Americans started new households, moved out to the suburbs, and adopted a car-oriented lifestyle. Today, we are still driving, but spending on motor vehicles and parts has gone down to 4 percent of personal consumption. Instead, Americans have boosted their spending on items such as medical care, while adding new products such as personal computers. The car is no longer king.

Nonresidential Investment

Another important GDP spending category is nonresidential investment. That's the total of outlays by businesses on the structures, equipment, and software they need to run their operations. Nonresidential investment includes computers on workers' desktops, office chairs, factory machinery, office buildings, power plants, wires to power plants, hospitals, medical equipment, and airplanes–anything that is used in production and that lasts for more than one year. Nonresidential investment also includes the research and development necessary to create new products and services.

The pattern of nonresidential investment has changed over time. In the 1950s and the 1960s, U.S. businesses put their money mostly into industrial and transportation equipment. Manufacturers were building and expanding factories, making everything from steel and cars to clothing and toys; as a result, they needed heavy machinery. At the same time, transportation companies were buying truck fleets to carry the raw materials to the factories and then shipping the finished goods to customers across the country.

The pattern of nonresidential investment has changed over time, reflecting the shift to a more global and information-based economy. Now many factories that feed U.S. stores are in China or other countries. As a result, U.S. companies have much less need to invest in industrial equipment at home.

That's why the biggest category of business investment spending in 2022 was research and development, followed by software, both of which count as investment. The next biggest category in 2022 was industrial equipment, including the forklifts and robots used in many e-commerce fulfillment centers, followed by communications equipment and computers. Information technology investment–which includes computers, communications equipment, and software–accounted for almost 26 percent of nonresidential investment spending in 2022, up from 5 percent in 1960 (**Figure 7.1**).

Figure 7.1 Information Technology's Share of Nonresidential Investment
What items are businesses spending money on? For many businesses, their biggest single investment is in the category of information technology equipment and software, which now accounts for almost 26 percent of nonresidential investment.
Source: Bureau of Economic Analysis, www.bea.gov (as of February 2023).

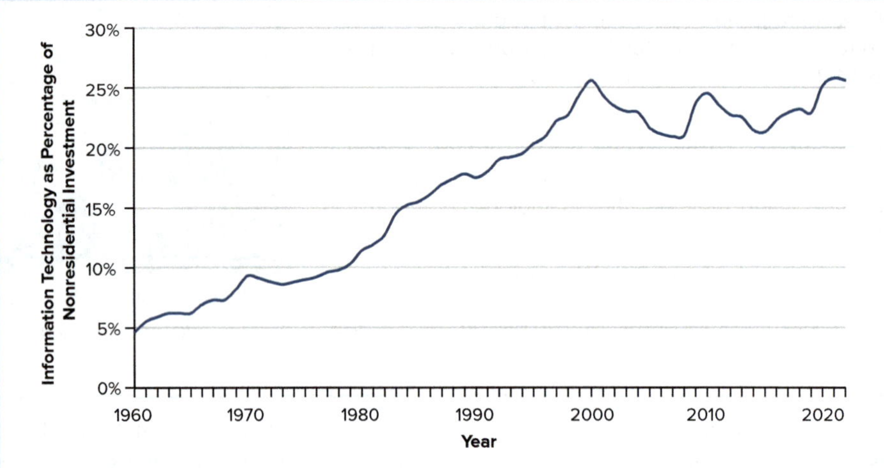

Keep in mind a couple of important points. First, business investment counts toward U.S. GDP only if it happens in this country. So when a U.S.-based company like Intel spends billions to build a factory in Ireland, that does not count toward U.S. GDP. In contrast, when a foreign-based company such as Toyota lays out billions to build factories in Kentucky and Indiana, that *does* count toward nonresidential investment and GDP. Location–not ownership–matters for the calculation of GDP.

The other point is that most outlays by businesses are for intermediate inputs, so they don't count as part of nonresidential investment. When Amazon buys socks from manufacturers and sells them to consumers, the socks count as personal consumption. However, when Amazon builds a new fulfillment center or renovates an existing one, its construction expenses are part of nonresidential investment. Similarly, purchases of food by restaurants are not counted in GDP, but the meals bought by diners count as personal consumption.

Residential Investment

Spending on the building of new homes and the renovation of existing ones is called *residential investment*. If you just rebuilt your kitchen for $50,000, that's part of residential investment. The construction of that eyesore of a home down the street also counts as residential investment. However, if you buy an existing home for $500,000, that does *not* count as residential investment because no actual production or construction occurred–the house was already there. Remember, GDP calculates production of new goods and services.

SWNS/Alamy Stock Photo

Residential investment is highly volatile, which means it can quickly swing from high to low and back again. Take a look at **Figure 7.2**, which measures residential investment as a share of GDP. That chart clearly shows the wide swings of homebuilding, including the housing boom years of the mid-2000s, which were followed by a deep bust and a slow recovery.

Figure 7.2 The Volatility of Residential Investment
Spending on construction of new homes and renovation of existing homes goes through big swings. This chart shows residential investment as a share of GDP.

Source: Bureau of Economic Analysis, www.bea.gov (as of February 2023).

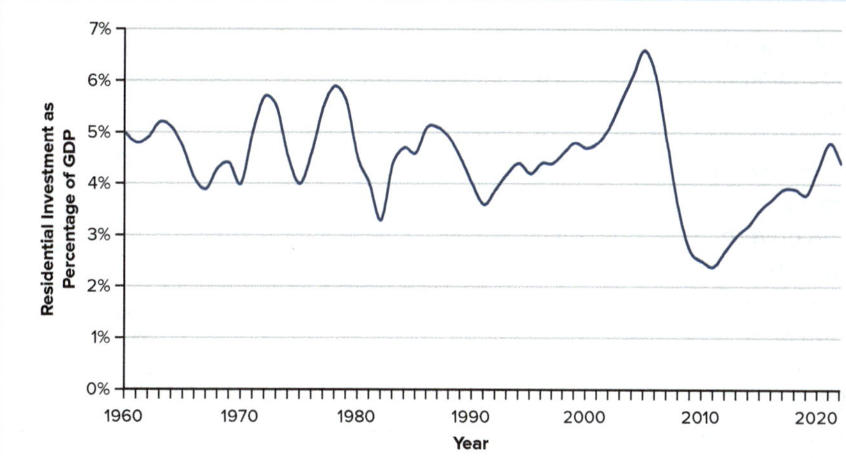

Government Consumption and Investment

Now we come to government. Clearly, the federal, state, and local governments in the United States are an important part of the economy, spending a total of $7.3 trillion in 2019. That rose to $9.1 trillion and $9.6 trillion in the pandemic years of 2020 and 2021, before falling slightly to $8.7 trillion in 2022.

In a typical non-pandemic year, roughly half of government spending is paid out directly to individuals in the form of **transfer payments,** also known as government social benefits. Government social benefits include Medicare, Social Security, unemployment insurance, education grants, veteran benefits, food stamps, welfare payments, and housing subsidies.

transfer payments
Government social benefits paid to individuals, including Social Security, Medicare, and unemployment benefits.

Government social benefits are typically used to fund personal consumption by individuals, or perhaps residential investment. Veteran benefits, Social Security, and unemployment insurance provide cash that can be used for food, televisions or to pay for rent or even home renovations. Medicare and food stamps are used to fund particular types of consumption.

output of government
The government's purchases of goods and services. Also called *government consumption and investment.*

During the pandemic, transfer payments to individuals were much higher than usual, because of the pandemic-related relief legislation discussed in **Table 6.2** in **Chapter 6**. These pandemic transfer payments included "economic impact payments" directly to individuals, child tax credits, and extra pandemic-related unemployment, among other items.

The other big category of government spending is called *government consumption and investment*, which includes all government purchases of goods and services, such as salaries paid to government employees. These goods and services are also called the **output of government.** In 2022, government consumption and investment totaled $4,447 billion, as shown in **Table 7.1**.

Government *consumption* includes all the salaries paid to government workers, such as teachers, police, military personnel, U.S. senators, and the president. It also counts all purchases by the government for immediate use, including food for government cafeterias, pencils for government offices, and fuel for nuclear submarines.

Government *investment,* on the other hand, reports all purchases of long-lived assets such as tanks and planes, government buildings, and software. It also includes money the government spends on building and maintaining highways and airports. The purchase of a new fire truck is counted as government investment, while the salaries paid to firefighters reflect government consumption.

The output of government is thus equal to government consumption plus government investment. One major output of government is spending on national defense. **Figure 7.3** shows how government's outlays for defense goods and services, nondefense goods and services, and government social benefits have changed over time. Since the 1960s, defense spending has dropped as a share of GDP. Nondefense government spending on goods and services, measured as a share of GDP, was trending down somewhat in recent years, with a bump during the pandemic. Government social benefits–propelled mainly by Social Security and government health care spending–have steadily risen as a share of the economy, also with a spike in pandemic-related benefits in 2020 and 2021.

Figure 7.3 Three Types of Government Spending
This chart shows government spending on nondefense goods and services, spending on defense goods and services, and spending on government social benefits. All three are measured as percentages of GDP and include all levels of government.
Source: Bureau of Economic Analysis, www.bea.gov (as of February 2023).

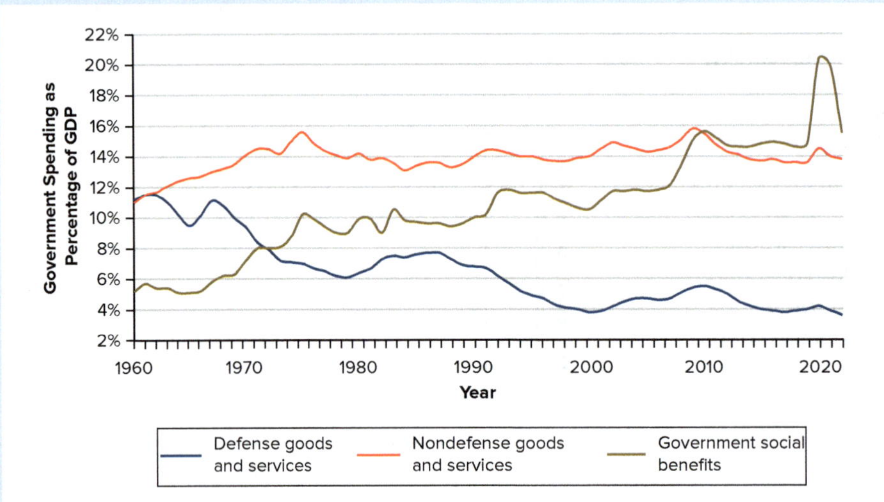

Change in Private Inventories

The change in private inventories is a small but important component of GDP. This category represents the increase or decrease of inventories held by manufacturers, wholesalers, and retailers. Goods that are produced but are not immediately sold–like cars–go into inventories. When companies add to their inventories, this change contributes positively to GDP because the goods count as production even if no one has bought them yet. When companies draw down their inventories by selling goods, the change in this category is subtracted from GDP.

Inadequate inventory management used to play a significant role in making economic downturns worse. Before the information revolution, companies had a hard time tracking sales and inventories in real time. In fact, it was a ritual for many manufacturers and retailers to physically count their inventory once a year. The problem was that when the economy slowed, inventories would build up unrecognized. And when manufacturers finally realized their mistakes, they would need to work off these inventories by cutting back production and laying off factory workers.

But today, information technology lets companies keep much better track of their inventories. In addition, many firms now manufacture cars, computers, or other products only when they actually have customer orders in hand and thus build up little or no unsold inventory. What's more, many goods consumed in the United States are now imported. As a result, when sales slow, inventories build up in foreign factories, where they do not count as part of U.S. GDP. As a result, inventory swings have become less important to the overall U.S. economy.

Net Exports

In this era of globalization, foreign trade is more important than ever. One measure of the contribution of the global economy to GDP is measured by *net exports,* which equal exports minus imports. **Exports** are goods and services produced in one country–in this case, the United States–and sold outside that country, so they count as part of GDP. If a company builds a tractor in the United States for sale overseas, that's part of GDP.

exports
The goods and services produced in a country and sold outside that country.

In contrast, **imports**, which are goods and services produced outside a country and consumed within that country, are considered in the GDP calculation with a negative sign. So, if you buy a toy for $5 that was made in China, it's counted as $5 of personal consumption–but it's also counted as −$5 of imports. Thus, the net impact on GDP is zero. (Actually, that's an oversimplification. Usually, a retailer would import that toy for $5, and sell it for something like $10. The difference of $5 would be the retailer's contribution to GDP.)

imports
Goods and services that are produced outside a country and consumed within that country.

In 2022, the United States imported about $3,954 billion of goods and services, and exported $2,980 billion of goods and services. Because imports today exceed exports, net exports are negative (−$974 billion). Let's stop here for a moment. The fact that net exports are negative doesn't mean that global trade is bad for the United States. As we will see in **Chapter 14**, the United States benefits in many different ways from trade, including lower prices and faster innovation.

supply chain
The network of suppliers needed to make a particular product.

HOW IT WORKS: TRACKING THE GLOBAL CORPORATION

Successful U.S.-based companies such as Apple, Google, Pfizer, IBM, Boeing, Intel, and GE have become increasingly global in recent years. For example, in 2022 aircraft maker Boeing got 41 percent of its revenue from customers located outside of the United States.

The planes that Boeing sells are assembled in the United States and exported to other countries. However, Boeing uses a global **supply chain**, so parts for its planes come from many different countries. For example, the 787 Dreamliner included major parts from Japan, Italy, England, France, and Sweden. That's not unusual. Many products that are exported from the United States contain parts that were originally made in other regions of the world.

Similarly, a product imported into the United States may contain parts from multiple countries. One famous study took apart the Apple iPhone 4, assembled in China, and found that it contained components from Japan, Korea, Taiwan, Europe, and the United States. The interconnection of the global economy is a reality.

Source: "Dreamliner: Where in the World Its Parts Come From," *CNNMoney*, January 18, 2013.

However, the fact that net exports are negative means that the United States is consuming more than it produces. **Gross domestic purchases** indicate the amount spent within the United States on final goods and services by consumers, businesses, and government. That is, it represents the *spending* activity of the whole country. In comparison, GDP is the amount of final goods and services *produced* in the United States. When gross domestic purchases are greater than GDP, as is the case now, that means net exports are negative.

gross domestic purchases
The amount spent within the United States on final goods and services.

YOUR ECONOMIC LIFE: Just Another Day for GDP

As you move through your day, almost everything you do is counted in GDP in one way or another. Your first cup of coffee counts as personal consumption. When you go online via your smartphone, the mobile fees count as personal consumption, and the nearby cell towers that give you the connection count as nonresidential investment. The software that powers the mobile apps you use also counts as nonresidential investment. Your clothing counts as personal consumption, though it may count as imports as well if it was made abroad. The building you live in counted as residential investment when it was built, though it still may be contributing to residential investment today if there are substantial repairs or renovations going on.

The street outside your home was likely built and maintained by the local government, so it counts as government consumption and investment. The car you drive counts as personal consumption, though depending on where it was made, it may count as an import as well.

If you eat lunch at a restaurant, the building housing the restaurant counts as nonresidential investment. The trucks that deliver the food and the software that run the cash register also count as nonresidential investment.

Your spending on education counts as personal consumption, even if it is partly financed by government grants or loans. The lecture hall either counts as nonresidential investment or government consumption and investment, depending on whether the educational institution is private or public. Indeed, GDP touches every part of your life.

WHAT GDP DOES NOT INCLUDE (LO7-3)

LO7-3 Explain what GDP does not include.

> **nonmarket economy**
> The part of the economy where people perform productive work without getting paid. Includes child-rearing and volunteer work.

GDP focuses primarily on the market economy–the part of the economy in which people get paid for the work they do. However, it does not cover the **nonmarket economy**, in which people may work just as hard but not get paid. For example, a stay-at-home parent is not given credit in the national income accounts for all the time and effort that go into raising children, cleaning house, and cooking food. That nonmarket labor disappears completely from GDP as if children magically raise themselves and homes stay clean without effort. All the hard work put in by volunteers at hospitals, schools, and religious organizations is not counted as part of GDP either.

The annual time use study by the BLS shows that, on average, U.S. adults spent 2.7 hours per day on unpaid work in 2021. That includes housework, lawn care, child care, and volunteering. By comparison, Americans devoted an average of 3.5 hours per day to paid work. (The reason that number seems low is that it includes weekends and the time of people who don't hold paid jobs, such as stay-at-home parents and the retired.)

If we counted those hours of unpaid work in GDP, how much would they be worth? Let's suppose we compensated all the unpaid hours at the low figure of $10 per hour. Then, unpaid work would be worth roughly $27 a day ($10.00 times 2.7 hours). With 365 days in a year, that means the unpaid work is worth about $10,000 per person, or about $2.8 trillion for the 280 million people in the United States who are 15 and older.

The omission of unpaid work from GDP creates some odd situations. For example, if a hospital moves an unpaid volunteer worker onto the payroll, GDP goes up even if the person is doing exactly the same amount of work as before. Similarly, if a mother who has been staying home to take care of her children takes a job outside the home and hires a nanny to watch the children, those child care activities move from the unpaid to the paid sector and now show up on the GDP ledger.

> **underground economy**
> The portion of the economy that does not pay taxes or otherwise get reported by government.

One final note: GDP also does not measure the **underground economy**, the portion of the economy that does not pay taxes or otherwise gets reported to the government. That includes illegal activities such as drug dealing and off-the-book transactions such as the babysitter or the landscaper who gets paid in cash and does not report it to the Internal Revenue Service. Estimates vary widely, but the size of the underground economy in the United States could be as large as 10 percent of GDP.

INTERNATIONAL COMPARISONS OF GDP (LO7-4)

LO7-4 Compare GDP and GDP per capita across countries.

So far we've been looking at the GDP of the United States, which has the largest economy in the world. Other countries calculate their own GDP using roughly the same rules and principles. That allows us to see how the U.S. economy stacks up against the production of other countries.

An international comparison of GDP tells us which countries have the most production. It can also indicate which countries have the highest living standards. And of course, we can still fulfill one of the original purposes of GDP, which is to calculate military capabilities. (Countries with higher GDP can generally produce more military ships, planes, and other equipment.) Today, the largest economy in the world still belongs to the United States, followed by China, Japan, and Germany.

GDP per Capita

GDP tells you how big an economy is—that is, how much it can produce. However, if we want to know which countries have higher living standards and which have lower, we need to look at population too. India, for example, has a bigger GDP than does Sweden, but India also has many more people.

The key concept here is **GDP per capita**, or GDP per person. GDP per capita is the economic output of a country divided by the size of its population. In other words, GDP per capita measures the amount of output each person would get if the economic pie were sliced evenly.

> **GDP per capita**
> The economic output of a country, divided by the size of its population.

Figure 7.4 shows the GDP per capita for selected countries, adjusting for different price levels in different countries. At the top are Switzerland, Norway, the United States, Sweden, and Germany. Other industrialized countries such as Canada, France, the United Kingdom, Korea, and Japan trail somewhat behind, followed by middle-income countries such as Russia, Mexico, China, and Brazil. Bringing up the rear are poor countries such as Bangladesh and Ethiopia.

Figure 7.4 An International Comparison of GDP per Capita
This figure compares estimated GDP per capita in 2022 for selected countries. Numbers are adjusted to reflect different price levels in different countries.

Source: International Monetary Fund, October 2022.

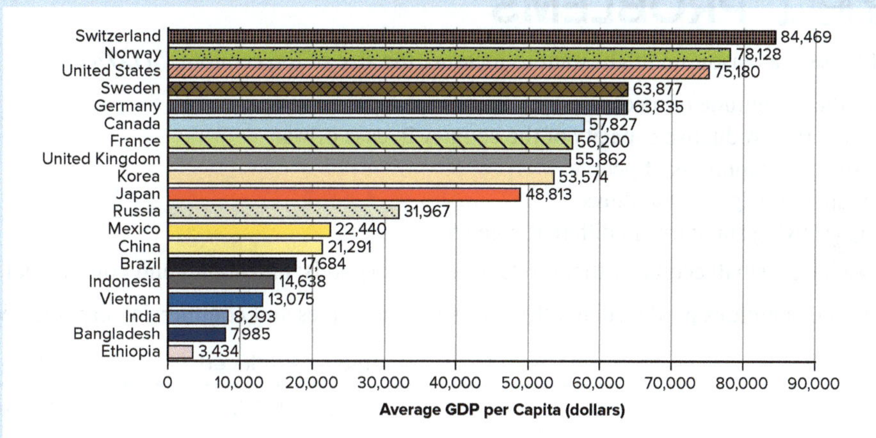

These numbers should be viewed a bit skeptically because it's hard to make economic comparisons across countries. What is true, though, is that looking at GDP per capita tells us that much of the world still has a long way to go before reaching the living standards of the United States and the big European countries.

CONCLUSION

Measuring the size of the economy is the essential first step in macroeconomics. The key measure is GDP, which enables us to put a dollar value on the output of the economy. We can also use GDP to compare different economies.

However, GDP is just a snapshot at a moment in time. In the next two chapters, we will go further and look at how the economy changes over time.

07 SUMMARY

1. The Great Depression and World War II forced economists to invent new tools for measuring an economy. They came up with GDP, which is the dollar value of the output of an economy. GDP counts only purchases of final goods and services, not purchases of intermediate inputs. ***(LO7-1)***
2. GDP includes personal consumption, nonresidential investment, residential investment, government consumption and investment, inventory investment, and net exports. ***(LO7-2)***
3. GDP does not include the nonmarket economy, such as the work done by stay-at-home parents and volunteers. It also does not include the underground economy of illegal and off-the-book activities. ***(LO7-3)***
4. GDP and GDP per capita allow economists to compare living standards across countries. ***(LO7-4)***

KEY TERMS AND CONCEPTS

macroeconomics
gross domestic product (GDP)
system of national accounts
personal consumption
nonresidential investment
residential investment
change in private inventories
government consumption and investment
net exports
final goods and services
intermediate inputs
transfer payments
output of government
exports
imports
gross domestic purchases
supply chain
nonmarket economy
underground economy
GDP per capita

connect PROBLEMS

1. Which of these is a reason we might want to measure the size of the economy? *(LO7-1)*
   a) To track the magnitude of recessions.
   b) To estimate the productive capacity of the country in case of war.
   c) To measure the happiness of people.
   d) To estimate the height of buildings.
   e) To compare living standards in different countries.
2. Suppose we have a small economy that produces only two goods: pineapples and commercial airplanes. *(LO7-1)*
   a) Here are the quantities produced and the prices for pineapples and commercial airplanes. What is the GDP of this country?

	Amount Produced	Prices
Pineapples	40,000,000 lbs	$1.00 per lb
Commercial airplanes	10 airplanes	$10 million per airplane

   b) Suppose five additional planes were produced and sold overseas. Does that change GDP, and if so, how?
3. Indicate whether each of the following transactions is a part of final goods and services or an intermediate input. If it is part of final goods and services, indicate which GDP component it belongs to: personal consumption, nonresidential investment, residential investment, government purchases of goods and services, inventory investment, or net exports. *(LO7-1)*
   a) A restaurant purchases chopped meat to use in hamburgers.
   b) A restaurant buys new chairs for its dining room.
   c) A family on vacation in the United States rents a car.
   d) The local school district pays the salary of a first-grade teacher.
4. Consider a private detective agency that does investigations for hire. In which category of GDP, if any, does each of the following spy expenditures belong, assuming that all purchases take place in the United States? *(LO7-2)*
   a) Purchases of miniature cameras for use in investigations.
   b) Purchases of Diet Coke for the agency cafeteria.
   c) The purchase of a new cell phone for the head of the agency.
   d) The purchase of a full set of James Bond movies for personal use by one of the agency's employees.
5. Indicate whether each of the following events causes GDP to increase, decrease, or stay the same, all other things remaining equal. *(LO7-2)*
   a) Consumers pay for fewer haircuts, and use the extra money to buy laptop computers that are made in China.
   b) Toyota builds a new car plant in the United States, and a same-size car plant run by Ford shuts down.
   c) Apple hires engineers and programmers in the United States to help design the next generation of iPads.
   d) Toyota builds a new car plant in the United States and reduces imports of its cars from Japan.
6. Government outlays for Social Security can be reported in which of the following categories of GDP? *(LO7-2)*
   a. Personal consumption
   b. Government consumption and investment
   c. Nonresidential investment
   d. Residential investment

7. Which of the following is not included in GDP? ***(LO7-3)***

   a) The value of the time of a stay-at-home parent.
   b) The purchase of a ticket to a Lady Gaga performance.
   c) The salary of a public school teacher.
   d) A new cell phone.

8. The rise of fast-food restaurants, such as McDonald's, made it easier for families to go out to eat rather than preparing their food at home. All other things being equal, the shift of food preparation from the home to the fast-food restaurant had the effect of ________ ***(LO7-3)***

   a) lowering GDP.
   b) raising GDP.
   c) not changing GDP.

9. The following table gives the gross domestic product (in dollars), adjusting for different price levels in different countries. ***(LO7-4)***

Country	GDP per capita in 2022 (Thousands of Dollars per Person)
United States	75.2
Mexico	22.4
India	8.3

Source: International Monetary Fund, October 2022.

   a) Calculate Mexico's GDP per capita as a percentage of U.S. GDP per capita.
   b) Calculate India's GDP per capita as a percentage of U.S. GDP per capita.

CH 08

INFLATION

Jake Rajs/Getty Images

LEARNING OBJECTIVES

After reading this chapter, you should be able to:

LO8-1 Define *inflation*, and calculate the inflation rate using the consumer price index (CPI).
LO8-2 Explain the difference between relative price shifts and the overall inflation rate.
LO8-3 Calculate and show how incomes and wages can be adjusted for inflation.
LO8-4 Discuss the impact of unexpected and expected inflation.

Everything has a price—that is, everything that is bought and sold in a market economy. In the United States, there are billions of different prices. Some businesses, like airlines, change their prices every day, raising ticket prices on some routes and lowering them on others. Gas stations post their price on electric signs that can be easily changed. Meanwhile, most colleges set their tuition price once a year.

To get a clearer picture of what's happening to prices in the economy as a whole, we need to be able to average those billions of prices together. We want to know whether the *overall* level of prices is falling or rising, and how fast.

That rise in overall prices—also known as *inflation*—is a key measure of the health of an economy. If prices are rising too fast (rapid price declines do happen, though rarely), that's bad news for consumers and businesses. In 2022, the inflation rate in the United States hit 8 percent, the biggest price increase since 1981. In fact, a main goal of economic policymakers around the world—particularly the people who run the central banks of each country—is to keep inflation under control.

In this chapter, we take the next big step into macroeconomics by defining the idea of an average price level for a whole economy. We'll explain how we can use this average price level to calculate the inflation rate. We'll also compare a rise in the overall price level and a shift in relative prices, and show how inflation is adjusted for changes in quality. We'll look at the difference between expected and unexpected inflation and identify who gets helped or hurt by each. Finally, we'll end with a discussion of falling prices, which is known as *deflation.*

THE BASICS OF INFLATION (LO8-1)

LO8-1 Define *inflation*, and calculate the inflation rate using the consumer price index (CPI).

Suppose you were walking down the street, and every 10 feet a thief stole a nickel or a dime out of your pocket. The first few times it might be funny, but then you would start getting annoyed. After a while, you'd realize that the steady theft of nickels and dimes was really making you poorer.

That, in a nutshell, is how inflation works. As prices rise, it's as if the money in your pocket were shrinking and becoming capable of buying less. Over the past 30 years, the overall price level in the United States has doubled. That means $50,000 in 1992 had the buying power of $104,000 in 2022. Or to put it a different way, if your parents earned $50,000 in 1992, and you are earning $104,000 in 2022, you are not doing any better than they were.

The Average Price Level

At any moment in time, consumers will see the prices of some goods and services rising while other items are becoming cheaper. In February 2023, the prices of eggs, rent, and airline fares, among other things, rose significantly compared to a year earlier. Meanwhile, in the same month, the prices of major appliances, televisions, and used cars and trucks were lower compared to a year earlier. In other words, that month was good for someone who was buying a dishwasher, and bad for someone who had to fly a lot.

When we talk about inflation, though, we're concerned with what is happening to prices *across the entire economy*, not to any particular item or even category of items. The **average level of prices** in the economy measures how much it costs to buy a **market basket** of common goods and services. The U.S. Bureau of Labor Statistics (BLS) picks the contents of the market basket to represent the pattern of expenditures by a typical U.S. household and gives each item a certain weight to represent its relative importance in the typical budget (see **Table 8.1**).

average level of prices

A measure of how much it costs to purchase a market basket of goods and services.

market basket

The typical household pattern of expenditures on goods and services that is used to calculate the average price level.

Table 8.1 Some Big Contributors to the Consumer Market Basket

This table shows the relative importance of different categories of goods in the market basket used to calculate the consumer price index. For a particular individual, of course, the percentages could be much different.

Category of Spending	Percentage of Market Basket, 2022	Includes
Owners' equivalent rent of primary residence	24.0	Owner-occupied homes
Food at home	8.7	Food bought for consumption at home
Medical care	8.1	Drugs, hospitals, physicians, insurance
Rent of primary residence	7.5	Rented homes and apartments
Recreation	5.4	Consumer electronics, sporting equipment, pets, tickets to sporting events
Food away from home	4.8	Restaurants, fast food, school cafeterias
New vehicles	4.3	Cars, SUVs, trucks
Communication	3.6	Postage, computers, telephone service, Internet service

Category of Spending	Percentage of Market Basket, 2022	Includes
Gasoline	3.2	Gasoline
Apparel	2.5	Clothing
Education	2.3	Tuition and books

Source: Bureau of Labor Statistics, www.bls.gov (as of December 2022).

The single biggest part of the market basket is "owners' equivalent rent of primary residence," which is a measure of the cost of owning your home. The second-largest part of the market basket is food consumed at home, followed by medical care and rent of primary residence. Some items that get the most attention in the media, such as gasoline, account for only a small portion of the market basket.

Any particular person or household may have a pattern of expenditures different from the market basket. For example, if you are young, you will tend to spend more on education and less on health care than an elderly household. But the basket is reasonably representative of the typical expenditures of an average U.S. household.

consumer price index (CPI)

A measure that tracks the average price level, starting from a base year.

To make comparisons between years easier, the BLS has chosen 100 to represent the average 1982–1984 price level, and it now measures all other years relative to this base year. This measurement gives us the **consumer price index *or* CPI**, which tracks the average price level in the United States.

For example, the CPI in 1992 was 140.3. That means the average price level in 1992 was 40.3 percent above the average price level in 1982–1984. In **Figure 8.1**, we can see the CPI for the United States from 1950 to 2022.

Figure 8.1 The Consumer Price Index, 1950–2022

The consumer price index (CPI) represents the average level of consumer prices based on a market basket of goods.

Source: Bureau of Labor Statistics, www.bls.gov.

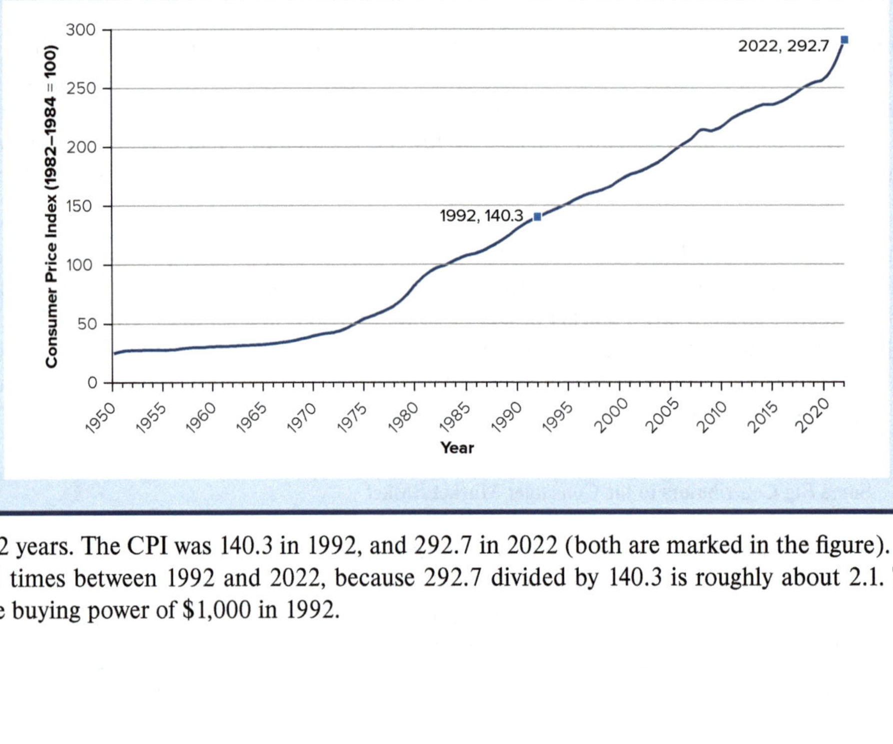

For another example, we will look at 2 years. The CPI was 140.3 in 1992, and 292.7 in 2022 (both are marked in the figure). That means the average price level rose about 2.1 times between 1992 and 2022, because 292.7 divided by 140.3 is roughly about 2.1. This in turn means $2,100 in 2022 has roughly the buying power of $1,000 in 1992.

The Inflation Rate

inflation

A sustained upward movement in the average level of prices.

inflation rate

The annual percentage change in the average price level.

We formally define **inflation** as a sustained upward movement in the average level of prices. The **inflation rate** is the annual percentage change in the average price level, or a measure of how much the average price level changes over a year. Because the CPI tracks the average price level, the inflation rate is also the annual percentage change in the CPI. For example, the inflation rate for 2022 is the percentage change in the CPI from 2021 to 2022.

As **Figure 8.2** shows, the annual inflation rate was low through most of the 1960s. In 1962, for example, the inflation rate was 1 percent, equivalent to the price of a $1.00 soft drink today going up by a penny in one year. On the other hand, the figure shows that inflation skyrocketed in the late 1970s and early 1980s, hitting 13.5 percent in 1980. In fact, inflation was generally identified as the biggest economic problem in those years. (Later in this chapter, we'll explain why high inflation is so disturbing.)

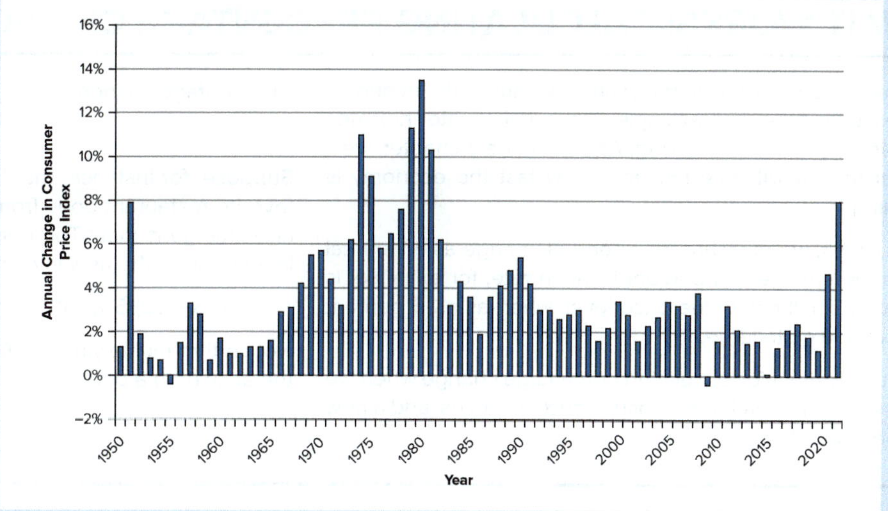

Figure 8.2 Annual Consumer Inflation Rate, 1950–2022
This figure shows the percentage increase of the average price level from one year to the next as measured by the consumer price index.

Source: Bureau of Labor Statistics, www.bls.gov.

SPOTLIGHT: WHY INFLATION SURGED IN 2021 AND 2022

As the United States gradually emerged from the pandemic in 2021, inflation began to accelerate. Consumer prices rose by 4.7 percent, the biggest jump since 1990. One problem was glitches in global supply chains. For example, it was harder for the U.S. automakers to get the right kind of computer chips from Asian factories, which were still battling the pandemic. As a result, vehicles were in short supply, and their prices went up sharply.

The inflation problem got worse in early 2022 when Russia invaded Ukraine. To attempt to get Russia to pull back, the United States and other Western countries put restrictions on trade with Russia. Since Russia was a major oil and natural gas exporter, these economic sanctions cut the supply of energy to world markets. As we saw in **Chapter 3**, a decrease in supply typically increases prices. Indeed, the price of gasoline skyrocketed.

At the same time, the invasion helped reduce Ukraine's exports of key products such as wheat, corn, and barley. That meant rising prices for these agricultural commodities, helping fuel inflation even more.

All these disruptions took place in the context of trillions of dollars of government spending to help individuals and businesses, as described in **Chapter 6**. As we will see in **Chapter 11**, this spending help keep up demand and provided the conditions under which inflation could accelerate.

As a result, consumer inflation jumped to 8 percent in 2022, the highest level since 1981. forcing the Federal Reserve to raise interest rates to attempt to slow down inflation. We'll read more about the Fed's fight against inflation in **Chapter 12**.

Source: Bureau of Labor Statistics, www.bls.gov.

From 1990 until the pandemic, the annual inflation rate remained under 4 percent. In 2009, the annual inflation rate was actually negative: The CPI fell from 215.3 in 2008 to 214.5 in 2009 (see **"How It Works: Calculating Percentage Change"**). Then, of course, inflation accelerated again in 2021 (see **"How It Works: Why Inflation Surged in 2021 and 2022"**).

The CPI and the consumer inflation rate are published each month by the BLS, which surveys 22,000 retail establishments and 6,000 housing units to update the prices in its market basket. The BLS then calculates how much the average price level changed that month. The BLS also calculates how much the average price level changed over the past year.

A related measure, also published by the BLS, is **core inflation**. That's the consumer inflation rate *without* taking food and energy into account. Why would we want to leave out food and energy? One reason is that those two categories happen to be volatile, sometimes spiking and then coming back down again. For example, if there's a frost in Florida, the prices of vegetables and fruit can jump and push up the overall inflation rate. But when the next growing season starts, those prices drop. Similarly, we've seen large fluctuations in energy prices that quickly reversed themselves.

> **core inflation**
> A measure of consumer inflation that omits the changes in food and energy prices.

These big movements in food and energy prices can sometimes obscure what's happening to inflation in other goods and services. For example, from February 2022 to February 2023, the overall inflation rate was 6.0 percent, but the core rate was 5.5 percent.

Which number matters more? If we expect food and energy prices to come back down to "normal," then we should keep an eye on the core inflation rate. But if we expect food and energy prices to stay low, then the overall inflation rate is the one to watch.

HOW IT WORKS: CALCULATING PERCENTAGE CHANGE

Economics is concerned, in part, with how rapidly the economy changes over time. For example, the inflation rate indicates how fast the price level is rising. And in the next chapter, we'll see that the growth rate indicates how fast the economy is expanding.

In both cases, we measure the speed of change as an annual percentage change. A 1 percent inflation rate, for example, is a relatively small rise in the price level, whereas a 20 percent rise would be quite large.

Here's the formula for calculating percentage change when we know the original level of a measure, such as prices, and a new level measured later:

Percentage change = [(Original number – New number)/ Original number] × 100

Suppose, for instance, that the price of dinner for two at your favorite restaurant goes from $50 to $55. How big a percentage change is that? The percentage change from the original level of 50 to the new level of 55 is

$$[(55 - 50)/50] \times 100 = [5/50] \times 100 = 0.1 \times 100 = 10\%$$

Notice that multiplying by 100 in the last step simply converts the answer to a percentage.

Table 8.2 Shifts in Relative Prices, 2000-2022

This table shows some goods and services where prices have been rising much faster than the overall rate of inflation, and some for which prices have been rising much more slowly or even falling.

Selected Consumer Goods and Services	Average Annual Inflation Rate, 2000–2022 (%)
College tuition	4.7
Gasoline	4.6
Medical care	3.4
Rent of primary residence	3.2
Alcoholic beverages away from home	3.0
Admission to sporting events	2.9
Owners' equivalent rent of primary residence	2.8
Haircuts and other personal services	2.6
All items	2.4
New vehicles	0.9
Airline fares	0.8
Apparel	–0.1
Sports equipment	–0.9
Wireless phone service	–2.1
Toys	–5.6
Personal computers and peripherals	–10.6
Televisions	–15.3

Source: Bureau of Labor Statistics, www.bls.gov.

RELATIVE PRICE SHIFTS (LO8-2)

LO8-2 Explain the difference between relative price shifts and the overall inflation rate.

The inflation figures that get the most attention each month are the overall inflation rate and the core inflation rate. The BLS also reports the inflation rate for subcategories of goods and services, narrowing the figures down to such individual fruits as apples, bananas, and oranges (including tangerines). Funeral expenses get their own price index, as do college textbooks, food from vending machines and mobile vendors, and "beer and other malt beverages away from home."

A **relative price shift** happens when the inflation rate of a good or service is significantly higher or lower than the overall inflation rate. If it's higher, then that good or service is getting more expensive over time relative to other possible purchases. If the inflation rate of a good or service is lower than the overall inflation rate, it's getting relatively cheaper.

If we look at the long-term inflation statistics in **Table 8.2**, we can see some large relative price shifts in items important to college students. The annual inflation rate for all items averaged 2.4 percent in the 22 years between 2000 and 2022. But the prices of goods such as apparel, toys, televisions, and sports equipment actually dropped over the same period. These goods have become relatively cheaper.

relative price shift

A situation where the inflation rate of a good or service is significantly higher or lower than the overall inflation rate.

What other items have become relatively cheaper? The biggest declines have come in the technology area (not surprisingly), where televisions, wireless telephone services, personal computers, and related items have dropped dramatically in price.

In contrast, the relative prices of many services have risen as well; their inflation rates have been significantly higher than overall inflation. For example, looking at **Table 8.2**, we see that admissions to sporting events rose at a 2.9 percent annual rate between 2000 and 2022–far faster than the overall inflation rate and probably due to the soaring pay of athletes. Other services with fast-rising prices included medical care and college tuition. (For an example of a recent relative price shift, see "**Spotlight: The Price of Air Travel.**")

SPOTLIGHT: THE PRICE OF AIR TRAVEL

Air travel plunged during the pandemic. But the number of passengers has rebounded, planes are packed full, and delays are common because airports are so congested.

But have airplane tickets become cheaper or more expensive? According to the BLS, the average price of plane tickets rose at an 0.8 percent annual rate between 2000 and 2022. However, over the same period, the overall price index rose at a 2.4 percent annual rate. In other words, air travel became a lot cheaper during that stretch compared with other goods and services. That helps explain why the number of air passengers rebounded so quickly after the pandemic.

Globalization and Inflation

One key reason some goods have become relatively cheaper is globalization. The production of many goods has shifted from the United States and the developed countries of Europe to lower-cost developing countries such as China. That's certainly kept down prices for things like clothing and consumer electronics, which are mostly imported.

In contrast, it is much harder to shift the production of services overseas. When you get your hair cut, the person holding the scissors generally has to be at the same location as you. As a result, it is difficult to import haircuts. Medical care, too, has proven tough to outsource because much of it, from surgery to nursing to physical rehabilitation, has to be delivered in person.

ECONOMIC MILESTONE

1994: The Great Coffee Crunch

Coffee drinkers were hit by a very large relative price shift in 1994 because of a spate of disasters in coffee-growing countries that made coffee beans scarce: insects in Colombia, frost in Brazil, and civil war in Rwanda. A pound of ground roast coffee rose from $2.50 in January of that year to $4.50 by August—a much bigger rise than the overall price level.

But gradually companies are figuring out how to "offshore" parts of service industries. In theory, for example, you could do your homework assignments online and they could be graded by someone in India or the Philippines. Your X-rays can be read by technicians overseas, though that is still not common. As events like these become feasible, the trend for goods to become cheaper relative to services could slow down—or even reverse if the prices of services were to fall low enough.

Quality Improvements and Inflation

When is a price increase not really a price increase? The inflation rate is supposed to measure price changes of a fixed market basket of goods and services. But in the real world, products are always changing. Companies introduce new products and improve their old ones.

Sometimes, the price of a good or service rises because of an **improvement in quality**, which is a change in the nature of a good or service that increases its value for buyers. In that case, we don't count that price increase as part of the inflation rate. Suppose a car manufacturer decides to install antilock braking as a standard feature in all its cars and raises prices by $100 at the same time. According to BLS statisticians, that price increase should not enter into the calculation of inflation because it represents a quality improvement and not merely a price change.

improvement in quality
A change in the nature of a good or service that increases its value for buyers.

When the quality or features of a product change slowly over time, it's relatively easy for the BLS to get a sense of how much of a price increase is related to changes in the product and how much represents a **pure price change**. A pure price change is simply a change in price without any change in the quality or nature of a product.

pure price change
An increase in the price of a good with no change in its quality or characteristics.

The Walkman was an enormous hit in 1979.
Comstock Images/Alamy Stock Photo

However, in areas of the economy where rapid technological change is taking place, an existing product or service can be replaced by one that's different and hard to compare to the original. For example, each generation of personal computers is faster than the one before. That makes the job of measuring inflation more difficult because even when the price seems to stay the same, the actual power of the computer is increasing, which makes computer power cheaper over time.

The same is true of consumer electronics. Consider, for example, the Sony Walkman, which was an enormous hit when it was introduced in 1979. It retailed for about $200 and held one audiocassette's worth of music, or roughly 15 songs. For the first time, people could bring their music with them.

Compare that to the first iPod, which sold for $399 but held about 1,000 songs when Apple introduced it in 2001. If we are calculating the inflation rate for consumer electronics, should the difference between the Walkman and the iPod be counted as a price increase or a price decrease? The first iPod cost a lot more than the first Walkman, but the iPod had a much lower price per song stored (roughly 20 cents compared to about $1.30 for the Walkman).

Today, many people store and play their music on their smartphones. These devices can store about 300 songs per gigabyte of memory. Because the newest smartphones can have 64 gigabytes of memory or more, in theory, they can store 15,000 or more songs. However, it doesn't make sense to compare the cost per song for a smartphone versus an iPod, because smartphones do many more things than simply play music.

The price comparison between the Walkman and the iPod is difficult enough, but at least they perform the same function: playing music on a portable device. Measuring inflation is even harder when technological change is disruptive—that is, when it enables us to do things that weren't realistically possible before.

YOUR ECONOMIC LIFE: The Relative Price of Housing

Where you live will be affected by the relative price of housing. Between 2000 and 2022, the price of rental housing has gone up by 101 percent, compared to a 70 percent increase in the overall price level. That means rental housing has become relatively more expensive compared to everything else.

But even then, some areas are worse than others. Data from the BLS shows the following rental data: Miami (142 percent increase in rental housing prices since 2000), Los Angeles (138 percent increase), Seattle (124 percent increase), San Francisco (108 percent increase), Washington, DC (108 percent increase), and New York (104 percent increase). In all cases, these figures are for the metro area of these cities, rather than just the core city.

On the other hand, if you want a location with a low inflation rate for rental housing, you might want to check out the whole Midwest, with only a 75 percent increase in rental housing prices since 2000. St. Louis had only a 73 percent increase, Detroit a 76 percent, and Atlanta, in the Southeast region, only a 85 percent increase. That's a much smaller increase than national rents.

Of course, when you make your location decision, you'll want to think about jobs as well. The problem, of course, is that the cities with more job growth—like Miami and Seattle—also tend to have bigger price increases for rental housing, as the strong job growth drives the demand curve for rental housing to the right. As with everything else in economics, your housing choices are about making trade-offs.

ADJUSTING FOR INFLATION (LO8-3)

LO8-3 Calculate and show how incomes and wages can be adjusted for inflation.

In 1979, the typical U.S. household had an income of about $16,461. As of 2021, the typical household had an income of about $70784 (where *typical* is defined as the median household, so half of U.S. households receive less than this household and half receive more). At first glance, it looks as though incomes have more than quadrupled over this 42-year stretch.

But, in fact, most of that apparent gain in income is canceled out by inflation. Over that same 42-year period, the average price level has more than tripled as well. Some items have risen even more. College costs have skyrocketed: A year of tuition, room, and board at Yale University was $8,140 in the 1979-1980 school year. As of the 2023-2024 school year, it was about $84,000, an increase of more than 10 times.

So, if you merely compared household income over time without looking at changes in prices, you would run the risk of suffering from **money illusion**. Money illusion is the mistake that we make when we compare dollar amounts in different periods without adjusting for inflation.

> **money illusion**
> The mistake of comparing dollar amounts in different time periods without adjusting for inflation.

Here's an example of money illusion. From 1955 to 1960, on a television show called *The Millionaire,* an eccentric old industrialist supposedly gave away a million dollars each week to a lucky person (it was staged, though). In 1999, a new television show called *Who Wants to Be a Millionaire* debuted, on which contestants answered Regis Philbin's questions with the ultimate goal of winning a million dollars. But when we look at the statistics published by the BLS, we see that inflation has taken its toll on the prize: The average price level rose by more than six times between 1955 and 1999. So, Regis would have to have given away more than $6 million to match the purchasing power of that anonymous (and fake) 1955 millionaire.

Avoiding Money Illusion

Suppose we have a quantity measured in dollars over time, such as our salary, the budget of our city or state, the price of our home, or the amount of money we have in the bank. To avoid money illusion, we must compare the change in these dollar figures with the inflation rate.

For example, suppose you are working and earning $50,000 per year. Your boss offers you a 3 percent raise of $1,500. Is that good news? It depends on the inflation rate. If inflation is running at 2 percent per year, then your 3 percent raise gives you an increase in purchasing power. But if the inflation rate is 4 percent, you are actually losing purchasing power because even with the increase, your income is going up more slowly than the average price level.

To avoid money illusion, the solution is to use the **real change**, which is the change in the money value after removing the effects of inflation (this is also sometimes called the **inflation-adjusted change**). A good rule of thumb for calculating the real change is to take the percentage change in dollars minus the inflation rate (there is a more precise formula for calculating the real change, which we show in the next section). We call the increase or decrease in a money value without adjusting for inflation the **nominal change**. So, if your nominal percentage change in wages is 3 percent, and the inflation rate is 2 percent, then your real increase in wages is 3 percent minus 2 percent, or 1 percent.

> **real change**
> The change in a quantity adjusted for inflation. See *inflation-adjusted change.*

> **inflation-adjusted change**
> The change in a money value after removing the effects of inflation.

> **nominal change**
> The increase or decrease in a monetary value over time without adjusting for inflation.

We can apply the same principle to any other economic quantity measured in dollars. For example, it's important to adjust for inflation when we're looking at government budgets. Spending by a government agency may rise—but if it doesn't go up as fast as inflation, then the real value of the budget is falling and the agency is actually spending less, not more.

One example is federal spending on elementary and secondary education, which includes direct grants to the states, as well as things like the early education program Head Start, which assists children from low-income families. Federal spending on elementary and secondary education rose from $39.7 billion in 2006 to $40 billion in 2007; that was an 0.8 percent increase. But with inflation running at about 2.5 percent in 2007, real federal education spending actually declined by 1.7 percent (0.8-2.5%).

Real versus Nominal Dollars

The rule of thumb for calculating the real increase works well in most situations. But the most precise way to avoid money illusion is to transform the original dollar figures (also called *nominal* dollars) into *real* dollars (also called *inflation-adjusted* dollars).

How do we do this? We pick a base year—say, 2022. We then use the CPI to adjust the nominal dollar figures for any other year to get real figures that eliminate the effects of inflation. The result is reported in "2022 dollars" or whatever the base year is.

Let's give a simple example first. Suppose that you earned $100,000 in 2021. Your boss decides to give you a raise of 8 percent in 2022, or $8,000 (that's 8 percent × $100,000). That seems like a fair amount of money.

But then you realize that the inflation rate in 2022 is 8 percent also, which cancels out your entire raise. In other words, your 2022 salary, expressed in 2022 dollars, is still $100,000. There's been no change in your real salary at all!

SPOTLIGHT: WHICH MOVIE EARNED MORE MONEY?

In 2022, the top-grossing film was *Top Gun: Maverick,* with domestic ticket sales of $700 million. We can compare that to the first *Star Wars* film, which earned a seemingly far less impressive $307 million in domestic ticket sales in 1977 when it was first released in movie theaters, according to *Box Office Mojo.*

But it turns out that, when we adjust for inflation, the young Han Solo and Luke Skywalker soundly beat Top Gun. Measured in 2022 dollars, the first *Star Wars* took in an astounding $1.5 billion in domestic ticket sales in its first movie theater run.

Source: www.boxofficemojo.com, Bureau of Labor Statistics.

Table 8.3 Calculating Real Wages

This table shows how we can use the consumer price index to transform nominal hourly wages into real hourly wages.

	Consumer Price Index	Inflation Adjustment to "2022 Dollars"	Nominal Average Hourly Wage in Dollars	Real Average Hourly Wage in 2022 Dollars
2007	255.7	292.7/255.7 = 1.144	27.99	$32.02
2018	292.7	292.7/292.7 = 1	32.25	$32.25

Source: Bureau of Labor Statistics, www.bls.gov.

Here is a formula for transforming a nominal amount into a real amount:

Real money amount = Nominal money amount × (Consumer price index for base year/Consumer price index for current year)

For example, suppose we wanted to calculate real wages in 2022 dollars. According to the BLS, in 2019, just before the pandemic, the average hourly wage for all workers was $27.99. By 2022, the average hourly wage had risen to $32.25. At first glance, that seems like a pretty good increase.

But, over the same stretch, the CPI rose from 207.3 in 2019 to 251.1 in 2022. So, the real hourly wage in 2019, expressed in 2022 dollars, is:

Real hourly wage in 2019 = $27.99 × (292.7/255.7)

This calculation is outlined in **Table 8.3**. The third column reports the nominal wage for the 2 years. The fourth column reports the real wage, which is obtained by multiplying the second column–the inflation adjustment–by the nominal wage in the third column.

As shown in **Table 8.3**, the real hourly wage in 2019 was $32.02, measured in 2022 dollars. That's just a bit lower than the $32.25 average hourly wage in 2022. So, shifting to real dollars has shown us that wages, adjusted for inflation, went up between 2019 and 2022, but far less than it appeared at first.

EXPECTATIONS AND INFLATION (LO8-4)

LO8-4 Discuss the impact of unexpected and expected inflation.

expected inflation
The inflation rate that consumers and businesses expect will happen over the next year or longer.

wage-price spiral
A situation that occurs when businesses and workers boost prices and wages to try to stay ahead of rising expected inflation.

So far, we've been discussing how the average price level has changed over time. In effect, we've been looking backward and comparing different years. Now we will look forward into the future and introduce the intriguing idea of **expected inflation**. Expected inflation, as the name implies, is the inflation rate that consumers and businesses expect will happen over the next year or even further into the future.

Expected inflation forms the basis for pricing and wage decisions that businesses make. For example, if you are a company manager, and you expect a 1 percent inflation rate over the next year, you know your workers will need a 1 percent raise to stay even with inflation, and you will need to raise your prices by 1 percent to cover your increased costs of doing business. Or if you are proposing a budget for a government agency and the expected rate of inflation is 3 percent, you start with the assumption that the agency will need a budget increase of 3 percent if it is to deliver the same services next year.

Businesses and individuals form their inflation expectations based on their recent experience. So, if inflation has been running at only 2 percent a year, people generally expect that low rate to continue. If inflation is 10 percent a year, that gets built into expectations as well. There's a certain amount of inertia in expectations.

Expected inflation can be changed by events. For example, if the price of gasoline soars from, say, $2 a gallon to $6 a gallon, there's a risk that people will now expect that this higher rate of inflation will continue. A **wage-price spiral** occurs when businesses and workers boost prices and wages faster and faster to stay ahead of higher expected inflation. An economy stuck in a wage-price spiral is like a dog chasing its own tail. Expected inflation rises, so everyone boosts prices and wages more, which drives up expected inflation even faster.

SPOTLIGHT: THE OIL TRIGGER

What starts a wage–price spiral? One cause, at least in the United States, is a sharp rise in oil prices. Because every industry needs energy, an oil price increase affects every part of the economy. That puts pressure on many companies to raise prices.

The biggest oil price shock came in 1973 after Egypt and Syria invaded Israel. While the war was still going on, the Arab oil-producing countries—led by Saudi Arabia, Kuwait, Iran, and Iraq—announced a sharp cut in oil production. In addition, these companies put an embargo on oil exports to the United States and some other western European countries that were supporting Israel.

The oil embargo sent prices leaping—not just the prices of gasoline and heating fuel, but all sorts of other prices, too. Businesses of all kinds had to pay higher energy costs to run their factories, heat and cool their offices, and transport their goods. As a result, they hiked the prices for their products. On top of that, companies had to invest a lot of money to buy more energy-efficiency equipment to try to use less energy.

The results were a big jump in the general price level (inflation) and a corresponding rise in expected inflation. What followed was a wage–price spiral that sent the inflation rate over 10 percent. Another oil price shock in 1979 followed the Iranian Revolution that deposed the Shah of Iran. Again, energy prices soared, and both inflation and inflation expectations rose. As we will see in **Chapter 12**, the wage–price spiral did not end until the Federal Reserve took drastic action.

More recently, oil prices spiked in 2022 because of the Russian invasion of Ukraine. As of the revision of this textbook in early 2023, it's not certain whether the latest oil shock has caused a wage–price spiral.

Hyperinflation

In the extreme case, inflation turns into **hyperinflation**—where prices soar at 20 percent, 50 percent, or more per year. The United States has not seen hyperinflation in recent memory, but other countries have. When hyperinflation hits, businesses and workers have no choice but to start building expected inflation into prices and wages, and inflation gets deeply embedded into the economy. If you were running a restaurant, you would no longer print menus. Instead, you might put up a chalkboard with prices on it and raise the prices every day—or even twice a day.

hyperinflation
A very rapid increase in the average price level.

Governments fervently want to avoid hyperinflation because it completely undercuts citizens' faith in the value of their money. In this situation, if workers are paid for their jobs in the morning, the value of the money has substantially fallen by the afternoon. People stop thinking about the future.

The most famous hyperinflation episode occurred in Germany in the 1920s. In 1919, one dollar was worth 8.9 German marks (a *mark* was the German currency at the time). By 1923, one dollar was worth *1 trillion* marks. In effect, German money was worth nothing, and barter became the order of the day. People's savings, pensions, and life insurance became valueless. Most economic historians believe that the economic devastation from this hyperinflation was one factor that, by disrupting the German economy and undermining faith in the government, laid the groundwork for the Nazi takeover of Germany in the 1930s.

Brazilian cruzados replaced cruzeiros to cope with hyperinflation.

Ben Molyneux/Alamy Stock Photo

More recently, several South American countries have experienced hyperinflation, though not as bad as the German case. From 1989 to 1994, Brazil endured several years of inflation greater than 1,000 percent, which means that prices rose by 10 times in a year. In 1985, Bolivia's inflation rate was more than 11,000 percent. That means average prices went up by more than 100 times over the year. Or to put it a different way, a dollar would be worth a penny by the end of the year, and if a newspaper cost $1 at the beginning of the year, it would cost $100 by December.

To cope with hyperinflation, countries have to keep issuing currency in bigger and bigger denominations. For example, during its period of hyperinflation, Bolivia issued currency bills worth 10 million bolivianos each (the boliviano was the Bolivian currency then). Another alternative is to change the name of the currency and replace old bills with new ones. For example, in 1986 Brazil replaced its former currency, the cruzeiro, with the cruzado. The conversion formula was that each cruzado replaced 1,000 cruzeiros (in 1986, $1 was worth about 13 cruzados).

The latest country to experience hyperinflation was Venezuela. Inflation started accelerating in 2016 and went over 100,000 percent per year in 2018.

The Harm from Unexpected Inflation

What damage does inflation do? We'll examine two different cases. In this section, we'll look at the impacts of *unexpected inflation*, when the actual inflation rate is much higher than expected. In the next section, we'll consider more downsides of *expected inflation*.

unexpected inflation
The sudden acceleration of the rate of price increases above expected inflation.

Unexpected inflation happens when the rate of price increases suddenly accelerates well above what businesses and individuals were expecting. For anyone who is locked into a long-term contract of any sort, that makes a big difference. If you are supposed to *receive* money, unexpected inflation is bad for you. If you are supposed to *pay* money, unexpected inflation is good for you.

HOW IT WORKS: WHY UNEXPECTED INFLATION HURTS LENDERS

To understand how unexpected inflation hurts lenders, let's consider the simple example of a candy economy. Amanda has $10, which can buy a nice box of chocolates. But, instead, she lends Sam the $10 for a month, expecting to get back $10 plus $2 in interest (she figures the $2 will allow her to buy a soda to go along with the chocolate).

Unfortunately, over the month, there is a sudden shortage of cocoa, and the price of a box of chocolate doubles to $20. So, at the end of the month, when Sam gives Amanda $12 (the $10 plus interest), she can no longer afford the nice box of chocolates. Instead, she has to settle for some M&Ms. As a lender, she has become the victim of an unexpected surge of candy inflation. If she had known this was coming, she would have asked for more interest or simply bought the chocolate before its price went up.

For example, consider the situation of lenders. A loan involves a transfer of money from lender to borrower, plus a promise from the borrower to pay back the money with interest some time in the future. For example, the bank might lend you $100 with the requirement that you will pay back the money, plus $10 in interest, next year.

The problem for the lender is that if the price level unexpectedly jumps, that means borrowers get to pay back their loans with less valuable dollars. Suppose inflation unexpectedly turns out to be 10 percent for the year. When the bank receives repayment of its loan, the repayment is worth 10 percent less. In fact, if the inflation rate is high enough, the bank may actually lose money on the loan. Unexpected inflation helps borrowers, at least temporarily, because they are paying back their loans with inflated dollars (see "**How It Works: Why Unexpected Inflation Hurts Lenders**").

But the benefits to borrowers from unexpected inflation evaporate as soon as lenders realize that prices are rising. At that point, they start raising their interest rates to compensate for the fact they are getting paid back in inflated dollars. That's what happened in the early part of the 1980s, when lenders kept interest rates high because they worried about a recurrence of the inflation of the 1970s.

The Harm from Expected Inflation

expected inflation
The inflation rate that consumers and businesses expect will happen over the next year or longer.

cost-of-living adjustments (COLAs)
An automatic rise in wages to compensate for inflation.

What happens if everyone expects the same rate of inflation that actually occurs? What is the harm from **expected inflation**? We've already mentioned hyperinflation. But what if inflation were only 7 percent or so? It might seem that expected inflation would be harmless if wages and salaries rise at the same rate as prices. If prices go up by 7 percent and wages go up by 7 percent, everyone is in the same relative situation they were in before, and nothing has really changed. In fact, one response to the high-inflation era of the 1970s was to put **cost-of-living adjustments (COLAs)** into many union contracts and government programs such as Social Security. A COLA automatically raises wages to compensate for inflation so that if inflation is 7 percent, wages rise by 7 percent. Similarly, Social Security recipients have been protected from inflation since 1972: Their payments rise along with consumer prices.

However, over time, even expected inflation is a problem. First, if employers automatically bump up wages for inflation, they will have to raise prices to compensate for their increased costs. Thus, COLAs build inflation into the economy and make a wage-price spiral more likely.

Second, economists have learned that higher levels of inflation are less predictable. If inflation is running at 2 percent this year, you can be pretty sure it will be close to 2 percent next year. But an inflation rate of 7 percent could be 12 percent or 3 percent next year. This makes it hard for businesses and households to make good decisions.

Finally, high levels of inflation increase the **cost of transactions**–the time and effort that go into managing your spending. If inflation is low, you can keep spending money in your checking account, where it is easy to get to, because you don't have to worry about it losing value. But if the average price level is rising quickly, you don't want to keep much money in cash or checking accounts because it quickly loses value. So, you have to spend a lot of time making sure your money is in money market funds or someplace else where it will earn a high enough return to compensate for inflation.

cost of transactions

The time and effort that go into managing spending.

The consensus among most economists is that policymakers should aim to keep inflation low–in the words of former Federal Reserve Chairman Alan Greenspan, "so low and stable over time that it does not materially enter into the decisions of households and firms." That level is generally accepted to be around 2 percent a year.

Deflation

If inflation is undesirable, why not strive for *deflation*? **Deflation** is an actual fall in the average price level. Don't confuse it with *disinflation,* which is a reduction in the inflation rate. If the inflation rate is 5 percent one year and 4 percent the next, that's disinflation. But if the inflation rate is −1 percent, that's deflation.

deflation

An actual fall in the average price level.

After the inflation shocks of the 1970s, economists were much more worried about inflation than deflation. However, until the pandemic, inflation had slowed in most industrialized countries, in some cases getting close to zero. In Japan, the average price index in 2019 was barely above year 2000 levels.

Economists generally agree that sustained deflation is not good for an economy. First, deflation usually means demand is so weak that businesses cannot raise their prices and workers cannot ask for higher wages. In order words, deflation is a sign of a poorly functioning economy.

The second problem with deflation has to do with loans. Remember that inflation hurts lenders because borrowers pay back loans in dollars that are worth less than expected. In the same way, deflation hurts borrowers because they are paying back loans with dollars that are worth more than expected. Indeed, if deflation hits wages as well as prices, your income may drop, but the size of that loan you took out stays the same. That's not a recipe for a happy life.

In the aftermath of the Great Recession of 2008-2009, avoiding deflation became a major goal for economic policymakers in the United States, Japan, and Europe. However, after the pandemic, inflation once again became more of a concern than deflation.

CONCLUSION

We've seen how inflation can change our picture of the economy. A high rate of inflation can eat away at the value of household income, wages, and any other monetary quantities.

But prices are not the only things that change over time. In the next chapter, we will see how the economy's output changes over time as well.

08 SUMMARY

1. Inflation is a sustained upward movement in the average level of prices. The inflation rate is the annual percentage change in the average price level or its equivalent, the Consumer Price Index (CPI). The inflation rate in 2022, for example, was the percentage change in the CPI from 2021 to 2022. ***(LO8-1)***
2. A relative price shift happens when the inflation rate of a good or service is significantly higher or lower than the overall inflation rate. Some goods or services have been getting relatively cheaper over time, whereas others have been getting relatively more expensive. ***(LO8-2)***
3. Money illusion occurs when we compare dollar amounts in different periods without adjusting for inflation. To avoid money illusion, we need to adjust nominal changes in dollar amounts by the rate of inflation to get real changes. ***(LO8-3)***

4. Expected inflation is the inflation rate that consumers and businesses expect will hold over the next year. Unexpected inflation happens when the rate of price increases suddenly accelerates above expected inflation. Unexpected inflation hurts lenders and anyone who is supposed to receive money under a long-term contract. Unexpected inflation helps anyone who is supposed to pay money under a long-term contract. A high level of expected inflation is harmful because it makes a wage-price spiral more likely, because it is unpredictable, and because it increases the cost of transactions. *(LO8-4)*

KEY TERMS AND CONCEPTS

average level of prices

market basket

consumer price index (CPI)

inflation

inflation rate

core inflation

relative price shift

improvement in quality

pure price change

money illusion

real change

inflation-adjusted change

nominal change

expected inflation

wage-price spiral

hyperinflation

unexpected inflation

expected inflation

cost-of-living adjustments (COLAs)

cost of transactions

deflation

connect PROBLEMS

1. Which of the following statements is not true? *(LO8-1)*
   a) When the average price level rises, the price of all goods and services goes up.
   b) Owners' equivalent rent of primary residence is the biggest part of the market basket in the consumer price index (CPI).
   c) The market basket for the CPI represents the expenditures of a typical person.
   d) The CPI tracks the average price level.
2. The following table gives the value of the CPI for 2011 through 2022. *(LO8-1)*

Year	Consumer Price Index
2011	224.9
2012	229.6
2013	233.0
2014	236.7
2015	237.0
2016	240.0
2017	245.1
2018	251.1
2019	255.7
2020	258.8
2021	271.0
2022	292.7

   a) Use the data in the table to calculate the inflation rate in 2013.
   b) Use the data in the table to calculate the inflation rate in 2017.
   c) What was the percentage increase in the average price level from 2011 to 2022?

3. The following table reports the average prices of gasoline and apples, as well as the CPI for 3 years. ***(LO8-2)***

	Gasoline (Price per Gallon)	Red Delicious Apples (Price per Pound)	Consumer Price Index (1982–1984 = 100)
1995	$1.15	$0.83	152.4
2005	$2.30	$0.95	195.3
2015	$2.45	$1.36	237.0

a) What was the percentage increase in the price of gasoline from 1995 to 2005?
b) Did the relative price of gasoline rise or fall from 1995 to 2005? (Remember that the relative price of a product rises if its percentage increase in price is bigger than the percentage increase in the CPI.)
c) Did the relative price of gasoline rise or fall from 2005 to 2015?
d) Did the relative price of apples rise or fall from 1995 to 2005?

4. Say whether each of the following represents a pure price change or an improvement in quality. ***(LO8-2)***

a) The price of a home goes up.
b) The price of a home goes up after a complete renovation.
c) The latest model of a car is more expensive than the previous model, but it also has more features.
d) The price of a peach rises.

5. Suppose you are a Social Security recipient. In 2022, you receive $1,600 per month in Social Security benefits. In October of that year, the Social Security Administration announces that the cost-of-living adjustment for 2023 will be 8.7 percent, roughly matching the inflation rate***(LO8-3)***

a) How much will your 2023 monthly benefits be?
b) In real terms, do your benefits go up, go down, or stay the same?

6. One of the biggest decisions most of us have to make is which industry to look for work in. Compensation matters, but it also matters whether pay is rising or falling. The following table gives the annual average pay in five major industries for 2011 and 2021 (the figures include the pay of all workers, including top managers). ***(LO8-3)***

Average Annual Wages and Salaries (Dollars)*

Industry	2011	2021
Manufacturers	61,687	79,465
Retail trade	32,572	46,279
Finance and insurance	91,987	134,108
Computer systems design and programming	102,641	151,790
Hospitals	58,539	78,034

*Per full-time worker.

Source: Bureau of Economic Analysis.

a) Calculate the percentage increase in pay for each industry from 2011 to 2021.
b) What was the real percentage increase in pay for each industry from 2011 to 2021, using the rule of thumb that the real percentage increase is roughly the nominal percentage increase minus the inflation rate? (The CPI in 2011 was 224.9, and the CPI in 2021 was 271.0.)
c) Which industry had the biggest increase in real wages?

7. The sports pages are always filled with news of the latest big contract an athlete has received. The following table shows the average price for major league baseball tickets for 4 years, the average player salary, and the CPI for those years. ***(LO8-3)***

	Average Ticket Price for Major League Baseball (Dollars)	Consumer Price Index (1982–1984 = 100)	Average Player Salary (Millions of Dollars)
2001	17.64	177.1	$2.14
2010	26.74	218.1	$3.31
2015	28.94	237.0	$4.25
2018	32,44	251.1	$4.52

Source: Team Marketing Report, Associated Press, USA Today.

a) Calculate the real percentage increase in ticket prices from 2001 to 2015, and from 2015 to 2018.
b) Calculate the real percentage increase in player salaries from 2001 to 2015, and from 2015 to 2018.
c) Between 2001 and 2015, total attendance at major league baseball games grew from 72.5 million to 73.8 million, despite the increase in real ticket prices. Using what you learned from **Chapter 3**, state whether this increase in attendance is more likely to represent a supply shift or a demand shift in the market for baseball tickets.
d) From the information provided below, do you think the rise in player salaries is the main cause of the rise in ticket prices? Explain.

8. Suppose the annual inflation rate has been 3 percent for several years. Then, without warning, it soars to 10 percent a year. Will each of the following individuals or businesses win or lose from such unexpected inflation? ***(LO8-4)***

   a) A tenant renting an apartment with a lease that fixes the rent for the next 3 years.
   b) An automobile dealer who has leased a car to a buyer for 3 years with fixed payments.
   c) A bank that has lent money to a family to buy a home with interest rates fixed for the next 30 years.

9. Which situation would most economists prefer? ***(LO8-4)***

   a) An unexpected drop in the inflation rate from 5 percent to 0 percent.
   b) A steady 2 percent inflation rate.
   c) An unexpected climb in the inflation rate from 3 percent to 6 percent.
   d) An expected decline in the inflation rate from 3 percent to −2 percent.

CH 09

GROWTH

Barrett Hedges/Getty Images

LEARNING OBJECTIVES

After reading this chapter, you should be able to:

LO9-1 Explain the benefits of economic growth.
LO9-2 Calculate the economic growth rate.
LO9-3 Discuss the short-term and long-term change in living standards, and calculate real GDP per capita.
LO9-4 List the forces driving economic growth.
LO9-5 Explain the role of government in economic growth.
LO9-6 Discuss the history of U.S. productivity growth.

Here's the most important fact about modern economies: Almost without exception, they grow over the long run. True, in 2020, the United States was hit by a pandemic-related economic downturn that temporarily cut the production of goods and services. But the general trend is still upward, both in the United States and in most other countries. For example, as of 2022, the global economy was about 34 percent larger than it was in 2012, 10 years earlier.

This record of success is encouraging and challenging at the same time. It's encouraging because when a country produces more goods and services, almost everyone is better off. An expanding economy almost always boosts living standards for the poor; frees up resources for the public sector, including dealing with emergencies like the pandemic; and lets the middle class enjoy more luxuries. But an expanding economy can be challenging because economic growth in a market economy often requires change and turmoil that make people uncomfortable.

In this chapter, we will look at the benefits of economic growth. We will explore how growth is defined and measured. Finally, we will look at the key factors that help drive a country's economic growth over the long run.

THE SIGNIFICANCE OF GROWTH (LO9-1)

LO9-1 Explain the benefits of economic growth.

economic growth
The increase in an economy's production of goods and services. Usually measured by the growth in gross domestic product adjusted for inflation.

What does it mean for an economy to grow from one year to the next? Simply put, an economy experiences **economic growth** if its production of goods and services increases. For example, suppose we have a simple economy that produces only one product: haircuts. This economy grows if its barbers and hairdressers begin providing more haircuts than in the past. (When an economy is growing, we also say it is "getting bigger.")

Improved Living Standards

Of course, actual economies usually produce a much wider range of goods and services than just haircuts. In general, a growing economy usually produces more necessities, such as more food, better housing, and easier access to education and health care. A growing economy also generates more resources for leisure, recreation, and entertainment. In other words, economic growth makes most people better off in many different ways, both tangible and intangible.

What does this mean in concrete terms? Here's a simple comparison. Today, thanks to economic growth, virtually all homes in the United States have complete plumbing facilities (defined as hot and cold running water, a bathtub or shower, and a flushable toilet). But as recently as 1940, almost half of all U.S. homes lacked one or more of these essentials. That means a big change has occurred in the quality of daily life.

Or take something essential like the survival rate of newborns. In 1950, there were 29 infant deaths for every 1,000 live births in the United States. Over the next half century, the U.S. economy grew enough to make it possible to devote more resources to better health care for pregnant women and newborns. As a result, the infant mortality rate plunged to only 5.4 infant deaths per 1,000 live births in 2020. That's still not as low as in some other industrialized countries, but it's far better than in the past.

On the lighter side, a bigger economy can also provide more variety in entertainment. In the 1960s, a typical household had access to fewer than 10 broadcast television channels. Then cable television raised the number of available channels to 100 or more. Today, the Internet opens a vast number of entertainment choices. And at least before the pandemic, people were not just sitting in front of screens—they were going more places as well (see **"Spotlight: Growth and Travel"**).

SPOTLIGHT: GROWTH AND TRAVEL

The pandemic interrupted a long boom in international travel (see **Figure 9.1**). The number of passengers on international flights to and from the United States rose from about 156 million in 2007 to 240 million in 2019, an increase of more than 50 percent.

That was an amazing rise, reflecting both international business travel and increased overseas tourism. Overseas travel is expensive, requiring enough money for a plane ticket, hotel rooms, and shopping. So, a sure sign of economic growth in a country is when people have enough money and leisure time to travel overseas.

As the chart shows, the pandemic sent international travel plummeting in 2020 and 2021, before a decent revival in 2022 (the latest data available as this textbook is updated). If no other disasters intervene, we would expect the number of international passengers to keep climbing as the world economy keeps growing.

Figure 9.1 Passengers on International Flights to and from the United States (millions)

The growth of international travel was interrupted by the pandemic but has since rebounded.

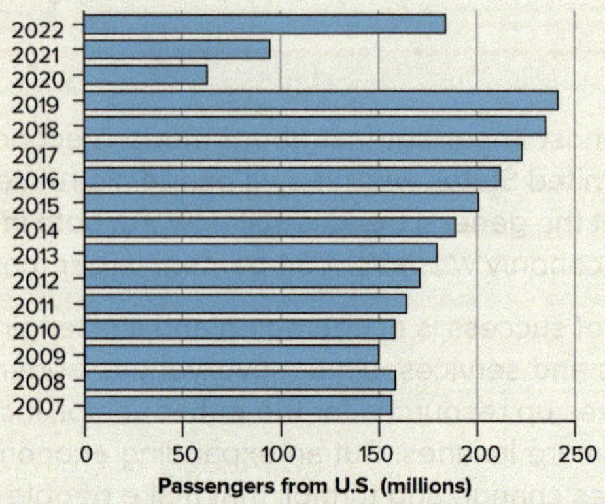

Source: Bureau of Transportation Statistics. Data include a small number of passengers carried on U.S. carriers between foreign airports.

Production Possibility Frontier

One consequence of economic growth is that it gives us more choices. To see this, we will define the **production possibility frontier (PPF)** as all the combinations of different goods and services the economy is capable of producing at a particular time, assuming full use of all resources. To illustrate, let's look at a PPF for two outputs: health care and entertainment, as shown in **Figure 9.2**. The PPF shows the different combinations of health care and entertainment the economy can achieve given our current state of knowledge and physical inputs. (Of course, we could draw a PPF with any other two goods and services the economy can produce, like food and cars, or haircuts and homes.)

production possibility frontier (PPF)
All the combinations of different goods and services the economy is capable of producing at a particular time, assuming full use of all resources.

Figure 9.2 The Production Possibility Frontier (PPF)
This example of a PPF shows all the combinations of entertainment and health care the economy can produce in a year. Point *A* shows one possible combination, as indicated by the dotted lines.

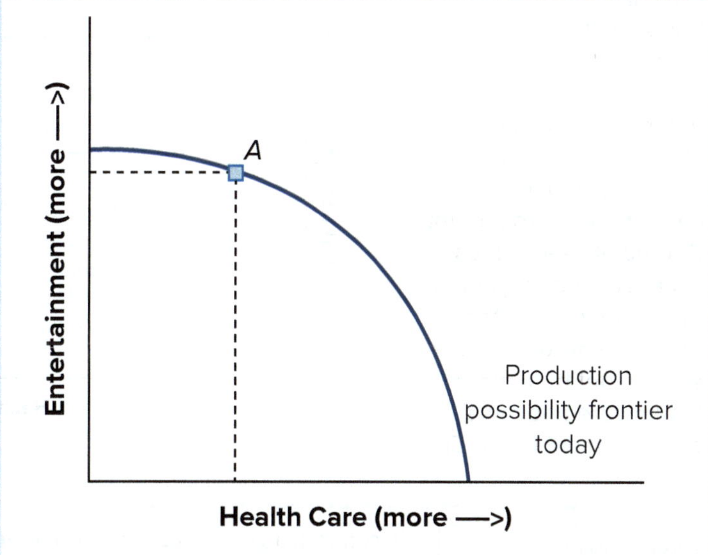

In this figure, the vertical axis measures the amount of entertainment the economy can produce, whereas the horizontal axis measures the amount of health care the economy can produce. The curved line shows all the different combinations of health care and entertainment that are possible. We can build hospitals, or movie studios, or some combination of them. Point *A* in the figure shows one possible combination of health care and entertainment that the economy can produce in a year.

If the economy grows, the PPF moves outward, as shown in **Figure 9.3**. That is, the economy has a greater capability of producing more health care, more entertainment, or both. Point *B* is one possible combination of health care and entertainment, but the economy is capable of producing any other combination on the PPF.

Figure 9.3 Growth and the PPF
As the economy grows, the production possibility frontier shifts outward. In this figure, growth means that it's possible to get more of both health care and entertainment. Point *B* corresponds to more health care and entertainment than point *A*, as the dotted lines show.

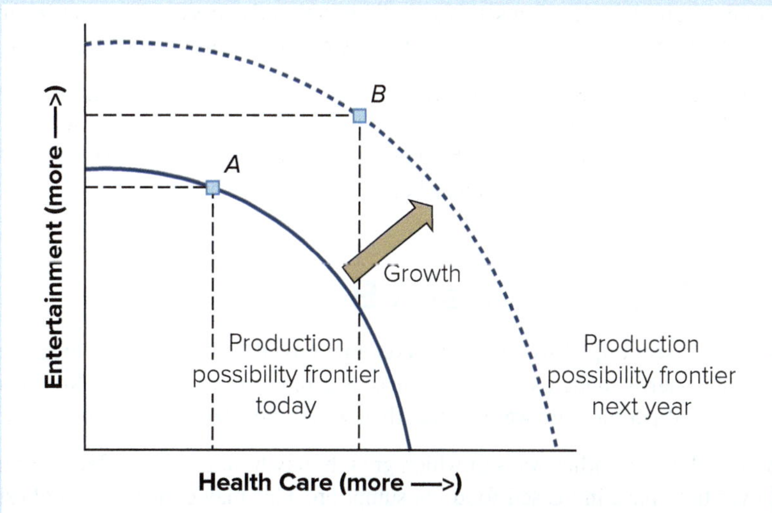

Growth versus the Zero-Sum Economy

zero-sum economy
When the only way an economy can produce more of something is to produce less of something else.

If there is no growth, we have a **zero-sum economy**. This means if we want the economy to produce more of something—say health care—we have to accept less of something else—perhaps entertainment. In **Figure 9.4**, if we are stuck on the same PPF (that is, no growth), then moving from point *A* to point *C* gives us more health care and less entertainment.

Figure 9.4 A Zero-Sum versus a Non-Zero-Sum Economy
Suppose there is an economy that produces only health care and entertainment. In the absence of growth, getting more health care—moving from point *A* to point *C*—requires accepting less entertainment. However, if the economy grows, it's possible to get both more health care and more entertainment (point *B*).

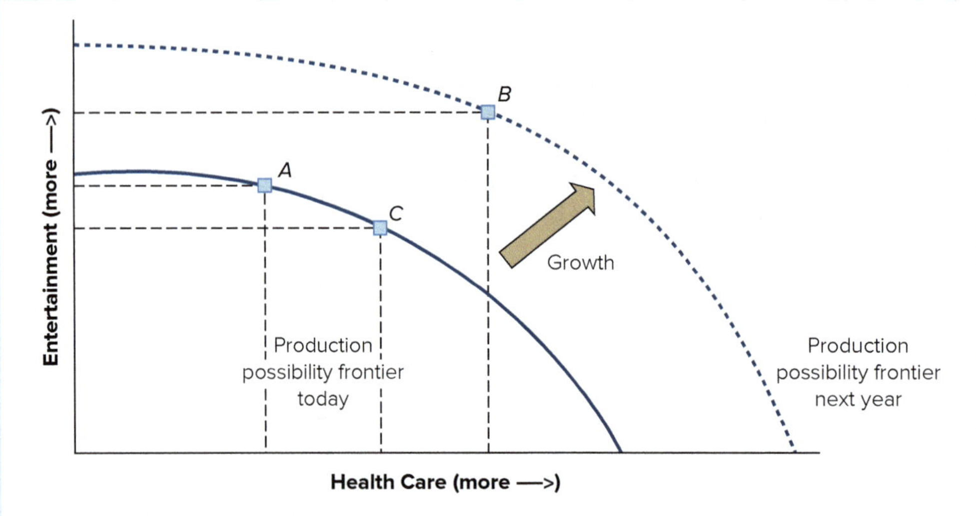

non-zero-sum economy
Occurs when an economy can produce more of one good or service without having to curtail production of another.

In contrast, a growing economy is **non-zero-sum**. So, as the PPF moves outward, we could potentially get more of both health care and entertainment (point *B* in **Figure 9.4**).

This argument can be extended to income distribution. In an economy without growth, the only way for someone to get more goods and services is for someone else to get less—like kids squabbling over a piece of cake. More specifically, without growth, the only way to make low-income households better off is to take money away from middle-income or high-income households. (We'll examine income distribution in more detail in **Chapter 17**.)

On the other hand, it is possible for everyone to see their incomes rise if the economy gets bigger. In a growing economy, both rich and poor can enjoy a rising standard of living.

In fact, that is what has happened in the United States over the past 75 years. As the U.S. economy expanded after World War II, the living standard of poor people in the United States improved as well. Fewer people went hungry, the quality of housing rose, and virtually everyone acquired a television set. Now cell phones and access to the Internet are fast spreading into low-income households. As of 2022, roughly 90 percent of U.S. households had a wired broadband connection at home.

In the poorest countries, economic growth can make a tremendous difference for the people at the bottom of the income ladder—even in something as basic as whether they have enough food to eat. As we will see later in this chapter, China was able to maintain strong growth from the early 1980s until the pandemic hit, and India from the early 1990s. The result has been a sharp fall in the proportions of their populations that are undernourished.

What Growth Doesn't Buy

To finish this section, let us be clear: Economic growth is not the only measure of a successful society. As we saw in **Chapter 7**, growth has not necessarily made us happier, at least judging by recent surveys. No one did such surveys back in 1900, but we cannot dismiss the possibility that people then were poorer than we are now but just as happy.

Moreover, there are other ways in which growth may have negative effects. Economic research suggests that the falling relative prices of food over time have increased food consumption. This may contribute to obesity—one of the key health issues facing the United States today. (We'll discuss the economics of health care in **Chapter 18**.)

Finally, as we'll see in **Chapter 19**, published figures on economic growth leave out the issue of its impact on the environment, including global warming. Some of the impacts are quite serious, but we do not account for them when measuring growth.

Still, all other things being equal, economists generally believe that economic growth is a positive event. Few people cheer if government statisticians announce a low growth number.

MEASURING GROWTH (LO9-2)

LO9-2 Calculate the economic growth rate.

A typical economy produces a wide variety of goods and services, such as food, homes, cars, haircuts, and television shows. From **Chapter 7**, we already know we can combine these different goods and services into one number, *gross domestic product* (GDP), which measures the output of an economy in dollars. An increase in GDP over time can indicate economic growth.

However, we have to be careful here. There are two reasons the dollar amount of output might rise, and only one of them counts as economic growth. First, an economy may actually be producing more food, homes, cars, haircuts, and so forth. Or it may be producing the same amount of goods and services–or even less–but prices have gone up. That is, inflation may make it look as though the economy has grown more than it really has. How do we know the truth?

The solution is to adjust GDP growth for inflation. In practice, that's a challenging task. Each quarter, statisticians at the Bureau of Economic Analysis (BEA) in Washington estimate the average price level for the whole economy, using hundreds of thousands of pieces of data. This is not the consumer price index with its basket of typical goods, but a broader measure that covers the prices of *all* items that go into GDP, including business investment, government consumption and investment, and foreign trade.

The BEA then adjusts GDP for inflation, using its estimate of the average price level for the whole economy. The result is called **real GDP**, which is GDP adjusted for inflation. For the U.S. economy, real GDP is usually measured in 2012 dollars (as we defined in **Chapter 8**). When real GDP is increasing, that means that the output of the economy, adjusted for inflation, is increasing as well. As a result, economic growth is measured by the growth in real GDP over time.

real GDP
Gross domestic product, adjusted for inflation.

When real GDP growth is positive, the economy's production of goods and services is increasing, and the economy is growing. For example, in 2004, the economic growth rate of the U.S. economy was 3.9 percent. That means the economy produced 3.8 percent more goods and services in 2004 than in 2003.

Looking at **Figure 9.5**, we can see clear signs of the Great Recession and the pandemic. Real GDP growth was negative in 2008 and 2009, and then again in 2020. When growth is negative, that means the economy is shrinking.

Figure 9.5
Economic Growth, 1960–2022
This figure shows the economic growth rate for each year. Note the years of negative growth.

Source: Bureau of Economic Analysis (as of February 2023), www.bea.gov.

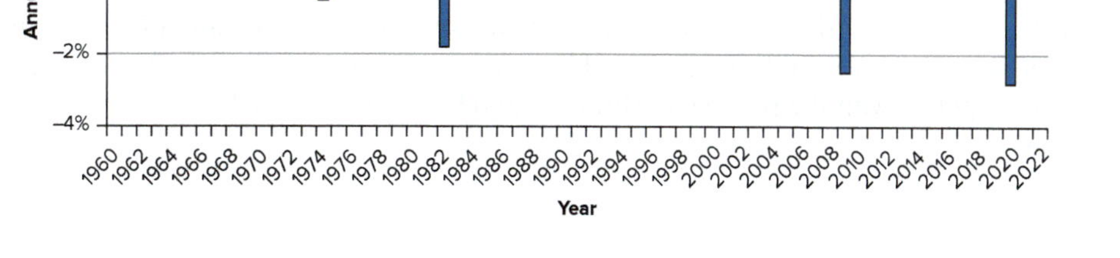

GDP versus Real GDP

The BEA publishes figures for both GDP and real GDP, because they serve different purposes. The GDP for a year reveals the amount that consumers, businesses, and government actually spent that year, measured in dollars. The comparable real GDP figure adjusts for price increases since 2012. **Table 9.1** shows the relationship between GDP and real GDP in recent years. For example, the figure for real GDP in 2022 is lower than the figure for GDP in the same year, because real GDP removes the effects of price increases since 2012.

Similarly, the growth rate of GDP includes both economic growth and the effects of inflation. In contrast, the growth rate of real GDP removes the effects of inflation (see "**How It Works: Calculating the Growth Rate**").

HOW IT WORKS: CALCULATING THE GROWTH RATE

The BEA regularly reports the growth rate of the U.S. economy, which represents the percentage increase in *real* GDP. For example, in 2021, real GDP was $19,610 billion, measured in 2012 dollars. In 2022, real GDP was $20,015 billion, measured in 2012 dollars. The growth rate from 2021 to 2022 was 2.1 percent.

Data: Bureau of Economic Analysis, www.bea.gov (as of February 2023).

	Billions of 2012 Dollars
Real GDP in 2021	$19,610
Real GDP in 2022	$20,015
Growth rate (20015/19610) − 1 = 0.021 = 2.1 percent	

Table 9.1 GDP versus Real GDP

Real GDP is measured in 2012 dollars, which removes the effects of inflation. The third column shows the growth rate of GDP, including inflation. The fourth column shows the growth rate of real GDP, which is adjusted for inflation.

	GDP (Billions of Dollars)	Real GDP (Billions of 2012 Dollars)	Growth Rate of GDP (%)	Growth Rate of Real GDP (%)
2012	16254	16254	4.2	2.3
2013	16843	16553	3.6	1.8
2014	17551	16932	4.2	2.3
2015	18206	17390	3.7	2.7
2016	18695	17680	2.7	1.7
2017	19477	18077	4.2	2.2
2018	20533	18609	5.4	2.9
2019	21381	19036	4.1	2.3
2020	21060	18509	-1.5	-2.8
2021	23315	19610	10.7	5.9
2022	25464	20015	9.2	2.1

Source: Bureau of Economic Analysis (as of February 2023), www.bea.gov.

A Word of Warning

Keep in mind that a rise in real GDP for a whole economy doesn't mean the quantity of any particular good or service is also rising. Similarly, the economy as a whole can be shrinking while some parts are expanding. In 2020, for example, the overall economy shrank as Americans were grappling with the pandemic. However, purchases of items such as furniture and televisions soared, as people spent more time at home.

THE INCREASE IN LIVING STANDARDS (LO9-3)

LO9-3 Discuss the short-term and long-term change in living standards, and calculate real GDP per capita.

So far in this chapter, we've been talking about the growth rate of real GDP–that is, the rate at which the production of the whole economy is expanding. Now let's bring growth down to the level of the individual consumer. Remember that **Chapter 7** defined GDP per capita as the GDP divided by the population of the country–in other words, the amount of economic output each person would get if we split up the entire economy evenly and gave everyone a piece. As we saw, this is a rough measure of the average standard of living in the economy.

Now we can ask, "How fast is the average standard of living rising?" To answer this, we want to look at the change in GDP per capita. Of course we have to adjust for the effects of inflation. That means we're interested in the growth in **real GDP per capita**.

Table 9.2 Calculating Real GDP per Capita

Dividing real GDP by the size of the population gives us real GDP per capita. From 2021 to 2022, real GDP per capita grew by 1.7 percent.

	Real GDP (Billions of 2012 Dollars)	Population (Millions of People)	Real GDP Capita (Real GDP ÷ Population) (2012 Dollars)
2021	19610	332.4	58995
2022	20015	333.6	59998
Percentage change from 2021 to 2022	2.1%	0.4%	1.7%

Source: Bureau of Economic Analysis (as February 2023), www.bea.gov.

For example, in 2021, real GDP was $19610 billion measured in 2012 dollars, as shown in **Table 9.1** and reproduced in **Table 9.2**. The U.S. population was 332.4 million. Thus, the real GDP per capita in 2021 was $58,995 (in 2012 dollars). If we divided real GDP equally among every man, woman, and child in the country, that's how much each person would get. In **Table 9.2**, we also do the same calculation for 2022 and come up with a real GDP per capita equal to $59,998 in year 2012 dollars. The growth rate of real GDP per capita equals the percentage change from 2021 to 2022, which in this case is 1.7 percent.

real GDP per capita
Real GDP divided by the number of people in a country. Serves as a measure of the standard of living.

short-term growth
Economic growth over a single year.

long-term growth
The average economic growth over longer periods such as 5 or 10 years.

Short-Term versus Long-Term Growth

So far we have been looking at yearly growth, which falls into the category of **short-term growth**. But it's also useful to look at **long-term growth**, which is the average growth rate over 5 or 10 years or longer. In particular, we can look back and see how real GDP per capita has changed over history, which gives us some insight into how the standard of living has changed. The chart of U.S. real GDP per capita in **Figure 9.6** shows how much living standards have risen over more than two centuries.

Figure 9.6 Real GDP per Capita throughout U.S. History
In most years since the country was founded, real GDP per capita has climbed.
Source: Louis D. Johnston and Samuel H. Williamson, "What Was the U.S. GDP Then?" MeasuringWorth.Com, 2023.

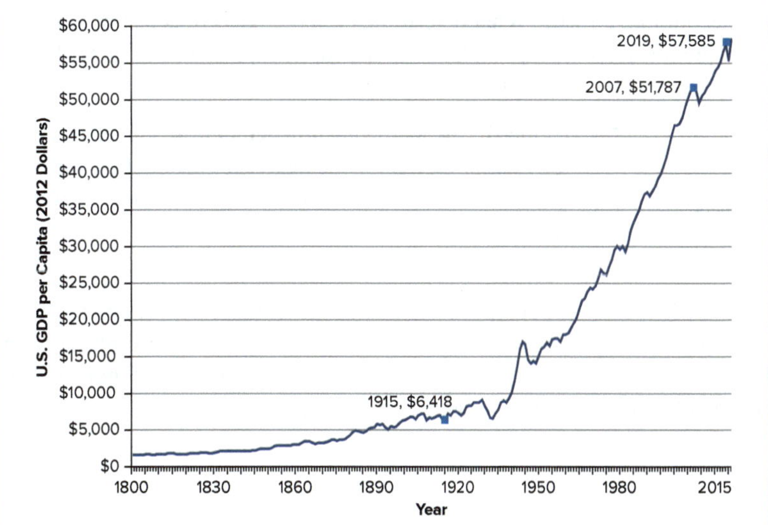

With only a couple of major interruptions, real GDP per capita has been on a steady upward climb since the United States was founded. For example, let's look at 1915 on the chart. The president was Woodrow Wilson, Russia was still ruled by a czar, and India was a British colony. Back then, real GDP per capita in the United States in inflation-adjusted 2012 dollars was $6,418. Jump forward a century: In 2019, the last year before the pandemic, real GDP per capita was $57,585 in 2012 dollars. That's a more than eightfold increase in a century, or an average real growth rate of roughly 2.1 percent per year.

Here's another way to think about this. The much lower real GDP per capita in 1915, compared to 2019, reflects the lack of many goods and services that we take for granted today. In 1915, you couldn't take an airplane trip, listen to the radio, watch television, or use a computer because none of these technologies were in commercial use or even existed. Automobiles were rare, and antibiotics were not part of the medical toolkit. Without weather satellites or radar, it was impossible to forecast tornadoes or hurricanes, so death tolls from severe weather were much higher. And when the "Spanish Flu" pandemic hit in 1918, killing perhaps 25–50 million globally, there was no capability of developing the sort of vaccines that lessened the impact of the COVID-19 pandemic. In effect, the productive capability of the 1915 economy was far lower–and so were living standards.

YOUR ECONOMIC LIFE: How Growth Helps You

Of course, these examples are all in the distant past. What do you, personally, get from economic growth today? Economic growth shows up in your life in two ways: More and better.

"More" means you can buy a larger quantity of the goods and services you already consume. Economic growth translates into higher incomes, which enables you to eat out more often; go to more concerts; take more vacations; and buy more clothes. You can pay off your student debt faster, afford a bigger place to live, and donate more money to worthy causes.

"Better" means you can buy goods and services that either didn't exist before or were far too expensive. The best example is your smartphone, which was only introduced in 2007 and has become absolutely indispensable since then. You may end up driving an electric car, especially if it becomes much more affordable. That's another aspect of economic growth. Equally important, the hope is that medical scientists will come up for improved treatments for common health problems such as diabetes and Alzheimer's, not to mention Covid vaccines.

Growth has its downsides, as we will see in later chapters. But without economic growth, your life would be much more of a struggle.

WHAT DRIVES GROWTH? (LO9-4)

LO9-4 List the forces driving economic growth.

What forces drive economic growth? What determines whether growth is fast or slow? In **Chapter 4**, you learned the production function of a business has five inputs: labor, capital, land, intermediate inputs, and business know-how. Given the levels of the different inputs, the production function tells us the output level of the business.

aggregate production function
The link between the inputs to an economy and its outputs.

Similarly, the **aggregate production function** tells us the output, or GDP, of the economy, given its inputs. The list of inputs for the aggregate production function includes the number of workers in the country (*labor*); the education and skill levels of these workers (what economists call *human capital*); equipment and structures (*physical capital*); raw materials, such as oil and iron ore (which come from the *land*); and a final category we will call *knowledge* (which includes both technology and business know-how).

The economy grows when these inputs grow. That is, as the number of workers increases, the output of the economy tends to rise. Similarly, output rises as workers become more educated and skilled, as more physical capital is used, as more raw materials are mined and used, and as the economy accumulates more knowledge, as shown in **Figure 9.7**. In other words, the forces driving growth are the increases in the five different inputs to the aggregate production function.

Figure 9.7 The Forces Driving Economic Growth
The economy grows when the inputs to the aggregate production function increase, all other things being equal.

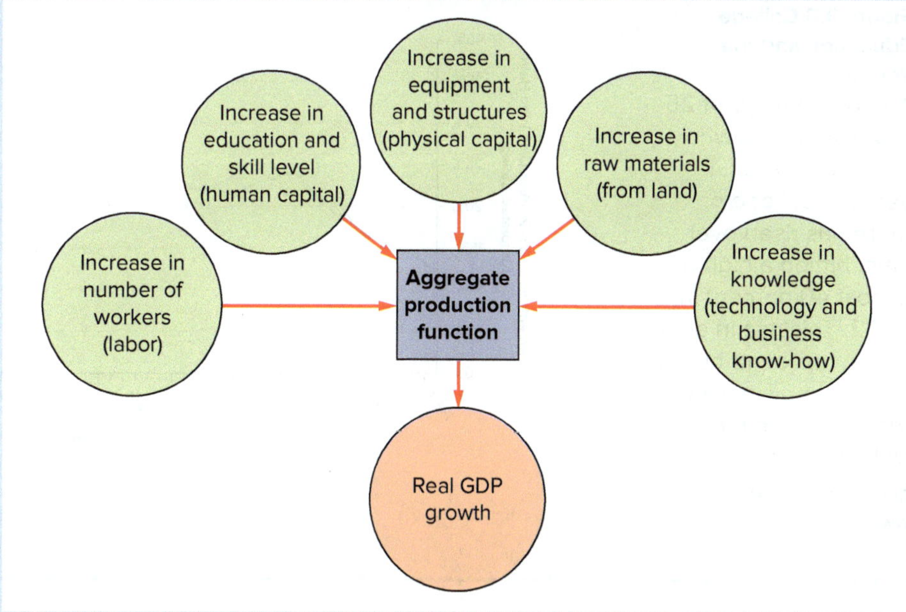

Increase in Labor

As the number of workers increases, output increases, too, even if nothing else changes. That makes sense. A country like the United States experiences some growth simply because the number of workers generally increases over time.

In 2012, for example, the U.S. **labor force**—the number of people either working or actively looking for jobs—was 155.0 million. In 2022, the labor force was 164.3 million. On average, the U.S. labor force has grown roughly 0.6 percent per year over the past decade, despite the impact of the pandemic.

labor force
The part of the adult population that is either working or actively looking for a job.

The Census Bureau—the government agency that does population projections—expects the working-age population of the United States to keep growing as today's young people reach working age and as the country continues to attract immigrants.

human capital
The education and skill level of a workforce.

Increase in Education and Skills

Another way to boost aggregate production is to increase the skills or education levels of the workforce—that is, to increase **human capital**. In general, better-trained and educated workers can produce more. Education helps future workers develop critical skills. Equally important, educated workers seem to have an easier time adapting to new technology.

An increase in physical capital can help an economy grow.
Cultura/Image Source

The education level of the U.S. workforce is much higher than it was in the past. **Figure 9.8** shows that, in 1965, only about 12 percent of U.S. adults between the ages of 25 and 29 had a college education. Back then, it was more common for people to graduate from high school and go directly into a factory job. As of 2022, almost 40 percent of U.S. adults aged 25-29 had completed four years of college or more.

Equally important, it's become far more common to have at least some exposure to post-high school education. This change is related to the dramatic rise of two-year colleges, which enrolled almost 5 million students as of 2020 (see "**Spotlight: Community Colleges and Economic Growth**").

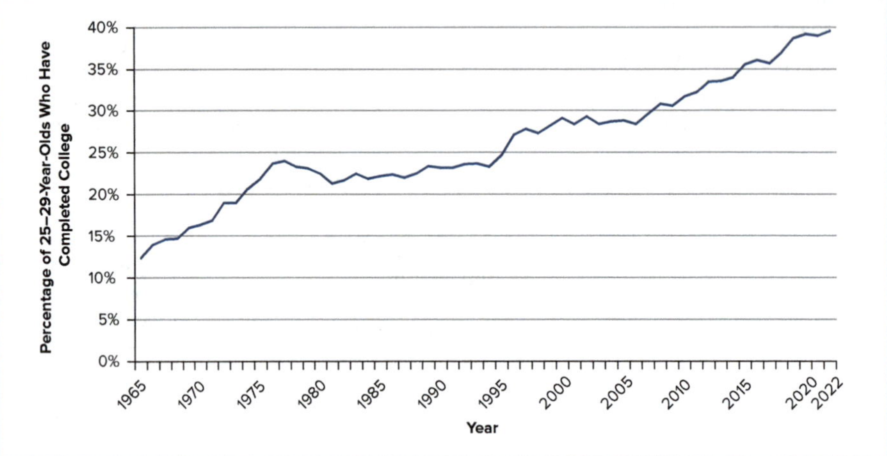

Figure 9.8 College Education and the Young

The percentage of 25- to 29-year-olds who have completed 4 years of college or more has risen over time, hitting a high of almost 40 percent in 2022. This rise in education has contributed to growth by making the workforce more skilled.

Source: Census Bureau, www.census.gov.

SPOTLIGHT: COMMUNITY COLLEGES AND ECONOMIC GROWTH

One essential force in the growth of human capital over the past several decades has been the community college system. Community colleges have been around for at least a century, but enrollments soared in the 1960s and 1970s. In 1963, enrollment in two-year colleges was 850,000. By 1970, this figure was 2.3 million, and by 1985, it had risen to 4.5 million, peaking at 7.7 million in 2010. As of 2020, 4.9 million students were enrolled in two-year colleges across the country.

The top fields for associate degrees in 2020–2021 were liberal arts, health professions, and business. These three fields together accounted for 67 percent of all associate degrees nationally. Following behind are protective services (such as law enforcement and homeland security) and computer and information sciences. As people graduate from community colleges and enter the workforce, their new education and skills contribute directly to the growth of GDP.

Investment in Physical Capital

Economists have long focused on investment in physical capital–firms' purchases of equipment and buildings for production–as an essential ingredient for growth. Almost nothing can be done in today's economy without relying on or using physical capital in some way. You can't take goods or passengers across the ocean without a ship or a plane; you can't employ workers comfortably without putting a roof over their heads; and you can't build computers without factories to make microprocessors, memory chips, and video screens.

Generally, if we give a worker more and better equipment to use, we can assume that once the worker learns which buttons to press, he or she will be able to produce more output than with less useful equipment. A driver with a truck can deliver more packages than a messenger on a bicycle. A construction worker with a giant crane can lift more material faster than the same worker with a hand truck.

The positive impact of increased investment in physical capital is very strong in poor countries, where rural farmers and low-end workers have poor access to any machinery or equipment, and adding even a little can make a big difference. But investment in new equipment, software, and buildings is also an important driving force for growth in a developed country such as the United States. For example, if you order a shirt online, you are relying on the wires and fiber optic connections that link you to the retailer. You are also relying on the retailer's computers, which are housed in a building somewhere; on the designers and marketers of the shirt, who presumably work in an office building in the United States; and on fleets of ships and trucks that eventually bring the shirt from the factory, which may be located in another country. Without all this physical capital, none of this would happen (see "**Spotlight: Capital Investment in the Age of the Internet**").

SPOTLIGHT: CAPITAL INVESTMENT IN THE AGE OF THE INTERNET

We usually think of the Internet as the ultimate intangible service. After all, the steady stream of data that feeds our mobile apps and laptop screens can't be seen or touched.

But it turns out that telecom companies such as AT&T and Comcast spend billions each year on building and maintaining the cables and cell phone towers that connect us to the Internet. Meanwhile, companies such as Alphabet, Amazon, Meta, and Microsoft spend billions each year to build massive data centers around the world to execute nearly instantaneously all those searches, shopping requests, or photo uploads. In fact, these data centers are essential for competing in today's information economy—even if your product is as intangible as an Internet search.

All told, in 2021, the information sector of the U.S. economy, including telecom and Internet companies, spent about $190 billion on equipment and buildings, even leaving aside the outlays for better software. All that money shows up in faster Internet connections, better coverage for mobile phones, and a wider variety of useful Internet services.

Source: Bureau of Economic Analysis.

Increase in Raw Materials

One essential input to growth is raw materials, which include everything from oil to iron ore to water. The importance of raw materials is obvious: You can't put up a building without iron ore, which is used to make the steel beams that hold up the building. Water is essential for drinking and agriculture. The list goes on and on.

Historically, economies have consumed more raw materials as they have grown. For example, the United States used roughly 7.4 billion barrels of crude oil and petroleum products in 2022, up from 5.9 billion barrels in 1981. It's possible, however, that environmental considerations may slow this increase in raw material use in the future.

Increase in Knowledge

Increase in knowledge plays a crucial role in economic growth, especially in developed countries such as the United States. Why? Because better **knowledge** means we have learned how to do something new, or learned how to produce something faster, better, or cheaper. In other words, we get smarter: We can produce more goods and services with the same amount of resources. For instance, food production has dramatically improved over the past 50 years because of enhancements in agricultural tools and techniques, seeds, fertilizers, and all sorts of related things.

knowledge

A category of input in the aggregate production function that includes both technology and business know-how.

Increases in knowledge include progress in science and technology, by which we learn more about the laws of nature and how to apply them. The results include better medicine, faster computers, and quieter airplanes that use less fuel.

Increases in knowledge also include improved business know-how: our greater understanding of how to arrange economic activities. For example, the invention of the credit card is important to our daily lives–but this has less to do with technology and more about realizing that people needed an easy way to make purchases on credit. As knowledge expands, more things become possible, and the economy grows. We will delve deeper into technological change and innovation in **Chapter 15**.

GOVERNMENT AND GROWTH (LO9-5)

LO9-5 Explain the role of government in economic growth.

As we saw in **Chapter 6**, the market economy does not function in a vacuum. The government plays an important role, setting laws and rules for everything from foreign trade to how mortgages are issued. (**Laws** are the actual legislation passed by Congress and state and local governments, whereas **rules** are the regulations issued by various government agencies.)

laws

Acts of legislation.

rules

Regulations issued by various government agencies.

Some laws and rules encourage growth by making markets work better. On the other hand, some laws and rules, even if well-intended, can end up discouraging growth by making markets work less efficiently.

Most economists favor less government interference in the marketplace as the strategy most likely to produce steady growth. The idea behind this preference is that corporations and individuals are in a better position than the government to know what kinds of investments are most likely to pay off. After all, they reason, the government should not tell Apple what kind of phones to make.

Sometimes, it's pretty clear that government is on the right track, exercising its power for the greater good. For instance, when a company is putting up a new structure such as an office building or a factory–an investment in physical capital–local governments often impose a long list of building code requirements, such as mandating a certain degree of resistance to fire, earthquakes, and storms. These requirements increase the cost of buildings and, therefore, slow down investment, but most people would agree that they are necessary.

Or consider the example of education. By law, everyone has to get an elementary and a high school education. That's the minimum amount of human capital that U.S. families are required to invest in. However, legislators could just as easily require everyone to pass at least two years of college–if they were willing to spend billions of dollars to build and staff new community colleges. For now, however, most people agree that completion of high school is an acceptable minimum.

In many cases, however, exactly where we want to draw the line on government interference is a subject of intense political and economic dispute. Immigration is one important example. Some people favor very tight government controls on the border, and a policy that allows only very few immigrants into the country. Alternatively, others support relaxed controls on immigration, with relatively generous annual quotas. In the short run, allowing more immigration might have a positive effect on growth because the population and the workforce would rise. But that's clearly unacceptable to a large proportion of citizens–and it would probably impose much bigger costs on local governments for education and health care. We'll discuss immigration further in **Chapter 16**.

We could keep offering examples because almost everything the government does–or doesn't do–can affect growth. But as we proceed through the following chapters, we will see other ways in which the government has an impact on growth. (For an example, see "**Spotlight: The Chinese Government and Growth.**")

SPOTLIGHT: THE CHINESE GOVERNMENT AND GROWTH

China illustrates how a shift in government policy can alter the long-term growth rate of a country. Until the late 1970s, the Chinese economy was tightly run by the Communist Party. Farms were managed collectively, which means farmers did not own their production; instead, it was owned by the whole group. Most manufacturing was done in state-run factories with names like Beijing No. 7 Paper Mill. The combination of the largest population in the world and an inefficient economy made China one of the poorest countries in the world. In 1980, its GDP per capita was only about $400, which ranked China 144 out of around 150 countries.

All that changed under Deng Xiaoping, leader of the Chinese Communist Party from 1978 to the early 1990s. Deng instituted a series of economic reforms that included a move away from collective agriculture to more autonomy for individual households, such as deciding what to plant, choosing where to sell it, and getting much of the gains. Local officials and plant managers were given more freedom to run factories and businesses for profit instead of producing to meet government quotas.

Under President Xi Jinping, the Chinese government has taken more of an active role in the economy in recent years. Nevertheless, the importance of markets in China is a example of the kinds of changes in laws and regulations that make an economy work better. In addition, the Chinese have been investing in human capital and knowledge at a high rate. The number of college graduates continues to skyrocket, and China ranks below only the United States in spending on research and development.

As a result, the Chinese economy has grown at an average rate of 8 percent per year for the past 25 years. It has struggled during the pandemic to maintain its rapid pace of growth. But at least for now, it's still a role model for other developing countries.

PRODUCTIVITY (LO9-6)

LO9-6 Discuss the history of U.S. productivity growth.

productivity
Economic output divided by the number of labor hours worked.

How can we summarize all these forces driving economic growth? Remember from **Chapter 4** that we defined the *average product* for a business as output per worker. **Productivity** is the equivalent concept for the whole economy. That is, the productivity of an economy is its output for a given year divided by the total number of hours worked in that year, counting all workers. We use total hours, rather than number of workers, to adjust for the fact that not everyone puts in the same amount of time on the job.

A sales clerk in a department store may work 20 hours in a week, whereas a highly motivated factory worker may put in overtime and work 60 hours a week; a corporate lawyer might work 90 hours.

Productivity is a key concept for measuring the health and prosperity of an economy. The higher the productivity, the more output an economy can produce with the same number of workers. For example, China has more workers than the United States does, especially if we count farmworkers. But the United States has a much bigger economy because U.S. workers are more productive–they can produce more with the same or fewer inputs as Chinese workers can.

The **growth rate of productivity** is the percentage increase in productivity over a year, and it is among the economic statistics that economists watch most closely. If productivity growth is rapid, the same number of workers can produce more goods and services. That's good news: Companies can afford to pay higher wages and still make a profit. Periods of solid productivity growth are usually also periods of rising living standards.

growth rate of productivity
The percentage increase in productivity over a year.

In contrast, persistent low productivity growth is bad news for workers. Without productivity gains, businesses can't afford to raise real wages. Eras of slow productivity growth are generally dismal.

The History of U.S. Productivity Growth

Since the end of World War II, the United States has experienced periods of both strong and weak productivity growth. Look at **Figure 9.9**, which shows the average rate of productivity growth for four different periods since 1947. One important note here: The productivity number reported by the Bureau of Labor Statistics focuses on the output of the "nonfarm business sector," which leaves out government, housing, agriculture, and nonprofits.

Figure 9.9 The Four Eras of Productivity Growth After World War II, the United States experienced rapid productivity growth until the mid-1970s. Then, productivity growth slowed for roughly two decades, followed by a speed-up as businesses learned how to use information technology and globalization increased. Finally, in recent years, productivity growth has slowed, for as yet unexplained reasons.

Source: Bureau of Labor Statistics, www.bls.gov. Data downloaded March 2023.

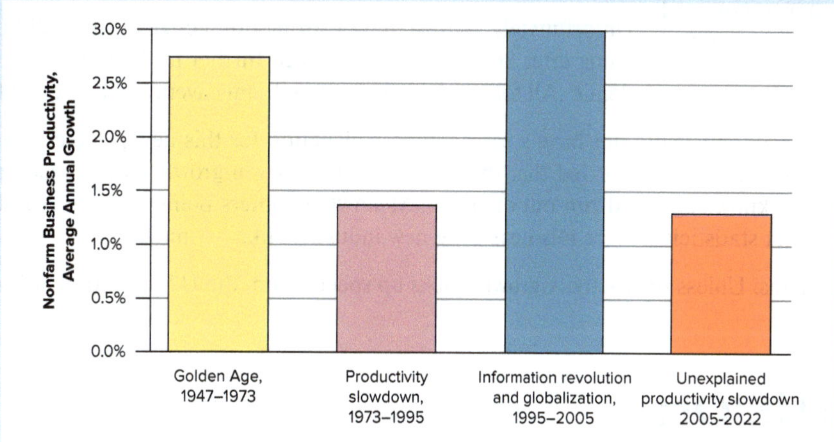

The first period, from the end of World War II to roughly 1973, was the **Golden Age** of U.S. growth. Productivity–output per hour–rose at an average of 2.8 percent per year. Not surprisingly, with that kind of productivity growth, everyone prospered. Real wage growth was strong, inflation was low, and living standards rose rapidly for most people.

Golden Age
The period from the end of World War II to roughly 1973 characterized by rapid increases in productivity and a rising standard of living.

This stretch of rapid productivity growth was also the period of government expansion described in **Chapter 6**. The construction of the interstate highway system, the massive program to put people on the moon, the creation of Medicare–it's no coincidence that these massive federal spending efforts came while productivity was growing quickly. With output per hour rising steadily, the economy was producing enough spare resources to expand government spending into new areas.

The era of rapid productivity growth ended around 1973. The immediate cause was the big jump in oil prices we described earlier, which made energy a lot more expensive and hurt the transportation and utility industries. But even after businesses learned to cope with more expensive energy, the earlier rate of productivity growth did not return.

productivity slowdown

The period from 1973 to 1995 in which productivity grew at a much slower pace than in the Golden Age.

Economists suggested a variety of possible explanations for the **productivity slowdown** from 1973 to 1995. One theory was that as the baby boom generation entered the workforce, these workers were young, inexperienced, and not highly productive. Another theory was that the environmental regulations passed in the late 1960s and early 1970s—such as the creation of the Environmental Protection Agency in 1970—were dragging down growth. Yet another theory proposed that U.S. workers were not saving and investing enough, which was holding back productivity. And still another theory suggested that there simply were not enough new products and innovation. Businesses were churning out the same old cars and washing machines.

All of these factors probably contributed to the productivity slowdown. But no matter which reason was the most important, the total impact was clear: From 1973 to 1995, productivity growth slowed to only 1.4 percent per year, which was roughly half the previous rate. This meant that real wage gains for many workers were much smaller or even nonexistent. It also meant that U.S. consumers, strapped for money, were much less willing to pay high tax rates.

information revolution

The application of additional processing capacity of new generations of computers to a wide variety of new uses. Enabled businesses to produce more output with fewer workers.

globalization

The increasing exchange of goods, services, ideas, and people among countries.

This productivity slowdown lasted until around 1995, when two things happened more or less simultaneously. First, the **information revolution** finally kicked in. Businesses learned how to use computers to produce more output with fewer workers, even as the rise of the Internet helped tie all those computers together. At the same time, there was a great expansion of **globalization** as businesses learned how to use foreign suppliers to cut their costs (we'll discuss globalization more in **Chapter 14**).

Together, the combination of the information revolution and globalization propelled a new productivity boom. Between 1995 and 2005, productivity growth rebounded to 3.0 percent, faster than during the Golden Age.

Unfortunately, that stretch of strong productivity growth did not last. Productivity growth started weakening after 2005 and then slumped further in the years after the Great Recession and during the pandemic. All told, productivity growth only averaged 1.4 percent annually from 2005 to 2022.

As of early 2023, economists did not have a satisfactory explanation for this new productivity slowdown. Some saw it as merely a temporary pause. Other economists worried that the forces that had driven growth in the past—specifically, investment in physical capital, human capital, and knowledge—had run out of steam. Meanwhile, others pointed to the possibility that government was overregulating the economy, or that statisticians were mismeasuring new industries like e-commerce.

Still, the fact remains: Unless productivity growth picks up speed again, the U.S. economy will remain stuck in a rut.

CONCLUSION

Economic growth is one of the most important things we can know about an economy. If we can measure how fast real GDP is rising, then we can tell whether the typical standard of living in the country is increasing. Rapid economic growth cannot be taken for granted—it depends on increasing the inputs to the aggregate production function.

However, in any particular year, the economy may shrink rather than grow. That means economic growth is negative rather than positive, and it's bad news for consumers and for businesses. As we will see in the next chapter and afterward, trying to avoid periods of negative economic growth—a shrinking economy—is one of the main goals of economic policymakers.

09 SUMMARY

1. Economic growth leads to higher living standards. It also offers more choices. By pushing out the production possibility frontier, economic growth increases the productive capabilities of an economy. *(LO9-1)*
2. As we saw in **Chapter 7**, gross domestic product (GDP) measures the output of an economy. Economic growth, or real GDP growth, is the increase in nominal GDP, adjusted for inflation. *(LO9-2)*
3. An increase in living standards can be measured by the increase in real GDP per capita, which is real GDP divided by the size of the population. In the United States, real GDP per capita has risen more or less steadily since the founding of the country. *(LO9-3)*
4. Economic growth is driven by several factors, including the number of workers, their education and skill, the amount of equipment and buildings, the availability of raw materials,

and the amount of knowledge. Increases in any of these can help propel growth on a macro level. *(LO9-4)*

5. Government has an important role in promoting growth through laws and rules. However, there's much disagreement about where to draw the line between government and the private sector. *(LO9-5)*
6. Productivity is the average output per hour of work. Fast productivity growth is an indicator of the health and prosperity of an economy. *(LO9-6)*

KEY TERMS AND CONCEPTS

economic growth
production possibility frontier (PPF)
zero-sum economy
non-zero-sum economy
real GDP
real GDP per capita
short-term growth
long-term growth
aggregate production function
labor force
human capital
knowledge
laws
rules
productivity
growth rate of productivity
Golden Age
productivity slowdown
information revolution
globalization

connect PROBLEMS

1. Which of the following statements is not true? *(LO9-1)*
   a) In a growing economy, the production possibility frontier (PPF) moves inward.
   b) Two of the forces driving growth are increases in knowledge and increases in labor.
   c) The Golden Age of productivity growth ran from roughly the end of World War II to the mid-1970s.
   d) The arrival of the Internet helped spur an increase in productivity growth.
2. The following figure shows a PPF, today and next year, for an economy that makes food and cars. *(LO9-1)*

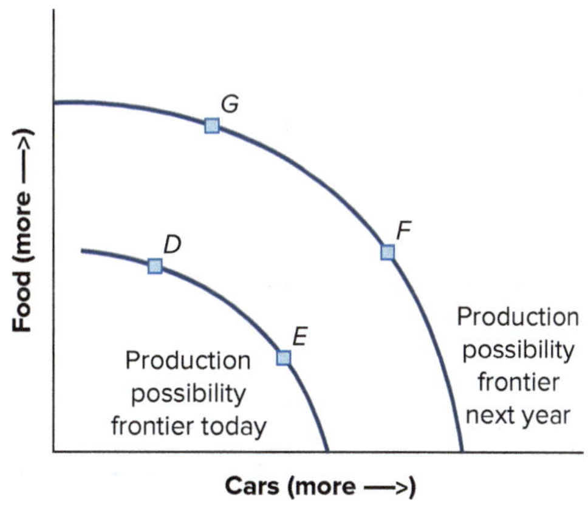

   a) Based on today's PPF, which point offers the higher production of cars?
   b) Which point on next year's PPF offers higher production of both cars and food compared to point *E?*
   c) Which point on next year's PPF offers lower production of cars compared to point *D?*
3. *Zero-sum* means that one person's gain is someone else's loss. *Non-zero-sum* means that it is possible for everyone to gain. Say whether each of the following represents a zero-sum or a non-zero-sum situation. *(LO9-1)*
   a) Three kids sharing a cookie.
   b) Two college students collaborating on a class project.
   c) Two baseball teams playing a game.
   d) A director and several actors making a movie.
   e) Two hotels competing for customers in a resort town where the total number of tourists stays the same.

4. The accompanying table shows real GDP from 2012 to 2022 for Italy, measured in billions of 2012 dollars. *(LO9-2)*

	Billions of 2012 Dollars
2012	2172
2013	2132
2014	2132
2015	2149
2016	2177
2017	2213
2018	2233
2019	2245
2020	2042
2021	2179
2022	2248

a) By what percentage did the Italian economy grow between 2012 and 2022?
b) Which year showed the fastest growth rate?
c) Which year showed the slowest growth rate?
d) Plot the real GDP of the Italian economy.

5. Suppose we are looking at an economy that produces only toys. In 2021, the country's toy factories produced 5 million toys, which it sold on the international market for $10 per toy. In 2022, the country produced 6 million toys, which it sold for $12 per toy. *(LO9-2)*

a) What was the percentage increase in the production of toys from 2021 to 2022?
b) What was the GDP of this economy in 2021? What was the GDP in 2022? (Remember that GDP is the monetary value of the economy's output, valued at the market price.)
c) What was the percentage increase in nominal GDP?
d) What was the growth rate of the economy from 2021 to 2022? Explain.

6. The following table shows real GDP (in billions of 2012 dollars) for Japan from 2012 to 2022, along with the population in each year. *(LO9-3)*

	Real GDP (Billions of 2012 Dollars)	Population (Millions of People)	Real GDP per Capita (Thousands of 2012 Dollars)
2012	4,800	127.6	—
2013	4,896	127.3	—
2014	4,910	127.1	—
2015	4,987	127.0	—
2016	5,025	127.0	—
2017	5,109	126.7	—
2018	5,142	126.5	
2019	5,123	126.2	
2020	4,887	125.8	
2021	4,968	125.5	
2022	5,054	125.2	

a) Calculate real GDP per capita for each year.
b) Is Japan's population rising or falling?
c) In what year did real GDP per capita rise by the biggest percentage?
d) By what percentage did real GDP per capita change from 2012 to 2022?
e) Plot real GDP per capita on a graph.

7. Say whether each of the following is likely to make real GDP for the United States rise or fall. *(LO9-4)*

a) An increase in the number of college graduates.
b) A war in the Middle East that cuts off the supply of oil to the rest of the world.
c) A new technology that speeds up the construction of homes.
d) A pandemic that forces people to stay home from work.
e) The local fast-food restaurant buys equipment to make more french fries at a time.

8. Identify which input (labor, human capital, physical capital, raw materials, or knowledge) is affected in the following scenarios. *(LO9-4)*

   a) An investment in new airports that cuts the number of flight delays.
   b) An earthquake that destroys a factory.
   c) Improved cash registers in stores.
   d) More immigrants entering the country.
   e) The discovery of natural gas under Pennsylvania.

9. For each of the following government laws and rules, identify whether it affects growth by influencing labor, human capital, physical capital, raw materials, or knowledge. *(LO9-5)*

   a) A new rule opening up more areas for oil drilling.
   b) A new law that provides more funds to support college scholarships.
   c) A new rule restricting how high an office building can be built.
   d) A new law that makes immigration into the United States more difficult.

10. Which of the following factors can contribute to a slowdown in productivity? *(LO9-6)*

    a) Tighter environmental regulations.
    b) Low levels of savings and investments.
    c) Lower oil prices.
    d) Lack of innovation.

11. One country (call it A) can make 1,000 shirts with 50 hours of labor. A second country (call it C) can make 1,000 shirts with 75 hours of labor. *(LO9-6)*

    a) Calculate productivity for countries A and C. Which one is higher?
    b) Suppose workers in country A get paid $30 per hour and workers in country C get paid $10 per hour. In which country is it more expensive to make a shirt (assuming that all other costs are the same between the two countries)?

CH 10

BUSINESS CYCLES, UNEMPLOYMENT, AND INFLATION

Mario Tama/Getty Images

LEARNING OBJECTIVES

After reading this chapter, you should be able to:

LO10-1 Compare and contrast potential GDP and real GDP.
LO10-2 Define the unemployment rate, and distinguish between the different types of unemployment.
LO10-3 Explain the trade-off between unemployment and inflation.
LO10-4 Define *recession,* and discuss the impact of recessions on workers and businesses.
LO10-5 List the possible causes of recession.

Life would be much easier if everything were predictable. We could plan a trip to the beach and know it wouldn't rain. We could drive to work and pick the highway that didn't leave us stuck in traffic for an hour behind a stalled truck. And best of all, in an ideal and stable world, we could be sure we'd never unexpectedly lose our job.

But as we have all learned, market economies are subject to distressing turbulence. In some cases, there's a clear external shock that causes a slowdown. The start of the pandemic in 2020 resulted in a short and unusual downturn, where many businesses temporarily closed down or reduced services to help protect workers and customers from being exposed to the virus.

The Great Recession of 2008–2009 was a longer and deeper economic decline. Unemployment soared, millions of Americans lost their jobs and homes, banks were closed, and major companies such as General Motors were forced to declare bankruptcy. Some state and local governments had trouble paying their bills. The crisis was worldwide, hitting Europe and Japan as well as the United States.

Over the years, economists have devoted enormous time and effort to understanding what causes economic fluctuations. In some ways, modern economics began with the Great Depression of the 1930s (described in **Chapter 6**), when production and employment plunged in a very short time—not just in the United States but around the world. With one out of every four workers jobless and many factories closed down, the nation looked to economists to take a central role in setting government policy. They had to explain why the Depression happened, how it could be ended, and how the United States could prevent something similar from happening in the future.

Since the 1930s, there have been plenty of economic downturns or *recessions* in the United States and other industrialized countries. However, one of the great triumphs of modern economics is that no industrialized country has ever again suffered a depression of the same horrifying magnitude. Part of the reason that the economic impact of the pandemic was so short-lived was that economists and policymakers had learned important lessons from the past. The government stepped in with large stimulus programs, as described in **Chapter 6**.

In this chapter, we will look at the ups and downs of economies. We will show how an economy can deviate from a smooth upward path of potential gross domestic product (GDP). We will define *unemployment,* one of the key measures of an economy's health, and examine the balance between unemployment and inflation. And we will look at recessions: what they are, what kind of damage they can do, and what causes them. Then in the two chapters that follow, we will show how a government can use the tools of fiscal and monetary policy to help moderate the swings of an economy. In particular, we'll discuss the details of government anti-pandemic stimulus programs.

POTENTIAL VERSUS REAL GDP (LO10-1)

LO10-1 Compare and contrast potential GDP and real GDP.

Imagine you're driving along a smooth highway, moving at the same speed as the other cars on the road, so there's no pressure to speed up or slow down. You're listening to music, talking with your friends in the car, and enjoying the ride. Life is good.

Or you could be driving like a maniac—speeding up to 90 miles per hour to pass other cars, then suddenly jamming on the brakes just before you crash into the back of a truck or run into a pothole.

An economy is not a car, but it is useful to think about what it would mean for an economy to move along a smooth and sustainable path. If an economy is not jarred by outside shocks, if workers are fully employed but not overworked, if companies can sell everything they make without strain, and if there are no sudden stops and starts, then output will generally rise smoothly over time. **Potential GDP** is the output of an economy along this smooth path of growth, which assumes no strains on production or unused resources (a bit later in this chapter, we'll explain more precisely what we mean by this). Potential GDP is measured in inflation-adjusted dollars like real GDP, and the rate at which it rises is the **potential growth rate**.

potential GDP
The output of the economy along a smooth path of growth, assuming no strains on production or unused resources.

potential growth rate
The rate at which potential GDP increases; also the combination of the long-term growth rate of the labor force plus the long-term growth rate of productivity.

Potential Growth

The potential growth rate is driven by the factors we saw in the preceding chapter: growth of the labor force, availability of better-educated and more highly skilled workers, investments in physical capital, availability of raw materials, and increases in knowledge. We can also think of the potential growth rate over the long run as the combination of the long-term growth rate of the labor force and the long-term growth rate of productivity:

Potential growth rate = Long-term labor force growth rate + Long-term productivity growth rate

So, if the labor force is growing at 1 percent per year, and productivity per worker is rising at 2 percent per year, then potential GDP (which is adjusted for inflation) is rising at 3 percent per year.

Estimating potential GDP is like drawing a line on a map to show where you are going. Economists project potential GDP into the future to forecast the sustainable growth path for an economy. If we plot potential GDP on a graph (see **Figure 10.1**), it generally looks like a smooth line.

The Output Gap

But the real GDP of an economy need not follow the same smooth path as potential GDP at all. At any moment, real GDP may be higher or lower than potential GDP, just as a car may be moving faster or slower than the flow of traffic on a road. The **output gap** is the difference between real and potential GDP. The output gap is negative when real GDP is less than potential GDP, and it is positive when real GDP is greater than potential GDP (see **Figure 10.2**).

output gap
The difference between real and potential GDP.

Figure 10.1 The Path of Potential GDP
As time goes on, potential GDP rises smoothly, reflecting the growth of productivity and the growth of the labor force.

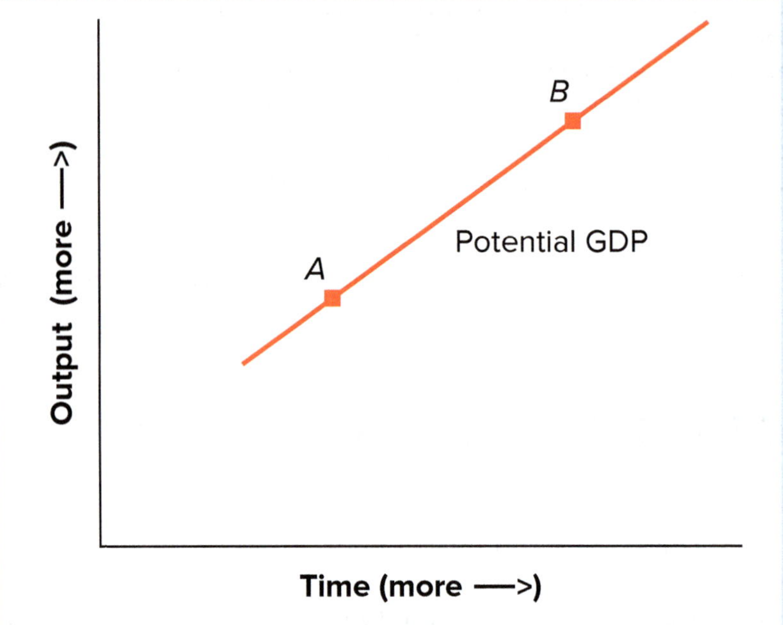

Figure 10.2 Potential versus Real GDP
The output gap measures the difference between potential and real GDP. When real GDP is greater than potential GDP, the output gap is positive. When real GDP is less than potential GDP, the output gap is negative.

Michael Mandel

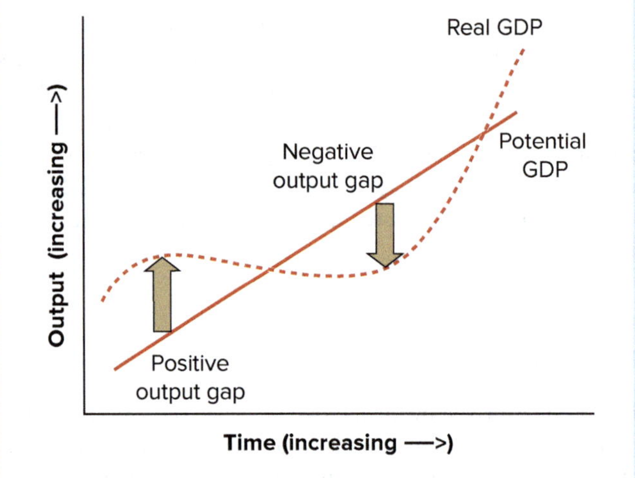

Real GDP can be lower than potential GDP if there are unused resources in the economy, such as workers who don't have jobs, or workers who have jobs that don't use their education (like a PhD flipping hamburgers). Other unused resources include idle machines and empty office buildings.

In 2009, the output gap expanded to approximately −5 percent of GDP. The output gap was negative because real GDP was less than potential GDP. In the second quarter of 2020, as the pandemic took hold, the output gap expanded to a stunning −10 percent of GDP, as many workers and productive resources were idled.

To understand how the output gap works, imagine a simple economy consisting of five students. In theory, they could study at an even pace all semester. That would be the path of potential GDP. However, in reality, three of these students don't work very hard–they wake up late and spend more time at parties than they do studying. In this economy, the actual output of work will fall short of potential, and the output gap will be negative.

But it's also possible for real output to exceed potential GDP. How? Suppose at the end of the semester, the three slackers pump themselves full of caffeine and stay up around the clock to finish their assignments and study for exams. The output gap is positive during this period because their output exceeds their potential. As a result, their output is very high, but it's not sustainable. As we will see, there is a parallel between these students and the economy.

UNEMPLOYMENT (LO10-2)

LO10-2 Define the unemployment rate, and distinguish between the different types of unemployment.

When real GDP drops below potential GDP, it means economic activity has slowed. Companies lay off workers or just don't hire. As a result, more workers become **unemployed**–that is, they don't have jobs but are actively looking for work.

unemployed
A description of individuals who do not have jobs but are actively looking for work.

Unemployment is a key measure of the ups and downs of an economy. The Bureau of Labor Statistics (BLS) estimates the number of unemployed workers each month based on a nationwide survey of 60,000 households of various demographic characteristics. The BLS also estimates the number of employed workers each month. The **labor force** is the sum of the employed workers and the unemployed workers.

labor force
The part of the adult population that is either working or actively looking for a job.

The **unemployment rate** is the percentage of the labor force that is unemployed. Note that the unemployment rate doesn't count people who are not looking for jobs because they have become discouraged and given up. Nor does it count people who are not working because they are going to school, taking care of children, or simply goofing off. Finally, the unemployment rate does not count the **underemployed**–people who are working part-time because they can't find a full-time job or people who take jobs below their skill or education levels while they look for something better.

unemployment rate
The percentage of the labor force that is unemployed.

underemployed
Individuals who take jobs below their skill or education levels or who are working part-time involuntarily.

In February 2023, the unemployment rate was 3.9 percent, meaning that 3.6 percent of the labor force did not have jobs. With 166 million people in the U.S. labor force (as of February 2023), a 3.6 percent unemployment rate translates into about 5.9 million unemployed Americans.

Figure 10.3 shows how the unemployment rate has varied since 1960. Over that stretch, the annual average unemployment rate has gone as high as 9.7 percent in 1982 and as low as 3.5 percent in 1969. Despite the severity of the Great Recession, the annual unemployment rate was only 9.3 percent in 2009 and 9.6 percent in 2010. (These are the annual averages; in particular months, the unemployment rate may have been higher or lower.)

Figure 10.3 Unemployment Rate, 1960–2022
This chart shows the percentage of the labor force that did not have jobs but was actively looking for work.

Source: Bureau of Labor Statistics, www.bls.gov.

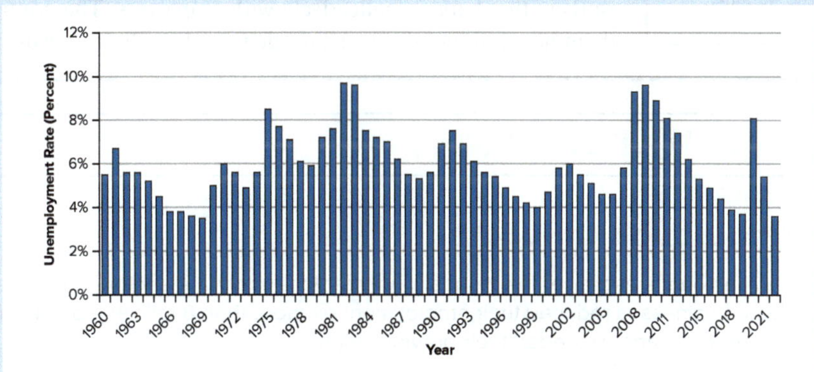

Types of Unemployment

As we saw in **Chapter 3**, markets typically tend toward an equilibrium in which the quantity supplied equals the quantity demanded. If that were true in the labor market, everyone would have a job who wanted one. But the unemployment rate never falls to zero in this way–not in the United States or in any other country.

frictional unemployment
Periods of temporary unemployment that correspond to short gaps between jobs.

Economists have long puzzled over this fact and have come up with a variety of explanations. One reason unemployment is never zero is that the unemployment rate includes **frictional unemployment**– periods of temporary unemployment that correspond to short gaps between jobs. Frictional unemployment arises because there are usually at least a couple of weeks between the end of one job and the beginning of the next one or between graduating from school and finding your first job. Even in the tightest labor market–or maybe *especially* in a tight labor market–people who are searching for work may actually turn some jobs down in hopes of getting a better one. This type of unemployment is also considered frictional unemployment.

structural unemployment
A situation in which there is a mismatch between the skills of unemployed workers and the needs of employers with unfilled jobs.

Another reason unemployment persists is **structural unemployment**. Structural unemployment occurs when there is a mismatch between the skills of unemployed workers and the needs of employers with unfilled jobs. For example, if a local factory is closing, the laid-off workers are probably not immediately qualified to take jobs as nurses even if the local hospital is hiring. The faster the economy changes, the more structural unemployment there will be.

Many people are concerned that automation and increased use of information technology would eliminate the need for many kinds of workers. For example, it is possible that self-driving or autonomous trucks may reduce the demand for truck drivers and increase structural unemployment.

cyclical unemployment
Large jumps in the unemployment rate that are tied directly to business cycles.

But frictional and structural unemployment do not fully explain some of the big swings we see in the unemployment rate. Especially striking are the big jumps upward in some years, which we call **cyclical unemployment**–large jumps in unemployment tied directly to slowdowns in economic growth. For example, in **Figure 10.3**, we see the annual unemployment rate remained above 6 percent for 6 years, from 2009 to 2014.

The people who lost their jobs because of the pandemic are an unusual case. Consider restaurant workers, for example, in the initial stages of the pandemic, many restaurants were closed, leading to a type of cyclical unemployment for restaurant servers and cooks. But even as the overall economy bounced back, some restaurants did not reopen, especially in downtown office districts where many office workers who used to go out for lunch were now working from home. Thus, a portion of pandemic-related unemployment became structural.

The Unemployment Puzzle

sticky wages
Wages that don't change much in the short term in response to economic conditions.

union
A group of workers who bargain collectively with employers for wages, benefits, and working conditions.

In general, when the quantity supplied exceeds the quantity demanded in a market, the price falls. In the labor market, the price is the wage. So the unemployment puzzle is really a wage puzzle: When the unemployment rate is high, why doesn't the wage drop? One possible answer is **sticky wages**. That is, wages are sticky when they don't change much in the short term in response to economic conditions. For one thing, workers might not want to accept wage cuts in periods of high unemployment because they expect the labor market to quickly recover. In **Figure 10.3**, we see that the unemployment rate often goes up and then does, in fact, come down within a couple of years. Another reason for sticky wages is that roughly 10.1 percent of the workforce in 2022 belonged to **unions**, which are organized groups of workers that bargain collectively with employers. The contracts set the wages for the workers, making them harder to cut if things turn down. (We will further discuss labor markets in **Chapter 16**.)

ECONOMIC MILESTONE

2020: Biggest Job Cutbacks

Sometimes, a milestone is negative; the biggest one-year loss in private-sector jobs since the Great Depression came in 2020. That year, private businesses reduced their employment by more than 8 million jobs because of the pandemic. By 2022, private-sector jobs had reached and exceeded their previous high.

The next biggest one-year loss in private-sector jobs, almost 6 million cuts, came in 2009, during the Great Recession of 2008–2009. It took the economy much longer, 5 years, to regain its previous high.

HOW IT WORKS: LOCAL UNEMPLOYMENT

The unemployment number that's usually quoted is the unemployment rate for the entire country. But the BLS also publishes the unemployment rates for many local areas. These give the percentages of the local labor force who are out of work and looking for a job.

Some areas have unemployment rates that are much lower than the national average. For example, in December 2022, the unemployment rate in Madison, Wisconsin, was only 1.6 percent. Madison has a recession-resistant economy because it is the home of the University of Wisconsin, as well as a wide variety of other businesses. In contrast, El Centro, California, a poor metropolitan area near the border with Mexico, had an unemployment rate of almost 15 percent in December 2022.

To see the local unemployment rate for your area, go to the BLS website (www.bls.gov/news.release/pdf/metro.pdf).

Source: Bureau of Labor Statistics.

THE TRADE-OFF BETWEEN UNEMPLOYMENT AND INFLATION (LO10-3)

LO10-3 Explain the trade-off between unemployment and inflation.

We just looked at the case in which actual GDP falls *below* potential GDP and more people end up without jobs. But what about the opposite case? As actual GDP rises *above* potential GDP, economic activity increases and unemployment falls. That's good. But the problem with increased economic activity is that inflation can rise; that is, prices and wages can start increasing at a faster rate.

Why should high GDP and low unemployment be linked to rising inflation? Here's one way to think about this: If the number of unemployed workers is low, it's harder for employers to find people to fill job openings. As a result, workers feel they have more power to ask for wage increases. Those wage increases drive up costs for companies and force them to raise prices. The higher prices eat away at the value of wages, and workers have to demand even bigger wage increases to keep up with inflation. The result is the sort of wage-price spiral described in **Chapter 8**.

In other words, if an economy runs too "hot"–that is, if GDP is too high relative to potential GDP–we get rising inflation. If an economy runs too "cold"–if GDP is too low relative to potential GDP–we get unemployment. As we will see in **Chapters 11** and **12**, one of the most important tasks for economic policymakers such as the chair of the Federal Reserve is to find the right balance between inflation and unemployment.

Inflation and Potential GDP

Earlier in this section, we gave a basic description of potential GDP. Now that we have seen the link among inflation, GDP, and unemployment, here is a more precise definition:

Potential GDP = The maximum economic output an economy can sustain without increasing the inflation rate

When the economy is operating at potential, the rate of inflation is neither rising nor falling. This level of potential GDP is the point at which the forces of supply and demand are well balanced, given the existing labor force, technology, and stock of capital. That is why the potential growth rate is sometimes called the *speed limit* of the economy. If actual growth exceeds potential growth for too long, the economy overheats and inflation rises.

The Natural Rate of Unemployment

Inflation tends to rise if the unemployment rate is below the NAIRU. Inflation tends to fall if the unemployment rate is above the NAIRU.

Historically, the unemployment rate provides useful information about whether economic output is approaching a level that causes inflation to accelerate. Milton Friedman, a University of Chicago economist who won the Nobel Prize in Economics in 1976, defined the **natural rate of unemployment** as the level at which inflation is more or less stable. When the unemployment rate is below the natural rate, inflation tends to increase, and when the unemployment rate is above the natural rate, inflation tends to fall. Another, rather long name for the natural rate of unemployment is the **nonaccelerating inflation rate of unemployment**, or **NAIRU** for short.

natural rate of unemployment
The level of unemployment in the economy at which inflation is more or less stable. Also called *NAIRU*.

Nonaccelerating inflation rate of unemployment (NAIRU)
The level of unemployment in the economy at which inflation is more or less stable. Also called *NAIRU*.

NAIRU, or natural rate, has been a key indicator throughout history of how hot an economy can run without pushing up inflation. For example, in 1983, the NAIRU was about 6 percent and the actual unemployment rate was 9.6 percent. With so many people out of work and cutting back on their spending, demand was weak and businesses found it difficult to raise prices. In fact, the inflation rate fell sharply in 1983.

In recent years, however, the association between the unemployment rate and inflation became not so clear-cut. Before the pandemic, the unemployment rate dropped below 4 percent in 2019, but both price and wage inflation stayed surprisingly low. On the other hand, when the unemployment rate dropped below 4 percent in 2022, inflation surged, as we saw in **Chapter 8**. As of early 2023, economists are still not sure whether the NAIRU concept is useful.

RECESSIONS (LO10-4)

LO10-4 Define *recession,* and discuss the impact of recessions on workers and businesses.

recession
A significant decline in economic activity spread across the economy, lasting more than a few months.

peak
The date a recession starts–the high point of an economy before its decline.

trough
The date on which a recession ends and the economy starts heading up again.

expansion
The period of time from a recession trough all the way to the next peak.

business cycle
The recurring pattern of recession and expansion.

Small deviations of real GDP from potential GDP or of the unemployment rate from the NAIRU don't matter much–just as you can drive slightly faster or slower than the flow of traffic on a highway without causing any big problems.

But large deviations from the potential growth path–especially deviations downward–are a problem. Think about what happens if your car stalls in the middle of a busy highway. Similarly, if GDP is running below its potential, everything in the economy suffers. It's harder to find a job, profits aren't as high, malls are empty, and tax revenues fall short of predictions. The world is a gloomier place.

If a downward deviation from potential growth becomes bad enough, an economy can actually shrink. A **recession** is defined as a significant decline in economic activity spread across an economy, lasting more than a few months. (Who identifies the official date when a recession starts? See "**How It Works: Calling the Recession.**")

The Business Cycle

Although all recessions are different, all display similar patterns. The **peak** is the date on which a recession starts–that's when the economy hits a high point and starts heading downward. The date on which the recession ends and the economy starts heading up again is called the **trough**. The **expansion** is the time from the trough, through recovery, and all the way to the next peak. This pattern of recession and expansion is known as the **business cycle**; see **Figure 10.4** for a closer look at a typical cycle.

Figure 10.4 A Typical Business Cycle
The peak marks the start of the recession, and the trough marks its end. A full business cycle runs from one peak to the next.

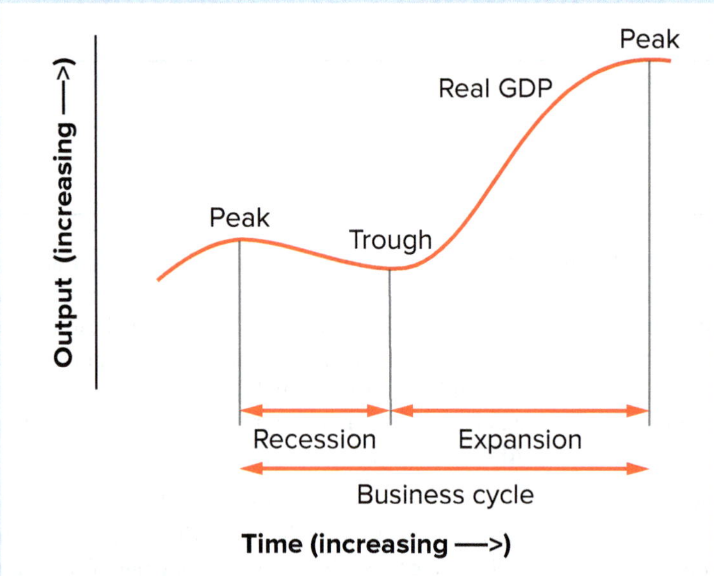

Despite its unusual severity, the Great Recession shows the same basic pattern as past downturns. The Great Recession officially started in December 2007, even though housing prices started dropping as early as 2006. The recession officially ended in June 2009, 18 months after it started, making it the longest, nastiest downturn since the Great Depression.

By contrast, the recession connected with the initial stages of the pandemic was the shortest downturn on record, lasting only two months from February 2020 to April 2020.

Figure 10.5 tracks real GDP through both recessions. The graph shows the differences. The peak of the Great Recession of 2008-2009 came in the fourth quarter of 2007, and the initial stages of the downturn were fairly mild. But after Lehman Brothers went bankrupt in mid-September 2008, the U.S. economy went into a steep plunge.

Figure 10.5 The Great Recession of 2008–2009 and the Pandemic Recession of 2020: Real GDP

The figure shows the peak and trough of the two latest business cycles, as measured by real GDP.

Source: Bureau of Economic Analysis, www.bea.gov.

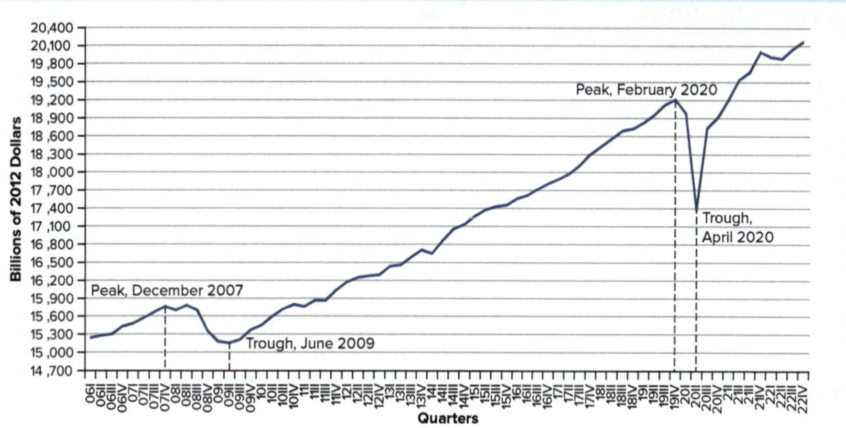

HOW IT WORKS: CALLING THE RECESSION

When is the U.S. economy in recession? That is, when is a decline in the nation's economic activity significant enough to qualify for this official designation? Oddly, government statisticians do not make this decision. Instead, a private research group—the National Bureau of Economic Research (NBER)—decides the official dates on which a recession starts and ends.

The NBER is a Cambridge, Massachusetts–based organization that was founded in the 1920s to study the ups and downs of business cycles. Today, whenever there is an economic downturn, the Business Cycle Dating Committee of the NBER—made up of several prominent economists—meets to decide the official beginning and end dates of a recession, based on key figures like employment and retail sales.

The low point for real GDP came in the second quarter of 2009, as shown in **Figure 10.5**. We can see that real GDP, a measure of the output of the economy, did not exceed its previous peak until 2011.

The pandemic recession had a very different pattern. Real GDP plunged quickly from its peak in the fourth quarter of 2019 and then rebounded equally rapidly. By early 2021, real GDP had regained its previous high.

One important reason why the pandemic recession was so short was the trillions of dollars of government stimulus pumped into the economy, including direct checks to many American households, beefed-up unemployment compensation payments and programs that effectively paid businesses not to lay off workers. These programs were briefly described in **Chapter 6**, but we will go into more detail in **Chapter 11**, which covers fiscal policy.

The Impact of Recessions on Workers

Who suffers the most from a recession? Without question, unemployed workers and their families suffer the most pain, especially those who do not have a savings cushion. From economic, political, and human points of view, a lengthy and deep recession can be a major disaster for individuals who lose their jobs.

The reason is simple: During a recession, if you lose your job, it's hard to find a new one. As the economy shrinks, factories close and companies stop hiring. And even after a recession is over, it can take months or years for the labor market to revive. As a result, people who lose their jobs in recessions can find themselves unemployed for months or even years. That's long enough to outlast their savings and their ability to hold on to their homes (see **Figure 10.6**).

Figure 10.6 The Great Recession and the Pandemic Recession: Private-Sector Jobs

The figure shows the path of private-sector employment during the Great Recession of 2008–2009, the Pandemic Recession of 2020 and the recoveries that followed.

Source: Bureau of Labor Statistics, www.bls.gov.

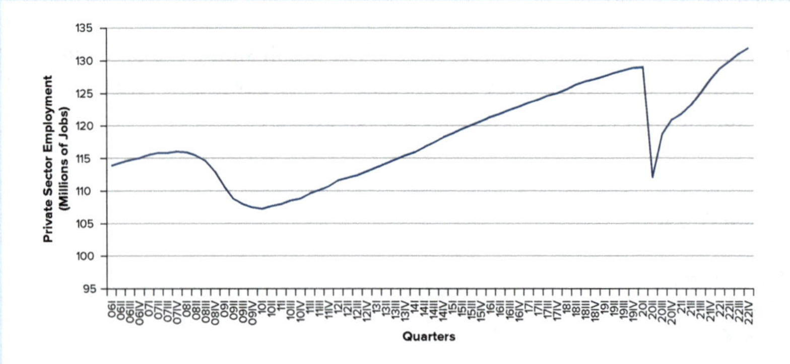

The Impact of Recessions on Businesses

Recessions hurt businesses as well as workers. As an economy slows, the demand schedules of most businesses shift to the left. For the same price, the quantity demanded falls, and therefore the quantity supplied also falls.

Figure 10.7 shows the supply and demand schedules for a market in an economy–say, for cars. During a typical recession, consumers have less money to spend on new cars, and that causes the demand schedule to shift to the left. As a result, production of cars falls from *Q* to *Q'*. The auto companies are forced to offer discounts and special deals, so the price falls from *P* to *P'*. In fact, this is exactly what happened in the Great Recession of 2008-2009. Motor vehicle sales collapsed to the point where General Motors and Chrysler were forced to declare bankruptcy and accept bailouts from the federal government. (During the unusual pandemic recession, consumers temporarily paused their spending on motor vehicles. But they had a lot of cash from government anti-pandemic stimulus programs, plus the money they saved on public activities such as eating out, and then started putting their extra cash into new and used vehicles).

Figure 10.7 The Effect of a Typical Recession on Car Companies

In a typical recession, demand for cars falls, and the demand curve shifts left. That reduces the quantity demanded and supplied for cars and typically causes car companies to offer customers better deals—that is, cheaper prices.

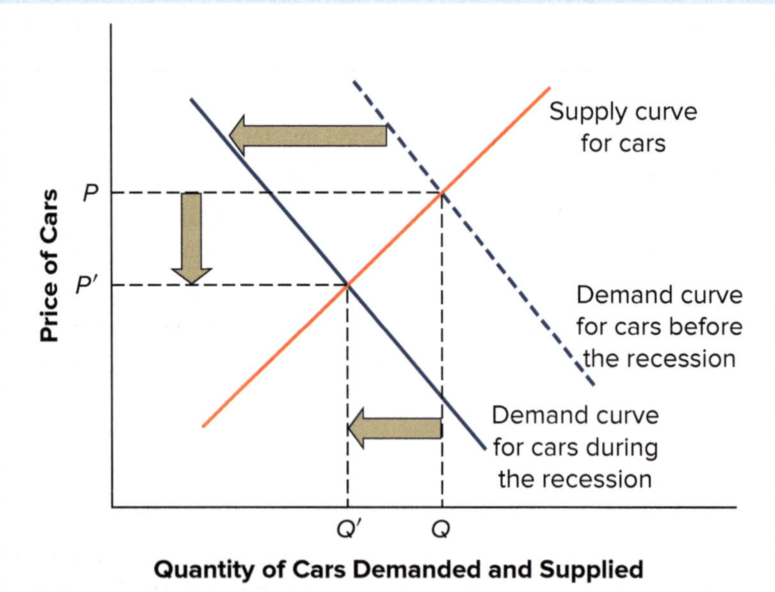

But companies don't simply cut back on current production in a typical recession. In fact, all sorts of businesses–big banks, the mom-and-pop store at the corner–also cut back sharply on expansion and their plans for upgrades in recessions. Any spending they can postpone, they will.

That's why recessions are usually accompanied by a rapid drop in purchases of capital equipment, such as machinery and computers, and an equally noticeable decline in the construction of commercial office buildings, factories, and other nonresidential structures.

In fact, an essential characteristic of a recession is that it is *broad based*, so that the slowdown is spread across most of the economy. **Table 10.1** lists some of the typical areas that are hit by recessions, including home construction and business profits. True, some industries tend to hold up better than others in most recessions (see "**Spotlight: Recession-Resistant Industries**"). Note that, as always, the pandemic recession is the exception to the rule.

Table 10.1 What Typically Falls in Recessions

A recession is a broad decline in economic activity. In addition to the fall in real GDP, here are some other aspects of the economy that typically decline in most recessions.

Aspect of the Economy	What Happens in a Typical Recession
Employment	Businesses lay off workers and cut back on hiring.
Retail sales	Many stores see falling sales and some close.
Home construction	Fewer homes are built.
Housing prices	Home prices drop.
Household income, adjusted for inflation	Many households see their real incomes drop.
Business profits	Businesses make less money.
Business investment	Businesses spend less on physical capital, such as trucks, computers, and buildings.
Industrial production (the output of factories)	Factories produce less.
Tax revenues	Governments collect less tax.

SPOTLIGHT: RECESSION-RESISTANT INDUSTRIES

In any recession, a few sectors usually avoid the general downturn and keep expanding. For example, entertainment spending is typically recession-resistant because people want to have fun to take their minds off their economic problems. Movie ticket sales held up well during the recession years of 2008 and 2009, spurred by the release of films such as *The Dark Knight* (though ticket sales did fall off in 2010, when the top-grossing film was the less-than-stellar *Toy Story 3*).

Another typically recession-resistant industry is health care. People keep getting sick whether the economy is up or down. Moreover, much of health care spending is funded by the federal government, which can keep spending even in a downturn by borrowing money.

As a result, health care employment typically keeps increasing even when other parts of the economy are shrinking. From December 2007 to December 2010, for example, hospitals, physicians' offices, and other health care businesses added roughly 800,000 jobs, while the rest of the private sector lost 7.5 million jobs.

The pandemic recession, of course, was not at all typical, spending on entertainment industries like movies and spectator sports fell sharply because people couldn't gather in large groups. Employment in health care declined because nonessential procedures were cut back to reduce the chances of infection.

Conversely, the industries which expanded the most during the pandemic recession were related to e-commerce and delivery, Companies such as Amazon and Walmart opened many e-commerce fulfillment centers across the country employing hundreds of thousands of workers, while the number of businesses providing local delivery vastly expanded. A conservative count suggests that e-commerce and delivery added more than 800,000 workers between February 2020, before the pandemic started, and February 2023. Brick-and-mortar retail employment stayed about the same, as job gains at building materials stores and supermarkets balanced out losses elsewhere.

Mark Agnor/123RF

WHY DO RECESSIONS HAPPEN? (LO10-5)

LO10-5 List the possible causes of recession.

If you see a car broken down by the side of the road, you don't know what happened. It could be that the driver was unlucky and hit a bad pothole. Or perhaps the driver neglected essential maintenance and the vehicle overheated. Or maybe the car simply ran out of gas.

We face the same uncertainty when it comes to recessions. An economy may stall for a number of different reasons. The question of what causes recessions is one of the longest-running debates among economists, going back to the Great Depression. For our purposes here, we just need to realize that recessions can have different triggers, as **Table 10.2** shows. Let's look at some of these: problems in financial markets, negative supply shifts, negative demand shifts, and inflation fighting.

Table 10.2 Recent Recessions and Their Causes

This table lists some of the causes of recent recessions.

Recession Start Date	Type of Recession	Main Cause
November 1973	Negative supply shift	Sharp rise in oil prices
January 1980	Negative supply shift, inflation fighting	Sharp rise in oil prices combined with interest rate hikes by the Federal Reserve
July 1981	Inflation fighting	Interest rate hikes by the Federal Reserve
July 1990	Negative supply shift, inflation fighting	Oil price hike caused by Iraqi invasion of Kuwait, combined with interest rate hikes by the Federal Reserve
March 2001	Negative demand shift	Decline in tech spending by business
December 2007	Financial crisis	Excess borrowing
February 2020	Negative supply shift, negative demand shift	COVID pandemic

Problems in Financial Markets

Recessions caused by a financial crisis are rare but challenging. Financial markets let individuals and businesses borrow money to finance everything from homes and cars to college educations. When financial markets stop working well, it becomes harder to borrow. When it becomes harder to borrow, the economy slows.

The Great Recession was caused, in large part, by problems in financial markets. As we'll see in **Chapter 13**, many consumers borrowed more than they should have, especially to buy homes. In particular, low-income homebuyers borrowed more than they could afford to pay back–the so-called subprime loans. And many banks lent more than they should have, helping fuel the housing boom.

But, eventually, the boom came to an end and was followed by a bust. Several big Wall Street firms either failed or were forced to sell themselves. Many homebuyers could not pay their mortgages.

After the bust, most banks tightened up their lending standards. As it became harder for consumers to borrow, there was less money available to buy homes and cars. It became harder for small businesses to raise the money they needed to operate and expand. The result was a sharp slowdown in the economy.

Negative Supply Shifts

Another significant cause of recessions is an unexpected negative supply shift, which moves the supply curve to the left for a broad array of markets. The pandemic recession was an unusual example of a negative supply shift, as many businesses were forced to temporarily close their doors, either because of government public health orders or because workers and business owners simply did not want to get exposed to an unknown and potentially fatal virus.

A much more typical example of a negative shock supply shock is a sudden rise in the price of oil. For example, the 1973 oil price shock, described in **Chapter 6**, helped trigger the recession of 1973-1975. Similarly, Saddam Hussein's invasion of Kuwait in 1990, which pushed oil prices up, was one of the main reasons the U.S. economy slipped into recession that year. And the oil price increase of 2007 and 2008 helped slow the U.S. economy going into the early stages of the Great Recession.

An oil price increase is particularly harmful because it is a broad supply shift that affects most markets in an economy. By making energy and transportation more costly, the higher price of oil causes the supply schedule in many individual markets to shift left.

Consider, for example, the market for grocery items. These items are shipped to supermarkets from all over the country, so an increase in the cost of fuel translates directly into rising costs for supermarkets. As **Figure 10.8** shows, a negative supply shift in a market tends to decrease the quantity demanded and increase the price.

Figure 10.8 The Impact of a Typical Negative Supply Shift
A rise in the price of oil can increase transportation costs for groceries and cause a shift in the supply curve to the left. That, in turn, reduces the quantity demanded and supplied. If this affects enough markets, it can cause overall economic output to decline.

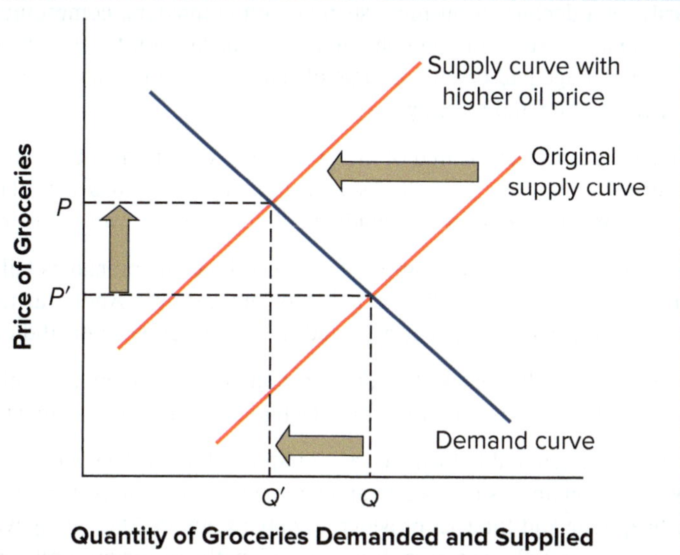

If the higher price of oil affected only the grocery market, that would not cause a recession by itself. After all, grocery purchases, even though they account for billions of dollars of sales each year, are just a small part of the economy.

To cause a recession, a negative shift has to affect many markets simultaneously. In that case, it can decrease the output of the whole economy *and* push up inflation. That's exactly what happened after the oil price shock of 1973: The economy went into a combination of recession and inflation called *stagflation*. In every market where energy was an important cost, the supply curve shifted to the left—including the labor market because higher gasoline prices made commuting more expensive for most people.

Another example of a negative supply shift is a terrorist attack that forces businesses and governments to adopt tighter security measures. For example, suppose every box and container imported into the United States had to be checked for bombs. Such measures would make both shipping and transportation more expensive. The result would be a leftward shift in supply schedules over a broad range of markets, with the resulting fall in quantity and increase in prices that precipitate a recession. (To see an example of a narrow supply shift, take a look at "**Spotlight: Do Hurricanes Cause Recessions?**")

SPOTLIGHT: DO HURRICANES CAUSE RECESSIONS?

Can a natural disaster such as a hurricane or an earthquake cause a recession? Perhaps, but history suggests that it is not likely in the United States. The worst recent natural disaster to hit the United States was Hurricane Katrina in 2005, which almost completely flooded New Orleans and much of the Mississippi coast. The storm caused at least $40 billion in losses and perhaps a lot more. At the same time, damage to the oil wells and refineries along the Gulf Coast drove gasoline prices up across the country.

But despite the devastation in New Orleans, GDP growth for the United States barely slowed in the third and fourth quarters of 2005. There are several reasons for the lack of overall economic impact. First, New Orleans, although a major city, contributed only a relatively small share to the whole U.S. economy. Second, many businesses with operations in New Orleans were able to move their production to other parts of the country. And third, the rebuilding effort, which included billions for repairing and upgrading dikes and levees, actually *added* to the level of economic activity in the United States.

Negative Demand Shifts

A sudden and unexpected drop in demand can also cause a recession. Once again, the pandemic gives us an example of an unusual negative demand shift. During the early months of the pandemic, many people stayed home as much as possible, responding to government public health mandates and voluntarily choosing to minimize their exposure. The reduction in demand meant that many businesses that might have been willing to stay open were forced to cut back or temporarily close.

Looking back a bit further, another example of a recession driven by a negative demand shift was the recession of 2001, which was caused primarily by a decline in business spending on computers, communications equipment, and other information technology gear. Until 2000, companies' spending on computers and information technology had been soaring for several different reasons. First, the dawning of the Internet age had created a surge of start-up dot-com companies, all of which had to spend heavily on computer equipment to get their operations up and running.

Second, businesses were scared of the "Y2K bug," which was the threat that older computer systems and programs would crash when the clock turned to January 1, 2000. As a result, many companies spent large sums of money replacing their old computers and programs. Third, telecom companies were spending billions laying down new fiber-optic cable to handle all the future online traffic they expected.

But these sources of demand evaporated. Most dot-com companies failed. January 1, 2000, came and went (without a major hitch, as it turned out), and the need to fix the Y2K problem was over. And it turned out that the telecom companies had overspent because Internet traffic did not rise as fast as they expected (though Internet traffic did eventually soar).

So businesses, which spent $225 billion on computers and communications equipment in 2000, cut back sharply in 2001 and kept cutting. By 2003, their spending on information technology hardware was down to $160 billion.

This decline in demand helped trigger widespread layoffs. The unemployment rate in the San Jose, California, area–where major Silicon Valley tech companies such as Sun and Cisco are based–jumped from 2.5 percent in 2000 to 8.5 percent just 2 years later. WorldCom, a major telephone and Internet provider, went bankrupt in 2002, along with a host of smaller companies. All told, the "tech bust," as it was called, led to the 2001 recession. It was not a lengthy recession–only eight months–but it took a long time for jobs to recover.

Inflation Fighting

Let's come now to the final important cause of the recession: inflation fighting. If you run too fast and get overheated, you have to slow down for a while to catch your breath. Sometimes, the economy gets into a similar situation: If output runs above potential for too long, the economy overheats and inflation rises, as discussed earlier. When that happens, economic policymakers at the Federal Reserve–the country's central bank–have to take inflation-fighting steps to slow growth. Sometimes, they slow growth so much that the result is a recession.

For example, in 1980 and 1981, the inflation rate was running at 13.5 percent and 10.3 percent, respectively. That was way too high. So Paul Volcker, who was chairman of the Federal Reserve at that point, applied the brakes. To bring down inflation, he needed to get the unemployment rate *above* the NAIRU–which was about 6 percent at the time. That is, he had to intentionally force unemployment way up to reduce inflation.

That's exactly what Volcker did. He raised interest rates so high that businesses and consumers pulled back from borrowing. Purchases of homes and cars plunged, and the unemployment rate skyrocketed. He achieved his goal of reducing inflation–but the result was a deep recession that put millions of people out of work.

As this textbook is being revised in early 2023, the Federal Reserve has been raising interest rates to deal with the inflationary surge described in **Chapter 8**. The economy is still growing, but the jury is still out on whether the Fed's rate hikes will lead to the first recession caused by inflation fighting since 1981-1982.

YOUR ECONOMIC LIFE: Should You Be Worried about a Recession?

By the time you read this textbook, a recession will either be underway or will happen sometime in the next few years. It's inevitable: Market economies occasionally go through downturns, and the United States is no exception.

The bad news: People who graduate during recessions have a harder time finding jobs and end up accepting lower wages. These negative career effects tend to last for years, unfortunately.

The good news: Recessions do end relatively quickly these days, and the recoveries that follow are long. When you look at a graph like **Figure 10.5**, you see the economy steadily climbing out of its low point.

Another piece of good news: Education protects against the worst effects of recession. In the Great Recession, the unemployment rate for high school grads peaked at 11 percent, while the unemployment rate for college grads never got over 5 percent. That's a big difference.

The bottom line is that recessions are tough on everyone, but there's less need to be fearful of them if you have a good education.

Additional Reading: Emily Bianchi, "People Who Graduate During Recessions Earn Less Money – but They're Happier," *Harvard Business Review,* September 21, 2018, https://hbr.org/2018/09/people-who-graduate-during-recessions-earn-less-money-but-theyre-happier.

CONCLUSION

Market economies don't always grow at a steady rate. Sometimes, they grow too fast for a period, creating the conditions in which inflation can get out of control. Other times, market economics shrink, turning into the unpleasant stretch that economists call a recession.

The ups and downs of economies described in this chapter will never go away. But they can be made less harmful by appropriate policy responses, as we will see in the next two chapters.

10 SUMMARY

1. Potential GDP is the output of an economy along a smooth path of growth, which assumes no strains on the economy or unused resources. Real GDP can be higher or lower than potential GDP. The difference between the two is known as the output gap. ***(LO10-1)***
2. When real GDP drops below potential GDP, businesses cut back on hiring. The result is a rise in the unemployment rate–the percentage of the workforce that wants to work but cannot find jobs. Three types of unemployment are frictional, structural, and cyclical. ***(LO10-2)***
3. If the unemployment rate rises above the natural rate of unemployment–also called the NAIRU–the inflation rate falls. If the unemployment rate drops below the NAIRU, the inflation rate rises. ***(LO10-3)***
4. A recession is a significant decline in economic activity spread across an economy, lasting more than a few months. The beginning of a recession is called the peak, and the end of a recession is the trough. Recessions can hurt both workers and businesses. ***(LO10-4)***
5. Recessions can have several different causes. These include problems in financial markets, negative supply shifts, negative demand shifts, and inflation fighting. ***(LO10-5)***

KEY TERMS AND CONCEPTS

potential GDP

potential growth rate

output gap

unemployed

labor force

unemployment rate

underemployed

frictional unemployment

structural unemployment

cyclical unemployment

sticky wages

unions

natural rate of unemployment

nonaccelerating inflation rate of unemployment (NAIRU)

recession

peak

trough

expansion

business cycle

connect PROBLEMS

1. Are the following situations more consistent with a positive output gap or a negative output gap? ***(LO10-1)***

   a) Workers at an e-commerce company are putting in lots of overtime shipping packages.
   b) Many new homes were built but not sold.

c) The roads are so crowded during rush hour that you have to leave early for work.
d) You apply for a new job listed online, and there are plenty of other applicants.
e) Workers stay home during a pandemic because of fear of infection.

2. Do the following events increase or decrease potential GDP? *(LO10-1)*

a) New government policies that restrict the number of educated immigrants entering the country.
b) A decrease in the purchases of new computers by businesses.
c) Expansion of funding for higher education.
d) The discovery of a new oil field in Pennsylvania.
e) The discovery of a cheaper way of generating energy from sunlight.
f) A safe COVID vaccine that eliminates the chances of getting infected.

3. The following table gives the potential GDP and real GDP for a very small economy, both measured in 2012 dollars. *(LO10-2)*

Year	Real GDP (2012 Dollars)	Potential GDP (2012 Dollars)	Output Gap
2016	100	100	—
2017	107	105	—
2018	110	110	—
2019	113	115	—

a) Fill in the column for the output gap.
b) Plot the lines for real GDP and potential GDP on a graph.
c) Would you expect the unemployment rate to be higher in 2017 or 2019? Explain.
d) In which year would you expect it to be easiest to find a job? (Assume that the NAIRU is the same each year.)

4. A man used to work for pay, but he is currently attending community college in the evening to get a degree, while taking care of his children during the day. We would count him in the category of ______________ *(LO10-2)*

a) unemployed.
b) underemployed.
c) employed.
d) neither employed nor unemployed.

5. Say whether each of the following is more likely to be a case of frictional, structural, or cyclical unemployment. *(LO10-2)*

a) You graduate from college, and it takes you a month to find a job.
b) A slowdown in the economy means that restaurants are hiring fewer workers.
c) A furniture maker closes a factory in North Carolina and moves production to China. The laid-off factory workers have trouble finding new jobs because other furniture companies are closing their U.S. factories as well.
d) The rise of e-commerce causes the local department store to lay off workers.
e) There are plenty of job advertisements for nurses but few for factory workers.
f) Restaurants in downtown office districts close permanently because more people are working from home after the pandemic.

6. Suppose the NAIRU is 5 percent, and the current unemployment rate is 4.5 percent. Are the following statements true or false? *(LO10-3)*

a) The inflation rate is likely to fall in future months.
b) Real GDP is likely higher than potential GDP.
c) We can find jobs for more people without increasing inflation.

7. Some historic inflation and unemployment figures for the United States are presented here. *(LO10-3)*

Year	Inflation Rate (%)	Unemployment Rate (%)
1996	3.0	5.4
1997	2.3	4.9
1998	1.6	4.5
1999	2.2	4.2
2000	3.4	4.0
2001	2.8	4.7

a) In what years does the inflation rate rise compared to the previous year?
b) What are the unemployment rates for the years when inflation rises?
c) Based on these data, was the NAIRU greater or less than 5 percent during this period? Explain.

8. The following table gives real GDP for a small economy going through a business cycle. *(LO10-4)*

Year	Real GDP (2012 Dollars)
2017	101
2018	103
2019	104
2020	102
2021	103
2022	105

a) Plot the line for real GDP on a graph.
b) What are the starting and ending dates of the recession?
c) How many years does the expansion last after the recession?

9. Recessions affect many aspects of the economy. For each of the following economic quantities, say whether it rises or falls during a typical recession. *(LO10-4)*

a) Construction of new hotels.
b) Tax revenues.
c) Airline workers.
d) Workers who are overqualified for their current jobs.

10. Here are several economic events that could potentially help trigger a recession. Say which category each one falls into: negative supply shift, negative demand shift, inflation fighting, or problems in financial markets. *(LO10-5)*

a) War in the Middle East destroys oil fields in Saudi Arabia.
b) China suddenly cuts off exports to the United States.
c) Inflation accelerates sharply to 10 percent a year.
d) Mortgages become much harder to get because banks become less willing to lend.

11. The pandemic recession was unusual. Which of the following helped cause the recession *(LO10-5)*:

a) Government public health requirements restricting nonessential travel.
b) High oil prices.
c) Problems in the banking system.
d) Workers who feared getting infected.

CH 11

FISCAL POLICY

Pixtal/AGE Fotostock

LEARNING OBJECTIVES

After reading this chapter, you should be able to:

LO11-1 Identify key differences between the private sector and government.
LO11-2 Describe the short-term impacts of increased government spending, and use the multiplier effect to calculate the effect of fiscal stimulus.
LO11-3 Summarize the limitations of using increased government spending to stimulate growth.
LO11-4 Discuss the ways that changes in tax rates affect the economy.
LO11-5 Explain how the budget deficit affects the economy in the short run and in the long run.

> fiscal policy
> Decisions about government spending, taxes, and borrowing in the short and long run.

In 2020 and 2021, the federal government used its financial muscle to combat the economic impact of the COVID pandemic. President Donald Trump signed multiple bills to help support individuals and businesses in the face of virus-induced disruptions, and President Joseph Biden followed with legislation that provided additional pandemic relief.

These unprecedented increases in federal spending and transfer payments helped cushion the economic impact of the pandemic. But in 2022, as the pandemic eased and inflation surged, attention turned to reducing the federal budget deficit, leading President Biden to sign the Inflation Reduction Act of 2022.

In this chapter, we will analyze the economic effects of **fiscal policy**—that is, decisions about government spending, taxes, and debt in both the short run and the long run. In the short term, fiscal policy consists of the government's budget decisions that affect employment, output, and inflation over the next couple of years. That includes the spending increases and tax cuts that the government enacted to fight the Great Recession of 2008–2009, and the huge government programs put in place to deal with the pandemic. In the long term, fiscal policy creates the link between government spending and taxation decisions and the country's economic growth.

Fiscal policy is probably the most politically charged area of economics. Each year, lawmakers and government officials in Washington decide how to allocate trillions of dollars. The result is a federal budget hundreds of pages long in which every sentence can make a big impact on someone's life or company. And of course, members of Congress get elected in part because of their ability to influence the budget in favor of individuals and companies that donated money to campaigns.

But leaving politics aside, reputable economists disagree about the right way to run fiscal policy. Some favor a larger role for the government, especially when the economy is in a slump or faces a major emergency like the pandemic. Others argue for shrinking government spending and taxation because they prefer less government interference and oversight. And a third group of economists focuses on reducing the size of the budget deficit, which is the difference between spending and revenue.

In this chapter, we will lay out the basics of fiscal policy. We will discuss both the positive and negative impacts of government spending, taxes, and borrowing on the rest of the economy, presenting the different perspectives in an unbiased fashion. We will end this chapter by examining long-term fiscal policy.

THE GOVERNMENT AND THE ECONOMY (LO11-1)

LO11-1 Identify key differences between the private sector and government.

In 2022, government at all levels–federal, state, and local–spent $4.4 trillion for the salaries of government workers and for goods and services provided to the government. This is what we called "government output" in **Chapter 7**. Another $980 billion went for interest payments on government debt, while another $3.9 trillion went to **transfer payments**–government payments to individuals such as Social Security, Medicare, welfare, and other payments such as subsidies to businesses. In other words, one of government's most important roles is to act as a pipeline, shifting money from some people to others.

transfer payments

Government social benefits paid to individuals, including Social Security, Medicare, and unemployment benefits.

HOW IT WORKS: LEVELS OF GOVERNMENT

In this chapter, we often talk about government as if it were one big entity. But there are three separate levels of government, each of which has different patterns of spending and taxation. The federal government, based in Washington, DC, spends mostly on national defense, Medicare, Medicaid, and Social Security.

In contrast, the 50 state governments and the more than 30,000 county and municipal governments have different priorities. Their big expenses are education and local services such as police, fire protection, and waste collection. State governments also pay quite a bit toward Medicaid—the medical care for the poor.

Take the city of Springfield, Massachusetts, which has a population of over 150,000 and is also home to the Basketball Hall of Fame (which, naturally, is shaped a bit like a basketball). In 2023, the city had a budget of $819 million. Out of that, 65.1 percent was spent on education and 10.4 percent on public safety (police and fire). This is a very different spending pattern from that of the federal government.

In many ways, a dollar spent by the government contributes as much to economic output as a dollar spent in the private sector. Paying a schoolteacher's salary, fixing a bridge, or providing medical care for the elderly can be just as important–or perhaps even more important–to the economy than your neighbor's purchasing an expensive sports car.

However, there *is* a big difference between government and the private sector. In the private sector, businesses and individuals collect and spend money by means of market transactions. They exchange money either for goods and services, in the case of businesses and their customers, or for labor, in the case of workers and employers. All transactions are voluntary, so presumably all parties benefit.

What's more, as we saw in **Chapter 5**, private businesses are always under pressure to cut costs and find ways to become more efficient. If they don't do that, they are at risk of being put out of business by competitors.

taxation
The main way the government raises revenue from individuals and businesses.

Governments, in contrast, are not under the same kind of market pressure to be efficient and innovative. Nobody is going to put the federal government out of business or take away its customers. Instead, the level of government spending is set by political negotiation rather than market transactions. That government spending is then funded through a combination of **taxation** and borrowing. Taxation, the main way the government raises money, is a legally mandated transfer of funds from individuals and businesses to the government.

Governments also raise money by borrowing. Like private borrowers, governments have to pay interest on their debts. But unlike private borrowers, they can pay back their debts by raising taxes if necessary. For these reasons, the government has a special role in the economy.

THE SHORT-TERM IMPACT OF GOVERNMENT SPENDING (LO11-2)

LO11-2 Describe the short-term impacts of increased government spending, and use the multiplier effect to calculate the effect of fiscal stimulus.

federal budget
The detailed list of the federal government's spending and revenue plans for the year.

The **federal budget** is the detailed list of the federal government's spending and revenue plans for the year. Each year, the federal budget is set through a complicated and exhausting process beginning in February or March, when the president proposes a budget for the next fiscal year (which starts on October 1 of each year). The detailed budget document is more than 1,000 pages long.

For the next nine months, various congressional committees and the executive branch wrangle over everything from the overall level of spending down to the smallest details, such as the funding for the Marine Mammal Commission (total 2022 budget: $4 million).

Eventually, Congress and the president agree on which government activities will be funded, for how much, and what the tax rules will be. What's important here is that the level of spending and the priorities for the year are set through political negotiations, not through market transactions. If emergencies arise–like the pandemic, a natural disaster, an economic crisis, or a national security threat–Congress can add money to the budget, with the president's signature.

The decisions made by Congress and the president have a huge impact on the rest of the economy. Let's say Congress and the president agree to boost spending by allocating an extra $100 million to repair a bridge that has been damaged in a flood the previous year. We will ignore for the moment the important question of where the extra $100 million will come from (though we'll see later in the chapter that this makes a big difference to the economy). We'll also ignore for the moment the positive benefits of travel from repairing the bridge (so that cars and trucks can take a shorter route).

The government spends some of the money on labor: architects and engineers to draw up the repair plans, truck drivers to move the supplies, construction workers to assemble the parts, and police officers to supervise the site. It spends some money on equipment: cranes, drilling equipment, and trucks. Other money goes for materials: steel, concrete, and paint.

Repairing the bridge creates more demand for labor, materials, and equipment. The demand schedule for labor and the demand schedule for construction materials and equipment both shift to the right, as we see in **Figures 11.1** and **11.2**.

The effect of the increase in government spending is to push up the quantity of labor from L to L' and to push up the quantity of construction materials from Q to Q'. In other words, unemployment falls because more workers are employed. And production increases because more construction materials are being demanded and supplied.

A similar process of boosting employment and production took place during the pandemic when the government wrote checks directly to individuals and businesses. In 2020 and 2021, the federal government sent out three rounds of pandemic stimulus checks, otherwise known as "Economic Impact Payments," totaling as much as $1200, $600, and $1400 per income tax filer. Moreover, the government greatly expanded unemployment insurance benefits, as well as creating the Paycheck Protection Program, which essentially paid businesses to keep their workers on payroll.

Some of the flood of government money went into household savings, but the rest was used to buy necessities like food, and to purchase motor vehicles and other goods and services. Notably, many families could afford to renovate and expand their homes, a necessity at a time when kids and parents were stuck at home. This renovation boom then increased the demand for construction workers.

Figure 11.1 The Impact of Government Spending on the Labor Market
An increase in government spending pushes the demand curve for labor to the right, which boosts the quantity of labor supplied and demanded from *L* to *L'*.

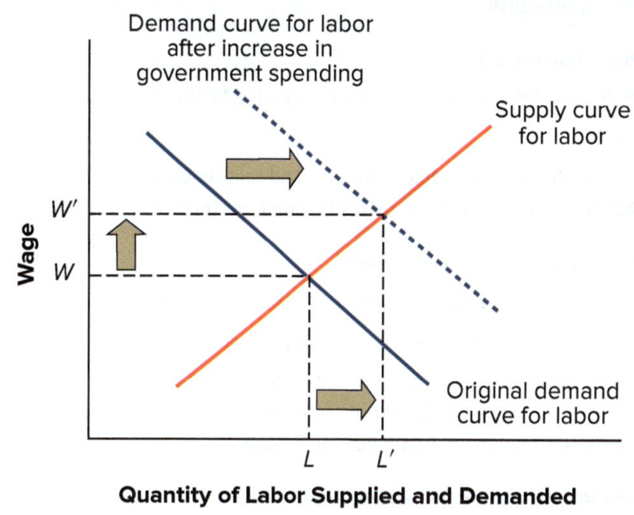

Figure 11.2 The Impact of Government Spending on the Market for Construction Materials
When the government spends money to repair a bridge, that pushes the demand curve for construction materials to the right, which boosts the quantity of construction material supplied and demanded from *Q* to *Q'*.

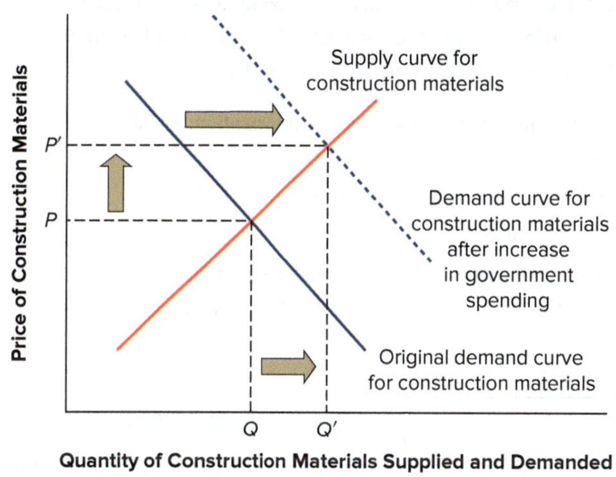

This brings us to the following general principle: In the short term, an increase in government spending lowers unemployment and increases gross domestic product (GDP), all other things being equal. This principle is the essence of the **Keynesian approach** to macroeconomics, which uses increases in government spending and cuts in taxes (as we will see later in this chapter) to combat the effect of recessions. Such increases in government spending and cuts in taxes are called **fiscal stimulus** because they involve changes in fiscal policy. Economist John Maynard Keynes originally proposed the use of government spending to stimulate the economy in the 1930s during the Great Depression. He argued that the reason for the steep decline in GDP during the Depression was the lack of demand–a problem the government could correct by spending more.

Keynesian approach
An approach to macroeconomics that uses increases in government spending and cuts in taxes to combat recessions.

fiscal stimulus
Increases in government spending and cuts in taxes designed to boost the economy.

Since then, economists have had long and complex disputes about the validity of the Keynesian approach. Over time, they have come to better understand many of its limitations, which we will discuss later in this chapter. However, when the economy faces an emergency, most economists agree it is important for the government to support demand. That was true during the pandemic, as we saw in **Table 6.2** in **Chapter 6**, which listed the major pieces of pandemic stimulus legislation signed by President Donald Trump and President Joseph Biden. And it was true during the Great Recession of 2008-2009, when President George W. Bush and President Barack Obama signed several pieces of legislation intended to stimulate growth and job creation by boosting demand (see **Table 11.1**).

Table 11.1 Major Fiscal Stimulus Legislation of the Great Recession, 2008-2010

Economic Stimulus Act

Date: February 2008, signed by President George W. Bush

Amount: $152 billion

Key aspects: Provided tax rebates for low- and middle-income households and investment incentives for some businesses.

Troubled Asset Relief Program (TARP)

Date: October 2008, signed by President George W. Bush

Amount: $410 billion invested, virtually all paid back

Key aspects: Gave the federal government authority to prop up the economy by investing up to $700 billion in troubled financial institutions and selected nonfinancial businesses.

American Recovery and Reinvestment Act (ARRA)

Date: February 2009, signed by President Barack Obama

Amount: $787 billion

Key aspects: Gave a wide range of tax reductions, including tax credits for college tuition, first-time home buyers, and home owners who invest in energy efficiency. Increased spending on health care and education, including aid to local school districts and Pell grants. Invested in highway, bridge, rail, and air projects.

Tax Relief, Unemployment Insurance Reauthorization, and Job Creation Act

Date: December 2010, signed by President Barack Obama

Amount: $858 billion

Key aspects: Extended tax reductions that were going to expire as of December 2010. Extended unemployment benefits. Temporarily cut payroll tax.

The Multiplier Effect

Now let's continue our story of repairing the bridge. With more workers employed, the demand for consumer products goes up. Workers now have money to buy necessities like food, consumer durables like cars, and luxuries like occasional dinners out. That boosts spending, which increases sales across the whole range of businesses, including grocery stores, auto dealers, and restaurants.

Think about auto dealers, for example. Remember, the government itself doesn't buy any extra cars because it's repairing the bridge, but the newly hired construction workers do. If the government hires 1,000 construction workers, and 100 of them buy new cars with their paychecks, that's 100 cars that weren't sold before.

The rise in sales across the board encourages private-sector businesses to hire more workers as well: more car sales staff, more supermarket checkout clerks, and more restaurant cooks. What's more, if sales go up enough, the auto dealers may be tempted to add another building to accommodate the new demand. And guess what? The construction company that builds the new auto dealership probably has to hire new workers too.

In other words, the initial government hiring effort creates enough additional purchasing power in the economy to induce another round of hiring in the private sector. And those extra workers, in turn, boost the economy with their purchases as well.

Taken together, this **multiplier effect** is the short-term boost in economic activity that flows from the government's spending increase (or tax cut, as we will see later in the chapter). A similar multiplier effect occurs for any type of government spending. For example, writing a pandemic stimulus check to poor households raises the demand for food, leading grocery stores to hire more cashiers. A purchase order for military submarines increases employment at the shipyards that keeps local stores humming, boosts construction of new homes for the shipyard workers, and perhaps even increases jobs at beach resorts as the workers can afford more family vacations.

multiplier effect
The short-term boost in economic activity that flows from the government's spending increase (or tax cut).

We can state the multiplier as a **job multiplier**, which gives the total number of jobs created by one additional government-funded job. A job multiplier of 2 means that each new government job creates one new private-sector job. A job multiplier of 1 means no additional private-sector jobs are created.

job multiplier
The total number of jobs created by one additional government-funded job.

Alternatively, we can state the multiplier as a **spending multiplier**, which gives the increase in GDP created by one additional dollar of government expenditures. Suppose the government spends an additional dollar on hiring workers or buying supplies. By itself that would boost GDP by $1 because government spending on goods and services is one component of GDP (as we saw in **Chapter 7**). But that dollar could have an additional effect as that new worker uses the new income to increase his purchases. A spending multiplier of 1.4 means that GDP goes up by $1.40 in response to the initial spending increase: $1 from the bigger government component and $0.40 extra in the private sector.

spending multiplier
The increase in GDP created by one additional dollar of government expenditures.

To put things in a wider perspective, suppose the government boosts spending by $200 billion. If the spending multiplier is 1.4, GDP will rise by $28 billion, including both the initial spending and its follow-up effects. That seems like a lot of money. However, with national GDP in 2022 running at about $25 trillion per year, a $280 billion increase is equivalent to only about a 1.1 percent increase in GDP (1.1 percent = $280 billion/$25 trillion).

Economists use the multiplier to help estimate the impact of fiscal stimulus (see "**Spotlight: Measuring the Impact of Stimulus Legislation**"). The multiplier can work at either the national or the local level. A clear example of the multiplier effect on the local level plays out in Washington, DC. The main employer in the District of Columbia is, of course, the federal government, which accounts for about 30 percent of all the area's workers. In fact, if it weren't for the federal government, most private-sector businesses in Washington wouldn't be there, including many law firms and trade associations that lobby legislators and regulators. Without the government and the multiplier effect, Washington might be a small and sleepy village.

The Marginal Propensity to Consume

What determines the size of the multiplier? One factor is the **marginal propensity to consume (MPC)**, which is the portion that households spend of each additional dollar they receive. Think about a construction worker being hired to build the bridge. When she gets the pay from her new job, she has the choice to spend the money or put it in the bank. If her MPC is 0.6, she'll spend 60 cents of that additional dollar and save the remaining 40 cents.

marginal propensity to consume (MPC)

The portion that households spend of each additional dollar they receive.

SPOTLIGHT: MEASURING THE IMPACT OF STIMULUS LEGISLATION

The pandemic was a unique event, with economic implications that will take years to play out. As a result, if we want to understand and measure the economic impact of fiscal stimulus, it's better to look a bit further back, at the legislation enacted to deal with the Great Recession of 2008–2009. From the beginning, President Barack Obama and his team tried to track the impact of the American Recovery and Reinvestment Act (ARRA) on output and jobs. They required recipients to report on job creation and set up a website to offer the public this information.

Tracking the job creation, though, turned out to be more difficult than expected. Part of the problem was the sheer diversity of projects. ARRA-funded projects included everything from $23 million to help complete biking and walking trails near Philadelphia and Camden, New Jersey; to $73 million for the construction of "Warriors in Transition Barracks" for military personnel who were wounded in Iraq or Afghanistan; to $1.6 billion for cleaning up the Savannah River nuclear weapons site in South Carolina.

In the end, the best estimates of the economic impact of ARRA came from the spending multipliers used by the Congressional Budget Office (CBO). For example, in a February 2015 report, CBO estimated that spending on infrastructure had a spending multiplier of as little as 0.4, or as much as 2.2, spread over several quarters.

Based on this assumption, CBO estimated that the stimulus program raised GDP by as little as 0.4 percent or as much as 1.8 percent in 2009, by 0.7 percent to 4.1 percent in 2010, and by 0.4 percent to 2.3 percent in 2011.

What's remarkable is how wide these ranges are. Despite the best efforts of economists, macroeconomic policy is still an inexact science.

Source: The Congressional Budget Office, https://www.cbo.gov/sites/default/files/114th-congress-2015-2016/reports/49958-ARRA.pdf.

The higher the marginal propensity to consume, the bigger the multiplier will be, all other things being equal. If those newly hired construction workers run right out and buy cars, they'll give a big boost to the rest of the economy. More autoworkers will be hired, who in turn will go out and spend their wages on renovating their homes, say. That will lift the employment of carpenters, and so forth.

But if the newly hired construction workers sock all their money away in the bank, the short-term boost to the economy will be much smaller. Car sales won't go up, extra autoworkers won't be hired, and employment won't rise as much.

At one end of the scale, poor individuals typically have a marginal propensity to consume of close to 1. They are generally short of money for necessities. So, given an extra dollar, they are forced to spend it all (a survey by the Federal Reserve suggests that only about one-third of low-income households do any saving).

In contrast, the richest individuals don't spend all their income, so if you give them an extra dollar, it's not likely to affect their spending habits much. Consider Elon Musk, CEO of Tesla, and one of the richest persons in the world. If you give him an extra $1000, he's not likely to go on a buying spree. As a result, the rich have a very low marginal propensity to consume–perhaps close to zero.

The implication? The multiplier is higher if government spending goes, directly or indirectly, to people with a high marginal propensity to consume. That's why the pandemic stimulus checks were designed with income limits, so that they were more likely to go to households that would spend the money. Similarly, a government project that hires unemployed workers into long-term jobs generally has a big multiplier effect because these workers are likely to spend a lot of their wages. But a program that hands out money to rich Americans is unlikely to have the same immediate impact on GDP.

Overseas Leakage

Another factor affecting the multiplier is the amount of money that's spent on goods and services produced in the United States versus the amount spent on imports. Government spending, if it is to boost output, needs to encourage production and employment in the United States. But in a world where so many products are made overseas, it becomes more likely that fiscal stimulus will lead to increased imports rather than to faster growth at home. This transfer of domestic economic stimulus to foreign markets is known as **overseas leakage**.

overseas leakage

A situation where fiscal stimulus leads to increased imports rather than to faster growth at home.

Leakage was less important in the past. In the 1960s, for example, imports of goods and services equaled only 4 percent of gross domestic purchases. As of 2022, imports of goods and services made up 15.5 percent of gross domestic purchases. For some types of goods, such as clothing and toys, imports supply more than half of all U.S. purchases.

As overseas leakage grows, the multiplier from fiscal stimulus shrinks. That's especially true when the government purchases directly from overseas suppliers, which completely skips any job creation in the United States (see "**Spotlight: Fiscal Stimulus and the Buy American Provision**").

SPOTLIGHT: FISCAL STIMULUS AND THE BUY AMERICAN PROVISION

Policymakers are naturally concerned with using fiscal stimulus to create jobs for Americans. To that end, several pieces of pandemic-era legislation contained provisions requiring money to be spent on goods produced mainly in the United States.

Will these provisions achieve their intended goal? Based on past experience, perhaps not. The American Recovery and Reinvestment Act (ARRA), the 2009 stimulus legislation, included a "Buy American" provision—public works projects funded by the legislation had to be built using only "iron, steel, and manufactured goods . . . produced in the United States."

Seems clear, right? Except that the legislation contained several large exceptions to the Buy American rule. The government was allowed to waive the rule if it cost too much to buy American, if American-made goods were not available in sufficient quantities, or if the agency overseeing a project said that requiring American-made products would be "inconsistent with the public interest."

For example, ARRA included funding for making high-speed broadband available to more people. But because most broadband equipment uses components from all over the world, the government had to issue a broad waiver of the Buy American requirement to achieve its goals. Another example: The Air Force wanted to construct housing for military families at an Alaskan base using ARRA funds. But the Air Force waived the Buy American requirements when it couldn't find domestic-made versions of a "Residential Style Polished Chrome Toilet Paper Holder" and other similar items.

In the end, it's hard to say how much impact the Buy American requirements had or how much of the fiscal stimulus leaked overseas. In a global economy, buying American is easier to say than to accomplish.

Source: https://innovationandgrowth.wordpress.com/2011/04/18/air-force-certifies-the-weakness-of-domestic-manufacturing/

The Size of the Multiplier

With all the different factors affecting the impact of government spending on the economy, there is much disagreement among economists about the size of the job and spending multipliers.

But as the next section shows, the exact size of the multiplier usually depends on where we are in the business cycle. What's more, the use of government spending to boost the economy comes with some troubling negative consequences, including inflation and debt. These, too, will be discussed in the next section and the rest of the chapter.

THE LIMITATIONS OF SPENDING STIMULUS (LO11-3)

LO11-3 Summarize the limitations of using increased government spending to stimulate growth.

So far, we've focused on one aspect of fiscal policy: how increased government spending can boost employment and GDP. In the short run, this seems to imply that if the spending and job multipliers are greater than 1, a clear strategy exists for creating widespread prosperity: Ramp up government budgets and watch the economy improve.

An increase in government spending tends to raise wages and prices in the short term.

In fact, in the 1960s, many economists and politicians believed that the government could get rid of unemployment and reduce poverty by stimulating the economy. In August 1964, for example, President Lyndon Johnson signed a bill that created the Job Corps, an agency that trained and found jobs for poor young people who might otherwise not be employed. The stated goal was to drive the unemployment rate down to 4 percent or less.

But economists gradually learned that there were plenty of downsides to stimulating the economy through fiscal policy. In fact, those downsides greatly limited the situations in which the government could use spending as an economic strategy.

The Perils of Inflation

Let's start with inflation. In the previous section, we showed how the bridge repair effort by the government would increase the quantities demanded of labor, construction materials, and all sorts of other goods and services. But if we look again at **Figures 11.1** and **11.2**, we also see something else: an increase in wages and prices.

In other words, an attempt to use government spending to boost the economy also tends to create inflation. The extra government spending pushes up demand, and prices and wages rise faster than they would otherwise.

This makes sense. In the bridge example, the government would need to hire a lot of skilled construction workers. If they already had jobs in the private sector, the government would need to offer higher wages to lure them away. Similarly, the need for steel for the bridge is likely to raise the price of steel. As a result, in the short term, an increase in government spending raises wages and prices.

Which effect of government spending is likely to be stronger–the impact on output or the impact on inflation?

It depends on where we are in the business cycle. Remember from **Chapter 10** that the business cycle consists of recession and expansion. During a recession, the unemployment rate rises above the natural rate. Real GDP drops and falls beneath potential GDP until the economy reaches a trough. Then the process reverses itself.

In the depths of a recession, when things seem miserable, there are plenty of underutilized resources–workers, factories, buildings, equipment. At that point, an increase in government spending can provide an effective boost to the economy. The job and spending multipliers will be relatively high, and the effect on inflation will be relatively low. For example, if there are many unemployed skilled construction workers, a new government bridge-building project can lower unemployment without depriving private companies of their workforce.

But what if the economy is already doing very well? Then, most available resources and workers are already being used by private industry. So, if the government comes in and boosts spending, there will be a big effect on inflation and relatively small job and spending multipliers. Returning to the bridge example, if most skilled construction workers are already employed in private jobs, the government's need for help with the new bridge will bid up the cost of workers rather than adding to employment.

In other words, an increase in government spending is more likely to have a positive impact on jobs and output when the economy is well into a recession so that the unemployment rate is above the natural rate and real GDP is below potential GDP. An increase in government spending is more likely to lead to higher inflation when the unemployment rate is below the natural rate and real GDP is above potential GDP.

Here's another way to think about it: In some respects, a recession is like a big pothole in a highway. It makes the ride bumpier, slower, and more dangerous. And just as a paving crew fills in the pothole with asphalt, the government can fill in the recession "pothole" by increasing spending. That gives business and individuals a smoother ride.

But what if the paving crew keeps pouring on asphalt after the pothole is filled? The cars don't move faster. Instead, we just get a big bump in the road that may even cause more problems than the original pothole did. Similarly, if the government continues to boost spending after the recession is over, we get more inflation rather than faster growth.

This helps explain why inflation accelerated in 2021 and 2022. Government fiscal stimulus continued to boost the economy after the pandemic recession was over. In addition, supply chain problems and the Russian invasion of Ukraine in early 2022 also helped lift prices, as we noted in **Chapter 8**.

stimulative

A government policy action, such as a tax cut, that pushes up output and reduces unemployment in the short run.

Lags in Policy

That brings us to the next problem: figuring out the right time for the government to boost spending in response to a downturn. When an economy goes into recession, unemployment rises and real GDP falls below potential GDP. So, according to the analysis we've just seen, boosting government spending in a recession should be **stimulative**–that is, it should have a good chance of pushing up output and reducing unemployment in the short run. But now here's a question: When an economic downturn hits, can Congress and the president increase government spending quickly enough to do any good?

lag

The length of time between recognizing that the economy is in recession and getting fiscal stimulus or monetary stimulus into effect.

income tax
A tax collected on individual income.

property tax
A tax collected on the value of residential and commercial real estate.

payroll tax
A tax collected on wage payments, paid by both employees and employers to fund Social Security and Medicare.

This may seem like an odd issue, but it's tougher for them to do so than you might think. There are big **lags** in the government response. First, it takes time to recognize that the economy is in a recession. Moreover, any major project–like a new bridge–takes months or years to get going. The money has to be approved by Congress and signed by the president, which does not happen quickly. Then the construction contracts have to be given out, which is also not a quick process. Given that the recession of 1990-1991 and the recession of 2001 both lasted only eight months, the stimulative spending may not actually take effect until after the recession has ended.

If the spending comes when the economy is already out of recession, it is worse than simply being late: It typically adds to inflation. For that reason, in past downturns, recession-fighting policy has focused on tax cuts (to be covered in the next section) and changes in monetary policy (to be covered in the next chapter).

The Great Recession lasted long enough for Washington to react with fiscal stimulus. The downturn started in December 2007, and ARRA was not passed until February 2009, 14 months later. However, the recession was still going on, and the stimulus was much welcomed. Policymakers learned from these experiences, and were able to utilize that knowledge when the pandemic recession occurred.

TAXATION (LO11-4)

LO11-4 Discuss the ways that changes in tax rates affect the economy.

corporate income tax
A tax collected on corporate profits.

sales tax
A tax collected on retail sales.

excise tax
A tax collected on particular items such as gasoline, tobacco, and alcoholic beverages.

Up to this point, we've focused on the impact of government spending. But remember that the money the government spends has to come from somewhere. Either the government raises funds through taxes, or it borrows.

Let's first look at the economic effects of tax increases or tax cuts. Then in the next section, we'll examine government borrowing.

The Basics

The main source of money for government spending is *taxation*. Taxes include a diverse collection of ways in which the government raises money: **income tax**, **property tax** on the value of homes and commercial buildings, **payroll tax** that funds Social Security and Medicare, **corporate income tax**, **sales tax** on retail purchases, and **excise tax** on gasoline, tobacco, and alcohol. In addition, there are all sorts of smaller taxes, such as taxes on hotel rooms, airline tickets, and sporting events (often called an *amusement tax*). **Table 11.2** lists the major taxes in the United States.

Table 11.2 Major Types of U.S. Taxes

The biggest revenue source for the government is the federal income tax.

Name of Tax	What It Taxes
Income tax	All individual income, including wages, gains from investments, tips, and lottery winnings
Property tax	The value of residential and commercial real estate
Payroll tax	Wage payments (paid by both employees and employers to fund Social Security and Medicare)
Corporate income tax	Corporate profits
Sales tax	Retail sales
Excise tax	Particular items such as gasoline, tobacco, and alcoholic beverages

We often complain about being overtaxed, and certainly the government collects a lot more tax than it used to. But compared to the size of the economy, tax collections have not changed much in the past 500 years or so.

In 1970, governments at all levels collected taxes totaling roughly 25 percent of GDP. Surprisingly, taxes were only 27 percent of GDP in 2021–taking just a slightly larger share of the economy compared to their level almost 50 years earlier. The reason? Tax collections have risen enormously since 1970, but so has GDP.

Changes in the Tax System

The single biggest tax is the federal personal income tax. **Figure 11.3** shows the income tax as a share of GDP, along with key changes in tax policy.

Figure 11.3 Federal Personal Income Tax as a Share of GDP, 1972–2022

Despite ups and downs, the federal income tax as a share of GDP shows no long-term trend.

Source: Bureau of Economic Analysis, www.bea.gov.

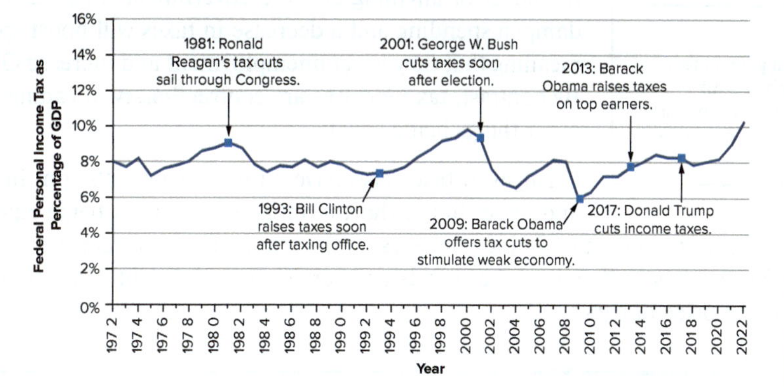

When the tax share rises, as it did in the late 1970s and the late 1990s, political pressure for tax cuts mounts. For example, the federal income tax as a share of GDP peaked at 9.1 percent in 1981, the year President Ronald Reagan proposed and got Congress to approve deep tax cuts. Similarly, the federal income tax share of GDP reached a peak of 9.8 percent in 2000, making it easy for President George W. Bush to make a case for cutting taxes.

But when the income tax share falls as it did in the early 1990s, it becomes easier for the legislature to pass tax increases. For example, the tax share reached a low of 7.3 percent in 1992, the year Bill Clinton was elected president. Once in office, Clinton proposed an income tax increase.

The big exception to this general pattern, however, is 2009. Despite the relatively low share of GDP going to the personal income tax, President Obama did not push to raise tax rates because of the weakness of the economy. Instead, he waited until 2013, when the economy had improved, to raise taxes on top earners.

In December 2017, President Donald Trump cut taxes on individuals, effective in 2018. However, federal personal income tax revenues continued to rise as a share of GDP, peaking at over 10 percent in 2022. As a result, Congress was then unwilling to raise personal taxes.

In the short run, tax cuts are stimulative and tax increases are contractionary, all other things being equal.

So far, we have focused on the personal income tax. However, big shifts have occurred in other kinds of taxes. For example, the corporate income tax shrank for many years as a share of the total tax pie. President Trump's 2017 tax package reduced the top marginal rate on corporate profits from 35 percent to 21 percent.

However, the pendulum may be swinging back. In 2022, President Biden signed legislation that required large, profitable corporations to pay at least a minimum tax. Moreover, tax authorities in different countries are getting better at taxing corporations with operations in many places.

The international angle is important when looking at the corporate tax. In part, the corporate tax rate was reduced in 2017 because corporations had good lobbyists, who helped rewrite the tax code to favor them. But there is a solid argument in favor of reducing the corporate tax rate. The United States is competing with other countries for corporate investment. So, lower corporate tax rates give companies more incentive to expand their business in the United States, which generates jobs at home. (We will discuss international implications in **Chapter 14**).

In comparison, a much bigger proportion of tax revenue now comes from payroll taxes–the taxes on wages that pay for Social Security, Medicare, unemployment insurance, and the like. Payroll taxes have been hiked several times as policymakers struggle to ensure that these programs are well funded. Currently, employees pay 6.2 percent of their wages for Social Security, on income up to a maximum of $160,200 in 2023, and 1.45 percent of wages for Medicare, with no upper limit. Employers chip in the same amount. (We will discuss Social Security and Medicare further in **Chapter 18**.)

The Direct Impact of Taxes

> **disposable income**
> The amount of income people have left after paying taxes.

> **contractionary**
> A description of a government policy action, such as a tax increase, that reduces output and pushes up unemployment in the short run.

Obviously, if you pay a dollar to the government in taxes, that's a dollar you don't have available to spend. **Disposable income** is defined as the amount of income people have left after paying taxes.

Naturally, tax cuts tend to boost disposable income, whereas tax increases tend to lower it (leaving out the effect of anything else the government might do). As a result, an increase in taxes will generally dampen spending and a decrease in taxes will boost spending. In other words, tax cuts are stimulative, meaning that they lower unemployment and increase GDP in the short run, all other things being equal. By contrast, tax increases are **contractionary**, meaning they tend to reduce output and employment, all other things being equal.

Changes in taxes also have an impact on inflation. In particular, a decrease in taxes will boost wages and prices in the short term, all other things being equal. To see why, look at **Figure 11.4**, which shows the short-term impact of a reduction in income taxes on the market for cars. As taxes are cut, disposable incomes go up, which shifts the demand curve for cars (as well as for other goods and services) to the right. As a result, the new quantity demanded in the market is higher, and so is the price of cars.

Figure 11.4 The Stimulative Effect of a Tax Cut
A tax cut boosts the disposable income of consumers, which causes their demand curve for goods and services (such as cars) to shift to the right. This boosts the quantity supplied and demanded of cars while raising their prices.

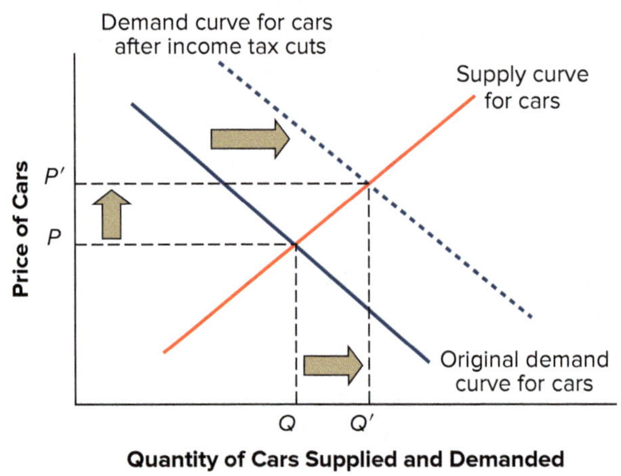

Using Tax Cuts to Fight Recession

> **tax multiplier**
> The increase in GDP from a $1 cut in taxes.

If the economy goes into recession, the government can cut taxes as a way of putting money into the hands of people who may otherwise be struggling financially and unable to spend. In some ways, this is similar to the argument in favor of boosting spending to fight recessions. As shown in **Figure 11.4**, a tax cut is stimulative.

What's more, as the effect of a tax cut spreads through the economy, economists can estimate the **tax multiplier**, which is the increase in GDP from a $1 cut in taxes. The tax multiplier depends on the marginal propensity to consume and overseas leakage, among other things.

However, for fighting recession, a tax cut has a big advantage over a spending increase: The tax cut can be put into effect more quickly. For example, in January 2008, President George W. Bush proposed a tax rebate–a type of one-time tax cut. The rebate was quickly passed by Congress. The first rebate checks were in the hands of Americans by May 2008, while the economy was still struggling. That's fast enough to be effective.

Incentives and Taxes

However, fighting recession is not the only reason why some economists and politicians favor lowering taxes. In the 1970s, a group of economists began to focus on the negative **incentive effects** of taxes. That is, higher taxes discourage whatever activity is being taxed. So, if labor income is heavily taxed, you are less likely to work hard. A high sales tax on clothing would make you less likely to buy clothing and more likely to buy something else. And a heavy tax on profits, which lessens the benefit of being successful in business, would make it less likely for you to start a new company.

incentive effect
When a tax discourages the economic activity being taxed.

supply-side economics
A school of economic thought that emphasizes the importance of low marginal tax rates.

marginal tax rate
The tax a person pays on the last dollar of income earned.

This link between taxes and incentives is the essential insight of **supply-side economics**. Supply-side economics focuses on the **marginal tax rate**: the tax you pay on the last dollar of income you earn. For example, when the marginal tax rate is 30 percent, if you earn an extra dollar, the government gets 30 percent of it and you get 70 percent.

Different people may have different marginal tax rates, depending on their level of income and the tax code. The marginal tax rate is important because it determines your incentives for working a bit more. If your marginal tax rate were 95 percent, for example, it would not pay for you to increase your hours of work because the government would be taking 95 cents of every additional dollar you made. But if your marginal tax rate were 10 percent, the federal government's share would be close to zero.

Supply-side economics argues that cutting taxes gives people an incentive to work and invest more. Over the past 30 years, many economists and politicians have accepted the proposition that cutting marginal tax rates can be beneficial. In the 1950s, as shown in **Figure 11.5**, the top marginal tax rate (the rate paid by those in the highest income brackets) was actually around 90 percent. To pick just one year–say, 1955–the tax code called for a 91 percent tax rate on a married couple with a taxable income greater than $400,000 (adjusting for inflation, that $400,000 would be worth about $3 million today). That's an amazingly high tax rate.

Figure 11.5 Top Marginal Tax Rates, 1913–2022
The top marginal tax rate paid by Americans has fallen from 91 percent in the 1950s to 37 percent today.

Source: Tax Policy Center, www.taxpolicycenter.org.

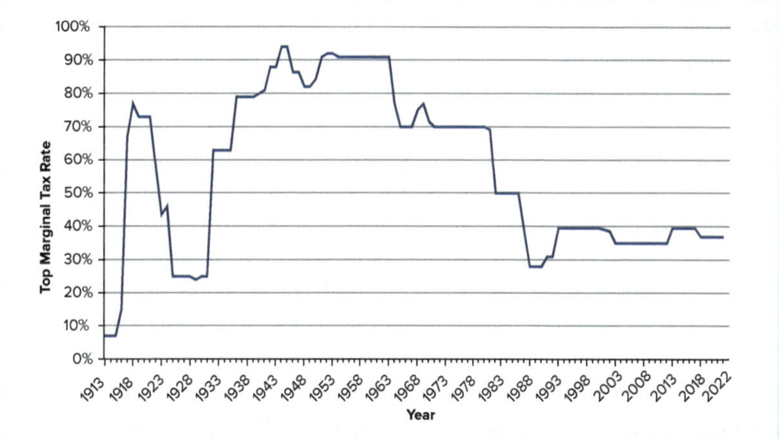

But the top marginal rate was repeatedly lowered over time. As of 2022, the top marginal rate for the federal income tax was down to 37 percent for married couples with taxable income greater than $647,850.

One extreme version of supply-side economics argues that cutting taxes can stimulate enough work and investment to actually *increase* tax revenues. That has been one argument given in favor of tax cuts, starting with Ronald Reagan's 1981 cuts and continuing through to George W. Bush's tax cuts in 2001 and 2003, and Donald Trump's tax cuts in 2017. However, most economists today accept that cutting marginal tax rates simply decreases tax revenues.

BORROWING (LO11-5)

LO11-5 Explain how the budget deficit affects the economy in the short run and in the long run.

If there is a gap between spending and tax revenues–as there was in 2022–the government has to borrow money to make up the difference. On one level, borrowing by the federal, state, or local government is no different from an individual or company taking out a loan. But the government borrows on a scale that is unimaginable for an individual or a business–and this has an impact on the whole economy.

Budget Deficits and Surpluses

budget deficit
The excess of the federal government's spending over its revenues.

public debt
The total of government borrowing.

surplus
A situation where government revenues exceed government spending.

The excess of the federal government's spending over its revenues is the **budget deficit**. In fiscal year 2022 (which ended September 30, 2022), the federal government spent \$6.3 trillion and took in \$4.9 trillion. The difference between the two (\$4.9 trillion − \$6.3 trillion) was the budget deficit, which totaled roughly \$1.4 trillion, coming to 5.5 percent of GDP.

To pay for a budget deficit, a government borrows money from investors. (In **Chapter 13**, we'll discuss government bonds, which are how the government borrows.) The total of all the government's borrowing is called the **public debt**. If the government runs a deficit, then the public debt increases. As of early 2022, the public debt was \$24 trillion.

We see in **Figure 11.6** that from year to year, the budget deficit rises and falls, getting as deep as 14.9 percent of GDP in fiscal year 2020, when the pandemic first hit (in the figure, negative numbers represent deficits and positive numbers represent surpluses). There were several years, including 1999 through 2001, when the budget was in **surplus**–that is, revenues exceeded spending. Overall, the budget has mostly been in deficit in recent decades.

Figure 11.6 Federal Budget Surplus or Deficit, 1969–2022
This chart shows the federal budget surplus or deficit as a share of GDP. Negative numbers are deficits, in which spending exceeds revenues. Positive numbers are surpluses.

Source: Congressional Budget Office, www.cbo.gov.

Before we go on, here's an important note about terminology. We say that the budget deficit *increases* when the gap between revenues and expenditures gets wider. That is, a budget deficit increases when it goes from \$100 billion to \$200 billion. Similar, the budget deficit *decreases* when the gap between revenues and expenditures gets narrower.

Why does the deficit swing so much? One reason is the state of the economy. Generally, the deficit widens during recessions because workers and companies earn less income. As a result, less tax revenue comes in; because unemployment is higher, the government also has to pay out more for unemployment insurance. During good times, the deficit narrows because tax revenues rise along with the economy.

An increasing budget deficit stimulates the economy in the short run, all other things being equal.

The deficit is also affected by changes in tax rates. The big tax cut put through by President Ronald Reagan in 1981 was one reason the deficit was so large in fiscal year 1983. Similarly, President George W. Bush's tax cuts helped flip the budget from a surplus in 2001 to deficits in subsequent years. President Donald Trump's tax cuts nearly doubled the size of the budget deficit from 2015 to 2018.

Finally, deficits usually rise during emergencies like wars, major natural disasters, and pandemics, as happened in 2020 and 2021. The United States, like other countries, is willing to borrow to finance national defense or to protect its citizens against unexpected events.

The Stimulative Effect of Bigger Deficits

In the short run, increasing the federal budget deficit has a stimulative effect on the economy. A bigger deficit could occur if the government boosted spending without raising taxes by the same amount, or if it cut taxes without a matching cut in spending. In either case, more money would stay in the pockets of U.S. consumers, and the government would have to borrow more.

For example, in 2001, President George W. Bush proposed a sharp tax cut, which Congress passed. Three things happened as a result. First, the federal budget went from $128 billion in surplus in 2001 to $158 billion in deficit in 2002. Second, the disposable income of U.S. consumers–that is, the income they had left after taxes were taken out–rose in 2002, even though employment was weak and the economy was sluggish. Third, consumer spending continued to rise as well.

These three facts are related. In general, an increase or decrease in the budget deficit serves as a rough-and-ready measure of the amount of fiscal stimulus applied to the economy. In this case, the total fiscal stimulus was roughly equal to $286 billion ($128 billion plus $158 billion, or the size of the swing from surplus to deficit).

An increasing budget deficit pushes up interest rates and crowds out private investment, all other things being equal.

Of course, the 2002 stimulus was dwarfed by the Great Recession of 2008–2009, when the budget deficit went from $459 billion in 2008 to $1,413 billion in 2009. And the 2020 stimulus was even bigger, with the budget deficit tripling in one year from $984 billion in 2019, to a staggering $3,133 billion in 2020 and an almost equally stunning $2,775 billion in 2021. These huge deficits were an enormous stimulus to the economy.

automatic stabilizer
The tendency of the budget deficit to increase during recessions because tax revenues slow and certain types of spending, such as unemployment insurance, increase. The result is a fiscal stimulus for the economy.

During a recession, the budget deficit generally increases because tax revenues weaken while expenditures rise. That increase in the deficit is known as an **automatic stabilizer** because the widening budget deficit pumps stimulus into the economy without the need for the government to change tax rates.

Crowding Out

However, government borrowing does have negative effects on the rest of the economy. When the budget deficit rises, the increased borrowing pushes the demand schedule for loans to the right, as we see in **Figure 11.7**. That, in turn, pushes the interest rate up from r to r'.

Figure 11.7 The Impact of Government Borrowing on Interest Rates
As the government borrows more money, it pushes up demand for loans and raises the interest rate. That, in turn, discourages private borrowing.

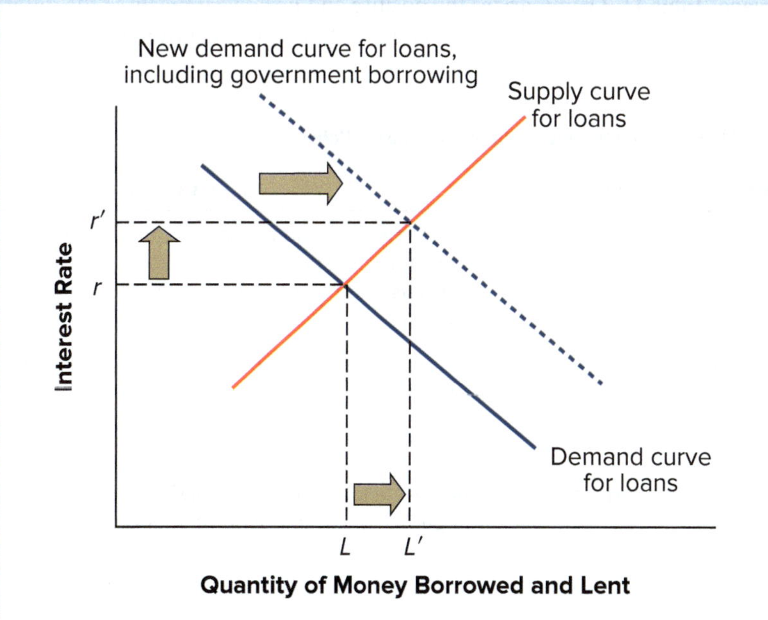

The law of demand tells us that if something is more expensive, the market will buy less of it. So, when the government's increased borrowing makes capital more expensive, business will be able to afford less investment in equipment and structures, and consumers can spend less on consumer durables such as homes and cars.

crowding out

A decline in private investment that results from an increase in government borrowing that pushes up interest rates.

This phenomenon is known as **crowding out**. In effect, the government competes with the private sector for capital and elbows the private sector out of the way. Crowding out is bad in the short run because it lessens the stimulative effect of a bigger budget deficit. The fiscal stimulus may generate jobs and income, but it is accompanied by a reduction in private investment. Crowding out is also bad because with less capital investment, businesses are less productive. Over the long run, that means economic growth will be slower.

The damage done by crowding out is not as apparent as the pain of taxation. You can see how much the government is taking from you in taxes just by looking at your paycheck or tax returns. It's much harder to see how much government borrowing has raised the interest rate.

The Impact of Budget Deficits in the Long Run

No discussion of the budget deficit would be complete without a mention of its long-term impact. As of 2022, the federal budget deficit shrank a lot compared 2021, but was still 5.5 percent of GDP. Out of that total, almost half the deficit comes from interest payments on federal debt. In other words, the federal government is borrowing in part to pay interest on existing debt.

Going forward, the CBO projects that the deficit will rise as a share of GDP. Part of that is due to increased obligations to care for an aging population. But the CBO also projects that the federal government will get stuck in a self-feeding cycle, where it has to keep borrowing more money to pay interest on its debt–but the more money it borrows, the more interest it has to pay in the future.

This is definitely not a desirable outcome. Therefore, it is necessary to get the long-term budget deficit under control, which means doing something about controlling the cost of Medicare, Medicaid, and Social Security. That's an issue we will cover in more detail in **Chapter 18**.

Putting It All Together

As we have seen, there are a lot of things going on simultaneously in fiscal policy. Congress and the president can raise or lower government spending. They can raise or lower taxes. Then the combination of these two decisions can lead to a bigger or smaller budget deficit, which changes the amount of borrowing.

All the fiscal policy actions put together can affect employment, output, inflation, and interest rates. It's useful to see all the impacts in one place. **Table 11.3** summarizes the positive and negative impacts of the different actions the federal government can take. For example, lowering taxes can create jobs, boost GDP, and provide incentives for work and investment–but it can also widen the budget deficit and pump up interest rates.

Table 11.3 Summarizing the Impacts of Fiscal Policy

Fiscal Policy Action	How It Can Help	How It Can Hurt
Increase government spending.	Can create jobs and boost GDP, and perhaps do something useful with the spending–for example, build new bridges and highways and fund pandemic relief for individuals and businesses.	Can boost inflation and widen the budget deficit, leading to higher interest rates and lower private investment.
Lower taxes.	Can create jobs and boost GDP, and provide incentives for work and investment.	Can boost inflation and widen the budget deficit, leading to higher interest rates and lower private investment.
Accept wider budget deficit.	Can create jobs and boost GDP. Other impacts depend on the particular combination of spending and tax changes.	Can lead to higher interest rates and lower private investment. Over the long run, can lower productivity and GDP growth.

The effects listed in the table work in the opposite direction as well. Suppose the government raised taxes. That would have a contractionary effect on employment and GDP while potentially reducing inflation and interest rates because the government would be borrowing less, all other things being equal.

What **Table 11.3** does *not* include is a summary of the relative sizes of the different effects. That's partly because they depend on where we are in the business cycle. It's also because economists disagree about which impacts are bigger. Is the incentive effect of a tax cut more or less important than its direct effect on jobs and GDP? You could poll 10 economists and get 10 different answers. That's what makes fiscal policy one of the most hotly disputed areas in economics.

YOUR ECONOMIC LIFE: Should You Care about the National Debt?

You learned from this chapter that the federal government is $24 trillion in debt (and is adding more to that every day). This is the equivalent of 335 million Americans, each being in debt for more than $70,000. That's a lot of money. Should you be personally concerned?

The answer, for now, is no. First, the debt is only one side of the national balance sheet. Along with the debt, the United States has 3.5 million square miles of land; $78 trillion worth of buildings, equipment and intellectual property assets like software; and the productive capacity of more than 160 million of some of the best-educated and creative workers in the world.

Second, the debt is ultimately backed up by the power of the federal government to levy taxes on the largest economy in the world. Third, foreigners who have lent the U.S. government more than $7 trillion believe that the United States is a better and safer borrower than almost any other country in the world.

The danger, of course, is that we could squander all of our advantages. We could stop investing in our businesses and in our workforce. We could lose our reputation for stability. And worst of all, we could keep borrowing until it exceeded the ability of a country even as large as the United States to pay it back. However, until that happens, you don't need to be personally concerned.

CONCLUSION

We've seen in this chapter that fiscal policy can affect the economy. In the short term, the spending and taxation decisions of the government can influence output, employment, prices, and wages. That's especially important when the economy is going into a recession or facing an emergency like a pandemic.

However, economists usually regard monetary policy–which is controlled by the Federal Reserve–as a more effective tool for adjusting the economy. That's what we will discuss in the next chapter.

11 SUMMARY

1. Fiscal policy is composed of decisions about government spending, taxes, and borrowing. The level of government spending is set by the political system, and that spending is funded through a combination of taxation and borrowing. ***(LO11-1)***
2. In the short term, an increase in government spending lowers unemployment and increases GDP, all other things being equal. This is the essence of the Keynesian approach to macroeconomics, which uses increases in government spending and cuts in taxes to fight recessions. The multiplier effect is the overall boost in economic activity that flows from the spending increase. The size of the multiplier is determined, in part, by the marginal propensity to consume and the amount of overseas leakage. ***(LO11-2)***
3. Stimulating the economy by government spending has a downside as well. In the short term, an increase in government spending can raise wages and prices and boost inflation. That's more likely if lags in policy make the fiscal stimulus show up after the recession is over. ***(LO11-3)***
4. In the short term, a decrease in taxes lowers unemployment and increases GDP, all other things being equal. That same decrease in taxes tends to boost wages and prices, all other things being equal. Supply-side economics argues that changes in marginal tax rates affect incentives to work. In response to these arguments, marginal tax rates have come down substantially over time. ***(LO11-4)***
5. Increasing the budget deficit can stimulate the economy, boosting employment and GDP. However, government borrowing can push up interest rates and crowd out private-sector investment. ***(LO11-5)***

KEY TERMS AND CONCEPTS

fiscal policy
transfer payments
taxation
federal budget
Keynesian approach
fiscal stimulus
multiplier effect
job multiplier
spending multiplier
marginal propensity to consume (MPC)
overseas leakage
stimulative
lag
income tax
property tax
payroll tax
corporate income tax
sales tax
excise tax
disposable income
contractionary
tax multiplier
incentive effect
supply-side economics
marginal tax rate
budget deficit
public debt
surplus
automatic stabilizer
crowding out

connect PROBLEMS

1. Identify whether each of the following government expenditures is a payment for goods and services or a transfer payment. *(LO11-1)*
   a) A local public school hires a new teacher.
   b) The Coast Guard orders a new ship.
   c) Medicare pays for a knee replacement for a 66-year-old.
   d) A poor family gets food stamps.
   e) The local Social Security office buys a new computer.
   f) The government writes a pandemic stimulus check to a household.
   g) The government purchases 100 million doses of COVID vaccine.
2. The federal government hires an extra worker in the Department of Homeland Security, but makes no other changes in taxation or spending. Identify whether each of the following is likely to rise or fall in the short term. *(LO11-2)*
   a) Federal government spending.
   b) Unemployment.
   c) Wages.
   d) Real GDP.
   e) The budget deficit.
3. The accompanying diagram shows the supply and demand curves for desktop computers. Suppose the federal government decides to boost the economy by buying more computers. *(LO11-2)*

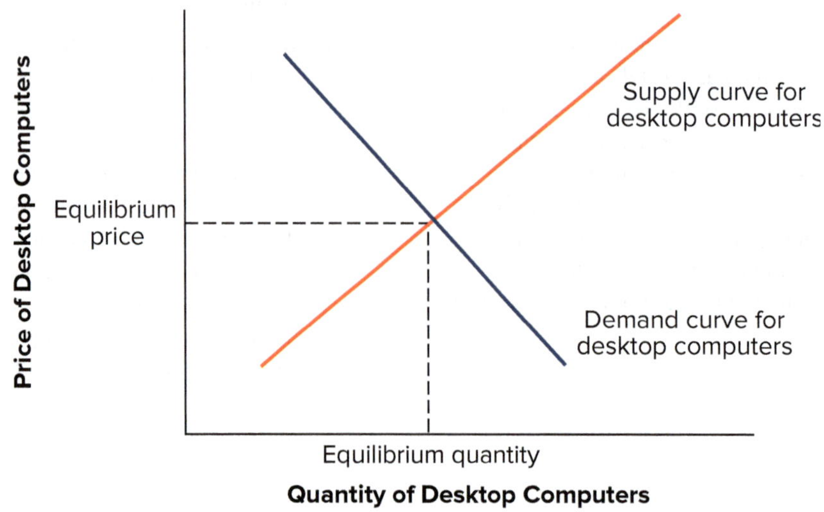

a) Draw the new demand curve, and label the new equilibrium.
b) Does the federal government purchase increase or decrease the price of computers?
c) Does the federal government purchase increase or decrease the quantity of computers sold?

4. Suppose the job multiplier is 0.7. The government hires 20,000 workers to give COVID vaccine shots to Americans who want them. *(LO11-2)*

a) How much does total employment rise or fall?
b) How much does private-sector employment rise or fall?
c) Would you regard this outcome as a success? Explain why.

5. Suppose you knew that the NAIRU (the nonaccelerating inflation rate of unemployment) was 5.5 percent. The current unemployment rate is 5 percent. *(LO11-3)*

a) Is an increase in government spending more likely to increase real GDP or to increase inflation?
b) Now the unemployment rate rises to 6.5 percent, but the NAIRU stays the same. Is an increase in government spending more likely to increase real GDP or to increase inflation?

6. Fiscal stimulus using increased government spending is best suited for ______________ *(LO11-3)*

a) fighting a short and shallow recession.
b) fighting a long and deep recession.
c) keeping an expansion from ending.

7. The federal government decides to impose a 3 percent sales tax on the purchase of new motor vehicles. *(LO11-4)*

a) Will the tax increase or decrease the number of motor vehicles sold?
b) As the result of the tax, the government collects more revenue. What happens to the budget deficit, assuming spending doesn't change?
c) What is the effect of the tax on interest rates?
d) Most states charge a fee to register a motor vehicle. If the fee was reduced, would the number of motor vehicles sold increase or decrease?

8. Over the last century, the top marginal tax rates in the United States have ______________ *(LO11-4)*

a) fallen to a low of 10 percent after supply-side economics was introduced.
b) remained stable at 35 percent.
c) ranged from a low of 10 percent to a high of 90 percent.
d) averaged out at about 45 percent.

9. Suppose that the economy is going into a recession. *(LO11-5)*

a) Is a spending increase or a tax cut more likely to be an effective response to the recession? Explain.
b) What effect will the tax cut have on the budget deficit?

10. The following table reports on GDP and government budget surplus or deficit for the country of France (measured in dollars). *(LO11-5)*

Year	French GDP (Billions of Dollars)	French Government Budget Surplus or Deficit (–) (Billions of Dollars)	Surplus or Deficit as Percentage of GDP
2013	2,609	–107	—
2014	2,662	–104	—
2015	2,719	-99	—
2016	2,864	–104	—
2017	2,997	-89	—
2018	3,125	-72	—
2019	3,241	-99	—
2020	3,021	-268	—
2021	3,359	-216	—
2022	3,668	–188	—

Data: International Monetary Fund, author calculations. Dollars are adjusted for differences in price levels.

a) For each year, calculate the French government budget surplus or deficit as a percentage of GDP.
b) In which year was the French budget deficit the biggest as a percentage of GDP?
c) In which year was the deficit the smallest as a percentage of GDP?
d) How much did the pandemic boost the French budget deficit, measured as a share of GDP?

CH 12

MONETARY POLICY

Paul Philippe Cret (American architect, 1876–1945)/Photov.com/Pixtal/age fotostock

LEARNING OBJECTIVES

After reading this chapter, you should be able to:

LO12-1 List the three uses of money.
LO12-2 Describe the history and structure of the Federal Reserve System.
LO12-3 Identify the major goals of monetary policy and list the policy tools used by the Federal Reserve.
LO12-4 Explain how changing the Fed funds rate can affect the economy.
LO12-5 Discuss how the Federal Reserve can use direct lending to fight financial and economic crises.
LO12-6 Compare and contrast monetary policy and fiscal policy.

The Federal Reserve, the nation's central bank, is the most important economic institution in the country. During normal times, its policies help determine the level of interest rates. But when a crisis hits, the Federal Reserve—also known as "the Fed"—can use a wide array of policy tools to support the financial system and the economy as a whole.

In response to the financial crisis of 2008–2009, then-Chairman Ben Bernanke and the Fed lent more than a trillion dollars to banks and other financial institutions that were in danger of failing. At the same time, the Fed cut its key interest rate, the Fed funds rate, to nearly zero. Combined with the fiscal policy measures described in **Chapter 11**, the Fed's actions helped prevent the Great Recession from turning into another Great Depression. In essence, the Fed did what it had been originally created to do: be the "lender of last resort" and preserve the stability of the financial system. Then under Bernanke and his successors, Janet Yellen and Jerome Powell, the Fed pursued policies to help the financial system heal from the crisis and to keep the broader economy growing.

But the Fed and Chair Powell faced a new challenge in 2020, when the Covid pandemic hit. First, the Fed had to help the financial system and the economy navigate the possibility of a deep Covid-induced recession. Then as the pandemic was easing in 2022, the inflation rate soared, putting the Fed into inflation-fighting mode, and triggering sharp interest rate increases.

This episode highlights the range of the Fed's responsibilities, including making sure the inflation rate does not get too high or too low. In this chapter, we will look at the history of the Fed and the reason for its creation almost a hundred years ago. We'll explain the Fed's main goals and how it conducts **monetary policy**, using control over interest rates, direct lending to financial institutions, and other policy tools to influence the economy.

> **monetary policy**
> The Federal Reserve's use of interest rates, direct lending to financial institutions, and other policy tools to influence the economy and support the financial system.

We'll look at the economic consequences of monetary policy, and we'll discuss some recent issues and problems faced by the Fed, both during the Great Recession and in the recovery that followed.

THE USES OF MONEY (LO12-1)

> **LO12-1** List the three uses of money.

There are more ways to invest and make money today than ever before–and more ways to lose it too. We'll look at some of them in detail when we discuss the financial markets in the next chapter, but here we're concerned with the question, What is money?

On the simplest level, **money** is made up of the bills and coins you have in your pocket, which have been printed or minted by the U.S. government (these are called **currency**). But money also includes the funds stored as electronic entries in your checking accounts and savings accounts.

> **money**
> A medium of exchange that also serves as a store of value and a standard of value.

> **currency**
> Bills and coins used as money.

Money serves three purposes. First, it is a **medium of exchange**. You can use money to buy goods and services and accept money in exchange for the goods and services you provide. A market economy would be impossible without money.

> **medium of exchange**
> The property of money that can be used to buy goods and services.

Second, money is a **store of value**. You can hold onto money to use later. So, when you put your money into a bank, you expect that you will be able to take it out sometime in the future and that it will still be able to buy goods and services.

> **store of value**
> The property of money that can be used for purchases in the future.

Third, money is a **standard of value**. It lets you make comparisons between different goods and services. If two houses sell for the same amount of money, then–at that moment–they are equally valuable. If you are willing to pay more for one car than another, then–at that moment–the first car is more valuable to you.

> **standard of value**
> The use of monetary values to make comparisons between different items.

For all three uses of money, it doesn't matter whether you have cash in your pocket, write a check, or pull some money out of your savings account. All three are equivalent, which is why we call them all *money* (see **"Spotlight: How Much Money Is There?"**).

However, money–whether it's a $10 bill or an entry in a bank database–always has an element of trust built in. When you work, you accept money for your labor, trusting that businesses you frequent will be willing to accept your tens and twenties in exchange for goods and services. And when you put your hard-earned cash in the bank, you trust that it will be worth something in the future when you take it out. If we lose trust, money can turn worthless in a moment. Those bills in your pocket would be nothing but pieces of green paper, and those electronic entries at the bank would have nothing to back them up.

Maintaining public trust in the value of a currency is paramount for a well-functioning economy. As a result, even the most free market-minded economists agree that a financial system needs a strong regulator with enormous powers. Therefore, in most countries, including the United States, the government is the sole issuer of currency.

Government-issued currency has several advantages. First, everyone knows which bills are valid. Imagine if Sam down the street could issue his own "Sam" money, with a picture of Sam and Sam's signature. Then you would have to worry if "Sam" money would be accepted at the local store, or if Sam would flee the country next year, leaving you with worthless bills. There's also no need to try and figure out whether those twenties with a picture of Sam on them are worth more or less than the twenties issued by the "Bank of Sally."

money stock

A measure of the amount of money in an economy.

Second, having a single source of currency under government control makes it easier for policymakers to guide and control an economy. That is, the government can print currency–and destroy it, if need be–to influence output, employment, inflation, and interest rates. Finally, having control over the money supply helps a government maintain trust in its money. The U.S. dollar is backed by the "full faith and credit" of the U.S. government–and, ultimately, that is a very powerful thing.

SPOTLIGHT: HOW MUCH MONEY IS THERE?

Lm Otero/AP/Shutterstock

You might think it would be easy to figure out how much money there is. After all, the government knows the amount of currency—how many bills it prints and how many coins it mints. As of February 2023, there was about $2.3 trillion in currency in circulation. Out of that amount, the largest share was in $100 bills.

But the definition of money is actually broader than that because people generally have only a small amount of cash in their pockets. Instead, they keep their money in checking and savings accounts or earn interest in a certificate of deposit or a money market fund (we will describe these further in **Chapter 13**). Checking deposits are not much different from cash because they can be easily accessed by writing checks or using a debit card. It's a bit of a slower process to get at savings accounts, certificate of deposits, or money market funds, but the money is still accessible and spendable.

The Fed keeps track of two measures of the **money stock**, called M1 and M2. M1 includes currency and checking accounts, basically, whereas M2 adds in savings accounts, certificates of deposits, and money market funds. As of February 2023, M1 was $19.3 trillion and M2 was $21.1 trillion. M1 and M2 used to be of great importance, but these days they are rarely mentioned by economists or by members of the Fed.

THE HISTORY OF THE FEDERAL RESERVE (LO12-2)

LO12-2 Describe the history and structure of the Federal Reserve System.

Federal Reserve System

The central bank of the United States.

central bank

The official institution that controls monetary policy in a country.

In the United States, the prime guardian of the financial system is the **Federal Reserve System**, also known as the country's **central bank**. Congress founded the Federal Reserve System in 1913 in response to a financial panic in 1907. That panic–which few people except economists and historians remember today–wiped out several big banks and sent the stock market plummeting by nearly 50 percent. To avoid a repetition of this near disaster, it became clear that a strong central bank was needed to step in and help support the financial system when things went bad.

The creation of the Federal Reserve was a milestone in U.S. economic history. The Fed, as it is often called, had the power to issue currency, set key interest rates, and lend directly to banks–the first time a government agency was given such strong tools for directly influencing the economy.

The Structure of the Fed

The Federal Reserve was set up as a system of banks, not as a single bank. At the head is the Federal Reserve Board, based in Washington, consisting of a seven-person Board of Governors. The Federal Reserve Board is housed in an impressive building in Washington, DC, with very tight security. Congress also created 12 regional Federal Reserve Banks around the country, in part to gain the support of western and southern politicians. But creation of the regional banks also reflects the fact that the Fed was set up in 1913, when communication and travel were not as easy as they are today. As a result, having local branches, so to speak, was essential.

As the country's central bank, the Fed was designed to have quite a bit of independence. True, the U.S. president appoints the members of its Board of Governors, including the chair. But the Fed funds its own operations, so it doesn't need budget allocations from Congress. And members of the Board of Governors serve 14-year terms, which end in different years, so a single president can't replace the whole board. The chair of the board of governors, who holds most of the power, is appointed for a four-year renewable term. Alan Greenspan, for example, was first appointed chairman in 1987 and, through reappointments, served until 2006, when Ben Bernanke became chairman. Bernanke was followed by Janet Yellen in 2014, who was succeeded in turn by Jerome Powell in 2018. Powell was originally appointed by President Donald Trump and then reappointed in 2022 by President Joseph Biden.

goals of monetary policy
The main goals of monetary policy are controlling inflation, smoothing out the business cycle, and ensuring financial stability.

If the central bank were not independent, it could come under pressure to adopt monetary policies that benefit the political party in power but are not necessarily good for the country as a whole. For example, the central bank could cut interest rates just before an election to gain votes for the party in power.

THE GOALS AND TOOLS OF MONETARY POLICY (LO12-3)

LO12-3 Identify the major goals of monetary policy and list the policy tools used by the Federal Reserve.

The Federal Reserve was created in response to a crash in the financial markets. Not surprisingly, its original purpose was to maintain financial system stability and people's trust in the currency. Although that aim is still important, over time the Fed has taken on a wider variety of objectives and concerns.

In 1978, Congress passed the Humphrey-Hawkins Act, which clearly specified a broad set of goals for the Fed:

> The Board of Governors of the Federal Reserve System and the Federal Open Market Committee shall maintain long-run growth of the monetary and credit aggregates commensurate with the economy's long-run potential to increase production, so as to promote effectively the goals of maximum employment, stable prices, and moderate long-term interest rates.*
>
> Federal Reserve System

In other words, the Fed was supposed to strive for high job creation, low inflation, and low-interest rates—something for everyone!

controlling inflation
One key goal of the Federal Reserve, which tries to keep inflation below a certain level.

smoothing out the business cycle
One key goal of the Federal Reserve, which tries to keep the economy from dropping into a steep recession.

ensuring financial stability
One key goal of the Federal Reserve, which tries to keep the financial system functioning well.

In reality, the Fed today does not follow the exact list of objectives in the 1978 legislation. Instead, it has taken a slightly different form. Today, the main **goals of monetary policy** are **controlling inflation**, **smoothing out the business cycle**, and **ensuring financial stability** (**Table 12.1**). We'll look at each of these in turn.

Table 12.1 The Three Goals of Monetary Policy

Goal	Signs of Success
1. Controlling inflation	The inflation rate stays in the neighborhood of 2 percent.
2. Smoothing out the business cycle	Recessions are short and mild, and the unemployment rate stays relatively low.
3. Ensuring financial stability	Most borrowers are able to get access to loans relatively easily with little fear that financial institutions will go out of business.

Controlling Inflation

Under most circumstances the top goal of monetary policy is to keep inflation under control. Central bankers have always worried about inflation because rising prices eat away at the value of money, as we saw in **Chapter 8**.

* Federal Reserve System

But that concern intensified after the experience of the 1970s, when the inflation rate spiked into the double digits. When Paul Volcker became chairman of the Fed in August 1979, the inflation rate was almost 12 percent–far too high to be acceptable–and Volcker's aim was to get it down in any way possible. As we will see later in this chapter, he succeeded–but at the price of a deep recession.

ECONOMIC MILESTONE

1998 Creation of the European Central Bank

The Federal Reserve has been a role model for central banks in other parts of the world. The European Central Bank (ECB) was set up in 1998 to manage the euro, the European currency. Based in Frankfurt, Germany, the ECB is independent of political control, like the Fed. However, the ECB places more emphasis on controlling inflation than the Fed does.

Alan Greenspan, who followed Volcker as Fed chairman in 1987, repeatedly argued that a low, stable inflation rate was the best way to achieve strong economic growth. In 1988, he told Congress, for example, that the right goal for monetary policy was to guide the economy to

> a situation in which households and businesses in making their saving and investment decisions can safely ignore the possibility of sustained, generalized price increases or decreases.*
>
> Federal Reserve System

In other words, the Fed should keep the rate of inflation contained so that no one really pays attention to it. How low a rate is that? Depending on whom you ask, it can be anywhere between zero and 2 percent per year.

One important point: You might think that if low inflation is good, then deflation–falling prices–must be better. But central bankers see deflation as a bad thing. As we saw in **Chapter 8**, falling prices hurt debtors because loans become harder to pay back.

Smoothing Out the Business Cycle

In the United States, the Federal Reserve has the primary responsibility for fighting recessions. So, when the economy slows and the unemployment rate starts to rise, economists, businesspeople, and politicians want to know what the Fed is going to do about it.

In response to rising unemployment, the main thing that the Federal Reserve can do is cut interest rates (we'll see how that works in the next section). Lower interest rates stimulate purchases of things like cars and homes, thus boosting the economy.

Ensuring Financial Stability

Under ordinary circumstances, people don't worry that their bank or other financial institution will go out of business overnight. However, in times of crisis, there's an understandable fear that your investments could suddenly vanish. When that happens, the role of the Fed is to calm things down by making sure banks and other financial institutions have the money they need to function.

lender of last resort

The Fed's role of lending to financial institutions to keep them in business and to keep the financial markets functioning in a time of crisis.

In fact, the Fed is the **lender of last resort** during a financial crisis. Having a lender of last resort is essential for a well-functioning market economy because a meltdown in the financial markets would bring most transactions to a halt. In the worst case, businesses wouldn't be able to accept credit cards or pay their employees, individuals wouldn't be able to get access to their stock market accounts or other investments, home buyers wouldn't be able to get mortgages, and state and local governments might not be able to fund their daily operations.

Unfortunately, this devastating scenario seemed possible in fall 2008 and early 2009. In one weekend in September 2008, the Wall Street firm Lehman Brothers went bankrupt because of risky investments and real estate loans. And the giant insurance company AIG had to be rescued with an $85 billion loan from the Federal Reserve. Many economists were worried that an economic collapse was right around the corner. Similarly, in the early days of the pandemic, there was concern that the rapid spread of the Covid virus could cause an economic and financial disaster.

* Federal Reserve System

Monetary Policy Tools

The Federal Reserve has four types of monetary policy tools available to help meet its goals (**Table 12.2**). For dealing with inflation and the normal ups and downs of the business cycle, the Fed can use its control over short-term interest rates. As we will see, this policy tool is effective for influencing the behavior of both consumers and businesses.

Table 12.2 The Main Monetary Policy Tools

1. Control over short-term interest rates.
2. Quantitative easing.
3. Direct lending to banks, other financial institutions, and non-financial institutions such as businesses and state and local governments.
4. Changes in financial regulations.

The second type of policy tool, called "quantitative easing," or QE for short, is another way to pump money into the financial system when the economy is struggling. The Fed uses QE when lower short-term interest rates are not enough by themselves to deal with a financial crisis or a recession. Later in this chapter, we'll discuss the policy actions that the Federal Reserve took to preserve the stability of the financial system and to promote recovery in the financial crisis of 2008-2009 and the pandemic.

The third type of policy tool is direct lending to banks, other financial institutions, and non-financial institutions such as businesses and state and local governments. This is a potentially big hammer in the Fed's toolbox. Chairman Bernanke used it extensively during the financial crisis of 2008-2009 to help struggling banks and other financial institutions survive. During the early stages of the pandemic, Chairman Powell was ready to lend billions to both financial and non-financial institutions if such actions were necessary.

Dodd-Frank

The Dodd-Frank Wall Street Reform and Consumer Protection Act was enacted in 2010 to improve regulation of the financial system and reduce the chance of another financial crisis.

The final policy tool includes changes in financial regulations. Traditionally, the Fed has great regulatory power over many financial institutions, which it can use to influence the financial system. In 2010, Congress passed the Dodd-Frank Wall Street Reform and Consumer Protection Act, designed to reduce the chances of another financial crisis. This legislation, usually just called **Dodd-Frank**, greatly expanded the Fed's regulatory power in some ways and limited it in others. We will further discuss financial regulation in the next chapter.

CONTROL OVER SHORT-TERM INTEREST RATES (LO12-4)

LO12-4 Explain how changing the Fed funds rate can affect the economy.

In this section, we will look at how the Fed controls short-term interest rates and the impact of this control on the economy.

Open Market Operations

The Fed's most-used policy tool is its ability to control short-term interest rates. You already know that interest rates affect the cost of borrowing. Short-term interest rates are relevant for loans with a relatively short length for repayment, like credit card balances and auto loans, and for adjustable-rate mortgages (these are home loans whose interest rates are allowed to rise at set times). Long-term interest rates, on the other hand, are relevant for loans such as 30-year fixed-rate mortgages and long-term corporate borrowing.

The Federal Reserve can influence short-term interest rates via **open market operations**, which increase or decrease the amount of money available to banks for lending out (see **"How It Works: Behind the Scenes at the Fed"**).

open market operations

The process by which the Federal Reserve affects short-term interest rates.

Suppose the Fed wants to cut short-term interest rates. It executes an open market operation to make more money available for banks to lend. As a result, the supply curve for loans shifts right, as shown in **Figure 12.1**. The interest rate falls from r to r', and the quantity of loans made increases. This works the opposite way, too, of course. If the Fed reduces the amount of money available to banks to lend, the supply curve for loans shifts left. Interest rates rise, and the quantity of loans made falls.

fed funds rate

The short-term interest rate controlled by the Federal Reserve. Also, the rate banks charge each other for lending reserves overnight.

Historically, the Fed has not tried to directly control interest rates on mortgages, credit cards, or auto loans. Instead, the Fed targets a particular short-term interest rate called the **Fed funds rate**. The Fed funds rate is the rate banks charge each other for lending reserves overnight.

Figure 12.1 How the Fed Cuts the Short-Term Interest Rates
Making more money available to banks to lend shifts the supply curve for overnight loans to the right, which in turn reduces interest rates.

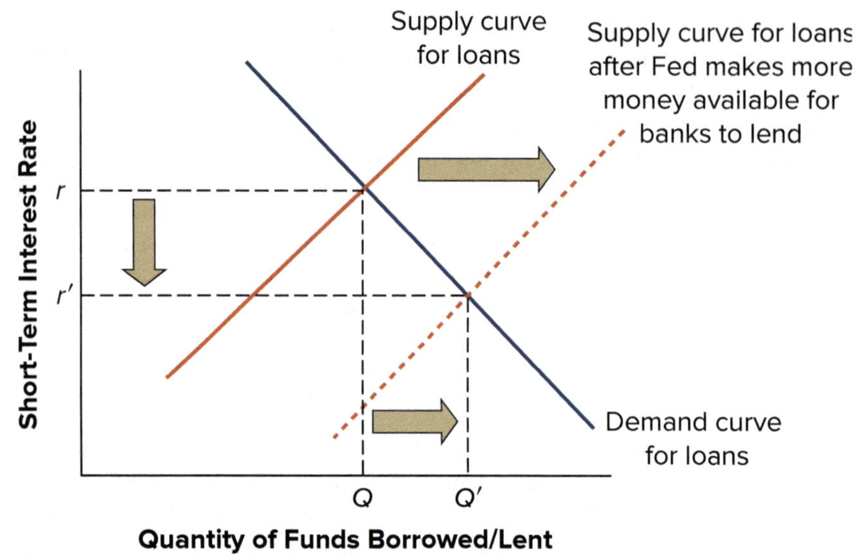

Federal Open Market Committee (FOMC)
The 12-member group at the Federal Reserve that votes on monetary policy.

The Fed funds rate is set by a vote of the **Federal Open Market Committee (FOMC)**, which includes all seven members of the Board of Governors and presidents of 5 out of the 12 Federal Reserve banks on a rotating basis. The FOMC meets eight times a year, or roughly every six weeks or so, to discuss the economy and decide on monetary policy; it typically issues a short statement after each meeting explaining its decision.

At each meeting of the Open Market Committee, the Fed tries to set the Fed funds rate at a level that moves the economy in the right direction. Generally speaking, if the economy is running above potential GDP and inflation is too high, the Fed will raise the Fed funds rate to slow the economy down. If the economy is running below potential and inflation is tame, the Fed will lower the Fed funds rate to stimulate growth.

Which Interest Rates Can the Fed Affect?

You, as a consumer, will never pay the Fed funds rate because it's an interest rate that banks charge each other. However, the Fed's control over the Fed funds rate affects all other short-term interest rates, including those of credit cards, auto loans, and adjustable-rate mortgages, as well as rates on money market funds. True, they don't necessarily move in lockstep with the Fed funds rate. General Motors and Ford might offer their customers a better interest rate on their cars even if the Fed funds rate goes up. But, in general, most short-term rates move more or less together.

HOW IT WORKS: BEHIND THE SCENES AT THE FED

The Fed chairman doesn't have two desk buttons that say "lower" and "raise" to control interest rates. Instead, when the Fed wants to change monetary policy by lowering or raising short-term interest rates, it takes a more roundabout route.

The first thing to realize is that banks are required to keep a portion of their deposits either in cash in their vaults or on reserve with the Fed (hence the name *Federal Reserve*). The more reserves they have, the more they can lend.

So, to lower interest rates, the Fed wants to make sure the banks have access to more reserves. That's what an *open market operation* does. In an open market operation, the Fed buys government bonds or other securities, usually from a big bank or other financial institution, and electronically credits the financial institution with more reserves. The previous owner of the securities now has money that didn't exist before, just as if the Fed had printed currency. The bank can now lend this extra money to borrowers, driving down short-term interest rates. Or it can lend the extra money to other banks, which then do more lending themselves.

Open market operations also work in reverse. If the Fed wants to raise rates, it sells some government securities it already owns. Then it reduces the money in the account of the purchaser. The net effect is that less money is available to be lent out and interest rates rise.

For example, look at **Figure 12.2**, which reports two interest rates: the Fed funds rate and the average interest rate on new car loans. You can see the rate on auto loans (the top line) more or less rises and falls in unison with the Fed funds rate (the bottom line). In particular, at the right side of the graph, you can see that a sharp increase in the Fed funds rate in 2022 helped push up the rate on new car loans as well.

Figure 12.2 New Car Loans and the Fed Funds Rate
Changes in the Fed funds rate affect many other kinds of short-term interest rates. This figure shows how the interest rate on new car loans rises and falls with the Fed funds rate.

Source: The Federal Reserve, www.federalreserve.gov.

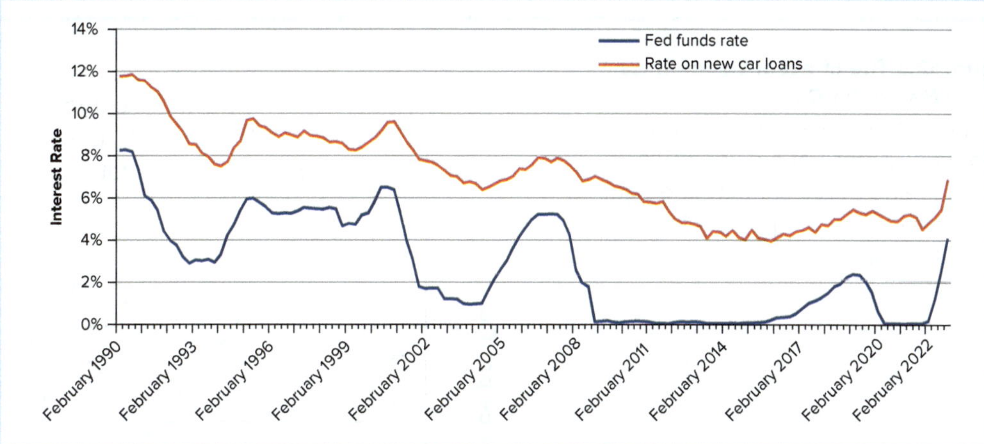

The same pattern is seen for the interest rates on credit cards and many other types of short-term consumer and business loans. As the Fed funds rate goes up and down, so do most other short-term interest rates.

HOW IT WORKS: THE CONSUMER BENEFIT FROM RATE CUTS

When the Fed cuts the Fed funds rate, other interest rates drop. And when other interest rates go down, you pay less if you need to borrow for a purchase.

Let's work through an example. Suppose you buy a $50,000 new car and take out a loan for the entire amount. In 2021, the Fed funds rate was close to zero, and a bank would have charged you a roughly 5 percent interest rate for a four-year (48-month) loan. But as of late 2022, the Fed funds rate was much higher—just above 4 percent—and the rates on auto loans had followed along. So in late 2022, the comparable rate on the same auto loan was roughly 7 percent.

That rate decline would have increased your monthly payment on the car from $1151 to $1197—a 4 percent increase. To think about this another way, that increase in payments is roughly equivalent to paying $52,000 for the car rather than $50,000.

Shutterstock / Greentellect Studio

Effect of Rate Changes on the Economy

As the Fed pushes short-term interest rates up or down, the effects of its actions are felt most directly by interest rate-sensitive sectors of the economy. These include motor vehicles sales, housing, and anything consumers buy with credit cards. These are the sectors of the economy dependent on short-term borrowing, so a rate change by the Fed affects the cost of their purchases.

In general, a decrease in the Fed funds rate boosts spending and GDP, whereas an increase in the Fed funds rate diminishes spending and GDP. Let's see how this operates; we'll start with motor vehicle sales. Most car buyers finance their purchases either by borrowing money for their new vehicles or by taking out leases. The monthly payments vary according to the prices of the cars, the length of the loans or leases, and the interest rates. The higher the interest rate, the higher the monthly payment; the lower the interest rate, the lower the payment (see "**How It Works: The Consumer Benefit from Rate Cuts**").

Figure 12.3 shows what happens in the car market when there is a decline in the interest rates on auto loans. Even if the prices of cars don't change, the quantity of cars demanded goes up when interest rates go down because the loan payments are lower. In the supply and demand diagram, that means the demand curve for cars shifts right when interest rates fall.

Figure 12.3 The Effect of Lower Rates on the Market for Cars
As the interest rates on car loans fall, people buy more at a given price. The demand curve shifts to the right, and the equilibrium quantity in the market rises.

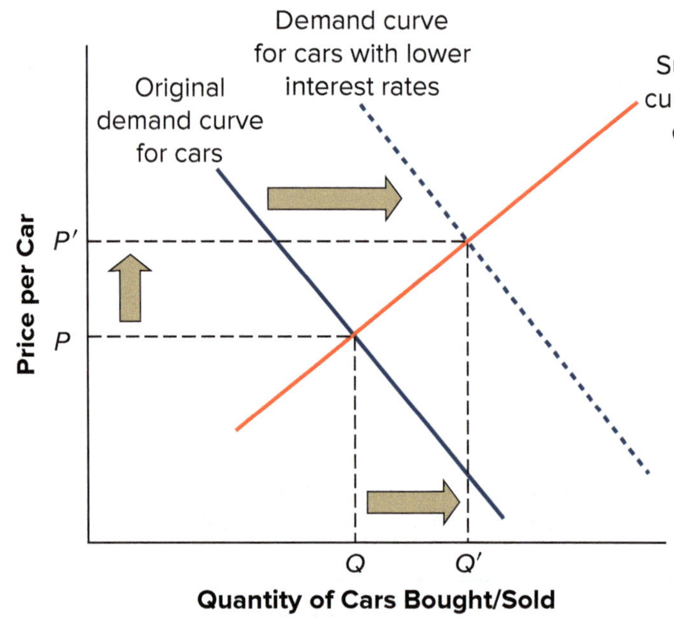

The result of these lower interest rates is that the quantity of cars demanded rises from Q to Q'. Similarly, if interest rates on auto loans rise, the demand schedule shifts left, and the quantity of cars sold drops.

Of course not only car sales are affected by changes in the Fed's interest rate policies. Let's think about credit cards, which consumers use to charge everything from groceries to tuition. Some people pay their charges off right away, but many others leave balances on their cards for a month or more. In fact, as of the end of 2022, U.S. consumers were carrying more than $1 trillion in revolving (credit card) debt.

If you have credit card debt, you have to pay interest on it. As we will see in the next chapter, credit card companies vary the rates they charge according to the creditworthiness of borrowers. But on average, credit card rates move up and down when the Fed funds rate increases or decreases. As a result, a decline in the Fed funds rate is likely to reduce the cost of using your credit card, assuming you don't pay off all of your credit card bills right away. So, we could draw a diagram like **Figure 12.3** for all goods and services bought with credit cards. As interest rates fall, the demand schedule shifts to the right, boosting overall sales.

Finally, we come to housing, one of the most important–and most complicated–markets in the economy. Most people buy their homes by borrowing through either a fixed-rate or an adjustable-rate mortgage. Interest rates on fixed-rate mortgages are tied to long-term interest rates, which are not usually directly affected by the Fed. But the interest rate on a one-year adjustable mortgage (in which the rate can change once every year) moves up and down with the Fed funds rate. When the Fed funds rate heads down, so does the one-year mortgage rate. And when the Fed funds rate rises, so does the one-year mortgage rate. As a result, the Fed can directly affect the affordability of housing through monetary policy.

So, taking it all together, the Fed funds rate affects auto sales, retail credit card purchases, and the housing market. That explains why cutting the Fed funds rate can boost GDP, at least in the short run. And it explains why raising the Fed funds rate has the potential to significantly slow the economy. When it's more expensive to borrow, people make fewer purchases that require borrowing.

monetary policy lags
The amount of time a monetary stimulus requires before it will have an effect on the economy.

It's important to note here that monetary stimulus requires about 12 to 18 months for its full effect. These **monetary policy lags** have a big influence on how monetary policy is conducted. For example, if the economy is coming out of a recession, the Fed usually needs to start raising rates before the economy is back to full employment.

Effect of Rate Changes on Inflation

Take another look at **Figure 12.3**. When interest rates decrease, the demand schedule moves to the right. This pushes up the price of cars from *P* to *P'* while the quantity demanded rises from *Q* to *Q'*. That means a price increase is associated with a monetary stimulus.

> In general, a cut in the Fed funds rate will put upward pressure on prices, while an increase in the Fed funds rate will put downward pressure on prices.

In general, cuts in the Fed funds rate put upward pressure on prices. Increases in the Fed funds rate put downward pressure on prices. However, the exact link between monetary policy and inflation depends on the overall economic situation, just as we saw in **Chapter 11** for fiscal policy. Suppose actual GDP is below potential GDP and the unemployment rate is above the NAIRU (the nonaccelerating inflation rate of unemployment). In that case, an interest rate cut will likely boost output without much fear of triggering inflation.

However, if actual GDP is above potential GDP or if the unemployment rate is below the NAIRU, an interest rate cut runs the risk of encouraging inflation. That's a great fear of central bankers.

Example: Volcker's Fight against Inflation

The modern era of monetary policy began when Paul Volcker became chairman of the Federal Reserve in 1979. Before that, the people who chaired the Fed did not fully understand that running an excessively loose monetary policy could lead to runaway inflation. Nor did they understand that the central bank had prime responsibility for bringing down high inflation.

In particular, Arthur Burns, who chaired the Fed from 1970 to 1978, believed that monetary policy was not an effective tool against inflation. In 1979, after leaving the Fed, he gave a speech called "The Anguish of Central Banking," in which he said,

> It is illusory to expect central banks to put an end to the inflation that now afflicts the industrial economies . . . their practical capacity for curbing an inflation that is driven by political forces is very limited.*
>
> Federal Reserve System

As a result, when inflation accelerated in the mid-1970s after the oil price shock, Burns did not see it as the Fed's role to stamp it out. Instead, he focused on cushioning the effects of the recession on unemployment–a seemingly compassionate maneuver that, instead, had the effect of letting inflation grow.

Volcker came into office with a different perspective: that the central bank has not only the power but also the responsibility to reduce inflation. He quickly tightened monetary policy, sending interest rates skyrocketing and throwing the United States into the short recession of 1980 and the deep and nasty recession of 1981-1982 (see **Figure 12.4**).

But this shock therapy worked. Inflation, which had been running sky-high, plummeted faster than almost anyone expected. Core inflation–leaving out food and energy–dropped from about 12 percent in 1980 to only 4 percent in 1983. The Fed's single-minded focus on inflation paid big dividends.

Example: Greenspan's Response to the 2001 Recession

Let's look at an example of how interest rates can be used to fight unemployment and boost growth. From 2000 through 2003, the United States experienced a sharp drop in business spending on information technology–the so-called tech bust. Over the same stretch, the stock market plummeted because people realized that the value of some stocks had raced too high. The economy was also buffeted by the terrorist attacks of 2001, which destroyed the World Trade Center towers in New York.

In response, Greenspan cut the Fed funds rate from 6.5 percent in 2000 to only 1 percent in 2003. Other short-term interest rates, such as auto loans, followed down as well. The point of such low rates was to encourage businesses and consumers to borrow and to keep the economy going when it was sluggish.

Greenspan succeeded in the sense that the recession ended in 2001. The economy grew in every year that followed. However, low rates did not help the job market much. The unemployment rate kept rising–from 5.3 percent in November 2001 to 6.3 percent by July 2003.

* Federal Reserve System

Figure 12.4 Fed Funds Rate, 1970–2022
This chart shows the Fed funds rate since 1970. Note that in late 1970s and early 1980s the Fed jacked up interest rates to fight inflation. Conversely, the Fed cut rates to nearly zero in 2008 and 2009 to fight the financial crisis, and then cut rates again in 2020 to deal with the pandemic. The right side of the chart shows the Fed starting to raise rates in 2022 to keep inflation in check, an effort that continued into 2023.

Source: The Federal Reserve, www.federalreserve.gov.

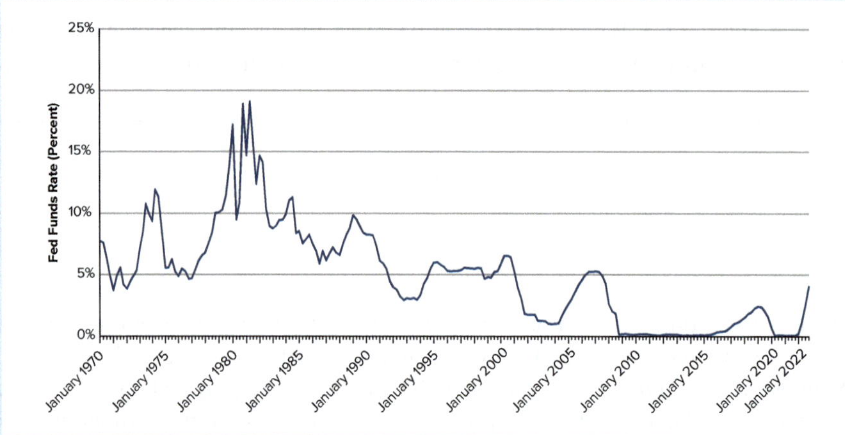

Example: Bernanke's Response to the Financial Crisis

As we have described in early chapters, the U.S. economy sharply contracted in 2008 and 2009. The response of Chairman Bernanke and the Fed was to rapidly cut the Fed funds rate to effectively zero, as shown in **Figure 12.5**.

Unfortunately, the deep financial crisis meant that banks were reluctant to lend to consumers and businesses, even with the Fed funds rate at nearly zero. The Fed's control of short-term rates was not enough to ensure recovery. As we will see in the next section, the Fed had to develop a new tool to stimulate the economy.

Example: Powell's Response to Pandemic and Inflation

When the pandemic unexpectedly hit in early 2020, Chairman Powell used all the tools that the Fed had developed to deal with earlier crises. For one, he rapidly cut the Fed funds rate to effectively zero, as shown in **Figure 12.5**. In addition, Powell utilized quantitative easing, direct lending, and regulatory changes to keep the financial system and the economy afloat during the very uncertain first few months of the pandemic, when it wasn't clear how bad things would get.

But in 2022, Powell and the Federal Reserve faced a different problem: the return of inflation. In a later section of this chapter, we will explore how the Fed balanced its different goals.

QUANTITATIVE EASING, DIRECT LENDING, AND OTHER TOOLS (LO12-5)

LO12-5 Discuss how the Federal Reserve can use direct lending to fight financial and economic crises.

Under ordinary circumstances, the Fed uses control of short-term interest rates as its main tool. But in times of financial crisis, the central bank has to dig deeper into its toolbox.

Quantitative Easing

The Fed had cut the Fed funds rate to near zero by the end of 2008, but the economy kept deteriorating. Despite everything the Fed was doing, the unemployment rate continued to rise until well into 2009 and then stayed stubbornly high.

The Fed was facing a tough problem: It couldn't push short-term interest rates any lower than zero. What's more, banks were reluctant to lend to businesses and consumers.

In response, the Fed employed a relatively new tool: It used open market operations, as described in the previous section, to influence long-term interest rates, such as mortgage rates, rather than short-term rates. This tool, known as **quantitative easing (QE)**, is too complicated to describe here in detail. But it had the effect of pumping more money into the financial system, even with the Fed funds rate at close to zero. As one Fed publication wrote:

> **quantitative easing (QE)**
>
> The use by central banks of open market operations to bring down long-term interest rates, such as mortgage rates.

> From the end of 2008 through October 2014, the Federal Reserve greatly expanded its holding of longer-term securities through open market purchases with the goal of putting downward pressure on longer-term interest rates and thus supporting economic activity and job creation by making financial conditions more accommodative.
>
> Source: Federal Reserve Bank, "Open Market Operations," www.federalreserve.gov/monetarypolicy/openmarket.htm

Quantitative easing was a very important part of the Fed's response to the pandemic. Lower long-term interest rates meant that it was easier for consumers to finance home purchases and renovations during the pandemic. In addition, companies could more easily borrow money to make investments, including much-needed improvements in broadband capacity.

When inflation accelerated in 2022, the Fed began to do the reverse of quantitative easing, sometimes called "quantitative tightening"—that is, pumping money out of the financial system to reduce inflationary pressures. We'll discuss this balancing act further in the next section.

Direct Lending

When two planes hit the World Trade Center on September 11, 2001, they destroyed the two towers and killed almost 3,000 people. The attack also shut down Wall Street, the biggest financial center in the world, and paralyzed the New York operations of many banks and other large financial institutions. The danger: a chain of massive bankruptcies that could devastate the global financial system.

To prevent this economic disaster from happening, the Federal Reserve immediately lent banks more than $45 billion to make sure they didn't run out of money. In fact, no banks failed in the aftermath of the terrorist attacks, and the economy kept functioning.

The response to the 9/11 attacks illustrates a crucial role of the central bank: to serve as the ultimate safeguard for the financial system when an unexpected crisis hits. To accomplish this role, the Fed can lend vulnerable financial institutions as much money as they need–money that's backed by the full faith and credit of the federal government. This usually ensures that banks and other financial institutions will have enough money to meet their financial obligations to depositors or to any other creditors.

To provide money to struggling financial institutions, the Fed has historically used a monetary policy tool called the **discount window**. (Although this isn't what actually happens, you can think of bank executives lined up at a teller's window.) In fact, a few hours after the September 11, 2001, terrorist attacks, the Fed announced, "The Federal Reserve System is open and operating. The discount window is available to meet liquidity needs."

> **discount window**
>
> A monetary policy tool that allows the Fed to lend money to financial institutions that are running short of funds.

The purpose of the discount window is to give financial institutions access to funds if they run short. To use the discount window, a bank would come to the Fed and ask to borrow money. It would then be charged the **discount rate**. The Fed usually sets the discount rate for banks 3/4 to 1 percentage point higher than the Fed funds rate and adjusts them both at the same time. (The bank also has to put up collateral to prove that it can pay back the loan.) Under normal circumstances, the use of the discount window is usually viewed as a sign that a bank is mismanaged, so banks are reluctant to use it. But in a financial crisis, it is an indispensable tool for getting money into the financial system quickly.

> **discount rate**
>
> The interest rate at which the Fed lends money to financial institutions through the discount window.

Example: The Fed's Response to the Financial Crisis

In 2007, the housing boom turned to bust–in part because too many homes had been built and because too many loans had been made to borrowers with low incomes or bad credit histories–the so-called subprime mortgages. Home prices started to plunge, and many people with subprime mortgages couldn't afford to pay them back. The falling housing prices meant that residential construction dropped sharply. Home owners also had to cut back on their spending because they could no longer easily borrow against the value of their homes.

The Fed addressed these problems by cutting the Fed funds rate from 5.25 percent in summer of 2007 to 2 percent by April 2008. That helped the economy by making borrowing cheaper.

But interest rate cuts weren't enough. As people started to have trouble paying back their loans, banks and other large financial institutions began reporting big losses. People feared that the troubles would spread and that a big bank might fail. There was an enormous amount of worry in the financial markets.

In response, Fed Chairman Ben Bernanke opened the discount window by encouraging financial institutions to borrow from the Fed as needed. But the discount window, in its usual form, was not enough to deal with the developing financial crisis either.

So, the Fed came up with several new ways to lend to financial institutions, with complicated names like the *term auction facility* (TAF), the *primary dealer credit facility* (PDCF), the *money market investor funding facility* (MMIFF), and the *term securities lending facility* (TSLF). With one exception, these new ways of lending were all closed down by 2010 after the crisis subsided (so you don't have to remember the names). But while they were in place, they enabled the Fed to get financially stressed banks and other financial institutions the funds they needed to stay afloat. **Figure 12.5** shows the total of all the crisis-related lending by the Fed, which peaked at about $1.5 trillion at the end of 2008.

Then when the pandemic struck in 2020, the Fed quickly opened up lending windows for various types of financial institutions, which were facing unprecedented stresses. In addition, the Fed created new ways to lend to nonfinancial institutions such as large, medium, and small businesses; nonprofits such as hospitals; and state and local governments. The total outstanding under all of the lending programs (also known as "liquidity facilities") peaked at just under $500 billion in 2020. In addition, their mere existence–and the sense that the Fed was putting its financial muscle behind the entire economy, and not just the financial system–may have helped reduce any pandemic-related panic.

Figure 12.5 Fighting the Financial Crisis and the Pandemic: The Fed Extends Credit to the United States and the World, 2007–2023
To fight the financial crisis, the Fed lent dollars to a wide variety of financial institutions, both in the United States and abroad. In addition, the Fed provided other central banks with dollars to help stem the crisis in other countries. The amount outstanding peaked at about $1.5 trillion at the end of 2008. Then the Fed resorted again to direct lending in the early days of the pandemic, with the amount outstanding peaking at almost $500 billion. (The figure shows the Fed's "liquidity facilities")
Source: The Federal Reserve, www.federalreserve.gov.

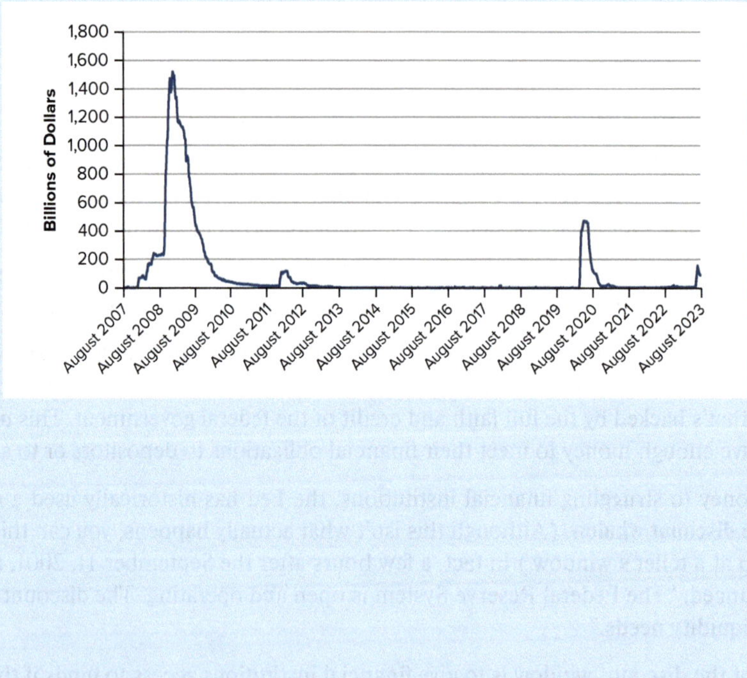

Financial Regulations

Increasingly over time, the Federal Reserve has taken the lead role in setting the regulations by which financial institutions can borrow and lend. By tweaking these, the Fed can exert control over the economy.

Four important regulations that the Fed controls are the reserve requirement, the interest on reserves, the capital requirement, and the margin requirement. Historically banks had to keep a portion of their deposits either in cash in their vaults or on reserve with the Fed. For most banks, this **reserve requirement** was 10 percent of deposits. In theory, the Fed could exert influence over bank lending by controlling the reserve requirement. The more money they had to keep on reserve, the less money banks had available to lend. Less lending by banks meant less spending by borrowers, which helps slow the economy.

reserve requirement
The requirement that banks keep a portion of their deposits either in cash in their vaults or on reserve with the Federal Reserve.

However, in March 2020, the Fed reduced the reserve requirement to zero. Instead, the Fed influences the level of reserves by controlling the **interest rate on reserves** that it pays banks. Cutting the rate on reserves should make banks more willing to use their funds for lending.

interest rate on reserves
The interest rate that the Federal Reserve pays on reserves held by banks.

The **capital requirement** is the amount of low-risk assets a bank or other financial institution has to hold to protect against possible losses. It's the equivalent of keeping money in your low-interest but totally safe savings account to guard against the possibility of losing your job. Higher capital requirements make it more difficult for banks to make potentially risky loans. During the early stages of the pandemic, the Fed adjusted capital requirements to make it easier for banks to lend.

capital requirement
The amount of low-risk assets a bank or other financial institution has to hold to protect against possible losses.

Finally, the **margin requirement** determines how much people can borrow when they buy stock. The higher the margin requirement (now at 50 percent for most stock purchases), the higher the percentage of cash down payment a purchaser must make when borrowing to buy securities. Raising the margin requirement makes it harder for investors to buy stock, and this has the effect of holding down the stock market.

margin requirement
The regulation that determines how much money a person can borrow when buying stock.

THE PRACTICE OF MONETARY POLICY (LO12-6)

LO12-6 Compare and contrast monetary policy and fiscal policy.

Some other important issues come up around monetary policy. These include how much to raise rates when unemployment is low, inflation is high, but the economy seems fragile; how monetary policy compares to fiscal policy; and the question of what monetary policy can do over the long term.

How Much Should Rates Be Increased When Unemployment Is Low, Inflation Is High, but the Economy Seems Fragile?

As this textbook is being revised in early 2023, the U.S. economy seems in an odd place. Inflation is running at a disturbing 6 percent, measured over the past year, and the unemployment rate is below 4 percent. Yet large states such as Ohio, Michigan, and New York are only now reaching pre-pandemic levels of employment. How much and how fast should the Fed raise interest rates to control inflation?

Recall that the trade-off between unemployment and inflation was discussed in **Chapter 10.** On the one hand, controlling inflation is a primary goal of the Federal Reserve. No self-respecting Fed Chair would allow 6 percent inflation to stand without taking action. So, even if some states are lagging economically, it makes sense to raise rates and accept the possibility of a mild recession in order to dampen inflation.

On the other hand, as we discussed in **Chapter 8**, the inflationary surge that began in 2022 was at least partly due to one-time events, like the Russian invasion of Ukraine and pandemic-related supply chain disruptions, as well as large doses of pandemic fiscal stimulus. So as these inflationary factors fade away, it's possible that the Fed can steer the economy to a "soft landing" with low inflation and no recession.

By the time you read this section, we'll have a better idea of whether the Fed has been successful in its balancing act. Alternatively, it may be that the Fed is in the process of making policy mistakes, as it has in the past (see "**Spotlight: The Fed's Biggest Mistakes**").

Monetary versus Fiscal Policy

Monetary policy is more flexible and less political than fiscal policy.

What are the similarities and differences between monetary and fiscal policy? Both can speed up or slow down the economy. The Fed can cut or raise rates, and Congress can boost or cut spending, or cut or raise taxes.

But several differences favor monetary policy as a tool when it comes to fighting inflation or smoothing out the business cycle. In particular, monetary policy is both more flexible and less political than fiscal policy. First, the Fed can act more quickly than Congress and the president because it doesn't have to go through the lengthy political process of passing legislation. In fact, if the need is great enough, the top decision makers at the Fed can raise or lower interest rates with just a telephone conference.

A second advantage is that the Fed, when it does act, can take action in baby steps. That means it can cut or raise rates a little bit at a time and see how the economy reacts before it goes further. In 2017 and 2018, for example, the Fed raised rates in seven very small steps of 0.25 percentage points each. The Fed was behaving like a cook adjusting the temperature of a stove, turning it up a little bit more each time. In contrast, Congress has to expend so much political energy to pass a big tax or spending bill that it can be done just once a year (or sometimes not at all). That makes monetary policy much more flexible than fiscal policy.

Finally, when the economy recovers from a downturn, the Fed can take back a monetary stimulus more easily than Congress can take back a tax cut or added spending. Think about it: When the Fed raises interest rates, making borrowing more expensive, people may complain. But the chair of the Fed is not going to be fired because of that. In comparison, if a member of Congress votes to take back a tax cut, she can be sure her next election opponent will accuse her of having voted for a tax increase.

SPOTLIGHT: THE FED'S BIGGEST MISTAKES

Fed mistakes contributed to bank failures in the Great Depression.
Library of Congress Prints & Photographs Division [LC-USZ62-130861]

One problem with being the most powerful economic agency in the world is that when you make a mistake, it's a big one.

The Fed's first mistake came during the Great Depression, the first major crisis the Fed faced. After the initial stock market crash in October 1929, the Fed loosened monetary policy, which was the right thing to do. By 1931, when the economy was just starting to recover, the Fed decided it would be a good idea to raise interest rates. The tightening continued on and off until 1933, helping contribute to an enormous number of bank failures and a widespread industrial collapse.

From this mistake, the Fed learned its first important lesson: Don't raise interest rates when the economy is collapsing. In the 1970s, however, the Fed made the opposite error. We saw in **Chapter 10** how the oil price shock of 1973 helped create a deep recession. When that happened, the Fed cut rates, which was the right thing to do. However, it then made the mistake of keeping rates too low for too long after the recession was over. That fueled a tremendous surge in inflation. So, the Fed's second lesson was this: Don't cut interest rates when inflation is accelerating. Finally, many economists argue that the Federal Reserve made a big mistake by keeping short-term interest rates too low for too long after the 2001 recession. This enabled a bubble to develop in the housing market and set the stage for the financial crisis.

Long-Term Effects of Monetary Policy

So far, we've been discussing the short-term impacts of monetary policy. Can Fed actions have any long-term impact on unemployment and growth? Can the Fed lower the NAIRU or raise the long-term potential rate of growth?

Economists generally agree that monetary policy affects the long-term rate of inflation but has little direct effect, over the long term, on the rate of unemployment or the potential rate of growth. That is, if the Fed stimulates the economy in an attempt to keep unemployment below the NAIRU or actual GDP above potential GDP over the long term, the main result will be accelerating inflation. Workers will push up wages and businesses will push up prices, potentially leading to a wage-price spiral.

The best way to improve long-term growth has nothing to do with the Fed. Instead, the country has to invest in physical and human capital and in the creation of knowledge, as we saw in **Chapter 9**. These sorts of investments can help cut unemployment as well because firms that are growing and succeeding can hire plenty of workers and keep them employed.

However, there are two indirect pathways by which effective monetary policy can improve long-term outcomes. Low inflation makes the future more predictable, making it easier for businesses and individuals to plan and make good decisions. That tends to improve growth and employment in the long run. So, if the Fed can hold inflation to around 2 percent or so, that's a plus for long-term growth.

In addition, if the Fed does a good job of smoothing out the business cycle, recessions will be few and mild. That makes it easier for businesses to take more risks in terms of investing in new technologies and opening up new business lines. In other words, the Fed's best long-term contribution to the economy is to manage it well by minimizing its ups and downs rather than stimulating it excessively.

YOUR ECONOMIC LIFE: How the Federal Reserve Can Affect You

Let's start first with some things that the Federal Reserve cannot affect. It can't help your car get better gas mileage. It can't help your favorite sports team win. And it can't help you lose weight.

On the other hand, if you've charged a health spa visit to your credit card, the Fed's actions can affect how much interest you are paying on that purchase. If you want to buy a Tesla or other electric vehicle, the Fed can influence the interest rate on the loan for that car. And if your favorite sports team needs to borrow money to build a new arena, stadium, or ballpark, they care about whether the Fed is raising or lowering rates.

Moreover, the Fed's actions influence your odds of being unemployed. High rates slow the economy and cause businesses to hire fewer workers. Low-interest rates give the hiring an extra boost (including hopefully you!).

Even the interest rates on your student loan are affected by the actions of the Federal Reserve. Just remember: There's no hiding from the Fed.

CONCLUSION

The U.S. Federal Reserve was founded in 1913. Since that time, economists have become much more adept at using monetary policy to accomplish important goals, such as controlling inflation, smoothing out the business cycle, and ensuring financial stability. Most recently, to deal with the financial crisis, the Fed had to find new ways of getting funds to vulnerable financial institutions.

But the economy is still evolving. In the next three chapters, we will explore the key driving forces for change in today's world: financial markets, international trade, and technological change.

12 SUMMARY

1. Money includes currency as well as the contents of checking and savings accounts. Money serves three purposes: a medium of exchange, a store of value, and a standard of value. *(LO12-1)*
2. The Federal Reserve was set up to support the financial system when things go bad. It was given the power to issue currency and set key interest rates–the first time a government agency was given such strong tools for directly influencing the economy. *(LO12-2)*
3. The goals of monetary policy include controlling inflation, smoothing out the business cycle, and ensuring financial stability. To accomplish these goals, the Fed has several policy tools, including control over short-term interest rates, quantitative easing, direct lending to financial and nonfinancial institutions, and changes in financial regulations. *(LO12-3)*
4. The main interest rate that the Fed controls is the Fed funds rate, using open market operations. Changes in the Fed funds rate influence other short-term interest rates, such as the interest rates on auto loans, credit card debt, and adjustable-rate mortgages. *(LO12-4)*

5. The Fed uses its control over short-term interest rates to fight inflation and smooth out the business cycle. When the Fed funds rate is cut, that encourages borrowing and spending in the economy and puts upward pressure on prices. An increase in the Fed funds rate discourages borrowing and spending in the economy and puts downward pressure on prices. *(LO12-4)*
6. The Fed's prime weapon against a financial crisis is its ability to lend vulnerable financial institutions as much money as they need. To do this, it uses the discount window. During the financial crisis, the Fed created several new ways to lend money to hard-pressed banks and Wall Street firms. In the early months of the pandemic, the Fed extended direct lending to nonfinancial institutions as well. The Fed also has the power to change the interest rate on reserves, capital requirements, and margin requirements. *(LO12-5)*
7. The advantages of monetary policy over fiscal policy as a tool for influencing the economy are that monetary policy is more flexible and less political. The Fed can react more quickly, take action in small steps to see how the economy reacts, and change direction if needed. *(LO12-6)*

KEY TERMS AND CONCEPTS

monetary policy
money
currency
medium of exchange
store of value
standard of value
money stock
Federal Reserve System
central bank
goals of monetary policy
controlling inflation
smoothing out the business cycle
ensuring financial stability
lender of last resort
Dodd-Frank
open market operations
Fed funds rate
Federal Open Market Committee (FOMC)
monetary policy lags
quantitative easing (QE)
discount window
discount rate
reserve requirement
interest rate on reserves
capital requirement
margin requirement
nonaccelerating inflation rate of employment (NAIRU)

connect PROBLEMS

1. Money has three roles: a medium of exchange, a store of value, and a standard of value. Which role is money playing in each of the following? *(LO12-1)*
   a) You go to the store and buy groceries.
   b) You put your money into a savings account.
   c) You write a check to make a purchase.
   d) You receive a paycheck from your employer.
   e) You have money taken out of your paycheck for your retirement account.
   f) You choose between two televisions, one costing $200 and the other costing $300.
2. You are playing a game of poker with some friends, using poker chips to bet and to keep track of who is winning. At the end of the evening, the chips are cashed in for money. Are these poker chips serving as a medium of exchange, a store of value, or a standard of value? *(LO12-1)*
3. The Federal Reserve was originally founded with the purpose of _______ *(LO12-2)*
   a) fighting inflation.
   b) fighting financial crises.
   c) printing money.
   d) controlling the economy.
   e) fighting pandemics.

4. One important goal of the Federal Reserve is controlling inflation. Which of the following policy actions are likely to help the Fed meet that goal? *(LO12-3)*

   a) Cutting the Fed funds rate to zero.
   b) Setting an inflation target of 2 percent.
   c) Raising the interest rate on reserves.
   d) Making a large loan to a big financial institution that is about to fail.
   e) Raising the discount rate.

5. Another important goal of the Federal Reserve is ensuring financial stability in the face of an emergency such as the pandemic. Which of the following policy actions are likely to help the Fed meet that goal? *(LO12-3)*

   a) Encouraging troubled banks to use the discount window.
   b) Reassuring investors that the Federal Reserve is standing behind the banking system.
   c) Raising the Fed funds rate.
   d) Lowering the Fed funds rate.
   e) Direct lending to troubled Wall Street firms and large nonfinancial corporations.

6. Suppose the Fed raises the Fed funds rate. *(LO12-4)*

   a) How will this increase affect the interest rates on credit cards?
   b) Suppose you are the sort of person who buys clothing on your credit card and pays off the balance over time. Will the increase in the Fed funds rate raise or lower your purchase of clothing?
   c) On a supply-demand graph for the clothing market, show how the increase in the Fed funds rate shifts the demand curve for clothing. Label the new equilibrium point.

7. People borrowing to buy a home usually have to borrow a large sum of money. Explain how monetary policy is likely to affect the demand for homes. *(LO12-4)*

8. Suppose there is a sharp rise in oil prices that sends the price of gasoline to $6 per gallon. *(LO12-4)*

   a) If the output gap is large and positive, the Fed should _______ the Fed funds rate.
   b) If the output gap is negative, the Fed should _______ the Fed funds rate.
   c) If the inflation rate is already 6 percent per year, the Fed should _______ the Fed funds rate.

9. The Fed's tool for helping financial institutions that are running short on money, even when the economy is not in crisis, is _______ *(LO12-5)*

   a) opening the discount window.
   b) lowering capital requirements.
   c) lowering the Fed funds rate.
   d) raising the Fed funds rate.

10. Monetary policy has little effect on which of the following economic outcomes? *(LO12-6)*

    a) Unemployment rate.
    b) Inflation.
    c) Technological change.
    d) Stability of the financial system.
    e) Long-term productivity growth.
    f) Development of a Covid vaccine.

11. Compared to fiscal policy, monetary policy is the preferred tool to fight inflation and smooth out business cycles, because _______ *(LO12-6)*

    a) monetary policy is more sensitive to politics.
    b) monetary policy can be adjusted more easily when economic conditions change.
    c) fiscal policy can be reversed faster.
    d) monetary policy is less transparent.

APPENDIX

DELVING DEEPER INTO MACROECONOMICS

LEARNING OBJECTIVES

After reading this appendix, you should be able to:

LO12A-1 Define *aggregate supply* and *aggregate demand.*
LO12A-2 Describe the effect of an aggregate supply or demand shift on prices and output.

In this appendix, we will explore aggregate supply and aggregate demand. This will give us a general framework for predicting the impact of various economic events—such as a sharp drop in home prices—on output and prices.

AGGREGATE DEMAND AND AGGREGATE SUPPLY (LO12A-1)

LO12A-1 Define aggregate supply and aggregate demand.

So far in this textbook, we've used supply and demand diagrams to analyze individual markets. But economists also use supply and demand diagrams to think about the whole economy. In particular, we talk about *aggregate demand* and *aggregate supply.*

Aggregate Demand

aggregate demand
The sum of the quantities demanded from all sectors of the economy.

Aggregate demand is the sum of the quantities demanded from the different sectors of the economy: *personal consumption* (C), *nonresidential investment* (NR), *residential investment* (R), *government consumption and investment* (G), *change in private inventories* (I), and *net exports* (NX). These are the same sectors that make up gross domestic product, as we saw in **Chapter 7**, but now we have given them labels. The value of net exports, for example, is NX.

The equation for aggregate demand (AD) is, therefore:

$$AD = C + NR + R + G + I + NX$$

aggregate demand curve
The link between the average price level of the whole economy and the aggregate quantity demanded.

The **aggregate demand curve** links the average price level of the whole economy with the aggregate quantity demanded. Obviously, as we've seen in earlier chapters, both the price level and output are almost always rising over time. Thus, we can think of the aggregate demand curve as a snapshot of the economy at a particular moment.

The aggregate demand curve is downward-sloping (see **Figure 12A.1**), which means that a higher overall price level means a lower quantity demanded by consumers, businesses, and government. This seems to make sense: We've seen over and over again in this textbook that in individual markets, higher prices mean lower quantities demanded.

Figure 12A.1 Aggregate Demand
The aggregate demand curve is downward-sloping. A higher price level *P* means a lower quantity demanded *Q*.

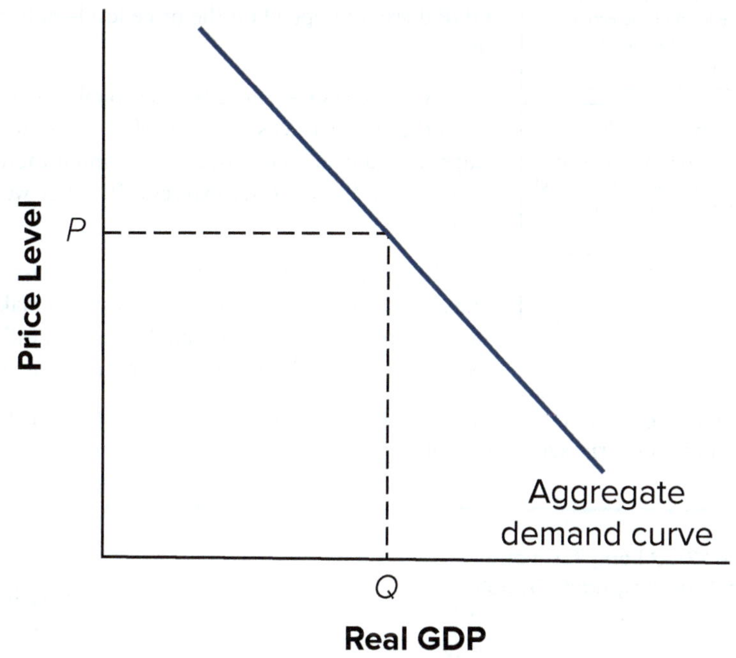

But the aggregate demand curve really doesn't work the same way as a market demand curve, even though it looks similar. The difference is that aggregate demand takes into account the price level for the entire economy. If that price level is higher, all prices are higher on average, including wages. Thus, while the price of a restaurant meal may have gone up by 10 percent, your wages have gone up by 10 percent, too–so that increase wouldn't stop you from buying a meal.

Economists have, instead, identified several other reasons a higher price level means less aggregate quantity demanded. Two of these are the **wealth effect** and the **interest rate effect**. First is the *wealth effect*: If prices are higher, the cash in your pocket and your bank account is worth less. In other words, your real wealth (adjusted for prices) drops. If prices are lower, the cash in your pocket and your bank account is worth more. For example, if you have a $10 bill, and the price of a cup of coffee falls from $2 to $1 per cup, you can buy 10 cups with that money instead of only 5 cups. So, a lower price level means that the buying power of your wealth increases, which in turn leads to more consumption.

wealth effect
One reason aggregate quantity demanded falls as the average price level rises. Also, the phenomenon in which higher wealth leads to more consumption.

interest rate effect
One reason aggregate quantity demanded falls as the average price level rises.

Second, rising prices also boost interest rates, and higher interest rates hold down business investment, residential construction, and consumer spending on things like automobiles, which are usually bought on credit. The link between prices and interest rates runs something like this: If prices are higher, you need to keep more cash on hand and in your checking account to pay your month-to-month bills. But that's money you can't deposit in your savings account, so it's not available for banks to lend out. With less money to lend out, the supply curve for loans moves to the left, and interest rates rise. This is the *interest rate effect.*

Aggregate Supply

Aggregate supply is the quantity of goods and services that the economy produces. Now let's look at the **aggregate supply curve**, which links the average price level of the economy with the aggregate quantity of goods and services produced. As in the case of the aggregate demand curve, we can think of the aggregate supply curve as a snapshot of the economy at a particular moment. In the long term, when prices rise, so do wages and all the other costs of production, such as rent and the costs of materials. From the perspective of a business, then, nothing much has changed–higher prices are balanced by higher costs. As a result, in the long run, a rise in the overall price level does not change the quantity supplied, so the **long-term aggregate supply curve** is vertical–that is, suppliers produce the same amount no matter what the price level is.

aggregate supply
The quantity of goods and services that the economy produces.

aggregate supply curve
The link between the average price level of the whole economy and the aggregate quantity of goods and services produced.

long-term aggregate supply curve
The long-term link between the average price level of the economy and the quantity of goods and services produced.

short-term aggregate supply curve
A curve that shows the short-term link between the average price level and the quantity of goods and services produced.

sticky wages
Wages that don't change much in the short term in response to economic conditions.

Here's another way to think about the long-term aggregate supply curve. In the language of **Chapter 10**, long-term aggregate supply *Q* at any moment is the same as potential GDP at that moment. Potential GDP does not depend on the price level–rather, it reflects the economy's sustainable productive capacity.

However, the **short-term aggregate supply curve** is upward-sloping. If prices rise, it takes time for wages and other input prices to react. Here's one way to think about this: In most businesses, salaries and wages are adjusted only once a year (and if there's a union and a signed labor contract, it may be several years before the contract expires). In other words, wages are **sticky**, meaning they don't change right away.

So, there's a period–after prices start to rise, and before wages respond–when labor gets relatively cheaper. During that period, a business can make more money by hiring additional workers and expanding. As a result, in the short run, businesses will boost their production in response to an increase in the overall price level. You can interpret this as real GDP temporarily exceeding potential GDP.

But, over time, wages catch up with prices, and the economy returns to the long-run aggregate supply curve. **Figure 12A.2** shows both the short-term and long-term aggregate supply curves.

Figure 12A.2 Long-Term and Short-Term Aggregate Supply
As the price level rises from *P* to *P*′, output increases from *Q* to *Q*′ in the short term as output rises above potential. Over time, however, output falls back to *Q*, which can be interpreted as a return to the path of potential GDP.

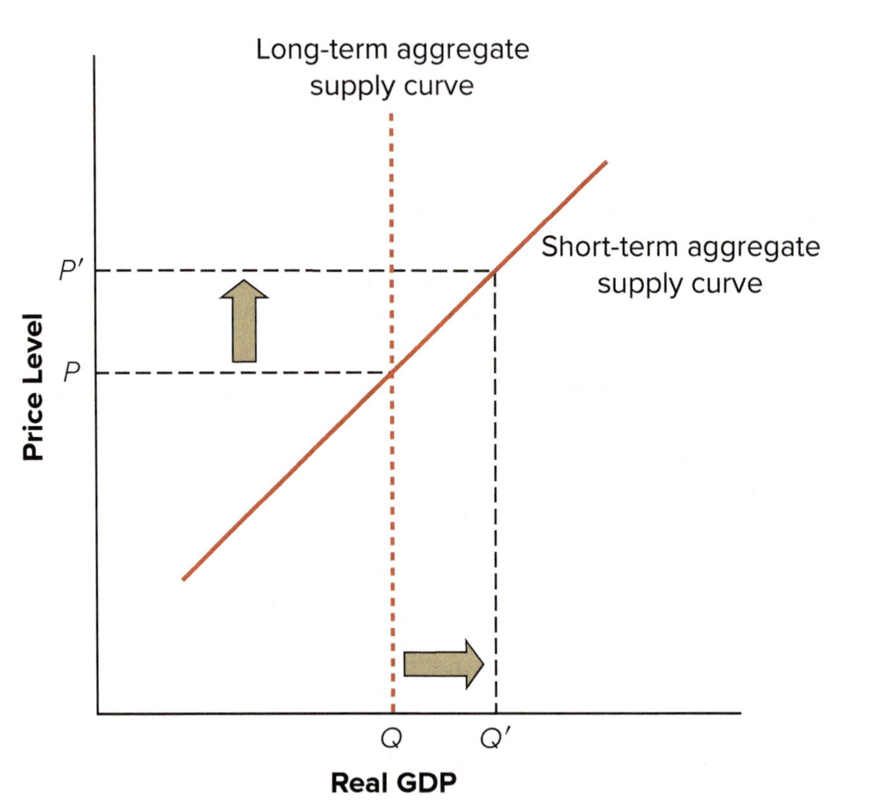

Long-Term Aggregate Equilibrium

aggregate equilibrium
The price where aggregrate quantity demanded equals aggregate quantity supplied.

In **Figure 12A.3**, the long-term **aggregate equilibrium** occurs at the point where long-term aggregate quantity supplied is equal to aggregate quantity demanded–that is, where the aggregate supply and demand curves cross. That gives us an equilibrium price level *P* for the economy and an equilibrium output *Q*.

Figure 12A.3 Aggregate Demand and Supply
The aggregate demand curve is downward-sloping, and the long-term aggregate supply curve is vertical. The equilibrium price *P* and output *Q* are shown at the point where the aggregate supply and demand curves intersect.

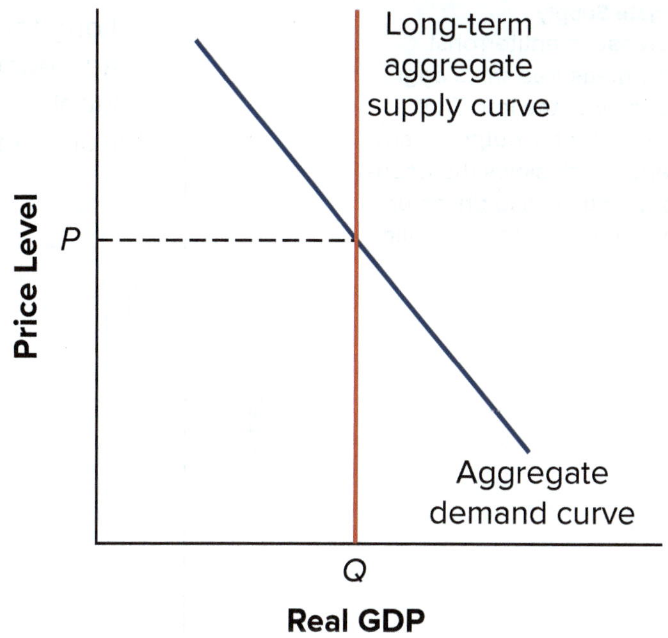

In aggregate equilibrium, demand is just strong enough to get the maximum output from businesses without creating upward pressure on prices. An economy at long-term aggregate equilibrium is, therefore, on the path of potential GDP, where there are no strains on production or unused resources.

REACTING TO EVENTS (LO12A-2)

LO12A-2 Describe the effect of an aggregate supply or demand shift on prices and output.

The whole point of developing the aggregate supply-aggregate demand framework is to understand what happens when the economy is hit by a big event, like a sharp rise in oil prices, a fall in housing prices, or a terrorist attack. We can also use the aggregate supply-demand framework to assess the impact of different government policy actions. Finally, we'll combine our understanding of aggregate supply and demand shifts to understand the impact of the pandemic.

Shifts in Aggregate Supply

Let's look first at events that cause a shift in aggregate supply–that is, a movement of the aggregate supply curve either left or right. The clearest example of a shift to the left is a terrorist attack that forces businesses and government to divert resources–money and people–to increased security. Every extra person working as a security guard or guarding the border is one less person available for productive work in a factory or an office. Every dollar put into security cameras is not available for new machinery and computers.

These resources are not available for production, which causes the long-term aggregate supply curve to shift to the left, as in **Figure 12A.4**. The result is that equilibrium output falls from *Q* to *Q′*. This decline can be interpreted as a reduction of potential output, which has the effect of slowing growth.

At the same time, all else being equal, the price level rises from *P* to *P′*. This can be interpreted as faster inflation because the price level takes an extra bump up. In other words, anything that reduces the level of potential output pushes up inflation (by raising the general price level), which in turn holds down output and slows growth.

Figure 12A.4 A Decline in Aggregate Supply
An increase in antiterrorist security measures shifts aggregate supply to the left. That reduces potential output at any moment, which slows the economy's growth. It also drives up the price level, increasing inflation.

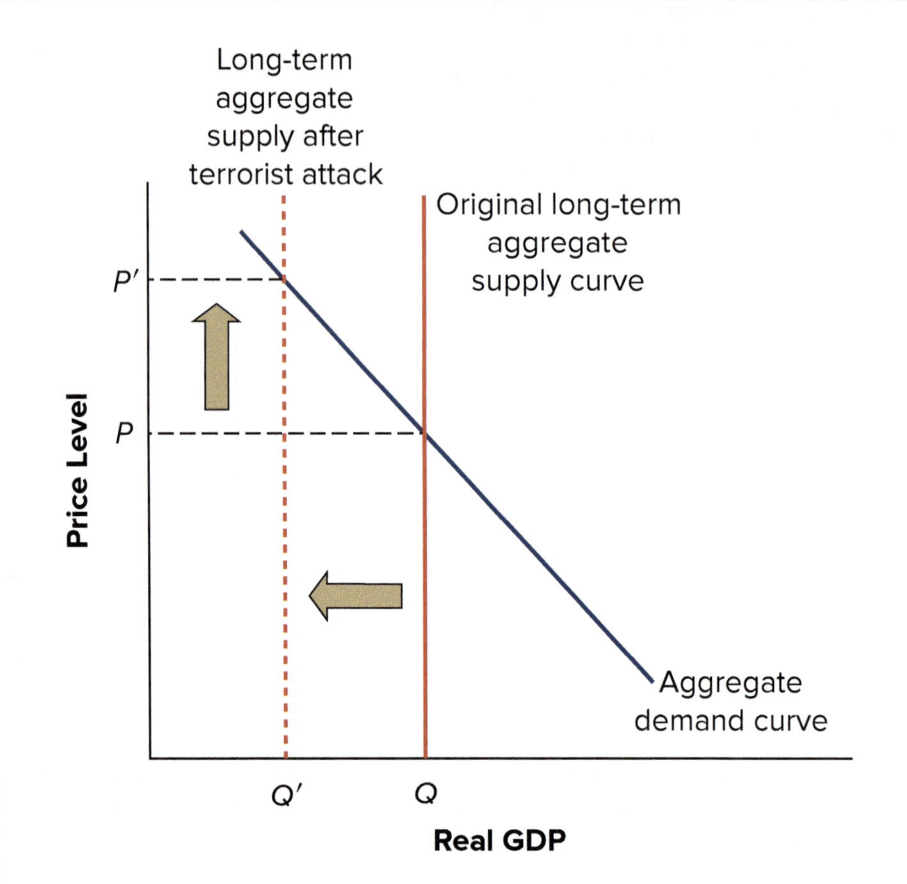

We would draw a similar diagram to illustrate the impact of rising oil prices, of the kind we saw in 2022 with the Russian invasion of Ukraine. So, as the price of oil rises, the amount that the United States has to pay oil-exporting countries goes up. That leaves less money to invest in new equipment at home. What's more, some pieces of equipment that use a lot of energy may be unprofitable to use with fuel prices so high.

stagflation
A combination of slow economic growth and rapid inflation.

As a result, rising oil prices cause the aggregate supply curve to shift to the left (similar to **Figure 12A.4**). That gives us what is known as **stagflation**–the combination of slow growth and inflation that we last saw in the 1970s. The bigger the rise in oil prices, the further that the aggregate supply curve shifts to the left. That means a bigger rise in overall prices and a deeper slowdown in growth.

Conversely, falling energy prices cause the aggregate supply curve to shift to the right. That boosts growth, while keeping inflation low. Part of the recovery since the financial crisis has been fueled by a deep decline in the price of energy as new techniques were developed to locate and produce oil and natural gas, as will be described in **Chapter 15** and **Chapter 19**.

Another change that has increased the level of potential output and shifted the aggregate supply curve to the right is the *information revolution*, later described in **Chapter 15**. Broader use of computers, the Internet, and mobile communications has led to an increase in productivity as more and more businesses integrated information technology into their operations. This is illustrated in **Figure 12A.5**. As the aggregate supply curve shifts to the right, equilibrium output increases from Q to Q', which can be interpreted as an upward boost to potential output, increasing the growth rate.

Figure 12A.5 also shows a drop in the price level from P to P'. This does not indicate actual deflation but rather should be seen as a slowing of the inflation rate. This is what happened in the second half of the 1990s–rapid growth without inflation, or the opposite of stagflation.

There might be other reasons the aggregate supply curve shifts to the right. Any significant technological change can increase aggregate supply. And many economists believe that cuts in marginal tax rates can increase the incentives to work and invest (as discussed in **Chapter 11**). That would increase output and produce a diagram much like **Figure 12A.5**. However, there is great disagreement about how big an impact a marginal tax cut might have.

Figure 12A.5 An Increase in Aggregate Supply
The information revolution shifted long-term aggregate supply to the right. That increased potential output at any moment, boosting growth. It also pushed down the price level, reducing inflation.

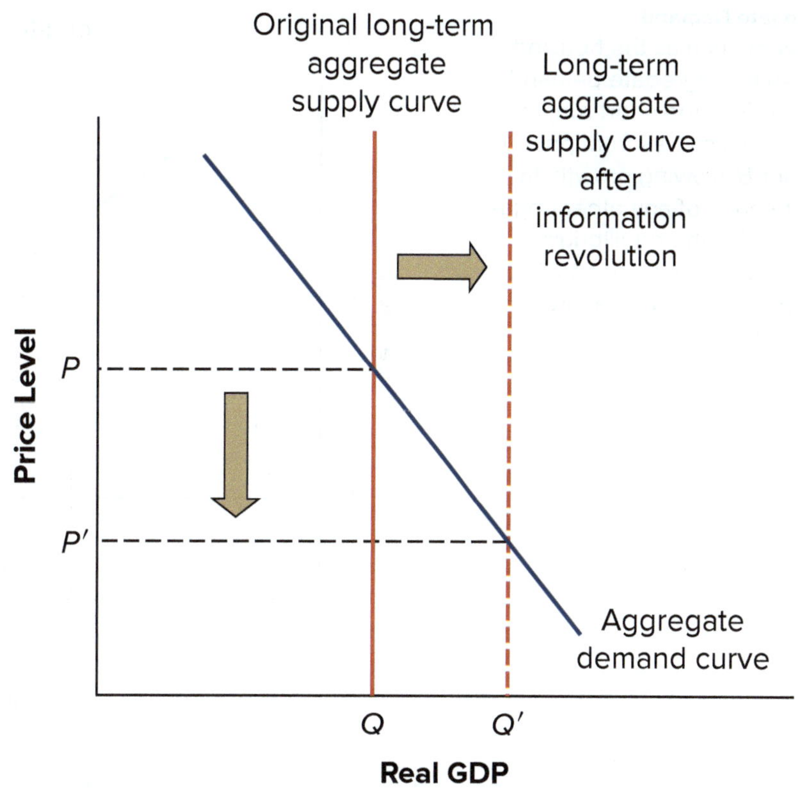

Shifts in Aggregate Demand

Many of the events that have hit the economy in recent years have affected the aggregate demand curve rather than the aggregate supply curve. Consider the financial crisis of 2008-2009. As home prices dropped, many households saw a large part of their personal wealth evaporate. What's more, it became harder for households to take out home equity loans because their homes were worth less and banks were more reluctant to lend. And falling home prices meant a lot less construction of new homes by builders.

The result is lower personal consumption (C) and residential investment (R)–and because personal consumption and residential investment are both components of aggregate demand, that means the aggregate demand curve shifts to the left.

Take a look at **Figure 12A.6**. The first thing that happens when aggregate demand falls is that the equilibrium shifts from point *A* to point *B* along the short-term aggregate supply curve. Assuming nothing else changes, demand falls, the average price level decreases from *P* to *P'*, and businesses drop their output from *Q* to *Q′* because they are less profitable. They hire fewer workers, the unemployment rate rises, and growth slows.

But over time, sticky wages and input prices fall along with the overall price level. Business profitability goes up because firms are paying lower wages, so they hire more workers. The result is that output (and the unemployment rate) returns to the original level of *Q*. This can be interpreted as a return to the path of potential GDP. But the price level *P'* is now much lower than the original price level *P*.

The implication is that the fall in housing prices leads to slow growth and to less inflation, with the economy eventually recovering, which means a return to the path of potential GDP.

What about events that increase aggregate demand? For example, in the second half of the 1990s, the information revolution caused businesses to spend heavily on information technology, boosting nonresidential investment (NR) and lifting aggregate demand. The housing boom that ran until 2006 stimulated both personal consumption and residential investment.

Aggregate demand can also be increased by government intervention. Using fiscal and monetary policy, as described in **Chapters 11** and **12**, government policymakers can increase demand by cutting interest rates, cutting taxes, or boosting government spending. For example, President Obama's fiscal stimulus package of 2009 created jobs and put money into the pockets of Americans, much of which they spent. Similarly, President Trump's tax cuts, which took effect in 2018, served to stimulate the economy.

Figure 12A.6 A Decrease in Aggregate Demand
An event such as the housing bust shifts aggregate demand to the left. In the short run, the equilibrium moves from point *A* to point *B*, slowing growth. In the absence of any other negative shocks, the equilibrium would eventually move to *C*, on the long-term potential growth path but with lower levels of inflation.

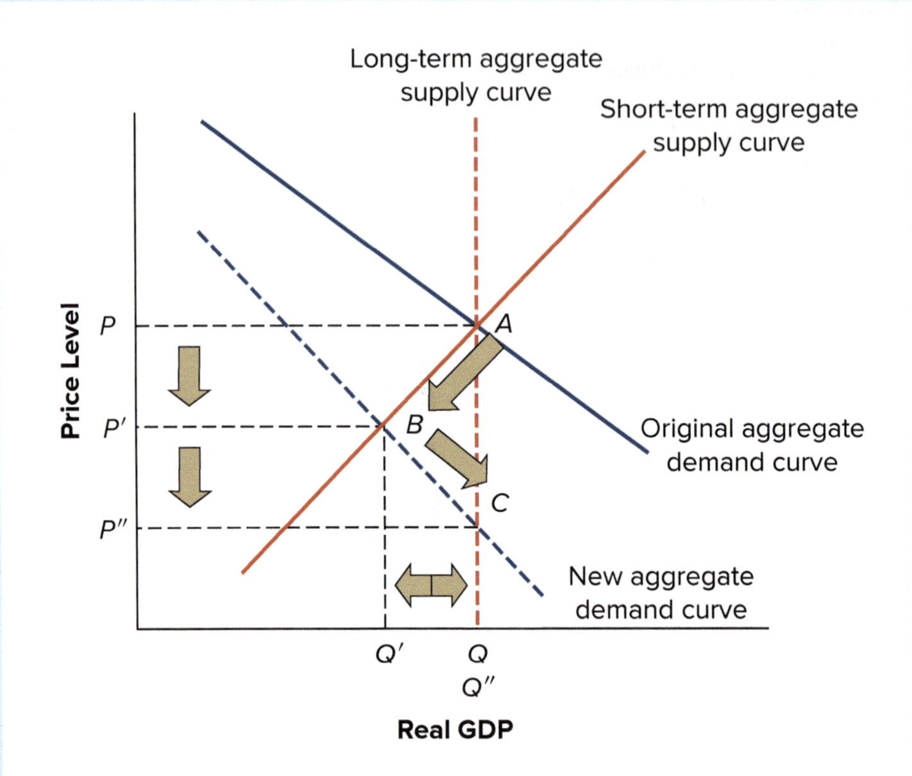

Let's see how we would represent a fiscal stimulus on an aggregate supply–aggregate demand diagram. Take a look at **Figure 12A.7**. The first thing that happens when aggregate demand rises is that the equilibrium shifts from point *A* to point *B*. Demand increases, the average price level increases from *P* to *P*′, and businesses boost their output from *Q* to *Q*′ because it's profitable for them to do so. They hire more workers, and the unemployment rate falls.

But then wages rise, catching up to prices. Employers lay off some of their additional workers or cut back on hours. Output falls back from *Q*′ to the original *Q*, returning back to potential GDP, and a higher price level, *P*′. That's a sign of potential inflation.

We can draw two conclusions from this analysis. First, attempts by the government to stimulate the economy and boost output above its long-term equilibrium level may succeed temporarily. In the long run, however, the main outcome of government stimulation is to increase prices (and inflation). In other words, there is no sustainable way to drive unemployment down below its natural rate.

The second conclusion, though, is more optimistic. Suppose the economy suffered a negative demand shock, such as turmoil in the financial markets that made it hard for people to get mortgage loans. Then policies designed to stimulate demand–such as cutting interest rates, cutting taxes, or boosting government spending–could get the economy back to long-term equilibrium faster.

Using Aggregate Supply and Demand to Analyze the Pandemic

Within the aggregate supply-demand framework, the pandemic can be thought of as a combination of several shifts or shocks. First, the pandemic resulted in aggregate supply shifting to the left. Many businesses had to close down, and global supply chains were disrupted.

Second, the pandemic initially shifted aggregate demand to the left as well, as consumers stayed home in many areas except for essential travel and shopping. They could not go to restaurants, or sporting events, or movie theaters.

The combination of aggregate demand and aggregate supply both shifting to the left would clearly reduce output Q, while having an uncertain impact on the price level P. That's what happened in the pandemic recession.

But the initial impact of the pandemic was quickly matched by a large amount of fiscal and monetary stimulus, as we saw in **Chapter 11** and earlier in this chapter. This stimulus tended to shift the aggregate demand curve back to the right again. Moreover, as the vaccine was introduced, business and travel restrictions were gradually lifted, allowing aggregate supply to shift back to the right as well.

Figure 12A.7 An Increase in Aggregate Demand
Fiscal or monetary policy stimulates the economy by shifting aggregate demand to the right. In the short run, the equilibrium moves from point *A* to point *B*, boosting growth. But eventually the equilibrium moves to *C* on the original long-term growth path but with higher inflation.

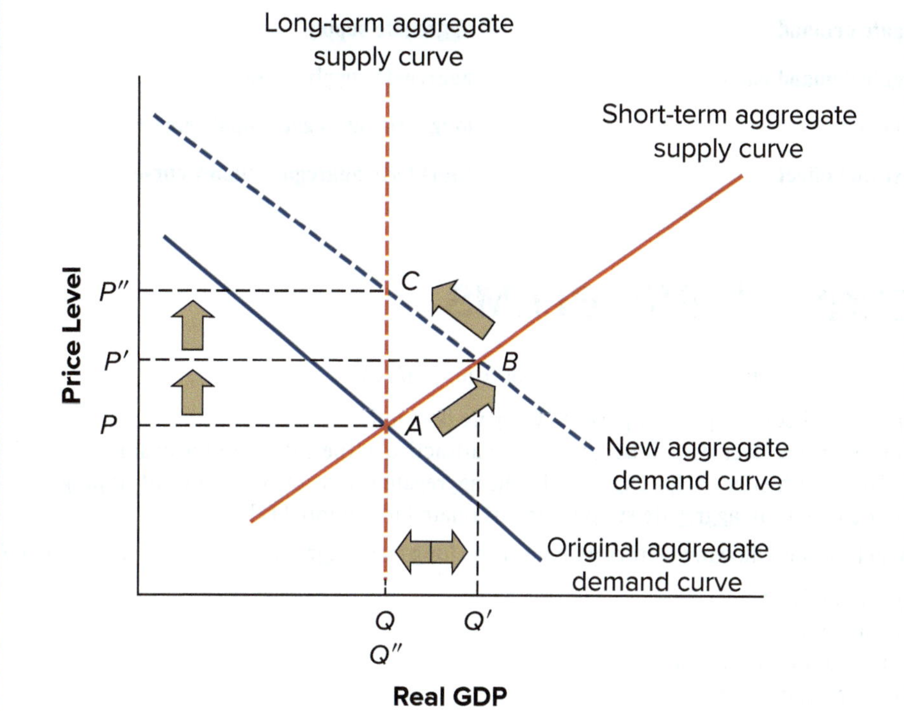

This analysis suggests that we would see a gradual return to the original aggregate supply and demand curves, with the addition of fiscal and monetary stimulus perhaps shifting aggregate demand to the right. The eventual result would look something like **Figure 12A.7**, with a rise in the price level. That would translate into an inflationary surge as the pandemic eased, which is of course exactly what happened in 2022.

SUMMARY

1. Aggregate demand is the sum of the quantities demanded from the sectors of the economy. The aggregate demand curve links the average price level of the whole economy with the aggregate quantity demanded. ***(LO12A-1)***
2. The aggregate supply curve links the average price level of the economy with the quantity of goods and services produced. The long-term aggregate supply curve is vertical, meaning that price changes have no effect on the quantity produced. The short-term aggregate supply curve is upward-sloping because price increases will induce businesses to produce more and hire more workers. ***(LO12A-1)***
3. A shift of the long-term aggregate supply curve to the left will reduce output and boost the price level. This can be interpreted as a reduction in potential GDP and an increase in the inflation rate. A shift in the long-term aggregate supply curve to the right will increase output and hold down the price level. This can be interpreted as an increase in potential GDP and a decline in inflation. ***(LO12A-2)***
4. In the short run, a rightward shift in aggregate demand–say, because the government boosts spending–will increase output and prices. This can be interpreted as a boost to growth and inflation. In the long run, output will fall back to the long-term aggregate supply curve, but the average price level will remain higher. ***(LO12A-2)***
5. In the aggregate supply-demand framework, the pandemic can be thought of as a combination of several types of shifts. Leftward shifts in aggregate supply and aggregate demand were counteracted by fiscal and monetary stimulus. ***(LO12A-2)***

KEY TERMS AND CONCEPTS

aggregate demand
aggregate demand curve
wealth effect
interest rate effect
aggregate supply
aggregate supply curve
long-term aggregate supply curve
short-term aggregate supply curve
sticky wages
aggregate equilibrium
stagflation

connect PROBLEMS

1. Which of the following statements is not true? *(LO12A-1)*
   a) Personal consumption is part of aggregate demand.
   b) If the price level rises, it becomes more attractive in the short run for businesses to hire workers.
   c) The wealth effect helps explain why the aggregate supply curve is upward-sloping.
   d) The long-term aggregate supply curve is related to potential GDP.
2. Which of the following factors will affect the long-term aggregate supply curve? *(LO12A-1)*
   a) Productivity.
   b) Unemployment rate.
   c) Education of the workforce.
   d) Government spending.
   e) The pandemic
3. From 2014 to 2015, the average price of crude oil plunged from $100 per barrel to $50 per barrel. *(LO12A-2)*
   a) Did the decline in the price of oil cause a shift in the aggregate supply curve or the aggregate demand curve?
   b) Draw an aggregate supply-aggregate demand diagram to illustrate the impact of the oil price decline. Label the original aggregate equilibrium and the new aggregate equilibrium. Does output Q rise or fall?
4. Suppose that the Federal Reserve lowers the Fed funds rate to fight the negative impact of the pandemic. *(LO12A-2)*
   a) Does the decrease in rates cause a shift in the aggregate supply curve or the aggregate demand curve?
   b) Draw an aggregate supply-aggregate demand diagram to illustrate the impact of the interest rate cut. Label the original aggregate equilibrium and the final aggregate equilibrium.
   c) All other things being equal, does output rise or fall in the short run because of the rate cut? Does output rise or fall in the long run?
5. The aggregate supply-aggregate demand framework can be used to understand the impact of the financial crisis that hit the U.S. economy in 2007-2009. *(LO12A-2)*
   a) As part of the financial crisis, banks tightened lending standards for consumers, making it harder to borrow to buy a car or home. Did that cause the aggregate demand curve to shift to the left or right?
   b) Assuming everything else stays constant, does the shift in the aggregate demand curve cause the equilibrium output to rise or fall? Does it cause the equilibrium price level to rise or fall?
   c) Another effect of the financial crisis was that many businesses found it harder to borrow money to buy new equipment or pay for raw materials, so their production slowed. Did that cause the aggregate supply curve to shift to the left or right?
   d) Assuming everything else stays constant, does the shift in the aggregate supply curve cause the equilibrium output to rise or fall?
   e) Based on your answers to (a) through (d), did the financial crisis raise the equilibrium price level, lower the equilibrium price level, or have an ambiguous effect?
6. Some people continue to have symptoms months after being infected by the Covid virus. These symptoms, known as “long covid,” can make working more difficult. Would you expect long covid to affect aggregate supply, aggregate demand, or both?

CH 13

THE FINANCIAL MARKETS

bartsadowski/123RF

LEARNING OBJECTIVES

After reading this chapter, you should be able to:

LO13-1 Discuss the demand and supply curves for loans and list some factors affecting interest rates.
LO13-2 Explain the role of a financial intermediary and discuss how banks work.
LO13-3 Describe the risk–return principle and explain how it applies to the stock market.
LO13-4 Review the benefits of the diversity of financial intermediaries.
LO13-5 Summarize the key causes of the financial crisis that started in 2007.

The first half of this textbook explored the basics of microeconomics and macroeconomics. Now, we shift gears and focus on critical trends driving the economy into the future. In this chapter, we will cover the financial markets, followed by discussions on globalization and technology in the next two chapters. The ups and downs of the stock market and other financial markets in response to the pandemic and other economic events; the rapid growth of technology companies; and the huge volume of trade with countries such as China and India are economic events that influence each of our lives.

In this chapter, we will take a good look at financial markets. Over the past 25 years, the financial markets and the businesses that participate in them—including high-profile financial institutions such as JPMorgan Chase and Goldman Sachs—have taken an increasingly central role in our economy. More and more, the financial markets influence where we live, what we drive, and what our retirement will look like.

We've already encountered interest rates and how the Fed can control rates to fight the economic drag from events like the pandemic and to deal with inflation. Now, we will review some basics of borrowing and lending. Then we'll introduce the important ideas of financial intermediaries, the risk–return principle, and diversification. (Don't worry! We'll explain all these terms.) Along the way, we'll describe some key institutions of the financial markets, such as the stock market and the bond market. We'll also explain how financial markets can go wrong, what happened in the financial crisis that started in 2007, and how regulations were tightened to reduce the chances of a similar event happening.

THE MARKET FOR LOANS (LO13-1)

LO13-1 Discuss the demand and supply curves for loans and list some factors affecting interest rates.

loan
A sum of money that a lender gives a borrower, which is expected to be repaid with interest.

principal
The sum of money in any loan that the lender gives the borrower.

term
The length of a loan; the period of time during which a borrower repays principal back to a lender.

In earlier chapters, we looked at simple lending and borrowing. Let's quickly review some terms and define some new ones. In any **loan**, a lender gives a borrower a sum of money called the **principal**. The price of the loan is its *interest rate,* which says how much the borrower has to pay the lender in exchange for the use of the money. For example, if the annual interest rate is 5 percent, the borrower has to pay the lender 5 percent of the principal in exchange for borrowing the money for a year. After some period of time, the borrower repays the principal to the lender, in addition to the interest already paid. The length of a loan is called its **term**.

Suppose a real estate developer wants to make money by building and selling some new houses in a previously rural area. Before she can sell the homes, the developer has to lay out a lot of money buying farmland, clearing the land with bulldozers, putting in the infrastructure (electricity, water, roads, sewer system), and actually building the homes. The process might take $3 million and a year or more.

Rather than taking this money out of her own pocket, the developer takes out a $3 million loan from a local bank–say, at a 5 percent interest rate–to finance the construction. A year later, she's built and sold the homes and has made enough money to repay the $3 million principal to the bank. In addition, she has to pay the bank 5 percent interest on the $3 million, which amounts to $150,000. So, in total, she pays the bank $3,150,000.

Table 13.1 Some Common Types of Loans

Individual Loans	Explanation
Credit card	When a consumer charges a purchase on a credit card, the credit card company is effectively lending the consumer the money to make the purchase.
Student loan	Many students borrow to pay for their college or graduate education.
Home mortgage	The biggest single category of household borrowing is loans to buy homes.
Home equity	Home owners can borrow money for any purpose, based on the value of their home.
Business Loans	**Explanation**
Business expansion	Businesses use loans to buy the equipment and resources they need to expand.
Commercial mortgage	Businesses take out loans to buy industrial property and office buildings.
Inventory and accounts receivable loans	Sometimes companies borrow to finance the materials and services they need to make their products. They pay back the loans after they've sold the products and gotten paid.

Because the borrower is actually a type of buyer who pays the lender–the seller–for the use of the principal for some length of time, we can think about this transaction in terms of the supply-demand framework we developed in **Chapters 2** and **3**. The interest rate is the price of using the money. The higher the interest rate, the higher the price.

Why Borrow?

Before we go further in our examination of the market for loans, let's ask a simple question: Why borrow? Most typical households don't have enough cash on hand to afford the cars, the homes, the college educations, or the vacations they want. In theory, they can save until they have enough money to pay cash, though that could take a while. Or they can borrow the money now and pay it back over time, either by taking out loans or by charging the purchases on their credit cards (this is just like taking out a loan from the credit card company, only usually at a higher interest rate than you would pay at a bank). About three of every four U.S. families have some debt.

The biggest single type of household debt by far is mortgage debt, used to buy or renovate homes. The second-biggest type of debt is student loans. In 2022, outstanding student loans totaled almost $1.8 trillion.

future-oriented activities
Activities intended to bring in profits over the long term.

When businesses borrow, their typical goal is to finance their expansion–another building, more machines, more workers. An airline, for example, might borrow money to buy more planes or spare parts. A doctor's office might take out a loan to finance a new computer system. An electric utility might borrow to build a new power plant. These are all **future-oriented activities** intended to bring in profits over the long term, as opposed to buying supplies for immediate use (see **Table 13.1** for some common types of loans).

The ability to borrow is important for healthy market economies. Without borrowing, there would be many fewer new businesses because potential entrepreneurs would have to save all the necessary money before their ideas could even get off the ground. Airlines could not buy new planes unless they had millions of dollars in cash to pay for them (which they almost never do). JetBlue, an airline that started flying in 2000, borrowed hundreds of millions of dollars to buy planes. Trucking companies generally take out loans to pay for their fleets. And most office buildings, warehouses, and factories would not be constructed without borrowed money. In fact, the flow of borrowed funds nourishes productive capacity in every part of the economy.

The Demand Curve for Loans

Interest rates matter. The willingness of consumers and businesses to borrow rises as the interest rate falls–that is, the *law of demand* holds for loans. If the interest rate is low, both businesses and consumers are more likely to take on debt. But if the interest rate rises, the quantity of loans demanded will fall.

For example, the real estate developer in our previous example has to pay interest on the money she borrows to pay for the land and the construction. If a bank is willing to lend her the money to buy the land at only 1 percent interest per year, she'll probably have the bulldozers roaring tomorrow. But if the interest rate is 10 percent per year, she'll be paying 10 times as much interest, and the loan to buy the land looks much less attractive.

In general, the willingness to borrow falls as the interest rate rises.

Table 13.2 illustrates in more detail how higher interest rates can discourage borrowing. As before, it costs the developer $3 million to buy the land and construct the homes. As a result, she needs a $3 million loan. She hopes to sell the homes for $3.2 million, which will generate a $200,000 gain ($3.2 million minus her $3 million costs).

Table 13.2 An Example of the Law of Demand in a Loan Market

This example shows why the quantity of loans demanded falls as the interest rate rises. A real estate developer is considering borrowing $3 million to buy land and build new homes. The process would take a year, after which she would sell the homes for $3.2 million. Here are her calculations under three different interest rate scenarios. As the interest rate goes up, it makes less sense to pursue the project.

	Low-Rate Scenario (Dollars)	Medium-Rate Scenario (Dollars)	High-Rate Scenario (Dollars)
Total Loan Needed to Purchase Land and Build Homes	**3,000,000**	**3,000,000**	**3,000,000**
Interest Rate on Loan	1%	5%	10%
Interest Cost	30,000	150,000	300,000
Total Amount to Be Repaid	**3,030,000**	**3,150,000**	**3,300,000**
Revenue from Selling the Homes	3,200,000	3,200,000	3,200,000
Profits	**170,000**	**50,000**	**−100,000**

But wait! The developer also has to pay interest on the loan. If the interest rate is 1 percent, as shown in the first column of **Table 13.2**, her interest payment is $30,000 (1 percent of $3 million). That gives her a net profit of $170,000, so it makes sense to take out the loan.

Now take a look at the second column, where the interest rate is 5 percent. The interest payments are higher, and the net profit is lower. Still, the developer will go ahead.

But if the interest rate is 10 percent, as shown in the third column of the table, the interest payment is $300,000. Even after earning revenue of $3.2 million, her total costs have gone up to $3.3 million, and she actually makes a net loss of $100,000 on the deal. So being a smart entrepreneur, she doesn't take out the loan or build the homes. As others face the same situation, the higher interest rate ends up reducing the amount of borrowing.

ECONOMIC MILESTONE

2021: A Low for the Mortgage Rate

In January 2021, in the middle of the pandemic, the average interest rate on 30-year home mortgages dropped to only 2.65 percent, the lowest since official statistics started being collected in 1971. These low rates helped fuel a pandemic housing boom.

Households have the same response to high-interest rates. If you are considering buying a new car, you're much more likely to go through with the purchase if you can get an auto loan at 1 percent per year rather than 10 percent. For example, if the car costs $30,000, a loan at 1 percent per year will cost roughly $300 in interest payments the first year. If the loan is at 10 percent, the first year's interest payments will come to $3,000. That's a big difference.

Because borrowing follows the law of demand, the demand curve for loans is downward-sloping, as we see in **Figure 13.1** (we first saw the downward-sloping demand curve for loans in **Chapter 3**, but it's worth repeating). As interest rates rise, the quantity of loans demanded falls, all else being equal.

Figure 13.1 The Basic Market for Loans
As the interest rate increases, the quantity of loans demanded goes down and the quantity of loans supplied goes up.

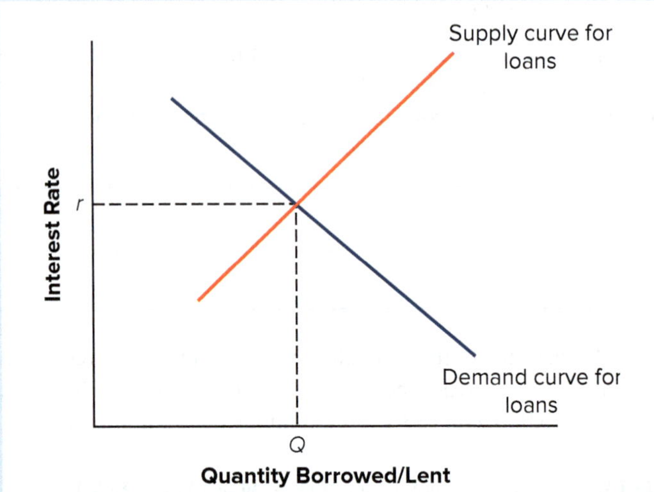

The Supply Curve for Loans

Why should anyone lend money? On one level, the answer is obvious. Lenders have more money than they can use right away, so they lend it to someone else who is willing to pay for the privilege of using it.

As interest rates rise, lenders are willing to supply more loans, all other things being equal.

But step back for a moment and imagine you have some spare money—that is, you are a potential lender. A friend or a relative wants to borrow the money and is even willing to pay interest. Why might you be reluctant to lend?

default
Failure of a borrower to pay back a loan to the lender on time, or at all.

First, if you lend someone money, there's a risk the borrower may **default**, or fail to pay you back on time (or at all). The possibility of not getting paid back on a loan is known as the *risk of default* (see **"Spotlight: What Happens after a Borrower Defaults?"**).

SPOTLIGHT: WHAT HAPPENS AFTER A BORROWER DEFAULTS?

When a borrower can't repay a loan, the lender will want to cut its losses. If the loan is a mortgage, the lender will foreclose on the home, which means it will take the property back from the owners, who will be forced to leave. The lender will then sell the home to get back whatever cash it can. If the loan is for a car, the lender will repossess the car and sell it.

Student loans that go into default are a bit different, because the loan paid for an asset—the education—cannot be repossessed and sold off. Instead, the lender may send a collection agency after the person who defaulted.

What about when a well-known retailer like Toys "R" Us can't pay back its loans? Under pressure from low-price competitors such as Walmart and Amazon, the giant toyseller declared bankruptcy in September 2017, eventually closing its last two stand-alone stores in 2021. However, as of early 2023, a new company bought the rights to the brand name Toys "R" Us, and is opening stores under that name which are housed within Macy's department stores around the U.S.

Smith Collection/Gado/Getty Images

Second, if you make a loan to someone, you don't have to use your money for the term of the loan. For example, if you lend your best friend or brother-in-law $10,000 to start a new business, that's $10,000 you don't have available for other purposes until he pays the money back. You may have unexpected medical costs, or you may want to buy a car, or you may want to put your money in a savings account where it could earn interest—but that money is not available to you.

The opportunity cost of not having your money available is known as the **time value of money**. Charging interest on the loan to your friend or brother-in-law is compensation for the fact that you don't have the money available for other uses.

time value of money

The opportunity cost of not having one's money available for use for some period.

For you to want to make a loan, the interest rate has to be high enough to compensate you both for sacrificing the time value of money and for bearing the risk of default. As a result, you are more likely to make a loan if you can charge a higher interest rate, all other things being equal. If rates get too low, it may be more worthwhile for you to put the money under a mattress or even spend it on yourself.

All lenders go through the same type of calculation. The result is an upward-sloping market supply schedule for lending, as shown in **Figure 13.1**. As the interest rate rises, lenders are willing to supply more loans, all other things being equal. This is the law of supply as applied to the loan market.

Some Factors Affecting Interest Rates

As we saw in **Chapter 3**, the price in any competitive market is set at the point where quantity supplied and quantity demanded are equal. The market for loans is no different. The interest rate in the loan market can be found at the point where the quantity supplied of loans is equal to the quantity demanded of loans. We look at the downward-sloping demand schedule for borrowing and the upward-sloping supply schedule for lending. The point where these two lines cross is the market equilibrium.

The equilibrium interest rate is determined by a host of factors. These include monetary and fiscal policy, which we looked at in **Chapters 11** and **12**. However, here we will pick out two other influences on rates: the strength of the economy and the borrowers' risk of default.

When the economy is stronger, businesses are more likely to invest because they expect they can make money. They anticipate rising demand for their output, so they borrow to build factories, open new offices, and buy more airplanes and trucks.

So, a growing economy—or more precisely, an economy that is expected to keep growing—will cause the demand curve for loans to shift to the right. As we see in **Figure 13.2**, the equilibrium amount of loans increases from Q to Q', and the equilibrium interest rate increases from r to r'. In other words, interest rates are more likely to be higher in good times and lower in tough times, all other things being equal.

Figure 13.2 The Impact of a Stronger Economy on the Loan Market
If businesses are seeing their revenues rise, that pushes the demand curve for loans to the right. The equilibrium quantity of loans increases from *Q* to *Q*′, while the equilibrium interest rate rises from *r* to *r*′.

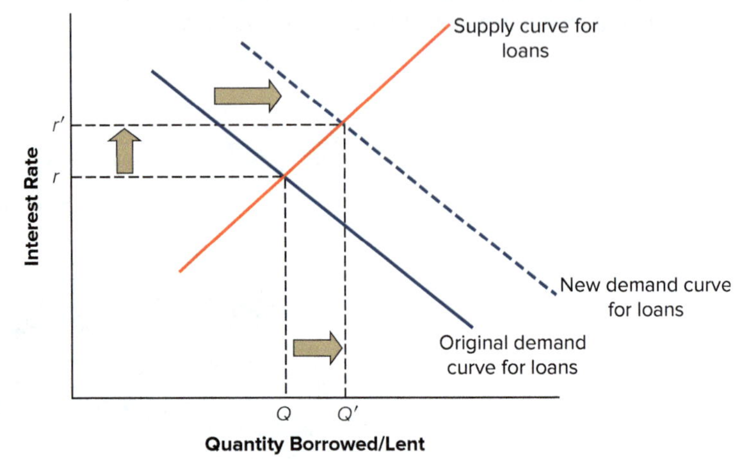

In tough times, the process operates in reverse. If businesses are having trouble selling their products or services, they are less likely to borrow to expand. All other things being equal, the interest rate will fall.

Now let's look at a different factor influencing rates. Not every loan is paid back in full: Some borrowers default, which means they cannot pay back the full amounts of their loans. Some borrowers have a higher risk of default than others. For example, someone who has a hard time holding a job is more likely to default than someone with a steady employment history. A well-established firm is less likely to default than one just starting up. Some industries, like restaurants, are notorious for their high number of failures, which leads to a high number of defaults on loans.

All other things equal, lenders are less willing to advance money to borrowers who are more likely to default. After all, lenders are in business to make money, not lose it when a borrower defaults. As a result, at the same interest rate, the quantity of loans made to high-risk borrowers is lower than the quantity of loans made to safer borrowers. This is equivalent to saying that the supply curve for borrowers at a high risk of default is to the left of the supply curve for loans to low-risk borrowers (as we see in **Figure 13.3**). As a result, the market equilibrium for high-risk borrowers has a higher interest rate (see "**Spotlight: Credit Scores**").

Figure 13.3 Why High-Risk Borrowers Pay a Higher Interest Rate
The supply curve for loans to high-risk borrowers lies to the left of the supply curve for low-risk borrowers. Thus, the equilibrium interest rate *r*′ charged to high-risk borrowers is higher than the rate *r* charged to low-risk borrowers.

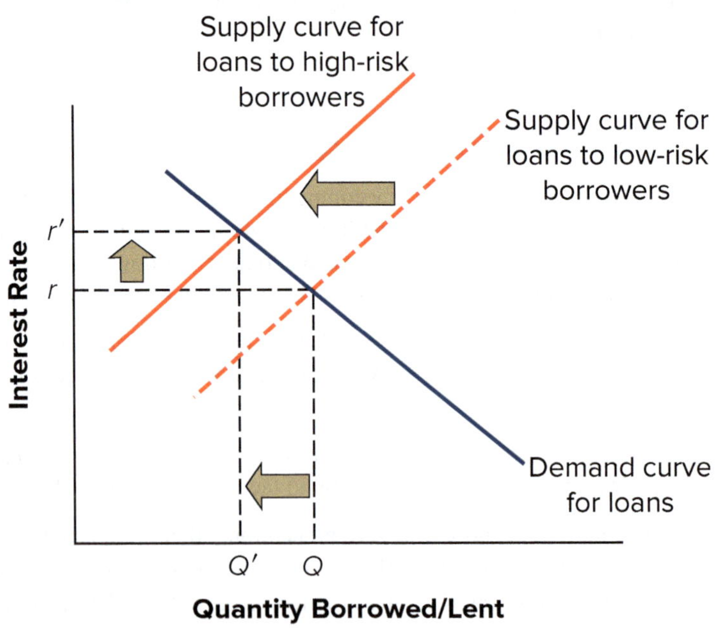

SPOTLIGHT: CREDIT SCORES

How do lenders determine which borrowers are at high risk of default? Consumers receive a *credit score* based on payment history, amounts owed on other loans and credit cards, length of time those accounts have been open, and number of new accounts. Credit scores range from 300 to 850, with the highest numbers being the best. The safest households, with no history of late payments and not much debt, get offered the best rates. But even borrowers with spotty credit histories can usually get loans if they are willing to pay high enough rates. For example, in the fourth quarter of 2022, the interest rate on a new car loan could run from as low as 4.75 percent to roughly 13 percent, depending on your credit score, as **Table 13.3** shows.

Table 13.3 How Credit Scores Affect Interest Rates

The higher your credit score, the lower the interest rate you have to pay.

Credit Score	Average Interest Rate for New Car Loan (%)
781–850	4.75
661–780	5.82
601–660	8.12
501–600	10.79
300–500	13.42

Source: Experian Information Solutions, as of fourth quarter 2022.

YOUR ECONOMIC LIFE: Thinking about Your Student Loans

If you haven't taken out loans to pay for your education, you've probably thought about it. Does borrowing for your education make financial sense?

You have to balance the economic benefits of more education against the cost of paying back the loan with interest. That means doing the same sort of calculation that the real estate developer did in **Table 13.2**. She weighed the gains from the project against the cost of the loan, including the interest payments. Lower interest rates made the project more economically beneficial.

You can do the same calculation for your student loan. Direct federal loans from the Department of Education generally have lower interest rates and better repayment terms than private loans. You can calculate or ask someone else to calculate the total amount of interest you will have to pay over time.

On the plus side, all the studies show that workers with bachelor's or associate degrees earn much more than those with high school diplomas. For example, Hispanic workers who are 25–34 years old earn 50 percent more with a bachelor's degree, on average, compared to similar workers with only a high school diploma.

However, what's important to remember is that you have to actually get a degree or certificate in order to get the future economic benefit of education. Simply attending school without finishing your program does not raise your future earnings very much, but it may leave you with a sizable debt.

So, if you don't finish your program, you may end up with a loan that doesn't have a positive return. That would not be an economically sensible thing to do.

FINANCIAL INTERMEDIARIES (LO13-2)

LO13-2 Explain the role of a financial intermediary and discuss how banks work.

In the loan example we've been discussing so far, we did not ask one key question: Where does a lender get money to lend out? Or to put this in more specific terms, when a bank makes a $10 million loan to a real estate developer to build some new homes, where do those funds come from? After all, most of us don't have $10 million in our pockets.

Banks are financial intermediaries.

Nikreates/Alamy Stock Photo

For the most part, the funds a bank lends come from its depositors. Individuals put their hard-earned cash into savings and checking accounts and certificates of deposit (certificates of deposit, also called CDs, are similar to savings accounts except that you agree to keep your money in the bank for a fixed time). The bank then lends those deposited funds to other consumers and to businesses. The bank pays interest to its depositors and receives interest payments from its borrowers. The loans are mostly mortgages, loans to established businesses, and consumer credit such as auto loans.

How do banks make profits? They generally charge higher interest rates on their loans than they pay on their deposits. For example, suppose a bank pays 3 percent annual interest on a $1,000 deposit, or $30 for a year (3 percent of $1,000). It then lends out that $1,000 and charges the borrower 5 percent interest, receiving $50 for a year (5 percent of $1,000). As a result, the bank makes $20 in profit. In addition, banks often charge sizable fees for various services; for example, if you try to write a check when you don't have enough money in your checking account, most banks will hit you with a fee of $25 or more.

Banks as Intermediaries

A bank, therefore, is both a buyer and a seller in the market for money. It collects money from depositors and funnels the funds to the individuals and businesses that borrow from the bank (see **Figure 13.4**).

Figure 13.4 Banks as Intermediaries
Banks take deposits from savers and then lend the money to borrowers.

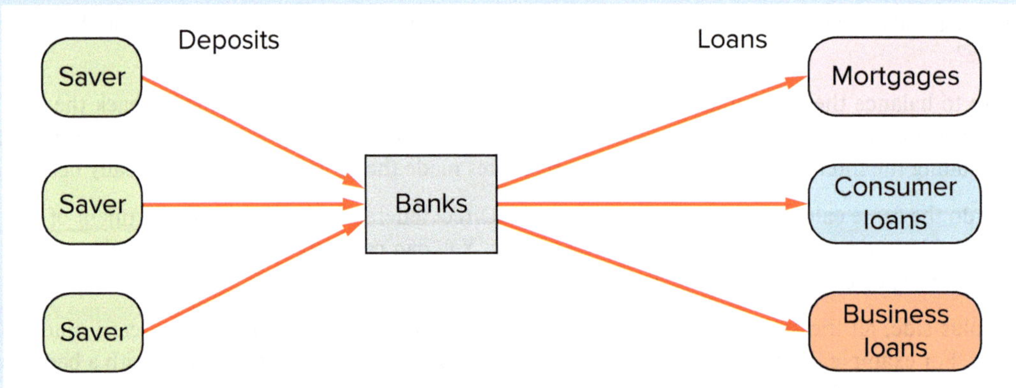

financial intermediary
Any institution, such as a bank, that collects money from suppliers of capital and funnels the funds to users of capital.

suppliers of capital
The investors who provide the funds. In the banking system, for example, the suppliers of capital are the depositors in the bank.

users of capital
The eventual recipients, such as borrowers, of funds from a bank or other financial intermediary.

A bank is one example of what economists call a **financial intermediary**. A financial intermediary is any institution that collects money from people or organizations, such as pension funds, with money to invest–what we will call the **suppliers of capital**. The financial intermediary then directs the funds to users of capital–people, businesses, or governments that are willing to pay for its use. In the case of the banks, the depositors are suppliers of capital and the businesses and individuals that borrow from the bank are **users of capital**.

In the following sections of this chapter, we will talk about other financial intermediaries in the economy. But note here that banks have a special protected status. Banks are tightly regulated by the federal and state governments, and they are required to keep a certain amount of cash reserves. What's more, the Federal Deposit Insurance Corporation (FDIC), a government agency created during the Great Depression, insures bank deposits up to a certain size (currently $250,000 per depositor). So even if your bank closed, the FDIC guarantees you would get your money back up to the insured limit. As a result, savings accounts and CDs have virtually no risk for the ordinary depositor.

Another Example: Venture Capital

venture capital firms
Financial intermediaries that provide funds to risky start-ups.

venture capital
The funds provided to risky start-ups by venture capital firms.

Let's look now at a very different kind of financial intermediary, **venture capital firms**. Whereas banks lend money to established companies, venture capital firms provide funds to risky start-ups in their early years when no one else will give them money. The investment in these new companies is called, naturally, **venture capital**.

Well-known companies that received venture capital in their start-up days include Intel, Apple, Google, Facebook, Cisco, Federal Express, Yahoo!, and Amazon. More recently, Twitter, Snapchat, Instagram, Dropbox, Uber, and Airbnb all received venture capital funding, as did OpenAI, the creator of ChatGBT. Such risky start-ups are the users of venture capital, and many would not exist if they had not received critical money at an early stage.

Venture capital firms are sometimes willing to fund ideas that look crazy at the time. Take Instagram, for example, the photo-sharing app now owned by Facebook. When Instagram was started in 2010, it had no users. But venture capitalists were still willing to invest money because it seemed like a good idea. Two years later, Facebook bought Instagram for $1 billion, making the founders–and early investors–rich.

Where does the money for venture capital come from? As shown in **Figure 13.5**, the suppliers of capital to the venture capital firms are pension funds, universities with big endowments, and other large institutions that can afford to take chances, as well as rich individual investors. They invest in venture capital firms such as Benchmark Capital, Sequoia Capital, and Kleiner Perkins. These venture capital firms are the financial intermediaries–they take the money from their suppliers and decide which start-ups to invest it in.

Figure 13.5 Venture Capital Firms as Intermediaries
Venture capital firms raise money from investors and invest it in small start-up companies.

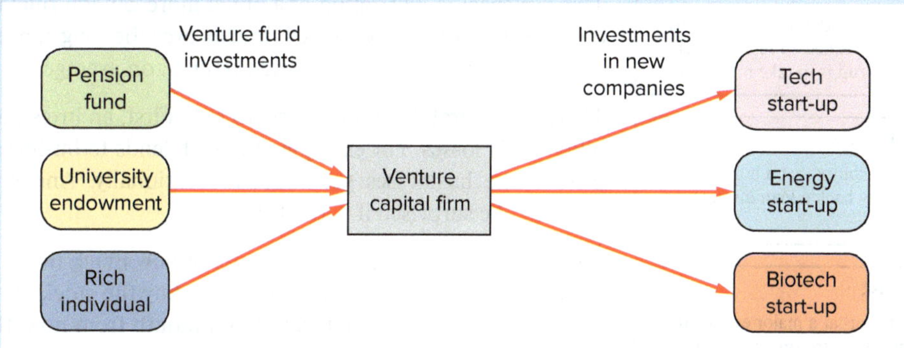

cryptocurrency
A digital currency, such as Bitcoin, where records of transactions and wealth are held in a decentralized database.

fintech
Companies that use information technology to provide new and cheaper forms of financial services

Like banks, venture capital firms offer a path by which funds can move from suppliers of capital to users of capital (like a pipe for money). However, the goal of venture capital firms is to find new companies that are going to be big winners. A rule of thumb is that only 1 out of 10 venture-funded start-ups will be a spectacular success. Only 3 out of 10 will even be profitable. The rest will fail or just barely continue to operate.

Sometimes venture-funded start-ups fail because they are a bad idea. A company called Juicero raised $120 million to make juicing machines that produced juice from packets, just like coffee machines produce coffee from packets. The machines, which were originally priced at $700, became an object of mockery when people learned that the juice packets could be squeezed by hand, without the expensive machine. Juicero closed down in September 2017 with a complete loss of money. But unlike banks, venture capital firms expect quite a few of their investments to fail. That's part of the cost of doing business.

HOW IT WORKS: CRYPTOCURRENCIES AND FINTECH

The financial system is full of innovation, as people try to figure out new and more efficient ways to raise money and direct it to the best uses. Two of the most important innovations in recent years are *cryptocurrencies* and *fintech*. A cryptocurrency, like Bitcoin, is a digital currency where records of transactions and wealth are maintained in a decentralized database. Originally cryptocurrencies were thought of as a possible private replacement for government-issued currency, but so far, they haven't turned out that way. Cryptocurrencies are so far subject to big swings in value which make them closer to a risky investment than to a stable store of value.

Fintech firms, short for "financial technology," are companies that use information technology to provide new and cheaper forms of financial services. One example of a fintech company is Square, which applies innovative infotech to help small merchants, like vendors at street fairs, take credit cards.

RISK AND RETURN (LO13-3)

LO13-3 Describe the risk–return principle and explain how it applies to the stock market.

risk
The possibility that something unexpected, either good or bad, will happen to an investment.

return
The gain on your investment in a year, measured as a percentage of original investment.

expected return
The average return that you can expect on an investment over the long run.

risk–return principle
The concept that the only way to get higher expected returns over the long run is to take more risks.

default risk
The possibility that a borrower won't pay back a loan on time, or at all.

event risk
The odds that a major event will affect the return on an investment.

inflation risk
The danger that inflation will suddenly accelerate.

stock
A piece of ownership in a company. Also called *equity*.

public companies
Businesses that have sold shares of stock (also called *equity*) to the general public.

The difference between banks and venture capital illustrates a key principle of financial markets: the link between risk and return. **Risk** is the possibility that something unexpected, either good or bad, will happen to your investment. **Return** is the gain on your investment in a year, measured as a percentage of the original investment. And **expected return** is the average return that you can expect over the long run.

For example, a savings account is a very low-risk investment, so you can sleep well without worrying about the safety of your funds. The return is the annual interest rate on the account (perhaps a 1 percent as of early 2023). If you left $1,000 in a savings account for a year, it would earn just 10 dollars in interest (1 percent = 0.01 = $10/$1,000). That's not even enough for a cup of coffee.

By contrast, venture capital is a much riskier investment, but it has a much higher expected return or average return over the long run. In any particular year, there's a chance that start-ups will fail, leading to a very low return that year. But the average return on venture capital is generally thought to be about 25 percent per year. That means an investment of $1,000 would return $250 per year, on average, because the big winners, such as Facebook (now called Meta), more than compensate for the losses.

This is a specific illustration of a much more general rule: the **risk–return principle**, which says that the only way to get higher expected returns over the long run is to take more risks. The flip side is that safe investments will get lower expected returns, on average.

There are several different aspects to risk. First, an investment can be risky if there's a substantial possibility of big losses. For example, if a bank lends to businesses in a flood-prone area, it will not be a surprise if the businesses get flooded occasionally. And someone who invests in start-up companies shouldn't be surprised if a lot of them fail.

We can also think of risk as a measure of how much the value of your investment bounces around from week to week or month to month. If you buy the stock of a big company like Microsoft, there's almost no chance it will completely fail. But a month from now, the value of your investment could be 10 percent higher or 10 percent lower.

Finally, here's a third way of looking at risk. An investment or loan is riskier if it is likely to lose value at the same time your other investments or loans do. That is, a bank that makes most of its mortgage loans in one city is probably exposed to higher-than-usual risk if the real estate market in that city crashes because so many loans might default at the same time.

Risk also has different sources. **Default risk** is the possibility that a borrower won't pay back a loan on time, or at all. **Event risk** measures the odds that a major event, such as a terrorist attack, a big earthquake, or a hurricane, will affect the return on an investment. **Inflation risk** is the danger that inflation will suddenly accelerate, so you are being paid back in dollars that are worth less, as we saw in **Chapter 8**.

Still, no matter what kind of risk we are talking about, the basic principle is the same: It's tough to make big gains over the long run without taking risks. In economics, as we have mentioned before, there is no such thing as a free lunch. We'll return to this principle later in this chapter when we discuss the causes of the financial crisis.

The Stock Market and the Risk–Return Principle

equity
Shares of stock.

dividend
A portion of a company's profits that it pays out to shareholders each quarter.

To see the risk–return principle in action, we will turn our attention to the stock market. First, we'll discuss the basics of the stock market, including how to calculate the total return on a stock. Then, we'll show how the stock market offers both higher risks and higher expected returns than putting your money into a savings account or another safe investment.

A share of **stock** in a company is a piece of ownership in that business. **Public companies** are businesses that have sold shares of stock (also called **equity**) to the general public. Each share represents a very small piece of the company. Facebook, for example, now has more than 2 billion shares.

What does an investor get from buying a share of stock? Buying one share of Amazon, say, makes you a part owner of Amazon–of a very small part, certainly, but still an owner. Shareholders elect corporate boards of directors and vote on major actions such as mergers and acquisitions. If enough shareholders vote together, they can influence what a company does. Recent shareholder proposals at some companies have included limitations on the pay of top executives and requests for environmentally sound policies.

Share ownership also entitles you to a **dividend**, which is a portion of the company's profits that it pays out to shareholders each quarter. Some companies, like Meta (Facebook), are profitable but don't pay their shareholders any dividends. Other companies may continue paying dividends even if they report a big loss in a quarter or a year.

Perhaps most important, owning a share of stock gives you the right to sell it to someone else for a higher price than you paid for it–and that's where stock markets and stockbrokers come in. A **stock market**, as the name implies, is a market where shares of stocks are bought and sold. The main U.S. stock markets are the New York Stock Exchange (NYSE) and the NASDAQ, but there are stock markets in most major countries (see "**How It Works: Initial Public Offerings**").

stock market

A market in which shares of stocks are bought and sold.

initial public offering (IPO)

The first time a company sells shares to the public.

investment banks

The financial intermediaries that handle the initial public offerings and secondary offerings of companies.

stockbrokers

The financial intermediaries that handle the buying and selling of shares between investors.

HOW IT WORKS: INITIAL PUBLIC OFFERINGS

What do companies get by selling shares of themselves? The short answer is that they get money for expansion or new equipment, or even for planned purchases of other companies. The first time a company sells shares to the public, it's called an **initial public offering *or* IPO**. When the ride-sharing company Lyft had its IPO in March 2019, it raised $2.3 billion from the sale of its shares.

Investors don't typically buy their shares directly from the company that issued them. Instead, they go through financial intermediaries such as **investment banks**, the stock market, and **stockbrokers**, which all make it possible for companies to sell their shares and for investors to buy and sell shares easily. Investment banks such as Goldman Sachs handle the initial public offerings of companies. Stockbrokers such as Merrill Lynch (now part of Bank of America), T.D. Ameritrade, and Charles Schwab handle the buying and selling of shares between investors.

Wall Street may go completely digital in the future.

Mario Tama/Getty Images

At any given moment, the **market price** of a stock is the price at which it most recently traded. If there are many potential buyers of a stock, they have to be willing to pay a higher price to get all the shares they want, and the market price rises. If there are many potential sellers of a stock, they have to be willing to accept a lower price to get rid of their shares, and the market price falls.

market price

The typical price at which a good or service sells in a market. Also, the current price at which a share of stock can be bought or sold.

Share prices also react to changes in the future prospects of companies. If you think solar power is going to be the next big thing in the energy industry, you'll want to invest in companies that make solar cells because they'll be doing a lot of business in the future. If you believe oil prices will keep going up, you might invest in oil companies because they'll continue to be profitable. Rising share prices are therefore a guide–though an indirect and hardly a perfect one–to areas of the economy that investors expect to grow.

CALCULATING THE TOTAL RETURN

It should be obvious that people buy stocks hoping to get back more than they put in. **Price appreciation** is the change that occurs in the price of a stock. The **total return** on a share of stock is the change in the stock price, plus the dividend, divided by the original price.

price appreciation

An increase in the price of a stock.

total return
The total return on a share of stock is the change in the stock price, plus the dividend, divided by the original price.

Table 13.4 shows how to calculate the total return on three widely held stocks: Ford, McDonald's, and Merck (a large pharmaceutical company). For example, on the last trading day of 2021, the price of a share of Ford Motor Company was $20.77. On the last trading day of 2022, a year later, the price had plunged to $11.63 per share, a loss of $9.14 per share. However, over the same period, Ford had also paid out 50 cents in dividends per share during the year. That means price appreciation plus dividends in 2022 equaled −$8.64 per share. As a result, the return on the stock in 2022 was −$8.64 divided by the share price at the beginning of the period: $20.77. That gives a return of −42 percent.

Table 13.4 Calculating Total Return: Three Examples

The total return on a share of stock over a year is the change in the stock price, plus the dividend, divided by the original price. Here, we calculate the total return in 2022 for three widely held stocks: Ford, McDonald's, and Merck.

Company	Stock Price on December 31, 2021	Stock Price on December 30, 2022	Price Appreciation per Share in 2022 (Column 3 − Column 2)	Dividend Payment per Share in 2022	Price Appreciation + Dividend in 2022 (Column 4 + Column 5)	Total Return in 2022 (Column 6/Column 2)
(1)	(2)	(3)	(4)	(5)	(6)	(7)
Ford	$ 20.77	$ 11.63	−$9.14	$0.50	−$8.64	−42%
McDonald 's	$268.07	$263.53	−$4.54	$5.66	$1.12	0.4%
Merck	$76.64	$110.95	$34.31	$2.80	$37.11	48%

Table 13.4 also illustrates how dividend payments can help balance out the fall in the price of a stock. A share of McDonald's stock fell in price by $4.54 in 2022. But each share earned a dividend of $5.66 per share, giving a total gain of $1.12 in 2022, or a percentage gain of 0.4 percent. That means if you had invested $1,000 in McDonald's stock at the end of 2021 and sold it at the end of 2022, you would have received roughly $1,004 (less stockbroker fees), a profit of $4–not much, but better than a loss. Finally, Merck is an example of a stock that was a big gainer in 2022.

STOCKS AND RISK

diversification
The process of splitting one's money across different investments to help reduce risk without reducing expected return.

The share price of any single company can swing widely from day to day or month to month. This unpredictability makes an investment in the stock market much riskier than, say, depositing the same money in a savings account. But common sense and economic research suggest that holding a larger number of stocks, especially in a wide range of industries, may help smooth out the swings in the value of your overall investment because it's unlikely your stocks will all rise or fall at the same time. In fact, **diversification**–splitting your money across different investments–is a central principle of financial economics. Diversification can help you reduce risk without reducing expected return. We might also call this the "don't put all your eggs in one basket" rule.

Economists have spent many years exploring which investment mix offers the best trade-off between risk and expected return. One approach is to buy a wide basket of stocks, such as the 500 large companies which make up the S&P 500 Stock Index (see **"How It Works: Tracking the Market"**).

HOW IT WORKS: TRACKING THE MARKET

On any day, some stocks are up while others are down. That's why we use a stock index to summarize the performance of the market. The two major stock indexes reported by the press and followed by financial professionals are the Dow Jones Industrial Average and the Standard & Poor's (S&P) 500 Index. The Dow, as it is called, is based on the average share price of 30 stocks including Microsoft, McDonald's, and Home Depot. The S&P 500 Index, as the name suggests, includes 500 of the largest and best-known U.S. companies. The sets of companies in the two stock indexes are regularly readjusted to account for mergers, acquisitions, and growth (remember, a company has to be big to be in the S&P 500).

For example, the company Keurig Dr Pepper, a provider of coffee and other beverage products, was added to the S&P 500 in June 2022, replacing Under Armour, a maker of athletic shoes and other sportswear which has the basketball star Stephen Curry as its top spokesperson. But despite Curry's prominence, Keurig Dr Pepper got the nod for the S&P 500 because it has more than twice the revenue as Under Armour.

But the stock market is still risky even if you diversify. In good years, investments in the stock market can return 20 percent or more, as measured by the S&P 500. But in bad times the stock market can plunge quickly. Between February 2008 and February 2009, the market dropped by roughly 45 percent.

This unpredictability makes an investment in the stock market much riskier than, say, depositing the same money in a savings account. But as the risk-return principle says, along with the risk comes a higher expected return, based on the long-run history. For example, if you look at the S&P 500 Stock Index in **Figure 13.6**, you see that it zigs and zags, but the general trend over time has been upward. From January 1961 to March 2023, the S&P 500 Index rose an average of roughly 7 percent per year. That's just price appreciation. If we include dividends, the total return on S&P 500 stocks has averaged around 10 percent per year. The inflation-adjusted total return is about 6 percent per year.

Figure 13.6 The S&P 500 Stock Index, 1961–2023
This chart shows the monthly values of the S&P 500 Stock Index from January 1961 to March 2023, without adjusting for dividends or inflation.

Source: S&P Global.

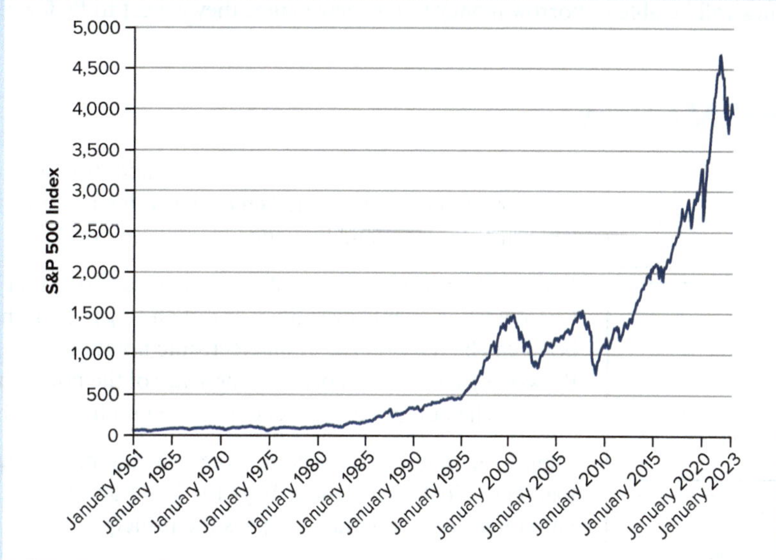

One final point: As the financial markets become more thoroughly international, diversification increasingly means putting some money into foreign stock markets as well. While the New York Stock Exchange and the NASDAQ are still the largest stock exchanges in the world, they have challengers. Other large stock exchanges include Euronext, a pan-European exchange; Shanghai; London; Tokyo; Hong Kong; and Mumbai.

THE DIVERSITY OF FINANCIAL INTERMEDIARIES (LO13-4)

LO13-4 Review the benefits of the diversity of financial intermediaries.

So far, we've talked about three very different financial intermediaries: banks, venture capital firms, and the stock market. But the full list of financial intermediaries is much longer. For example, the **mortgage market** raises money for home loans and then funnels it to home buyers. Another crucial financial intermediary is the bond market, which is the main way that big companies and governments raise money. We'll discuss this market in the next section.

mortgage market
The market for home loans.

Multiple types of financial intermediaries lead to more competition and make it easier for businesses and individuals to raise money.

The fact that there are so many different ways to raise money is one of the strengths of the U.S. economy. It leads to more choices and more competition. For example, if you wanted to start a new business, you could charge your credit cards up to the limit, as some entrepreneurs do. Or you could borrow against your home through a home equity loan. Or if you were starting a technology business, you might be able to go to a venture capital firm for funds.

Visualize a large concert hall. If only one door is open, it will take a long time to get everyone in. Opening more doors speeds the process. In effect, having multiple ways to raise money removes bottlenecks from the financial system by opening up routes for individuals and firms to get funds.

These gains in the financial markets help other sectors of the economy that need to raise money–and that includes nearly everyone. A corporation has more options for raising money to erect a new factory that is expected to earn profits in the future, or to put up a new office building that will be filled with rent-paying tenants. Producers will find it easier to raise money from private investors to finance multimillion-dollar movies they hope will be big hits. Start-up companies will be more likely to get the money they need to develop new products. Airlines will be able to borrow money to buy new planes they expect to fly for years to come.

The Bond Market

bond market
One of the main ways corporations and governments borrow.

bond
A loan that entitles the lender to get regular interest payments over time, and then to get back the principal at the end of the loan period. Also called a *fixed-income security*.

bondholder
The purchaser of a bond.

Let's apply the principles of risk, return, and diversification to one of the main ways that corporations and government borrow: the **bond market**. It's essential to know at least a bit about the bond market if you want to understand how today's economy works.

Let's start with some terminology. A **bond** is a loan that entitles the lender–the **bondholder**–to get regular interest payments over time, and then to get back the principal at the end of the loan period. (The bond can be represented by an electronic notation or an actual piece of paper; in either case, the idea is the same.) We call the borrower the *seller* of the bond; thus selling bonds is the same thing as borrowing money. The bondholder, or lender, is the purchaser of the bond.

Figure 13.7 shows how a bond works. At the beginning, the borrower sells the bond and receives the loan (principal). The lender buys the bond and pays out the principal. Then, over time, the borrower pays interest and eventually repays the principal.

Figure 13.7 How a Bond Works
In this diagram, the arrows represent the direction in which money moves. In the beginning the borrower sells the bond and receives money in return. The borrower has to pay interest and then pay back the principal.

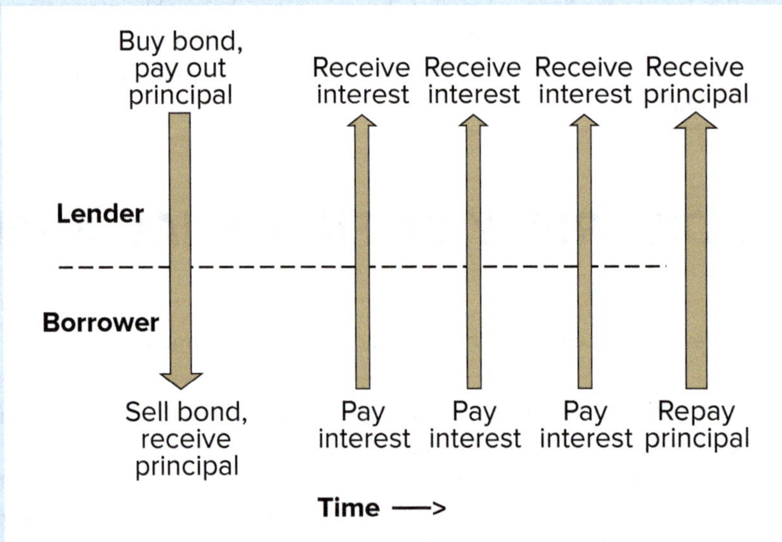

fixed-income securities
Bonds that entitle the lender to receive regular interest payments over time.

Most bond sellers promise to pay a fixed amount of interest per quarter or per year for the length of the loan. For that reason, bonds are also known as **fixed-income securities**. Bond terms usually range from 1 to 30 years, though some companies like Walt Disney and Coca-Cola have issued 100-year bonds.

The suppliers of capital in the bond market are generally big institutions such as pension funds, life insurance companies, and mutual funds. In addition, U.S. bonds are often bought by foreign investors. The users of capital in the bond market are the borrowers, the bond sellers.

All other things being equal, borrowing by selling bonds is typically cheaper than taking a loan from a bank. One reason has to do with diversification. A bank that gives a big loan to a company has to consider the possibility, however minuscule, of a default. In the bond market, however, that big loan can be broken down into a lot of smaller bonds that are sold to many different investors. And each of those investors can hold bonds from different corporations. As a result, they are diversified, so any single default has only a small impact. That makes investors more willing to buy bonds of even riskier companies, so the supply curve is pushed to the right–keeping the interest rate lower than it would have been. Thus, companies have been steadily relying more on the bond market than on borrowing from banks.

Government Borrowing

In **Chapter 11**, we talked about government borrowing and debt without discussing the precise way in which the federal government borrows. In fact, the federal government–or more specifically the Treasury Department–issues many securities each year to fund the budget deficit. It sells **Treasury bonds** with terms of 10 years and 30 years. The Treasury also issues securities with terms as short as one month; these are known as **Treasury bills**. When long-term interest rates are quoted in the press, they are usually the interest rates on 10-year Treasury bonds. The U.S. federal government is the biggest borrower in the world.

Treasury bonds
Securities the federal government issues each year to fund the budget deficit with terms as long as 10 years and 30 years.

Treasury bills
Securities the federal government issues with terms as short as one month.

However, the federal government is also probably the safest borrower in the world. Its power to tax allows it to draw on the wealth of the entire U.S. economy to pay back any bonds it sells. As a result, the interest rates on Treasury bonds are lower than the rates corporations or individuals pay to borrow money for a comparable term. This is another application of the risk-return principle.

Bonds are also issued by state and local governments. Typically, they borrow to fund long-term projects such as the construction and renovation of highways, airports, parking lots, sports stadiums, and schools.

In recent years, there have been relatively few instances in which local governments defaulted on bonds. Detroit went bankrupt in 2013, but since then no other major American city has filed for bankruptcy. Even during the pandemic. This track record of safety enabled state and local governments to pay relatively low interest rates, though not as low as the federal government.

THE CAUSES OF THE FINANCIAL CRISIS (LO13-5)

LO13-5 Summarize the key causes of the financial crisis that started in 2007.

The financial crisis that started in 2007 is 15 years or so in the past, but it still carries important lessons for us today. Now that we have developed an understanding of how financial markets work, we can ask some key questions: What caused the **financial crisis**? How did the housing market, the stock market, and indeed the whole economy crash so suddenly? And can anything be done to avoid such crises in the future?

financial crisis
An economic disruption that starts in the financial sector.

The first thing to realize is that financial markets are historically prone to **bubbles**. A bubble occurs when prices in a financial market rise for an extended period, and investors convince themselves that the increases aren't going to stop. At that point the bubble becomes self-feeding–believing that prices will go up, investors put more money into the market, which drives the prices well above a level that is sustainable over the long run.

bubble
A situation where the price of an asset, such as housing, rises far above sustainable levels.

For example, in the late 1990s, there was a bubble in technology stocks. Many investors convinced themselves that the Internet was an unstoppable force that was going to keep driving up the stock price of both existing technology firms and start-ups. For example, the stock price of Corning–one of the world's biggest makers of fiber-optic cable, used for high-capacity data transmission–went from $16 per share at the beginning of 1999, up to more than $100 per share in 2000, and then down to less than $2 a share in 2002. Fortunes can be made–and lost–with price movements like this.

The financial crisis that started in 2007 was the result, in large part, of a bubble as well. This time, the bubble occurred in the whole U.S. housing market, which represents a large part of the wealth of the country. From 1997 to 2006, the increase in housing prices far outstripped the rate of inflation. That increase, in turn, led to home buyers paying ridiculous prices for homes because they thought they would make a profit when they sold, home builders constructing more and more expensive new homes because they thought they would make a profit when they sold, and banks making questionable mortgages because even poor people could pay back their loans if they sold their homes in a rising market.

Weaknesses in financial regulation also helped contribute to the financial crisis. Regulatory agencies such as the Federal Reserve did not pay close enough attention to the rapidly evolving markets in complicated financial instruments known as derivatives. Using these derivatives, many large financial institutions were able to place big bets on the housing market, which would pay off as long as housing prices didn't fall. The financial institutions thought they had history on their side, because housing prices hadn't fallen nationwide since the Great Depression.

In the end, of course, the housing bubble burst, home prices went down, and everyone was left holding the bag. Some financial institutions, like Lehman, went bankrupt, while others came close. And the U.S. government had to borrow trillions of dollars to stimulate demand and keep the economy afloat.

Dodd-Frank
The Dodd-Frank Wall Street Reform and Consumer Protection Act was enacted in 2010 to improve regulation of the financial system and reduce the chance of another financial crisis.

In response, policymakers strengthened the regulation of the financial system. In particular, Congress passed the **Dodd-Frank** Wall Street Reform and Consumer Protection Act in 2010, which President Obama signed into law. Dodd-Frank, as it is commonly called, was 848 pages long and touched every aspect of finance and insurance, including mortgages, student loans, and credit cards. In particular, the new law made special provisions for dealing with very large banks in times of crisis.

Overall, Dodd-Frank probably reduces the odds of another financial crisis. Nevertheless, there are no guarantees. Financial bubbles have happened before, and they will happen again. Indeed, one fear is that the large amounts of monetary and fiscal stimulus that was used to fight the pandemic in the United States and globally may have created a bubble of its own.

CONCLUSION

The financial markets are extremely important to the economy. Without them, businesses would not be able to raise money for future-oriented activities, such as expansion. Governments would not be able to borrow to fund budget deficits and investment in infrastructure. Individuals would not be able to afford to buy as many big-ticket items such as homes and cars.

The next chapter will cover an equally critical feature of today's world: globalization. While financial markets are about transactions involving money, globalization is about movements of goods, services, and money across national borders. As we will see, such international trade brings up a whole new set of issues.

13 SUMMARY

1. The market for loans is essential for financing household consumption and business investment. The market for loans typically follows the laws of demand and supply. Higher interest rates reduce the quantity of borrowing, all other things being equal. Higher interest rates also increase the quantity of lending. ***(LO13-1)***
2. Banks are examples of financial intermediaries. That means they collect money from suppliers of capital and funnel it to users of capital. Venture capital firms are other examples of financial intermediaries. They collect money from investors and funnel it to start-up companies. ***(LO13-2)***
3. The risk-return principle says that in a well-functioning financial market the only way to get higher expected returns over the long run is to take more risks. The flip side is that safer investments will get lower expected returns, on average. For example, an investment in the stock market, on average, has higher risks and higher expected returns than putting your money into a savings account. Diversification, which means splitting your money across different investments, can help you reduce risk without reducing expected return. ***(LO13-3)***
4. The U.S. economy has many different kinds of financial intermediaries. That's an advantage because it leads to more choice, more competition, and a lower cost of funds. One important financial intermediary is the bond market, which lets corporations and governments raise money by issuing bonds instead of borrowing from banks. ***(LO13-4)***
5. The financial crisis that started in 2007 was the result, in large part, of a bubble in the housing market. In addition, weaknesses in financial regulation enabled financial institutions to take too many risks. Since then, improved regulation has lessened but not eliminated the possibility of another financial crisis. ***(LO13-5)***

KEY TERMS AND CONCEPTS

loan
principal
term
future-oriented activities
default
time value of money
financial intermediary
suppliers of capital
users of capital
venture capital firms
venture capital
cryptocurrency
fintech
risk
return
expected return
risk-return principle
default risk
event risk
inflation risk
stock
public companies
equity
dividend
stock market
market price
initial public offering (IPO)
investment banks
stockbrokers
price appreciation
total return
diversification
mortgage market
bond market
bond
bondholder
fixed-income securities
Treasury bonds
Treasury bills
financial crisis
bubbles
Dodd-Frank

connect PROBLEMS

1. Suppose a company borrows $20 million for a year at an interest rate of 6 percent annually, with all interest and principal to be paid at the end of the year.
(LO13-1)
   a) How much money will the company give the lender at the end of the year?
   b) How much is the principal, and how much is the interest payment?
2. In each of the following scenarios, identify the borrower and the lender.
(LO13-1)
   a) A corporation sells $1,000,000 in bonds to investors.
   b) A family takes out a mortgage from a bank for $250,000.
   c) A foreign investor buys $10 million in Treasury bonds.
   d) You buy a new coat with your credit card issued by your local bank.
3. Your brother-in-law wants to borrow $100,000 to start a new business selling T-shirts online. Will each of the following events make you more or less likely to lend him the money? Give the appropriate reason for each answer (time value of money or risk of default). *(LO13-1)*
   a) The interest rate on savings accounts goes up.
   b) Your teenager wins a full scholarship to college.
   c) You discover that your brother-in-law has started a business before and failed.
   d) Economists predict a recession for next year.
   e) Your neighbor comes to you with a hot stock tip.
4. For each of the following, identify the main suppliers of capital, the main users of capital, and the financial intermediary. *(LO13-2)*
   a) A bank credit card.
   b) An investment in a new mobile game company.
   c) A mortgage loan from a local bank.

5. Are the following statements true or false? *(LO13-2)*

 a) Venture capital goes to established companies such as General Motors and Procter & Gamble.
 b) Venture capital is a high-risk investment.
 c) The suppliers of capital in the venture capital market are ordinary individuals.
 d) Venture capital firms expect that most of the companies they invest in will be big successes.
 e) The venture capital market helps accelerate the adoption of new technology.

6. Two restaurants are on the same block. One has been open 10 years and is a thriving business. The other one has been open for only a year. They both want to expand. When the two owners go to the local bank looking for a loan, which one is likely to get a lower interest rate? Explain in terms of the risk-return principle. *(LO13-3)*

7. Following are the actual stock prices for the hotel chain Marriott at the end of four different months, starting before the pandemic, along with dividend payments. *(LO13-3)*

Month	Price of a Share of Marriott Stock (at end of month)
December 2019	$151.43
December 2020	$131.92
December 2021	$165.24
December 2022	$148.89
	Dividends Paid on a Share of Marriott Stock
Paid in 2020	$0.48
Paid in 2021	$0 (dividend suspended)
Paid in 2022	$1.00

 a) What was the price appreciation in Marriott stock from December 2019, before the pandemic, to December 2020?
 b) What was the price appreciation from December 2020 to December 2021, in dollars?
 c) Marriott stopped paying dividends once the pandemic started, and did not resume until spring of 2022. What is the most likely reason for this suspension?
 d) What was the total return from December 2021 to December 2022, in dollars?

8. If you use a credit card, have you looked carefully at how much the credit card company can charge you for your unpaid balances? Probably not—but you might be surprised to find that the maximum interest rate on a typical card can go up to 25 percent or higher. True, virtually all states have usury (excess interest) laws that appear to limit interest rates. For example, in Michigan the usury limit is 7 percent. However, these laws are riddled with loopholes. They do not apply to national banks, including the ones that issue most credit cards. Nor do they apply to car financing companies or to late fees. In fact, the usury laws generally apply only to loans made between individuals or nonfinancial businesses, which of course are relatively rare. *(LO13-3)*

 a) What would happen if state governments tightened their usury laws so that nobody could charge more than 5 percent on any kind of debt? Would that restriction increase or decrease the quantity of loans demanded? Explain.
 b) Would tighter usury laws increase or decrease the quantity of loans supplied? Explain.
 c) Would tighter usury laws make it harder or easier to get a credit card? Explain.

9. A large company needs money to construct a new headquarters building. Which of these funding sources is the least likely source of financing for the construction? *(LO13-4)*

 a) Venture capital.
 b) The bond market.
 c) The mortgage market.
 d) The stock market.

10. When a company borrows money in the bond market, that means it ______ *(LO13-4)*

    a) buys bonds.
    b) sells bonds.
    c) collects interest.
    d) sells stock.

11. If financial regulation had been stricter in the years leading up to the financial crisis, in all likelihood mortgage loans would have been harder to get. That would have meant that ______ *(LO13-5)*

    a) housing prices would have gone even higher.
    b) the housing bubble would have been less pronounced.
    c) the financial crisis would have been more severe.

CH 14

INTERNATIONAL TRADE

John W Banagan/Getty Images

LEARNING OBJECTIVES

After reading this chapter, you should be able to:

LO14-1 Explain why global trade has increased so much in recent years.
LO14-2 Summarize the main gains to trade.
LO14-3 Compare and contrast absolute advantage and comparative advantage.
LO14-4 Discuss the winners and losers from trade and analyze the arguments for protectionism.
LO14-5 Describe what it means for a currency to appreciate or depreciate.
LO14-6 List explanations for why the United States consistently runs a trade deficit.

Foreign trade has been an increasingly controversial political topic in recent years. Virtually every reputable economist would agree that most countries have received big gains from trade. These include lower product prices, faster growth, better use of resources, and generally higher living standards.

Indeed, over the past 25 years, foreign trade has soared, jamming the sea lanes with enormous cargo ships and filling ports around the world. The freight is coming by plane as well, such as special cargo Boeing 747s with giant front nose doors that flip open for big cargo. And undersea cables are sizzling with the flow of bits and bytes as European car companies hire American software developers, while U.S. companies rely on customer service agents in countries such as India. Moreover, big U.S.-based tech companies like Google and Facebook have millions of users around the world.

This is **globalization**, 21st-century style—the increasing exchange of goods, services, ideas, and people among countries. More and more, local and national markets are going global as communication has become cheaper and easier and many trade barriers have been lowered.

globalization
The increasing exchange of goods, services, ideas, and people among countries.

Developing countries have embraced trade as the road to prosperity after seeing how exports helped China become a manufacturing powerhouse—and how India used service exports to jump-start its economy.

On the other hand, trade and globalization can also be very disruptive. Workers and companies face increased competition and uncertainty, along with a frightening flow of jobs to overseas labor markets, with nothing immediately apparent to replace them.

FABRICE COFFRINI/Staff/Getty Images

Moreover, there are downsides to being dependent on overseas sources for crucial supplies in the event of emergencies like pandemic or war. In the early days of the pandemic, it was difficult to get hospital-grade N95 masks because they were mostly manufactured overseas. In 2021 and 2022, shortages of semiconductor chips made in China and other Asian countries meant that crucial parts were missing from new automobiles. And national security experts have grown increasingly worried about the U.S. dependence on China-made parts for U.S. weapons and telecommunications systems.

As a result, distrust of international trade has grown in recent years. Shortly after taking office in January 2017, President Donald Trump pulled the United States out of negotiations for a new trade treaty to cover Pacific Rim countries such as Japan and Vietnam. He later imposed new tariffs on some categories of imported goods from China and other countries. President Joseph Biden implemented controls on the export of certain advanced semiconductor technologies to China.

In this chapter, we will examine some key issues and concepts connected with globalization, including the nature of international trade, the benefits from trade, the logic behind comparative advantage, and the winners and losers in globalization. We'll finish with a discussion of exchange rates and the trade deficit.

THE NATURE OF INTERNATIONAL TRADE (LO14-1)

LO14-1 Explain why global trade has increased so much in recent years.

The 40-year boom in international trade may be unprecedented in recent history. With almost no interruptions, the volume of global trade, adjusted for inflation, has grown sevenfold since 1980, as **Figure 14.1** shows. That's equivalent to an average annual growth rate of 5 percent for more than 40 years.

Figure 14.1 Growth of Global Trade
The figure indicates how much the volume of global trade, adjusted for inflation, has grown since 1980. The global financial crisis of 2008 and 2009 and the pandemic were only temporary pauses.
Source: International Monetary Fund as of October 2022.

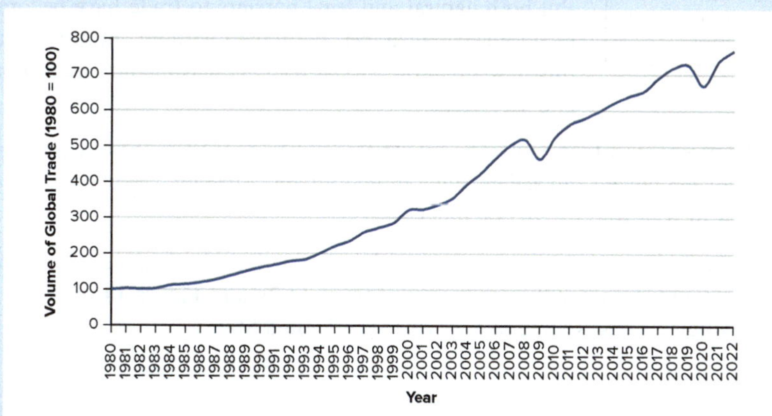

trade in goods
Exchanges that occur when sellers physically ship items to another country.

trade in services
Exchanges that occur when a person or a company in one country provides a service to a resident of a different country.

Both **trade in goods** and **trade in services** have been soaring. Trade in goods happens when items are physically shipped from one country to another. These include commodities such as oil and copper; manufactured products such as clothing, furniture, and automobiles; and high-tech products such as computers and airplanes. When a product crosses the border, it becomes an *export* of the originating country and an *import* of the destination country.

Trade in services is becoming increasingly important to many countries. You might be wondering how we can trade a service. Service trade happens when a person or a company in one country provides a service to a resident of a different country. Let's start with service exports. When a foreign student comes to study at a college in the United States, the tuition payments count as payments for a U.S. service export (because the student, although physically in the United States, is still a resident of a different country). In other words, the United States is exporting education to the foreign country. Here's another example: When a television network in another country broadcasts a U.S. television series–say, *Game of Thrones,* which is one of the most popular TV shows ever–it usually pays a fee to the U.S. owner of the show. That fee is reported as payment for service-sector exports. The service category of exports of U.S. "movies and television programming" was worth about $13.5 billion in 2021, compared to $7 billion in imports in the same category.

What about service imports? One example of service imports is spending by U.S. residents on foreign travel: If a U.S. consumer travels to Paris, her hotel and meals there count as payment for a service import to the United States. Another example: When you call the help desk of a computer company and are connected to a customer service representative in India, that's a service export for India and a service import for the United States.

Health care services, too, can be exported or imported. If someone who lives in a foreign country travels to a top U.S. hospital for special treatment, that is an export of health care services from the United States. Alternatively, health care services are imported when more and more patients without medical insurance are trying to cut costs by having expensive procedures performed in other countries. A knee replacement operation, for example, might cost $10,000 to $13,000 in Singapore or even less in India or Mexico, compared to roughly $50,000 in the United States. Such medical tourism could be the wave of the future.

Finally, cross-border flows of data have been soaring. When you connect to a website, you often have no idea whether the server is based in your city, in another state, or in another country. Videos, games, news, and financial data all easily cross international borders at the push of a button. For example, typing https://www.ecb.europa.eu into your browser will bring you to the website for the European Central Bank, located in Frankfurt, Germany. You can download European financial and economic data, if you want, and it will travel across multiple national borders without charge to get to you.

Falling Natural Barriers to Trade

natural barriers to trade
Obstacles to trade that include distance and differences in cultures.

legal barriers to trade
Tariffs, quotas, and other government actions that limit trade or make it more expensive.

Why has trade risen so much in recent years? To answer, we first have to understand why trade *between* countries is different from trade *within* countries. Historically, businesses that wanted to sell to buyers in another country faced both **natural barriers to trade** and **legal barriers to trade**. The natural barriers include such obstacles as distance, differences in culture and values, and the difficulty of delivering services remotely. The legal barriers include tariffs, quotas, and other government actions that limit trade or make it more expensive.

But both natural and legal barriers to trade have become less important in recent years. That's due to technological advances, combined with a commitment among major countries to foster freer trade. In this new situation, global trade is feasible among a broader range of countries, involving more goods and services.

Let's start with the most important natural barrier to trade: distance. Distance obviously raises the cost of shipping. Distance also makes communication between buyers and sellers much more difficult. After all, if you have a problem with your purchase, would you rather be dealing with a seller in your town or 10,000 miles away?

As a result, countries have tended in the past to trade most with their close neighbors, which for the United States meant Canada and Mexico. These two countries are still important, as **Figure 14.2a** and **Figure 14.2b** show. However, in 2022, China, on the other side of the globe, was the single biggest source of imports to the United States.

Figure 14.2a Top 10 Purchasers of U.S. Goods Exports, 2022
These countries were the top purchasers of exported goods from the United States in 2022.

Source: U.S. Census Bureau, www.census.gov.

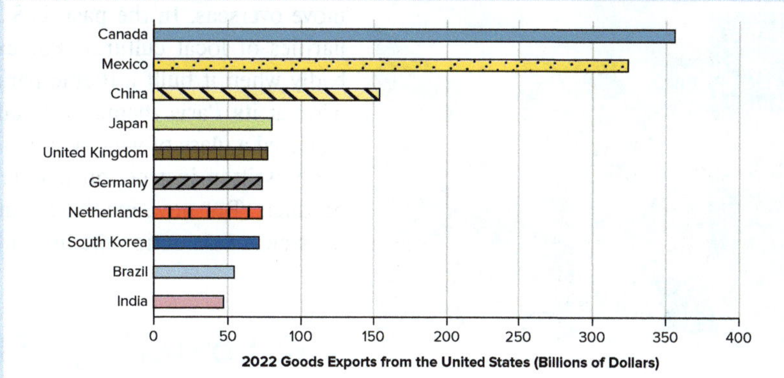

Figure 14.2b Top 10 Sellers of Imported Goods to the United States, 2022
These countries were the biggest shippers of goods to the United States in 2022 (these figures include commodities such as crude oil).

Source: U.S. Census Bureau, www.census.gov.

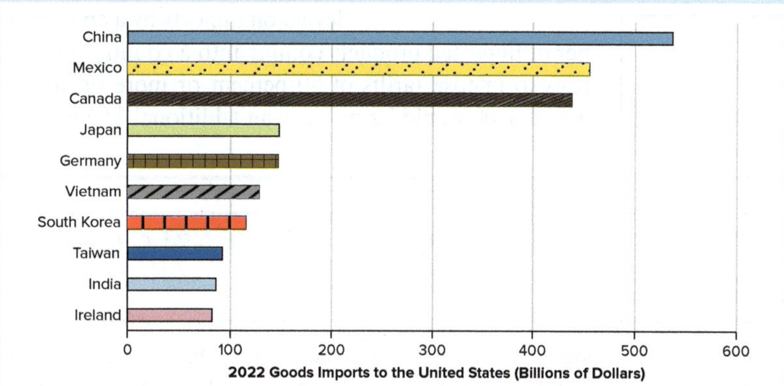

There are several reasons distance has become less important. One key factor is that the cost and time of shipping have become less onerous. The use of shipping containers–those 20-foot or 40-foot metal boxes that dominate ports–has dramatically reduced the amount of labor needed for ocean freight transportation (not to mention cutting the amount and cost of pilferage). The containers are packed at factories, trucked to ports, loaded onto ships, unloaded at their destinations, and trucked to stores or warehouses–all without needing to be unpacked again. Exporters and importers are also making much more active use of air freight to move high-value items such as semiconductors and perishable items such as seafood.

At the same time, the Internet and better technology have made communication over long distances much easier. When a factory in China or Germany is directly linked to the computer system of the U.S. retailer of its products, information about customer tastes and preferences can flow in real time, and coordination of production becomes almost as easy as if the factory were down the block.

The same ease of communication means that increasingly we live in a single global culture. That makes it easier to overcome problems with selling to customers who have a different language and different preferences. Following the lead of MTV, many television networks, such as CNN and BBC, now offer international or foreign language versions (see "**Economic Milestone: How TV Went Global**"). Large tech companies such as Google, Meta, Apple, and Amazon have a global presence. And because more and more people travel internationally, foreign countries are no longer as foreign.

ECONOMIC MILESTONE

1987: How TV Went Global

The music video channel MTV was the first TV network to make the big jump across borders, starting with its first broadcast on a European channel in 1987. The company's channels now include MTV China, MTV Sweden, and MTV Vietnam, which have helped create a shared global youth culture. Thus, besides being a service export itself, MTV also was one factor in lowering the cultural barriers to trade.

We should note that not all television programming travels across borders. Sporting events, especially, are frequently restricted by country. Europeans often complain that they cannot easily find telecasts of their home soccer teams if they are in a different country.

The use of shipping containers has facilitated long-distance trade.

Prasit photo/Getty Images

As a result, cultural barriers are less of a problem for companies that want to move overseas. In the past, U.S. companies often didn't understand the peculiarities of local cultures. For example, the Walt Disney Company stumbled badly when it built a theme park in France in the early 1990s. It didn't serve wine at its Paris theme park–an unpleasant surprise to French tourists who expected a glass of wine with lunch. Similarly, for years people made fun of the badly written instruction manuals that came with many imported electronics products. But now, machine translation programs make a much easier to produce clear instruction manuals in many languages.

The Lowering of Legal Barriers

Another important reason for the increase in trade is the reduction of legal barriers. Historically, countries have put tariffs and quotas on imported goods to raise money and protect their own industries. **Tariffs** are extra charges or taxes levied on imports by a country, whereas **quotas** are numerical limits on the number of imported products coming into a country. For example, at one time, it was not unusual for countries to impose tariffs of 50 percent or more on imports, meaning that a company importing a shirt worth $100 would have to pay an additional $50 to the U.S. government.

tariffs
Extra charges or taxes levied on imports by a country.

SPOTLIGHT: HOW A SPANISH–GERMAN COMPANY CREATES AMERICAN JOBS

To see another aspect of globalization, go to the little town of Fort Madison, Iowa, next to the Mississippi River. At a time when manufacturing jobs were disappearing all over America, Fort Madison saw the opening of a new factory in 2007. The factory makes the blades for "wind turbines"—the official name for the giant windmills that are increasingly generating electricity all around the country.

The surprise: The plant is owned and operated not by a U.S. company but by a large Spanish-German firm—Siemens Gamesa. The blades are an astounding 148 to 160 feet long, depending on the model, and drive wind turbines in California, Washington, Iowa, North Dakota, and Texas. When in place, the turbines themselves are higher than a 20-story building.

The plant closed down temporarily in 2022 because of a lack of orders and then restarted again in early 2023.

Sources: http://www.siemens.com/press/en/pressrelease/?press=/en/pressrelease/2016/windpower-renewables/pr2016010122wpen.htm. https://www.iowapublicradio.org/ipr-news/2022-12-07/siemens-gamesa-plant-reopening-in-fort-madison

quotas
Government-imposed disincentives to trade that include numerical limits on the number of imported products coming into a country.

Since the end of World War II, most countries–led by the United States–have made a concerted global effort to reduce tariffs, quotas, and other legal trade barriers. The first step came in 1947, when 23 countries signed the General Agreement on Tariffs and Trade (GATT). Successive rounds of negotiations reduced tariffs from an average of 50 percent to less than 5 percent among developed countries. In the following years, more countries joined GATT as members.

In 1995, the members of GATT converted it into the World Trade Organization (WTO), with 150 members and a better procedure for resolving disputes. China joined the WTO in 2001–a big step. The WTO's rules governing world trade include about 550 pages of agreements, plus another 30,000 pages (!) that spell out in detail what each country has agreed to do to reduce tariffs and make trade cheaper and easier.

Why did the reduction of tariffs increase trade? The effect of a tariff is similar to the effect of a tax. The difference between what the consumer pays and what the importer receives is the tariff–so a 50 percent tariff, for example, adds 50 percent to the price of the import, and the consumer pays a higher price than the importer receives.

Another version of a tariff is a fixed dollar amount for each item imported. For example, a country could impose a $500 tariff on each imported car. That would add $500 to the price of the car, over and above the amount received by the importer.

Take a look at **Figure 14.3**. In the presence of such a fixed tariff, a consumer pays more than he or she would otherwise, which reduces the quantity demanded (point *A* in the figure). Meanwhile, the importer receives less than it would have received without the tariff (point *B*).

Figure 14.3 Eliminating a Tariff Increases the Quantity of Imports
A tariff on imports creates a gap between what consumers pay (point *A*) and what the importer–the business actually importing the good–receives (point *B*). If the tariff is repealed, the market shifts to the equilibrium level (point *C*). The quantity of imports increases, the price paid by consumers decreases, and the price received by importers increases.

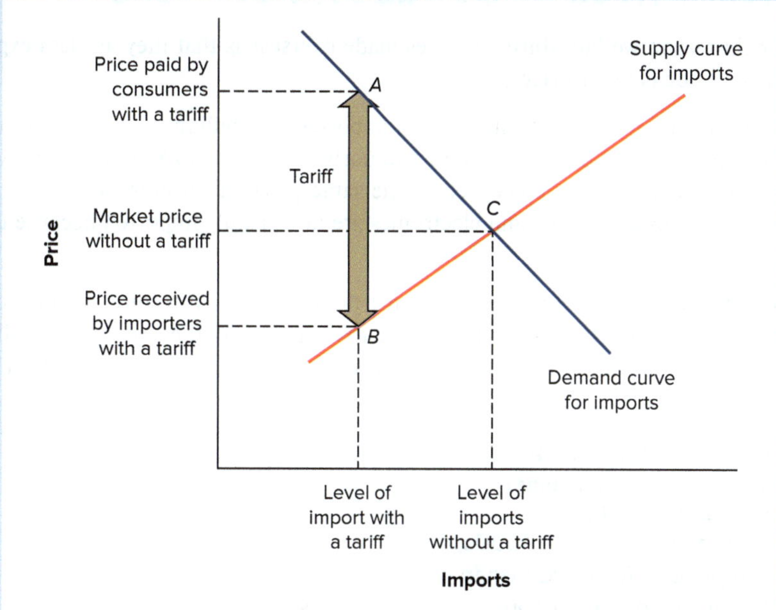

When the tariff is removed, the price the consumer pays goes down. The revenue the importer gets to keep increases, and the quantity of imports supplied goes up (point *C*).

Trade negotiators have also worked hard to get rid of quotas, which are numerical limits on imports. In effect, quotas artificially restrict the quantity supplied to below the equilibrium level, which drives up the price. For example, in 1981, Japanese car makers accepted a "voluntary restraint agreement" limiting the number of cars they could ship to the United States. Even though it was "voluntary," this agreement was the equivalent of a quota because Japanese car makers abided by the limits. But because consumers were clamoring to buy Japanese-made cars, a waiting list grew for the hottest models. With Japanese cars in short supply in the United States, dealers could sell them for more–up to $1,000 more, by one estimate.

As tariffs and quotas have been reduced or eliminated, trade has become much easier. True, countries can still put up plenty of legal or practical trade barriers if they want. For example, China blocks access to Facebook.

Moreover, in recent years the trend toward easier trade has slowed. Under President Donald Trump, the United States pulled out of negotiating two large trade treaties: one with Pacific Rim countries such as Japan, Vietnam, and Mexico, and the other with the European Union. In addition, in 2018 President Trump raised tariffs on steel and aluminum imports from most countries, as well as some categories of goods imported from China. And under President Biden several large pieces of pandemic stimulus legislation contained provisions designed to encourage spending on American-made goods and services.

Nevertheless, imports were higher in 2022 than they were in 2019, after adjusting for inflation. The forces of trade are difficult to stop.

THE GAINS FROM TRADE (LO14-2)

LO14-2 Summarize the main gains to trade.

Now that we have seen the growing importance of trade, the next question is a simple one: Why do countries trade? Why go to all the trouble of hauling washing machines, cars, and all sorts of other goods halfway around the world?

gains from trade
The benefits from participating in trade relationships with other countries.

Obviously, a small country cannot produce everything it needs, so it must trade with others. But why did a large country like the United States–which can produce almost everything it needs within its own borders–import $4 trillion worth of goods and services in 2022? And why did countries from Austria to Zambia import $3 trillion worth of goods and services from the United States in the same year?

The answer is that there must be big enough **gains from trade** to justify the expenses and challenges of foreign trade. Let's look at what some of these gains from trade might be.

Lower Prices of Goods and Services

The main reason we buy shirts or shoes made overseas is that they are less expensive than comparable domestic products. Thus, a key gain from trade is lower prices.

For example, in 2002, the United States imported $18 billion worth of furniture and related products from countries such as China, Canada, and Italy. As of 2022, furniture imports had soared to $58 billion per year, with much of this increase coming from China. The reason? Chinese factories could deliver the same piece of furniture at a lower price than a U.S. furniture factory. Similarly, consumer items such as toys, clothing, and electronics are now mainly imported because they can be made much more cheaply outside the United States.

Look at **Figure 14.4**. It shows the consumer price index for furniture, compared to the consumer price index for all goods and services. Until the late 1990s, the price of furniture rose at roughly the same rate as all consumer prices. But starting around 1997, something changed: The price of furniture began to fall while overall consumer prices kept heading up.

Figure 14.4 Furniture Prices versus Overall Consumer Prices, 1990—2022
Starting with the late 1990s, the price of furniture began to fall, while overall consumer prices kept rising. Even with the inflationary surge during the pandemic, the price of furniture in 2022 is only slightly higher than it was in 1990.

Source: Bureau of Labor Statistics, www.bls.gov.

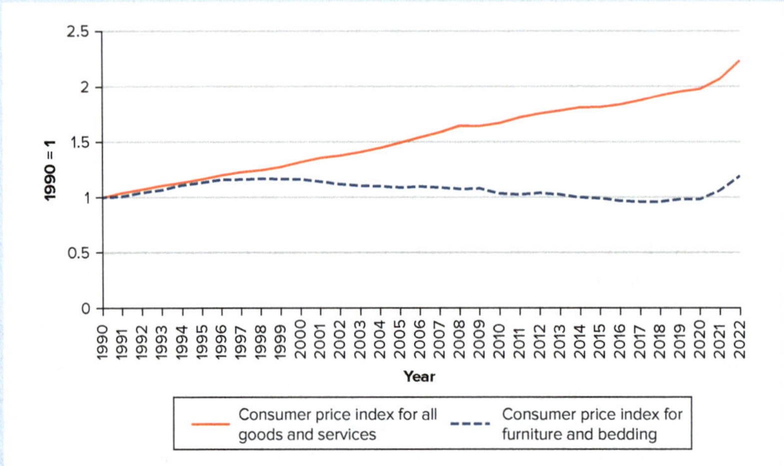

Today, more than two-thirds of U.S. fresh flower purchases are imported.

MediaWorldImages/Alamy Stock Photo

What changed? Imports of furniture into the United States started skyrocketing. In particular, China became a much bigger source of everything from tables to bedroom sets. The imported furniture was considerably less expensive than its domestic-made counterparts–perhaps about two-thirds the price, according to people in the industry. As a result, consumers benefited.

In addition, the competition from imports forced domestic manufacturers to hold down their prices. Remember from **Chapter 5** that a company with few competitors–a monopolist or an oligopolist–has market power and thus can keep prices higher than the competitive equilibrium. When an industry faces competition from imports, however, it's harder for businesses to exert market power.

Here's another example. At one time, all the fresh flowers sold by florists, supermarkets, and gardening centers were grown in the United States. More recently, however, more than two-thirds of U.S. floral needs are imported, mainly from Colombia and Ecuador. The climate and long days in these countries, both of which are on the equator, let producers grow flowers such as roses and carnations all year long without expensive hothouses. In other words, these countries have relatively abundant resources of the type needed to grow flowers.

As a result, the price of indoor plants and flowers has risen much slower than the overall rate of inflation over the past 25 years. The United States could replace imports with domestic flowers–but that would require growers to build expensive hothouses to yield a similar supply of blooms year-round. Domestic flowers would cost more, and the large investment of labor and capital required to build and maintain the hothouses would draw resources away from the rest of the economy.

Access to Natural Resources

Another gain from trade is access to natural resources that either are too expensive to be produced domestically or are not available in sufficient quantities. An obvious example is crude oil, which is essential for running a modern economy. As we will see in **Chapter 19**, the United States produces far more oil domestically than just a few years ago. Nevertheless, cutting off the flow of imported oil would be enough to send gasoline prices sky-high. Other industrialized countries, such as Japan and Germany, have no oil resources of their own and, therefore, have no choice but to import oil from other countries where petroleum is abundant, no matter what the price.

Meanwhile, there is a long list of important minerals that the United States does not produce at all. Niobium, for example, is a metal you may never have heard of. It's used to make superconductors and heat-resistant steel for items like jet engines and rockets. The United States has some low-grade niobium deposits in places like New Mexico, Idaho, and Alaska. But the last active U.S. niobium mine closed in 1959 because production was so expensive compared to other countries. So, today, the United States imports all its niobium, mainly from Brazil and Canada. The large-scale manufacture of batteries for electric vehicles requires access to supplies of minerals such as lithium and cobalt, which mostly must be imported from other countries.

Access to Global Markets

Yet another gain from trade is that it gives companies access to global markets. Why is this important? The global market is bigger than any single national market, including that of the United States. So, if you are running a company that has spent a lot of money developing a new product, you want to get the maximum benefit from your investment by selling it in the biggest market possible–that is, the global one.

A good example is the film industry. Big-budget movies with famous actors and lots of special effects are generally very expensive to produce. But once a film is done, the cost of making copies and showing the film around the world is quite low. That's why movie companies try as hard as they can to export movies to other countries–especially action films, which attract a broad global audience. As a result, a typical successful Hollywood movie earns 60–70 percent of its box office revenues outside the United States, and its earnings from foreign distribution count as service exports.

For instance, *Avengers: Infinity War,* released in April 2018, cost about $300–$400 million to produce. However, over the next year it took in $2 billion in ticket sales around the world, with 67 percent of that coming from outside the United States.

Movies are an example of a business with high fixed costs and low marginal costs, as defined in **Chapter 4**. Such businesses make more profits by selling to a bigger market, so they are more profitable if they can sell globally.

Other industries also have large development costs for new products, making a global sales strategy essential. Consider the pharmaceutical industry. The cost of developing and testing a new drug is very high, ranging anywhere from $650 million to more than $2.7 billion, depending on which study you believe. In order to cover those costs, it is necessary to sell the drugs globally.

Access to New Ideas

A final gain from trade is access to new ideas from outside a country. Remember from **Chapter 9** that knowledge is a critical factor driving growth. When countries trade, they not only exchange goods and services, but they also trade ideas, information, and new ways of doing things. That accelerates the development of new products.

Today, many new U.S. products are either designed in countries other than the United States or are the result of cross-country collaboration. One of the most successful COVID vaccines was the result of the American pharmaceutical giant Pfizer partnering with a small German company, BioNTech. The most advanced semiconductor chips use a combination of technologies from the United States, Europe, and Asia. Looking further back, the flat-panel LCD television became a commercial product because of work done in multiple countries (see "**Spotlight: The Development of the Flat-Panel Television**").

SPOTLIGHT: THE DEVELOPMENT OF THE FLAT-PANEL TELEVISION

Walk into an electronics store and you'll see row after row of flat-panel LCD (liquid crystal display) televisions. The televisions themselves are all imported, but the idea for flat-panel TVs that could hang on walls originally came from a young U.S. researcher, George Heilmeier, in the 1960s.

Heilmeier expected to be able to make flat-panel TVs right away. But it took 25 years—and concentrated research efforts by major companies in the United States, Europe, and Japan—before a flat-panel TV became a reality.

The process of producing a workable LCD TV would probably have been much slower if U.S. researchers had tried to do it alone. Today, LCD screen manufacturers—mainly Japanese, Taiwanese, and Korean firms—are pouring billions of dollars into building mammoth TV factories in China and elsewhere. The result is that televisions keep getting cheaper, larger, and thinner.

Source: H. Kawamoto, "The History of Liquid-Crystal Displays," *Proceedings of the IEEE* 90, no. 4 (April 2002), pp. 460–500.

filadendron/iStock/Getty Images Plus/Getty Images

Many of the top console, desktop, and mobile games originated outside the United States. For example, the spectacularly successful Minecraft, now owned by Microsoft, was developed by Mojang Studios, in Stockholm, Sweden. The best-selling game Fortnite was created by Epic Games, an American company with employees all around the world, including the United Kingdom, Finland, and China. Pokémon Go, released in 2016, was based on characters created in Japan, even though the game itself was developed by the American company Niantic. Candy Crush Saga, a big hit, was developed by King Digital Entertainment, a Swedish-headquartered company with game developers in places like Barcelona, Berlin, Shanghai, London, and Bucharest. And going back a decade, Angry Birds, which first became a hit in 2010, came from a Finnish game developer, Rovio.

ABSOLUTE ADVANTAGE VERSUS COMPARATIVE ADVANTAGE (LO14-3)

LO14-3 Compare and contrast absolute advantage and comparative advantage.

Now that we understand the gains from international trade, let's examine who produces what. For example, why is so much furniture produced in China, while aircraft are produced in the United States?

Absolute Advantage

absolute advantage

A situation in which one country can produce a particular good or service with less labor, capital, and other inputs than another country.

If it takes less labor, capital, and other inputs to produce the same good in one country than in another, the first country has an **absolute advantage** in that good. Saudi Arabia has an absolute advantage over the United States in oil production because U.S. oil reserves require much more complicated and expensive methods of extraction. Colombia has an absolute advantage over the United States in flower production because of its location. Colombia is on the equator, with more hours of intense sunlight, making it easier to raise flowers there.

Let's look at another example. If one country has better and faster software programmers than another country does, the first country has an absolute advantage in software. The same software project will require fewer people; that is, the first country has higher *productivity* in software (remember that productivity was defined in **Chapter 9** as output per hour of labor).

Sometimes absolute advantage is something that can be held for a long time, as in the case of Saudi oil. Sometimes it's fleeting. In the software example, it's possible for another country to train good programmers. If that happens, the absolute advantage disappears.

The Theory of Comparative Advantage

comparative advantage

The tendency of countries to specialize in the goods or services in which they have the biggest productivity advantage or the smallest productivity disadvantage.

You might think that any country will produce and export the products in which it has an absolute advantage. Sometimes that's true. Saudi Arabia exports oil, for example, and Colombia exports flowers.

However, in general, what gets exported is determined by a more complicated set of factors than simply absolute advantage. Patterns of trade are determined by **comparative advantage**. That means a country will tend to specialize in the goods or services in which it has the biggest productivity advantage compared to other countries, or the smallest productivity disadvantage.

A country will tend to specialize in the goods or services for which it has the biggest productivity advantage or the smallest productivity disadvantage compared to other countries.

The easiest way to understand comparative advantage is with a simple example from daily life. Suppose that you are taking a car trip with a friend. You are slightly better at reading maps than your friend, but you are a much better driver. In theory, you could take on both tasks: drive and then stop occasionally to read the map. But you will probably get to your destination faster if you take the role where you have the biggest advantage–driving–and let your friend take care of the navigating.

Now let's look at a similar sort of trade example. Imagine two countries. One country, *D*, has good dress designers and workers who are fast at sewing dresses. The other country, *P*, has poor dress designers and workers who are just a bit slower at sewing than their counterparts in country *D*. From this description, country *D* has an absolute advantage in both dress design and sewing.

offshoring
The movement of manufacturing and service sector jobs to lower-wage countries.

reshoring
The movement of manufacturing and service sector jobs back to the United States.

nearshoring
The movement of manufacturing and service sector jobs to nearby countries such as Mexico.

The theory of comparative advantage says that a trade between the two countries will make both countries better off. In particular, country *D* will probably specialize in dress design, where it has a big advantage. Country *P* will probably specialize in sewing the dresses, where it has only a small disadvantage. Country *D* can export dress designs to country *P* and get back inexpensive dresses in return.

Here's another way to think about comparative advantage. Suppose one country has a large pool of low-cost labor. Another country excels at innovation and the creation of cutting-edge companies. And a third country has a history of solid manufacturing and engineering. Comparative advantage then suggests that each country should specialize in what they do best, relative to the other two.

These three countries, of course, are China, the United States, and Germany, respectively. China's cost advantage in manufacturing helped turn it into the manufacturing hub for the world (see "**Spotlight: Offshoring, Reshoring, and Nearshoring**"). Meanwhile, Germany, with very well-paid factory workers, is still a manufacturing powerhouse. German companies such as BMW, Mercedes, and Siemens are the envy of the world.

SPOTLIGHT: OFFSHORING, RESHORING, AND NEARSHORING

Every economic era has its own new vocabulary. The current wave of globalization has brought us several words: **offshoring**, **reshoring**, and **nearshoring**. Offshoring means the movement of manufacturing and service sector jobs to lower-wage countries. Reshoring means the movement of jobs back to the United States. Nearshoring, a relatively new term, means the movement of jobs to nearby countries such as Mexico.

Economists who study offshoring have difficulty coming up with an estimate of the number of U.S. jobs affected. Overall, there were 17.3 million manufacturing jobs in the United States in 2000, compared to 12.8 million in 2022. Some portion of those 4.5 million lost manufacturing jobs certainly went to other countries such as China, but we don't know how many.

Recently there have been early signs of some jobs returning to the United States, especially in critical industries such as semiconductor production and electric vehicles. In order to avoid the sort of supply chain disruptions that happened during the pandemic, companies have been looking at moving some of their production domestically. In addition, recent legislation provides incentives to produce some goods in the United States.

However, the companies producing in the United States don't necessarily have their headquarters in the United States. Figures from the Bureau of Economic Analysis suggest that, as of 2020, affiliates of foreign multinationals employed almost 8 million workers in the United States who work in a wide range of industries from manufacturing, to professional services, to finance.

At the same time, companies are considering shortening their supply chains by moving production from Asia to closer countries, such as Mexico, which already trade heavily with the United States. One goal is to lessen dependence on China.

The United States, by comparison, has specialized in the creation and nurturing of innovative companies such as Google, Apple, Amazon, and Facebook. As we will see in **Chapter 15**, fostering innovation and technological change requires certain expensive investments that are not easy to duplicate, such as R&D and venture capital.

One final note to emphasize: A country's comparative advantage can change over time. Consider India, which got its start with customer call centers because it had a relative abundance of English-speaking college graduates who had no other good opportunities in the Indian economy. Therefore, these skilled workers were relatively inexpensive to hire. However, as India develops other industries that employ college graduates, such as consulting and programming, it may no longer have a relative abundance of college graduates. The wages of college graduates will go up, and India may lose its comparative advantage in call centers.

Similarly, China's comparative advantage in low-cost manufacturing could be challenged by countries such as Vietnam and Mexico. Germany's comparative advantage in high-end manufacturing and the United States' comparative advantage in innovation could slip away as well, as other countries get better. As we have seen from earlier chapters, the threat of competition is an important motivation.

WINNERS AND LOSERS (LO14-4)

LO14-4 Discuss the winners and losers from trade and analyze the arguments for protectionism.

One of the most politically contentious issues in the United States today is the impact of trade on individuals. The impact of globalization was a central theme of the 2016 and 2020 presidential elections and is likely to play an equally large role in future presidential elections.

The theory of comparative advantage says that international trade will benefit an entire economy. That is, on average, living standards should go up in an economy that is open to global markets. Consumers have access to cheaper goods and services, and workers who once might have toiled in factories are now available for other industries.

However, it's quite possible for particular people or companies to be hurt by trade. In fact, there will almost always be losers, at least in the short run–the people whose jobs are displaced and who have to move to other parts of the economy. This sort of displacement and movement is not just a side effect of trade, however–it's part of the key mechanism by which trade raises overall living standards.

In this section, we will look at the winners and losers from international trade, and we will consider the problems with protectionism.

Winners: Consumers

As we discussed earlier, many benefits of trade show up as lower prices for all sorts of goods and services. So, when you go to the store and buy an inexpensive shirt or a cheap piece of electronics, you are reaping the benefits of trade. An iPhone, if made in the United States, would be too expensive for most people to buy.

We already mentioned that inexpensive imports help hold down the price of furniture to consumers. Similarly, the average price of clothing actually fell from 2000 to 2022, as did the price of televisions, appliances, toys, and sports equipment. These are goods where most of the production is coming from overseas.

Equally important, these gains from trade are broadly distributed. Anybody who goes into a store or who purchases online–that is, basically everyone–is benefiting from low-priced imports.

Winners: Workers Who Don't Compete with Imports

Let's think about a consumer buying a new dining room table that was made in a Chinese factory, not one in North Carolina. The table costs a lot less–let's say, $500 less–which is good news for the consumer.

That's not the end of the story, though. A household that buys an imported dining room table now has an extra $500 to spend. Where does it go? Recreation, perhaps. Or eating out, college tuition, a massage, a visit to the doctor, or any one of a thousand different domestic goods and services.

In other words, the money freed up by inexpensive imports of clothing, furniture, and electronics has enabled Americans to spend more on items such as live entertainment and sports, hairdressing salons and personal grooming establishments, and veterinary and other services for pets. Cheaper imports also give Americans more money to pay for the rising cost of health care and higher education. All of these are primarily supplied domestically.

This extra money leads to new jobs in the United States. Take pets, for example. Americans love their pets, and the money freed up by cheap imports has enabled Americans to more than quadruple the amount they spend on veterinary and pet care services since 2000, according to the BEA. As a result, the number of people employed in businesses that provide veterinary and pet care services doubled from 2000 to 2022. In 2022, there were about 83,000 veterinarians, roughly 150,000 veterinary technologists and technicians, and around 70,000 veterinary assistants (including laboratory animal caretakers!).

Winners: Innovative Companies and Their Employees

Earlier in this chapter, we gave examples of how entertainment companies boosted sales and profits by selling their highest-rated shows and movies around the world. Similarly, U.S. technology companies have been able to prosper by investing in new products and innovative applications and then expanding to other countries.

And it's not just the companies that benefit–workers gain as well. As innovative U.S. companies expand to take advantage of global markets, they hire workers at home. A globally successful company like Microsoft will tend to add employment in the United States as well.

The rule of thumb is simple: All other things being equal, globalization benefits people whose skills are relatively scarce in world markets. It hurts people whose skills are relatively common. In general, better-educated workers should do better in a globalized economy because most countries have a smaller proportion of college graduates among their citizens than the United States does.

Losers: Unemployed Workers

Now we come to one of the most distressing aspects of international trade: the transition costs. In the short run, imported goods and services sometimes displace domestically produced goods and services, resulting in lost jobs. Factories close, research facilities move overseas, and home-grown fruits and vegetables are replaced by ones from other countries.

As we have just seen, new jobs are created as well by trade. But that's a slender consolation to workers who have lost their jobs to overseas competitors and who may not have the skills to switch careers.

When a factory closes, some workers retire early; the rest have to retrain themselves for new jobs and move to other parts of the country if necessary. Many displaced workers have to return to school to qualify for new jobs, which can be an expensive and time-consuming proposition, even if the new jobs pay more.

Moreover, certain states and regions have taken a deeper blow than others (see "**Spotlight: The Biggest Losers**"). With many people in the same area suffering at the same time, it becomes harder to find new work. In the 2016 presidential election, many of the states hit hard by imports voted for Donald Trump, who spoke about the negative impact of trade on American workers.

SPOTLIGHT: THE BIGGEST LOSERS

Table 14.1 Manufacturing Job Loss by State, 2000–2022

	Change in Manufacturing Jobs (Thousands), 2000–2022
California	–520
Ohio	–340
New York	–326
Illinois	–302
Pennsylvania	–301
North Carolina	–285
Michigan	–283
New Jersey	–170
Massachusetts	–164
Texas	–145

Source: Bureau of Labor Statistics.

Table 14.1 lists the 10 states that had the biggest manufacturing job losses since 2000. Some big losers of manufacturing jobs, such as California and Massachusetts, were able to prosper because they had other industries, such as tech, to pick up the slack. In New York, the upstate counties have struggled, while New York City did well. Other states, such as Ohio and Michigan, are still looking for new engines of growth.

The Adjustment Process

Let's step back and look at the big picture. **Figure 14.5** traces the bad and the good sides of trade.

From the perspective of the factory workers displaced from their jobs, the import boom was terribly disruptive, forcing them out of work and requiring them to get added training or education to move into a new career. But from the perspective of the whole economy, the surge of imports lowered consumer prices and freed up millions of workers for gainful work in other parts of the economy.

To put this a different way, if the closed factories were to reopen tomorrow, millions of workers would have to be pulled from the rest of the economy to run them. Presumably, they are working at new jobs and would be missed if they were gone. The gain from international trade is that we not only get to consume the imported goods—we also get the benefit of all the labor freed from the manufacturing sector.

But there are ways of easing the pain of transition. That's why the government has a role in assisting people who have lost their jobs retrain for new ones (see "**How It Works: Helping the Losers**").

Figure 14.5 Imports and Jobs
The arrows on the right show how a purchase of imported furniture destroys manufacturing jobs in the United States. The arrows on the left show how that same purchase creates jobs in other industries.

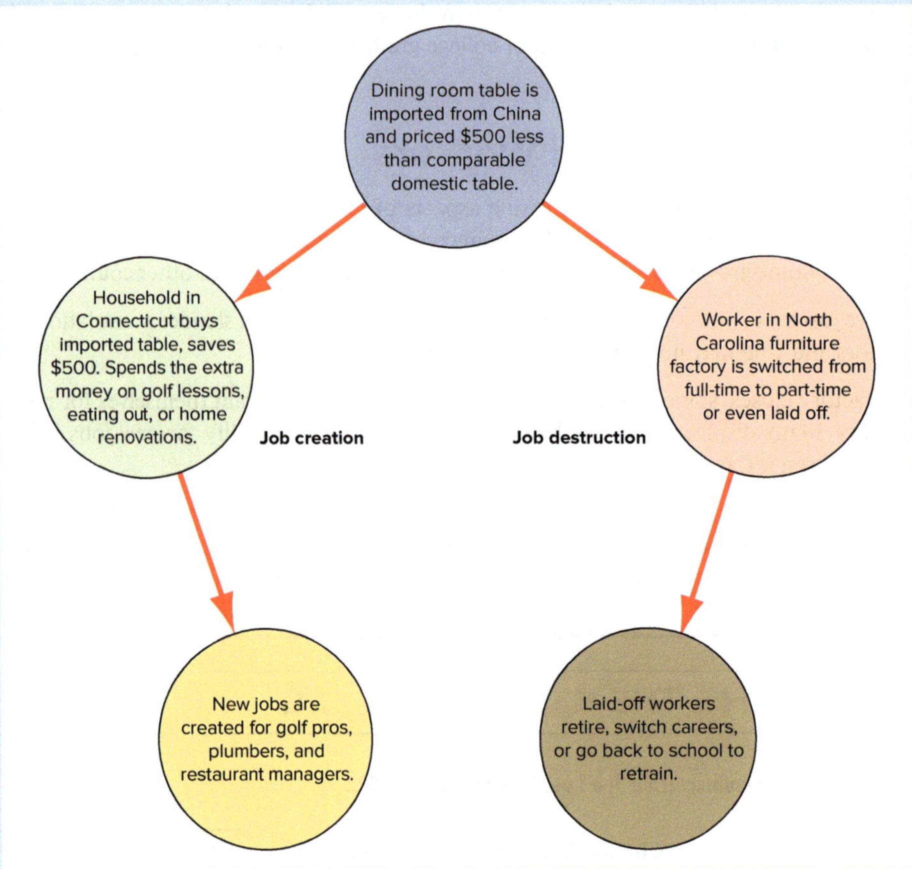

HOW IT WORKS: HELPING THE JOB LOSERS

The overall economy benefits from trade, but some individuals and companies are almost inevitably going to be hurt. As a result, there's a logical role for some form of trade adjustment assistance to compensate the losers.

Trade adjustment assistance can include support for retraining; income support during a transition from one career to another; relocation assistance; temporary government payments for health insurance; and incentives to businesses to help create new jobs.

Since at least the 1970s, the United States has tried various forms of trade adjustment assistance. However, there's little evidence that the programs have been successful. Depending on which economist you talk to, the reason is either that the programs were underfunded or that it's hard for the government to intervene in labor markets (or both).

Arguments for Protectionism

Most economists believe, and the evidence shows them to be correct, that international trade is beneficial to any economy. As a matter of history, countries that have been open to international trade seem to do better, in terms of growth, than ones that have been more closed off.

For example, China, India, and Germany have done well in recent decades–largely because they are participating actively in the global economy. They followed different strategies: China has become an important source of manufacturing goods, shipping all sorts of toys, machinery, clothing, and other manufactured goods to the United States. India has concentrated on exporting business services, such as computer programming and customer service call centers. Germany has gone for high-end manufacturing. But the continued growth of each rests on trade with the rest of the world.

Yet globalization is regularly attacked by politicians who believe it harms too many workers and too many domestic businesses. There are often demands for a return to **protectionism**—the use of tariffs, quotas, or other trade barriers to protect domestic jobs and businesses.

protectionism
The use of tariffs, quotas, or other barriers to trade to protect domestic jobs and businesses.

Are there good arguments for protectionism? Some economists point out that trade can sometimes be **disruptive**, which means that it can impose big economic and social adjustment costs. In developed countries, small towns are often organized around local factories. So, when that factory moves to China, it affects everyone in the town, not just the workers in the factory.

disruptive trade
Trade that imposes big economic and social adjustment costs.

The problem of disruptive trade is bigger in developing countries that have a large agricultural subsistence sector composed of poor farming households who survive by selling small amounts of crops locally. The danger here is that foreign competition in agriculture could leave whole villages and regions like these without a livelihood. For that reason, trade treaties typically allow poor countries to protect at least some of their agricultural industries.

infant industry
A new or a small industry that is vulnerable to being crushed by better-funded and more mature foreign competitors.

Another reason given for protectionism, the **infant industry** argument, is simple: An infant industry is a new or a small industry in a country, which is vulnerable to being crushed by better-funded and more mature foreign competitors. Given a chance to grow while protected, however, the new industry could be a viable global competitor (see "**Spotlight: How Canadians Nurture Their Music**").

SPOTLIGHT: HOW CANADIANS NURTURE THEIR MUSIC

The Canadian government has mounted a determined effort to protect and foster Canadian culture, which it regards as vulnerable to being overwhelmed by its giant U.S. neighbor. This effort includes setting rules for the kind of music radio stations can play to ensure that Canadian musicians get enough exposure to do well.

The regulations require that most broadcasters devote at least 35 percent of their popular music selections to Canadian songs. And what makes a song Canadian? Well, it's not enough that the performer is Canadian—either the music or the lyrics have to be written by a Canadian as well, or the song has to be recorded in a Canadian studio. There are other possibilities, but that's the basic idea. (These regulations are in the process of being revised as of early 2023).

The biggest winners from the Canadian content rule are young bands who get more airtime than they would otherwise. Well-known bands that benefited from this exposure in their earlier days include Nickelback and Barenaked Ladies.

Source: "Canadian Content Requirements for Music on Canadian Radio," Canadian Radio-Television and Telecommunications Commission, http://www.crtc.gc.ca/eng/cancon/r_cdn.htm.

In theory, this argument makes sense. But in practice, it rarely seems to work because it reduces competition. In the 1980s, Brazil wanted to develop its own computer industry. So, the government imposed restrictions on the use of imported computers and software and set up regulations that forced domestic computer makers to use domestically made parts.

The result was to cut Brazil off from the rapid technological progress being made in the global computer industry. As a result, Brazil's computers lagged several years behind those in the rest of the world and were more expensive, too. What's worse is that the rest of the Brazilian economy suffered because of the country's inability to use the fastest, cheapest computers available.

Another justification for protectionism is **unfair competition**. This usually refers to cases in which a foreign country subsidizes its exporting industries by lowering their taxes, offering them low-cost loans, or just giving them money. Armed with such a subsidy, the foreign industry can afford to price its products more cheaply. The result is that subsidized industries can get a bigger share of the global marketplace.

unfair competition
In global trade, cases in which a foreign country favors its own exporting industries by lowering their taxes or giving them some other subsidy.

For example, Airbus, the European airplane manufacturer, has access to low-cost loans from European governments. In effect, this is a subsidy because Airbus can borrow money at a lower interest than it could as a "normal" company. Boeing, its U.S. competitor, has complained that these loans give Airbus an unfair advantage.

On the face of it, unfair competition looks a bit like cheating. However, if one country subsidizes its exports, that may benefit consumers in other countries. Suppose the government of Fiji decides to subsidize its tourist industry by giving anyone who comes to the island a free room and meals. Obviously, this will attract travelers who might have gone elsewhere. For example, some tourists who might have spent time in Hawaii will go to Fiji instead, hurting the Hawaiian tourist industry.

But the tourists themselves will be better off: Free room and meals in Fiji—what could be better? In fact, the gains to consumers will exceed the losses to domestic industries, as in any other form of trade. However, losing jobs to unfair competition seems, well, unfair, because it comes about as the result of government decisions rather than pure economic competition.

Probably the most compelling reason to maintain some trade barriers is concern about protecting important industries in case of an emergency such as war or pandemic. During normal times, it doesn't matter whether factories are in the same country as their goods' ultimate consumers. It's in the interest of the exporting countries to keep shipping their goods. After all, what else are the factories for?

But a major national emergency changes these calculations. In the early days of the pandemic, countries that were major manufacturers of N95 masks and other "personal protective equipment" naturally prioritized their own citizens. Countries like the United States that mostly relied on imported medical protective gear found themselves with shortages.

The threat of war is even more daunting. Once shooting starts, you don't want to find out that all your bullets are made in the country you're fighting. Or that all the special steel in your missiles and all the electronics in your fighter planes are made in a neutral country that can't provide any more supplies because the shipping lanes are closed by war. Or even that the supply of computer and communications equipment, so essential for running a modern economy, starts drying up because so much of it is produced abroad.

For example, the U.S. military, in recent years, has begun to raise concerns about whether it is a good idea to rely too heavily on electronics produced in China. The worry has been that Chinese companies might create "back doors" that would allow the Chinese military to eavesdrop on U.S. communications. More generally, non-U.S. countries, including China, have become a major source of the semiconductor chips that go into both U.S. military systems and civilian products like automobiles.

National security requires balancing the economic benefits of trade against the potential vulnerabilities of a global supply chain during war. In ordinary times, outsourcing cuts costs and enables the defense dollar to go further. But it may take too much time to rebuild factory capacity during war.

For that reason, recent legislation has focused on upgrading the U.S. capability to produce some semiconductor chips domestically. However, the United States has still not figured out the right balance between low cost and national security.

YOUR ECONOMIC LIFE: What Globalization Means to You

Today, globalization is a fact of life. Look around you. The appliances in your kitchen, the clothes in your closet, the smartphone in your pocket–all were likely made overseas, or contain substantial components from outside the United States. If you tried to buy U.S.-made versions of these products, they would be far more expensive, if you could even find them.

But globalization means more than cheaper goods. Globalization is also about the ability and desire to travel freely to other countries. In 1990, only 11 million Americans had passports. In 2022, 152 million Americans had passports, an almost inconceivably large jump, and a sign that more Americans are traveling abroad in the aftermath of the pandemic.

Globalization is also about access to creativity and culture from other countries. This shows up most clearly in mobile games, which come from around the world. But other forms of creativity, such as cooking, are also influenced by other cultures.

However, some people feel like their national identity is challenged by globalization. How can they feel American if their physical possessions, their music, and even their food is coming from other countries? Fear of immigration, as we will see in **Chapter 16**, is part of the mix as well.

We acknowledge that globalization can be challenging and disruptive, but as we have seen in this chapter, it brings tremendous positives as well.

EXCHANGE RATES (LO14-5)

LO14-5 Describe what it means for a currency to appreciate or depreciate.

If you travel outside of the United States, one of the first things that you notice is that the bills and coins are different. Mexico uses the peso, Canada's currency is called the Canadian dollar, while Costa Rica uses the colón.

The most important currencies today are the dollar (United States), the euro (which is used by 23 European countries including France and Germany), the yen (Japan), the pound (Great Britain), and the yuan (China). But there are currencies for small countries that receive almost no attention, including the Albanian lek, the Bangladesh taka, and the Paraguay guarani.

For two countries to trade, they need to be able to convert one currency to another. Suppose Honda makes a motor scooter in Japan and ships it for sale in Los Angeles. The workers in Japan are paid in yen, but the U.S. consumers who buy the motorcycles pay dollars for them. At some point, if Honda wants to keep operating its factories and paying its workers, it has to turn those dollars into yen.

The **exchange rate** is the rate at which one currency can be converted into another. For example, on April 2, 2019, one dollar was worth 111 yen. That same dollar could also be turned into 0.89 euro or 23,200 Vietnamese Dong.

exchange rate
The rate at which one currency can be converted into another.

These numbers can be flipped around. For example, if 1 dollar is worth 0.89 euro, then 1 euro is worth 1.12 dollars (1.12 = 1/0.89).

In most cases exchange rates between currencies are **floating**, which means they are set in the foreign exchange markets. Currency traders buy and sell dollars for yen, or yen for euros, or euros for the Thai baht or the Indonesian ringgit. The exchange rate is determined by the outcome of market transactions, and it can swing dramatically.

floating exchange rate
An exchange rate between two currencies that is set in the financial markets.

Some currencies do not float; instead, their exchange rate is **pegged**, which means the government of the country manages the exchange rate to keep it fixed relative to another currency. For example, some Caribbean countries, including Aruba and the Bahamas, peg their currencies to the dollar (e.g., one Bahamian dollar equals one U.S. dollar). Some African countries, such as Chad and Senegal, peg their currencies to the euro.

pegged exchange rate
Occurs when the government of one country manages its exchange rate to be fixed in relation to another currency.

For many years, China pegged its currency, the yuan, to the U.S. dollar at a rate of 8.3 yuan to the dollar. Starting in July 2005, the Chinese government began allowing the exchange rate to change slowly (**Figure 14.6**). As of March 2023, a dollar was worth only 6.9 yuan.

Figure 14.6 The Exchange Rate of the Yuan versus the Dollar The chart shows the number of yuan a dollar can buy. As that number has fallen over time, the dollar has depreciated against the yuan.

Source: The Federal Reserve, www.federalreserve.gov.

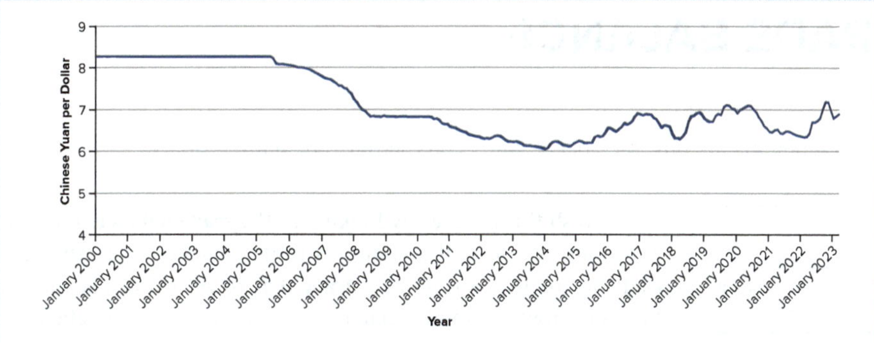

When an exchange rate changes so that one currency can buy more of another, we say the first currency is **appreciating** and the second currency is **depreciating**. For example, based on **Figure 14.6**, we can say that the yuan appreciated against the dollar between July 2005 and March 2023. That's equivalent to saying that the dollar depreciated.

currency appreciation
A change in an exchange rate allowing one currency to buy more of another.

currency depreciation
A change in an exchange rate allowing one currency to buy less of another.

Effects of Appreciation and Depreciation

What happens when one currency depreciates relative to another? To make this concrete, let's suppose the dollar depreciates relative to the euro: One dollar buys fewer euros, and one euro buys more dollars. This affects the price of imports and exports.

Consider what happens when a U.S. maker of construction equipment ships a massive construction crane to Europe that is priced (in dollars) at $100,000. If the exchange rate is one dollar for each euro, that crane sells for 100,000 euros, as line A in **Table 14.2** shows. But if the dollar depreciates to $1.30 for each euro, the crane sells for roughly 77,000 euros (€) to European buyers. The crane is the same price in dollars, but it becomes cheaper for European buyers, as line B shows.

Table 14.2 How Depreciation Works

A depreciating dollar raises the price of imports to domestic buyers and cuts the price of exports to foreign buyers.

A construction crane is exported from the United States to Europe. After the dollar depreciates, the price of the crane in euros falls.

	Original Price in Dollars	Dollars per Euro	Price in Euros
A	100,000	1.00	100,000
B	100,000	1.30	76,923

A car is imported from Germany to the United States. After the dollar depreciates, the price of the car in dollars goes up.

	Price in Dollars	Dollars per Euro	Original Price in Euros
C	40,000	1.00	40,000
D	52,000	1.30	40,000

Here's another example, also from **Table 14.2.** Consider a German-made car priced at 40,000 euros. If it is shipped to the United States at a time when the exchange rate is one dollar for one euro, its price would be $40,000, as shown in line C. Now suppose the dollar depreciates, so one euro is worth $1.30. That same €40,000 car would cost roughly $52,000 in the United States, as shown in line D.

The bottom line is that imports become more expensive when a currency depreciates. Similarly, exports become cheaper when a currency depreciates. If imports become more expensive, the law of demand suggests that purchases of imports will fall. And when exports become cheaper, purchases of exports should rise. As a result, when a currency depreciates, its trade deficit should eventually shrink over time, all other things being equal.

The other thing that happens when a currency depreciates is that assets in that country–real estate, stocks, and so forth–become cheaper for foreign investors to buy. Think about this. Suppose you have a U.S. home selling for $300,000. If the dollar-euro exchange rate is one for one, then a European buyer would have to pay 300,000 euros (€). But if the dollar depreciates to $1.30 for each euro, the price of that home in euros falls to only $230,000. Suddenly, U.S. real estate looks much cheaper to European investors, even if nothing has changed about their price in dollars.

THE TRADE BALANCE (LO14-6)

LO14-6 List explanations for why the United States consistently runs a trade deficit.

trade balance
The difference between exports and imports of goods and services.

trade deficit
Occurs when a trade balance is negative so that imports exceed exports.

Let's finish this chapter by looking at the **trade balance**, the difference between exports and imports of goods and services. If a country's trade balance is negative–that is, if imports exceed exports–we say that the country is running a **trade deficit**. As we will see in this section, the amount that the United States borrows is closely related to the size of its trade deficit.

The U.S. trade deficit as a percentage of GDP widened sharply in the 1990s and the first half of the 2000s as **Figure 14.7** shows. Between 2006 and 2019, the trade deficit narrowed as a percentage of GDP, first because of the recession (which reduced the amount of imports) and then due to declining payments for foreign oil. Then the trade deficit widened again during the pandemic.

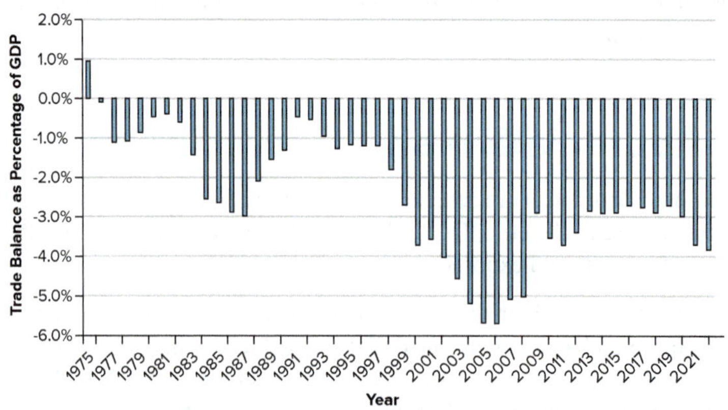

Figure 14.7 Goods and Services Trade Balance as Percentage of GDP, 1975–2022
In this chart, when the trade balance is negative, the United States is running a trade deficit. In 2022, for example, imports exceeded exports by $978 billion, or almost 4 percent of GDP. Because the trade balance is negative, the bars stretch downward.

Source: Bureau of Economic Analysis, www.bea.gov.

As of 2022, the United States continues to run a substantial trade deficit that does not appear to be disappearing. Indeed, the U.S. trade deficit is by far the largest in the world, measured in dollars.

Economists disagree about how to interpret the U.S. trade deficit. They offer several different explanations, which fall into three general categories: "It's our fault"; "It's their fault"; and "It's no one's fault" (see **Table 14.3**).

Table 14.3 Explanations for the U.S. Trade Deficit

"It's Our Fault"
U.S. consumers borrow too much.
The U.S. government borrows too much.
U.S. manufacturers can't compete.
"It's Their Fault"
Other countries restrict imports from the United States.
Other countries unfairly subsidize their exports.
"It's No One's Fault"
The United States is a successful rich economy, able to afford imports.
The United States is a successful rich economy, making it a magnet for lending from other countries.

Some Explanations for the Trade Deficit

Let's start with "It's our fault." Because the big trade deficits started in the 1980s, some economists have put the blame solidly on the actions of U.S. manufacturers, consumers, and governments. The deficit was caused, some say, because U.S. manufacturers are incompetent and unable to compete with overseas rivals, which is why U.S. consumers have been buying imports. Others blame the trade deficit on overspending by U.S. consumers. If consumers would cut back on their purchases instead of borrowing heavily to buy imported goods such as cars, toys, and electronics, the trade deficit would shrink or even vanish. Along the same line, many economists argue that the big trade deficit is the result of overspending by the federal government. According to this explanation, the expansion of the trade deficit from 2019 to 2022 was the result of the big increase in pandemic-related stimulus spending.

What about "It's their fault"? Some economists, politicians, and business leaders blame the trade deficit, at least in part, on decisions made by foreign countries. For example, during the 1980s, the United States ran big trade deficits with Japan, which seemed to be using nontariff barriers to keep out U.S. exports. More recently, the Chinese government has been accused by some of making it harder for U.S. companies to sell to Chinese consumers. In 2018, President Donald Trump raised tariffs on some imports from China in an attempt to get the Chinese government to open up its domestic markets to more U.S.-made goods.

Finally, some economists believe the United States trade deficit may simply reflect the strength of the U.S. economy, rather than its weakness. People in the United States have high enough incomes to be able to afford high levels of consumption, including imports. Moreover, the United States, the largest and most stable economy in the world, is a magnet for lending from other countries. Ask yourself this: If you were a Chinese billionaire, would you like to keep all of your wealth in China, or would you prefer to move half of it to the comparative safety of the United States?

ECONOMIC MILESTONE

1975: The Last Trade Surplus

In 1975, the United States ran a small excess of exports of goods and services over imports, as a weak economy cut consumer demand. That was the last U.S. trade surplus. Since then, the United States has registered 40 straight years of trade deficits, with no end in sight.

The truth is, all these explanations have an element of truth. The trade deficit does reflect U.S. overspending in part, decisions by other countries in part, and the wealth and health of the U.S. economy in part.

Paying for Trade

But no matter what explanation for the trade deficit you accept, this is true: If you buy an imported toy, bottle of wine, or car, you have to pay for it, one way or another. As economists say, there is no such thing as a free lunch. A country must pay for its imports somehow. There are four ways to do this (see **Table 14.4**).

Table 14.4 Four Ways to Pay for Imports

- Sell exports to foreign purchasers.
- Borrow money from foreign investors.
- Sell assets such as stock or real estate to foreign investors.
- Allow foreign companies to build factories or other facilities in the United States.

One way to pay for our imports is to send back exports of our own goods and services. Saudi Arabia sends us oil, and we send aircraft, machinery, and arms and ammunition. Australia sends us wine, uranium, and beef, and we send excavating machinery, agricultural machinery, drugs, and medical equipment.

But what if we are running a trade deficit with a country? When China sends us a containership full of toys, what do we send China in return? One possibility is that China and other countries can give us the goods and services on credit, like a bar that lets its patrons run tabs. As of the end of 2022, the United States government had borrowed more than $7 trillion from the rest of the world, plus another $1 trillion in debt backed by the federal government.

From one perspective, more than $8 trillion seems like a lot of money. Paying back that much debt may decrease the amount of money available for our future consumption.

On the other hand, if our economy is growing fast enough, even a high level of obligations may not be a problem. A fast-growing country will likely have enough future income to pay back accumulated debt–much as a family with a rising income can pay back the mortgage it used to buy a house.

Alternatively, we can pay for imports by selling other countries valuable U.S. assets. These can be stock shares in U.S. companies, for example; as of the end of 2022, foreigners owned more than $10 trillion in U.S. stocks. Or we can sell some of our buildings or homes or other real estate to foreigners to help pay for our imports.

A fourth way of paying for imports is to encourage foreign companies to invest directly in the United States by building their factories and office buildings here. Such "foreign direct investment" includes foreign investment in the Fort Madison plant making wind turbine blades, mentioned earlier in this chapter. According to a report from the International Monetary Fund, the United States was the top destination for foreign direct investment in 2021, the most recent data available.

CONCLUSION

In the past, you might not have given a moment's thought to China, India, or any other faraway country. Today, however, globalization is one of the key driving forces of the economy, and there's no way to understand your future without some knowledge of international trade.

Still, globalization would not be possible without breakthroughs in communication and transportation. That's what has enabled national economies to be tied closer together. It's these sorts of technological improvements that we will discuss in the next chapter.

14 SUMMARY

1. The current boom in international trade may be unprecedented in recent history. Both trade in goods and trade in services have expanded. The increases are due to falling natural barriers to trade, such as distance, and falling legal barriers to trade, such as tariffs. *(LO14-1)*
2. The gains of trade include lower prices of goods and services, access to natural resources, access to global markets, and access to new ideas. For example, international trade allows consumers and businesses to buy lower-priced imports. *(LO14-2)*
3. If it takes fewer resources to produce the same good in one country than in another, the first country has an absolute advantage in that good. However, patterns of trade are determined by comparative advantage rather than absolute advantage. Comparative advantage means that countries specialize in the products or services for which they have the biggest productivity advantage–or the smallest productivity disadvantage. *(LO14-3)*
4. The theory of comparative advantage says that there always is a trade between two countries that makes both better off. You cannot identify a country's comparative advantage by just looking at its own economy. You also have to know how it compares to its trading partners. *(LO14-3)*
5. Economists believe that the gains from trade are broadly distributed. However, particular people and companies may be hurt by trade. In the short run, the transition costs of adjusting to trade can be large. Arguments for protectionism include the disruptive effects of trade, the desire to protect infant industries, concerns about unfair competition, and the need to protect important industries in case of emergencies such as pandemic or war. *(LO14-4)*
6. The exchange rate is the rate at which one currency can be converted into another. If the exchange rate changes so that one currency can buy more of another, we say that the first currency is appreciating and the second is depreciating. A depreciating currency makes imports more expensive to domestic buyers and exports cheaper to foreign buyers. *(LO14-5)*

7. There are several explanations for why the United States has been running big trade deficits. These include overconsumption by the United States, policies by foreign countries that keep out U.S. exports, and the strength of the U.S. economy. *(LO14-6)*

KEY TERMS AND CONCEPTS

globalization
trade in goods
trade in services
natural barriers to trade
legal barriers to trade
tariffs
quotas
gains from trade
absolute advantage
comparative advantage
offshoring
reshoring
nearshoring
protectionism
disruptive trade
infant industry
unfair competition
exchange rate
floating exchange rate
pegged exchange rate
currency appreciation
currency depreciation
trade balance
trade deficit

connect PROBLEMS

1. Identify each of the following transactions as an import, an export, or neither, from the perspective of the United States. *(LO14-1)*
   a) You purchase a new BMW made in Germany.
   b) You purchase a Toyota Camry made in Toyota's Kentucky plant.
   c) Thailand purchases a 5 million doses of COVID vaccine from Moderna, a U.S-based pharmaceutical company.
   d) You call customer service for your computer and are connected to a service representative in India.
   e) You study in another country for a year.
2. Americans have a choice between buying U.S.-made motorcycles and imported motorcycles. *(LO14-1)*
   a) Draw a supply-demand diagram for the market for U.S.-made motorcycles. Label the equilibrium point.
   b) Show how a drop in the price of imported motorcycles affects the demand curve for U.S.-made motorcycles. Label the new equilibrium point.
   c) Will the quantity of U.S.-made motorcycles rise, fall, or stay the same? Will the price of U.S.-made motorcycles rise, fall, or stay the same?
3. The U.S. imposes a new tariff of $50.00 on every imported kitchen appliance. *(LO14-1)*
   a) Does imposing the tariff raise or lower the prices U.S. consumers pay?
   b) Does the tariff raise or lower the prices foreign appliance producers receive for the appliances they sell in the United States?
   c) Does imposing the tariff increase or decrease the quantity of imported appliances?
   d) Does the tariff make U.S. consumers better off or worse off?
4. This chapter identifies four categories of gains from trade: lower prices of goods and services, access to natural resources, access to global markets, and access to new ideas. For each of the following situations, identify which category of gain from trade is the most important and explain why. *(LO14-2)*
   a) In 2022, Microsoft received roughly half of its revenue from customers outside the United States.
   b) The United States imports almost all of the platinum that it uses.
   c) The Wii video game machine, designed in Japan by Nintendo, was a big hit in the United States.
   d) The price of furniture to U.S. consumers has dropped over time because of imports from China.
5. One important gain to trade is access to global markets. That's likely to be important for U.S. companies if ______ *(LO14-2)*
   a) U.S. wages are rising.
   b) the United States is growing faster than other countries.
   c) other countries are growing faster than the United States.
   d) wages in other countries are falling.

6. Suppose that because of climate or some other reason, Country A's wheat farmers have higher productivity than Country B's wheat farmers. That is, on the same size farm, Country A can grow twice as much wheat as Country B with the same amount of labor. ***(LO14-3)***

   a) Is this an example of absolute advantage or comparative advantage? Explain.
   b) Does this mean Country A will necessarily export wheat to Country B? Explain.

7. Suppose that a massive oil field was discovered in Michigan. If it was large enough, we would expect that ______ ***(LO14-3)***

   a) oil imports would increase.
   b) the United States would become a net exporter of oil.
   c) oil consumption would fall.
   d) the United States would lose its comparative advantage in oil drilling.

8. Suppose that Chinese manufacturers develop the ability to build an electric car that costs only $5,000. They start shipping it to the United States. For each of the following groups, say whether they are likely to win, lose, or not be affected much by the Chinese imported cars. ***(LO14-4)***

   a) Low-income American families.
   b) High-income American families.
   c) U.S. autoworkers.
   d) U.S. auto companies.

9. Sometimes exchange rates change rapidly over a short period of time. For example, at the end of 1993, the exchange rate between Mexico and the United States was 3.1 pesos to the dollar. By the end of 1994, the exchange rate was 5 pesos to the dollar, and at the end of 1995, it was 7.7 pesos to the dollar. ***(LO14-5)***

   a) Over this period, did the dollar appreciate or depreciate against the peso?
   b) A $1,000 piece of construction equipment made in the United States would have cost ______ pesos in 1993. It would have cost ______ pesos in 1995.
   c) Would you expect exports from the United States to Mexico to rise or fall over this period?
   d) Suppose it cost 1,000 pesos to make a television set in Mexico in the early 1990s. That was equivalent to ______ dollars in 1993 and ______ dollars in 1995.
   e) Would you expect imports from Mexico to the United States to rise or fall over this period?

10. The currency of Iceland is called the krona. In July 2007, the exchange rate was roughly 60 krona to a dollar. In April 2023, the exchange rate was roughly 135 krona to a dollar. ***(LO14-5)***

    a) Over this period, would you expect exports from the United States to Iceland to get cheaper or more expensive in Iceland?
    b) Would you expect living standards in Iceland to rise or fall?
    c) Is the krona appreciating or depreciating against the dollar?

11. In 2022, the United States ran a trade deficit equal to almost 4 percent of GDP. Suppose that the government imposed tariffs of 100 percent on all imported goods, effectively doubling the price of imported goods such as electronics and clothing. ***(LO14-6)***

    a) Would the quantity demanded of imported goods rise or fall?
    b) Would the size of the trade deficit shrink or increase?
    c) Would U.S. consumers be better off or worse off because of the tariffs?

CH 15

TECHNOLOGICAL CHANGE

Halfpoint/Shutterstock

LEARNING OBJECTIVES

After reading this chapter, you should be able to:

LO15-1 Explain the importance of technological change, including the information revolution.
LO15-2 List three types of innovation.
LO15-3 Explain the link between innovation and innovative activities.
LO15-4 Identify and discuss the factors that affect the supply curves for innovative activities.
LO15-5 Identify and discuss the factors that affect the demand curves for innovative activities.

What's next? The growth of the modern market economy is, in many ways, the story of technological change. Science—the urge to understand nature—has been harnessed to the profit motive, and the combination has been exceptionally potent.

Finding the next big innovation is a good way to make money. James Watt invented the steam engine in the 1700s to pump water out of mines and became rich in the process. Henry Ford invented the assembly line and the Model T automobile and created one of the greatest fortunes in U.S. history. Larry Page and Sergey Brin invented a better search engine, and the result—Google—made them both billionaires.

But that's not where technological change stops. Artificial intelligence and chatbots are popping up everywhere. Self-driving cars and trucks seem just around the corner. Pharmaceutical companies quickly developed new vaccines to tame COVID and are working on innovative treatments for cancer, obesity, arthritis, and other major health problems. Scientists are working on new materials for clothing and roadways.

It's a virtuous circle. Economic incentives encourage people and businesses to create and commercialize new technology, and then technological change and innovation drive economic growth. In fact, one of the greatest advantages of the U.S. economy, compared to its rivals in Europe and Japan, has been its ability to take new ideas and commercialize them quickly.

In this chapter, we will use our tools of supply and demand to understand the economics of technological change. We'll describe the different kinds of innovation and look at the factors affecting the supply of and demand for innovation.

THE NATURE OF TECHNOLOGICAL CHANGE (LO15-1)

LO15-1 Explain the importance of technological change, including the information revolution.

technological change
An improvement in knowledge that increases the quantity and range of goods and services an economy can deliver.

As we saw in **Chapter 1**, **technological change** is an improvement in knowledge that increases the range of goods and services that the economy can deliver. By definition, technological change expands the limits of what we can produce, given today's natural resources and workforce. To use a term that we defined in **Chapter 9**, technological change pushes out the **production possibility frontier (PPF)**.

Technological change expands the limits of what we can produce, given today's natural resources and workforce.

production possibility frontier (PPF)
All the combinations of different goods and services the economy is capable of producing at a particular time, assuming full use of all resources.

innovations
New products and processes.

Technological change leads to **innovations**, which are new products and processes. Without technological change, it's impossible to get sustained increases in living standards. Imagine, if you would, today's world with the technology from a century ago. No antibiotics or television–they didn't exist in 1910. No commercial air travel, although by 1919 airplanes had already played a role in World War I, including the invention of the first fighter plane. The first transcontinental phone call came in 1915, but there was no Internet. As of 1919, the average life expectancy at birth was only 56 years for men and 58 years for women, and air conditioning had not been invented.

Since those days, a century ago, technological progress has proceeded in waves. One wave came in the first half of the 20th century, with amazing breakthroughs like antibiotics, radio, air travel, television, widespread use of electricity, cars, plastics, and other new materials that had never existed before. For example, nylon, the first synthetic fiber, was invented in 1935.

Innovation took flight starting with the Wright brothers.

Library of Congress Prints and Photographs Division [LC-DIG-pprs-00699]

The next stretch–from roughly 1950 to 1975–had fewer big breakthroughs. Instead, it was a productive period of building on earlier innovations. Companies refined and improved their new products, in some cases in major ways. For example, the shift from black-and-white to color television happened in the 1960s and 1970s (in 1966, NBC became the first network to broadcast its shows in color). Airlines introduced widespread use of jets, which replaced propeller-driven planes and improved speed and passenger comfort.

However, in the 1970s, it became clear that two highly touted breakthrough technologies were failing to deliver much in the way of economic benefits. The first was space travel. Putting a person on the moon in 1969 and making five additional landings over the next three years was a great public relations achievement. But despite all the hoopla, the manned space program, including today's space shuttle launches, has generated relatively few economic returns so far. Our major economic uses of space today, including the launching of weather and communications satellites, mainly predate the beginning of the manned space program.

The second big failure from an economic perspective was nuclear energy, which was supposed to be a limitless source of cheap power. When the first nuclear power plants were built after World War II, utility companies expected the cost would fall, just as other new technologies had become cheaper over time. Instead, nuclear power plants became more expensive to operate and build, and safety considerations loomed larger–especially after the 1979 accident at Three Mile Island in Pennsylvania and the 1986 Chernobyl disaster in Russia. U.S. utility companies, which stopped ordering nuclear power plants after Three Mile Island, had planned to build a dozen more. But nearly all were canceled after the 2011 Fukushima incident in Japan and because of rising construction costs.

The Information Revolution

While space travel and nuclear power have fallen short of expectations, there has been one source of innovation that has transformed our world: information technology. In 1971, Intel created the first microprocessor–a computer on a chip–for use in a Japanese calculator.

Apple, led by Steve Jobs and Steve Wozniak, introduced the Apple II in 1977, the first real mass-market personal computer. IBM produced the IBM PC in 1981, using an operating system from Microsoft, then a small, unknown company.

These events created enormous excitement and press attention at the time. The new companies and their inventions also produced a generation of billionaires and multibillionaires, led by Bill Gates, the founder of Microsoft. Yet economists were justifiably skeptical about the impact of personal computers on the economy. At the time, there was no sign they were really changing how business was done or helping the United States compete better in global markets. They seemed more like toys.

Moore's law
The historical pattern that microprocessors double their performance every 18-24 months.

information revolution
The application of additional processing capacity of new generations of computers to a wide variety of new uses. Enabled businesses to produce more output with fewer workers.

But electronic devices grew smaller, faster, cheaper, and more powerful each year, following **Moore's law**. Named for Geoffrey Moore, one of the founders of Intel, Moore's law says that microprocessors double their performance every 18-24 months. That is, with the same resources, over time, we can do a lot more computing.

Sometime in the early 1990s, computers became powerful enough to make a real difference in the economy. This advance ignited the **information revolution**, which means the application of the additional processing capacity of the new generation of computers to a wide variety of new uses. These included sophisticated financial models for banks and Wall Street firms, corporate databases for retailers and manufacturers, and computer games of all sorts.

HOW IT WORKS: E-COMMERCE

One of the most important uses of the Internet is for e-commerce: buying and selling over the web. More and more retail sales are conducted via the Internet, and virtually every business of any size has a website.

Moreover, Amazon and other e-commerce retailers have made it much easier to buy online by offering rapid delivery and easy returns. Thus, consumers can purchase several pairs of shoes online and return the ones that don't fit.

E-commerce grew quickly during the pandemic, as people shopped from home rather than risk being exposed to the virus. Still, e-commerce remains a relatively small share of sales. According to the Census Bureau, e-commerce sales in the fourth quarter of 2022 came to only 16 percent of total retail sales. That makes sense: There are so many things, such as gasoline, that simply can't be bought online. Moreover, people like to touch and see what they are buying.

Perhaps most important, as **Figure 15.1** shows, faster computers also revolutionized communications. The Internet is based on the idea that information of any sort–a web page, an e-mail message, a picture–can be broken into little packets of information and routed to the right destination. This sort of networking would not be possible without very fast computers.

Figure 15.1 How Has the Information Revolution Changed Our Spending? In 1975, American households devoted 3.1 percent of their spending to landline phone service, televisions, music cassette players, and similar gear. In 2022, households put 4.7 of their spending into infotech and communications equipment and services.

Source: Bureau of Economic Analysis, www.bea.gov.

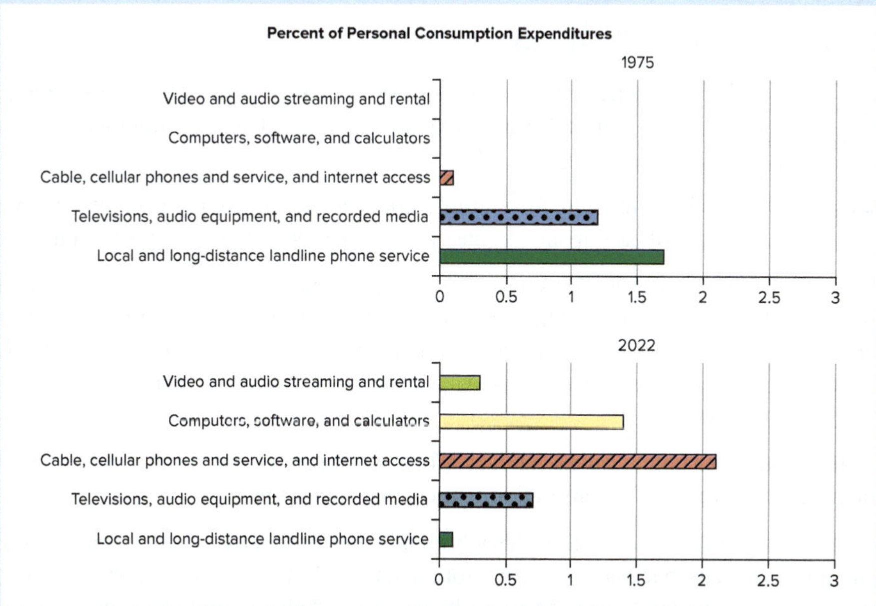

Similarly, fast and cheap computing was the essential factor behind the development of such innovations as the Google search engine, first available in 1998; the Facebook social network, founded in 2004; and the Apple iPhone, first launched in 2007. These innovations changed the way we communicate and interact with each other, and the way we learn about the rest of the world.

The latest big developments in the information revolution are artificial intelligence and machine learning. These concepts sound scary, but they simply mean using data to improve the performance of workers, programs, and physical objects. The new generation of artificial intelligence programs, for example, can help people write reports and database queries. In **Chapter 16**, we'll examine how artificial intelligence might affect the labor market.

THREE TYPES OF INNOVATION (LO15-2)

LO15-2 List three types of innovation.

Our society and our economy have been shaped by technological change and innovation. Yet not all innovations have the same degree of impact. In fact, we can identify three different channels by which technological change and innovations can affect businesses and consumers–and thus the economy.

Productivity Enhancements

productivity-enhancing innovation
Technological change that provides more of the same product while holding inputs constant. It has the effect of shifting the supply curve to the right.

Suppose Tesla figures out how to produce its electric cars with fewer parts or with fewer steps on the assembly line. Then, it can produce and sell the same number of cars as before at a lower cost. This is an example of a **productivity-enhancing innovation**.

Another example of a productivity-enhancing innovation is the ATM, which enables you to get money from your account and make deposits without having to wait in line for a teller. Yet another example is the use of prefabricated components such as doors, windows, and even walls to build homes. That reduces construction time and ultimately makes the home less expensive.

In general, a productivity-enhancing innovation in an industry gives you more of the same product, holding fixed the resources used. That has the effect of shifting the supply curve to the right. The reason is that businesses can afford to produce more output for the same cost, typically reducing the market price and increasing the quantity sold in the market.

Productivity-enhancing innovations are very common because businesses are always trying to improve the performance of their operations. The goal is to either cut costs or boost output.

New Goods and Services

creation of new goods and services
Technological change that allows people to do things they could not do before.

A second kind of technological change yields the **creation of new goods and services**, enabling people to do things that weren't possible before. These are not mere improvements but spectacular jumps forward that change daily life.

Television, for example–the beaming of live pictures into the home–had no analogue in the past. Now it eats up an average of more than two hours per day for adults (three hours per day on weekends!).

Or consider the cell phone. On one level, it's just another way to make a phone call, something that has been possible since 1876. But on another level, the portability of the cell phone lets us be permanently connected to the communications grid no matter where we are. That's a major change in how we live our lives, as evidenced by the number of people who walk through the streets with their phones pressed to their ears or eyes glued to their screens. Additionally, smartphones, such as the iPhone, are powerful enough to substitute for computers in many applications.

Another example: Multiplayer online games, such as World of Warcraft or Fortnite, could not have been developed before the Internet. They clearly fall into the category of an innovation that created something new.

Some innovations fit more than one category: They both enhance productivity and provide new goods and services. In the early part of the 20th century, as electricity became more common, it replaced other forms of power in factories. This was productivity-enhancing because electricity cut costs without changing what the factories produced. But electricity also created the opportunity for firms to produce new goods and services, such as elevators and escalators, that did not exist before. Similarly, the Internet both enhances productivity and also enables the development of new goods and services.

ECONOMIC MILESTONE

1935: First Synthetic Fiber

Scientists are always looking for new uses for old materials. One of the biggest success stories came in 1935, when chemists at DuPont learned how to turn coal into a silk-like fiber they called *nylon*. Within a few years, nylon and other synthetic fibers were being used in parachutes and women's stockings. In toothbrushes, they used it to replace boars' hair bristles. Soon, the production and use of synthetic fibers became a multibillion-dollar industry.

ECONOMIC MILESTONE

1941: First TV Commercial

Companies such as Google and Facebook make the bulk of their money by selling advertising, which helps support services such as Google Maps. But it's important to remember that video advertising is a relatively recent innovation. The Bulova Watch Company ran a short ad before the television broadcast of a Brooklyn Dodgers–Philadelphia Phillies baseball game in 1941. Bulova paid less than $10 for the 20-second spot, which was the first TV commercial. By providing television stations with a source of revenue, commercials turned the innovation of television into a rapidly expanding business. In 2017, advertisers paid $5 million for a 30-second ad in the Super Bowl.

Quality of Life

A **qualify-of-life innovation** does exactly what it says: enhances the quality of life for you and those around you. The clearest example is an improvement in health care technology that lets you or your loved ones live longer or better. For example, Alzheimer's disease–a debilitating form of dementia involving loss of memory and alterations to thinking–currently afflicts almost 6 million U.S. adults, mostly the elderly, and that number is likely to rise quickly as the population ages. Right now, there is no cure. But if medical science could produce a way of even reducing the severity of Alzheimer's, that would be a tremendous quality-of-life innovation.

quality-of-life innovation
Technological change that enhances the quality of life for you and those around you.

The latest quality-of-life innovation, of course, was the development of a COVID vaccine in record time (for a source of possible innovations in health care, see **"Spotlight: The Biotech Revolution"**).

SPOTLIGHT: THE BIOTECH REVOLUTION

The next big wave of innovation may come from *biotechnology*, which is the use of new techniques to modify living cells and biological molecules. Scientists have labored hard in recent years, and there have been enormous advances in this area. These include the decoding of the human genome, a much deeper understanding of how the human body works, and the ability to manipulate the internal workings of cells.

Biotech has the potential to create enormous breakthroughs in medical care, agriculture, and even energy. In theory, once we know the underlying workings of the human body, it should be possible to create drugs or treatments targeted directly at cancer, diabetes, or any one of a number of medical or genetic problems.

The Food and Drug Administration (FDA) has approved important new drugs over the past few years, including a cure for Hepatitis C. Many more potential treatments are currently being tested for safety and "efficacy" (i.e., do they actually produce results). Typically, it can take 10 years or more to transform promising scientific research into tested and approved products available to ordinary patients.

The mRNA COVID vaccines from Pfizer and Moderna were an important exception to the usual slow process. The highly effective and safe vaccines against COVID were developed, tested through extensive clinical trials, approved, and put into production in record time. Although some people were understandably concerned about the speed, the vaccines are in wide use around the world and appear to be as safe as the original clinical trials suggested.

Technological advances that reduce pollution also fall into the category of quality-of-life innovations. Less pollution does not necessarily show up in any of the usual measures of economic output (as we will see in **Chapter 19**). Nevertheless, most people prefer a cleaner environment for its health benefits, for the beauty of nature and the safety of wildlife it enhances, and for its beneficial impact on our planet's ecology.

What's the difference between a quality-of-life innovation you enjoy and an ordinary innovation that gives you pleasure–say a new generation of iPads? In the language of **Chapter 6**, a quality-of-life innovation generates positive externalities or reduces negative externalities. Diminishing pollution affects many people simultaneously. Similarly, an improvement in the health of a parent will improve our quality of life as well.

INNOVATIVE ACTIVITIES (LO15-3)

LO15-3 Explain the link between innovation and innovative activities.

innovative activities

Any economic activities primarily directed at creating and developing new products, processes, ideas, knowledge, and technology.

Where do innovations come from? They don't simply fall out of the sky. Instead, innovation and technological change are the direct result of **innovative activities**. Those are any economic activities directed primarily at creating and developing new products, processes, ideas, knowledge, and technology. One example of an innovative activity would be a scientist studying the biochemistry underlying cancer. Another example would be an automobile company devoting resources to developing a fully electric car. Still another example would be an entrepreneur starting a new company to develop a new type of microprocessor or a company employing programmers and artists to create a new video game.

research and development (R&D)

Money and resources–particularly human resources–that economies or businesses devote to science and technology.

The amount of money available for **research and development (R&D)** is the most important measure of the amount of innovative activities going on in an economy. R&D represents money and resources–particularly human resources–that economies or businesses devote to science and technology. It can be undertaken by corporations, by the government, or by scholars in academic settings. Corporate funding for the development of a new drug, for example, comes under the heading of R&D. So does a government research grant to a physics professor for the study of superconductors. In sum, R&D is anything that moves the frontier of science and technology forward.

Figure 15.2 shows that in 2019, the U.S. public and private sectors spent almost $700 billion on R&D. The next largest is China, followed by Japan and Germany, though there is debate about whether such Chinese spending is being correctly measured. Most countries spend little on R&D.

Figure 15.2 The United States Leads in R&D Spending, 2019
If research and development were a sport, the United States would be the gold medal winner. This chart shows the top seven countries in the world, ranked by spending on R&D.

Source: National Science Foundation. Spending adjusted for differences in price levels.

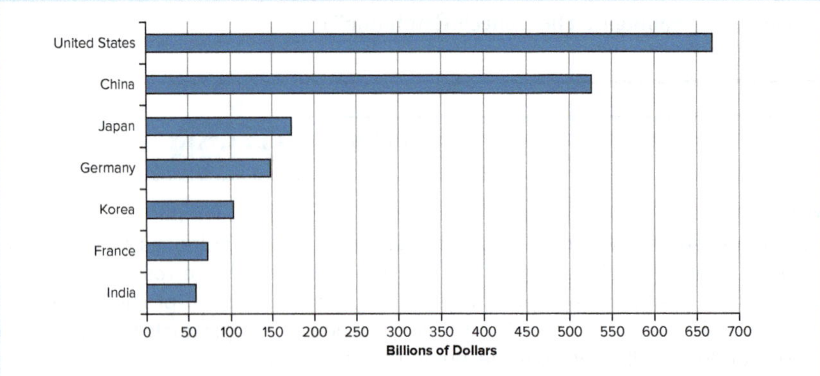

basic research

Scientific investigations that have no immediately obvious commercial applications.

One category of R&D is **basic research**, which is devoted to scientific investigations that have no immediately obvious commercial applications. In the past, big companies like AT&T and IBM did basic research in their labs. For example, two researchers at AT&T's Bell Labs–Arno A. Penzias and Robert W. Wilson–won the 1978 Nobel Prize in physics for their discovery of faint background radiation remaining from the "big bang" explosion that is believed to have given birth to the universe.

Today, however, basic research is performed mostly in universities and nonprofit institutions and is funded primarily by the federal government. Corporations, under much more intense competitive pressure, focus their resources on applied research and development. **Applied research** is scientific research focused on solving real-world problems, while **development** is aimed at creating commercial products. For example, if a pharmaceutical company spends heavily to test different approaches for fighting cancer, that is applied research. But testing a particular drug for safety counts as development. Similarly, when Tesla, the electric car maker, hires scientists and engineers to study new battery technologies, that counts as applied research. But working out the details of a new battery for a particular car counts as development spending.

applied research
Scientific research focused on solving real-world problems.

development
Innovative activities that are aimed toward creating a commercial product.

The Market for Innovative Activities

Traditionally, economists have treated technological change as a kind of black box, driven by nonmarket factors such as government funding for R&D. To some extent, that's still true. In particular, spending on basic R&D, which has no immediate economic payoff, is money that must come mainly from the government or from universities.

But, in many other cases, we can think about innovative activity as a service that can be bought and sold in a market, just like any other service (**Figure 15.3**). First, innovative activities have a price. The price of research, for example, might be the salary for a scientist for the year and the price of renting or buying the equipment. Or imagine that rather than trying to create new products by itself, a frozen-food business pays a scientific research laboratory to do its development. In that case, the price of innovative activities is the amount the frozen-food company pays per month to the scientific research firm.

Figure 15.3 The Supply and Demand of Innovative Activities
This figure shows supply and demand curves for innovative activities. The price might be the salary for a scientist, and the quantity might be the number of scientists employed.

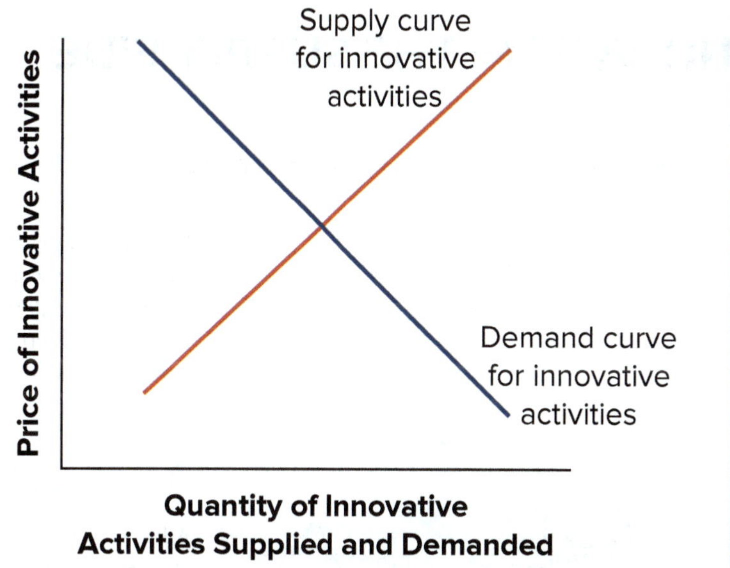

The **supply curve for innovative activities** tells us the quantity of innovative activities that are supplied, given their price. For example, given the wages paid to scientists, the supply curve tells us how many people will be available for science and engineering jobs, as opposed to law or other occupations.

supply curve for innovative activities
Reports the quantity of innovative activities that are supplied, given their price.

Similarly, the **demand curve for innovative activities** tells us the quantity of innovative activities businesses will want to fund, given the price. For example, given the wages paid to engineers and scientists, the demand curve tells us how many resources a business is willing to devote to creating a new product. The willingness to spend on knowledge creation, of course, depends on how much profit the business can expect to make from the new product and whether it's easy for competitors to copy.

demand curve for innovative activities
Reports the quantity of innovative activities businesses will want to fund, given the price of those innovative activities.

Consider, for example, the market for research into cancer-fighting drugs. The price of research is the amount of money a business pays for, say, one year's worth of research by a scientist. The greater the price, the more scientists will move into anticancer research, so the supply curve slopes up. Meanwhile, the higher the price of such research, the less of it drug companies will want to buy. Hence, the demand curve for innovative activities slopes down. For another example of the market for innovative activities, see **"Spotlight: Private Space Tourism."**

SPOTLIGHT: PRIVATE SPACE TOURISM

For an example of the market for innovative activities in action, consider private space travel. Since the first manned space flights in 1961, space travel had been solely the responsibility of government agencies, mainly in the United States and Russia. These agencies did not operate by markets. Instead, they were willing to spend tens of billions of dollars to put people into space for both prestige and research.

Private businesses could not afford that kind of money. For private space travel to become a reality, it had to become a lot cheaper than government-funded space travel—and just as safe. For years, that didn't seem possible.

But recently, two sets of market forces converged to make private space travel possible. First, there is suddenly greater demand for private space travel by a long line of rich individuals willing to pay big bucks to go into space. That made it more attractive to research relatively inexpensive space travel. Second, new materials made it possible to build a safe spacecraft more cheaply.

In other words, both the demand and supply curves for the development of relatively inexpensive space travel shifted to the right. The result was far more research into private space travel.

A milestone was reached in July, 2021 when Virgin Galactic—a company started by Virgin Atlantic owner Richard Branson—put Branson and several other passengers into a short flight into space. Later that same month, Blue Origin—a space company started by Amazon founder Jeff Bezos—put Bezos and other passengers into space as well. As of April 2023, Virgin Galactic is preparing to charge $450,000 to potential passengers for a short trip into space.

See Virgin Galactic, https://brochure.virgingalactic.com/pricing for more information.

How does this market-based view of innovation help us? It tells us that if we want more innovation, we should look at factors that shift the supply and demand curves for innovative activity. That's what we will look at in the next two sections.

INNOVATION: THE SUPPLY SIDE (LO15-4)

LO15-4 Identify and discuss the factors that affect the supply curves for innovative activities.

George Doyle/Stockbyte/Getty Images

In this section, we will look more closely at factors that can move the supply curve for innovative activities. These include the availability of scientists and engineers, availability of venture capital, and location of an innovation cluster. In the next section, we'll also examine the factors that can cause the demand curve for innovative activities to shift.

Availability of Scientists and Engineers

A key factor affecting the supply curve for innovative activities is the availability of scientists and engineers–the people who perform actual research and development. That's consistently a problem in the United States because the number of people getting PhDs in science and engineering has not kept up with demand.

Part of the problem is simply that wages for scientists and engineers have not risen as fast as the wages for other occupations a highly educated person can enter. According to the Bureau of Labor Statistics, the average salary of a biochemist or biophysicist was $113,000 in 2021, while the average salary for a chemist was $89,000. By contrast, the average salary of a lawyer was $148,000.

As a result, many members of the scientific and engineering workforce in the United States are originally from other countries. As of 2021, for example, roughly 50-60 percent of computer and mathematical scientists with advanced degrees were foreign-born. Some enter the United States as graduate students and remain here to work; others come because they are offered jobs.

There's a heated debate about whether the immigration of skilled scientists and engineers is a good thing for the United States. On the one hand, it pushes the supply schedule of the market for scientists and engineers to the right, lowering the pay of U.S. scientists and engineers, as shown in **Figure 15.4**. On the other hand, it raises the number of engineers and scientists, which pushes the supply schedule for innovation to the right and increases the amount of innovation, as shown in **Figure 15.5**. The net result, as is true for most types of foreign trade, is that the influx of foreign-born scientists and engineers is probably a good thing for the country as a whole but is problematic for a subgroup of the population.

Figure 15.4 How Immigration Affects the Market for Engineers and Scientists
An increase in immigrant engineers and scientists pushes the supply curve for engineers and scientists to the right and lowers their wage.

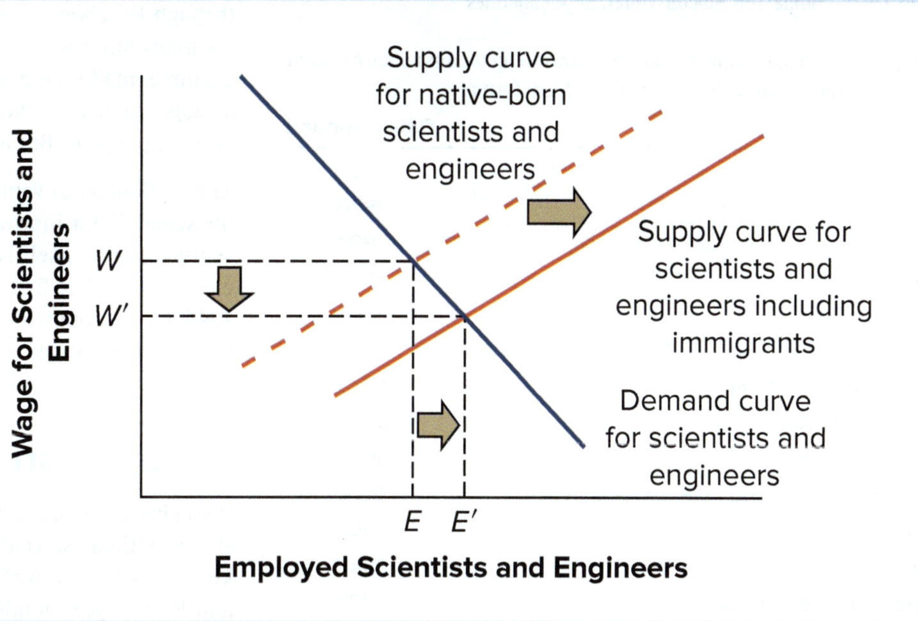

Figure 15.5 How Immigration Affects Innovation
Immigration increases the supply of engineers and scientists, which pushes the supply curve for innovative activities to the right. The result is more and cheaper innovation.

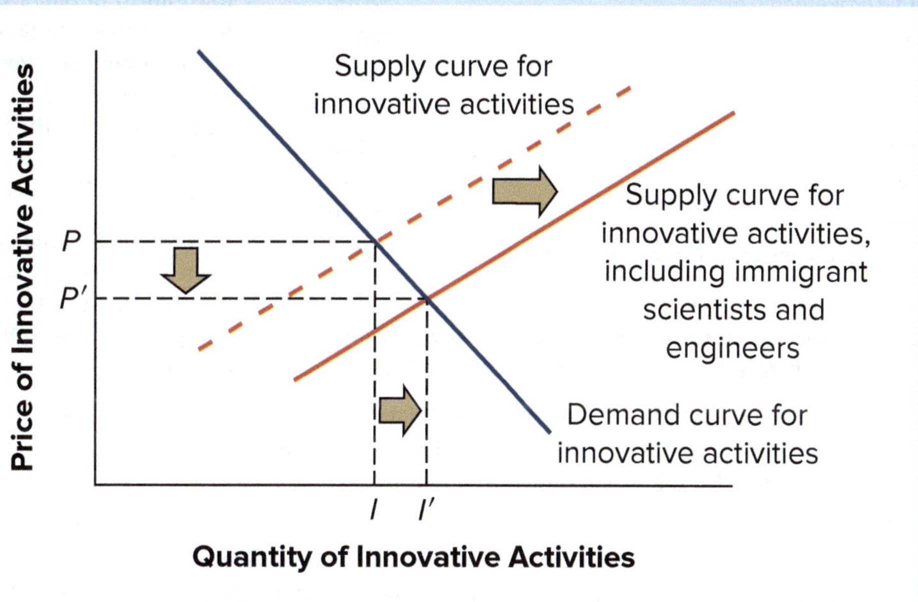

Availability of Venture Capital

It doesn't do any good to have a bright idea if you can't support yourself and a small staff to develop it. And banks typically won't lend money to brand new businesses without a track record of profits.

One solution to this problem is venture capital, which we discussed in **Chapter 13**. Venture capital funds collect money from insurance companies, pension funds, college endowments, and wealthy individuals, and they invest those funds in high-risk technology start-up companies. Venture capitalists closely monitor the start-up companies they invest in, help them with key strategic decisions, and even replace the company founders if it looks like they are not up to the task.

Venture capitalists expect that most of their investments will not create successful companies. In fact, they accept a failure rate that would make a banker's hair turn gray. Most companies funded by venture capitalists never become profitable and eventually close.

Table 15.1 Some Top Silicon Valley/SF Companies

This is a partial list of important or well-known tech companies based in the Silicon Valley/San Francisco region of California.

Company	Date Founded
Airbnb	2008
Apple	1976
Cisco	1984
Dropbox	2007
eBay	1995
Electronic Arts	1982
Facebook (now Meta)	2004
Google (now Alphabet)	1998
Hewlett-Packard	1939
Instagram (purchased by Facebook in 2012)	2010
Intel	1968
Intuit	1983
Linden Lab (Second Life)	1999
LinkedIn (purchased by Microsoft in 2016)	2002
Lyft	2012
Niantic (Pokémon Go)	2015
OpenAI	2015
Oracle	1977
Pinterest	2010
Twitter	2006
Uber	2009
Yahoo!	1994
YouTube (purchased by Google in 2006)	2005
Zoom	2011

However, the big successes–starting with Intel and running through Facebook and Google–are truly impressive and make up for many failures. Venture capitalists who invested in Google, for example, made quite a bit of money. As noted in **Chapter 13**, the average return on venture capital is thought to be about 25 percent per year. But any particular deal is extremely risky.

The availability of venture capital has the effect of shifting the supply schedule for innovation to the right. What's interesting is that venture capital itself is actually a relative innovation in the financial markets. The first modern venture capital fund was started in 1946. Other countries have some venture capital, but far less than in the United States.

Location in an Innovation Cluster

If you list some of the great tech companies of the world, a healthy share of them started in the area south of San Francisco now known as Silicon Valley. Two engineers named Gordon Moore and Bob Noyce founded Intel in 1968 in Santa Clara, California, then a sleepy little town about 20 minutes south of Stanford University. Google has its headquarters in Mountain View, the next town north of Santa Clara, and Facebook is based in Palo Alto, just a bit closer to San Francisco. OpenAI, the company that got so much publicity for releasing ChatGBT in November 2022, is actually based in San Francisco (which now is more or less treated as part of the Silicon Valley cluster). Zoom, the communications program that sprung to prominence in the pandemic, is based in San Jose (see **Table 15.1**).

It's not simply coincidence. The chances of innovations occurring seem to improve when innovative companies are clustered together because they can share ideas and workers. A pool of skilled and experienced labor moves from company to company. There are good resources, like lawyers who understand technology and start-ups. And there are sources of financial support, like nearby venture capital firms and successful entrepreneurs.

In addition, innovation is easier when there is a major university nearby. Google and Yahoo! were both started by Stanford students. Other technology hot spots include Cambridge, Massachusetts, which has become the world center for biotech, and Bangalore, which has become the center for software in India. New innovation clusters include New York City, London, and Berlin.

innovation cluster

A geographic region in which the resources for innovation are plentiful and the supply curve for innovative activities is shifted to the right.

In other words, an **innovation cluster** is a region where the resources for innovation are plentiful so that the supply curve for innovative activities is shifted to the right. As a result, innovation is easier for a business located in an innovation cluster like Silicon Valley. Moreover, once innovation clusters get started, they tend to persist. Silicon Valley, for example, has retained its magic. Some of the hottest new companies, like Zoom and OpenAI, have started there in recent years (see **Table 15.1**). The power of clustering continues.

INNOVATION: THE DEMAND SIDE (LO15-5)

LO15-5 Identify and discuss the factors that affect the demand curves for innovative activities.

The demand for innovative activities is a tricky thing to measure. Everybody likes the newest or best technology–unless your job is being eliminated by automation, or your home is threatened by pollution from a new factory down the street, or your scenic view is blocked by energy-generating windmills. The truth is that it's not unusual for new technologies to face opposition–from existing companies, from workers who feel their jobs are threatened, or simply from ordinary people who don't like change.

That's why technological change needs to be propelled by a strong force–which usually is the profit motive. What sustains innovation is the fact that businesses can make money from it. Although, in theory, the government can fund and encourage innovative activities, in practice no society has been able to sustain a commitment to innovation over a long period without the profit motive.

So, let's look at the factors that can determine the demand curve for innovative activities.

Return and Risk from Innovative Activities

return from innovative activities

The payback to spending on innovative activities such as R&D.

risk from innovative activities

The possibility that spending on innovative activities such as R&D will not pay off.

The demand for innovative activities is closely tied to their ability to create profits for companies and benefits for society. Economic studies repeatedly show that the **return from innovative activities**–that is, the long-term payback to businesses from spending on research, development, and all sorts of other activities that have the potential of producing innovations–is very high. For example, a dollar spent on R&D can yield an average return of 25–50 percent per year. That's excellent. By comparison, the average annual return from investing in the stock market is about 10 percent.

However, most corporate executives view R&D spending with trepidation because the chances of failure are so high. Although the return on R&D spending is high, all sorts of things can go wrong when you try something new. In other words, the **risk from innovative activities**–the possibility that spending on R&D and other innovative activities will not pay off–is high.

The pharmaceutical industry understands the risk of innovative activity well. Drug companies start with literally thousands of compounds they have reason to think might be good candidates to treat illness. Then each compound goes through a multistep, multiyear process that includes laboratory evaluation, animal testing, testing on humans, and then clinical trials to see whether the new drug safely does what it's supposed to do and is measurably more effective than existing treatments. At any step along the way, a proposed compound can fail expensively, and many do. In the end, very few successful new drugs are introduced each year. In 2022, the Food and Drug Administration (FDA) approved 37 new drugs, down from 50 in 2021. (The development, testing, and approval of the COVID vaccines was an unusual case, as explained in **Spotlight: Operation Warp Speed**).

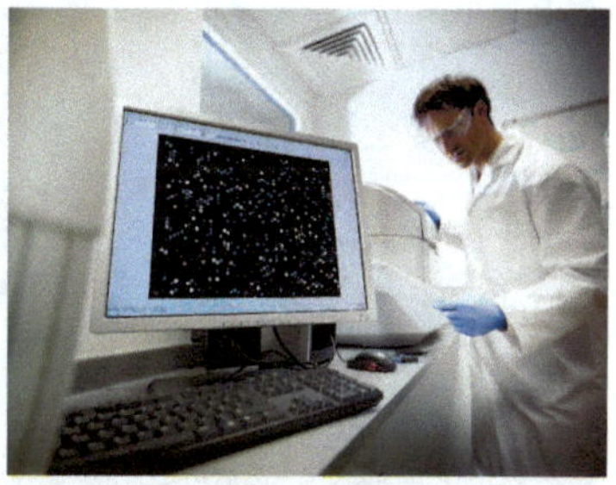

Monty Rakusen/Cultura RF/Getty Images

Corporate executives have another reason for being reluctant to put money into R&D and other innovative activities. In many cases, the company that pays for research may not get all or even most of the benefits. The private return from innovative activities is the gain to the original company sponsoring the research, while the social return from innovation is the benefit to the whole economy. In general, the social return will be much greater than the private return because it's difficult to keep good ideas fenced in.

Xerox is a classic example of a company that came up with great ideas but reaped little benefit from them. In the 1970s, the Rochester, New York-based company had a research facility in Palo Alto, California, that helped develop many great innovations for the personal computer, including the mouse and the graphical user interface. But Xerox, mainly focused on copiers at the time, was slow to take advantage of these innovations. Instead, Apple and Microsoft developed the graphical user interface and made big money from it. The social return to innovation was very high in this case, and the private return to the original inventor was low or practically zero.

SPOTLIGHT: OPERATION WARP SPEED

The goal of Operation Warp Speed, started under President Donald Trump in April 2020, was simple: To develop safe and effective vaccines against the new coronavirus pandemic, and to manufacture hundreds of millions of doses as quickly as possible. Under normal circumstances, even after a new vaccine was developed, it might take years to recruit volunteers for clinical testing. Then, if the vaccine was approved, new manufacturing facilities would need to be built. And if the vaccine was not approved, it might take years for the original company or a new company to try a different approach.

To save time, Operation Warp Speed did everything at once. First, the government started with several different vaccine candidates using different approaches, to raise the odds that at least one would provide an effective vaccine. Second, government funding meant that the pharma companies could set up their clinical trial sites and have their volunteers ready to go as soon as the safety of the vaccine candidates was established. Third, the government subsidized the construction of manufacturing facilities and the purchase of crucial materials before the clinical testing was done. Fourth, the government issued guaranteed advance purchase contracts for vaccine doses, reducing the financial risk for the pharma companies. Meanwhile, the FDA served in its usual role as an independent judge, promising only to approve vaccines that met its standards.

Operation Warp Speed worked, producing several safe and effective COVID vaccines in less than a year. And the economic and health benefits of those vaccines far outweighed the cost of the program.

Patents and Other Intellectual Property Protection

intellectual property protection

Laws that make it more difficult to copy innovations.

Companies are more likely to invest in creating innovative new products and services if they can make money with them. And making money is more likely if they can protect their innovation from being copied, at least for a while. For this reason, the United States and other developed countries have several different means of **intellectual property protection**–that is, laws that make it difficult to copy innovations.

patent

A protection against copying granted by the U.S. Patent and Trademark Office to inventors for their discoveries.

The most important means of protection against copying is a **patent**, granted by the U.S. Patent and Trademark Office (USPTO) to a person who "who invents or discovers any new and useful process, machine, manufacture, or composition of matter, or any new and useful improvement thereof."* Such a patent is a grant from the government that allows an inventor to control the use of his or her innovation for a set period, currently 20 years. In particular, the inventor has "the right to exclude others from making, using, offering for sale, or selling the invention throughout the United States."

Thomas Edison at work.

Everett Historical/Shutterstock

Inventions protected by patents run the gamut from very important to totally weird. In the 1800s, Thomas Edison patented the electric lightbulb, the microphone used in telephones, the phonograph, and the motion picture camera. AT&T patented the transistor, which was invented in AT&T's Bell Labs in 1948.

The technology in your smartphone is covered by hundreds of thousands of different patents. Many of the medicines you take are covered by patents as well.

Patents have two purposes. First, they allow an inventor to benefit from innovation by making it harder for others to duplicate it. If you have a patent on an invention, no one can use your invention without your permission until the patent runs out.

The second purpose of a patent is to encourage inventors to share ideas with the rest of society. You can license your invention to others, allowing them to use it, and collect royalties from them (a share in their profits). Without patents, you might be tempted to conceal your idea to protect it from imitators.

The transistor patent is an interesting case. The three scientists credited with inventing the transistor won a Nobel Prize for their achievement, but their employer, AT&T, never got any economic benefits. At the time, the company was fighting an antitrust suit, and it was sensitive about its public image. AT&T was, therefore, willing to license the patent rights to the transistor for a relatively low fee. Then, as part of the 1956 settlement of the antitrust suit, it let anyone use the transistor patent without charge.

Intensity of Competition

Remember from **Chapter 5** that in a competitive market, companies with a lower cost curve drive out ones with a higher cost curve over the long run. If you have an innovation that allows you to offer the same or better product at a lower cost, you'll be more successful in the marketplace.

Innovation is one of the key ways to get a competitive advantage. Boeing gets more orders by creating more fuel-efficient airplanes than the ones sold by Airbus. One computer manufacturer gets an advantage by designing a computer that is faster and cheaper than those of its rivals.

intensity of competition

The pressure on businesses to innovate to get a competitive advantage.

Thus, a key factor driving demand for innovative activities is **intensity of competition**. One of the most important benefits of economic competition is that it spurs faster creation and adoption of new technology by both existing firms and new firms. Let's be blunt: Most companies would avoid the risk of innovation activity if they did not face the threat of competition.

A note of caution here: If a market is close to pure competition, profits may be low. If so, no companies may have enough extra money to spend on long-run research. What's more, rivals may immediately copy any new ideas that one company comes up with. As a result, economists sometimes worry that too much competition may slow down technological change.

* Source: U.S. Patent and Trademark Office (USPTO).

The Diffusion of New Technologies

If you buy a sandwich and eat it, nobody else can eat it. In contrast, if you spend money developing a new technology, the knowledge you create can be used by someone else as long as it is not restricted by a patent.

Technological diffusion is the process by which new ideas spread from one person or business to other parts of the economy. It sometimes seems as if any successful idea is immediately picked up and imitated by competitors. The initial high ratings for shows like *Below Deck, The Bachelor, American Idol, Top Chef,* and *Real Housewives of Orange County* spawned many similar projects.

technological diffusion
The process by which new ideas spread from one person or business to other parts of the economy.

However, in most areas of the economy, technological diffusion takes longer than in entertainment. In medicine, for example, it takes a long time for doctors to adopt new and better treatments, even for common problems such as strokes and heart attacks.

The same thing is true in corporations. Economic studies show wide differences between the productivity levels of different factories making the same products. Some people and companies are more willing to take the risk of adopting a new technology, whereas others wait until that new technology is mature (see **"How It Works: Innovation and Youth"**). It can take 10, 20, even 30 years before an innovation spreads through the whole economy. The process of technological diffusion is slow and gradual.

HOW IT WORKS: INNOVATION AND YOUTH

It often seems as if young people adopt new technologies faster than middle-aged or older workers. In part, that's because the young have more malleable minds. But there are also economic reasons young workers get more benefits from spending time learning something new.

Think about it this way. A 25-year-old worker can expect to be in the labor force for another 40 years. A 55-year-old worker can expect to be employed for another 10 or so years. That means the young worker will get many more years of benefits from learning how to use, say, instant messaging. That's a big economic incentive.

In addition, the 55-year-old worker is typically paid more. That means the opportunity cost of his or her time is higher than for the 25-year-old. So, the older worker gets lower benefits and higher costs from spending time learning a new technology. That helps explain why many older workers seem to lag in adopting current innovations.

YOUR ECONOMIC LIFE: Innovation over the Next 10 Years

What innovations are likely to have the biggest impact on your life over the next 10 years? The past 10 years have seen a tremendous transformation in the way you use data. Mobile broadband, smartphones, social networks, and online entertainment allow you to be connected all the time, if you want to be.

But the next 10 years may very well bring changes in the way you relate to the physical world. Your car may be not totally self-driving, but it will become a lot smarter, able to sense potential collisions, and respond accordingly. Health care will increasingly rely on telemedicine: monitoring and diagnosis at home. Artificial intelligence papers will help you write e-mails and reports.

Your job possibilities will change as well. Some jobs will disappear, while new jobs will be created. For example, the rise of e-commerce has meant fewer minimum-wage jobs for cashiers, and more positions working in e-commerce fulfillment centers, which tend to pay better.

Similarly, the increased use of technology in construction–including robots and drones–will change the mix of workers and skills. Rather than needing manual labor to lay bricks and rivet beams, construction workers will be programming and monitoring automated machinery and supervising drone pilots.

If you work in health care, that industry will also change. The shift to electronic health records has been bumpy and difficult. Nevertheless, health care will increasingly become a digital industry, and jobs will require more knowledge of technology.

One final thought: You may be worried that technological change will make it harder to find good jobs. History, though, suggests that technological change actually creates more well-paid jobs, rather than fewer. The real issue is making sure you have the right education and training to take advantage of the opportunities.

CONCLUSION

It's impossible to imagine what today's economy would be like without technological change, globalization, and financial markets, the topics of this chapter and the previous two. The most vivid example is the Internet, which was tiny 15 years ago and now pervades our entire lives. At the same time, our ties to other countries have transformed the whole economy, while the ups and downs of the financial markets have had a pervasive impact.

In particular, change affects all of us in our working lives—what type of work we do, how we are paid, who hires us, and how we spend our days. In the next chapter, we will examine the labor market, which is one of the most important markets in the economy. That will help us better understand why some people are gaining from financial markets, globalization, and technological change, while others seem to be worse off.

15 SUMMARY

1. Technological change is the introduction to the market of new goods and services, or new processes of production, that did not exist before. Without technological change, it's impossible to get big increases in living standards. The most recent wave of technological change was the information revolution. Following Moore's law, electronic devices get smaller, cheaper, faster, and more powerful every year. ***(LO15-1)***
2. Three types of innovation are productivity enhancements, the creation of new goods and services, and quality-of-life improvements. ***(LO15-2)***
3. Traditionally, economists have treated technological change as a kind of black box, driven by nonmarket factors. But it has become clear in recent years that the creation of new knowledge is an economic activity or service that can be bought and sold just like any other service. Innovative activities are any economic activities directed primarily at creating and developing new ideas, new knowledge, and new technology. ***(LO15-3)***
4. Innovative activities can be bought and sold in the market. The supply curve for innovative activities tells us the quantity of innovative activities that are supplied, given their price. The supply curve for innovative activities can be affected by the availability of scientists and engineers, access to venture capital, and location. ***(LO15-4)***
5. Similarly, the demand curve for innovative activities tells us the quantity of innovative activities that businesses will want to fund, given the price. The demand curve for innovative activities can be affected by the return from innovative activities, by patents and other forms of intellectual property protection, and by the intensity of competition. Unlike ordinary goods and services—which can be consumed by only one buyer—new technologies and ideas can spread from one person or business to the rest of the economy. ***(LO15-5)***

KEY TERMS AND CONCEPTS

technological change

production possibility frontier (PPF)

innovations

Moore's law

information revolution

productivity-enhancing innovation

creation of new goods and services

quality-of-life innovation

innovative activities

research and development (R&D)

basic research

applied research

development

supply curve for innovative activities

demand curve for innovative activities

innovation cluster

return from innovative activities

risk from innovative activities

intellectual property protection

patent

intensity of competition

technological diffusion

connect PROBLEMS

1. Technological change is the surest route to higher living standards. For example, farmers can now use sensors in their fields to precisely identify the best times to plant, water, and harvest crops. This enables farmers to produce more food using the same amount of resources, such as land and fertilizer. *(LO15-1)*
   a) Draw a supply-demand diagram for food. In the diagram, show how technological change in farming affects the supply curve for food. Label the new equilibrium point.
   b) Does technological change in farming raise or lower the price of food? Does technological change in farming raise or lower the quantity of food demanded?
   c) Would you expect technological change in farming to reduce or increase the number of people who go hungry? Explain.
   d) Would you expect technological change in farming to reduce or increase the exports of food? Explain.
2. Moore's law says that microprocessor performance improves at a rapid pace. For each of the following statements, state whether Moore's law would make it more or less likely. *(LO15-1)*
   a) Cell phones getting smaller.
   b) The cost of Internet service rising.
   c) The creation of new companies like Facebook.
   d) Supermarkets charging a fee for using a credit card.
   e) More useful examples of artificial intelligence programs.
3. Say whether each of the following is mainly a productivity-enhancing innovation, a creation of new goods and services, or a quality-of-life innovation. *(LO15-2)*
   a) A car that emits less pollution.
   b) A car that uses less gasoline.
   c) A drug that cures lung cancer.
   d) Robot construction workers that can put up buildings.
   e) Passenger drones that can carry up to four people by air over short distances.
   f) A drug for treating COVID.
4. Which of the following represents an increase in innovative activity? Explain. *(LO15-3)*
   a) A drug company hires more scientists to work on a new cancer drug.
   b) A department store hires more sales clerks.
   c) A university buys faster computers for its research labs.
   d) An automobile manufacturer tells its engineers to figure out how to reduce the cost of car production.
5. Many U.S. companies opened research facilities in China and India, where the lower cost of labor let them hire more scientists and engineers. Consider a company trying to develop passenger drones. *(LO15-3)*
   a) Draw the supply and demand curves for innovative activities directed toward the development of passenger drones.
   b) Suppose the company moves some of the development of passenger drones to China and India. Does this affect the supply curve or the demand curve for innovative activities? Show the change on your supply-demand diagram.
   c) What happens to the quantity of innovative activity when new research centers open abroad? Do we get more or fewer new models of passenger drones?
   d) Suppose government agencies are banned from using drones designed in China, because of worries about the Chinese military being able to tap into data from the drones. How does this affect the supply and demand curve for drone innovation.
6. There's a very heavy concentration of biotechnology firms in the Boston area that are closely attached to the Massachusetts Institute of Technology. This concentration of biotech is usually considered one of the premier innovation clusters in the United States. If you were starting a new biotech company, which of the following would be an advantage of locating to the Boston area? *(LO15-4)*
   a) A large pool of well-trained scientists.
   b) Warm climate.
   c) Lack of competition from other companies in the same industry.
   d) Easy access to special technical equipment.
7. Suppose that a drug company spends $1 billion developing a new treatment that potentially cures cancer. *(LO15-4)*
   a) Is the private return from this innovative activity best measured by increased life expectancy for patients, or by higher profits for the drug company?
   b) Is the social return from this innovative activity best measured by increased life expectancy for patients, or by higher profits for the drug company?

8. Imagine that a company has a monopoly on video game sales in a country. That is, it is the only company allowed to develop and sell new video games. The company has a choice: It can spend $500,000 to slightly update its best-selling game or $100 million to write a completely new game, which might or might not be a success. ***(LO15-5)***

   a) As a monopolist, explain which choice the company might make.
   b) Now suppose the video game company faces new competition in the form of a hot new game imported from another country. Explain which choice the company might make.

9. Suppose workers are going to retire at a higher age and stay in the workforce longer. ***(LO15-5)***

   a) Does the higher retirement age increase or decrease the willingness of workers to learn new technology?
   b) Does postponed retirement affect the supply curve or the demand curve for innovative activities? What happens to the quantity of innovative activities?

10. Companies are putting large amounts of money into developing self-driving trucks (also known as "autonomous trucks"). Self-driving trucks are expected to save money by reducing labor costs. In addition, because self-driving trucks can travel all night, they can get cargo to its destination faster. Finally, self-driving trucks will reduce the occupational death rate for truckers, which today is quite high. ***(LO15-5)***

    a) Draw the supply-demand diagram for R&D spending on self-driving trucks. Suppose the wage of truck drivers rises. Show how that affects the demand curve for R&D spending for self-driving. Label the new equilibrium point.
    b) Does the amount spent on self-driving truck R&D go up or down?
    c) Suppose Congress passes a law imposing a big fine on trucking companies for each death of a truck driver. Show how that affects the demand curve for R&D spending for self-driving. Label the new equilibrium point.

CH 16

ECONOMICS OF THE LABOR MARKET

Purestock/Getty Images

LEARNING OBJECTIVES

After reading this chapter, you should be able to:

LO16-1 Define the labor supply and demand curves.
LO16-2 Identify factors affecting labor market equilibrium.
LO16-3 Explain why different workers may receive different wages.
LO16-4 Describe effects of government regulation on the labor market.
LO16-5 Identify the forces driving long-term labor supply, including immigration.

The *labor market*—the buying and selling of the time and effort of different kinds of workers—is the most important market in the economy. There is no productive activity that does not require some input of labor.

True, the nature of work has changed over time: Many people go to school now to become nurses and medical technicians, instead of finding a job in a factory just out of high school. There are literally tens of thousands of online want ads for "social media managers," a profession that barely existed in 2000. But, in the end, human input is essential for all productive activities.

As this textbook was being revised in early 2023, the unemployment rate was below 4 percent. That was good news, showing that new jobs were being created. Still, the Bureau of Labor Statistics reported that average real wages for private-sector workers in early 2023 were roughly at pre-pandemic levels, leaving many Americans with a sense of running in place.

Understanding the labor market, and how it evolves, is crucial for understanding the world we live in. In many respects, the labor market functions the same way as the basic markets we described in **Chapters 2** and **3**. *Wages*—the price of labor—are set by the interaction between supply and demand, just like prices in the market for fruit or for homes.

But there is, of course, a big difference between fruit and people: People have rights, and unlike fruit, they complain bitterly when they feel they've been unfairly treated. As a result, the labor market has some special characteristics, including rules regulating how many hours people can be required to work and the minimum wage they must be paid. In this chapter, we will explore the nature of the labor market in the United States and the global economy. We will discuss the labor market impact of immigration, as well as new factors such as artificial intelligence and working from home. In addition, we will explain the similarities and differences between the labor market and the other markets we've studied so far.

THE BASICS OF THE LABOR MARKET (LO16-1)

LO16-1 Define the labor supply and demand curves.

When you're looking for a job, it may feel as if the odds are against you. There are so few open positions, and so many applicants who want to be hired. A company advertising a desirable, high-paying job may receive hundreds or even thousands of résumés, especially when the economy is weak.

But turn the situation around, and imagine that you are a manager trying to fill an open position. You have a mental picture of the skills, experience, and personality the perfect job candidate will have. Yet that perfect person may be impossible to find, especially if you can't pay a high enough wage to get the sort of person you want. As a result, some positions may stay open for months or even years. In February 2023, U.S. businesses reported almost 10 million open positions, even though almost 6 million people were unemployed and searching for jobs.

In some ways, the labor market is a giant matching game in which job seekers hop from interview to interview, and managers roll prospective employees in and out of the office, with everyone looking for the right fit. The pain of matching is eased by such innovations as online job sites that make it easier to quickly scan many potential jobs and candidates (see **"Spotlight: The Rise of the Online Job Search"**).

SPOTLIGHT: THE RISE OF THE ONLINE JOB SEARCH

Employers with a job opening used to have limited options for filling it: They could put a help-wanted ad in the local newspaper, or they could ask friends and acquaintances whether they knew anyone who was qualified. Both avenues were chancy. Friends might not know anyone right for the job. And the best candidate might not read the newspaper that week—or worse, might live in a different city.

In 1994, a Boston area advertising executive named Jeff Taylor created an alternative: the Monster Board, an online site for matching job seekers with employers. At the beginning, it listed about 200 job openings, but, over time, it grew. In 1999, the site was renamed Monster.com.

Other job search websites, such as Indeed.com, soon followed. As of February 2023, Indeed, which calls itself "the world's #1 job site," covered more than 60 countries. Indeed.com and sites like it improve the job search process for employers and workers in several ways.

First, unlike newspaper classified ads, job search websites typically allow the job seeker to search for key job characteristics, such as desired skills. Second, a job seeker can potentially look at all national jobs or focus down on one geographic area. Economists agree that job search websites should result in faster, better job matches and a better-functioning labor market.

ECONOMIC MILESTONE

1969: The Shortest Stretch of Unemployment

In 1969, workers without jobs were unemployed for less than 8 weeks, on average. That's the shortest time on record. By contrast, in 2023, the average unemployed worker was searching for a new job for 19 weeks, despite the low unemployment rate.

The Labor Supply Curve

What happens before the job search? Let's focus on the worker's side of the labor market first. The worker's first and most important decision is a simple one–should I look for a job or do something else? In other words, what is the opportunity cost of working? (In **Chapter 2**, we defined *opportunity cost* as the value or benefit of the next-best alternative use of time or money.) Remember that people have alternatives to working a steady job. For example, they can go to college or graduate school. They can stay home with their kids or grandkids. They can be supported by their parents or other relatives, or they can receive Social Security checks from the government. Or, especially if they are young or retired, they can travel or simply be at loose ends.

The **labor force** is the part of the adult population that is either working or actively looking for a job. An individual chooses whether to be in the labor force or not. The **labor force participation rate** is the share of the adult population that is in the labor force. In the United States as of March 2023, 68 percent of men and 57 percent of women 16 years old or over were in the labor force. These numbers reflect the reality that, even today, it is still socially more acceptable for women than for men to take off time from paid work, especially when raising children.

labor force
The part of the adult population that is either working or actively looking for a job.

labor force participation rate
The percentage of the adult population in the labor force.

The labor force participation rate also reflects the willingness and physical ability of individuals to work. For example, in the wake of the pandemic, some percentage of the population appears to be suffering from "long COVID"–a continuation of symptoms after the initial infection seems to be gone. Economists are watching to see if long COVID has a significant impact on the labor force.

The **labor supply curve** tells us, given the wage, how many people are in the labor force–that is, working or looking for work (see **Figure 16.1**). Alternatively, it can tell us the total quantity of labor hours supplied (remember from **Chapter 4** that labor can be measured by either people or hours). Generally speaking, the labor force participation rate of men between 25 and 54 is not very responsive to changes in pay. However, young people, women, and senior citizens are more likely to make decisions about whether to look for work based on the available pay. For example, the high-paying tech jobs of the 1990s caused many young people to forgo graduate school and go directly to work for a tech firm. Then, when the economy went into recession in 2001 and information technology companies experienced a sharp drop in demand, young people started applying to graduate schools instead. Similarly, the Great Recession increased the number of people who wanted to go to business schools.

labor supply curve
Reports, for each level of wages, how many people are in the labor force, or the quantity of labor hours supplied.

Figure 16.1 Labor Market Supply and Demand
The intersection of the labor demand schedule and the labor supply schedule determines the equilibrium wage *W* and the equilibrium quantity of labor *L*.

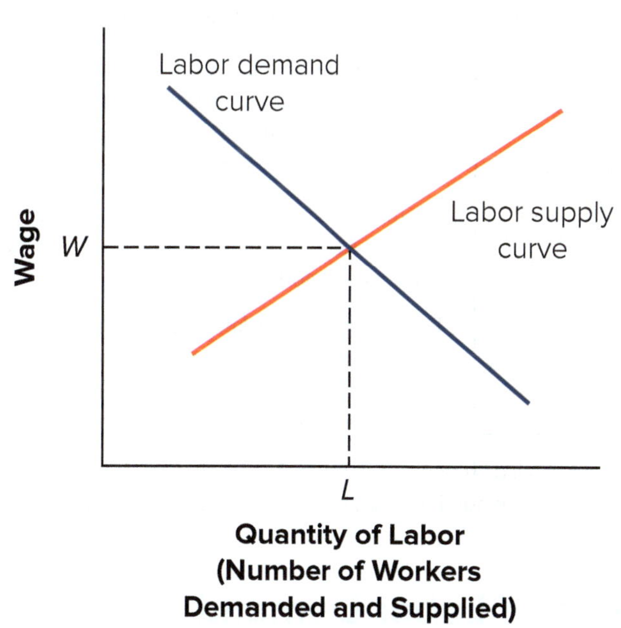

The labor force participation rate of adults over 65–a growing part of the workforce–is sensitive to the wages they might receive. That makes sense: They are already receiving Social Security benefits and have a bit more flexibility about whether they work.

In some jobs, such as retailing, it's also possible to choose whether you work full-time or part-time. In these types of jobs, it is natural to write the labor supply curve in terms of the total quantity of working hours that people are willing to supply. So, if three people are willing to work half-time–20 hours per week–at the going wage, that would be 60 hours per week of labor supplied.

job market decision
An individual's decision regarding what kind of job to look for.

The next decision is usually about what kind of job to look for. This is the **job market decision.** If you have an accounting degree, for example, you could look for a job as an accountant. Or you could try to get work as a cashier, or a computer programmer, or a journalist, or an actor. Each of these jobs is in a different labor market.

Each labor market has its own labor supply curve. In its simplest form, the labor supply curve for a given job reports how many people are looking for that kind of job at a particular wage. (Or, if we think of labor supply as measured in hours, the labor supply curve reports the total quantity of hours of labor people are willing to supply for that job at a particular wage.) The general rule is straightforward: If the wage for a job increases, more workers (or more hours) will be available for that job. This is the law of supply applied to the labor market.

Where do the additional workers come from? Some are lured into the labor market from other activities, such as schooling. Some switch from other lines of work. Schoolteachers sometimes become construction workers when the pay for construction climbs high enough. Economics and finance professors move into high-paying Wall Street jobs; journalists go into public relations. Government officials are hired at much higher pay by firms that lobby their former agencies.

The Labor Demand Curve

marginal product of labor
The extra amount of output a firm can generate by adding one more worker or one more hour of labor.

marginal revenue
The additional money a business gets from producing and selling one more unit of output; the additional money that a business gets from adding one more worker or one more hour of labor.

marginal cost of labor
The wage a firm must pay for an additional worker or for an additional hour of labor.

benefits
The part of worker compensation that includes employer-provided health care insurance and other supplements to the basic paycheck.

labor demand curve
Reports how many workers businesses will want to hire, or how many hours of labor they will want to pay for, given the market wage.

Recall from **Chapter 4** that businesses choose how many workers to hire because they have identified the number of employees that will help maximize their profit. This may seem obvious, but plenty of employers, like governments and nonprofits, such as most hospitals, have goals other than profit when they hire workers.

Let's look inside the mind of a manager at a profit-making business deciding whether to hire an additional worker. On the plus side is the increased production or output that an extra worker generates. This is called the **marginal product of labor**. For example, the marginal product of an added worker in a hair salon is the additional haircuts the salon can provide because of that worker. The marginal product of an extra stockbroker is the additional trades he or she brings into the brokerage house.

The **marginal revenue** of an additional worker is the extra revenue his or her efforts add to the business. In the simplest case, the marginal revenue is equal to the price of the output times the marginal product. For example, if the marginal product of an additional hairdresser is six haircuts per day, and the price of a haircut is $30, then the marginal revenue from hiring that added hairdresser is $180 per day.

To make the hiring decision, a manager must compare the added revenue generated by an additional worker to the added cost of hiring that worker. The **marginal cost of labor** is the wage the company must pay the additional worker. (We will think of the wage as including the cost of **benefits**, such as employer-provided health care insurance, and other supplements to the basic paycheck.)

In the short run, economic logic calls for the manager to keep hiring workers as long as the marginal revenue exceeds the wages paid to the workers (including benefits). As long as that's true, the additional workers will add to the profit of the business.

For jobs where workers are hired by the hour, such as retail sales clerks or waiters, the marginal revenue of labor is the extra revenue from one more hour of labor, while the marginal cost of labor is the hourly wage. The same rule applies: Managers will increase the quantity of hours demanded as long as marginal revenue exceeds marginal cost.

The **labor demand curve**, also shown in **Figure 16.1**, reports, for each level of wages, how many workers businesses will want to hire, or the quantity of labor hours demanded. Generally, as the wage rises, businesses will want to hire fewer workers or pay for fewer labor hours.

An Example of Labor Demand

Let's work through an example of labor demand, using the case of a hair salon, as mentioned back in **Chapter 2**. The first two columns of **Table 16.1** give the salon's production function. The first column shows the number of hairdressers employed by the salon, while the second column, labeled output, gives the number of clients the salon can serve in a day (and assuming one haircut per client). The first hairdresser can take care of six customers in a day, and so can the second. A third hairdresser is a bit less productive because he keeps bumping into the other two and has to wait to use some of the equipment. These problems get a little more severe with each added hairdresser. As a result, the marginal product per hairdresser falls as more hairdressers are hired.

Table 16.1 The Labor Demand Decision

Here's how the owner of a hair salon might decide how many workers to hire, given the price of each haircut and the amount each worker gets paid. The rule is to keep hiring more workers as long as marginal revenue is greater than marginal cost.

			If the Price Is $30 per Haircut		If Each Worker Gets Paid $119 per Day		
Labor (Number of Workers)	Output (Total Number of Haircuts per Day)	Marginal Product (Number of Haircuts per Additional Worker)	Total Revenue (Dollars)	Marginal Revenue (Dollars per Additional Worker)	Total Labor Cost (Dollars)	Marginal Labor Cost (Dollars per Additional Worker)	Profit (Dollars)
1	6	6	180	180	119	119	61
2	12	6	360	180	238	119	122
3	17	5	510	150	357	119	153
4	21	4	630	120	476	119	154
5	24	3	720	90	595	119	125

Suppose the market price for haircuts is $30 per cut; that's cheap for many areas of the country. The fourth column shows the total revenue of the salon, assuming each client pays $30 per cut. The fifth column shows the marginal revenue from adding each additional worker. We can see that marginal revenue declines as more workers are hired. The marginal revenue of the first worker hired is $180, whereas the marginal revenue of the fifth worker is only $90.

Jack Hollingsworth/Stockbyte/Getty Images

That's the revenue side; what about the cost side? The Bureau of Labor Statistics reports that the average national wage for hairdressers and cosmetologists was roughly $17 per hour. So, let's suppose the market wage for hairdressers is $119 for a seven-hour day ($17 × 7 = $119). The **market wage** is the prevailing normal wage for a particular type of job. Then, the marginal cost of each additional worker is $119 per day.

The salon owner will want to hire additional hairdressers as long as they increase his or her profit. In other words, the marginal revenue has to exceed the marginal cost. Looking down the table columns, we see that marginal revenue ($180) exceeds marginal cost ($119) for the first worker. The same is true for the second, third, and fourth workers. For the fifth worker, marginal revenue is less than marginal cost. So, the profit-maximizing owner hires the first four hairdressers and politely says no to the fifth.

market wage
The prevailing normal wage for a particular type of job.

We can check this conclusion by a different route. If we subtract total cost from total revenue, what's left is profit. That's the far right column of the table. We can see that the salon reaches its maximum profit with four workers–precisely the same conclusion as before.

So, now we know that if the wage is $119 per day, the firm will hire four workers. A similar calculation shows us that if the wage is $80 per day, the firm will hire five workers (because the marginal revenue of the fifth worker is $90, which is greater than the wage). And if the wage is $130 per day, the firm's labor demand will be three workers (because the fourth worker has a marginal revenue of only $120). Higher wages lead to less hiring, and lower wages lead to more.

LABOR MARKET EQUILIBRIUM AND WAGES (LO16-2)

LO16-2 Identify factors affecting labor market equilibrium.

We've seen that in the labor market managers are busy making hiring decisions, based on the going wage for a job. But where does that wage come from? In the world of economics, the answer is simple: The wage is set by the interaction of supply and demand in the labor market, just like any other market.

labor market equilibrium
The wage at which the quantity of labor supplied is equal to the quantity of labor demanded. Alternatively, the wage at which the number of workers available is equal to the number of workers businesses are willing to hire.

The basic mechanism is that the wage rises (or falls) to the point where the number of workers available for a particular type of job is just equal to the number of workers that businesses are willing to hire. That is the **labor market equilibrium** as shown in **Figure 16.1**. (We'll leave aside for the moment the fact that there are always some workers who are between jobs or unemployed.) Alternatively, for jobs that are hired by the hour, the labor market equilibrium is the wage at which the quantity of labor hours supplied is equal to the quantity of labor hours demanded.

The equilibrium wage W is affected by anything that affects the supply and demand curves, just as we described in **Chapter 3**. Consider, for example, the market for accountants in a city. The demand for accountants comes from accounting firms, companies that need accountants to do their books, ordinary people who need help with their taxes, and government agencies that need accountants to keep track of where the people's tax money is going. The supply of accountants includes people currently working as accountants, new graduates with accounting degrees, and people working in other lines of work who have accounting training.

Let's suppose that the government passes legislation requiring companies to document all their financial decisions more closely. In fact, in 2002 Congress passed the Sarbanes-Oxley Act (known as Sarbox for short), which requires public corporations to meet much more rigorous financial accounting standards. To implement Sarbox, companies had to hire more accountants, which shifted the demand curve for accountants to the right (see **Figure 16.2**). The result of such a shift? The equilibrium wage rises from W to W', and the quantity of accountants rises from L to L'. In reality, that's exactly what happened after the law was passed. Despite an overall weak labor market, the demand for accountants grew, pushing up salaries.

Figure 16.2 The Changing Labor Market for Accountants
The demand curve for accountants shifts to the right after the government increases requirements for financial reporting.

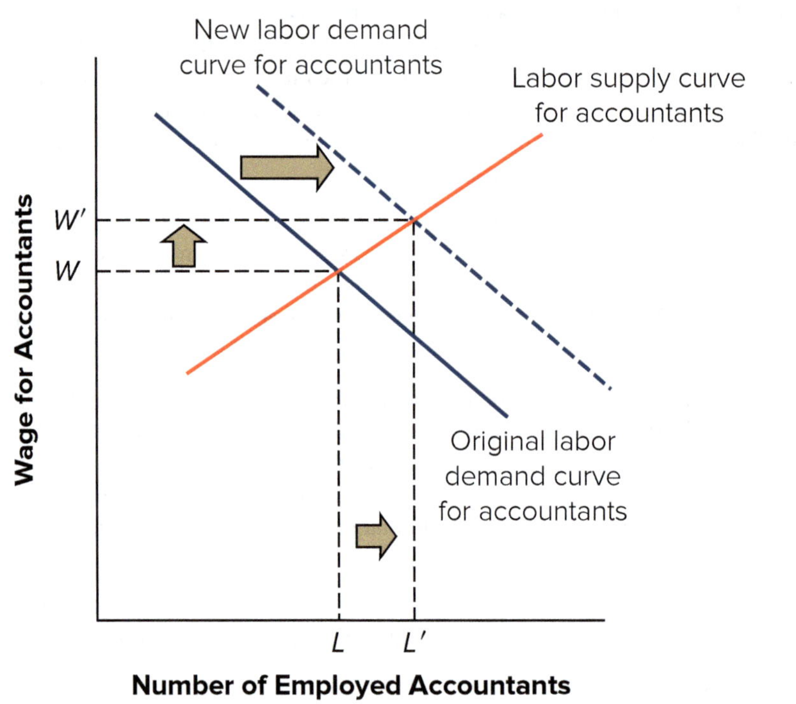

The Impact of Technological Change

Technological change can have a profound impact on both the labor supply schedule and the labor demand schedule. Think about the automobile, which came into widespread use in the early 1900s. As production ramped up, auto companies hired many thousands of workers to make the engines and other parts for the new cars, and assemble them into a working vehicle.

But that's not all. Automobiles were powered by gasoline, which was refined out of crude oil. That meant businesses had to find many new workers for jobs that barely existed before: Oil rig workers, to get the crude oil out of the ground; refinery workers, to help produce the gasoline from the oil; and gas station attendants, to pump the gas. The demand for skilled mechanics increased dramatically because workers were needed who could repair the new "horseless carriages," which were prone to regular breakdowns. At the same time, the increasing use of automobiles *decreased* demand for some types of jobs, such as making saddles and harnesses for horses.

More generally, technology can be either a substitute or a complement for labor. Technology is a substitute for labor if businesses hire fewer workers at the same wage. Technology is a complement for labor if businesses hire more workers at the market wage. For example, a bulldozer is a substitute for unskilled labor because, at any wage, it dramatically reduces the demand for workers with shovels.

The speed of technological change has benefited educated workers.

Or consider some more recent examples. The widespread use of automated telephone answering systems–voice mail–dramatically reduces the need for secretaries and phone operators because a caller can leave a message without talking to a person (see **"Economic Milestone: The First Voice-Mail System"**). However, new technology can also *increase* the demand for certain kinds of workers. In recent years, there has been a great need for app developers–the people who create the mobile applications that run on your smartphone.

ECONOMIC MILESTONE

1975: THE FIRST VOICE-MAIL SYSTEM

There was nearly a century between the invention of the telephone and the introduction of the first voice-mail system. Maybe that was too little time: In a 1997 survey, U.S. adults called voice mail the number-one technology that should never have been invented. Nevertheless, voice mail is one of the clearest examples of technology substituting for labor. It has transformed the staffing of many offices by reducing the need for assistants.

Going forward, driverless vehicles, such as the ones being tested by Google, Uber, and other companies, could lower the demand for truck drivers. At the same time, driverless vehicles could raise the demand for skilled mechanics to keep the driverless vehicles in very good shape.

In general, most recent technological innovations have acted as substitutes for less-skilled labor and complements for high-skilled labor. That is, the voice-mail system eliminated the job of the secretary, but not the job of the manager. Websites and mobile apps for buying airline tickets mean fewer reservation clerks are needed, but pilots are still in high demand.

The speed of technological change benefits educated workers. In eras of rapid change, businesses want workers who can learn new technologies quickly. That generally boosts the demand for educated workers, who find it easier to adapt.

But here's a question: Will future technological change continue to favor educated workers? Not necessarily. As this textbook is being revised in early 2023, a new generation of artificial intelligence programs have been getting attention for their ability to write speeches, reports, newspaper articles, and even college essays.

It's not clear yet which jobs will be affected by the new technology. In the past, technological innovation has opened up new opportunities for well-paid work even as some positions were eliminated. For example, the introduction of computers into the work environment greatly reduced the need for low-paid typists, while creating a new need for armies of software developers and help desk specialists. Going further back, the introduction of forklifts into warehouses reduced the need for people with muscles to lift heavy boxes, while creating the need for trained workers to operate the new machinery. This pattern of job destruction and creation is likely to operate the same way with artificial intelligence, but the exact implications are difficult to predict.

The Impact of Globalization

Historically most labor markets were local. After all, whether you were a manager, a factory worker, or a secretary, your employer expected you to physically show up at the place of business every day. But today, globalization and advances in communication technology make it possible for multinational companies to hire and communicate with workers across the country or on the other side of the world. And these are not just low-level production jobs. More and more U.S. companies are having their research and development work done in Korea, Taiwan, China, or India.

labor pool effect
A situation where the labor supply curve in a given market shifts to the right because there is a larger pool of workers available globally.

As a result, when U.S. companies look to hire, they face a labor supply curve that has shifted to the right because a larger pool of workers is available globally for any job. We will call this the **labor pool effect** of globalization (see **Figure 16.3**). Assuming no change in demand, the labor pool effect causes wages in the United States to drop because U.S. companies can now employ low-wage workers in China, India, and other developing countries.

Figure 16.3 The Labor Pool Effect of Globalization
Because a growing number of jobs can now be done overseas, U.S. companies face a supply curve for labor that has shifted to the right. Assuming no change in demand, that drives the equilibrium wage down from *W* to *W′*.

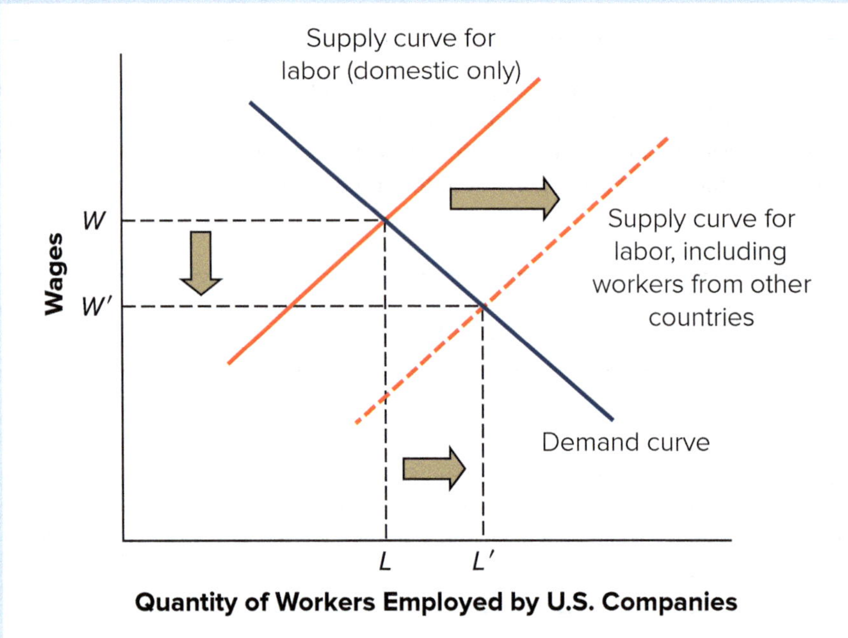

But globalization can also have a positive impact on labor demand because U.S. companies can produce not just for the U.S. market but for the German, Chinese, and Indian markets as well. As we saw in **Chapter 14**, most large U.S. companies, and many small ones, have tapped into overseas demand as a good way to increase sales.

market expansion effect
An increase in labor demand when businesses can sell to overseas customers.

We will call this the **market expansion effect** of globalization. Globalization means more potential customers, more potential sales–and potentially more labor demanded by U.S. companies. This translates into a rightward shift of the labor demand curve for U.S. companies, as shown in **Figure 16.4**. Assuming no change in labor supply, this can drive up the wage the companies pay.

Figure 16.4 The Market Expansion Effect of Globalization
Because companies have better access to growing overseas markets, the demand schedule for labor has shifted to the right. Assuming no change in labor supply, that boosts the equilibrium wage from *W* to *W′*.

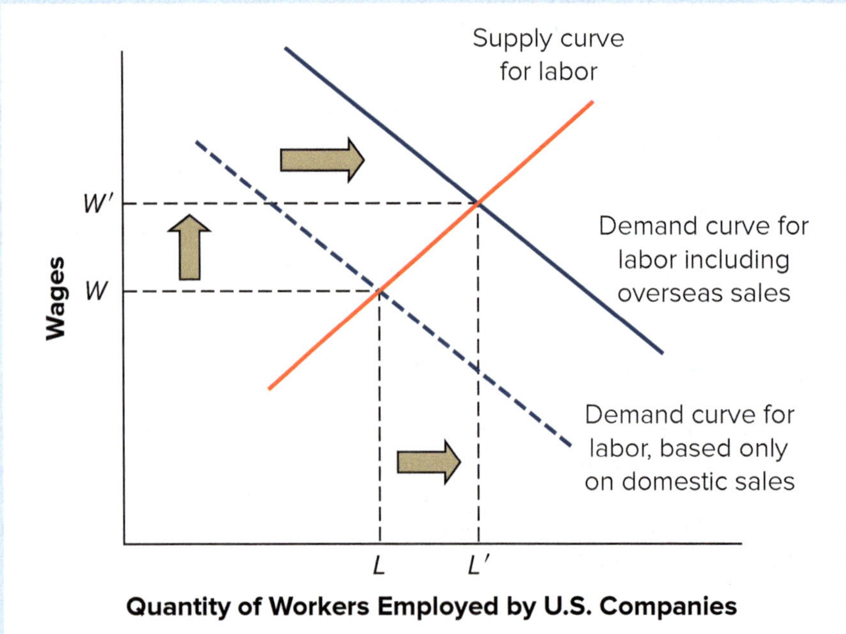

The overall impact of globalization on wages depends on whether the market expansion effect is stronger than the labor pool effect. For U.S. manufacturing workers, the labor pool effect has been greater than the market expansion effect. U.S. manufacturers are selling a lot of goods overseas, but they are using overseas factories to produce those goods. So, while total revenue for these firms is going up, the demand for U.S. factory labor is going down.

Construction equipment made by U.S-based Caterpillar is sold globally.

tlorna/Shutterstock

But plenty of workers in the United States have benefited from access to the global economy. For example, big Wall Street brokerages and investment banks, such as Goldman Sachs, have been very successful at operating abroad, and the resulting profits have created new jobs and higher wages at home. (See **"Spotlight: The Global Movie Star"** for another example of a winner from globalization.)

SPOTLIGHT: THE GLOBAL MOVIE STAR

Robert Downey, Jr. at the premier of an Avengers movie in Korea.

Ahn Young-joon/AP/Shutterstock

At least so far, some of the biggest winners from the market expansion effect have been U.S. movie stars. Consider Robert Downey, Jr., star of the *Iron Man* and *Avengers* movies. Over his career, his movies have taken in impressive box office revenues of $6 billion in the United States. But total worldwide box office revenues were an astonishing $16 billion, according to *The Numbers,* an online movie analytics firm. No wonder Downey now ranks as one of the best-paid U.S. actors.

So far, U.S. movie stars haven't suffered much from the labor pool effect. Stars like Downey don't fear competition from Indian film stars such as Shah Rukh Khan, who has won India's equivalent of the best actor prize eight times. (However, some immigrant actors have done well in the United States, such as English-born Daisy Ridley, one of the stars of *Star Wars: The Force Awakens,* and Arnold Schwarzenegger, originally from Austria.)

It's not impossible to imagine that Bollywood–India's equivalent of the Hollywood movie machine–or some other filmmaking region could start producing viable global stars. But it hasn't happened yet.

Finally, the pandemic had a complicated impact on global labor markets. On the one hand, people became much more accustomed to working remotely, using videoconferencing programs such as Zoom. This strengthened the labor pool effect of globalization, since it became easier to imagine hiring someone in another country and working virtually.

On the other hand, in earlier chapters, we have already mentioned the supply chain disruptions that the pandemic caused. Companies in the United States are now looking for suppliers that are closer to home to reduce their production risks in the event of future pandemics, natural disasters, or even wars.

WHY NOT ALL WORKERS ARE THE SAME (LO16-3)

LO16-3 Explain why different workers may receive different wages.

Suppose there is a sudden increase in the demand for experienced accountants. That will likely boost the wages for accountants, but it will probably not affect the pay for nurses. Similarly, an increase in the demand for nurses is unlikely to boost the pay for accountants.

Accountants and nurses are not competing for the same jobs. Each occupation requires different skills, qualifications, and experience. That's not to say an accountant can't retrain to be a nurse, or vice versa. But it's a slow process, and most people won't do it.

noncompeting labor markets
Occurs when the workers in one labor market do not seek jobs in another.

The labor markets for accountants and for nurses are **noncompeting labor markets**. Two labor markets are noncompeting if the workers in one market do not compete for jobs in the other.

In fact, the overall U.S. labor market is really a collection of many smaller labor markets. Surgeons don't compete for the same jobs as fast-food cooks. Airline pilots don't compete for the same jobs as major league baseball players.

This lack of competition helps explain the big differences in what different workers are paid. Surgeons got paid an average of $294,420 per year in 2021, whereas fast-food cooks made an average of $25,490–but a cook can't apply for a job as a surgeon, even if he or she is good with knives. Similarly, airline pilots and flight engineers earn, on average, $169,540 per year in 2021, whereas the average pay for major league baseball players in the 2021 season was $3.7 million–but no one would suggest that a highly skilled pilot would make a good second baseman.

Education

But why should there be separate labor markets? To put this another way, what's to stop any worker from competing for a highly paid job? Some labor markets, like those for professional athletes or opera singers, are walled off by the need to have particular skills that are rare and cannot be easily acquired.

More generally, in today's labor market, education has become the key qualification that workers need. Employers for many good jobs increasingly want to see a bachelor's or associate degree, depending on the position. There were once a sizable number of well-paid U.S. factory jobs that required at most a high school diploma, but those jobs have mostly melted away, and there is a much tighter link between education and income than before.

education premium
The added lifetime pay for getting a college degree.

Obtaining an education, especially a college or graduate degree, can be an expensive proposition, but it can also yield high returns in terms of better pay and benefits and lower unemployment. For example, according to the U.S. Census Bureau, the average full-time worker with a bachelor's degree earned $79,996 in 2017. A similar worker with only a high school diploma earned $48,037. The added pay for getting a college degree is the **education premium**. Over a 40-year work career, the average college graduate, whether male or female, earns far more than the average high school diploma holder.

To be sure, **Figure 16.5** shows that the education premium has not widened significantly since 2000. However, higher wages are not the only benefit of earning a college degree. Data from the Bureau of Labor Statistics show that better-educated workers also have a lower unemployment rate, as **Table 16.2** reveals.

Figure 16.5 Inflation-Adjusted Earnings by Education Level Holders of bachelor's and advanced degrees saw their earnings rise in the 1990s, adjusted for inflation. But since 2000, inflation-adjusted pay has stagnated for all education levels.

Source: Census Bureau, www.census.gov.

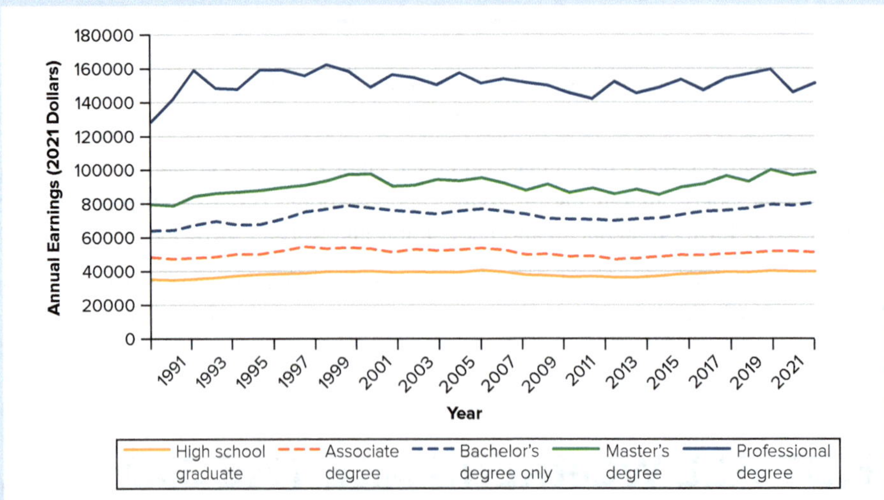

Why should college-educated workers get paid so much more? One possible reason is that college teaches skills and knowledge that make future workers more productive. That shifts the demand curve for college-educated workers to the right, driving up their wage *and* making them less likely to be unemployed.

But that's not the only possible explanation. Perhaps college doesn't teach much but, instead, provides a way of identifying smart people who are able to follow directions. That is, a college degree signals to future employers that you are smart enough and dedicated enough to pass four years' worth of classes. In essence, college is one long test.

But no matter what the explanation, the question remains: If going to college has such a big payoff, why doesn't everyone get a college degree? One reason, of course, is that going to school is an expensive proposition. The cost of tuition, textbooks, and other supplies can be sizable. (Room and board–the cost of housing and eating–would have to be paid whether or not the student is in school.)

Table 16.2 Education and Unemployment

Better-educated workers are less likely to be unemployed. In 2022, the unemployment rate for college graduates was only 2.1 percent, compared to 4.1 percent for high school graduates with no college education.

	Unemployment Rate, 2022 (%)
Less than a high school diploma	5.5
High school graduate, no college	4.0
Some college, no degree	3.5
Associate degree	2.7
Bachelor's degree and higher	2.0

Source: Bureau of Labor Statistics, www.bls.gov.

The biggest cost, though, is the value of the earnings you've lost because you are in school rather than working. This is the opportunity cost of education. If it takes 25 hours a week to complete a full-time program, you have 25 fewer hours a week to work for pay. So, the true economic cost of college is tuition and all its other costs *plus* forgone earnings.

Incidentally, the opportunity cost of education helps explain why it's easier to go to school when you're young. Your wage is lower when you're young, so you lose less money by going to school in your teens and 20s than you would if you went later. In other words, you might be giving up a $15,000-a-year job at McDonald's to go to college now rather than a $60,000-a-year job as a stockbroker.

Age and Experience

Does experience make a difference? Older workers do earn more than younger workers–up to a point. Data from the Census Bureau show that for full-time workers with a high school diploma only, average earnings generally hit their peak when workers are between 45 and 54 (see **Figure 16.6**). For workers with a bachelor's or advanced degree, average pay peaks when workers are 55-64 years old.

Figure 16.6 Average Earnings of Workers by Age and Education: 2021
For full-time workers with a high school diploma only, average pay rises with age up to a point, peaking when workers are 45–54 years old. For full-time workers with a bachelor's or advanced degree, average pay peaks when workers are 55–64 years old.

Source: Census Bureau, www.census.gov.

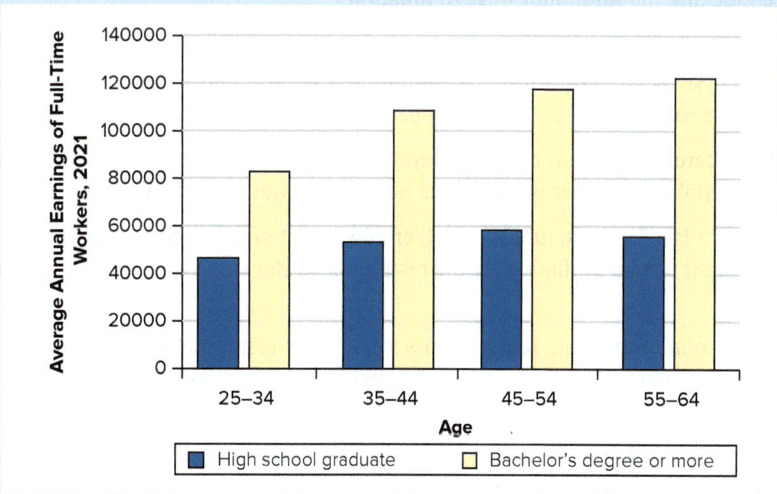

There are plenty of reasons pay should rise with age. Experience clearly improves performance, up to a point. Many jobs require a learning curve, often years long, before you achieve full proficiency. One suggestive fact is that it takes roughly 10 years to achieve expert competence in a game where strategy and analysis are important, such as chess. Moreover, the longer you work at a particular company, the more you build up firm-specific experience–knowledge of how to get things done within that company. Most firms value this knowledge in their employees.

Finally, research has shown that verbal and interpersonal skills stay at high levels as people age. In the 1984 presidential debates, Ronald Reagan, then 73 years old, quipped, "I will not make age an issue of this campaign. I am not going to exploit, for political purposes, my opponent's youth and inexperience."* At the time, his opponent, Walter Mondale, was 56 years old. In the 2016 presidential race, the candidates of the two major political parties, Hillary Clinton and Donald Trump, were 69 and 70 years old, respectively, on election day. In the 2020 presidential race, the candidates of the two major political parties, Joseph Biden and Donald Trump, were 77 and 74 years old, respectively, on election day.

But as workers age, other types of physical and cognitive capabilities decline. Reasoning abilities, mental speed, and the ability to remember events drop off significantly before 50 years of age. Painters, musicians, and writers seem to achieve their peak creative output in their 30s and 40s. Moreover, in a fast-changing economy, knowledge and experience depreciate quickly. As we saw in **Chapter 15**, young people have more incentive than do older workers to invest in learning new technologies because they have more time left in the workforce to use their new knowledge.

REGULATION OF THE LABOR MARKET (LO16-4)

LO16-4 Describe effects of government regulation on the labor market.

The labor market is one of the most intensely regulated parts of the economy. There are rules governing everything from work hours to child labor to the minimum wage to employment discrimination to retirement benefits. In **Chapter 6**, we discussed the role of government in the economy; here we'll explore some rules and laws that specifically govern labor markets.

The Minimum Wage

minimum wage
A wage floor set by the government that lifts the wages of the lowest-paid workers above their market wage.

Let's start with the **minimum wage**, the clearest case of government regulation. The minimum wage law sets a floor for hourly wages for most workers. When introduced in October 1938, the federal minimum wage was 25 cents per hour! But that wasn't as low as it sounds–the average wage in manufacturing at that time was 62 cents per hour. As of February 2023, the federal minimum wage was $7.25 per hour.

However, most states now set their minimum wage above the federal level, California's minimum wage as of February 2023 is $15.50 per hour, for example, while Missouri's minimum wage is $12.00 per hour. Florida's minimum wage, now at $11.00 per hour, is set to go up to $15.00 per hour by 2026. Moreover, 19 states and the District of Columbia are indexing the minimum wage to inflation.

What effect does the minimum wage have on the labor market? This is one of the most hotly debated topics in economics. The basic supply-demand analysis is straightforward: A minimum wage lifts the wages of the lowest-paid workers above their market wage. As a result, employers have to cut back on their hiring because the marginal revenue of some workers is below their wage.

A minimum wage creates a situation of excess supply in the labor market. The higher wage lowers the quantity of labor demanded and raises the quantity supplied. In other words, some people who want jobs can't get them.

The usual example is a fast-food restaurant, which employs a lot of low-paid young workers to stay open long hours. If the minimum wage were increased, it might not be profitable for the restaurant to stay open quite so late. The result would be fewer work hours, and perhaps fewer workers hired.

Alternatively, higher minimum wage requirements might spur restaurants to use more automation, both in the kitchen and in serving customers. "Robotic" restaurants have been opening in cities such as San Francisco and Tokyo. It remains to be seen, however, how successful they will be.

Figure 16.7 shows graphically the impact of instituting a minimum wage. L is the equilibrium employment without the minimum wage law, and W is the equilibrium wage. When a minimum wage law is imposed that raises the wage to W', that lowers the quantity of labor demanded from L to L'.

However, we don't know whether the drop from L to L' is big or small. A series of studies done in the 1990s suggested that raising the federal minimum wage by a moderate amount would have only a small negative effect on employment, if any. There are a few reasons. First, not many workers nationally actually earn the minimum wage. According to the Bureau of Labor Statistics, only 1.4 percent of hourly workers were paid at or below the federal minimum wage in 2021. Second, many employers seem to be relatively insensitive to small or moderate changes in the minimum wage when it comes to making hiring decisions. Third, the federal minimum wage in February 2023, adjusted for inflation, was still below its peak.

* Source: Ronald Reagan

Figure 16.7 Labor Supply and Demand with a Minimum Wage
The original equilibrium wage is *W*. The minimum wage raises the wage to *W′* while lowering the quantity of labor demanded from *L* to *L′*. With the minimum wage the quantity of labor supplied *L″* is higher than *L′*.

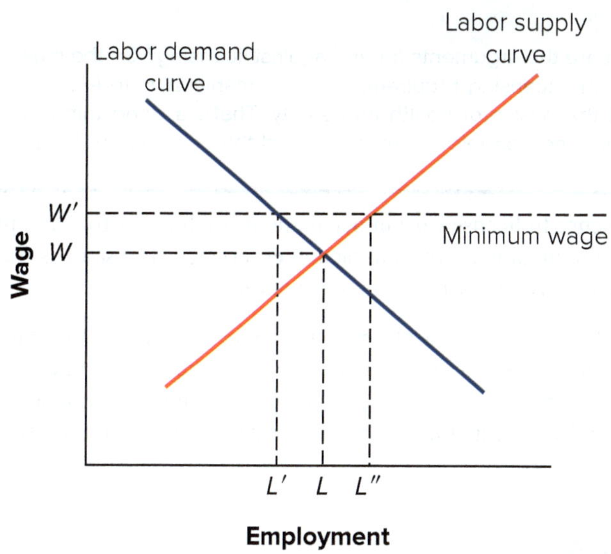

With some states and cities raising their minimum wage, we'll soon have more evidence about the trade-off between higher pay for some low-income workers and the possibility of some job loss. However, the correct level of the minimum wage will continue to be a controversial topic.

The Working Day

Of course, the minimum wage is not the only example of government regulating labor markets. Consider the length of the working day. Today, the 8-hour day and the 40-hour workweek are ingrained into our culture. But those conditions are the result of hard-fought and sometimes violent disputes between unions and employers. In 1886, nationwide demonstrations to shorten the workweek–which then averaged 60 hours–turned into riots around the country. And it wasn't until 1938 that the federal government passed effective rules to set a 40-hour workweek, with a requirement for overtime pay for many workers.

What effect does regulating the workweek have on the labor market? Suppose a new law reduces the legal workweek to 35 hours. Then the employer would have two choices. She could pay overtime wages to encourage everyone to work five more hours, which would obviously be more expensive. Or she could hire and train extra workers to make up for everyone else's reduced hours. Training is expensive; so is paying benefits such as health care to more workers. As a result, limitations on work hours impose extra expenses on businesses.

> **licensing requirements**
> Course and examination requirements that an individual must pass to be licensed to practice an occupation.

This is exactly what happened in France, which put a 35-hour workweek into effect at the beginning of 2000. Many companies struggled with the law, and by 2005, the government relaxed the standard, saying that it was making businesses less competitive.

Licensing

Government often intervenes in labor markets by setting **licensing requirements** for certain professions. That is, you need to receive permission from the government before doing certain jobs (see "**Spotlight: Licenses for Manicurists**").

SPOTLIGHT: LICENSES FOR MANICURISTS

To see how occupational licensing requirements work, let's take a look at manicurists, also known as "nail technicians." Most states prohibit someone from working as a manicurist unless he or she has passed certain hurdles. In Arkansas, for example, budding manicurists must take 600 hours of course instruction at an approved school of cosmetology. In addition, they have to pass both a written and a practical exam.

The licensing requirements are not trivial. A required manicurist course might cost $4,000 and consume the equivalent of 75 full working days, or more than three months. Studying for the written and practical exams requires time and materials as well.

What are the arguments for and against licensing? On the plus side, the licensing requirements force manicurists to learn at least the basics of health and safety. That's a good thing at a time when people are more worried than ever about being infected with something that is not easily treatable. Licensing also enforces some minimum of skill at doing nail care.

On the minus side, the licensing requirement reduces the supply of manicurists because it rules out people who don't have enough money or time to pay for the course. This, in turn, has the effect of driving up the wages paid to manicurists, which in turn raises the price of a manicure.

It makes sense to license certain occupations, such as doctors and pharmacists. You want to know that the doctor who treats you has at least a minimum amount of training and experience. The same is true for the pharmacist who fills your drug prescriptions. It can also be argued that restricting who can practice law makes sense.

But, sometimes, the oddest professions require licenses. In the state of California, for example, you need to be licensed to be a boxing matchmaker, a brake and lamp adjuster, or an esthetician (someone who works in a beauty salon). You need a license or permit to run a cemetery, sell bedding, or process anchovies. It's not hard to imagine that the true purpose of some licensing requirements is to restrict competition by making it more difficult for people to qualify for certain occupations.

Unions

union

A group of workers who bargain collectively with employers for wages, benefits, and working conditions.

A **union** is a group of workers that bargains collectively with employers for wages (including benefits) and working conditions. At one point, unions were extremely important in the economy. In the 1950s, for example, roughly one-third of workers belonged to unions, compared to 10.1 percent as of 2022. Only 6.0 percent of private-sector workers belonged to unions in 2022, compared to 33.1 percent in the public sector. Indeed, the largest union is the National Education Association, which has roughly 3 million members, mainly teachers.

Wage setting with collective bargaining is very different from wage setting in a competitive market like the ones we've discussed in this chapter so far. In collective bargaining, the employer talks with the representatives of the union to come up with an acceptable deal. The employer's ultimate resort is to fire the workers, and the ultimate threat of the union is to walk off the job or go on strike and deprive the employer of skilled and experienced labor.

Bargaining takes place against a backdrop of laws and regulations that determine what is acceptable: When is it legal for an employer to hire replacement workers? When is it legal for a union to picket a workplace? All this is governed in the United States by the National Labor Relations Act of 1935 and the Taft-Hartley Act of 1946. Compliance is monitored by the National Labor Relations Board, whose members are appointed by the president. In addition, individual states are allowed to pass "right-to-work" laws, which mean that employees cannot be compelled to join a union.

When they're effective, unions can raise pay and improve working conditions for current workers. By definition, that means pushing wages above the equilibrium market level, as **Figure 16.8** shows.

Under what conditions can unions be effective at raising wages? First, it has to be difficult for a company to hire replacement workers. In the airline industry, the pilots' union is generally more effective at raising wages than is the flight attendants' union. Planes can fly with substitute flight attendants, but it's much harder to replace trained pilots at short notice. That gives the pilots more leverage in bargaining for wage increases.

Second, unions are more effective when it is difficult for nonunion competitors to enter an industry. The public sector is heavily unionized, in part because there is little or no competition for most government functions. Private companies can do some government jobs, like waste collection, but it is much less usual to have a private company handle police or fire protection or even public school education. The scarcity of other options for getting the work done is another way in which unions gain bargaining leverage.

Why has private-sector unionization fallen sharply in recent years? Globalization is one key reason. When whole factories can move to other countries, the possibility of a union strike becomes much less threatening to employers. That helps explain why strikes have become far less common in recent years. **Figure 16.9** shows that work stoppages due to strikes have become both less common and shorter in the last 50 years. The only recent exception was in 2000, when actors working in radio and television commercials went on strike for half the year. Despite this strike, however, there is no evidence that fewer commercials were made or shown in that year.

Figure 16.8 The Impact of Union Membership on Wages
In some cases, unions can push up wages. However, the resulting employment level will be less than the competitive market equilibrium.

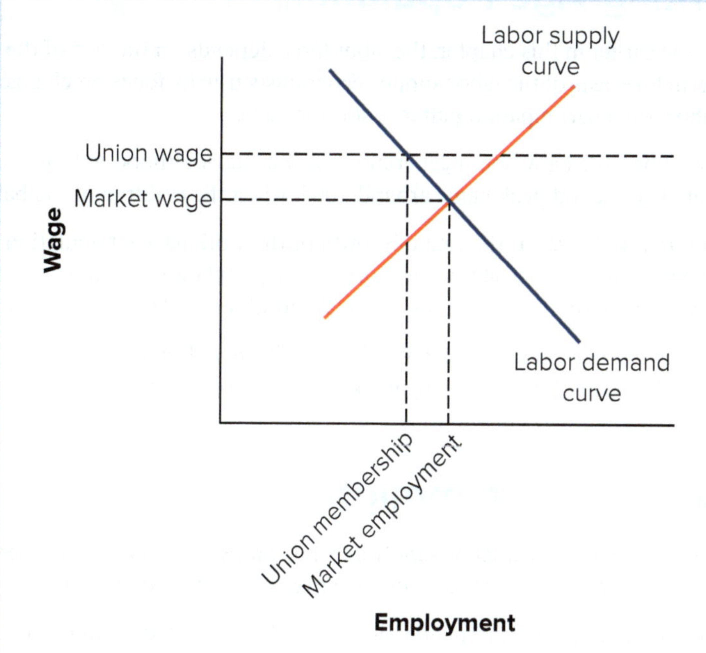

Figure 16.9 Days of Work Lost to Work Stoppages, 1965–2022
As unionization has become less important in the American economy, work stoppages due to strikes have become less common and shorter.

Source: Bureau of Labor Statistics, www.bls.gov.

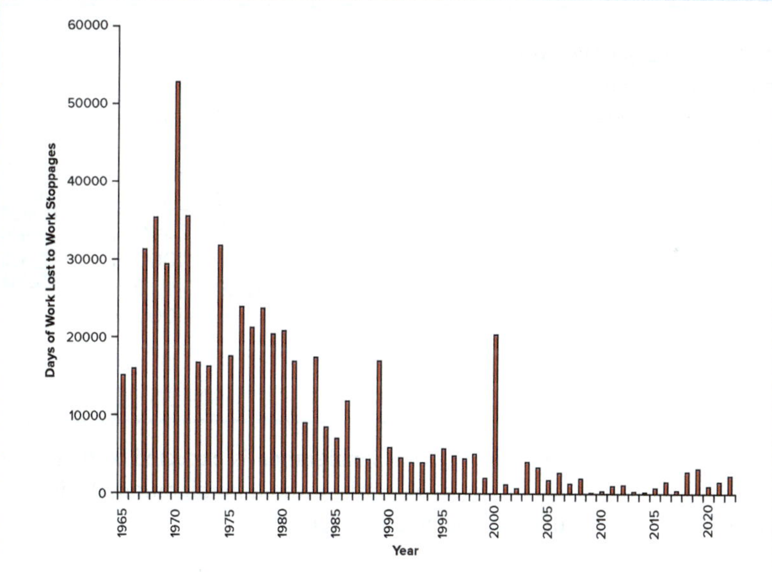

LONG-TERM LABOR SUPPLY (LO16-5)

LO16-5 Identify the forces driving long-term labor supply, including immigration.

To end this chapter, we will look at the **long-term labor supply**: the predicted size of the labor force in a country or a region at some point in the future. Economists and businesses worry about the long-term labor supply because it affects the growth rate of the economy, future tax revenues, and the ability of businesses to find workers. The long-term labor supply depends on the birth rate and on immigration, which has become an increasingly controversial subject.

long-term labor supply
The predicted size of the labor force in a country or a region in the future.

Working-Age Population

As we saw earlier in this chapter, the labor force depends on the size of the population and the labor force participation rate. However, for long-term forecasts of the labor supply, economists usually focus on changes in the size of working-age population (ages 20–64), assuming that labor force participation patterns stay the same.

In 1980, when the baby boom generation was hitting adulthood in large numbers, the working-age population was growing at 1.8 percent per year. The second peak came around 2005, when the children of the baby boom generation were entering the workforce.

Going forward, however, the rate of growth of the working-age population is expected to slow sharply. There are two implications of this slowdown in the growth rate of the working-age population. First, it may become difficult for businesses to find enough skilled and educated workers in the United States, especially as older workers retire. This will put more pressure on workers to get an education.

Second, as we will see in **Chapter 18**, this slowdown will make it harder to pay for Social Security and Medicare because these programs are funded by payroll taxes paid by workers. Fewer workers will mean less payroll tax available to help support retirees.

The Impact of Immigration

Ultimately, the long-term labor supply depends on two factors: the number of births and the number of immigrants from other countries. The fertility rate edged up slightly in recent years, but it is still near record lows.

Both before and during the pandemic, foreign-born workers have been an important contributor to labor force growth (**Figure 16.10**). Between 2007 and 2019, the foreign-born labor force rose by 4.4 million, compared to the 6 million increase in the native-born labor force. During the pandemic, from 2019 to 2022, the number of native-born workers in the labor force actually fell, while the number of foreign-born workers continued to rise.

Figure 16.10 Foreign-Born Workers Contribute to Labor Force
Growth: Foreign-born workers accounted for all the labor force growth during the pandemic.
Source: Bureau of Labor Statistics.

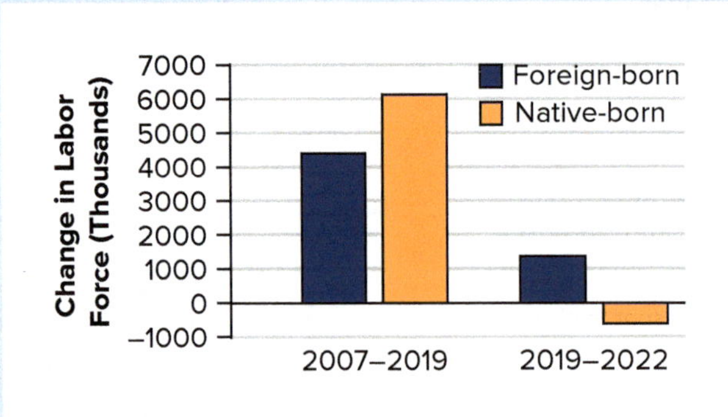

immigration
The entry of new people into a country, either temporarily or permanently.

Over the long run, **immigration** is expected to be the main driver of the long-term labor supply going forward. In other words, without immigration, the long-term growth rate of the labor force in the United States will be much slower.

Still, immigration is a highly controversial topic, not just in the United States but around the world. In 2015 Europe grappled with an influx of well over 1 million refugees and migrants from Syria and other countries. This surge generated heated political debate about the economic and cultural impacts of immigration. The Russian invasion of Ukraine led to millions of Ukrainian refugees seeking safety in European countries.

From the economic perspective, immigration clearly shifts the labor supply curve to the right–in a big way. All other things being equal, this decreases wages while increasing the level of employment in the host country. Economic research has not nailed down the size of this wage effect from immigration, though it's certainly real.

This concern about immigration driving down wages fuels much of the political debate over immigration policy. People are worried that the influx of foreign-born workers makes it harder for native-born workers to get paid well. Low-skilled workers worry about competition from low-skilled immigrants, while native-born workers with a college education are concerned about competition from immigrants who received college degrees in their own countries.

But that's not where the story stops. Immigration also shifts the national demand curve for labor to the right, which helps push up wages. Why? Immigrants are consumers as well as workers. They buy homes and furniture, use telephones and banks, and shop for cars and toys. As a result, immigrants not only increase the supply of labor, they increase the demand for goods and services and, therefore, the demand for labor. This may be especially true in cities such as New York and Los Angeles, which have vibrant immigrant communities.

These two opposing effects of immigration help explain why there is much disagreement among economists about the actual impact of immigration on wages. Reputable estimates range from a big negative impact to almost no impact at all.

Location

Another aspect of the long-term labor supply is location. People move around. They change jobs and relocate from one area of the country to another–from Texas to California or from Cleveland to New York City. They graduate from college and move to a city where they've landed a good job or where their spouse or friend has gotten a good job. Or they take a big leap and change countries–moving from Mexico to the United States or from the United States to China or some other country where the opportunities seem better.

As people move, the supply of labor in a region or country changes over months or years. If a region is attractive to enough people–because of climate, job opportunities, cost of living, or presence of cultural institutions–the local labor supply will grow. The development and widespread use of air-conditioning in the 1930s made warm-weather states like Florida and Georgia more attractive because people could be comfortable during the hot summers.

Meanwhile, certain areas of the country are losing working-age population because of their lack of jobs, combined with colder climates. That's especially true in the manufacturing areas of the U.S. Midwest and many rural counties. For example, the population of the city of Cleveland fell by 6 percent between 2010 and 2020. The 2020 Census showed that rural areas lost population between 2010 and 2020.

Gary John Norman/Getty Images

Where do they go? Young college graduates like to live where there are lots of other young college-educated people (if you are single, you certainly understand). Similarly, educated workers go where they can find cultural opportunities, which creates enough demand to attract even more cultural opportunities.

One important question is whether the rise of "work from home" arrangements during the pandemic will permanently change where people locate. In theory, many jobs can be done remotely, which would allow workers to live anywhere. Nevertheless, as this textbook is being revised, many employers are trying to convince workers to physically return to the office, at least part of the time. It's not clear yet what the outcome of this back-and-forth will be.

YOUR ECONOMIC LIFE: Should You Move?

When you decide where to live, what factors should you consider? Obviously, availability of work is important. And that, in turn, depends on what occupation you pick.

Some occupations are widely distributed. If you are a pharmacist or nurse, for example, you can find work almost anywhere. By contrast, half of all lawyers are concentrated in only 10 metro areas. In the aftermath of the pandemic, some employers are open to remote work, allowing people to locate anywhere there is a good Internet connection, while other employers are insistent that new employees regularly come into the office.

Another issue is cost of living. People who might want to live in a rapidly growing area like San Francisco have been priced out by the rapidly escalating price of homes and rental units. Moreover, local land use regulations often make it expensive to build new housing.

Commuting costs and time are important as well. In dense urban areas, people often trade off longer commutes for bigger homes, especially if they can choose to work at home part of the time. And, of course, the quality of the school system plays a role as well. Your choice of a place to work and live is an excellent opportunity for you to apply your skills in utility maximization.

CONCLUSION

Every worker, from the president of the United States to the housekeepers in the local hotel, participates as a seller in the labor market. Similarly, almost every business, from the largest down to almost the smallest, is a buyer in the labor markets. Indeed, labor markets are pervasive in today's economy.

But something else is pervasive as well: the sense that someone else is being paid more than you. In the U.S. economy, there's a very wide gap between the highest- and lowest-paid workers. That fact distresses many people and maybe a social problem–and that's why the next chapter will take up the tough problem of the distribution of income and inequality.

16 SUMMARY

1. The labor force is the part of the population that is either working or actively looking for a job. The labor force participation rate is the share of the population in the labor force. The labor supply curve tells us, given the wage, how many people are in the labor force or the total number of labor hours supplied. The labor demand curve reports how many workers businesses want to hire, given the wage. Businesses want to expand their employment as long as the marginal revenue from an additional worker exceeds the wage paid to the worker (including benefits). *(LO16-1)*
2. Labor market equilibrium is affected by various factors, including government legislation, technological change, and globalization. For example, the market expansion effect of globalization causes the labor demand curve to shift to the right, boosting equilibrium employment and wages. *(LO16-2)*
3. Workers differ by education, age, and experience. Higher-educated workers get paid more, but the education premium has not widened significantly since 2000. *(LO16-3)*
4. The labor market is heavily regulated. The minimum wage law sets a floor for hourly wages for most workers. This has the effect of raising wages for a small number of workers and somewhat reducing employment. Another regulation limits the workweek for many workers and requires the payment of overtime rates for anything above that. A union is a group of workers that bargains collectively with employers for wages (including benefits) and working conditions. An effective union can raise pay above the equilibrium level, which reduces employment. *(LO16-4)*
5. The long-term labor supply is expected to grow more slowly in coming years. That will affect the ability of businesses to find enough skilled and educated workers. One critical factor determining future labor supply is the number of immigrants. *(LO16-5)*

KEY TERMS AND CONCEPTS

labor force
labor force participation rate
labor supply curve
job market decision
marginal product of labor
marginal revenue
marginal cost of labor
benefits
labor demand curve
market wage
labor market equilibrium
labor pool effect
market expansion effect
noncompeting labor markets
education premium
minimum wage
licensing requirements
union
long-term labor supply
immigration

connect PROBLEMS

1. Identify which of the following statements is false. *(LO16-1)*
   a) The Internet makes it easier for employers to find potential job candidates.
   b) High unemployment means there are no job openings.
   c) The labor demand curve slopes down.
   d) The labor market is in some ways different from other markets.
   e) Women and men have the same labor force participation rate.

2. The following table shows the production function for a bicycle manufacturer. *(LO16-1)*

Number of Workers	Number of Bicycles Produced per Week
1	3
2	7
3	10
4	12
5	13

a) Suppose that the weekly wage is \$850. What is the marginal labor cost of the second worker per week?
b) Suppose that the price of a bicycle is \$450. What is the marginal revenue of the third worker, per week?
c) How many workers does the bicycle manufacturer employ if the price per bicycle is \$450 and the weekly wage is \$850?
d) If the price per bicycle drops to \$300, what happens to the number of employed workers?

3. Consider the labor demand curve for a city. For each of the following events, say whether the labor demand curve shifts to the left, shifts to the right, or stays in place. Explain. *(LO16-2)*
a) The local factory installs a robot assembly line.
b) The local wage increases.
c) The local factory is able to sell more products overseas.
d) A new department store opens in town to compete with existing retailers.

4. A restaurant installs an automated conveyor belt system for getting food from the kitchen to customers' tables faster, with fewer dropped plates. Is this technology a substitute or a complement for the following jobs? *(LO16-2)*
a) Waitress.
b) Conveyor belt mechanic.
c) Cook.
d) Cashier.

5. Identify whether each of the following situations is an example of the market expansion effect or the labor pool effect of globalization. *(LO16-2)*
a) A furniture maker shifts production from the United States to China.
b) Merck, a large U.S. pharmaceutical company, hires more scientists in the United States so it can develop drugs to sell in overseas markets.
c) A U.S. newspaper hires reporters in India to write about the U.S. stock market.
d) A U.S. magazine hires reporters in the United States to write about the Indian stock market.

6. Indicate whether each of these factors will increase or decrease the odds that a young person in the United States will choose to get a college education. *(LO16-3)*
a) An increase in the global number of unskilled workers.
b) Increased industry investment in technology.
c) Increased college tuition.
d) Increased pay for high school graduates.
e) Rising wages in India for college-educated workers.

7. Suppose a law is passed forcing everyone to work until age 69. *(LO16-3)*
a) In March 2023, the labor force participation rate of people aged 65–69 was 33 percent. After the law is passed, will the labor force participation rate of this group go up or down?
b) What will be the impact of the new law on the labor supply curve? Will it shift left, shift right, or stay in place?
c) Will the new law raise wages, cut wages, or leave them the same?

8. Suppose labor laws in China were changed to require a higher minimum wage for Chinese workers. *(LO16-4)*
a) What would happen to the price of Chinese-made products?
b) How would that affect the labor demand curve for U.S. factory workers?
c) What would happen to U.S. factory wages?

9. A town changes its zoning regulations to close down all its dance clubs because too many workers are staying out late and aren't able to come to work the next day. *(LO16-4)*
a) In the short run, does the labor supply curve shift to the left, shift to the right, or stay the same? What happens to production in the town?
b) The town develops a reputation as a boring place, so young people no longer want to live there. In the long run, does the labor supply curve shift to the left or the right?
c) In the long run, would you expect wages and employment to go up or down? Explain your reasoning.

10. Consider the long-term labor supply curve for a city. For each of the following events, say whether the labor supply curve shifts to the left, shifts to the right, or stays in place. Explain. ***(LO16-5)***
    a) The tuition of the local community college is raised.
    b) The local wage increases.
    c) The minimum wage in a neighboring city is increased.
    d) The city receives a sudden influx of immigrants from another country.
11. This chapter focused on individuals who work for an employer. But another alternative is to start your own business. This is a risky proposition, however. The upside is that successful business owners can make a lot of money. The downside is that many new businesses either fail or end up requiring a lot of work hours without much profit. ***(LO16-5)***
    a) What are the advantages of starting a new business when you are young? (*Hint:* Consider opportunity cost.)
    b) What are the disadvantages of starting a new business when you are young? (*Hint:* Think about the different skills you might need.)

CH 17

THE DISTRIBUTION OF INCOME

imging/Shutterstock

LEARNING OBJECTIVES

After reading this chapter, you should be able to:

LO17-1 Summarize the basics of income distribution.
LO17-2 Identify some reasons income inequality and poverty have risen in recent years.
LO17-3 List and discuss the arguments for and against government action to reduce inequality.
LO17-4 Explain how the tax system can be used to redistribute income.
LO17-5 Give examples of labor market discrimination.

In 2021, David Baszucki, chief executive officer of Roblox, a popular 3D game platform, was given a pay package worth more than $230 million. In the same year, 17 percent of all U.S. households had incomes of about $25,000 or less.

That gap—between $230 million and $25,000—demonstrates the wide spread of incomes in the U.S. economy. In recent years, the economy has produced a growing number of very high-income winners: corporate executives, athletes and entertainers, hedge-fund and private equity managers, and technology entrepreneurs. Mark Zuckerberg, founder of Facebook, went from college student to billionaire in just 3 years.

Unfortunately, there seems to be a growing gap between the people with very high incomes and everyone else. In particular, the country's overall prosperity seems to have missed a large number of low-income households. The percentage of U.S. citizens living in poverty in 2021—that is, with incomes below the official poverty line—is roughly about the same level as in the late 1970s.

This income gap is one of the most important topics in economics, yet it is also one of the most controversial. Does having such a wide spread between top and bottom provide an incentive to try harder, or does it discourage effort and create political resentment? Is it unfair that some people make millions of dollars and others earn very little, or is it unfair to take money away from people who have earned it to give it to others who have less?

In this chapter, we'll lay out the basic facts about the distribution of income in the United States. We'll discuss some reasons the income gap may have widened in recent years, and we'll examine the justifications for income redistribution. Then, we'll finish with a look at racial and gender discrimination in pay.

THE BASICS OF INCOME DISTRIBUTION (LO17-1)

LO17-1 Summarize the basics of income distribution.

income
The amount of money an individual receives in a year from various sources.

The starting point for any discussion of U.S. incomes is the data produced each year by the statisticians at the Census Bureau. Each year, the department asks a sample of American households about their **income**—that is, how much money they received in the previous year from various sources such as their jobs, the interest on their savings accounts, the dividends on their stocks, their Social Security payments, and their profits if they own businesses. This sample is large enough to let the statisticians draw conclusions about the whole population. Then, the Census Bureau reports its findings, together with information about the characteristics of the households (a *household* is a group of people living together in one housing unit).

income distribution
Share of households at different income levels.

Figure 17.1 shows some basic information about the **income distribution**—that is, a description of the share of households at different income levels. For each level of income in 2021, **Figure 17.1** reports two numbers: the share of households in that income category and their share of the country's total income. For example, 35 percent of households received between $0 and $50,000 in 2021. These households, taken together, received 9 percent of U.S. total income.

Figure 17.1 Income Distribution in the United States, 2021
For each income category, this figure shows the share of total households and the share of total household income. For example, households with income between $0 and $50,000 make up 36 percent of all households and receive 9 percent of all income.
Source: Census Bureau, www.census.gov.

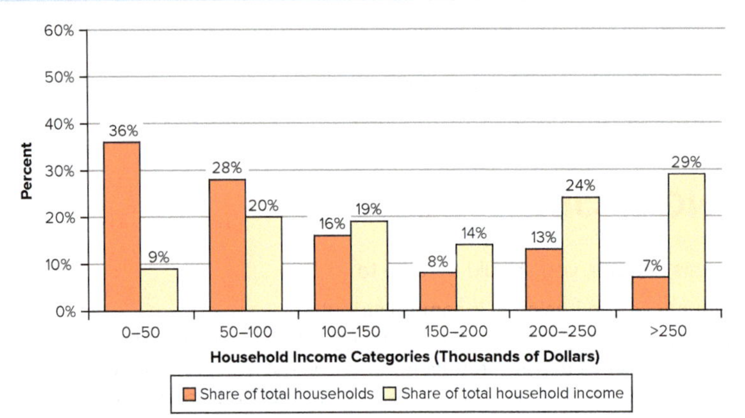

quintiles
20 percent of a group. Used when considering income distribution.

At the upper end of the distribution, roughly 7 percent of households in the United States had income greater than $250,000 in 2021. But that relatively small number of people also received 29 percent of the country's total income, much bigger than their share of the number of households.

Quintiles

Table 17.1 The Quintiles of Household Income, 2021

Each row shows the minimum income that a household needed to get into each group in 2021. For example, to be in the top 5 percent of households required an annual income of at least $286,304.

Income Quintiles, 2021	
Top 5%	$286,304
Top quintile	$ 149,131
Fourth quintile	$ 89,744
Third quintile	$ 55,000
Second quintile	$ 28,007
Bottom quintile	$ 0

Source: Census Bureau, www.census.gov.

Figure 17.1 looks at the distribution of income in terms of monetary ranges. But economists also like to think about income distribution in terms of **quintiles**. A quintile represents 20 percent of households. For example, the bottom quintile is the 20 percent of families with the lowest incomes. The top quintile is the 20 percent of families with the highest annual incomes (the top quintile is usually also subdivided into the top 5 percent and the top 1 percent).

Table 17.1 shows the minimum income needed to get into each quintile in 2021. If you worked full-time and earned the national minimum wage ($7.25 an hour at the end of 2021), your total earnings for the year would be $14,500, which is in the first quintile. A household income of at least $28,007 is needed to get you into the second quintile.

On the other hand, 5 percent of U.S. households earn annual incomes of $286,304 or higher. This category includes highly educated households. Many lawyers, successful small business owners, and doctors fall in the top 5 percent (the average salary of an obstetrician-gynecologist was in excess of $286,000 in 2021, according to the Bureau of Labor Statistics). Many highly paid corporate managers are in the top 5 percent as well. (See **"Spotlight: The CEO Pay Ratio"**).

SPOTLIGHT: THE CEO PAY RATIO

Among the best-paid workers in the United States are the chief executive officers (CEOs) of big companies. They typically get salary and bonuses, often running into the millions of dollars. In addition, they usually are granted stock in their companies, or the option to buy stock at a fixed price. This stock-related pay can be very valuable.

One important question is how much CEOs get paid relative to the workers in their company. Until recently, it was nearly impossible to get the data to calculate that number. But public companies are now required to report the annual pay of their "median employee"—that is, half the workers in the company get paid more, and half get paid less. That enables us to calculate the ratio of CEO pay to worker pay.

For example, in 2021 the CEO of Southwest Airlines earned $5.8 million, compared to median employee pay of $85,000, for a CEO pay ratio of about 70 to 1. At the other end of the scale, the CEO of Domino's Pizza received $7.1 million, compared to median employee pay of $17,782, for a CEO pay ratio of roughly 400 to 1.

Some companies have even bigger CEO pay ratios. Indeed, one of the biggest changes in the economy over the past 20 years has been the widening gap between pay for top corporate executives and the average pay of American workers.

What are large companies paying for? First, running a large multinational corporation successfully is a tough job. Corporate boards (who hire CEOs) perceive that few people have the experience and leadership ability to do this work. In other words, the labor supply is relatively skimpy. So, it's worth paying a lot to hire and retain a good CEO.

A second possible reason for high CEO pay could be called the *tournament effect.* By making the CEO job so lucrative and therefore desirable, high salaries in effect set up a tournament in which many middle-level managers compete hard to make it up the ladder. Thus, well-paid jobs at the top stimulate work effort throughout an entire organization

Another justification for huge pay packages—especially for pay in the form of stock and stock options—is the need to give corporate managers incentives to make decisions in the best interest of shareholders. A CEO who owns stock options or stock in his or her company will be more motivated to manage the firm so as to boost the company's share price, which is what shareholders want.

The final reason for high pay is simple. In many corporations, the CEO controls who gets to sit on the board of directors. And guess who votes on CEO pay? The board of directors. This sort of arrangement also helps explain why CEO pay keeps going up.

Source: Corporate financial reports; https://www.bloomberg.com/graphics/ceo-pay-ratio/

The top 5 percent also includes virtually all major league athletes. For example, the minimum annual salary for major league baseball players in 2022 was $700,000. That number would put a player and his family into the top 5 percent of households for sure.

Finally, the top 5 percent of households also includes quite a few two-earner families, in which both members of a couple work at good jobs. That is, if both people earn $150,000 a year, that would push a household into the top 5 percent.

One Way to Measure Inequality

Income inequality, generally speaking, is the disparity between high-income and low-income households or individuals. There are several different ways to measure the degree of income inequality, but here's one of the most widely used. Remember that a quintile represents one-fifth or 20 percent of households. The income level that marks the dividing line between the bottom quintile and the second quintile is called the 20th percentile because 20 percent, or one-fifth, of households fall below that level (see **Figure 17.2**). The income level that marks the dividing line between the top quintile and everyone else is called the 80th percentile because 80 percent of households have incomes below that level. In 2021, the income level for the 20th percentile was $28,007, and the income level for the 80th percentile was $149,131.

income inequality

The disparity between high-income and low-income households or individuals.

We can think of the households in the top quintile as "high-income" and the households in the bottom quintile as "low-income." From that perspective, we can calculate the **80/20 ratio**–that is, the 80th percentile of income divided by the 20th percentile of income. For **Figure 17.2**, the 80/20 ratio is $149,131/$28,007, which is roughly 5.3. In other words, high-income households have an income that is more than five times that of low-income households.

80/20 ratio

A measure of income inequality obtained by dividing the 80th percentile of income earners by the 20th percentile.

Figure 17.2 One Way to Measure Inequality
The spread between the 20th percentile and the 80th percentile of income indicates the degree of income inequality.
Source: Census Bureau, www.census.gov.

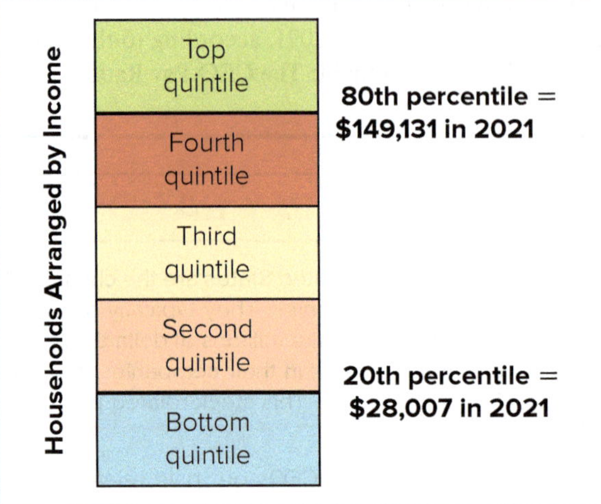

An 80/20 ratio of 5.3 means that high-income households earn a lot more than low-income ones. By contrast, if the 80/20 ratio is close to 1, high-income and low-income households have relatively similar incomes, and the degree of inequality is low.

CHANGING INCOME INEQUALITY (LO17-2)

LO17-2 Identify some reasons income inequality and poverty have risen in recent years.

Most economists believe the distribution of income has widened over the past 40 years. In other words, income inequality has increased. However, there is no consensus about whether the increase in inequality has been large or small. It depends on which data source you look at and which measure of inequality you use.

The 80/20 Ratio

Let's start by looking at the 80/20 ratio, which the Census Bureau calculates each year based on its survey of income. **Figure 17.3** shows that the 80/20 ratio has been rising over time, which means the spread between high-income and low-income households has been widening. In 1985, high-income households had incomes at least 4.4 times those of low-income households. By 2021, that difference had widened appreciably.

Figure 17.3 The 80/20 Ratio, 1985 versus 2021
The ratio of the 80th percentile to the 20th percentile is higher in 2021 than in 1985, suggesting an increase in inequality.
Source: Census Bureau, www.census.gov.

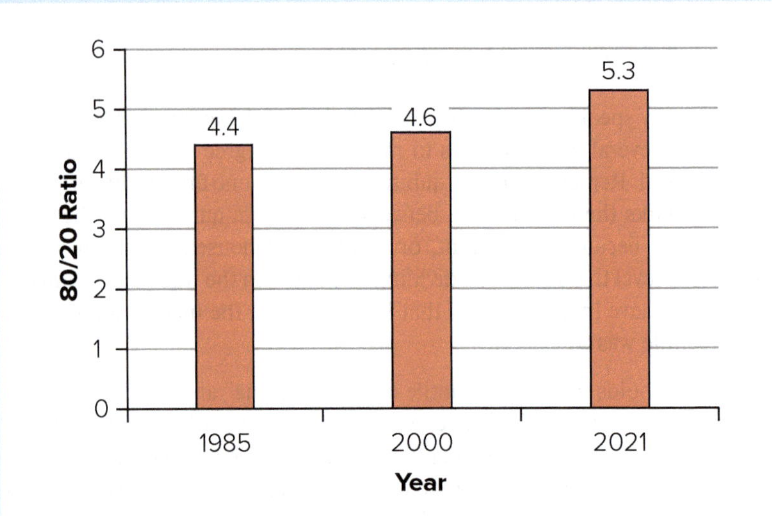

However, **Figure 17.3** does not indicate a dramatic increase in inequality. High-income households have seen their incomes rise faster than their low-income counterparts over the past 40 years, but the difference is not that great.

An Alternative View

Some economists have disputed this relatively benign view of slow-rising inequality. They look at tax return data from the Internal Revenue Service, under the reasonable assumption that people are more likely to be truthful to tax collectors about their incomes than to surveyors from the government.

Based on tax return data, the share of reported income going to the top 1 percent has risen sharply over the past 40 years. In the 1980s, the top 1 percent of taxpayers got about 11 percent of total income, as shown in **Figure 17.4**. By contrast, in the period 2010-2019, the top 1 percent of taxpayers were getting 20 percent of all income. That's a stunning increase.

Figure 17.4 Share of Reported Income Going to Top 1 Percent of Taxpayers, 1980–2019
Data from U.S. tax returns show an increasing concentration of reported income at the very top. The top 1 percent of taxpayers averaged roughly 20 percent of reported income between 2010 and 2019.
Source: The Tax Foundation, taxfoundation.org.

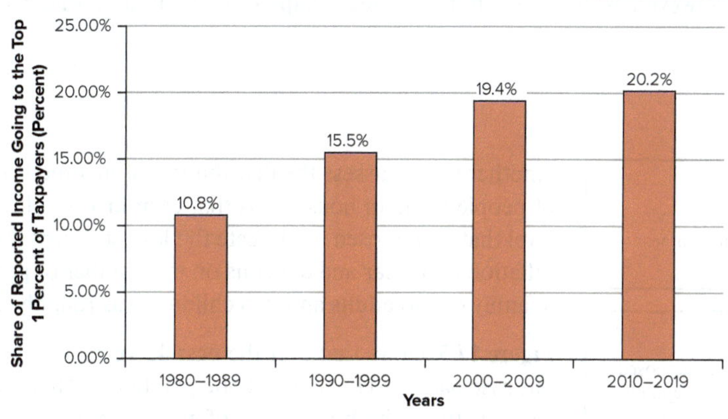

Not surprisingly, this view has itself been disputed by other economists, who argue that tax return data have all sorts of problems. In particular, they do not include Social Security payments, which are a large part of income for many elderly taxpayers. And tax return numbers may be distorted by tax evasion. Nevertheless, whether you trust the 80/20 ratio or the tax return data, it seems likely that income inequality has increased.

Reasons for Rising Inequality

Economists are still not sure what has caused the increase in income inequality since the 1970s. However, they have suggested several different reasons, each of which may explain part of the increase (see **Table 17.2**).

First, the introduction of computers into the workplace in the 1980s and the 1990s seems to have favored skilled and educated workers. Remember that before the early 1980s, virtually no one had a personal computer at work. By the end of the decade, personal computers were everywhere. The new technology eliminated or reduced the need for certain low-skilled jobs, and it put a premium on the ability to understand and use sophisticated equipment. The result was an increase in the *education premium* in the 1980s, as we saw in the previous chapter in **Figure 16.5**. As the pay gap between the college-educated and those with less education widened, it led to more income inequality.

Another cause for widening inequality, especially in recent years, is foreign trade. This explanation used to be controversial among economists, but it has become much more widely accepted. Prior to the 1980s, workers with a high school education could find well-paying jobs in manufacturing. Many of those jobs have now

Table 17.2 Possible Reasons for Increasing Inequality

Economists have come up with several different explanations for why the U.S. income distribution gap is widening.

Reason	Explanation
Rapid technological change	The increased use of information technology favors educated workers.
Growth of foreign trade	Competition from low-wage countries has hurt less skilled workers.
Shift to "superstar" markets	To a greater degree, the top people in a field do much better financially than everyone else.
Changes in government policy	The minimum wage has not risen as fast as inflation, while taxes have been cut for high-income households.

vanished because low-cost imports from China and elsewhere have reduced the size of the U.S. manufacturing sector. In other words, the *labor pool effect* of globalization has caused wages for low-skilled workers to fall (as described in **Chapter 16**). At the same time, highly skilled workers have benefited from the *market expansion effect* of globalization, at least until now.

superstar economy
Situations in which there is a widening gap in compensation between the top people and the merely competent.

Another cause of widening income inequality is what we might call the **superstar economy**. In many fields—sports, entertainment, consulting, academics, and law—there is a widening gap in compensation between the top people and the merely competent ones. As the economy evolves from local to national and even global markets, companies are reaching out to the best talent they can find. The reason is simple: If you are accused of a crime, you want the best criminal defense attorney if you can afford him or her, rather than the 10th best or a competent but average one. If you are a big company looking for help with a tough problem, you'd rather go to one of the top consulting firms rather than get a second stringer. This means that the top people in any field end up doing very well.

Finally, government action—or inaction—has probably played a role in increasing income inequality, though it's hard to say just how big this role is. For example, some economists believe that the minimum wage helps reduce income inequality by boosting the pay of low-income workers. However, as discussed in the previous chapter, the minimum wage has not kept up with inflation over the past 40 years.

Poverty

poverty rate
The percentage of people living in households that earn incomes below the poverty line.

poverty line
An income level that is supposed to indicate the lowest acceptable living standard in an economy; it depends on the number of people in the household and is adjusted for inflation each year.

Another way to assess the distribution of income is to look at the **poverty rate**, which is the percentage of people living in households that earn incomes below the poverty line. The **poverty line** is an income level that is supposed to indicate the lowest acceptable living standard in the economy. It is adjusted for inflation each year and depends on the number of people in the household. In 2021, the poverty line for a family of two adults and two children was roughly $26,500.

Figure 17.5 shows that over the past 45 years, the poverty rate has been as low as 10.5 percent in 2019, but rose back to 11.6% during the pandemic. This rise in the poverty rate would likely have been much worse without the broad array of government programs to cushion the impact of the pandemic, as we saw in **Chapter 6**.

Figure 17.5 The Poverty Rate, 1975–2021
The percentage of the U.S. population living below the poverty line rose after the Great Recession but has been declining in recent years.

Source: Census Bureau, www.census.gov.

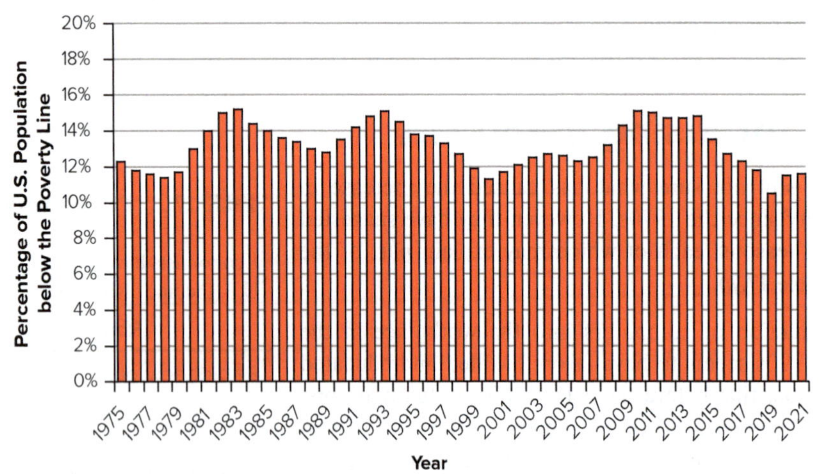

However, the official poverty rate does not tell the full story of how the people at the bottom of the income distribution are doing. One reason is that the government's calculations of the poverty rate exclude noncash benefits such as food stamps and health care programs such as Medicaid (a *noncash benefit* is any income support that the government provides other than a direct check to the recipient).

It's also important to remember that a household classified as poor in the United States may have a higher standard of living than the typical person in another country. Over time, some countries have closed the income gap with the United States, but it's a slow process. (See "**How It Works: Global Catch-Up**").

HOW IT WORKS: GLOBAL CATCH-UP

Are emerging countries catching up to the industrialized countries? **Figure 17.6** shows gross domestic product (GDP) per capita for four important emerging economies compared to the United States. If the line on the chart is rising, that means the country is catching up with the United States. If it's falling, it's losing ground. In this figure, incomes in China and India have gained significant ground in the United States, but incomes in Brazil and Mexico have not.

Figure 17.6 GDP per Capita: Four Important Emerging Economies

This figure shows the GDP per capita of four emerging countries as compared to the United States from 1990 to 2021, adjusting for price levels.

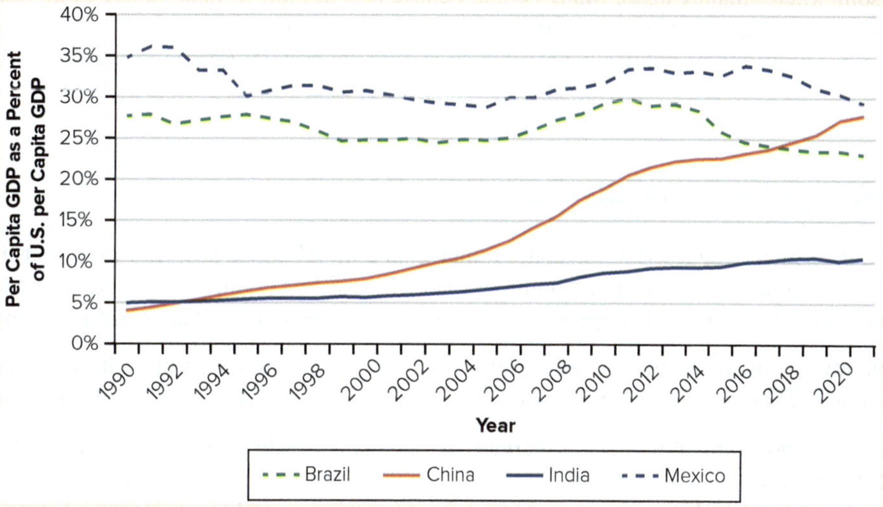

Source: International Monetary Fund, www.imf.org.

THE DEBATE OVER INEQUALITY (LO17-3)

LO17-3 List and discuss the arguments for and against government action to reduce inequality.

When we consider rising income inequality in the United States and what economists, politicians, and the public want to do about it, we find enormous and passionate differences of opinion. Virtually everyone would agree that a rich country like ours cannot allow its citizens to starve, no matter how poor they may be. Yet people argue about whether the government should act to reduce inequality and, if so, by how much. We summarize these ideas in **Table 17.3** and discuss them next.

Table 17.3 The Pros and Cons of Government Intervention to Reduce Inequality

For every argument in favor of government taking an active role to reduce inequality, there's an argument against government action.

	Arguments in Favor of Government Intervention to Reduce Inequality	Arguments against Government Intervention to Reduce Inequality
Fairness	A wide gap between rich and poor is unfair and immoral.	Taking money away from individuals who have earned it is unfair and immoral.
Growth	More equal societies experience stronger growth.	Allowing big rewards to go to the most successful performers helps motivate creativity, innovation, and hard work.
Politics	Big income differences cause political strife and eventually undermine support for a market economy.	A policy devoted to reducing inequality eventually leads to political control of the economy and an increase in rent-seeking behavior.
Data	Income distribution statistics understate inequality because they undercount high-income households.	Income distribution statistics overstate inequality because they do not include noncash benefits and fail to take economic mobility into account.

Two Competing Notions of Fairness

Supporters of government intervention argue that an economy with wide gaps between rich and poor is inherently unfair and immoral. It's not right, they say, for one person to live in a shack and go hungry while someone else lives in a mansion. The gaps between vast wealth and poverty in the same economy, or even the same city, are morally problematic for many people.

Those in favor of government action use this argument to support many different kinds of intervention, including using the tax system to even out incomes; offering subsidies for necessities like housing, food, education, and medical care; providing income support for families and children; and retraining workers for better jobs. These programs all exist today, though not funded to the level that their supporters want.

However, an appeal to fairness can also underpin an argument *against* government intervention. Income support programs cost money, which has to come from somewhere—mainly taxes. Many people believe it is not fair to take money away from those who have earned it: "I worked many hours to earn my money—why should the government take it away and give it to someone else?" Whether or not you agree with this argument, it has proven to be politically potent enough over the past 35 years to win support for tax cuts at both national and local levels.

Inequality, Growth, and Politics

Some supporters of government intervention use a pragmatic rather than a moral argument. They point out that big income gaps cause social stresses and political strife that impede the functioning of the economy. For example, if people in the bottom half of the income distribution are doing poorly, they are more likely to press for restrictions on foreign trade. That's bad for economic growth.

Moreover, in a global economy in which education is increasingly important, a national economy with many poor and unskilled workers is increasingly at a disadvantage. That's one reason many corporate executives are concerned about poverty and education.

On the other hand, opponents of government intervention argue that inequality could actually be good for growth. How so? In a market economy, you motivate effort and creativity by giving bigger rewards to the most successful performers. The economy functions better if people have an incentive to try as hard as they can, so a bigger gap between winners and losers means a bigger incentive to succeed.

This is one of the guiding principles of *supply-side economics,* discussed in **Chapter 11**. Starting with President Ronald Reagan, a significant number of politicians and economists have argued that taxing the rich too heavily lessens their incentive to work hard because they don't get to keep what they earn. From the same perspective, some people believe the fear of unemployment and poverty is important for motivating the poor to work rather than stay at home on welfare.

There's another reason government intervention might be a drag on growth. Remember that in **Chapter 6** we discussed *rent-seeking behavior,* which includes activities, such as lobbying, undertaken for the sole purpose of influencing government decisions. The more the government intervenes in the economy for good purposes such as helping the poor, the more tempting it is for lobbyists and special interest groups to try and get a share of the government pie for themselves. This can be an enormous burden on the economy; it diverts resources and leads to bad decisions.

Misleading Statistics

As we saw earlier in this chapter, economists do not agree about how much income inequality has risen. Supporters of government intervention argue that the official figures put out by the Census Bureau understate inequality. In fact, an analysis of income distribution based on tax returns—which are arguably more complete than the census survey—seems to show greater increases in income inequality (as shown in **Figure 17.4**).

income mobility
The change in an individual's income over his or her lifetime.

On the other hand, the figures may overstate inequality because they don't include noncash benefits such as Medicare and food stamps. The figures also don't take into account **income mobility**, which describes the changes in your income level over your lifetime. There may be years when you have very low income—when you are young, for instance—and times when your income is much higher. For example, imagine an economy in which all young workers earned $20,000 per year, and all middle-aged workers earned $100,000 per year. If we looked only at the figures for one year, we'd see a big gap between the poor and well-off households. But if we tracked people's income through their lifetimes, we'd see that this was a highly equal society in which everyone's income rose equally as they matured.

TAXES AND REDISTRIBUTION (LO17-4)

LO17-4 Explain how the tax system can be used to redistribute income.

We are going to focus here on the most common form of government intervention: the use of the tax system for **redistribution**. Redistribution is government action that transfers money from high-income to low-income households. Some amount of redistribution is essential for fixing the inequities produced by a market economy and for ensuring that poor people have enough money to live.

redistribution
The transfer of money from high-income to low-income households.

In theory, a tax system could be an effective mechanism for redistributing income. Suppose, for example, we imposed a high tax rate–say 90 percent–on anyone earning over $100,000. Then the **after-tax income distribution**–that is, what's left after the tax is taken out–would be much more equal than the **pretax income distribution**.

after-tax income distribution
The spread of incomes after taxes have been taken out.

pretax income distribution
The spread of incomes before taxes have been taken out.

We call the share of total income a household pays in taxes the **effective tax rate** (by contrast, the marginal tax rate is the share of the last dollar going for taxes). An income tax is **progressive** if high-income households pay a higher share of their income in taxes than do low-income households; that is, high-income households have a higher effective tax rate. For example, the federal income tax is progressive because the tax rate rises as household income rises. A progressive tax tends to make the after-tax income distribution more equal than the pretax income distribution.

effective tax rate
The share of income a household pays in taxes.

For example, **Table 17.4** shows how a progressive income tax can reduce inequality. Suppose the government collects a 10 percent tax on incomes up to $50,000 and then a 30 percent tax on everything a household earns above that (obviously, this is a simplified version of the actual tax system). Then a household with a $20,000 income will pay $2,000 in taxes (10 percent of $20,000). A household with a $200,000 income will pay $47,000 in taxes (10 percent of the first $50,000 plus 30 percent of the remaining $150,000).

progressive tax
A tax that requires high-income households to pay a higher tax rate than low-income households.

Table 17.4 An Example of a Progressive Income Tax

In this example, households pay a 10 percent tax on income up to $50,000 and 30 percent on everything over that. As a result, households with higher incomes pay a higher effective tax rate.

	Low-Income Household	High-Income Household	Ratio of High Income to Low Income
Before-tax income	$20,000	$200,000	10 to 1
10% tax up to $50,000	$ 2,000	$ 2,000	
30% tax on everything over $50,000	$ 0	$ 45,000	
Total tax	$ 2,000	$ 47,000	
Effective tax rate (as a percent-age of before-tax income)	10%	24%	
After-tax income	$18,000	$153,000	8.5 to 1

In this example, the high-income household pays about 24 percent of its income in taxes, and the low-income household pays 10 percent. This difference in tax rates tends to narrow income inequality. Before taxes, the high-income household has an income 10 times that of the low-income household as shown in the right column of **Table 17.4**. After taxes, the ratio falls to 8.5–still a big gap, but not as wide as before.

In contrast, a tax is **regressive** if it makes low-income households pay a bigger share of their incomes than high-income taxpayers. Consider a sales tax, for example. A sales tax is typically equal to some percentage of the money spent on purchases. That is, households pay the tax on the portions of their incomes that they spend but not on the portions saved.

regressive tax
A tax that requires high-income households to pay a lower tax rate than low-income households.

As a result, the sales tax is regressive. Most low-income households don't do much saving, so they pay sales tax on almost their entire incomes. However, high-income households don't spend all their incomes, so they pay a lower share of their incomes in tax. That is, if you earned $1 million per year but spent only $10,000, you could pay the same sales tax as a family earning $10,000 and spending $10,000.

Table 17.5 How a Regressive Sales Tax Works

In this example, households pay a 6 percent sales tax on all spending.

	Low-Income Household	High-Income Household	Ratio of High Income to Low Income
Before-tax income	$20,000	$200,000	10 to 1
Amount spent	$20,000	$100,000	
Amount paid on sales tax of 6%	$ 1,200	$ 6,000	
Percentage of before-tax income paid in sales tax	6.0%	3.0%	
After-tax income	$18,800	$194,000	10.3 to 1

Table 17.5 shows a more realistic example of a regressive sales tax in action. The tax rate is 6 percent on all purchases, so the low-income household–which spends everything–ends up paying a sales tax of $1,200 (6 percent of $20,000). But the high-income household, because it spends only half its income, pays $6,000 in taxes (6 percent of $100,000). That means the after-tax ratio of high income to low income actually *increases* from 10 percent to 10.3 percent because of the sales tax.

Adding It All Up

Figuring out whether the whole U.S. tax system is progressive or regressive is not easy because U.S. citizens pay a lot of different taxes, including income tax, sales tax, property tax, and payroll tax (for Social Security and Medicare). Some of these, like the income tax and property tax, are progressive. Others, like the sales tax and the payroll tax, are regressive.

What's more, there have been multiple recent changes to the tax code, including big tax cuts in 1981, 2001, 2003, and 2018, and big tax increases in 1990, 1993, and 2013. In fact, Washington has changed the tax law almost every year, in either big or small ways.

After all these changes, the federal tax system through 2019 was just somewhat less progressive than it was in 1979. For example, those in the top 1 percent income bracket paid 35 percent of their income in federal taxes in 1979 (including income taxes, payroll taxes, gasoline and other excise taxes, and their share of corporate income taxes). That's according to the nonpartisan Congressional Budget Office. After President Reagan cut taxes for high-earning households, the effective tax rate for the highest-earning 1 percent dropped as low as 24.7 percent. Tax increases by President Bill Clinton in 1993 pushed the effective rate at the top as high as 35 percent, which his successor, President George W. Bush, lowered again. Then, President Barack Obama pushed it back up again, followed by President Donald Trump pushing it down again with his 2018 tax cuts. The effective tax rate on top-income individuals in 2019, the last year for which data are available, was 30 percent (see **Figure 17.7**).

Figure 17.7 The Effective Federal Tax Rate for the Top 1 Percent of Taxpayers, 1979–2019
The effective federal tax rate for the top 1 percent in 2019 was somewhat lower than it was in 1979. These figures include federal income tax, payroll tax, gasoline and other excise taxes, and their share of corporate income taxes.

Source: Congressional Budget Office, November 2022.

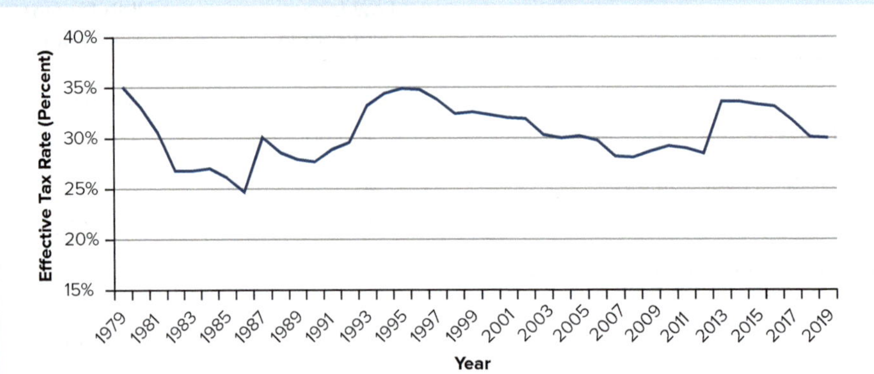

EARNINGS AND LABOR MARKET DISCRIMINATION (LO17-5)

LO17-5 Give examples of labor market discrimination.

Now we turn to another aspect of income inequality: the question of discrimination in labor markets. **Labor market discrimination** occurs when one person is paid less or treated worse on the job than an equally qualified person because of their race, gender, or some other characteristic. One government responsibility is to enforce workplace antidiscrimination laws. These may differ by city, by state, and by occupation. On the national level, for example, the Equal Employment Opportunity Commission (EEOC) enforces laws forbidding employment discrimination based on age, race, color, religion, gender, national origin, sexual orientation, or disabled status.

labor market discrimination
When an individual is paid less or treated worse on the job than an equally qualified person because of his or her race, gender, or some other characteristic.

Despite such laws, a reality of today's labor market is that some groups–notably women, blacks, and Hispanics–consistently earn less on average than others. Women earn less on average than men, while blacks and Hispanics earn less on average than whites. **Figure 17.8** provides some comparative figures for 2022, based on Bureau of Labor Statistics data. For example, the median weekly earnings of adult male workers were $1154 per week, compared to $958 for adult female workers (*median* means the midpoint–half the members of a given group earn more than the median, and half earn less).

Figure 17.8 Weekly Earnings by Gender and Race, 2022
This chart shows the median weekly earnings in 2022 for full-time workers in several gender, race, and ethnicity subgroups. For example, typical white male workers earned $1172 per week, compared to only $921 for black male workers.

Source: Bureau of Labor Statistics, www.bls.gov.

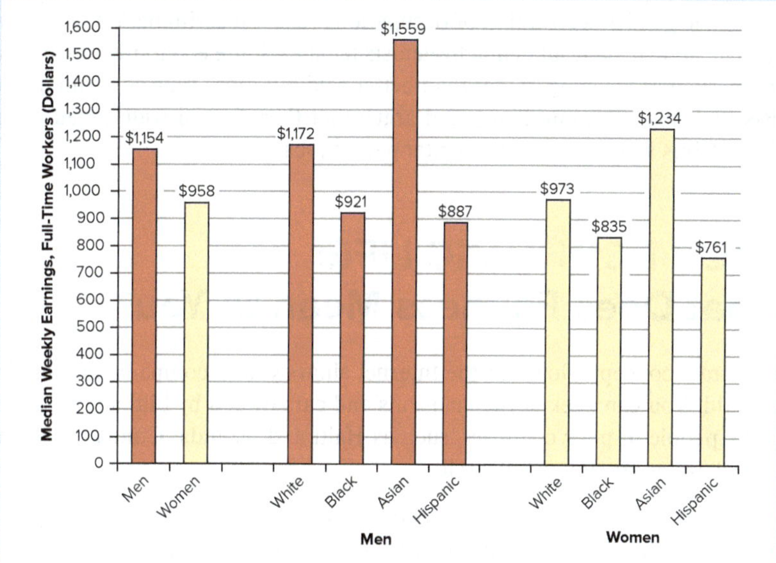

How much of these disparities comes from illegal discrimination, and how much from other sources? In addition to discrimination, there are three main reasons earnings could differ by gender and race: differences in education, differences in experience, and differences in occupational choices.

Let's start with education. As we saw earlier in the chapter, better-educated workers generally earn higher pay. Today, women have pretty much the same education levels as men, so education differences can't explain much of the gender pay gap. As of 2021, 39 percent of women 25 years and over were college graduates, slightly higher than the 37 percent of men. And if we look at men and women aged 25 to 34, there's a big difference in favor of women: 46 percent of women were college graduates compared to 36 percent of men.

However, education differences can explain part of the pay gap for blacks and Hispanics because non-Hispanic whites still have a much higher average level of formal education than do blacks and Hispanics in the same age group. For example, among 25- to 34-year-olds, only 27 percent of blacks and 23 percent of Hispanics were college-educated in 2021. In comparison, 48 percent of non-Hispanic whites in that age group were college-educated.

If we stopped here, it would look as though differences in education go a long way toward explaining why non-Hispanic whites earn higher wages than do blacks or Hispanics. But the full situation is more complicated. Some people argue that blacks and Hispanics may face unfair obstacles in attending and graduating from college. One reason is that these groups may come from families who may have a harder time paying for education, and because they face discrimination getting into and attending college. To the extent that these two factors are true, a difference in educational attainment can itself reflect economic inequality and discrimination.

Similar complications come up when we look at differences in pay between men and women working full-time. This pay gap has narrowed substantially over time, but it is still there. As **Figure 17.9** shows, in 2022 the median weekly earnings of full-time female workers were only about 83.0 percent of earnings of full-time male workers.

Figure 17.9 Women's Median Weekly Earnings as a Percentage of Men's

Women's wages have been catching up with men's, but there is still a gap.

Source: Bureau of Labor Statistics, www.bls.gov.

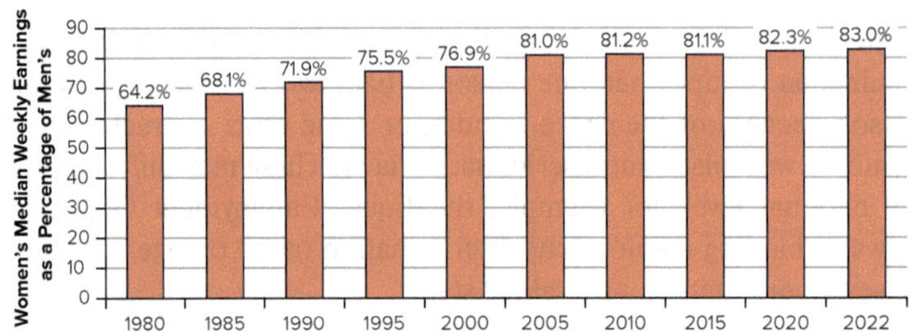

Part of this pay gap reflects the tendency of many occupations to be filled primarily by one gender, as reported to the BLS. Occupations that are mainly filled by people who identify as women tend to be paid less. For example, roughly 40 percent of lawyers are women as of 2022, but 83 percent of paralegals and legal assistants, who are paid much less, are women. About 37 percent of dentists are women, while 96 percent of dental hygienists, a lower-paid profession, are women.

To what extent does the gender segregation of occupations reflect discrimination, and to what extent does it reflect choice? Why should most dentists be male and virtually all dental hygienists female? Some economists assert that women choose lower-paid occupations with more flexible hours, such as teaching, rather than better-paid but more time-consuming occupations, such as being corporate executives. Other economists find this reasoning flimsy and argue that there is still widespread discrimination against women in traditional male occupations, which drives women away from better-paying jobs.

YOUR ECONOMIC LIFE: What Does Fairness Mean to You?

Inequality is an abstract concept. However, the Internet allows you to compare your life, in detail, with other people in the United States and around the world. You can peek at the mansions and cars owned by billionaires and rich athletes. Meanwhile, you can also see the difficulties faced by people in poor countries, such as Haiti and Uganda. Compared to those deeply impoverished nations, most of the people in the United States are doing quite well.

In that context, what does fairness mean to you personally? Does fairness mean taxing rich people in the United States to pay for better schools and homes in Haiti? Or would it be fairer to use that money to improve conditions for poor communities in the United States? Or is it unfair to tax the rich at a higher rate than everyone else?

These are not questions with obvious answers. Nor will you be tested on them. But they are important to think about.

CONCLUSION

Just by the numbers, there is clearly income inequality in the United States. Equally clearly, it has been increasing in recent years, with an increase in the share of income going to the top earners.

Similarly, labor market outcomes continue to reflect differences in pay and occupational choice by gender, and differences in pay and educational attainment by race and Hispanic ethnicity.

However, there is little agreement among economists about how to address inequality. Some argue that there is little that government can and should do. Others believe that taking action to reduce inequality is one of the most important responsibilities of government. This question is likely to be one of the more controversial ones in economics for many years to come.

17 SUMMARY

1. The Census Bureau tracks the nation's income distribution each year, based on a survey. A quintile represents 20 percent of all households. The 20th percentile is the income level that marks the dividing line between the bottom quintile and the second quintile, whereas the income level that marks the dividing line between the top quintile and everyone else is called the 80th percentile. One way to measure income inequality is the 80/20 ratio, which is the 80th percentile of income divided by the 20th percentile of income. A high 80/20 ratio means that high-income households earn a lot more than low-income households. *(LO17-1)*
2. Income inequality in the United States has been increasing over time. However, the size of the increase depends on what measure you use. The reasons for rising inequality include rapid technological change, the growth of foreign trade, a shift to superstar markets, and changes in government policy. Another way to assess inequality is to look at the poverty rate, which measures the percentage of the population living in households with incomes below the poverty line. *(LO17-2)*
3. Economists disagree about whether more government intervention is needed to reduce income inequality. These disagreements involve issues of fairness, growth, politics, and data problems. *(LO17-3)*
4. The tax system can be used to redistribute income from high-income households to low-income households, thus reducing inequality. A progressive tax like the income tax reduces inequality, whereas regressive taxes like sales or payroll taxes increase inequality. *(LO17-4)*
5. Another aspect of income inequality is discrimination in labor markets. That means one person is paid less or treated worse on the job because of his or her race, gender, or some other characteristic. *(LO17-5)*

KEY TERMS AND CONCEPTS

income
income distribution
quintiles
income inequality
80/20 ratio
superstar economy
poverty rate
poverty line
income mobility
redistribution
after-tax income distribution
pretax income distribution
effective tax rate
progressive tax
regressive tax
labor market discrimination

connect PROBLEMS

1. Look at **Figure 17.1**, which gives some basic information about the income distribution in 2021. *(LO17-1)*
   a) What percentage of households received between $100,000 and $150,000 in income in 2021?
   b) What percentage of total income did this group get?
   c) What percentage of households received between $0 and $100,000 in income in 2021? (Hint: You can add the percentages of different categories.)
   d) Look at the households with incomes greater than $250,000. What percentage of total income did this group get?
2. The following table gives eight occupations and their average annual wages in 2021, as determined by the Bureau of Labor Statistics (these are nationwide averages across all experience levels). *(LO17-1)*

Occupation	Average Annual Wage (Dollars)	Quintile
Compensation and benefits managers	$139,470	—
Elementary schoolteachers	64,870	—
Fashion designers	83,650	—
Network and computer systems administrators	91,250	—
Paralegals and legal assistants	58,330	—
Registered nurses	82,750	—
Security guards	35,835	—
Shampooers (in hair-cutting establishments)	25,160	—

a) Suppose that a worker is the only person employed in a one-earner household. For each occupation listed in the table, identify which quintile of income that puts their household into. Use the data in **Table 17.1.**
b) Suppose a fashion designer married a security guard, and they both kept working. Which quintile would their household be in?
c) Suppose a network administrator married a registered nurse. Which quintile would their household be in (assuming both keep working)?

3. Which of the following is not a reason for rising inequality? ***(LO17-2)***

   a) Widespread use of computers.
   b) Rising enrollments at community colleges.
   c) Increased global competition from China and other low-wage countries.
   d) The widening education premium.

4. Suppose that we have a country with a population of 30 million, where 3 million are below the poverty line. What would the poverty rate be? ***(LO17-2)***

   a) 10 percent.
   b) 30 percent.
   c) 3 percent.
   d) 15 percent.

5. Many CEOs of large corporations have enormous pay packages in the tens of millions of dollars per year. Such high pay helps contribute to income inequality because the vast majority of people earn much less. Suppose Congress passed a law that the annual pay for any job could not exceed $500,000 per year. What effect would this law have on the market for corporate executives? ***(LO17-3)***

6. It's sometimes said, half in jest, that the best antipoverty policy is to simply give the poor more money. Which of the following would be a disadvantage of such a policy? ***(LO17-3)***

   a) More equal societies tend to experience greater growth.
   b) People would have less incentive to work hard.
   c) Big income differences cause political strife.
   d) A wide gap in income is immoral.

7. Suppose our tax system imposed a 30 percent tax rate on income up to $50,000 and a 10 percent tax rate on income over $50,000. ***(LO17-4)***

   a) Would this tax system be progressive or regressive?
   b) The Social Security tax paid by workers is 6.2 percent of wages, up to a maximum of $160,200 in 2023. For incomes above that maximum, no additional taxes are paid. Is the Social Security tax progressive or regressive?

8. Which of the following situations most clearly represents labor market discrimination against women? ***(LO17-5)***

   a) A man earns $50,000 per year, and a woman in a different occupation and the same education and experience earns $40,000.
   b) A woman earns $75,000 and a man with less experience earns $70,000.
   c) A man earns $50,000 per year, and a woman in the same occupation with the same education and experience earns $45,000.
   d) A woman earns $100,000 and a man with less experience and more education earns $110,000.

CH 18

ECONOMICS OF HEALTH CARE AND RETIREMENT

Monkey Business Images/Shutterstock

LEARNING OBJECTIVES

After you have read this chapter, you should be able to:

LO18-1 Describe the basic economic features of health care in the United States.
LO18-2 Discuss possible reasons health care spending is rising so quickly.
LO18-3 Identify the three main approaches to health care reform and discuss the differences between them.
LO18-4 Describe the life cycle theory of retirement and identify the main sources of retirement funds.
LO18-5 Explain the difference between defined benefit and defined contribution retirement plans.
LO18-6 Summarize the demographic challenge facing Social Security and describe the possible solutions.

The biggest health-related event of our lifetimes was the COVID-19 pandemic. As of early 2023, the official U.S. death count from the pandemic was over 1 million. Americans are making the decision about whether or not to get vaccine booster shots to handle new variants. And an unknown number of people are suffering from "long COVID"—lingering symptoms from infection with the virus that can force workers to retire earlier than they planned.

Yet despite the sweeping pandemic-related impacts on the economy that we have already discussed in this textbook, what's striking is how little the basic economics of health care and retirement have changed. There are few certainties in life, but here are two scenarios that are inevitable. First, at some point, you will get sick and need the services of a doctor and perhaps a hospital. And second, you will eventually grow old and be ready to (or be forced to) retire.

Because these scenarios apply to everyone, the questions of how to pay for health care and retirement are two of today's most important economic issues.

Both require society to take care of people who may not be in a position to care for themselves. As a result, the normal market solution of letting individuals make their own decisions doesn't always work. It is not socially acceptable to let old or poor people suffer or die because they cannot afford medical care. And it is not socially acceptable to allow old people to live in poverty because they cannot work anymore.

Up to now, the United States has adopted a mixed private–public system to provide for both health care and retirement. Health care is paid for through a combination of funding sources: personal spending, employer-provided insurance, and government programs (mainly Medicare for the elderly and Medicaid for the poor). Retirement income comes from a combination of personal savings, employer retirement plans, and government programs (mainly Social Security).

However, this mixed public–private system is expensive, and it is getting more so as the population ages. What's more, many people believe the U.S. health care system does not work well and leaves too many people unprotected. That led President Barack Obama to sign health care reform legislation (the Affordable Care Act, or ACA) in March 2010. This bill transformed the health care sector and led to many more people being covered by health insurance.

This chapter covers the economics of health care and retirement. We start by describing today's health care system, and the potential reason why spending keeps increasing. Then, we discuss three broad approaches to reforming health care. Next, we examine retirement and lay out the basic life cycle theory, which explains how retirement would work in the absence of Social Security and pensions. Following that, we discuss the difference between defined benefit and defined contribution plans and examine the demographic challenges facing Social Security.

THE BASICS OF HEALTH CARE ECONOMICS (LO18-1)

LO18-1 Describe the basic economic features of health care.

employer health insurance plan
A health insurance plan set up by and partly paid for by an employer. Employees are usually required to pay a fraction of the cost in monthly premiums.

Affordable Care Act
The health care reform legislation signed by President Barack Obama in March 2010.

Health care today is the largest sector of the economy. In 2021, Americans spent $4.3 trillion on health care, including drugs, hospital care, and nursing homes. That's over 18 percent of the economy.

Health care's share of the economic pie has been growing, as **Figure 18.1** shows. If these trends continue, health care could equal 30 percent of the economy by 2075. Imagine a world where every third building is a hospital, nursing home, or doctor's office!

Moreover, compared to other countries, the United States spends far more on health care per person. (see **Figure 18.2.**) In 2021, health care cost Americans more than $12,000 per person, including all private and public sources of funds. Other major industrialized countries spent about half as much per person.

As a result, the question of how to slow the growth of health care spending, while still maintaining or even improving care for everyone, is one of the biggest issues facing policymakers.

Figure 18.1 National Health Expenditures as a Percentage of GDP
Spending on health care has consumed a growing share of the economy over the past half century.
Source: Centers for Medicare and Medicaid Services, www.cms.gov.

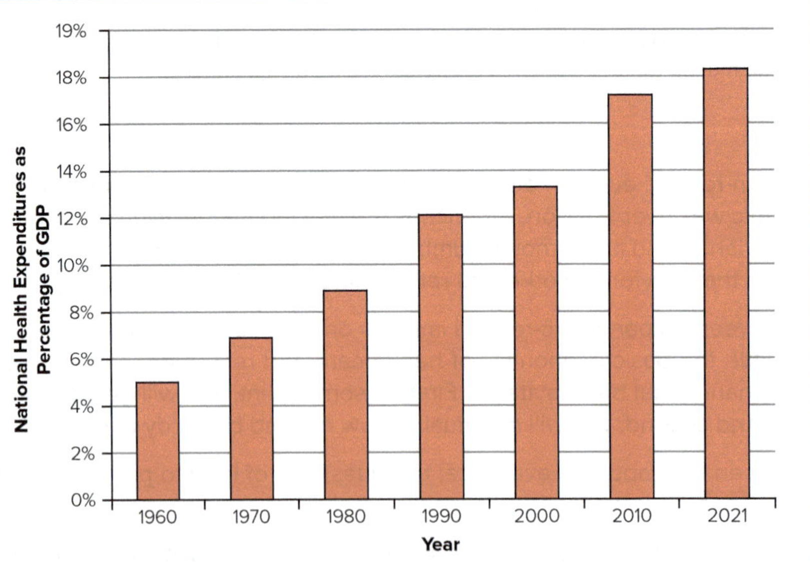

Who Pays for Health Care?

Where does the money for health care come from? (see **Table 18.1.**) First, as of 2021, the majority of Americans are covered through **employer health insurance plans**. The **Affordable Care Act** (ACA) of 2010 imposed certain rules on employer health insurance plans, including requiring insurers to cover preexisting conditions.

Figure 18.2 Per Capita Health Care Spending across the World, 2021 The United States spends far more on health care, per person, than other industrialized countries.

Source: The Organisation for Economic Cooperation and Development (OECD), www.oecd.org.

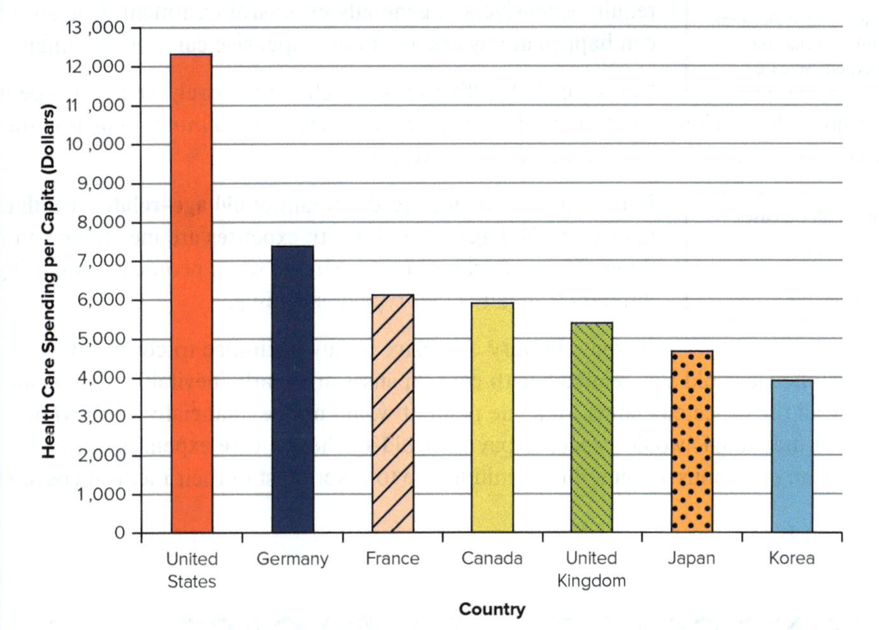

Low-income children, their parents, and individuals with disabilities are covered, not always completely, by **Medicaid**, which was introduced by President Lyndon Johnson in 1965. Some states took advantage of provisions in the ACA to significantly expand Medicaid coverage to all low-income households. Rules for Medicaid coverage were also relaxed for the duration of the pandemic emergency.

Medicaid

A government-funded health plan that helps cover health care costs of low-income children, parents, and others.

When Americans reach 65, the responsibility for covering health care costs is shifted to **Medicare**, another program introduced by President Johnson in 1965. Medicare is funded in part by payroll taxes paid by both workers and companies.

Medicare

A government-funded health plan that helps cover health care costs of older individuals.

Some people buy their own health insurance directly. That percentage increased after the ACA went into effect. All told, 92 percent of Americans were covered by insurance as of 2021.

How Health Events Drive Spending

Table 18.1 Types of Health Insurance, 2021

Roughly 92 percent of Americans were covered by at least one type of health insurance in 2021 (percentages add to more than 100 because some individuals have multiple coverage).

Type of Insurance	Individuals Covered (in %)
Employer health insurance	54.3
Medicaid	18.9
Medicare	18.4
Direct-purchase by individuals	13.7
Military health care	3.5

Source: Census Bureau, census.gov.

Why are there so many different types of health insurance? Part of the reason has to do with the basic economics of health care. In most markets, decisions to purchase and consume are voluntary. You choose when and how to buy a new car or a new home. That gives you, as a consumer, the opportunity to make informed choices, and to choose to spend less if you don't have the resources.

By contrast, in the health care market, consumption decisions are usually forced by an external health event such as getting sick, and there is much less opportunity for choice. From the economic perspective, we can divide health events into three categories. First, **ordinary health care expenses** are the more or less predictable annual physician visits when you are young and middle-aged: dental and vision costs, occasional visits to the doctor for the flu or sports-related injuries, and maternity-related visits.

ordinary health care expenses

The more or less predictable flow of minor health issues when you are young or middle-aged, including dental and vision problems.

Ordinary health care expenses are a bit like buying food. For most people, food expenses can be budgeted because they are predictable and involve a lot of choice. But if people are too poor, they may have trouble affording a good diet without subsidies such as food stamps. Similarly, ordinary health care expenses may be difficult for poor Americans to pay for without subsidies such as Medicaid.

catastrophic health events
Major health issues such as cancer or significant injuries that require extensive and expensive care.

Second, **catastrophic health events** are major health issues such as cancer or significant injuries that require extensive and generally expensive treatment. Catastrophic health events are unpredictable and can happen at any age, including expensive care for sick infants.

Catastrophic health events, which are relatively rare and expensive, have similar characteristics to auto accidents and home fires. These sorts of events are typically covered by *insurance,* which is the payment of regular small premiums in exchange for coverage in the case of an expensive but rare event.

old age-related health expenses
The inevitable health issues connected with aging, including expensive end-of-life care.

Finally, people incur a steady stream of **old age-related health expenses** as they move into their 60s and later years. Old age-related health expenses are inevitable and may include some very expensive procedures. They also come at a time in life when people are not bringing in other income. They are therefore different from any other type of spending.

It would be very expensive to buy insurance to cover old age-related health care expenses. The reason is straightforward: Because old age-related health care expenses are nearly inevitable, the insurance company would have to charge high premiums to pay all the expected claims. At some point, it would not be financially worthwhile for an older person to buy medical insurance. Middle-aged individuals would expect to pay their old-age health care expenses out of their own pockets. That means they would have to sock away an enormous amount during middle age to cover most of their medical costs. Hence, Medicare is provided through the government.

THE RISING COST OF HEALTH CARE (LO18-2)

LO18-2 Discuss possible reasons health care spending is rising so quickly.

A crucial fact about today's economy is that health care spending per person has consistently risen faster than income per person. In other words, the richer we get, the more we spend on doctor's visits, medical tests, mental health care, cosmetic surgery, and almost every other form of necessary or elective care.

Table 18.2 Six Reasons Health Care Costs Are Rising Quickly

Reason	Explanation
Demographic change	An aging population needs more health care.
Rising incomes	A richer population is willing to pay for more health care.
Third-party payments	Spending decisions are made by doctors and patients, but most of the payments come from insurance companies and the government.
Tax rules for employer health insurance plans	Workers are not taxed on company-funded health care spending.
The cost of better medical technology	New health care technologies are expensive.
Unnecessary medicine	The American health care system is wasting money on unnecessary and perhaps dangerous procedures.

For a few years in the 1990s, health care spending seemed under control. But in recent years, costs have jumped again. One measure of this increase is the consumer price index for medical care, which includes both health care services (doctors and hospitals) and health care products (drugs and equipment). Between 1997 and 2022, the price to consumers of medical care rose at an average annual rate of 3.4 percent. Meanwhile, the price of everything else rose at an annual average rate of only 2.4 percent. That difference sounds small, but it accumulates over time.

Why the disparity? Economists have explored several reasons why health care costs are so difficult to control. These reasons are summarized in **Table 18.2**. Let's look at them more closely.

Demographic Change

Demographic change—the changing distribution of age groups in the population—is an important explanation for rising health costs. As **Table 18.3** shows, the percentage of the population that is 65 years and older rose from 11.3 percent in 1980 to 16.8 percent in 2020. It will likely continue to rise as the American population ages, though the exact numbers depend on how long people live, how many children are born, and the number of (younger) immigrants who enter the country.

demographic change
A changing distribution of groups in a population.

As we saw in the previous chapter, old age-related health expenses are inevitable and high. Major health problems such as cancer or heart attacks become increasingly common as people age, and the cost of treatment is correspondingly high. So, the aging population is helping drive up health care costs.

Rising Incomes

However, demographic change by itself does not fully explain the rise in health care spending. Another reason for this is because health care is a *luxury good,* as defined in **Chapter 3**–one whose consumption goes up sharply when incomes rise. The argument runs something like this: We have all the physical goods we need–food, housing, transportation, and entertainment. So, as we get richer, we don't spend the extra money on a fourth car or a fifth television set. Instead, we spend it on health care.

In fact, U.S. adults seem willing to spend a bit extra to be able to quickly see a doctor rather than waiting months for an appointment. And they are willing to pay for additional tests just to have some peace of mind.

Table 18.3 The Aging American Population

Year	Population 65 Years and Older (in %)
1980	11.3
1990	12.5
2000	12.4
2010	13.1
2020	16.8
2030 (projected)	20.6
2040 (projected)	21.6

Source: Census Bureau, census.gov.

Third-Party Payments

Imagine that the store manager at your local supermarket was allowed to choose the foods you buy. He or she would make up the list, fill your shopping cart, and then bill your insurance company. You'd likely end up eating some tasty but expensive items that you otherwise would not have bought.

Similarly, when it comes to health care, the person making decisions is often not the patient but the doctor. Moreover, the great majority of health care spending is paid for by a **third party**–an employer health insurance plan, Medicare, or Medicaid. That means the normal constraints on purchases are not present. In theory, a doctor can order expensive tests and treatments without worrying about whether they are actually worth the money, and the patient can agree without worrying about whether she will have to pay for them. In fact, if the doctor is worried about being sued for malpractice by an unsatisfied patient, ordering extra tests for self-protection becomes a rational decision.

third party
In health care, a private or public insurance plan that pays for health care services for an individual.

This is different from the usual sort of market we discussed in earlier chapters. Typically, when we talk about buyers in a market, we assume the buyer is also the ultimate consumer of the good or service being purchased. So, when you buy a car, you'll pay for extra options like special shiny trim only if you think they're worth their cost.

In practice, both private and public health insurers closely scrutinize doctors' decisions and refuse to pay for care they think is excessive. However, many economists believe that if patients had to pay their own health care costs, they would spend more frugally.

Tax Rules for Employer Health Insurance Plans

> Health care is a luxury good because people spend a lot more on it as their incomes rise.

If a worker receives a dollar in wages from an employer, he or she has to pay federal, state, and local taxes on that money. But if the employer spends that same dollar on giving the worker a better health insurance plan, then the worker does not pay tax on that money.

To put it another way, employer contributions to health care plans are not counted as taxable income to workers. It's a general principle that, if something is untaxed, you receive more of it. In this case, workers might choose to receive part of their raises as better health insurance, which is untaxed, rather than as higher wages, which are taxed.

The Cost of Better Medical Technology

Over the past 10 years, private companies, academic institutions, and the federal government have poured perhaps $1 trillion dollars into medical research. The result has been all sorts of new medical technologies, pharmaceuticals, and procedures intended to improve health and save lives. One example is the death rate from heart disease, which has been steadily declining despite an aging population.

But this technological progress often comes with a big price tag. New drugs can be quite expensive when they are first introduced. Advanced equipment like robotic surgery can also be expensive.

Even some advances that save money in the long run end up adding to costs in the short run. For example, in 2014 a pharmaceutical company, Gilead, came out with a cure for hepatitis C, at that time the most common chronic bloodborne infection in the United States. People infected with hepatitis C would often develop chronic liver diseases, sometimes leading to expensive liver transplants 20 or 30 years down the road. The new drug reduced or eliminated those long-term expenses. But public and private insurance plans had to pay for the new drug right now. The result: a one-time spike in pharmaceutical costs in 2014 and 2015, as many people infected with hepatitis C were cured of their disease. Then, costs went way down because the pool of infected people was much smaller.

Unnecessary Medicine

life expectancy

The number of years an individual is expected to live, given his or her current age and available medical knowledge.

Researchers suspect that the American health care system is wasting money on unnecessary and perhaps dangerous medical procedures. For example, antibiotics are often prescribed when they are not necessary. Expensive tests are done even when the results won't make a difference to treatment. And back pain can often be reduced or controlled with physical therapy and pain medications rather than expensive surgery.

However, while everyone agrees that there is waste in the health care system, there is also resistance to dictating how doctors practice medicine. This will continue to be an important topic in years to come (see **"Spotlight: How Well Does the U.S. Health Care System Work?"**).

SPOTLIGHT: HOW WELL DOES THE U.S. HEALTH CARE SYSTEM WORK?

We spend an enormous amount on health care, but does all that money improve our health? With most purchases in a market economy, you know whether you received value for the money you paid. For example, when you buy a car, you know whether or not it runs well.

The simplest way to assess the quality of our health care system is to look at the change in our **life expectancy**, or expected years of remaining life, based on today's health care system. (Obviously, there is no way to predict future medical breakthroughs, so we must ignore them in this analysis.) Life expectancy for newborns—the usual number cited—has risen a lot because of better care for pregnant mothers and young children. In 1900, life expectancy at birth was only 47.3 years. In 2019, the latest year before the pandemic, life expectancy at birth was 78.8 years. That's a big gain.

However, we can also compare life expectancy in the United States with other industrialized countries, and that picture is not so rosy, as **Figure 18.3** shows. These data reflects the first year of the pandemic, but United States life expectancy was lagging other major countries even before COVID.

Why is the U.S. lagging? One hypothesis is that Americans have been taking worse care of themselves—getting less exercise and eating too much—even as medical science has gotten better. Alternatively, inefficiencies in the U.S. health care system may prevent the delivery of good medical care to many adults.

Figure 18.3 Life Expectancy at Birth for Selected Countries, 2020

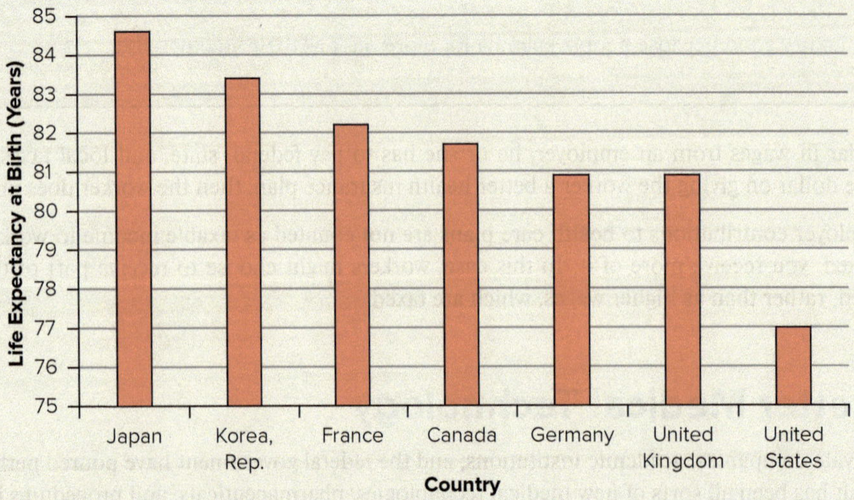

Source: World Bank

HEALTH CARE REFORM (LO18-3)

LO18-3 Identify the three main approaches to health care reform and discuss the differences between them.

In several places in this text, we have discussed the debate over the role of government in the economy. This debate is especially intense in the case of health care.

The pandemic, of course, saw massive health-related government interventions in the economy. In early 2020, many schools and businesses were closed by government order. The government-funded unprecedented safety nets for American families and businesses (Chapter 6), guided and financed emergency development of a COVID vaccine (Chapter 15), and originally mandated COVID vaccinations for many workers (Chapter 16), though there was resistance to those mandates.

These measures have turned out to be intensely controversial. But even before the pandemic, the appropriate approach to funding and administering health care has been hotly debated. For example, the Affordable Care Act of 2010 (ACA) made health care insurance available to more Americans, which was popular among voters. Yet even after its passage, opponents made repeated attempts to repeal or modify the ACA, objecting to government intervention into the private sector.

On the other hand, there is also substantial support for government to play an increased role in regulating and paying for health care. That could mean expanding Medicare or Medicaid. Some policymakers have even proposed a **single-payer system**, where the government pays for all health care through revenues raised by taxes. This would be more similar to the systems in other countries such as the United Kingdom, Canada, and Japan.

So, as this textbook is being revised in early 2023, the United States is likely getting ready for another round of bruising battles over the appropriate role of government in the health care system. There are three main approaches to health care reform: keeping and improving the current system, reducing government's role, and increasing government's role (see **Table 18.4**).

Table 18.4 Three Approaches to Health Care Reform

Approach	Description	Positives and negatives
Keeping and improving current system	Keep today's mixture of public and private insurance, while tweaking regulations to reduce costs and improve choice.	Positive: Most Americans have access to good medical care. Negative: Current system is complicated and leaves both patients and providers unhappy.
Reducing government's role	Reducing regulation of health insurance plans and cutting back on subsidies for poor.	Positive: Lower cost to taxpayers, at least in short run. Negative: More people would not have health insurance. More potential for *adverse selection.*
Increasing government's role	Offering individuals more options for government-provided health insurance. Some people have proposed a single-payer system	Positive: Everyone would have access to good health insurance, perhaps at a lower price. Companies would have lower health care costs. Negative: Taxes would likely rise. Government action has downsides such as the incentive problem.

single-payer system
A proposed health plan in which health care spending for everyone is paid for through the government.

Approach 1: Keeping and Improving the Current System

In many ways, the ACA achieved its main goals. The percentage of uninsured dropped from 13.3 percent in 2013, as the law was going into effect, to 8.0 percent in 2019, before the pandemic. Moreover, the large number of people with preexisting conditions could more easily get good health insurance.

JGI/Blend Images LLC

However, the ACA preserved and even expanded the patchwork of private and public health insurance plans. So, for patients, doctors, and hospitals, the process of obtaining, providing, and paying for care became more complicated. Moreover, many Americans objected to the high cost of medical care, including spending on pharmaceuticals. Thus, the Inflation Reduction Act of 2022 included a provision that was designed to hold down the price paid by Medicare for many important medications.

Approach 2: Reducing the Role of Government in Health Care

From the moment that the ACA was passed in 2010, it was attacked for giving the government too large a role in the health care system. Opponents called for a reduction in subsidies, and more choice in whether people were required to buy health insurance or not.

Reducing the role of government in the health care system has three main negatives. First, government-subsidized health care is essential for poor Americans, since they cannot afford to directly pay for insurance. Thus, a reduction in the role of the government is likely to leave more people uninsured.

adverse selection problem
The tendency of insurance–health insurance in particular–to be purchased by those who are more likely to make claims.

Second, if people can easily opt out of buying health insurance, health insurance is more likely to be purchased by people who are sick and less likely to be purchased by people who need it less–the ones who are healthy. This is what's known as the **adverse selection problem**. Adverse selection is the tendency for insurance to be purchased by those who are more likely to make claims. This drives up insurance rates because the plan must pay a lot more in claims (compared to how much it receives in premiums) than it would if everyone, including healthier people, were insured and paying premiums.

Third, in the absence of government regulation, any profit-maximizing health insurance plan will attempt to exclude people who might be expected to make a lot of claims. Thus, there is an incentive to weed out people with "preexisting conditions."

Approach 3: Increasing the Role of Government in Health Care

In most other industrialized countries, the government plays a bigger role in health care than in the United States. These systems appear to have lower costs and higher life expectancy than the United States.

As a result, at least some voters support expanding the government role in health care. One such proposal would make it easier for young and middle-aged workers to purchase health insurance from Medicare. A more extreme option would set up a single-payer system, where the government provides health insurance for everyone.

Increasing the role of government in health care would tend to improve access to good medical care for the poor. It would also reduce the adverse selection problem, especially if everyone was covered under the same system.

However, increasing the role of government is likely to be funded by higher taxes. That could reduce public support. Moreover, we also saw in **Chapter 6** that government action is accompanied by several downsides. These include the *incentive problem* because government managers don't have to worry about making a profit; *rent-seeking behavior,* which leads companies to divert resources to lobbying public officials rather than improving productivity; and *the lack of flexibility and innovation* that can occur because government officials may be too cautious about making big changes.

YOUR ECONOMIC LIFE: Are Health Care Jobs a Good Bet?

Should you look for a job in the health care sector? The prospects for health care careers depend on the balance between demand and supply for workers. On the demand side, as of 2022, the Bureau of Labor Statistics projected employment in the health care and social assistance sector to add 2.6 million jobs over the next 10 years, about one-third of all new jobs.

On the supply side, to become eligible for these jobs, you need education and training. Medical technicians require either an associate's or bachelor's degree, and perhaps some additional certifications. Similarly, registered nurses need an associate's or bachelor's degree, and perhaps additional education as well.

One big issue you should consider is whether financial pressures, technological change, and the pandemic have changed the desirability of health care jobs. Certainly, the need to take care of an aging population will only increase. However, hospitals and other providers are under increased pressure to be more productive, which means more investment in technology and more demands on health care workers.

THE BASICS OF RETIREMENT (LO18-4)

LO18-4 Describe the life cycle theory of retirement and identify the main sources of retirement funds.

Why do people retire? For some people, retirement is voluntary. They have enough income from investments and other sources that they can stop working and still live at their desired standard of living. But for many people, retirement is forced on them, because they slow down as they age and employers would rather hire younger people. As people age, it generally becomes harder for them to find paying employment.

life cycle theory of retirement

The pattern of spending and saving for retirement over an individual's lifetime in the absence of government and business-supported assistance for the elderly. Posits that people spend when they are young, save during the latter part of their working lives, and spend when they are retired.

Before we examine the current system of retirement, we should understand how individuals might finance their spending in old age by themselves, without any assistance from the government or from employer retirement plans. Remember, retirement means you no longer have income from work.

The Life Cycle Theory of Retirement

The **life cycle theory of retirement** describes the pattern of spending and saving for retirement over an individual's lifetime in the absence of government and business-supported assistance for the elderly. According to this hypothesis, young people have a low income and spend heavily on education and buying a home. Middle-aged individuals have a higher income, which is used to pay off mortgage and student loans and to build their wealth. Then, as people age and retire, they support their living standard by drawing down their accumulated savings.

net worth

Total household assets minus liabilities.

This life cycle theory is illustrated in **Figure 18.4**. The graph shows how your **net worth**–your total assets minus your debt–starts out negative as you borrow for a home and education. Your net worth turns positive as your income rises, followed by a decline after you leave the workforce. Whether your net worth actually drops to zero depends on how long you live after retirement and on how much you spend–and whether you want (or are able) to leave an inheritance to your heirs.

Figure 18.4 The Life Cycle Theory of Retirement

According to the life cycle theory of retirement, the young borrow for education and to buy homes. The middle-aged pay off their mortgages and student loans and build savings. Then, in old age, people use their savings to pay for medical and living costs.

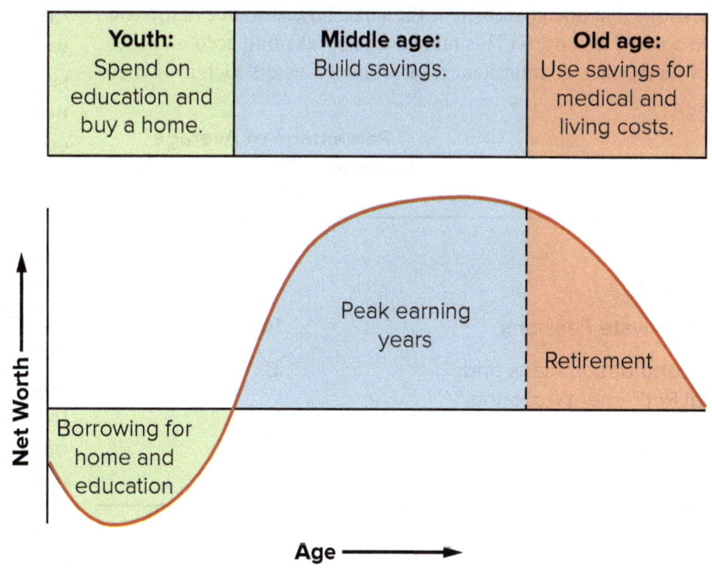

Problems with the Life Cycle Theory

In some ways, the life cycle theory seems reasonable as a prescription for action. It suggests a strategy for everyone to provide for their own retirement without the need for any government intervention. All that's required is the willingness to save for the future.

retirement poverty problem
The problem that poor people often don't have enough income to save for retirement.

retirement uncertainty problem
The problem that individuals don't know how long they will live after retirement.

four-legged stool
A metaphor for the four main components of retirement income: part-time work, individual savings, employer retirement plans, and Social Security.

employer retirement plan
Provisions for retirement that an employer contributes to on behalf of an employee.

Social Security
The government program that provides income support to older citizens who have contributed during their working years.

But at least two things can go wrong with this simple vision. First, poor people are often not in a position to save much for retirement. Because their incomes are low, all their earnings go for necessities such as food and housing. No savings accumulated when working means no savings available for old age. According to the Federal Reserve's 2019 Survey of Consumer Finances, only 59 percent of families save–that is, have income greater than their current spending. This is called the **retirement poverty problem**.

Second, it's difficult to know how much money to put away in savings to cover all the eventualities. For example, the amount of savings you need for retirement depends on how long someone will live after retirement. Based on pre-pandemic (2019) data, a person who is 35 years old can expect to live another 45.5 years on average, to 80 years old (slightly less for men, slightly more for women). However, at the current state of medical science, there's a 20 percent chance that a 35-year-old man will live until at least 90, and a 32 percent chance that a 35-year-old woman will live until at least 90.

Given these numbers, should you save enough to cover 15 years of retirement, 25 years, or even more? That's a hard question. This is called the **retirement uncertainty problem**.

The length of your life is not the only unknown making it difficult to plan the right amount of money to save for retirement. Depending on your assumptions, the amount of money you need can vary enormously. Will you or your spouse be stricken by an illness that requires expensive treatment and leaves you poor? Will the investments into which you put your savings do well or poorly? Will inflation be high enough to eat away at the value of your savings?

Because running out of money can leave you poor in old age, you need to save extra. The need to save extra money for retirement should lower your consumption and living standards during your working life.

Sources of Retirement Income

Table 18.5 Where U.S. Adults Aged 65 and over Get Their Income, 2020

This table shows that Social Security is the single biggest source of income for people aged 65 and over. (This table does not take into account other sources of funds, such as inheritance, or selling off assets such as homes or stock).

	Percentage of Average Income for People Aged 65 and Over
Earnings from Work	30
Social Security	32
Public and Private Pensions	14
Defined Contribution Plans and Individual Retirement Accounts	5
Income from Assets	12
All Other	7

Source: Census Bureau, www.census.gov.

The combination of the retirement poverty problem and the retirement uncertainty problem means that individual savings by themselves are not enough to provide for retirement. Today, economists talk about the **four-legged stool** of retirement income: part-time work, **employer retirement plans**, **Social Security**, and individual savings. Employer retirement plans, which we will discuss in the next section, are provisions for retirement that your employer contributes to on your behalf. And Social Security–which we will discuss at length later in this chapter–is income the government provides to older citizens.

Table 18.5 lays out the sources of income in 2020 for U.S. adults aged 65 and over. Their single largest source of support was Social Security, which accounted for 32 percent of their income. The next biggest source was earnings from current work, showing that many older people are still working part-time. Amazingly, income from assets–that is, the result of individual savings–accounted for only 12 percent of income for adults 65 and over. That's because most people reach old age without much savings.

In fact, if you did want to fund your retirement completely out of individual savings, you would require a truckload of money. The exact amount would depend on what assumptions you made about your return on investments and how long you would live. (see **"How It Works: How Much Do You Need to Save for Your Own Retirement?"**).

HOW IT WORKS: HOW MUCH DO YOU NEED TO SAVE FOR YOUR OWN RETIREMENT?

Suppose you had to fund your retirement entirely out of your own savings—that is, with no Social Security checks or payments from employers. How much would you need in savings when you retire?

The answer to this question is not simple: It depends on how much income you want, how long you will live, and what kind of risks you want to take with your investments. Obviously, the longer you live, the more savings you need. And if you want to put your money into safe investments, you will have to compensate for their low average rate of return by saving more.

For example, suppose you have saved $500,000 when you retire at age 67, and you decide that you want to take out $40,000 per year, adjusted for inflation (remember that Chapter 8 discussed how to adjust for inflation).

How long will your money last? It depends on where you invest it. If you invest your money in a savings account or money market account, it will be totally safe. However, you will be lucky if you get an interest rate that will barely keep up with inflation. In that case, you will end up drawing down your entire savings in 12 years or so.

Alternatively, you could put your money into the stock market, which historically has returned an average of 7 percent annually after adjusting for inflation. Then, assuming you get the average return, your money will last 25–30 years—but then you take the risk that the value of the market might fall and take some of your money with it. There are no guarantees.

EMPLOYER RETIREMENT PLANS (LO18-5)

LO18-5 Explain the difference between defined benefit and defined contribution retirement plans.

In some ways, the existence of employer retirement plans is a bit of a surprise. After all, why should employers care about what happens to their workers after they stop providing productive labor?

But, in fact, in the late 19th century, employers discovered that setting up a retirement plan was a good way of attracting and keeping high-quality workers. Today, there are two types of employer retirement plans, *defined benefit* and *defined contribution*. In this section, we will discuss the differences between the two and the limitations of employer retirement plans in general.

Defined Benefit versus Defined Contribution

A **defined benefit plan** gives you a predetermined amount of money monthly when you retire. The exact amount depends on how much you earned during your work life, how long you were employed with that company, and the age at which you retired. The amount received may or may not be adjusted for inflation. This is the classic employer-provided pension.

defined benefit plan

A retirement plan that pays retirees a predetermined amount of money monthly.

Defined benefit plans are funded primarily by the employer. In the case of private employers, the money comes from pretax profits (that is, the amounts a company contributes to a pension plan for its employees are not subject to the corporate income tax). The company invests the money in the stock market and in bonds. If the stock market goes up, the employer might be able to provide the pension without putting in any money of its own. But even if the investments fall short, the employer is responsible for making the promised future payments.

Defined benefit plans used to be common. In 1980, 84 percent of full-time employees in large and midsized private firms were participating in defined benefit plans. In particular, big companies such as General Motors and IBM almost always had generous defined benefit plans. Many government employees today still have good defined benefit plans.

In recent years, however, more and more private employers have been moving to **defined contribution plans**. Such plans require employees–and usually employers as well–to put money each month into an account, which the employer then invests. The actual monthly payment to the retired worker, however, depends on how the investment does over time. As a result, the retirement benefits are not guaranteed.

defined contribution plan

A retirement plan that pays retirees an amount of money that depends on the return on investments.

401(k) plan
A common type of retirement plan that allows employees to save pretax income, often matched in part by the employer.

The most important form of a defined contribution plan today is the **401(k) plan**, named for the corresponding section of the tax law. Generally, in a 401(k) plan, a participant will decide how much of his or her pretax income should be put into the retirement account (within government-set limits). The employer then matches the contribution, either partly or in full. For example, a worker earning $100,000 per year might put 5 percent of her pretax salary, or $5,000, into her 401(k) account. At the same time, her employer might match 3 percent of her pretax salary, or $3,000. The total contributions would be 8 percent of her salary, or $5,000 from the worker and $3,000 from her employer, per year.

Participants in 401(k) plans can generally choose whether to invest their funds in the stock market (in the United States or abroad), put them into interest-paying money market accounts, or put them into other kinds of investments. No taxes are imposed on those funds as long as they stay in the 401(k) account. They are taxed only when withdrawn to pay for retirement expenses.

The Limitations of Employer Retirement Plans

Employer retirement plans can be useful in raising individuals' retirement income, especially given new laws that expand coverage (see **How It Works: The Benefits of Auto Enrollment**)

HOW IT WORKS: THE BENEFITS OF AUTO ENROLLMENT

Historically, many people had access to defined contribution plans at work but chose not to participate. For example, in 2022, 43 percent of private sector, low-wage workers had access to a defined contribution plan in 2022, but only 21 percent participated in them. There were a variety of reasons. Some people didn't have any spare cash to save; some didn't think about the future; some didn't realize the company contributes to boost their savings; and some simply forgot to file the right forms.

To address this problem of nonparticipation, Congress passed the SECURE 2.0 Act, which was signed by President Joseph Biden in December 2022. Under the new law, most major employers will be required to automatically enroll workers in 401(k) plans. Workers can still opt not to contribute, but they have to make an active choice in that case. The expectation is that this will raise participation rates.

In addition, the new law will help workers who are still paying off student loans build up retirement savings. Under the previous rules, employers could "match" employee contributions to 401(k) plans. That effectively left out workers who were devoting all of their free cash to student loan repayments, and had no money left over for retirement plan contributions.

But the new law will enable employers to make "matching" contributions to the retirement plans of workers who are paying off student loans. This could be a big deal.

However, by themselves, employer retirement plans do not solve the retirement poverty problem. Better paid workers can still afford to contribute more to their defined contribution plans and build up better nest eggs.

Nor do employer retirement plans fully address the retirement uncertainty problem. If you participate in a defined benefit plan, in theory, it will pay you the same amount monthly as long as you live. That provides a certain measure of security. However, defined benefit plans have a big downside: They assume the company will be able to provide enough money to fund all future benefits. If a company goes bankrupt or fails, the money to fund the pension plan may not be there.

To avoid the heavy burden of defined benefit plans, many companies have been switching to defined contribution plans, which transfer the risk to individual workers. With a defined contribution plan, you still have to worry about how your investments will do and whether you will live long enough to exhaust your savings.

SOCIAL SECURITY (LO18-6)

LO18-6 Summarize the demographic challenge facing Social Security and describe the possible solutions.

Social Security was introduced as part of the New Deal in 1932 to help address the retirement poverty problem. It takes a different approach to retirement income than either individual savings or employer retirement plans. Both of those sources of income are based on the idea of saving now and building assets for the future.

In contrast, Social Security levies a tax on current workers to pay for the retirement of yesterday's workers. In other words, income is transferred from current workers to current retirees. At the same time, there is an implicit commitment that the next generation will do the same when current workers retire. **Figure 18.5** shows how Social Security modifies the life cycle model we described earlier in the chapter.

Figure 18.5 The Life Cycle with Social Security
The retirement life cycle changes once Social Security is introduced. Each generation is supported in retirement by the ones that come after.

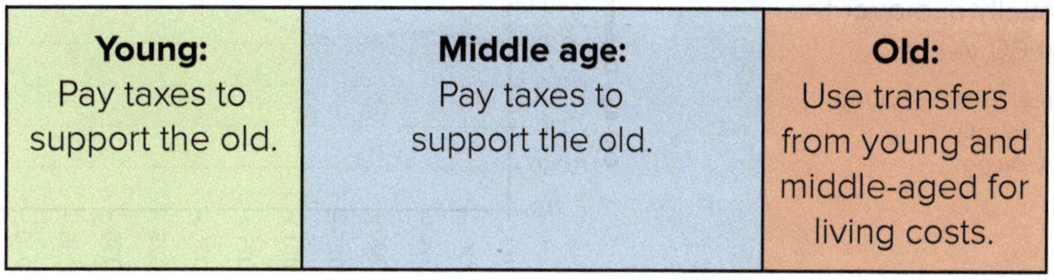

In principle, Social Security can solve both the retirement poverty problem and the retirement uncertainty problem. Because Social Security is funded by current taxes, it can offer a decent retirement income to low-income workers without requiring them to contribute that much during their careers. Indeed, Social Security has made a major contribution to lowering the poverty rate of older retirees.

Moreover, because Social Security draws on current taxes, it can offer people retirement benefits as long as they live. That means workers don't have to save up huge nest eggs to account for the possibility of living to age 80, 90, or more.

How Social Security Works Today

As we saw earlier in the chapter, Social Security provides 32 percent of the income of people aged 65 and over. Because of its importance to the economy, it's good to know how the program works today. First, the Social Security Administration, which runs the program, has a formula for determining your monthly benefits. That formula depends on the average of how much you earned during your lifetime, adjusted for the rise in average wages over time. The formula is **progressive** so that low-income workers get back higher percentages of their lifetime average incomes than do better-paid workers. The benefits are also indexed to inflation–so as prices rise, the benefits rise to keep pace with them.

progressive tax
A tax that requires high-income households to pay a higher tax rate than low-income households.

Second, there's a formula for determining how much payroll tax you and your employer pay each year to fund Social Security. As of 2023, you pay 6.2 percent of your wages up to a $160,200 wage cap, and your employer pays an equal amount. The cap is raised each year to account for inflation. These taxes are paid into the Social Security trust fund (officially the combined "Old-Age and Survivors Insurance and Disability Insurance Trust Funds"), invested in Treasury bonds, and then paid out in benefits to current retirees.

Third, and most important, there's no real link between the taxes you pay and the benefits you receive later in life. Congress can raise and lower the benefit formula as it likes–and it has done this many times. It can also raise and lower the tax rates as it likes–as it has done many times. There's no direct connection between the two, and there never has been. Early recipients received far more than they put in, whereas many current high-income workers are likely to get only a small return on their payroll taxes.

The Demographic Challenge Facing Social Security

The concept of Social Security works well when the population is expanding. In this scenario, a large working population has to support a smaller number of elderly people. Paying off the previous generation is cheaper than saving for yourself.

It also helps if real wages are rising over time, as has been true over the past 75 years. Then, the younger generation is better off than the older generation, making it easier for them to pay Social Security taxes.

But funding Social Security becomes more difficult when population growth slows. The clearest sign of the funding problem comes from the **old-age dependency ratio**, which is the ratio of the size of the older population (65 years and older) to the size of the working-age population (ages 20 through 64). For example, a ratio of 0.2 means there are five working-age people for every older person to support. The lower the old-age dependency ratio, the less tax burden each worker has to support the older population.

old-age dependency ratio
The ratio of the size of the older population (65 years and over) to the size of the working-age population (ages 20 through 64).

Figure 18.6 shows the history of the old-age dependency ratio, along with the projections of the Social Security Administration through 2086. The ratio goes from 0.2 to 0.4, which means instead of 5 workers supporting every retiree in 2086, there will be only 2.5 workers. The burden on each worker will double.

Figure 18.6 The Demographic Challenge of Social Security

The old-age dependency ratio will substantially rise over the next 60 years.

Source: Social Security Administration, www.ssa.gov.

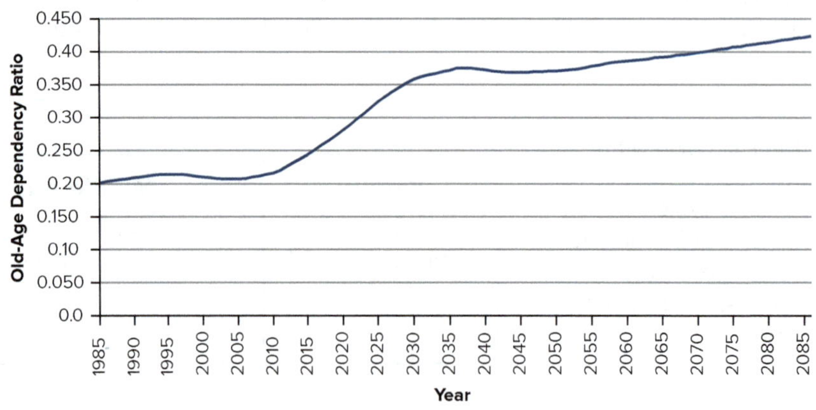

Will Social Security Run Out of Money?

You've probably heard this over and over again: "Social Security is going to run out of money." That's partly true, but it's also misleading. For many years, Social Security was running a surplus: The amount coming into the program from taxes and interest on assets exceeded the amount being paid out in benefits. As a result, as of the end of 2020, there was roughly $2.9 trillion in the Social Security trust fund, held in federal government bonds (these bonds are promises from the government to pay recipients in the future). In effect, the Social Security trust fund has lent the rest of the government its surplus.

financing gap

A mismatch between the amount of money coming in and the amount of money that needs to be paid out. In this book, the term *financing gap* refers to a long-term problem facing the Social Security system.

However, in 2021, Social Security ran a deficit for the first time since the 1980s: The amount being paid out in benefits to current retirees slightly exceeds the amount coming into the Social Security trust fund from taxes and interest on. From this point on, there will be a **financing gap** between Social Security taxes and benefits that will get larger over time. To meet the legal obligations to retirees, the Social Security trust fund will start cashing in its assets, which are Treasury bonds.

But here's the tricky part. The Treasury bonds in the trust fund are obligations of the U.S. government. So, when the Social Security trust fund starts selling its bonds, the purchaser is the rest of the government. That means as soon as the Social Security financing gap appears–which means now–Congress and the president have to come up with more money.

ECONOMIC MILESTONE

1940: THE FIRST SOCIAL SECURITY RECIPIENT

Ida May Fuller, a legal secretary in Ludlow, Vermont, received the first monthly Social Security retirement check in January 1940, three years after the program started collecting taxes. During that time, Fuller paid a total of $24.75 in payroll taxes. She lived until 1975, and she collected $22,889 in Social Security benefits. Not a bad deal!

Fixing the Retirement Shortfall

In the short run, the relatively small Social Security financing gap is just going to be rolled into the broader federal deficit. The federal government will raise a bit more money by issuing public debt, and then use that money to buy back bonds from the Social Security trust fund.

But as the old-age dependency ratio increases and the Social Security financing gap grows larger over time, policymakers will have four possible responses: cut Social Security benefits, raise payroll taxes, fund the gap from general revenues, or privatize Social Security. Let's look at the pluses and minuses of each of these, and whether and how they might be combined.

CUTTING BENEFITS

The most likely response to the financing gap is probably a reduction in Social Security benefits. Despite what is commonly believed, Social Security benefits will not disappear. However, a 20 percent reduction of benefits from their expected levels, starting today, would bring the cost of Social Security back in line with expected payroll taxes.

Policymakers have a choice about how to cut benefits in such a scenario. They can reduce payments to everyone, which would spread the pain. They can reduce benefits for people who have not yet retired, which would hurt younger people. They also have the option of raising the Social Security retirement age–that is, the age at which people receive full benefits. An increase in the retirement age might make sense, given that people are living longer. However, workers in physically taxing professions such as construction might find it difficult to continue the same type of job into their late 60s.

personal savings rate
Savings by households as a share of disposable income.

SPOTLIGHT: WHY DON'T AMERICANS SAVE MORE?

Social Security is not about to disappear, but its benefits are likely to be trimmed in the future. That means Americans should be saving more for retirement. The **personal savings rate** is equal to personal savings as a percentage of disposable personal income, which is income after taxes. **Figure 18.7** shows that the personal savings rate dropped from more than 10 percent in the early 1980s to a low of 3.2 percent in 2005. But the savings rate crept up after the financial crisis of 2008–2009 as households became a bit more frugal. It then soared during the pandemic years of 2020 and 2021 as Americans stayed home, cut back on discretionary spending, and saved the cash payments they received from the federal government. Finally, the savings rate plummeted again in 2022 as Americans opened their wallets again.

Despite the surge during the pandemic, most economists agree that Americans don't save enough compared to citizens of other countries. One reason is that, historically, U.S. consumers have had access to a lot more credit than consumers in other countries; this let them keep buying instead of saving. Second, the housing boom in the 2000s increased the value of homes around the country and made U.S. homeowners feel wealthier, encouraging them to consume beyond their incomes and driving down savings. Finally, Americans have to pay more for health care, which lowers the amount available for savings.

Sooner or later, Americans are going to have to boost their personal savings. That may mean buying smaller cars and homes or cutting back on personal entertainment expenses.

Figure 18.7 The Personal Savings Rate, 1980–2022

Personal savings as a percentage of disposable income hit a low in 2005 as Americans borrowed against their homes.

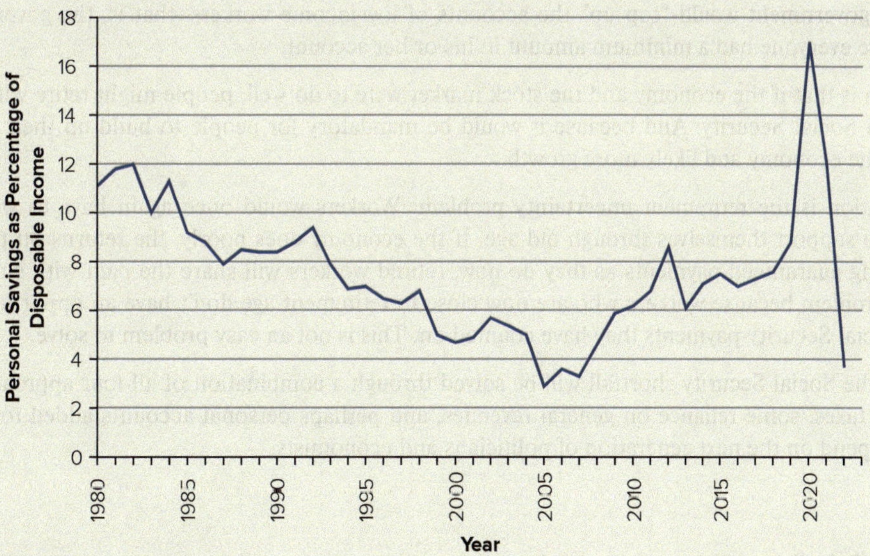

Source: Bureau of Economic Analysis, www.bea.gov.

Another possibility is a reduction in benefits for high-income workers. That would be less harmful because these people are expected to have good savings and alternative sources of income. But such a targeted reduction in benefits would be likely to erode the political support for Social Security because high-income voters would get less from the program, making them less likely to support it.

RAISING THE PAYROLL TAX

Another possible response–either by itself or combined with a benefits reduction–is an increase in the amount that Social Security receives from payroll taxes. One way to achieve this is to raise the Social Security payroll tax rate, which is currently 6.2 percent of wages from both workers and employers, or 12.4 percent of wages in total.

Another way to raise payroll taxes is to lift the Social Security cap–that is, the maximum amount of income that can be taxed. For example, in 2023 the Social Security cap was $160,200. If a worker made $200,000 that year, he or she paid Social Security tax on only the first $160,200 earned. Raising the cap faster than inflation, or eliminating it completely, would increase Social Security tax revenues.

FUNDING WITH GENERAL REVENUES

It is inevitable that at least a portion of the Social Security gap will be funded out of general revenues, which include personal and corporate income taxes. When the Treasury bonds in the Social Security trust fund are cashed in, that money will come out of the overall federal budget–in the form of higher taxes, lower spending, or both. When the trust fund has been completely depleted, Congress and the president will have the option to use the same flow of funds from general revenues–personal and corporate income taxes, primarily–to directly support Social Security benefits.

But will there be the political desire and will to do this? It probably depends on how well the economy is doing. If growth has been strong and real incomes have risen, workers may feel able to pay a bit more in taxes to support older citizens. But if growth has been weak, the natural tendency will be to force everyone to cut back–which includes cutting Social Security benefits.

PRIVATIZATION

privatization
The shifting of certain aspects of government programs, such as Social Security, to the private sector.

The first three responses to the Social Security shortfall keep the basic structure of today's retirement system. **Privatization**, in contrast, refers to an overhaul of the Social Security system that takes the radical step of moving more of the decisions and responsibility of retirement saving into the private sector while preserving a basic safety net for the poor and unlucky.

Many versions of privatization have been proposed. The most basic version is a defined contribution plan: The money from each individual's payroll taxes would go into a personal account rather than a national trust fund. Each individual would then be responsible for investing the money to have enough for retirement.

In this scenario, the government role would be to set rules for how much workers would have to contribute and how they would be allowed to invest. In addition, the government would "top up" the accounts of low-income workers–that is, the government would contribute enough money to make sure everyone had a minimum amount in his or her account.

The benefit of privatization is that if the economy and the stock market were to do well, people might retire with more money than they would have gotten through Social Security. And because it would be mandatory for people to build up their personal accounts, there would be more savings in the economy and likely more growth.

The downside of privatization is the retirement uncertainty problem: Workers would once again have to worry about whether they will have enough money to support themselves through old age. If the economy does poorly, the returns on personal accounts will be lower–and instead of having guaranteed payments as they do now, retired workers will share the pain with current workers. Moreover, there's a large transition problem because workers who are now close to retirement age don't have an opportunity to build up personal accounts to replace the Social Security payments they have counted on. This is not an easy problem to solve.

In the end, it's likely that the Social Security shortfall will be solved through a combination of all four approaches–some reductions in benefits, increased payroll taxes, some reliance on general revenues, and perhaps personal accounts added to the current system. The exact mix, however, will depend on the next generation of politicians and economists.

CONCLUSION

In the United States, health care expenses are funded through a mixture of employer and direct-purchase insurance plans and public programs, such as Medicaid and Medicare. Retirement expenses are funded through a combination of earnings from work, Social Security, public and private pensions, and personal savings,

The country's health care and retirement systems both face funding problems as Americans age. In both cases, there is widespread disagreement about the best way to fix these problems. One key issue is whether to rely less on government, or to increase the amount of government intervention.

The next and final chapter will focus on another issue likely to be debated for years: how to handle energy, pollution, and global warming. We will lay out the dimensions of the economic problem and discuss potential policy alternatives.

18 SUMMARY

1. Health care today is the largest sector of the economy, and its share of the economic pie has been growing. Moreover, compared to other countries, the United States spends far more on health care per person. In 2021, health care cost Americans more than $12,000 per person, including all private and public sources of funds. *(LO18-1)*
2. Roughly 92 percent of Americans were covered by at least one type of health insurance in 2022 These includc employer health insurance, Medicaid, Medicare, direct purchase by individuals, and military health care. These cover three types of health events: ordinary health expenses; catastrophic health events; and old age-related health expenses. *(LO18-1)*
3. Health care expenditures have been rising steadily as a share of GDP. The reasons include demographic change, rising incomes, third-party payments, tax rules for employer health insurance plans, the cost of better medical technology, and unnecessary medicine. *(LO18-2)*
4. As of early 2023, we are likely to see more battles over the appropriate role of government in the health care system. Three approaches to health care reform include keeping and improving the current system; reducing government's role in health care; and increasing government's role in health care. Each of these has positives and negatives. *(LO18-3)*
5. The life cycle theory of retirement says people spend when they are young, save during the latter part of their working lives, and spend while they are retired. Two things can go wrong in the life cycle model. First, poor people often cannot save much for retirement. Second, it's difficult to know how much money to put away in savings to cover all eventualities. The four components of retirement income are part-time work, individual savings, employer retirement plans, and Social Security. *(LO18-4)*
6. Employer retirement plans can be useful in raising individuals' retirement incomes. The two types of employer retirement plans are defined benefit plans and defined contribution plans. However, they do not solve the poverty problem. Meanwhile, defined contribution plans, although increasingly common, do not solve the uncertainty problem. *(LO18-5)*
7. Social Security levies a tax on current workers today to pay for the retirement of yesterday's workers. Currently, Social Security is the single largest source of support for U.S. adults aged 65 and over. The concept of Social Security works well when the population is expanding, but funding Social Security becomes more difficult when population growth slows. That means we will likely need some combination of benefit cuts, tax increases, funding with general revenues, and privatization. *(LO18-6)*

KEY TERMS AND CONCEPTS

employer health insurance plan
Affordable Care Act
Medicaid
Medicare
ordinary health care expenses
catastrophic health events
old age-related health expenses
demographic change
third party
life expectancy
single-payer system
adverse selection problem
life cycle theory of retirement
net worth
retirement poverty problem
retirement uncertainty problem
four-legged stool
employer retirement plan
Social Security
defined benefit plan
defined contribution plan
401(k) plan
progressive tax
old-age dependency ratio
financing gap
personal savings rate
privatization

connect PROBLEMS

1. In 2021, health care cost Americans an average of $12,318 per person, a figure that includes both private and public spending. Canadians spent $5,904 per person on health care. As of 2020, life expectancy at birth in Canada was 81.7 years, and life expectancy at birth in the United States was 77 years.
   In which country do people expect to live longer? In which country is health care more expensive? The Canadian health care system has universal coverage provided by the government, supplemented by private insurance. Wait times are long in Canada: One

report, by the Vancouver-based Fraser Institute, reported a median wait time of almost 20 weeks from referral by a general practitioner to treatment by a specialist. Out of the following, which are potential reasons why wait times might be longer in Canada? *(LO18-1)*

a) The Canadian health care system employs fewer specialists per patient than the United States health care system.
b) Canadians are sicker than Americans.
c) Canada spends less per person on health care than the United States does.
d) Canadians care less about waiting than Americans do.

2. In this chapter, we identify several reasons that might explain why health care costs have risen so rapidly. Fill in the blanks in the following statements. *(LO18-2)*

a) If a state's population is older than the rest of the country, health care costs would be ______ than the rest of the country.
b) If workers were forced to pay income taxes on the value of their employer-provided health care benefits, then the growth rate of health care costs would ______.
c) If we could identify health care practices that don't work, then the cost of health care would ______.
d) If patients were forced to pay a bigger share of their medical bills, that would lessen the ______ problem.

3. Cancer was the second-leading cause of death in 2020, resulting in an estimated 600,000 deaths. Suppose a drug was approved that immediately cured cancer. *(LO18-2)*

a) In the short run, is that drug likely to increase or decrease health care spending? Explain.
b) In the long run, is that drug likely to increase or decrease health care spending? Explain.

4. The United States is currently debating the appropriate role of government in the health care system *(LO18-3)*

a) Name the three approaches to health care reform.
b) Which approach to health care reform is likely to provide the most Americans with health insurance?
c) Which approach to health care reform is likely to reduce taxes?
d) Which approach to health care reform is likely to lead to an adverse selection problem?

5. Consider the life cycle theory of retirement. *(LO18-4)*

a) In which stage do workers accumulate savings for retirement?
b) An individual who comes from a long-lived family needs to pay special attention to which retirement life cycle problem?
c) Social Security payments are adjusted for inflation. That helps solve which retirement life cycle problem?

6. Suppose that you reach 65 years old and have $100,000 in an investment that pays a return of 5 percent per year. *(LO18-4)*

a) If you withdraw $10,000 at the end of each year for living expenses, how many years will it take before your investment is gone? (Hint: Go year by year and calculate the return on the investment and then the amount remaining after the withdrawal.)
b) If you withdraw $5,000 at the end of each year for living expenses, how many years will it take before your investment is gone?

7. Employer retirement plans are an important element of retirement income. *(LO18-5)*

a) Suppose that in addition to your salary, your employer invests a sum of money in the stock market each year in your name. Then, when you retire, you get the current value of the invested money. Is this a defined benefit or a defined contribution plan?
b) Suppose the plan is set up so that it is invested only in the stock of the company you work for. Which life cycle retirement problem does this *not* solve?

8. The labor force participation rate of an age group is the percentage of people of that age who are either working or actively looking for jobs. Would you expect the existence of Social Security to increase or decrease the labor force participation rate for people aged 65 and over? Explain your answer. *(LO18-6)*

9. Most economists agree that immigration helps improve the finances of the Social Security system. *(LO18-6)*

a) To benefit Social Security funding, would we prefer immigrants to be old or young? Explain.
b) Would the finances of Social Security benefit more from low-wage immigrants or high-wage, highly skilled immigrants?
c) Assume that about half of illegal immigrants actually pay Social Security taxes, but they are unlikely to collect benefits. Based on that assumption, do illegal immigrants help improve the finances of the Social Security system? Explain.

10. The following table gives the population at different ages for the city of Elizabeth, New Jersey, as of 2020. *(LO18-6)*

Age	Number of People
Under 10 years old	20,988
10–19 years old	18,415
Ages 20–64	81,107
Ages 65 and over	14,895

a) What is the old-age dependency ratio in Elizabeth in 2020?
b) Is the old-age dependency ratio in Elizabeth higher or lower than the country as a whole in 2020, based on Figure 18-6?

CH 19

ECONOMICS OF ENERGY, THE ENVIRONMENT, AND GLOBAL CLIMATE CHANGE

huyangshu/Shutterstock

LEARNING OBJECTIVES

After reading this chapter, you should be able to:

LO19-1 Characterize the basics of energy consumption, supply, and price.
LO19-2 Discuss energy sustainability and conservation.
LO19-3 List the types of damage done by pollution externalities.
LO19-4 Describe different approaches to controlling pollution.
LO19-5 Explain how a market-based approach could help mitigate global climate change.

Two key topics for us are the economics of energy and the economics of the environment. They are closely related to each other because much of the pollution emitted today is related to the production and use of energy.

In this chapter, we examine several key aspects of the economics of energy and the environment. First, we will look at the balance between supply and demand for energy in the short run. This is a topic of enormous importance, especially since we have seen big swings in the price of gasoline and oil in recent years. The latest surge in energy prices was driven by Russia's invasion of Ukraine in early 2022.

Second, we will consider the sustainability of our energy supplies in the long run. As countries such as China and India increase their output and improve their standards of living, they also increase their consumption of energy. How will the world economy meet those energy needs? Will the price of oil and other energy sources increase sharply? Is there a role for government intervention to either encourage the development of new sources of energy or to encourage energy conservation?

Then, we will examine the economic impact of pollution, including the economic consequences of global climate change. We look at this from an economic perspective, asking how we can cost effectively reduce pollution's effects on the environment. Finally, we examine the pros and cons of different approaches, including using the market as a tool for reducing pollution.

THE BASICS OF ENERGY CONSUMPTION AND SUPPLY (LO19-1)

LO19-1 Characterize the basics of energy consumption, supply, and price.

Let's start by looking at the basics of energy consumption and supply. Energy is one of the most important markets in the economy. Every family, every business, and every organization use energy, so any changes in the price of energy affect everyone simultaneously.

Energy Consumption

Economic history has been the story of rising energy consumption–energy to power factories, move vehicles, heat and cool homes, and so forth. **Figure 19.1** shows energy usage in the United States since 1949, measured as millions of British thermal units per person per year. (A British thermal unit, or BTU, is a measure of energy; 1 gallon of gasoline is equivalent to 124,000 BTUs.)

Figure 19.1 U.S. Energy Consumption per Person, 1949–2022

Per capita consumption of energy peaked in the 1970s and has been drifting down since then.

Source: Energy Information Administration and author calculations.

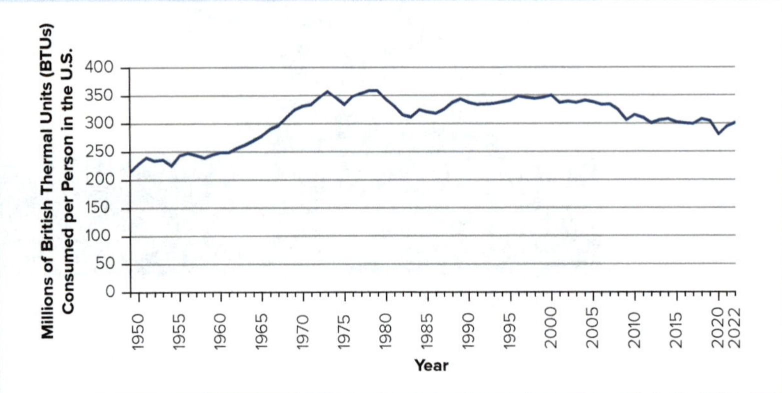

From 1900 (not shown on chart) to the 1970s, energy usage per person roughly tripled. However, the oil price shock of 1973 marked the end of unbridled energy use. Since then, energy use per person in the United States has been drifting down.

Still, the United States today uses more energy per person than most other countries. Data from the International Energy Agency show that the United States uses about 4.1 times the world average (see **Figure 19.2**). In contrast, the industrialized European Union uses only 1.7 times the world average energy per person.

Figure 19.2 Global Energy Consumption per Person, 2021

Consumption of energy per capita in the United States is 4.1 times the world average.

Source: International Energy Agency and author calculations.

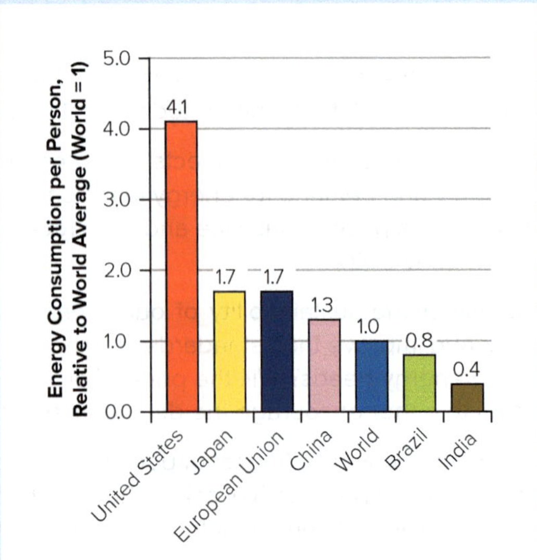

Why is the European Union's energy consumption per person so much lower than that of the United States? One reason is that, compared to Americans, Europeans tend to live in smaller homes that cost less to heat and cool. Perhaps most important, Europe is a much more compact region than the United States, so less travel–which consumes gasoline or jet fuel–is required to get from one point to another. The distance between the European Union's two largest cities, Berlin and Madrid, is 1160 miles. The two largest U.S. cities, New York and Los Angeles, are roughly 2,500 miles apart in contrast.

Developing countries such as China and India, although sprawling geographically, use much less energy per person than the United States. That's because they have less industry and are poorer. Over the long run, however, as these countries become richer and more heavily industrialized, they will almost inevitably use more energy.

Energy Supply: Fossil Fuels

Where does our energy come from? From an economic perspective, this is an important question because different fuels have different supply and demand characteristics. The most widely used energy source is **fossil fuels**, which include coal, crude oil, and natural gas. These are all found underground and have been produced over millions of years by the transformation of dead animals and plants. Fossil fuels are **nonrenewable**: There is a limited quantity of them (though no one knows how much–see **"How It Works: Growing Reserves of Fossil Fuels"**).

fossil fuels

Nonrenewable energy sources such as oil and natural gas that have been produced over millions of years by the transformation of dead animals and plants.

nonrenewable energy

Sources of energy like fossil fuels that have only a limited supply.

The combustion of fossil fuels releases large quantities of carbon dioxide, which is a **greenhouse gas**. As we will see later in this chapter, the emission of greenhouse gases contributes to global climate change.

greenhouse gas

Greenhouse gas, such as carbon dioxide and methane, contributes to global climate change.

To use fossil fuels, we must first locate them underground, which may be quite difficult. For years, it was necessary to hunt in nearly inaccessible areas–such as far offshore–to find new oil fields. More recently, companies have been able to use new technologies, such as hydraulic fracturing ("fracking") and horizontal drilling, to tap into new sources of oil and natural gas. This effort requires vast sums–in 2022, ExxonMobil, the mammoth U.S. oil company, spent $23 billion on exploration and capital investment.

Once the wells and mines are in place, the **marginal cost of extraction** is the amount of money it takes to get one more ton of coal, one more barrel of oil, or one more cubic foot of natural gas out of the ground. This can vary greatly. In some cases, the coal or oil lies close to the surface, so the marginal cost of extraction is low. For more inaccessible fields, the marginal cost of extraction may be high.

marginal cost of extraction

The amount of money that it takes to get one more ton of coal, one more barrel of oil, or one more cubic foot of natural gas out of the ground.

From our discussion of profit maximization earlier in the text, we might think that companies will mine coal or pump oil and gas as long as the marginal cost of extraction is less than the market price. After all, they make a profit on anything they can sell for less than the marginal cost.

However, when it comes to a nonrenewable resource, that's not quite true. The businesses will take into account the fact that the price of the coal, oil, or natural gas may rise in the future because there is only a limited amount in the ground. This implies that the energy companies may not produce as much as they possibly could. They may rationally want to leave some supply in the ground–even if it was profitable to extract today–because they expect the future price to rise. Suppose, for example, the marginal cost of extraction is $50 per barrel of oil, and the price of oil today is $55 per barrel. That sounds profitable, but if the company expects the price to rise to $100 per barrel next year, it makes sense to not pump everything today.

When they pump oil or mine coal, the companies will probably first want to take it from the oil fields or coal mines where the marginal cost of extraction is the lowest. So, we extract natural resources from the cheapest places. As those are exhausted, we get our energy from more expensive locations. Eventually, as the marginal cost of extraction rises, we shift to other energy sources.

HOW IT WORKS: GROWING RESERVES OF FOSSIL FUELS

In 2000, the world's proven reserves of oil were equal to about 1.3 trillion barrels. U.S. oil reserves were flat, and more and more economists were predicting that oil was about to become an increasingly scarce commodity.

Fast-forward to 2020. The world's proven oil reserves had grown by 33 percent to more than 1.7 trillion barrels. Similarly, proven natural gas reserves grew by 36 percent.

What happened? Remember from **Chapter 9** that the production possibility frontier can move out if technology improves. That's exactly what happened here. Petroleum engineers developed new extraction techniques such as hydraulic fracturing (fracking) and horizontal drilling that made it possible to extract oil and natural gas from places where no one thought it possible before.

From the economic perspective, the increase in fossil fuel reserves helps hold down the cost of energy, which is a positive for consumers and businesses. Moreover, without these additional supplies, the Russian invasion of Ukraine would have had an even bigger impact on global energy prices.

From the environmental perspective, the increase in fossil fuel reserves is a mixed blessing. As we will see later in this chapter, the use of fossil fuels contributes to global climate change, which is a huge problem. On the other hand, use of natural gas contributes much less to global warming than use of coal, another fossil fuel.

Energy Supply: Renewable and Nuclear

renewable energy
Energy sources such as wind and solar power.

nuclear power
An energy source using contained nuclear reactions to generate electricity.

Now we turn our attention to the two other main sources of energy: renewable energy and nuclear power. **Renewable energy** includes solar power, wind power, hydroelectric power, and the energy products made from newly grown plants and trees. This last category includes ethanol, a gasoline replacement, which can be made either from corn (corn ethanol) or from agricultural wastes and nonfood plants (cellulosic ethanol).

Renewable energy sources such as solar power have relatively low variable costs–after all, the sun is free, and so are wind and rushing water. These energy sources also emit much less greenhouse gases than using fossil fuels. Because they can be used to generate electricity, they can help power electric vehicles.

Solar power is one source of renewable energy.

Ververidis Vasilis/Shutterstock

On the other hand, solar panels have high fixed costs. Installing a solar power system that supplies most of the electricity for an average-sized house might cost $20,000 in an area with lots of sun. This means that solar power is not yet economically competitive with fossil fuels, though it is likely to be in the future.

The final category of energy source is **nuclear power**, which uses the contained nuclear reaction of uranium or some other radioactive element to power an electric generator. Nuclear power, like solar power, is likely to be a growing source of energy in the future, in part because nuclear power does not emit carbon and does not contribute to global climate change. However, the Fukushima nuclear disaster in Japan has made countries much more safety-conscious. (see "**Spotlight: Energy-Related Disasters**"). As a result, the cost of building and operating nuclear power plants, already high, is likely to rise.

SPOTLIGHT: ENERGY-RELATED DISASTERS

Unfortunately, 2010 and 2011 were big years for energy-related disasters. On April 20, 2010, the British Petroleum (BP) Deepwater Horizon oil rig exploded in the Gulf of Mexico and triggered the biggest accidental oil spill in history, a sea-floor oil gusher that flowed for three months until it could be successfully plugged. The spill damaged marine and wildlife habitats, hurting the Gulf's fishing and tourism industries.

On the other side of the globe, and nearly a year later (March 11, 2011), the Fukushima Daiichi nuclear power complex in Japan was wrecked by a mammoth tsunami from one of the largest earthquakes on record. The result was a partial meltdown of fuel, venting of radioactive gases and water, and an evacuation of the surrounding area. The combination of tsunami-related damage and high radioactivity means the utility that owns the facility is still in the process of clean-up as of 2023.

However, neither disaster is likely to derail the global need for more energy. After the oil spill, the Obama administration ordered a six-month moratorium on drilling, and BP paid out fines, penalties, and compensation of at least $69 billion. But companies still continue to drill for oil and move it via pipeline and train through the country.

Similarly, countries such as China and India are still planning to go ahead with their large-scale programs for building nuclear power plants, even though the ultimate scope of the Fukushima disaster is not yet clear. In addition to the direct costs of dismantling the damaged plants—which could require more than $100 billion and 40 years to complete—the people evacuated from the nearby regions will need to be compensated. Moreover, nuclear plants will need to meet ever-higher and more expensive safety regulations.

MC2 Justin Stumberg/U.S. Coast Guard

Still, it is difficult to see a way of meeting the energy needs of fast-growing economies without nuclear power, especially as nuclear power does not contribute to global climate change.

Distribution of Supply

Since the 1970s, the sources of the world's energy supply have shifted, as **Table 19.1** shows. Crude oil has become less important as an energy source while natural gas and nuclear energy have become more important.

Table 19.1 Where the World's Energy Comes From, 1973 and 2019

The world's sources of energy have remained relatively stable since the early 1970s.

Energy Source	Percentage of World's Energy Supply 1973	2019
Coal (including oil shale)	25	27
Crude oil and products	46	31
Natural gas	16	23
Nuclear	1	5
Hydro	2	3
Biofuels and other combustible renewables*	10	9
Solar, geothermal, wind, and other	0.1	2

*Wood and similar products.

Source: International Energy Agency, www.iea.org.

However, in other ways, the distribution of energy production has been surprisingly stable. In 1973, fossil fuels made up 87 percent of world energy production. As of 2019, that's fallen only a tad, to 81 percent. Renewable energy rose from 12 percent of production in 1973 to only 14 percent in 2019. In particular, solar, geothermal, and wind power still only make up a small share of global energy supply.

ECONOMIC MILESTONE

1885: The First Internal Combustion-Powered Vehicle

The internal combustion engines that still dominate the landscape are just over a century old. They were invented by Nicholas Otto of Germany in 1876. But it wasn't until 1885 that George Daimler, also of Germany, was the first person to use a gasoline-powered internal combustion engine to drive a vehicle. Daimler went on to found the auto company that now bears his name, Daimler, the maker of Mercedes-Benz vehicles.

The internal combustion technology has turned out to be remarkably persistent. About 14 million new vehicles were sold in 2022. Out of those, roughly 800,000 were fully electric. That's less than 6 percent of total sales.

One reason for the slow adoption of electric vehicles is that it is difficult to build batteries that are light enough, cheap enough, and hold enough charge. People worry that they won't be able to find a charging station when they need one on a long trip. However, it's expected that the share of electric vehicles will continue to rise.

The Price of Energy

What do we know about the price of energy? The easiest energy commodity to track is gasoline, which touches all of us. If the price of gasoline, adjusted for inflation, goes up, that means, as we saw in **Chapter 8**, that gasoline prices are rising faster than the overall price level. If the inflation-adjusted price of gasoline is falling, that means gasoline prices are rising more slowly than the overall price level.

Figure 19.3 shows that between 1960 and the late 1990s inflation-adjusted gasoline prices actually fell. True, there were several spikes in prices, most notably an enormous one in the late 1970s and early 1980s. But even that spike faded away relatively quickly.

One reason was that oil companies kept finding new oil fields. The second reason for the stability of oil prices was the very low marginal cost of extraction in the Middle East oil fields, where most of the world's reserves are located. That low marginal cost put a ceiling on all energy prices because oil can be used for producing electricity and heating, as well as transportation.

This was the era when Americans bought lots of fuel-guzzling cars and sport utility vehicles. Remember that consumers react to prices. With fossil fuel prices stable and relatively low, it makes perfect sense that consumption of fossil fuels remained high, and there was little impetus to switch to other forms of energy.

Figure 19.3 The Real Price of Gasoline, 1960–2022
In 1960, the price of gasoline, measured in 2022 dollars, was about the same level as 2019, before the pandemic.
Source: Energy Information Administration and author calculations.

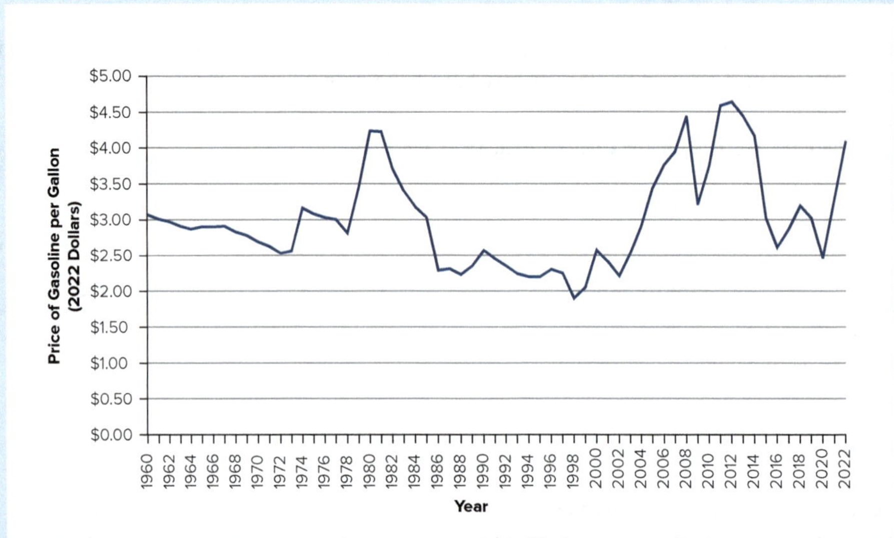

But starting in the late 1990s, the real price of gasoline begins to climb. With fits and starts, the climb continued after the Great Recession. At that point, some economists started worrying again that the global demand for oil was growing faster than the supply. There was more pressure to go for smaller, fuel-efficient vehicles.

What happened then? New technologies enabled the United States and other countries to boost oil reserves since 2000. (see again "**How It Works: Growing Reserves of Fossil Fuels**"). The price of gasoline dropped sharply, before rebounding again in 2022 because of the Russian invasion of Ukraine, as we see in **Figure 19.3**.

ENERGY SUSTAINABILITY (LO19-2)

LO19-2 Discuss energy sustainability and conservation.

What happens next? We can expect continuing improvements in both renewable and nonrenewable technologies for producing energy. For example, the cost of generating electricity from solar power is falling as solar panels become cheaper and more efficient. In other words, the supply curve for energy is likely to keep shifting to the right.

At the same time, the rapid growth of China, India, and other developing countries suggests that we can expect rising energy demands worldwide for the foreseeable future. So, the global demand curve for energy is shifting to the right as well.

Will our supplies of energy be up to the task? The main danger is not that we will suddenly run out of energy. Instead, one potential problem is a sharp and sudden increase in the *price* of energy sometime in the future that raises costs and impairs economic growth.

The Economics of Conservation

energy conservation
A shift in economic activities to reduce the use of energy.

As we look at the future of energy, we need to consider **energy conservation**, which is a shift in economic activities to reduce the use of energy.

There are three types of energy conservation. First, one type of conservation happens automatically because of the normal working of the market: When the price of something goes up, you use less of it. If the price of gasoline rises, you drive less or buy a more fuel-efficient car. More broadly, consumers and businesses respond to rising energy prices by reducing their consumption of gasoline, electricity, and other forms of energy.

Figure 19.4 illustrates this form of conservation in the gasoline market. Suppose something happens to shift the gasoline supply curve and drive-up prices–perhaps the Middle East oil fields are becoming depleted faster than expected, so the marginal cost of extraction rises. This causes the market equilibrium to shift from point *A* to point *B*. As the figure shows, this represents a *movement along the demand curve* for gasoline (remember that the concept of a movement along a demand curve was defined in **Chapter 3**). The price of gasoline rises, and the quantity of gasoline supplied and bought falls.

Figure 19.4 Energy Conservation in Response to a Supply Shift
If the supply curve for gasoline shifts to the left, the market equilibrium moves from point *A* to point *B*. The market quantity of gasoline falls from *Q* to *Q′*, and the market price rises from *P* to *P′*.

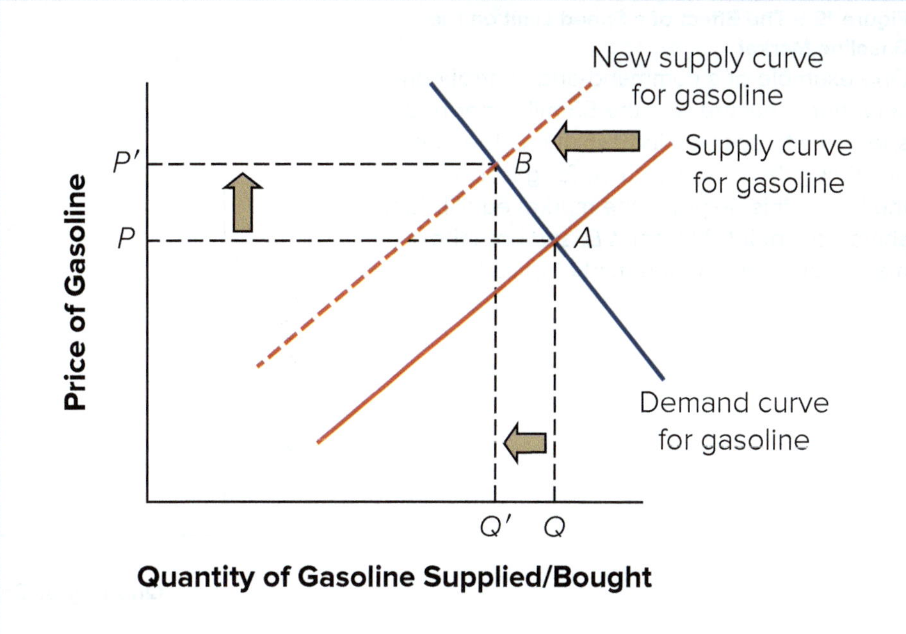

The second type of energy conservation does not depend on the normal workings of the market. Instead, it is the result of direct government intervention to control economic activity to achieve a desirable goal–the **command-and-control approach**, as we defined it in **Chapter 6**. One important example of command-and-control conservation is the fuel efficiency standard for motor vehicles (also known as the CAFE standards, an acronym for corporate average fuel economy). Since 1974, automakers selling in the United States have been required to meet an average "miles per gallon" target for all the cars they sell. The goal is to ensure that U.S. motorists are driving more fuel-efficient cars.

command-and-control approach
An approach to regulation that directly specifies certain market outcomes and activities to achieve desirable goals.

These standards have been steadily increased over the years. Under President Barack Obama, a rule finalized in 2012 would raise average fuel economy for new vehicles to 54 miles per gallon by 2025. Under President Donald Trump, that new rule was partly rolled back, to 40 miles per gallon. Under President Joseph Biden, the fuel economy standards were raised back again, to 49 miles per gallon for passenger cars and light trucks for the model year 2026.

Economists have debated the effectiveness and cost of the CAFE standards. On the plus side, the standards have encouraged automakers to put more money into the development of some new technologies for increased fuel efficiency. On the minus side, the need to raise fuel efficiency has probably raised the costs of new vehicles.

In addition to fuel efficiency standards, the government has tried a variety of different methods over the years to encourage conservation. One of the biggest moves was the passage of the National Maximum Speed Law in 1974, which forced states to reduce the maximum speed limit to 55 miles per hour. Economists disagree about how much fuel that restriction saved; in any case, the law was repealed in 1995.

Figure 19.5 shows how such speed limits affect the market for gasoline. The law shifted the demand curve to the left (unlike **Figure 19.4**, which was a movement along the demand curve). The equilibrium shifted from point *A* to point *B,* and the quantity of gasoline supplied and bought fell.

The third type of conservation is also the result of government intervention, but using a **market-based approach.** A market-based approach changes the price signals that consumers and producers face in order to move their behavior in the desired direction. However, rather than directly telling people what to do, a market-based approach gives them more options.

market-based approach
Government action to change the price signals faced by consumers and producers in order to move their behavior in the desired direction, such as polluting less or emitting fewer greenhouse gases.

One example of a market-based approach is raising the tax on gasoline. This discourages the use of gasoline by most drivers, but it allows people who really need to drive to get the fuel they need. **Figure 19.6** illustrates the impact of a gasoline tax. Remember from **Chapter 6** that a tax on a good or service generally lowers the quantity demanded and supplied in a market.

Figure 19.5 The Effect of a Speed Limit on the Gasoline Market
One example of a command-and-control conservation measure was the 55 miles-per-hour speed limit, repealed in 1995. It had the effect of shifting the demand curve for gasoline to the left. In this diagram, the market equilibrium shifts from point *A* to point *B*, and both the market quantity and the market price fall.

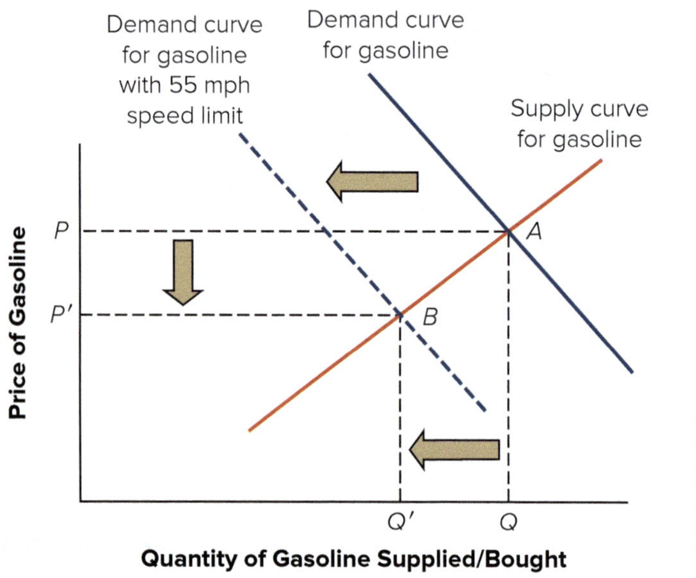

Figure 19.6 Energy Conservation with a Gas Tax
A tax on gasoline can reduce the quantity supplied and bought.

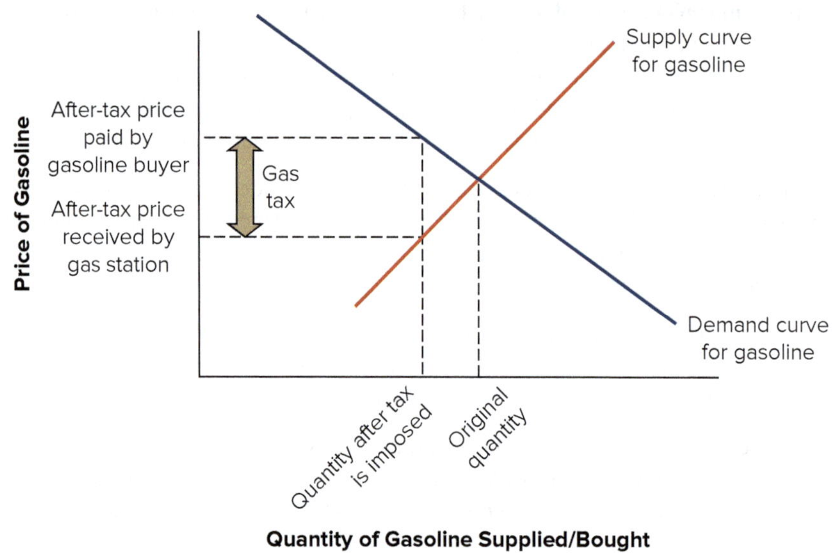

A market-based approach to energy conservation can also use carrots rather than sticks. That is, instead of taxing energy consumption, the government can offer tax credits for such actions as putting up energy-efficient buildings or improving the energy efficiency of existing homes. In 2018, for example, the New Jersey state government offered up to $75 rebates to people who bought energy-efficient washing machines.

Along these lines, the government has taken the important step of offering tax credits for the purchase of new electric vehicles. The Inflation Reduction Act of 2022 authorized tax credits of up to $7500 for a new electric vehicle, depending on its characteristics and whether it is substantially produced in the United States.

Let's finish up this section by asking a simple question: Why does the government need to *do anything* about encouraging conservation? Why not just let higher prices and the normal workings of the market do the work of bringing down energy consumption?

There are several reasons the government might want to intervene in energy usage. First, individuals sometimes put too little weight on the future. So, the price of oil or other forms of energy today may take insufficient account of the fact that there is a limited supply of oil in the ground. In that case, government intervention corrects for short-sightedness.

Second, government-led conservation measures can help accelerate the development of new energy technologies. For example, a tax on gasoline encourages car companies and other businesses to research alternatives to gasoline-powered internal combustion engines. By making existing energy sources more expensive, the government is sending a signal that it's worthwhile to take the risk of pursuing innovative activities in the energy area.

Third, energy usage of fossil fuels generates pollution, **greenhouse gases,** and other negative *externalities* (which were defined in **Chapter 6**). The measures used to encourage conservation also have the side benefit of reducing negative externalities, as we will see a bit later in this chapter.

Greenhouse gas

Greenhouse gas, such as carbon dioxide and methane, contributes to global climate change.

Alternatives to Fossil Fuels

If prices of oil and petroleum products such as gasoline were to continue to rise, would there be any good alternative fuel sources? The short answer is "yes, sort of." As **Table 19.2** shows, each alternative source of energy available today, while improving, has some key disadvantages, which explains why oil is still the most significant source of energy for the global economy.

Table 19.2 Alternatives to Fossil Fuels

Each alternative to oil has both advantages and disadvantages.

Alternative Source	What It Is	Economic Advantages	Economic Disadvantages
Solar	The use of energy from the sun to either generate electricity or heat water.	Very low operating costs. Efficiency is improving. No greenhouse gas emissions.	Initial cost of installing solar, while falling, is still high compared to fossil fuels; solar is more economical in locations with more sun.
Nuclear	The use of nuclear reactions to generate electricity.	Relatively low fuel costs. No greenhouse gas emissions.	High capital costs; high operating expenses for safety reasons; possibility of major disasters.
Ethanol and other biofuels	Fuels derived from plants or other biological products.	Can substitute directly for gasoline.	Corn ethanol competes with food crops for agricultural land. Cellulosic ethanol, made from agricultural wastes and nonfood plants, is still not economically viable.
Hydro	The use of running water to generate electricity.	Very low operating. costs. No greenhouse gas emissions.	Limited amount available; river dams endanger salmon and other fish populations.
Wind	The use of wind to generate electricity.	Very low operating costs. No greenhouse gas emissions.	Not always available; generators are large and highly visible in the landscape.
Fuel cells	The use of hydrogen to generate electricity.	Theoretically low operating costs.	Very high initial costs, and no infrastructure yet in place to generate and deliver hydrogen.

However, when we look at the list of alternatives in **Table 19.2**, we also need to consider the role of *technological change,* which we discussed at length in **Chapter 15**. History tells us that technological change is both important and unpredictable. Over the long run, the solution to rising energy prices is likely to include technological breakthroughs that make one or more of the alternatives in **Table 19.2** more compelling–or perhaps make it possible to commercialize an energy source that is not even in the table. Remember: In 1900, a list of serious competitors to trains would not have included airplanes, which had not yet been invented.

SPOTLIGHT: SHOULD THE UNITED STATES HAVE A HIGHER GASOLINE TAX?

Compared to other industrialized countries, the United States imposes very low taxes on gasoline. The combination of state and federal gas taxes came to an average of 50 cents per gallon in January 2023. By comparison, the average gasoline tax in Germany and France at the beginning of 2022 was about $3 per gallon, though that amount was cut somewhat later in 2022 after the Russian invasion of Ukraine drove up gasoline prices around the globe.

Many economists believe the United States should boost its gas tax to at least $1.00 per gallon. That would encourage energy conservation, as well as reducing the pollutants and greenhouse gases created by gasoline combustion. However, the political opposition to an increase in the gas tax is enormous, especially in large states whose residents drive long distances. What's more, a gas tax would be regressive because gasoline is a bigger portion of the budget of low-income families.

ECONOMICS OF THE ENVIRONMENT (LO19-3)

LO19-3 List the types of damage done by pollution externalities.

pollution
One important negative externality from economic activity.

Now let's turn our attention from the economics of energy to economics of the environment. In this section, we consider the negative impact of **pollution**, an unwanted side effect of economic activity.

Sources of Pollution Externalities

The key concept in environmental economics is *externalities*. A negative externality is a negative side effect from an exchange that affects someone other than the buyer and seller. For example, a loud car causes noise externalities for the people who live in the neighborhood of the driver. A sewage treatment plant causes odor externalities for people nearby.

One important source of pollution externalities is the production and use of energy. For example, a plant burning coal to generate electricity produces externalities in the form of various air pollutants such as sulfur dioxide and nitrogen dioxide. These pollutants help produce urban smog and acid rain, which damages forests. Vehicles burning gasoline also produce those pollutants, plus carbon monoxide and a variety of other problematic compounds. And virtually any process using fossil fuels produces greenhouse gases, such as carbon dioxide, which contribute to global climate change.

However, there are other sources of pollution beyond airborne-related ones. For example, manufacturing residues and chemicals create water pollution when they are dumped into rivers or onto the ground, from which they seep into nearby streams and aquifers. Old industrial sites can leave behind contaminated land. And derailments of trains carrying toxic chemicals, and crashes of tanker trucks, can create localized hazardous spills in surrounding areas.

SPOTLIGHT: WIND TURBINE POLLUTION

Glen Allison/Getty Images

Wind turbines would seem to be the perfect energy source for the 21st century. Apparently nonpolluting and with no by-products, they use a completely renewable resource—the wind—that no one else wants.

Yet many people find that wind turbines cause a kind of externality: visual pollution. Across the country, people and communities have opposed the construction of wind turbines for power. The reason is simple. Today's power-generating wind turbines are typically more than 400 feet high, or as tall as a 30-story building. Put 10, 20, or 50 of them on top of a hill to catch the winds, and they can be seen for miles. In other words, they harm environmental amenities.

The best-known fight against wind turbines occurred in Massachusetts, where one developer proposed in 2001 to put 130 wind turbines into Nantucket Sound, off the coast of Massachusetts. The local and summer residents of Martha's Vineyard and Nantucket fought the project, called "Cape Wind," for years. They cited a variety of reasons, including potential danger to navigation and to the local ecosystem. People complained about the spoiled views. Electric utilities also resisted buying Cape Wind's electricity, which was more expensive than from other sources. In December 2017, Cape Wind's developers abandoned the project after a 16-year effort.

The Impact of Pollution Externalities

Economists have identified many negative impacts from pollution. First, **health impacts** include loss of life and reduction of health caused by externalities. For example, air pollution increases asthma and bronchitis–killing people and causing them to miss work and be admitted to hospitals.

health impacts
(of pollution) The loss of life and reduction of health caused by pollution.

A second negative impact from pollution is **material and crop damage**, which represents the harm to buildings and to agriculture from pollution. If you see grime and soot covering a city building, that's material damage.

material and crop damage
Negative effects of pollution on human structures and agriculture.

Next is the **harm to environmental amenities**, which includes negative effects of pollution on natural resources that people enjoy. Examples include untreated sewage ruining an unspoiled beach and noise disturbing a quiet residential neighborhood (see **"Spotlight: Wind Turbine Pollution"**).

harm to environmental amenities
Negative effects of pollution on natural resources that humans enjoy, such as lakes, beaches, and clear skies.

Finally, pollution can cause **ecological damage**, which is damage done to the functioning of an ecosystem, including harm to plants and animals. An obvious example of ecological damage is an oil spill that kills thousands of fish and birds. But any kind of pollution can hurt an ecosystem.

ecological damage
Negative effects of pollution on the functioning of an ecosystem, including harm to plants and animals.

Measuring the Damage Done by Pollution Externalities

We'd like to be able to translate the costs of pollution externalities into monetary terms. That would make it easier to figure out which aspects of pollution do the most damage, helping us choose environmental policies with the biggest benefits.

Let's start with the health impacts of pollution. To put a monetary value on these negative externalities, regulators and economists use what they call the **value of a statistical life**. This odd phrase describes a monetary value we treat as the cost of an additional death from pollution. It is *not* what a person would pay to avoid dying. Rather, it represents the value that we as a society put on having one person not die from pollution.

value of a statistical life
A monetary value economists treat as the cost to society of an additional death–in this book, from pollution.

To estimate this number, the two main techniques that economists use are known as *revealed preference* and *stated preference.* **Revealed preference** is an approach that analyzes the choices people make in their daily lives to change their risk of death or injury. For example, if we look at patterns of job choice, how much of a lower salary are they willing to accept to take a job with a somewhat smaller chance of death or injury? How much are consumers willing to pay for a new automobile safety feature that slightly reduces the chance of dying in an accident? By analyzing consumption and labor market behavior, economists can calculate how much value people put on avoiding death or injury.

revealed preference
One way of putting a monetary value on the health impacts of pollution, based on analyzing the choices that people make in their daily lives to change their risk of death or injury. Also used to assess the monetary value of harm to environmental amenities.

The other technique is **stated preference**, which involves surveying individuals and asking how much they would pay to reduce their risk of death. One way is to simply ask them how much they would pay to reduce their chances of dying by 1 percent over the next 5 years.

stated preference
One way of determining the monetary value of the damage done by pollution, based on surveys of individuals or other direct queries.

But economists have found it's hard for people to answer that question directly. Instead, stated preference surveys usually set up a comparison between two situations and ask people to choose between them. For example, a question might go something like this:

> Suppose you have a choice between two jobs at companies A and B. The jobs are identical except for one fact: At company A you will be exposed to a chemical that has a 1 in 100 chance of causing a fatal illness over the next five years. The job at company A pays $100,000 a year, and the job at company B pays $50,000 a year. Which one do you choose?

This is not an easy question to answer–but it gives some insight into your trade-off between money and the odds of dying.

We can use similar techniques of revealed and stated preferences to judge the value of environmental amenities. For example, suppose that the breathtaking scenic views from the top of a mountain are being reduced by pollution, and we want to know the monetary value of the damages. One possibility is that we can look at records of home sales to see how much extra people are willing to pay for a home on that mountaintop versus one in a valley. This revealed preference helps estimate the value of a mountaintop view. Alternatively, we can survey people, asking how much they would pay to preserve the views.

The ecological damage done by pollution is usually addressed through stated preference methods because no one really has a direct monetary stake in ecology. For example, the Hawaiian hoary bat–found only in Hawaii–is on the endangered species list (www.fws.gov/Endangered/species). Suppose someone asked you how much you would be willing to pay to preserve its habitat. You might say 5 cents;

but if we multiply that 5 cents by the more than 300 million people in the United States, the total amount people would be willing to pay to help the hoary bat is $15 million ($0.05 × 300 million).

Finally, the monetary value of material and crop damage from pollution can usually be calculated directly. The loss of crops, for example, is simply what those crops would have brought on the open market. The damage to buildings is valued at what it would cost to repair them.

Taking these factors together, we can add the various costs of the externalities generated by a particular type of pollution to get a total cost figure. This figure may have a wide range, but as we will see in the next section, it is helpful in thinking about economic policy.

Costs in a Market with Externalities

In a typical market, a cost function sums up all the expenses of production borne by the seller. The marginal cost curve tells us the additional costs of producing one more unit. So, the marginal cost of a cell phone, say, is the additional cost to the phone maker of producing that phone.

However, the cost function for a business omits the externalities of production–that is, the costs imposed on people other than the seller. In particular, it does not include the negative externalities produced by the business, such as air, water, or noise pollution.

The fact that the cost function is missing the externalities makes a big difference. Let's think about the airlines that use an airport in a town. Each airline has a cost function, which depends on labor (pilots, flight attendants, mechanics), capital (airplanes, primarily), and jet fuel. The more flights into the town, the higher the costs. If the air travel market in this town is competitive, then each airline adds capacity until the price of a ticket is equal to the marginal cost of an extra passenger. This is the principle for profit maximization in a competitive market, as described in **Chapter 5**.

But notice what is *not* in the cost function: the extra noise pollution that hits the residents of the town because of the additional flights. One more daily 11 p.m. arrival, for example, can cause sleepless nights for thousands of people–but the airlines don't have that in their cost function.

Let's assume, using revealed and stated preference, that we've done all the calculations and surveys necessary to calculate the monetary value of the noise externality. For the sake of argument, let's say the noise externality caused by an extra flight is valued at $500. If we assume that the typical plane has 50 passengers and it flies completely full, then the *extra* marginal cost per passenger is $10.

If the airline was actually forced to pay the negative externality–that is, pay an extra $10 for each passenger–that would affect its decision about how many planes to fly into the town. It might be more reluctant to add capacity, and the price of the tickets would have to be higher.

Let's show this graphically in **Figure 19.7**. In a competitive market, the airlines will add seats up to the point where the price of a ticket equals the marginal cost of another passenger (leaving out the noise externality). That's point *A* on the diagram.

Figure 19.7 Effect of a Noise Externality
If airlines had to pay for the noise externalities generated by their flights to a town, then they would provide less service to that town. The number of passenger seats available, assuming that the price of a ticket stayed the same and all planes flew at capacity, would drop from Q to Q'.

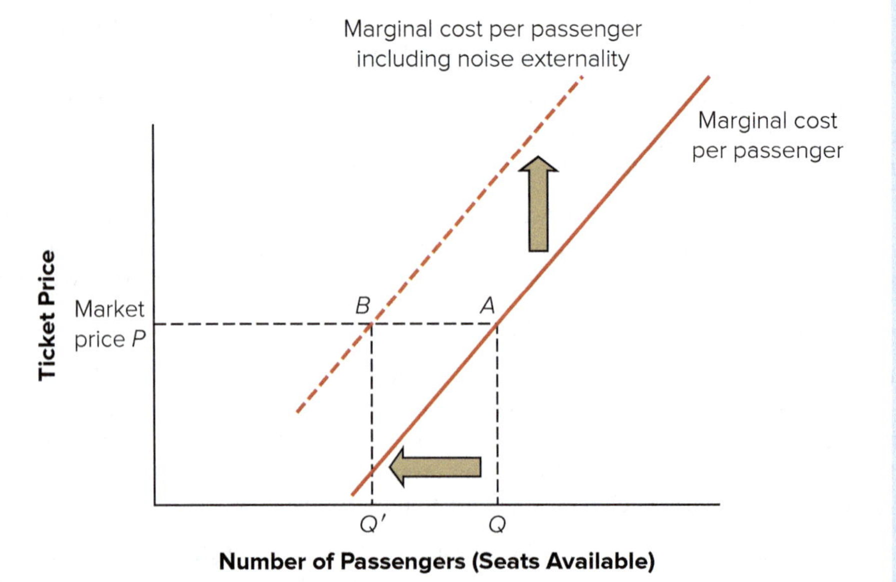

Now, let's suppose the price stayed the same, but the airline had to pay the $10 noise externality as well. Then, the marginal cost curve would shift upward because the cost would be $10 higher for each passenger. The result would be that the airline would want to fly fewer planes to the town. That's point *B* on the diagram.

This example is an oversimplification, of course. If the supply of flights into a town falls, that's likely to lead to higher ticket prices and a lower number of people who want to fly.

But despite the oversimplification, the basic intuition of this example is straightforward: In general, if sellers have to take into account the negative externalities produced by their good or service, then they probably will choose a lower level of output.

HOW IT WORKS: "GREEN" GDP

One of the goals of economic policymakers is to increase economic growth, which is the increase in real gross domestic product (GDP). But there's a problem—the official government calculation of GDP includes the output of factories, power plants, and refineries, but it does not subtract the environmental damage done by the pollution they produce. That means policy decisions may be distorted.

To get a more accurate accounting of the costs and benefits of growth, some economists have tried to calculate what is called *green GDP*. Green GDP counts the production of the country as a positive but subtracts damages to the environment. Such negatives include depletion of natural resources and harm to forests, water resources, and other parts of the environment.

Measuring green GDP turns out to be a difficult task because economists can't agree on what should be counted on the environmental side. Suppose, for example, that the amount of forested land increases, as it has in some countries. Should that be counted as a positive for GDP? That's a hard question to answer. Nevertheless, green GDP is an important concept.

CONTROLLING POLLUTION (LO19-4)

LO19-4 Describe different approaches to controlling pollution.

How do we get polluters to change their behavior to take account of the negative externalities that they generate? In the airline example, we made the assumption that the airlines had to pay for the negative noise externalities that they generated. But in the real world, it's not as easy as that.

Imagine, for example, a small town of people who live around a lake. They dump their wastewater in the lake, which ends up being severely polluted. The members of the town council vote and decide that these discharges into the lake need to be substantially reduced. How should they accomplish this change?

The most straightforward way is to issue regulations restricting how much waste each family or business can discharge into the lake and establish fines or jail sentences for the violators. That's how most pollution control is done today. However, as we will see in this section, economists have come up with alternative ways of controlling pollution that may produce better results.

Command-and-Control Approaches

As we saw in the section about energy conservation earlier in this chapter, the government can use a command-and-control approach to reduce pollution. That means the government tells businesses and consumers what to do and what not to do. Here are a couple of examples. In 1972, the Environmental Protection Agency banned the pesticide DDT because of concern about the harm it caused to the environment and both human and animal health. Similarly, in 1973, the EPA issued regulations forcing refineries to sharply reduce the amount of lead they put in gasoline to make car engines run better. Studies had shown that the lead from gasoline ended up in the air and on outdoor and indoor surfaces, and this lead was especially poisonous to children.

Overall, command-and-control regulations have helped reduce pollution in the United States and other developed countries. **Figure 19.8**, for example, shows the emissions of carbon monoxide, a toxic gas produced by internal combustion engines. The Clean Air Act, passed in 1970 by Congress, required that emissions of carbon monoxide be sharply curtailed. In response, the EPA issued strict regulations detailing how much carbon monoxide cars could produce. The result: Automakers installed catalytic converters in cars, which turn carbon monoxide into carbon dioxide. The amount of emitted carbon monoxide fell by 78 percent from 1970 to 2022, despite a large increase in the number of vehicles.

Figure 19.8 The Decline in U.S. Carbon Monoxide Emissions, 1970–2022
Regulation helped drive the decline in airborne pollutants such as carbon monoxide (omitting emissions from wildfires).

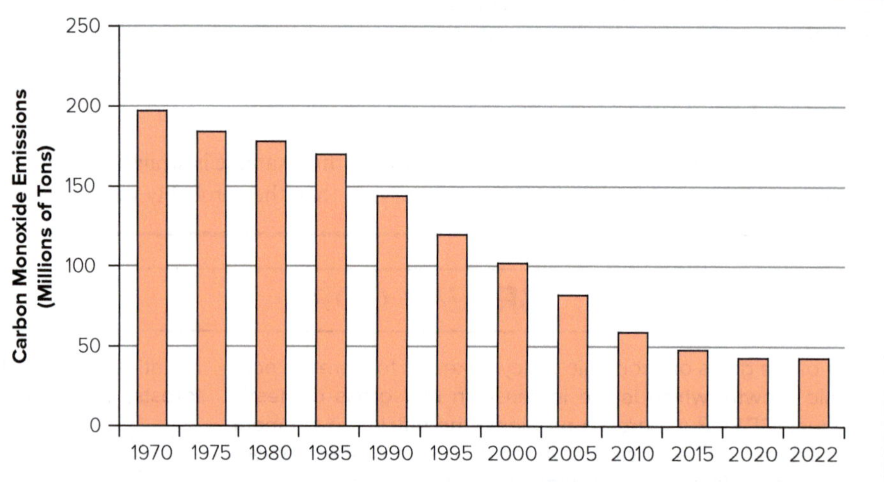

The benefit of the command-and-control approach is that you know what you're going to get as a result—in this case, less pollution. You can simply ban the offensive actions or substances or require the use of a particular antipollution technology. Command and control can be appropriate for pollutants that have large and immediate negative health effects because stopping their use is clearly the best strategy for safeguarding the public.

However, command-and-control approaches have a big disadvantage: They're inflexible and usually force all pollution emitters to meet the same standards or install the same equipment. That can be expensive and perhaps counterproductive, especially if the regulations take effect very quickly.

For example, let's go back to the problem of noise pollution at airports. Suppose that the federal government made a rule that all airlines could no longer use older, noisier planes, in order to address noise complaints from people living near airports. What would happen then? Suddenly, U.S. airlines would have to ground most of their fleet (because they all tend to have aircraft that average over 10 years old). The result: bankrupt airlines and sharply higher ticket prices for passengers. That's not a good idea at all.

Market-Based Approaches

As we saw for energy conservation, market-based approaches to controlling pollution work by changing the price signals that people and businesses face in the market. Such price signals give people and businesses incentives to produce less pollution while giving them more options than the command-and-control approach.

One example of using a market approach to reduce the amount of pollution is to tax the product or process causing the externality. The government can use that tax to make sure buyers and sellers take into account the externalities of their actions affecting third parties.

Let's see how this might work, using your computer as an example. Computers and monitors contain sizable amounts of toxic metals, such as lead, cadmium, and mercury. A typical computer monitor, for instance, can contain several pounds of lead, which can seriously damage children's brains if inhaled or ingested. When it's time to dispose of the computer, if it is simply thrown in a landfill, these toxic metals are released—harming human health and the environment.

Now suppose a tax is put on the computer according to the amount of toxic metals it contains. The more lead, cadmium, and other toxins in the computer, the higher the tax is. Faced with these incentives, computer manufacturers will look for ways to reduce the amounts of toxic metals. In other words, the tax forces the computer manufacturers to bear part of the externality.

tradable pollution permits
A government-endorsed "allowance" that gives a business the right to emit a particular amount of pollution. These permits can be traded or sold among private businesses.

In the air travel example, a similar solution for reducing the externality from noise would be to make the airlines pay a tax for each landing and takeoff. The exact amount of the tax would depend on the noisiness of the aircraft. Extremely noisy planes would pay a steep tax, while quiet planes would pay no tax at all. The result would be an extra encouragement for airlines to upgrade their fleets to quieter models.

Another market-based approach for reducing pollution is the use of **tradable pollution permits**. A pollution permit gives a business the right to emit a particular amount of pollution. For example, since 1995, electric utilities in the United States have needed pollution permits (also called *allowances*) to emit sulfur dioxide, the pollutant that causes acid rain.

The idea of issuing permits to pollute may seem like a funny concept. But they can be highly effective in reducing pollution. First, only a certain number of permits are issued, which provides a cap on the amount of pollution (that's why such programs are often called **cap-and-trade systems**). The cap can be reduced over time.

cap-and-trade system
See *tradable pollution permits.*

More important, these permits can be bought or sold. If a business has a permit to emit some amount of pollution, it has three choices. It can use the permit itself. It can decrease its own pollution and sell the permit to another business that needs it more. Or it can buy more permits if reducing its own pollution is too expensive.

The ability to sell permits for a profit gives firms an incentive to cut their own emissions more than required. In other words, there is a reward for virtue. And the permits are sold to companies that have the hardest time cutting their pollutants.

GLOBAL CLIMATE CHANGE (LO19-5)

LO19-5 Explain how a market-based approach could help mitigate global climate change.

Now we will focus on one important environmental problem: the growing amount of greenhouse gases, such as carbon dioxide, in the atmosphere. Greenhouse gases arise primarily from the combustion of carbon-based fossil fuels, such as coal, oil, and natural gas. The current strong scientific consensus is that the buildup of greenhouse gases from human activities will significantly warm the earth over the next several decades, and that the warming has already started. Moreover, there seems to be agreement that global climate change will lead to a significant rise in sea level in the coming years.

This is an economics textbook, so we will not address here the very important science of climate change. However, it is increasingly clear that global climate change is happening, and it will have significant economic impacts. We can look at potential policies to adapt to global climate change and to mitigate its effects.

The Potential Costs of Global Climate Change

Let's start by reviewing some of the potential economic costs of global climate change. First, the effects of global climate change on agriculture could be far-reaching. Higher carbon dioxide speeds the growth of some crops, while higher temperatures would change where certain crops could be grown. Crucially important would be the change in rainfall patterns. Certain food-growing regions could be turned into dust bowls, while other areas might become more productive.

Second, higher temperatures could decrease the livability of areas of the world that already have high average temperatures, while making currently cold areas more comfortable. Some researchers believe that global climate change will increase the likelihood of extreme weather events such as droughts and hurricanes, leading to the possibility of economically devastating natural disasters. And higher temperature will likely cause expansion of ocean waters and melting of the Greenland and Antarctica ice sheets, leading to rising sea levels that could threaten many of the world's largest cities, including New York and London.

adaptation
The response of consumer and business behavior to a change in conditions—for example, the alteration of behavior to reduce the negative impact of global climate change.

Still, one of the greatest uncertainties connected with global climate change is identifying which parts of the world would be hurt the worst and which parts might possibly be better off. This uncertainty makes it much harder to get countries to work together: It's harder to help the people who are going to be hurt if we don't know who they are ahead of time.

Policy Response: Adaptation

What can we do about global climate change? The responses fall into two broad categories: *adaptation* and *mitigation.* **Adaptation** is the alteration of consumer and business behavior to reduce the damage from global climate change. **Mitigation** includes policies to significantly reduce emissions of greenhouse gases. We'll look at adaption in this section and mitigation in the next section.

mitigation
The implementation of policies and programs designed to significantly reduce emissions of greenhouse gases.

In some ways, adaptation is similar to the usual demand response to a price change. Remember from the law of demand that as the price increases, the quantity demanded goes down. For example, if there is a drought in the coffee-growing regions of Colombia and the price of a cup of coffee goes up, you adapt by consuming less.

On a much larger scale, adaptation to global climate change represents the same sort of response. Suppose the rise in temperatures shifts the main wheat-growing region of the United States northward. Gradually, farmers will change the crops that they plant to take account of the new temperature and rainfall patterns. Similarly, a rise in the sea level will cause people to adapt, either by moving farther back from the coast, by building dikes or dams to hold back the water, or by altering the construction of large office and residential buildings to be water-resistant on the lower floors.

Adaptation is a useful strategy for a rich country like the United States, which can afford to rebuild homes and farms to take account of changing climate. But it is much more difficult for poorer countries, which do not have the resources to adapt. In particular, small island countries that are barely above sea level now could see most of their land disappear.

Moreover, even within the United States, the costs of adaptation fall very unevenly. Suppose you own a small home right along the New Jersey coast, or on North Carolina's Outer Banks. Then, a sustained rise in sea levels will make your home uninhabitable and unsellable.

SPOTLIGHT: CAN ISLAND COUNTRIES ADAPT TO RISING SEA LEVELS?

The U.S. coastal communities would be hurt by rising sea levels, but many island countries would lose significant portions of their land. For example, a sea rise of 1 meter (roughly 3 feet) would inundate many of the tourist resorts on the Bahamas. The Pacific Ocean nation of Kiribati, made of more than 30 small low islands, is worried that rising sea levels will reduce the amount of their land that can be inhabited or used for agriculture.

How can these small islands adapt? One solution: move. In 2014, the Kiribati government paid for almost 6,000 acres in Fiji, about 2,000 miles away, as a backup plan for either farming or for migration. Another solution, proposed in 2022: Physically raise the islands above the rising sea levels, which could cost billions. For more information, see "'No safe place': Kiribati seeks donors to raise islands from encroaching seas" (*The Guardian,* November 18, 2022).

https://www.theguardian.com/environment/2022/nov/18/cop27-kiribati-donors-raise-islands-sea-level-rise

The question, then, is whether the government should help the adaptation process in this case, perhaps by buying up homes. More generally, is there a role for government in speeding adaptation to global climate change by helping resettle people? In the extreme, could we imagine moving large numbers of people from tropical countries–which may become unbearable–to the now-comfortable temperatures of northern Canada and northern Russia? A difficult question, for sure–but one that could conceivably make economic sense.

Policy Response: Mitigation

If adaptation by itself is not enough, the question becomes how best to mitigate the harm caused by climate change. Can any of the policies we've suggested to control pollution work to slow the activities that contribute to global climate change? The command-and-control approach is too ponderous a solution for a goal as broad as controlling the emission of greenhouse gases. The government would have to regulate every use of fossil fuel. The resulting degree of control might harm the economy and would likely stifle much innovation.

carbon tax
A tax on fuels that depends on the amount of carbon in the fuel.

Instead, the preferred approach for mitigating global climate change is the effective use of price signals. The priority is to effectively slow the emission of greenhouse gases while doing the minimum possible damage to the economy. That means giving people and businesses maximum incentives to research and adopt new technologies.

One approach is to provide funding and tax credits to accelerate the adoption of clean energy technologies. We already mentioned one approach, which is tax credits for electric vehicles. The Infrastructure Investment and Jobs Act of 2021, and the Inflation Reduction Act of 2022, described in Chapter 6, also included investments in improving the power grid, tax credits for investments in clean energy production, and incentives to consumers to reduce energy use at home. Taken together, these programs are expected to have a large impact on greenhouse gas emissions in the United States.

Two other potential approaches seem to have less immediate chance of being adopted in the United States: a **carbon tax** and tradable permits. One proposed means for reducing the incentive to burn fossil fuels is a *carbon tax,* which would vary for different fuels according to their carbon content. Fossil fuels such as coal would bear the heaviest taxes because such fuels have a high carbon content, which means they emit the most greenhouse gases when they burn. Fuels with lower carbon content, such as natural gas, would be taxed at a lower rate.

Over the long run, a carbon tax would encourage less use of high-carbon fuels and more use of low-carbon fuels. It would also make fossil fuels more expensive across the board, thus reducing their consumption.

As a result, consumers and businesses would find it worthwhile to invest in energy efficiency. For example, it would become much more cost-efficient to improve the insulation in a house to retain heat rather than to use more fuel. The carbon tax would also encourage the development and use of alternative technologies, such as solar power, by boosting demand for them as the cost of fossil fuels rose.

There are problems related to the carbon tax, however. The first is that it's a tax, and no one likes taxes. Worse, it would be a *regressive* tax because poor families devote a larger share of their income to energy than do high-income families. That's why some economists propose using the proceeds from a carbon tax to reduce other taxes that hit the poor especially.

The other proposed alternative is to use a system of tradable pollution permits discussed earlier in the chapter. In the context of greenhouse gases, this is usually called a *cap-and-trade system*. Already in effect in Europe, a cap-and-trade system has the government issue a limited number of tradable permits for greenhouse gas emissions. The number of permits sets the total cap on emissions.

Then, each company has a choice in what it does with its permits. It can use its permits. It can buy more permits from other companies if it exceeds its carbon emission allowance. Or it can sell its permits if it's managed to reduce its emissions.

The buying and selling of permits allows companies to make extra money by reducing greenhouse gas emission further than required. In effect, it offers an incentive to be environmentally sound.

An International Problem

Probably the toughest part of creating a good mitigation strategy is that it's an international problem. As **Figure 19.9** shows, the top countries, in terms of greenhouse gas emissions, are a mixture of developing countries such as China, India, Brazil, and Indonesia and developed countries such as the United States, Japan, and Germany.

In theory, either a carbon tax or a tradable permit system should work to reduce greenhouse gas emissions. But it's not clear yet which one will be more politically acceptable or workable in the United States. Nor is it clear whether developing countries such as China and India will be willing to accept reductions in growth in order to hold down their greenhouse gas emissions.

YOUR ECONOMIC LIFE: The Importance of Global Climate Change

Over the course of the next 30 years, global climate change could be an important factor in your economic life or the economic life of your children. For instance, rising sea levels are likely to have a significant impact on coastal areas. Major port cities such as New York are already considering expensive infrastructure projects to protect them from storm surges, potentially creating a large number of new jobs.

This is only one example of how climate change could reshape the economy. Changes in temperature and rainfall could, over a period of decades, affect both supply and demand in many markets, including where businesses are located and where you might decide to live. Of course, there is still enormous disagreement about the size and speed of climate change effects.

Figure 19.9 Top 10 Countries: Share of World Greenhouse Gas Emissions, 2019

Source: World Resources Institute.

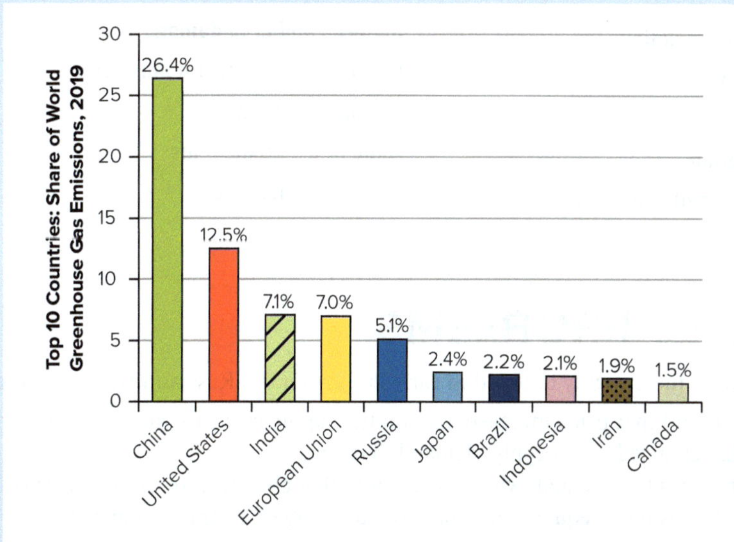

CONCLUSION

This chapter has discussed some of today's most important economic issues: energy, environment, and global climate change. With these topics likely to be at the top of the news for the next several years, economics is going to play a crucial role in the energy and environment debate.

We've come to the end of the text, but not the end of economic topics. New problems and questions are going to arise, and you now have the tools to understand them.

19 SUMMARY

1. Energy consumption per person has been flat in the United States since the mid-1970s. Nevertheless, on a per-person basis, the United States still uses 3.7 times the world average. About 81 percent of the world's energy comes from fossil fuels, which are nonrenewable. Crude oil is still the single largest energy source. The quantities supplied of crude oil and other nonrenewable energy sources depend on the market price, the marginal cost of extraction, and the amount thought to remain in the ground. Other energy sources include nuclear power, hydropower, and solar power. ***(LO19-1)***
2. There are three types of energy conservation. First, the normal response is to reduce the quantity demanded of energy when its price goes up. This is a move along the demand curve. The second type is command-and-control, which represents direct government intervention to reduce the use of energy. The third type is a market-based approach, which uses price signals to change the incentives of consumers and businesses. ***(LO19-2)***
3. Pollution produces negative externalities, which affect someone other than the buyer or the seller in a market. Pollution externalities can lead to health impacts, material and crop damage, harm to environmental amenities, and ecological damage. The monetary value of the damages done by pollution externalities can be estimated using revealed or stated preferences. ***(LO19-3)***
4. Pollution can be reduced by either the command-and-control approach or the market-based approach. One example of a market-based approach is a tax on pollution. Another example is the use of tradable pollution permits. ***(LO19-4)***
5. Global climate change, because of the buildup of greenhouse gases, is a critical environmental and economic issue. Possible policy responses include adaptation and mitigation. ***(LO19-5)***

KEY TERMS AND CONCEPTS

fossil fuels
nonrenewable energy
greenhouse gas
marginal cost of extraction
renewable energy
nuclear power
energy conservation
command-and-control approach
market-based approach
pollution
health impacts
material and crop damage
harm to environmental amenities
ecological damage
value of a statistical life
revealed preference
stated preference
tradable pollution permits
cap-and-trade system
adaptation
mitigation
carbon tax

connect PROBLEMS

1. The price of jet fuel roughly doubled in early 2022 after the Russian invasion of Ukraine. ***(LO19-1)***
   a) What effect did that price increase have on the supply curve for airplane travel?
   b) Show what changed on a supply-demand diagram.
   c) All other things being equal, what effect would that change have on the price of air travel tickets?
   d) All other things being equal, how would the quantity of air travel change?

2. In 2023, the Department of Energy (DOE) projected that the price of electricity, adjusted for inflation, would remain roughly flat for the next 25 years. Meanwhile, the price of gasoline, adjusted for inflation, was also expected remain roughly flat. *(LO19-2)*
   a) If the DOE is right, are these price trends likely to increase the demand for electric vehicles? Explain.
   b) Suppose the federal government increases the tax on gasoline. Draw a supply-demand diagram for electric vehicles and show how the curves shift as the tax on gasoline increases. Label the new equilibrium point.
3. It is common to use the tax system to help support new energy technologies. The Inflation Reduction Act of 2022 authorized tax credits of up to $7500 for a new electric vehicle, depending on its characteristics and whether it is substantially produced in the United States. *(LO19-2)*
   a) What effect does the tax credit have on the number of electric vehicles sold?
   b) Does the tax credit raise or lower the price charged by sellers of electric vehicles?
4. A potential negative impact of energy generated by wind turbines is _____ *(LO19-3)*
   a) visual pollution.
   b) negative health effects.
   c) ecological damage.
   d) crop damage.
5. The patrons at a local bar get rowdy on Friday and Saturday nights and wake up the 10 residents of the adjacent apartment building. The town economist surveyed the residents and found that each of the residents would be willing to pay $15 per night, on average, to not be woken. *(LO19-3)*
   a) Calculate the size of the negative externality per night.
   b) Calculate the size of the negative externality over the course of the year (assuming 50 weeks).
6. Suppose a town has lots of noisy restaurants that disturb their neighbors. The citizens would like to reduce the noise level without driving all of the restaurants away. *(LO19-4)*
   a) Suppose the town issues fines for exceeding noise limits. This is an example of the _____ approach to pollution control.
   b) Alternatively, the town decides to issue tradable "noise permits" that allow restaurants to make a certain amount of noise each night. This is an example of the _____ approach to pollution control.
   c) Suppose there are six restaurants making the same amount of noise each night, but the town would like to get the number down to three. Is the fine-based or the tradable permit approach likely to work better?
   d) If the town succeeds in reducing the number of noisy restaurants, is the price of a meal likely to rise or fall?
7. Every household produces garbage, some more than others. In town A, the local sanitation department will collect all the garbage that households put out. In town B, the residents have to pay per bag to have their garbage collected. In all other respects, the towns are identical. *(LO19-4)*
   a) In which town would the residents produce less garbage? Explain.
   b) Suppose town A finds itself with soaring garbage costs because too many households put out 5 or 10 bags of garbage per week. To solve this problem, the town imposes a new rule saying that households can put out only three bags of garbage. What type of households would be hurt by this rule?
   c) Would you prefer to live in town A (with the maximum number bag rule) or town B? Explain.
8. Economists regularly suggest that the United States needs to raise the gasoline tax. *(LO19-4)*
   a) The following table lays out the share of expenditures spent on gasoline and motor oil by households with different levels of income. Using the table, explain why a higher gasoline tax would be regressive or progressive.

Income Level	Spending on Gasoline and Motor Oil as a Percentage of Total Expenditures, 2021
Less than $70,000	3.8%
$70,000–$100,000	3.7%
$100,000–$200,000	3.1%
$200,000 and more	2.0%

Source: Bureau of Labor Statistics.

   b) People in the Northeast devote 2.5 percent of their spending to gasoline and motor fuels, compared to 3.3 percent in the Midwest, 3.5 percent in the South, and 3.3 percent in the West. Which region is most likely to favor raising the gasoline tax? Which region or regions are more likely to be opposed?
9. Consider the following actions for dealing with global climate change. Identify whether each represents adaptation or mitigation. *(LO19-5)*
   a) Building up tall levees to stop the rising ocean from flooding a town.
   b) Raising the tax on gasoline.
   c) Giving a subsidy for people to buy hybrid cars.
   d) Giving a subsidy for people to buy air conditioners for their homes.

GLOSSARY

401(k) plan A common type of retirement plan that allows employees to save pretax income, often matched in part by the employer.

80/20 ratio A measure of income inequality obtained by dividing the 80th percentile of income earners by the 20th percentile.

A

absolute advantage A situation in which one country can produce a particular good or service with less labor, capital, and other inputs than another country.

adaptation The response of consumer and business behavior to a change in conditions—for example, the alteration of behavior to reduce the negative impact of global climate change.

advance purchase discount A reduced price given for buying in advance, so that prices differ according to when purchases are made.

adverse selection problem The tendency of insurance—health insurance in particular—to be purchased by those who are more likely to make claims.

advertising Paid communication with potential customers through a public medium such as television, print, or a website.

Affordable Care Act The health care reform legislation signed by President Barack Obama in March 2010.

after-tax income distribution The spread of incomes after taxes have been taken out.

aggregate demand The sum of the quantities demanded from all sectors of the economy.

aggregate demand curve The link between the average price level of the whole economy and the aggregate quantity demanded.

aggregate equilibrium The price where aggregrate quantity demanded equals aggregate quantity supplied.

aggregate production function The link between the inputs to an economy and its outputs.

aggregate supply The quantity of goods and services that the economy produces.

aggregate supply curve The link between the average price level of the whole economy and the aggregate quantity of goods and services produced.

antitrust law Government regulation intended to maintain competitive markets and discourage unfair accumulation of market power.

applied research Scientific research focused on solving real-world problems.

Artificial intellligence Computer systems that perform tasks that normally require human intelligence, including sophisticated decision making.

automatic stabilizer The tendency of the budget deficit to increase during recessions because tax revenues slow and certain types of spending, such as unemployment insurance, increase. The result is a fiscal stimulus for the economy.

average level of prices A measure of how much it costs to purchase a market basket of goods and services.

average product The total output of a business divided by the number of labor hours or by the number of workers. Also *output per hour* or *output per worker.*

B

bar graph A graph where the height of vertical bars represents quantities.

barrier to entry Anything that makes it difficult for a new competitor to enter a market.

basic research Scientific investigations that have no immediately obvious commercial applications.

benefits The part of worker compensation that includes employer-provided health care insurance and other supplements to the basic paycheck.

bond A loan that entitles the lender to get regular interest payments over time, and then to get back the principal at the end of the loan period. Also called a *fixed-income security.*

bond market One of the main ways corporations and governments borrow.

bondholder The purchaser of a bond.

bubble A situation where the price of an asset, such as housing, rises far above sustainable levels.

budget constraint The combinations of goods and services an individual is able to buy, given prices and the amount of money available to spend.

budget deficit The excess of the federal government's spending over its revenues.

business cycle The recurring pattern of recession and expansion.

business know-how The knowledge and technology necessary for the production process.

buyers In a market, the consumers or businesses that exchange their money for goods and services from others.

C

cap-and-trade system See *tradable pollution permits.*

capital The long-lived physical equipment, software, and structures a business uses in its production process.

capital requirement The amount of low-risk assets a bank or other financial institution has to hold to protect against possible losses.

carbon tax A tax on fuels that depends on the amount of carbon in the fuel.

catastrophic health events Major health issues such as cancer or significant injuries that require extensive and expensive care.

central bank The official institution that controls monetary policy in a country.

centrally planned economy An economy in which most economic activities are controlled by the government.

ceteris paribus A Latin phrase meaning "all other things equal."

change in private inventories Increase or decrease of inventories at manufacturers, wholesalers, and retailers.

collusion An illegal practice in which two or more oligopolists work together to keep the prices of their products artificially high.

command-and-control approach An approach to regulation that directly specifies certain market outcomes and activities to achieve desirable goals.

comparative advantage The tendency of countries to specialize in the goods or services in which they have the biggest productivity advantage or the smallest productivity disadvantage.

competitive market A market that is characterized by *perfect competition.*

complements Two inputs that are used together, such that when the price of one goes up, a cost-minimizing business uses less of the other.

consumer price index (CPI) A measure that tracks the average price level, starting from a base year.

contractionary A description of a government policy action, such as a tax increase, that reduces output and pushes up unemployment in the short run.

controlling inflation One key goal of the Federal Reserve, which tries to keep inflation below a certain level.

core inflation A measure of consumer inflation that omits the changes in food and energy prices.

corporate income tax A tax collected on corporate profits.

corruption Bribery or other illegal activities intended to influence government actions.

cost function Reports the total cost of producing each level of output.

cost minimization The process of choosing the lowest-cost way of producing a given level of output.

cost of accumulating business know-how Outlays that increase a company's knowledge and capabilities.

cost of capital and land Outlays for buying or renting equipment, structures, and land.

cost of intermediate inputs Outlays for goods and services purchased from other companies.

cost of labor Monetary outlays for labor, including benefits.

cost of transactions The time and effort that go into managing spending.

cost-of-living adjustments (COLAs) An automatic rise in wages to compensate for inflation.

costs The money a business pays for its inputs.

COVID-19 pandemic The global pandemic that was officially declared in March 2020.

creation of new goods and services Technological change that allows people to do things they could not do before.

crowding out A decline in private investment that results from an increase in government borrowing that pushes up interest rates.

cryptocurrency A digital currency, such as Bitcoin, where records of transactions and wealth are held in a decentralized database.

currency Bills and coins used as money.

currency appreciation A change in an exchange rate allowing one currency to buy more of another.

currency depreciation A change in an exchange rate allowing one currency to buy less of another.

cyclical unemployment Large jumps in the unemployment rate that are tied directly to business cycles.

D

default Failure of a borrower to pay back a loan to the lender on time, or at all.

default risk The possibility that a borrower won't pay back a loan on time, or at all.

defined benefit plan A retirement plan that pays retirees a predetermined amount of money monthly.

defined contribution plan A retirement plan that pays retirees an amount of money that depends on the return on investments.

deflation An actual fall in the average price level.

demand curve A line on a graph showing the link between price and quantity demanded.

demand curve for innovative activities Reports the quantity of innovative activities businesses will want to fund, given the price of those innovative activities.

demand schedule The link between a buyer's quantity demanded and the price.

demand shift A change in the amount buyers want to purchase at a given price.

demographic change A changing distribution of groups in a population.

deregulation The process of reducing government control over markets.

development Innovative activities that are aimed toward creating a commercial product.

diminishing marginal product A situation where marginal product declines as a business adds workers without changing other inputs.

diminishing marginal utility The tendency for marginal utility to decline as the consumption of a good or service increases.

discount rate The interest rate at which the Fed lends money to financial institutions through the discount window.

discount window A monetary policy tool that allows the Fed to lend money to financial institutions that are running short of funds.

disposable income The amount of income people have left after paying taxes.

disruptive trade Trade that imposes big economic and social adjustment costs.

diversification The process of splitting one's money across different investments to help reduce risk without reducing expected return.

dividend A portion of a company's profits that it pays out to shareholders each quarter.

Dodd–Frank The Dodd–Frank Wall Street Reform and Consumer Protection Act was enacted in 2010 to improve regulation of the financial system and reduce the chance of another financial crisis.

downward-sloping A graph where higher values on the horizontal axis are generally associated with lower values on the vertical axis.

downward-sloping demand curve A demand curve that is consistent with the law of demand, so that an increase in price leads to a decline in quantity demanded. As a result, the line slopes down when read from left to right.

E

ecological damage Negative effects of pollution on the functioning of an ecosystem, including harm to plants and animals.

economic competition The effort by people and businesses to achieve a desirable outcome, given what everyone else is doing.

economic growth The increase in an economy's production of goods and services. Usually measured by the growth in gross domestic product adjusted for inflation.

economics The study of how individuals, businesses, and governments make decisions and trade-offs in the face of scarce resources.

education premium The added lifetime pay for getting a college degree.

effective tax rate The share of income a household pays in taxes.

elastic demand Intuitively, a situation in which a small change in price has a big impact on quantity demanded. More precisely, a situation in which the price elasticity of demand is greater than 1.

elastic supply Intuitively, a situation in which a small change in price has a big impact on quantity supplied. More precisely, a situation in which the price elasticity of supply is greater than 1.

elasticity The responsiveness of quantity supplied or quantity demanded to changes in price, income, or other economic variables.

employer health insurance plan A health insurance plan set up by and partly paid for by an employer. Employees are usually required to pay a fraction of the cost in monthly premiums.

employer retirement plan Provisions for retirement that an employer contributes to on behalf of an employee.

energy conservation A shift in economic activities to reduce the use of energy.

ensuring financial stability One key goal of the Federal Reserve, which tries to keep the financial system functioning well.

equilibrium price The price at which the quantity supplied in a market equals the quantity demanded.

equilibrium quantity The quantity corresponding to the equilibrium price. At that price, there's a match between what buyers want and what sellers are willing to supply.

equity Shares of stock.

event risk The odds that a major event will affect the return on an investment.

excess demand A situation in which quantity demanded exceeds quantity supplied at the current market price.

excess supply A situation in which quantity supplied exceeds quantity demanded at the current market price.

exchange rate The rate at which one currency can be converted into another.

excise tax A tax collected on particular items such as gasoline, tobacco, and alcoholic beverages.

expansion The period of time from a recession trough all the way to the next peak.

expected inflation The inflation rate that consumers and businesses expect will happen over the next year or longer.

expected return The average return that you can expect on an investment over the long run.

exports The goods and services produced in a country and sold outside that country.

externality The impact that the actions of an individual or business can have on others.

F

Fed funds rate The short-term interest rate controlled by the Federal Reserve. Also, the rate banks charge each other for lending reserves overnight.

federal budget The detailed list of the federal government's spending and revenue plans for the year.

Federal Open Market Committee (FOMC) The 12-member group at the Federal Reserve that votes on monetary policy.

Federal Reserve System The central bank of the United States.

final goods and services The goods and services that are bought by ultimate users.

financial crisis An economic disruption that starts in the financial sector.

financial intermediary Any institution, such as a bank, that collects money from suppliers of capital and funnels the funds to users of capital.

financial markets The parts of the economy connected with borrowing, investing, or transferring money. It is also called the *financial system*.

financial system See *financial markets*.

financing gap A mismatch between the amount of money coming in and the amount of money that needs to be paid out. In this book, the term *financing gap* refers to a long-term problem facing the Social Security system.

fintech Companies that use information technology to provide new and cheaper forms of financial services

fintech Companies that use information technology to provide new and cheaper forms of financial services

fiscal policy Decisions about government spending, taxes, and borrowing in the short and long run.

fiscal stimulus Increases in government spending and cuts in taxes designed to boost the economy.

fixed costs Costs that are difficult to change in the short run.

fixed-income securities Bonds that entitle the lender to receive regular interest payments over time.

floating exchange rate An exchange rate between two currencies that is set in the financial markets.

fossil fuels Nonrenewable energy sources such as oil and natural gas that have been produced over millions of years by the transformation of dead animals and plants.

four-legged stool A metaphor for the four main components of retirement income: part-time work, individual savings, employer retirement plans, and Social Security.

free-rider problem Occurs when individuals benefit from a public good that they have not helped to pay for.

frictional unemployment Periods of temporary unemployment that correspond to short gaps between jobs.

future-oriented activities Activities intended to bring in profits over the long term.

G

gains from trade The benefits from participating in trade relationships with other countries.

GDP per capita The economic output of a country, divided by the size of its population.

global market economy A collection of all the different participating markets in the world interacting simultaneously.

global market A market where buyers and sellers can be located anywhere in the world.

globalization The increasing exchange of goods, services, ideas, and people among countries.

goals of monetary policy The main goals of monetary policy are controlling inflation, smoothing out the business cycle, and ensuring financial stability.

Golden Age The period from the end of World War II to roughly 1973 characterized by rapid increases in productivity and a rising standard of living.

government consumption and investment The goods and services purchased by the government.

government intervention Actions taken by the government to affect the economy.

Great Recession of 2008–2009 The deep economic downturn that started in December 2007 and lasted through June 2009.

Greenhouse gas Greenhouse gas, such as carbon dioxide and methane, contributes to global climate change.

gross domestic product (GDP) The dollar value of the total output of an economy. Based on final goods and services produced in a year.

gross domestic purchases The amount spent within the United States on final goods and services.

growth rate of productivity The percentage increase in productivity over a year.

H

harm to environmental amenities Negative effects of pollution on natural resources that humans enjoy, such as lakes, beaches, and clear skies.

health impacts (of pollution) The loss of life and reduction of health caused by pollution.

horizontal axis A horizontal reference line on a graph, usually labeled to show values.

human capital The education and skill level of a workforce.

hyperinflation A very rapid increase in the average price level.

I

immigration The entry of new people into a country, either temporarily or permanently.

implicit collusion Occurs when oligopolists let one company—the market leader—set prices in the market without direct communication.

imports Goods and services that are produced outside a country and consumed within that country.

improvement in quality A change in the nature of a good or service that increases its value for buyers.

incentive effect When a tax discourages the economic activity being taxed.

incentive problem The potential lack of pressure on public-sector managers because governments don't need to make a profit.

income The amount of money an individual receives in a year from various sources.

income distribution Share of households at different income levels.

income inequality The disparity between high-income and low-income households or individuals.

income mobility The change in an individual's income over his or her lifetime.

income redistribution A policy of transferring income from high-income households to low-income households.

income tax A tax collected on individual income.

inefficiency of taxation The reduction of production and sales that typically results from imposing a tax on a good or service.

inelastic demand A situation where the quantity demanded does not change much even if the price changes significantly. More precisely, a situation where the price elasticity of demand is less than 1.

inelastic supply A situation where the quantity supplied of a good does not change much even if the price changes significantly. More precisely, a situation where the price elasticity of supply is less than 1.

infant industry A new or a small industry that is vulnerable to being crushed by better-funded and more mature foreign competitors.

inferior good A good for which the quantity demanded falls as income increases.

inflation A sustained upward movement in the average level of prices.

inflation rate The annual percentage change in the average price level.

inflation risk The danger that inflation will suddenly accelerate.

inflation-adjusted change The change in a money value after removing the effects of inflation.

information revolution The application of additional processing capacity of new generations of computers to a wide variety of new uses. Enabled businesses to produce more output with fewer workers.

initial public offering (IPO) The first time a company sells shares to the public.

innovation cluster A geographic region in which the resources for innovation are plentiful and the supply curve for innovative activities is shifted to the right.

innovations New products and processes.

innovative activities Any economic activities primarily directed at creating and developing new products, processes, ideas, knowledge, and technology.

inputs The goods and services a business or an economy uses to produce outputs.

intellectual property protection Laws that make it more difficult to copy innovations.

intensity of competition The pressure on businesses to innovate to get a competitive advantage.

interest rate The amount a borrower has to pay a lender each year in exchange for the use of the lender's money; given as a percentage of the loan.

interest rate effect One reason aggregate quantity demanded falls as the average price level rises.

interest rate on reserves The interest rate that the Federal Reserve pays on reserves held by banks.

intermediate inputs Any goods or services purchased from other businesses and used up in production.

investment banks The financial intermediaries that handle the initial public offerings and secondary offerings of companies.

invisible hand A term to describe a situation in which individual actions of buyers and sellers tend to result in a positive social outcome.

J

job market decision An individual's decision regarding what kind of job to look for.

job multiplier The total number of jobs created by one additional government-funded job.

K

Keynesian approach An approach to macroeconomics that uses increases in government spending and cuts in taxes to combat recessions.

knowledge A category of input in the aggregate production function that includes both technology and business know-how.

L

labor The inputs supplied by various types of workers. Measured by the hours of work or the number of workers.

labor demand curve Reports how many workers businesses will want to hire, or how many hours of labor they will want to pay for, given the market wage.

labor force The part of the adult population that is either working or actively looking for a job.

labor force participation rate The percentage of the adult population in the labor force.

labor market The market where workers sell time on the job in exchange for money.

labor market discrimination When an individual is paid less or treated worse on the job than an equally qualified person because of his or her race, gender, or some other characteristic.

labor market equilibrium The wage at which the quantity of labor supplied is equal to the quantity of labor demanded. Alternatively, the wage at which the number of workers available is equal to the number of workers businesses are willing to hire.

labor pool effect A situation where the labor supply curve in a given market shifts to the right because there is a larger pool of workers available globally.

labor supply curve Reports, for each level of wages, how many people are in the labor force, or the quantity of labor hours supplied.

lack of flexibility and innovation The lack of incentive in the public sector to put technological breakthroughs into widespread commercial use.

lag The length of time between recognizing that the economy is in recession and getting fiscal stimulus or monetary stimulus into effect.

laissez-faire economy An economy with few government regulations or laws.

land The actual ground used by a business. Distinct from the buildings on the land.

law of demand The tendency of quantity demanded to rise if the price falls, all other things being equal.

law of supply The tendency of quantity supplied to rise if the price rises, all other things being equal.

laws Acts of legislation.

legal barriers to trade Tariffs, quotas, and other government actions that limit trade or make it more expensive.

lender of last resort The Fed's role of lending to financial institutions to keep them in business and to keep the financial markets functioning in a time of crisis.

licensing requirements Course and examination requirements that an individual must pass to be licensed to practice an occupation.

life cycle theory of retirement The pattern of spending and saving for retirement over an individual's lifetime in the absence of government and business-supported assistance for the elderly. Posits that people spend when they are young, save during the latter part of their working lives, and spend when they are retired.

life expectancy The number of years an individual is expected to live, given his or her current age and available medical knowledge.

line graph A type of graph that uses a line to convey information.

loan A sum of money that a lender gives a borrower, which is expected to be repaid with interest.

local market A market where buyers and sellers are geographically close to each other.

long-term aggregate supply curve The long-term link between the average price level of the economy and the quantity of goods and services produced.

long-term cost function The link between the output of a business and the cost of producing that output, allowing for all inputs to be changed.

long-term costs See *fixed costs*.

long-term growth The average economic growth over longer periods such as 5 or 10 years.

long-term labor supply The predicted size of the labor force in a country or a region in the future.

long-term profit maximization Profit maximization by businesses, assuming that all inputs can be changed and that there is the option to shut down.

luxury good A good whose demand rises sharply as income increases.

M

macroeconomics The study of the overall economy.

margin requirement The regulation that determines how much money a person can borrow when buying stock.

marginal cost The added expense of producing one more unit of output.

marginal cost of extraction The amount of money that it takes to get one more ton of coal, one more barrel of oil, or one more cubic foot of natural gas out of the ground.

marginal cost of labor The wage a firm must pay for an additional worker or for an additional hour of labor.

marginal product of labor The extra amount of output a firm can generate by adding one more worker or one more hour of labor.

marginal propensity to consume (MPC) The portion that households spend of each additional dollar they receive.

marginal revenue The additional money a business gets from producing and selling one more unit of output; the additional money that a business gets from adding one more worker or one more hour of labor.

marginal tax rate The tax a person pays on the last dollar of income earned.

marginal utility The added amount of utility an individual gets from one more unit of consumption of a good or service, holding everything else constant.

market basket The typical household pattern of expenditures on goods and services that is used to calculate the average price level.

market demand schedule A sum of the demand schedules for all the individual buyers in a market.

market economy A collection of all the different markets in a given area.

market equilibrium A situation in which the quantity supplied and the quantity demanded in a specified market are equal. See *equilibrium price* and *equilibrium quantity*.

market expansion effect An increase in labor demand when businesses can sell to overseas customers.

market mechanism The process by which a market reaches equilibrium without a central planner. See *invisible hand*.

market power The ability to raise prices above the level that perfect competition would produce by restricting the quantity supplied.

market price The typical price at which a good or service sells in a market. Also, the current price at which a share of stock can be bought or sold.

market regulation The role of government in setting basic rules for market competition that businesses have to follow.

market shift A shift of the demand or supply curve to the left or right, often as the result of events external to the particular market; a change in the quantity demanded or quantity supplied at a given price.

market structure Market classification according to the number of buyers and sellers and the intensity of competition.

market supply schedule The sum of the supply schedules for all the individual suppliers in a market.

market transactions The activity of exchanging goods and services that other people are willing to pay for.

market wage The prevailing normal wage for a particular type of job.

market-based approach Government action to change the price signals faced by consumers and producers in order to move their behavior in the desired direction, such as polluting less or emitting fewer greenhouse gases.

markets A way for buyers and sellers to voluntarily exchange goods and services for money.

material and crop damage Negative effects of pollution on human structures and agriculture.

Medicaid A government-funded health plan that helps cover health care costs of low-income children, parents, and others.

Medicare A government-funded health plan that helps cover health care costs of older individuals.

medium of exchange The property of money that can be used to buy goods and services.

minimum wage A wage floor set by the government that lifts the wages of the lowest-paid workers above their market wage.

mitigation The implementation of policies and programs designed to significantly reduce emissions of greenhouse gases.

mixed economy An economy that is mainly market-based but also includes a significant role for government.

monetary policy The Federal Reserve's use of interest rates, direct lending to financial institutions, and other policy tools to influence the economy and support the financial system.

monetary policy lags The amount of time a monetary stimulus requires before it will have an effect on the economy.

money A medium of exchange that also serves as a store of value and a standard of value.

money illusion The mistake of comparing dollar amounts in different time periods without adjusting for inflation.

money stock A measure of the amount of money in an economy.

monopolistic competition A situation where a market has many sellers with similar but not standardized products.

monopoly A situation where a market has only one seller, and buyers have no good alternatives.

Moore's law The historical pattern that microprocessors double their performance every 18–24 months.

mortgage market The market for home loans.

movement along a demand curve The effect of a price change on the quantity demanded.

movement along a supply curve The effect of a price change on the quantity supplied.

multinational A business that operates in multiple countries.

multiplier effect The short-term boost in economic activity that flows from the government's spending increase (or tax cut).

N

national market A market where buyers and sellers can be in different parts of a country.

natural barriers to trade Obstacles to trade that include distance and differences in cultures.

natural monopoly An industry in which it may make economic sense to have only one supplier.

natural rate of unemployment The level of unemployment in the economy at which inflation is more or less stable. Also called *NAIRU.*

nearshoring The movement of manufacturing and service sector jobs to nearby countries such as Mexico.

negative externalities An undesirable impact that an economic activity can have on others.

negotiated price A price that is determined on a case-by-case basis as a result of negotiation between individual buyers and sellers.

net exports The difference between exports and imports.

net worth Total household assets minus liabilities.

network externality How the decision of a person to use a network affects the value of that network to other people.

New Deal A collection of public programs that President Franklin Roosevelt instituted to alleviate economic suffering during the Great Depression.

new entrants New businesses competing in an existing market, or existing businesses that are expanding into a new market.

new markets Markets with new products and services, or markets that include mostly new buyers and sellers.

nominal change The increase or decrease in a monetary value over time without adjusting for inflation.

non-zero-sum economy Occurs when an economy can produce more of one good or service without having to curtail production of another.

Nonaccelerating inflation rate of unemployment (NAIRU) The level of unemployment in the economy at which inflation is more or less stable. Also called *NAIRU.*

noncompeting labor markets Occurs when the workers in one labor market do not seek jobs in another.

nonmarket economy The part of the economy where people perform productive work without getting paid. Includes child-rearing and volunteer work.

nonprofit organizations Enterprises that focus on providing useful services to society rather than maximizing profits.

nonrenewable energy Sources of energy like fossil fuels that have only a limited supply.

nonresidential investment The buildings, equipment, and software that businesses purchase to use in production.

normal good A good whose demand rises more or less in step with income.

nuclear power An energy source using contained nuclear reactions to generate electricity.

O

offshoring The movement of manufacturing and service sector jobs to lower-wage countries.

oil price shock The events occurring in 1973 when the Organization of Petroleum Exporting Countries (OPEC) put an embargo on oil shipments to the United States and several European countries. Skyrocketing oil prices followed, which helped trigger an era of high inflation.

old age-related health expenses The inevitable health issues connected with aging, including expensive end-of-life care.

old-age dependency ratio The ratio of the size of the older population (65 years and over) to the size of the working-age population (ages 20 through 64).

oligopoly A situation where a market has only a small number of sellers producing similar products.

open market operations The process by which the Federal Reserve affects short-term interest rates.

opportunity cost The value or benefit of the next-best alternative use of money or time.

ordinary health care expenses The more or less predictable flow of minor health issues when you are young or middle-aged, including dental and vision problems.

output gap The difference between real and potential GDP.

output of government The government's purchases of goods and services. Also called *government consumption and investment.*

outputs The goods and services a business sells to customers.

outsourcing Shift of labor to third parties to handle tasks once done by a firm's own employees.

overseas leakage A situation where fiscal stimulus leads to increased imports rather than to faster growth at home.

P

Pandemic An infectious epidemic that crosses international borders.

patent A protection against copying granted by the U.S. Patent and Trademark Office to inventors for their discoveries.

payroll tax A tax collected on wage payments, paid by both employees and employers to fund Social Security and Medicare.

peak The date a recession starts—the high point of an economy before its decline.

pegged exchange rate Occurs when the government of one country manages its exchange rate to be fixed in relation to another currency.

perfect competition A situation in which all buyers and sellers in a market are price takers.

perfectly inelastic supply The quantity supplied does not change at all when the price changes.

personal consumption The goods and services bought by households.

personal savings rate Savings by households as a share of disposable income.

pollution One important negative externality from economic activity.

positive externality A desirable impact that an economic activity can have on others.

potential GDP The output of the economy along a smooth path of growth, assuming no strains on production or unused resources.

potential growth rate The rate at which potential GDP increases; also the combination of the long-term growth rate of the labor force plus the long-term growth rate of productivity.

poverty line An income level that is supposed to indicate the lowest acceptable living standard in an economy; it depends on the number of people in the household and is adjusted for inflation each year.

price The rate at which buyers and sellers exchange money for a good or service.

poverty rate The percentage of people living in households that earn incomes below the poverty line.

pretax income distribution The spread of incomes before taxes have been taken out.

price appreciation An increase in the price of a stock.

price elasticity of demand The percentage change in quantity demanded that results from a 1 percent change in price.

price elasticity of supply The percentage change in quantity supplied, given a 1 percent change in price.

price takers Buyers and sellers who take the market price as given and make their buying and production decisions accordingly.

principal The sum of money in any loan that the lender gives the borrower.

private sector The economy outside of government, including privately owned businesses.

privatization The shifting of certain aspects of government programs, such as Social Security, to the private sector.

product A good or service.

production The process of turning inputs into outputs.

production function The link between the inputs of a business and its outputs.

production possibility frontier (PPF) All the combinations of different goods and services the economy is capable of producing at a particular time, assuming full use of all resources.

productivity Economic output divided by the number of labor hours worked.

productivity slowdown The period from 1973 to 1995 in which productivity grew at a much slower pace than in the Golden Age.

productivity-enhancing innovation Technological change that provides more of the same product while holding inputs constant. It has the effect of shifting the supply curve to the right.

profit The difference between revenues and costs.

profit maximization The main objective of a business in a market economy: finding a way to achieve the largest difference between revenue and costs.

profit-maximizing rule A profit-maximizing business will increase production as long as marginal revenue exceeds marginal cost.

progressive tax A tax that requires high-income households to pay a higher tax rate than low-income households.

property tax A tax collected on the value of residential and commercial real estate.

protectionism The use of tariffs, quotas, or other barriers to trade to protect domestic jobs and businesses.

public companies Businesses that have sold shares of stock (also called *equity*) to the general public.

public debt The total of government borrowing.

public goods Goods and services that benefit many people in a city, region, or country.

public sector The portion of the economy that includes the federal, state, and local levels of government.

pure price change An increase in the price of a good with no change in its quality or characteristics.

Q

quality-of-life innovation Technological change that enhances the quality of life for you and those around you.

quantitative easing (QE) The use by central banks of open market operations to bring down long-term interest rates, such as mortgage rates.

quantity demanded The amount of a good or service that a buyer is willing to purchase at a given price.

quantity supplied The amount of a good or service that a seller is willing to supply at a given price.

quintiles 20 percent of a group. Used when considering income distribution.

quotas Government-imposed disincentives to trade that include numerical limits on the number of imported products coming into a country.

R

rational individual A person who maximizes his or her utility, subject to a budget constraint.

real change The change in a quantity adjusted for inflation. See *inflation-adjusted change.*

real GDP Gross domestic product, adjusted for inflation.

real GDP per capita Real GDP divided by the number of people in a country. Serves as a measure of the standard of living.

recession A significant decline in economic activity spread across the economy, lasting more than a few months.

redistribution The transfer of money from high-income to low-income households.

regressive tax A tax that requires high-income households to pay a lower tax rate than low-income households.

relative price shift A situation where the inflation rate of a good or service is significantly higher or lower than the overall inflation rate.

renewable energy Energy sources such as wind and solar power.

rent-seeking behavior Occurs when businesses spend money trying to influence the government.

research and development (R&D) Money and resources—particularly human resources—that economies or businesses devote to science and technology.

reserve requirement The requirement that banks keep a portion of their deposits either in cash in their vaults or on reserve with the Federal Reserve.

reshoring The movement of manufacturing and service sector jobs back to the United States.

residential investment The construction of new homes and the renovation of existing homes.

retirement poverty problem The problem that poor people often don't have enough income to save for retirement.

retirement uncertainty problem The problem that individuals don't know how long they will live after retirement.

return The gain on your investment in a year, measured as a percentage of original investment.

return from innovative activities The payback to spending on innovative activities such as R&D.

revealed preference One way of putting a monetary value on the health impacts of pollution, based on analyzing the choices that people make in their daily lives to change their risk of death or injury. Also used to assess the monetary value of harm to environmental amenities.

revenue The amount of money companies get from selling their products or services.

risk The possibility that something unexpected, either good or bad, will happen to an investment.

risk from innovative activities The possibility that spending on innovative activities such as R&D will not pay off.

risk–return principle The concept that the only way to get higher expected returns over the long run is to take more risks.

rules Regulations issued by various government agencies.

S

safety net Government programs that provide a measure of economic security for the poor, the sick, and the vulnerable.

sale price A price intentionally set below the market price to stimulate purchases.

sales tax A tax collected on retail sales.

satiation The point at which the value of additional consumption of a good or service goes to zero.

sellers Businesses or individuals who receive money in exchange for supplying goods and services.

shift in tastes A shift in the demand curve for a good or service based on a change in consumer preferences.

short-term aggregate supply curve A curve that shows the short-term link between the average price level and the quantity of goods and services produced.

short-term cost function The link between the output of a business and the cost of producing that output, assuming that fixed costs cannot be changed.

short-term costs See *variable costs.*

short-term growth Economic growth over a single year.

short-term profit maximization The process of running a business to achieve the greatest excess of revenues over costs, assuming that fixed costs cannot be changed.

shutdown decision A business decision to keep operating or not, based on the level of profits.

single-payer system A proposed health plan in which health care spending for everyone is paid for through the government.

smoothing out the business cycle One key goal of the Federal Reserve, which tries to keep the economy from dropping into a steep recession.

Social Security The government program that provides income support to older citizens who have contributed during their working years.

spending multiplier The increase in GDP created by one additional dollar of government expenditures.

stagflation A combination of slow economic growth and rapid inflation.

standard of value The use of monetary values to make comparisons between different items.

standardized products Outputs that differ from each other in only a small number of easily identifiable features.

stated preference One way of determining the monetary value of the damage done by pollution, based on surveys of individuals or other direct queries.

sticky wages Wages that don't change much in the short term in response to economic conditions.

stimulative A government policy action, such as a tax cut, that pushes up output and reduces unemployment in the short run.

stock A piece of ownership in a company. Also called *equity.*

stock market A market in which shares of stocks are bought and sold.

stockbrokers The financial intermediaries that handle the buying and selling of shares between investors.

store of value The property of money that can be used for purchases in the future.

structural unemployment A situation in which there is a mismatch between the skills of unemployed workers and the needs of employers with unfilled jobs.

substitute Two inputs are substitutes if a business will use more of one when the price of the other rises.

superstar economy Situations in which there is a widening gap in compensation between the top people and the merely competent.

suppliers of capital The investors who provide the funds. In the banking system, for example, the suppliers of capital are the depositors in the bank.

supply chain The network of suppliers needed to make a particular product.

supply curve A line on a graph showing the link between price and quantity supplied.

supply curve for innovative activities Reports the quantity of innovative activities that are supplied, given their price.

supply schedule The link between a seller's quantity supplied and the market price.

supply shift A change in the amount sellers produce at a given price.

supply-side economics A school of economic thought that emphasizes the importance of low marginal tax rates.

surplus A situation where government revenues exceed government spending.

system of national accounts All the statistics that feed into the process for estimating the quarterly and annual output of the U.S. economy.

T

tariffs Extra charges or taxes levied on imports by a country.

tax incidence The people or businesses who ultimately have to bear the burden of a tax.

tax multiplier The increase in GDP from a $1 cut in taxes.

taxation The main way the government raises revenue from individuals and businesses.

technological change An improvement in knowledge that increases the quantity and range of goods and services an economy can deliver.

technological diffusion The process by which new ideas spread from one person or business to other parts of the economy.

telemedicine The delivery of medical services at a distance using information technology.

term The length of a loan; the period of time during which a borrower repays principal back to a lender.

third party In health care, a private or public insurance plan that pays for health care services for an individual.

time value of money The opportunity cost of not having one's money available for use for some period.

total cost The sum of costs for each of the inputs used in production.

total return The total return on a share of stock is the change in the stock price, plus the dividend, divided by the original price.

tradable pollution permits A government-endorsed "allowance" that gives a business the right to emit a particular amount of pollution. These permits can be traded or sold among private businesses.

trade balance The difference between exports and imports of goods and services.

trade deficit Occurs when a trade balance is negative so that imports exceed exports.

trade in goods Exchanges that occur when sellers physically ship items to another country.

trade in services Exchanges that occur when a person or a company in one country provides a service to a resident of a different country.

transfer payments Government social benefits paid to individuals, including Social Security, Medicare, and unemployment benefits.

Treasury bills Securities the federal government issues with terms as short as one month.

Treasury bonds Securities the federal government issues each year to fund the budget deficit with terms as long as 10 years and 30 years.

trough The date on which a recession ends and the economy starts heading up again.

U

underemployed Individuals who take jobs below their skill or education levels or who are working part-time involuntarily.

underground economy The portion of the economy that does not pay taxes or otherwise get reported by government.

unemployed A description of individuals who do not have jobs but are actively looking for work.

unemployment rate The percentage of the labor force that is unemployed.

unexpected inflation The sudden acceleration of the rate of price increases above expected inflation.

unfair competition In global trade, cases in which a foreign country favors its own exporting industries by lowering their taxes or giving them some other subsidy.

union A group of workers who bargain collectively with employers for wages, benefits, and working conditions.

upward-sloping A graph where higher values on the horizontal axis are generally associated with higher values on the vertical axis.

upward-sloping supply curve A supply curve that is consistent with the law of supply, so that an increase in price leads to an increase in quantity supplied. As a result, the line slopes up when read from left to right.

users of capital The eventual recipients, such as borrowers, of funds from a bank or other financial intermediary.

utility A measure of the physical and emotional benefits a person gets from consumption.

utility function The link between the goods and services a person consumes and his or her utility.

V

value of a statistical life A monetary value economists treat as the cost to society of an additional death—in this book, from pollution.

variable costs Costs that managers can quickly raise or lower by decisions they make today.

venture capital The funds provided to risky start-ups by venture capital firms.

venture capital firms Financial intermediaries that provide funds to risky start-ups.

vertical axis A vertical reference line on a graph, usually labeled to show values.

volume discount A price set below the market price to reward buyers who purchase a large quantity of items.

W

wage–price spiral A situation that occurs when businesses and workers boost prices and wages to try to stay ahead of rising expected inflation.

wealth effect One reason aggregate quantity demanded falls as the average price level rises. Also, the phenomenon in which higher wealth leads to more consumption.

Z

zero price Occurs when an additional unit of a good or service is offered at no cost to buyers.

zero-sum economy When the only way an economy can produce more of something is to produce less of something else.

INDEX

Note: Page numbers followed by f refer to figures; page numbers followed by t refer to tables.

C

D

E

F

G

H

I

J

K

L

M

N

Q

R

U

V

W

X

Y

Z